4th Workshop on Gender Bias in Natural Language Processing (GeBNLP 2022)

Online
15 July 2022

ISBN: 978-1-7138-5633-7

Printed from e-media with permission by:

Curran Associates, Inc.
57 Morehouse Lane
Red Hook, NY 12571

proceedings.com

Some format issues inherent in the e-media version may also appear in this print version.

Association for Computational Linguistics
209 N. Eighth Street
Stroudsburg, Pennsylvania 18360

Phone: 1-570-476-8006
Fax: 1-570-476-0860

acl@aclweb.org

Additional copies of this publication are available from:

Curran Associates, Inc.
57 Morehouse Lane
Red Hook, NY 12571 USA
Phone: 845-758-0400
Fax: 845-758-2633
Email: curran@proceedings.com
Web: www.proceedings.com

GeBNLP 2022

The 4th Workshop on Gender Bias in Natural Language Processing

Proceedings of the Workshop

July 15, 2022

Order copies of this and other ACL proceedings from:

Association for Computational Linguistics (ACL)
209 N. Eighth Street
Stroudsburg, PA 18360
USA
Tel: +1-570-476-8006
Fax: +1-570-476-0860
acl@aclweb.org

Preface

This volume contains the proceedings of the Fourth Workshop on Gender Bias in Natural Language Processing, held in conjunction with the 2022 Conference of the North American Chapter of the Association for Computational Linguistics – Human Language Technologies (NAACL-HLT2022). This year, the organization committee changed membership: Kellie Webster made way for Christine Basta and Gabriel Stanovsky. Kellie has been one of the main reasons for the success of this workshop and we would like to thank her for her valuable and enthusiastic contribution to this workshop. We are glad to welcome our two co-organizers and look forward to sharing their insights and expertise.

This year, the workshop received 33 submissions of technical papers (12 long papers, 21 short papers), of which 28 were accepted (11 long, 17 short), for an acceptance rate of 84%. We are pleased to see an increased interest compared to our previous editions in the last three years: the submissions have increased this year to 33 papers compared to 18 papers last year and 19 papers in 2019 and 2020. Furthermore, the high quality of the submissions allowed us to have a higher acceptance rate this year of 84% compared to the previous years, where the acceptance rate was 63%, 68% and 67% respectively. Once more, we thank the Programme Committee members, who provided extremely valuable reviews in terms of technical content and bias statements, for the high-quality selection of research works.

The accepted papers cover a wide range of natural language processing research areas. From the core tasks of NLP, the papers include language modeling and generation, annotation, machine translation, word embeddings, and evaluation. New aspects regarding the analysis and the debiasing mechanisms are introduced and we are excited about the discussions these will inspire. Besides English, we have interesting studies targeting Inuktikut, Hindi and Marathi as well as Chinese, Italian, French and Spanish. All papers cover a variety of gender (and intersectional) bias studies as well as a taxonomy definition.

Finally, the workshop has two keynotes by speakers of high standing: Kellie Webster and Kevin Robinson, Google Research, and Kai-Wei Chang, University of California (UCLA-CS). We also have a panel under the theme of Evaluating gender bias in NLP and we are looking forward to the insights of this panel.

We are very pleased to keep the high interest that this workshop has generated over the last three editions and we look forward to an enriching discussion on how to address bias problems in NLP applications when we meet at a hybrid event on 15 July 2022!

July 2022
Christine Basta, Marta R. Costa-jussà, Hila Gonen, Christian Hardmeier and Gabriel Stanovsky

Christian Hardmeier was supported by the Swedish Research Council under grant 2017-930.

Organizing Committee

Organizers

Christine Basta, Polytechnic University of Catalonia and Alexandria University
Marta R. Costa-jussà, Meta AI
Hila Gonen, Meta AI and University of Washington
Christian Hardmeier, IT University of Copenhagen / Uppsala University
Gabriel Stanovsky, Hebrew University of Jerusalem

Program Committee

Chairs

Christine Basta, Universitat Politècnica de Catalunya
Marta R. Costa-jussà, Meta AI
Hila Gonen, Meta AI and University of Washington
Christian Hardmeier, IT University of Copenhagen/Uppsala University
Gabriel Stanovsky, The Hebrew University of Jerusalem

Program Committee

Gavin Abercrombie, Heriot Watt University
Jenny Björklund, Uppsala University
Su Lin Blodgett, Microsoft Research
Houda Bouamor, Carnegie Mellon University in Qatar
Ryan Cotterell, ETH Zürich
Hannah Devinney, Umeå University
Matthias Gallé, Naver Labs Europe
Mercedes García-Martínez, Pangeanic
Seraphina Goldfarb-Tarrant, University of Edinburgh
Zhengxian Gong, Computer science and technology school,soochow university
Nizar Habash, New York University Abu Dhabi
Ben Hachey, Harrison.ai
Svetlana Kiritchenko, National Research Council Canada
Shiyang Li, UC Santa Barbara
Tomasz Limisiewicz, Charles University in Prague
Gili Lior, The Hebrew University of Jerusalem
Sharid Loáiciga, University of Gothenburg
Inbal Magar, The Hebrew University of Jeruslaem
Maite Melero, BSC
Johanna Monti, L'Orientale University of Naples
Carla Perez Almendros, Cardiff University
Will Radford, Canva
Rafal Rzepka, Hokkaido University
Sonja Schmer-Galunder, Smart Information Flow Technologies
Bonnie Webber, University of Edinburgh
Lilja Øvrelid, Dept of Informatics, University of Oslo

Table of Contents

Program

Friday, July 15, 2022

08:30 - 08:40 *Opening Remarks*

08:40 - 09:25 *Keynote 1: Kellie Webster and Kevin Robinson, Google Research*

09:30 - 10:00 *Oral papers 1*

Challenges in Measuring Bias via Open-Ended Language Generation
Afra Feyza Akyürek, Muhammed Yusuf Kocyigit, Sejin Paik and Derry Tanti Wijaya

Looking for a Handsome Carpenter! Debiasing GPT-3 Job Advertisements
Conrad Borchers, Dalia Gala, Benjamin Gilburt, Eduard Oravkin, Wilfried Bounsi, Yuki M Asano and Hannah Kirk

10:00 - 10:30 *Break*

10:30 - 11:15 *Keynote 2: Kai-Wei Chang, UCLA Computer Science*

11:15 - 12:00 *Oral papers 2*

Fewer Errors, but More Stereotypes? The Effect of Model Size on Gender Bias
Yarden Tal, Inbal Magar and Roy Schwartz

Analysis of Gender Bias in Social Perception and Judgement Using Chinese Word Embeddings
Jiali Li, Shucheng Zhu, Ying Liu and Pengyuan Liu

On the Dynamics of Gender Learning in Speech Translation
Beatrice Savoldi, Marco Gaido, Luisa Bentivogli, Matteo Negri and Marco Turchi

12:00 - 13:30 *Lunch break*

13:30 - 14:30 *Poster session*

Analyzing Hate Speech Data along Racial, Gender and Intersectional Axes
Antonis Maronikolakis, Philip Baader and Hinrich Schütze

Friday, July 15, 2022 (continued)

Friday, July 15, 2022 (continued)

On Gender Biases in Offensive Language Classification Models
Sanjana Marcé and Adam Poliak

Gender Bias in BERT - Measuring and Analysing Biases through Sentiment Rating in a Realistic Downstream Classification Task
Sophie Jentzsch and Cigdem Turan

Occupational Biases in Norwegian and Multilingual Language Models
Samia Touileb, Lilja Øvrelid and Erik Velldal

Indigenous Language Revitalization and the Dilemma of Gender Bias
Oussama Hansal, Ngoc Tan Le and Fatiha Sadat

What changed? Investigating Debiasing Methods using Causal Mediation Analysis
Sullam Jeoung and Jana Diesner

Why Knowledge Distillation Amplifies Gender Bias and How to Mitigate from the Perspective of DistilBERT
Jaimeen Ahn, Hwaran Lee, Jinhwa Kim and Alice Oh

Incorporating Subjectivity into Gendered Ambiguous Pronoun (GAP) Resolution using Style Transfer
Kartikey Pant and Tanvi Dadu

14:30 - 15:00 *Oral papers 3*

HeteroCorpus: A Corpus for Heteronormative Language Detection
Juan Vásquez, Gemma Bel-Enguix, Scott Andersen and Sergio-Luis Ojeda-Trueba

Worst of Both Worlds: Biases Compound in Pre-trained Vision-and-Language Models
Tejas Srinivasan and Yonatan Bisk

15:00 - 15:30 *Break*

15:30 - 16:15 *Panel discussion*

Friday, July 15, 2022 (continued)

16:15 - 16:45 *Oral papers 4*

Evaluating Gender Bias Transfer from Film Data
Amanda Bertsch, Ashley Oh, Sanika Natu, Swetha Gangu, Alan W. Black and Emma Strubell

Choose Your Lenses: Flaws in Gender Bias Evaluation
Hadas Orgad and Yonatan Belinkov

16:30 - 17:00 *Discussion and closing*

Analyzing Hate Speech Data along Racial, Gender and Intersectional Axes

Antonis Maronikolakis* and **Philip Baader*** and **Hinrich Schütze**
Center for Information and Language Processing (CIS), LMU Munich, Germany
antmarakis@cis.lmu.de

Abstract

Warning: *This work contains strong and offensive language, sometimes uncensored.*

To tackle the rising phenomenon of hate speech, efforts have been made towards data curation and analysis. When it comes to analysis of bias, previous work has focused predominantly on race. In our work, we further investigate bias in hate speech datasets along racial, gender and intersectional axes. We identify strong bias against African American English (AAE), masculine and AAE+Masculine tweets, which are annotated as disproportionately more hateful and offensive than from other demographics. We provide evidence that BERT-based models propagate this bias and show that balancing the training data for these protected attributes can lead to fairer models with regards to gender, but not race.

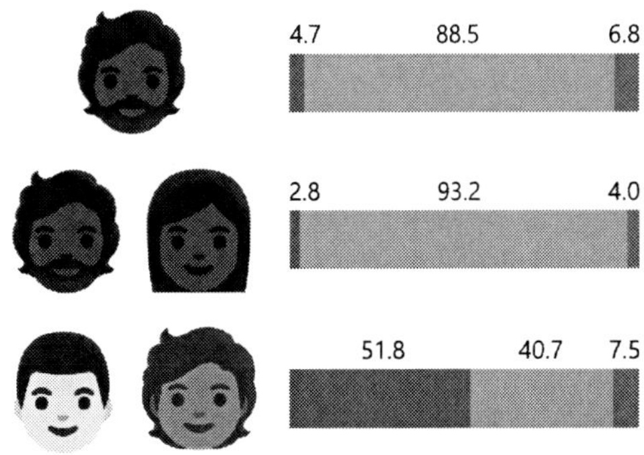

Figure 1: Distributions of label annotations on DAVIDSON (neutral, offensive, hateful) for AAE+Masculine, AAE and SAE (top-to-bottom). AAE has a higher ratio of offensive examples than SAE, while AAE+Masculine is both highly offensive and hateful.

1 Introduction

Hate Speech. To tackle the phenomenon of online hate speech, efforts have been made to curate datasets (Davidson et al., 2017; Guest et al., 2021; Sap et al., 2020). Since datasets in this domain are dealing with sensitive topics, it is of upmost importance that biases are kept to a (realistic) minimum and that data is thoroughly analyzed before use (Davidson et al., 2019a; Madukwe et al., 2020). In our work, we are contributing to this analysis by uncovering biases along the racial, gender and intersectional axes.

Racial[1], Gender and Intersectional Biases. During data collection, biases can be introduced due to–among other reasons–lack of annotator training or divergence between annotators and user demographics. For example, oftentimes the majority of annotators are white or male (Sap et al., 2020; Founta et al., 2018). An annotator not in the 'in-group' may hold (un)conscious biases based on misconceptions about 'in-group' speech which may affect their perception of speech from certain communities (O'Dea et al., 2015), leading to incorrect annotations when it comes to dialects the annotators are not familiar with. A salient example of this is annotators conflating African American English with hateful language (Sap et al., 2019).

Intersectionality (Crenshaw, 1989) is a framework for examining how different forms of inequality (for example, racial or gender inequalities) intersect with and reinforce each other. These new social dynamics need to be analyzed both separately and as a whole in order to address challenges faced by the examined communities. For example, a black woman does not face inequality based only on race or only on gender: she faces inequality because of both these characteristics, separately and in conjunction. In this work, we are analyzing not only the racial or gender inequalities in hate speech

*Equal contribution.

[1]While the correlation of race and African American English (AAE) is complicated (Anderson, 2015), in our work we consider AAE as a proxy for race, since it is a dialect overwhelmingly used by African Americans (Spears and Hinton, 2010; Spears, 2015).

Proceedings of the The 4th Workshop on Gender Bias in Natural Language Processing (GeBNLP), pages 1 - 7
July 15, 2022

datasets, but their intersectionality as well.

With research in the area of hate speech, the NLP community aims at protecting target groups and fostering a safer online environment. In this sensitive area, it is pivotal that datasets and models are analyzed extensively to ensure the biases we are protecting affected communities from do not appear in the data itself, causing further marginalization (for example, by removing AAE speech disproportionately more often).

Contributions. In summary, we **(i)** investigate racial, gender and intersectional bias in three hate speech datasets, Founta et al. (2018); Davidson et al. (2017); Mathew et al. (2021), **(ii)** examine classifier predictions on existing, general-purpose African/Standard American English (AAE/SAE) and gendered tweets, **(iii)** identify model bias against AAE, masculine and AAE+Masculine (labeled as both AAE and masculine) tweets, **(iv)** show that balancing training data for gender leads to fairer models.

2 Related Work

Hate speech research has focused on dataset curation (Davidson et al., 2017; Founta et al., 2018; Sap et al., 2020; Guest et al., 2021; Hede et al., 2021; Grimminger and Klinger, 2021) and dataset analysis (Madukwe et al., 2020; Wiegand et al., 2019; Swamy et al., 2019). In our work, we further analyze datasets to uncover latent biases.

It has been shown that data reflects social bias inherent in annotator pools (Waseem, 2016; Al Kuwatly et al., 2020; Davidson et al., 2019a,b). Work has been conducted to identify bias against AAE (Sap et al., 2019; Zhou et al., 2021; Xia et al., 2020) and gender (Excell and Al Moubayed, 2021).

Research has also been conducted in identifying disparities in performance across social groups, with machine learning algorithms underperforming for certain groups (Tatman, 2017; Buolamwini and Gebru, 2018; Rudinger et al., 2018).

Kim et al. (2020) investigated whether bias along the intersectional axis exists in Founta et al. (2018). While Kim et al. (2020) focused on bias within a single dataset, in our work we generalize to multiple hate speech datasets. We also examine classifier behavior and methods to mitigate this bias.

Research from a sociolinguistic perspective has shown that genders exhibit differences in online text (Gefen and Ridings, 2005) as well as general speech (Penelope Eckbert, 2013). In Bamman et al. (2014) and Bergsma and Van Durme (2013), gender classifiers for English tweets were developed with accuracy of 88% and 85% respectively. In our work, we develop a gender classifier of tweets as well, focusing on precision over recall, leading to a smaller but more accurate sample of gendered data.

Dataset	Neutral	Offensive	Hateful
DAVIDSON	0.92	0.85	0.53
FOUNTA	0.85	0.79	0.47
HATEXPLAIN	0.69	0.55	0.70

Table 1: F1-score of BERT for each label, evaluated on DAVIDSON, FOUNTA and HATEXPLAIN.

3 Datasets

Five English datasets were used: three hate speech datasets (DAVIDSON, FOUNTA and HATEXPLAIN), one dataset of tweets labeled for race (GROENWOLD) and one for gender (VOLKOVA). We adopt the definitions of Davidson et al. (2017) for hate speech (defined as speech that contains expressions of hatred towards a group or individual on the basis of protected attributes like ethnicity, gender, race and sexual orientation) and offensive speech (speech that contains offensive language but is not hateful).

DAVIDSON. In Davidson et al. (2017), a hate speech dataset of tweets was collected, labeled for neutral, offensive and hateful language.

FOUNTA. In Founta et al. (2018) a crowd-sourced dataset of tweets was presented, labeled for normal, abusive and hateful language. To unify definitions, we rename normal to neutral language and abusive to offensive language.

HATEXPLAIN. Mathew et al. (2021) presented a dataset from Twitter and Gab[2] passages. It has been labeled for normal (neutral), offensive and hateful language.

GROENWOLD. In Groenwold et al. (2020) a dataset of African American English and Standard American English tweets was introduced. The AAE tweets come from (Blodgett et al., 2016) and the SAE are direct translations of those tweets provided by annotators.

VOLKOVA. Volkova et al. (2013) presented a dataset of 800k English tweets from users with an associated gender (feminine/masculine).

[2]Gab is a social platform that has been known to host far-right groups and rhetoric.

Dataset	Masc.	Fem.	SAE	AAE	SAE+Masc.	SAE+Fem.	AAE+Masc.	AAE+Fem.
DAVIDSON	2716	2338	3534	8099	1279	1240	3157	1172
FOUNTA	26307	13615	43330	4177	13486	13257	971	787
HATEXPLAIN	4509	1103	10368	1103	4145	2376	250	240
GROENWOLD $_{AAE}$	586	613	0	1995	0	0	587	612
GROENWOLD $_{SAE}$	587	601	1980	0	587	601	0	0
VOLKOVA	41164	58836	37874	3755	16243	21631	1843	1912

Table 2: Protected attribute statistics for DAVIDSON, FOUNTA, HATEXPLAIN, GROENWOLD and VOLKOVA.

4 Experimental Setup

AAE Classifier. To classify tweets as AAE or SAE, we used the Blodgett et al. (2016) classifier. We took into consideration tweets with a confidence score over 0.5, which can be interpreted as a straightforward classifier of AAE/SAE (whichever class has the highest score is returned).

Gender Classifier. To classify tweets as masculine or feminine, we finetuned BERT-base[3] on Volkova et al. (2013), which includes gender information as self-reported from authors. We split the dataset into train/dev/test (50K/25K/25K) and employed a confidence score of 0.8 as the threshold for assigning gender to a tweet. For the tweets with a confidence over the given threshold, precision was 78.4% when classifying tweets as 'masculine' and 79.5% when classifying tweets as 'feminine'.

Hate Speech Classifiers. For each of the three hate speech datasets we finetuned BERT-base. We split each dataset into 80:10:10 (train:dev:test) sets, used a max sequence length of 256 and trained for 3 epochs, keeping the rest of the hyperparameters the same. Performance for the development set is shown in Table 1[4]. In DAVIDSON and FOUNTA, BERT performs well for neutral and offensive examples, performance drops for hateful content. In HATEXPLAIN, BERT overall performs worse, with slightly better performance for neutral and hateful examples over offensive ones.

Intersectionality. For our analysis, we classified tweets from all datasets for gender and race.

5 Intersectionality Statistics

In Table 2, we present statistics for gender, race and their intersection as found in the three examined hate speech datasets as well as in GROENWOLD and VOLKOVA.[5] We show that no dataset is balanced between AAE and SAE. In FOUNTA and HATEXPLAIN, AAE tweets make up approximately 1/10th of the data. In DAVIDSON, we see stronger representation of AAE, with the AAE tweets being almost twice as many as the SAE tweets. DAVIDSON is also balanced for gender. The other hate speech datasets, while still not balanced, are more balanced for gender than they are for race. FOUNTA has twice as many masculine than feminine tweets and HATEXPLAIN has four times as many.

In Table 3, we present a breakdown of protected attributes per class (neutral/offensive/hateful) for DAVIDSON, FOUNTA and HATEXPLAIN. A main takeaway for DAVIDSON and FOUNTA is the imbalance of AAE versus SAE. In SAE, the neutral class makes up 52% of the data for DAVIDSON and 81% for FOUNTA, while the respective numbers for AAE are 3% for DAVIDSON and 13% for FOUNTA.

In HATEXPLAIN, AAE and SAE are more balanced, but there is instead imbalance between genders. For masculine and feminine speech, passages are neutral at rates of 43% and 61% respectively. In DAVIDSON, SAE+Feminine speech is viewed as more offensive than SAE+Masculine (48% vs. 19%), while in HATEXPLAIN, SAE+Masculine is more hateful than SAE+Feminine (34% vs. 16%). Finally, when comparing genders in AAE speech, we see that while AAE+Feminine contains a larger percentage of offensive tweets (for example, in FOUNTA, 69% vs. 54% and in HATEXPLAIN, 50% vs. 21%), AAE+Masculine contains disproportionately more hateful speech (in DAVIDSON, 7% vs. 5%, in FOUNTA, 28% vs. 9% and in HATEXPLAIN, 19% vs. 6%).

Overall, AAE and masculine speech is annotated as more offensive and hateful than SAE and feminine speech. Further analyzing AAE, AAE+Masculine is viewed as more hateful than AAE+Feminine.

[3]https://huggingface.co/bert-base-cased

[4]Performance on the test set is similar, omitted for brevity.

[5]Race/gender for the hate speech datasets, gender for GROENWOLD and race for VOLKOVA have been computed as described in Section 4.

Dataset	Masc.			Fem.			SAE			AAE			SAE+Masc.			SAE+Fem.			AAE+Masc.			AAE+Fem.		
	N	O	H	N	O	H	N	O	H	N	O	H	N	O	H	N	O	H	N	O	H	N	O	H
Davidson	32.2	61.9	5.9	27.7	69.5	2.8	51.8	40.7	7.5	2.8	93.2	4.0	77.0	19.4	3.6	50.0	47.8	2.3	4.7	88.5	6.8	6.8	88.0	5.2
Founta	81.2	12.3	6.4	71.0	25.0	4.0	80.5	14.6	4.9	13.2	69.2	17.6	86.9	7.6	5.5	86.2	11.4	2.4	18.3	53.8	27.9	21.8	69.4	8.8
HateXplain	43.0	23.7	33.3	60.7	24.6	14.8	38.3	26.7	35.0	45.6	39.1	15.3	41.6	24.0	34.4	58.9	25.1	16.0	59.4	21.3	19.4	44.4	50.0	5.6

Table 3: Distribution of protected attribute annotations for neutral/offensive/hateful (N/O/H) examples.

Dataset	Masc.			Fem.			SAE			AAE			SAE+Masc.			SAE+Fem.			AAE+Masc.			AAE+Fem.		
	N	O	H	N	O	H	N	O	H	N	O	H	N	O	H	N	O	H	N	O	H	N	O	H
Random	33.8	63.2	3.0	27.7	71.2	1.1	53.1	40.5	6.4	4.9	94.1	1.0	77.3	19.3	3.4	45.6	53.2	1.2	6.4	91.2	2.4	3.0	94.3	2.7
Balanced	25.3	71.5	3.2	25.4	71.1	3.5	54.3	39.2	6.5	4.3	95.1	1.6	71.0	22.8	6.2	52.3	46.4	2.3	5.8	92.1	2.1	6.2	93.1	0.7

Table 4: Distribution of predictions for protected attributes on random and balanced datasets based on DAVIDSON. The balanced set is balanced on race (equal number of AAE and SAE tweets) and gender (equal number of feminine and masculine tweets). Shown are percentages for neutral/offensive/hateful (N/O/H) predictions.

Dataset	All	AAE
DAVIDSON	n*ggerize, subhuman, bastards, border, pigfucking, feminist, wetbacks, savages, wetback, jumpers	queer, n*gros, n*ggaz, racial, shittiest, wet, savage, skinned, darky, f*gs
FOUNTA	moron, insult, muslims, aggression, puritan, haters, arabs, coloured, ousted, pedophiles	white, killing, pathetic, n*gga, slave, n*ggas, sells, hell, children, violent
HATEXPLAIN	towelhead, muzzrat, muscum, n*gresses, n*ggerette, n*glets, musloid, n*ggerish, n*ggery, gorilla	spic, fuck, f*ggots, gorilla, towel, sandn*gger, zhid, c*ons, rag, fowl

Table 5: Top 10 most contributing words for DAVIDSON, FOUNTA and HATEXPLAIN as computed with LIME for hateful predictions.

6 Bias in BERT

We investigate to what extent data bias is learned by BERT. We compare our findings against a dataset balanced for race and gender, to examine whether balanced data leads to fairer models. Namely, we compare a randomly sampled with a balanced set the DAVIDSON dataset.[6] In the balanced set we sample the same number of AAE and SAE tweets (3000) and the same number of masculine and feminine tweets (1750). We also include 8000 neutral tweets without race or gender labels. For the randomly sampled set, for a fair comparison, we sampled the same number of tweets as the balanced set.[7] All sampling was stratified to preserve the original label distributions. Results are shown in Table 4.

In the randomly sampled set, there is an imbalance both for gender and race. For gender, while masculine tweets are more hateful (3% vs. 1%), feminine tweets are more offensive (71% vs. 63%). For race, AAE is marked almost entirely as offensive (94%), while SAE is split in neutral and offensive (53% and 41%). In the SAE subset of tweets, there is an imbalance between genders, with SAE+Feminine being marked disproportionately more often as offensive than SAE+Masculine (54% vs. 19%).

6.1 Balanced Training

In Table 4, before balancing, 34% of masculine and 28% of feminine tweets are marked as neutral. After balancing, these rates are both at 25%. There is an improvement in the intersection of AAE and gender, with the distributions of AAE+Masculine and AAE+Feminine tweets converging. For SAE, SAE+Masculine and SAE+Feminine distributions converge too, although still far apart. Overall, balanced data improves fairness for gender but not for race, which potentially stems from bias in annotation.

6.2 Interpretability with LIME

In Table 5, we show the top contributing words for offensive and hateful predictions in DAVIDSON,

[6] FOUNTA and HATEXPLAIN were not considered for this study as they do not contain enough AAE examples to make confident inferences.

[7] Experiments were conducted with the entirety of the original dataset with similar results. They are omitted for brevity.

FOUNTA and HATEXPLAIN. We see that for AAE, terms such as 'n****z' and 'n***a' contribute in classifying text as non-neutral even though the terms are part of African American vernacular (Rahman, 2012), showing that this dialect is more likely to be flagged. In non-AAE speech (which includes–but is not exclusive to–SAE), we see the n-word variant with the '-er' spelling appearing more often in various forms, which is correctly picked up by the model as an offensive and hateful term. On both sets, we also see other slurs, such as 'f*ggots', 'moron' and 'wetback' (a slur against foreigners residing in the United States, especially Mexicans) being picked up, showing the model does recognize certain slurs and offensive terms.

7 Conclusion

In our work, we analyze racial, gender and intersectional bias in hate speech datasets. We show that tweets from AAE and AAE+Masculine users (as classified automatically) are labeled disproportionately more often as offensive. We further show that BERT learns this bias, flagging AAE speech as significantly more offensive than SAE. We perform interpretability analysis using LIME, showing that the inability of BERT to differentiate between variations of the n-word across dialects is a contributing factor to biased predictions. Finally, we investigate whether training on a dataset balanced for race and gender mitigates bias. This method shows mixed results, with gender bias being mitigated more than racial bias. With our work we want to motivate further investigation in model bias not only for the usual gender and racial attributes, but also for their intersection.

8 Bias Statement

Research in the sphere of hate speech has produced annotated data that can be used to train classifiers to detect hate speech as found in online media. It is known that these datasets contain biases that models will potentially propagate. The **representational harm** that can be triggered is certain target groups getting their speech inadvertently censored/deleted due to existing biases that marginalize certain groups. In our work we investigate this possibility along intersectional axes (gender and race). We find that tweets written by female users are seen as disproportionately more offensive, while male users write tweets that appear more hateful.

9 Ethical Considerations

In our work we are dealing with data that can catalyze harm against marginalized groups. We do not advocate for the propagation or adoption of this hateful rhetoric. With our work we wish to motivate further analysis and documentation of sensitive data that is to be used for the training of models (for example, using templates from Mitchell et al. (2019); Bender and Friedman (2018)).

Further, while classifying protected attributes such as race or gender is important in analyzing and identifying bias, care should be taken for the race and gender classifiers to not be misused or abused, in order to protect the identity of users, especially those from marginalized demographics who are more vulnerable to hateful attacks and further marginalization. In our work we only predict these protected attributes for investigative purposes and do not motivate the direct application of such classifiers. Further, in our work we are using dialect (AAE) associated with African Americans as a proxy to race due to a lack of available annotated data. It should be noted that not all African Americans make use of AAE and not all AAE users are African Americans.

Finally, in our work we only focused on English and a specific set of attributes. Namely, we considered race (African American) and gender. This is a non-exhaustive list of biases and more work needs to be done for greater coverage of languages and attributes.

10 Acknowledgments

This work has been funded by the German Federal Ministry of Education and Research (BMBF) under Grant No. 01IS18036A. Antonis Maronikolakis was partly supported by the European Research Council (#740516). The authors of this work take full responsibility for its content.

References

Hala Al Kuwatly, Maximilian Wich, and Georg Groh. 2020. Identifying and measuring annotator bias based on annotators' demographic characteristics. In *Proceedings of the Fourth Workshop on Online Abuse and Harms*, pages 184–190, Online. Association for Computational Linguistics.

Kate T. Anderson. 2015. Racializing language: Unpacking linguistic approaches to attitudes about race and speech. In Green Lisa J. Bloomquist, Jennifer and Sonja L. Lanehart, editors, *The Oxford Handbook of Innovation*, chapter 42, pages 773–785. Oxford University Press, Oxford.

David Bamman, Jacob Eisenstein, and Tyler Schnoebelen. 2014. Gender identity and lexical variation in social media. *Journal of Sociolinguistics*, 18(2):135–160.

Emily M. Bender and Batya Friedman. 2018. Data statements for natural language processing: Toward mitigating system bias and enabling better science. *Transactions of the Association for Computational Linguistics*, 6:587–604.

Shane Bergsma and Benjamin Van Durme. 2013. Using conceptual class attributes to characterize social media users. In *Proceedings of the 51st Annual Meeting of the Association for Computational Linguistics (Volume 1: Long Papers)*, pages 710–720, Sofia, Bulgaria. Association for Computational Linguistics.

Su Lin Blodgett, Lisa Green, and Brendan O'Connor. 2016. Demographic Dialectal Variation in Social Media: A Case Study of African-American English. In *Proceedings of EMNLP*.

Joy Buolamwini and Timnit Gebru. 2018. Gender shades: Intersectional accuracy disparities in commercial gender classification. In *Proceedings of the 1st Conference on Fairness, Accountability and Transparency*, volume 81 of *Proceedings of Machine Learning Research*, pages 77–91. PMLR.

Kimberle Crenshaw. 1989. Demarginalizing the intersection of race and sex: A black feminist critique of antidiscrimination doctrine, feminist theory and antiracist politics. *The University of Chicago Legal Forum*, 140:139–167.

Thomas Davidson, Debasmita Bhattacharya, and Ingmar Weber. 2019a. Racial bias in hate speech and abusive language detection datasets. In *Proceedings of the Third Workshop on Abusive Language Online*, pages 25–35, Florence, Italy. Association for Computational Linguistics.

Thomas Davidson, Debasmita Bhattacharya, and Ingmar Weber. 2019b. Racial bias in hate speech and abusive language detection datasets. In *Proceedings of the Third Workshop on Abusive Language Online*, pages 25–35, Florence, Italy. Association for Computational Linguistics.

Thomas Davidson, Dana Warmsley, Michael Macy, and Ingmar Weber. 2017. Automated hate speech detection and the problem of offensive language. In *International AAAI Conference on Web and Social Media*.

Elizabeth Excell and Noura Al Moubayed. 2021. Towards equal gender representation in the annotations of toxic language detection. In *Proceedings of the 3rd Workshop on Gender Bias in Natural Language Processing*, pages 55–65, Online. Association for Computational Linguistics.

Antigoni-Maria Founta, Constantinos Djouvas, Despoina Chatzakou, Ilias Leontiadis, Jeremy Blackburn, Gianluca Stringhini, Athena Vakali, Michael Sirivianos, and Nicolas Kourtellis. 2018. Large scale crowdsourcing and characterization of twitter abusive behavior. In *11th International Conference on Web and Social Media, ICWSM 2018*. AAAI Press.

David Gefen and Catherine Ridings. 2005. If you spoke as she does, sir, instead of the way you do: A sociolinguistics perspective of gender differences in virtual communities. *DATA BASE*, 36:78–92.

Lara Grimminger and Roman Klinger. 2021. Hate towards the political opponent: A Twitter corpus study of the 2020 US elections on the basis of offensive speech and stance detection. In *Proceedings of the Eleventh Workshop on Computational Approaches to Subjectivity, Sentiment and Social Media Analysis*, pages 171–180, Online. Association for Computational Linguistics.

Sophie Groenwold, Lily Ou, Aesha Parekh, Samhita Honnavalli, Sharon Levy, Diba Mirza, and William Yang Wang. 2020. Investigating African-American Vernacular English in transformer-based text generation. In *Proceedings of EMNLP*.

Ella Guest, Bertie Vidgen, Alexandros Mittos, Nishanth Sastry, Gareth Tyson, and Helen Margetts. 2021. An expert annotated dataset for the detection of online misogyny. In *Proceedings of the 16th Conference of the European Chapter of the Association for Computational Linguistics: Main Volume*, pages 1336–1350, Online. Association for Computational Linguistics.

Anushree Hede, Oshin Agarwal, Linda Lu, Diana C. Mutz, and Ani Nenkova. 2021. From toxicity in online comments to incivility in American news: Proceed with caution. In *Proceedings of the 16th Conference of the European Chapter of the Association for Computational Linguistics: Main Volume*, pages 2620–2630, Online. Association for Computational Linguistics.

Jae-Yeon Kim, Carlos Ortiz, Sarah Nam, Sarah Santiago, and Vivek Datta. 2020. Intersectional bias in hate speech and abusive language datasets. *CoRR*, abs/2005.05921.

Kosisochukwu Madukwe, Xiaoying Gao, and Bing Xue. 2020. In data we trust: A critical analysis of hate speech detection datasets. In *Proceedings of the Fourth Workshop on Online Abuse and Harms*, pages 150–161, Online. Association for Computational Linguistics.

Binny Mathew, Punyajoy Saha, Seid Muhie Yimam, Chris Biemann, Pawan Goyal, and Animesh Mukherjee. 2021. Hatexplain: A benchmark dataset for explainable hate speech detection. *Proceedings of the AAAI Conference on Artificial Intelligence*, 35(17):14867–14875.

Margaret Mitchell, Simone Wu, Andrew Zaldivar, Parker Barnes, Lucy Vasserman, Ben Hutchinson, Elena Spitzer, Inioluwa Deborah Raji, and Timnit Gebru. 2019. Model cards for model reporting. In *Proceedings of the Conference on Fairness, Accountability, and Transparency*, FAT* '19, page 220–229, New York, NY, USA. Association for Computing Machinery.

Conor J. O'Dea, Stuart S. Miller, Emma B. Andres, Madelyn H. Ray, Derrick F. Till, and Donald A. Saucier. 2015. Out of bounds: factors affecting the perceived offensiveness of racial slurs. *Language Sciences*, 52:155–164. Slurs.

Sally McConnell-Ginet Penelope Eckbert. 2013. *Language and Gender*. Cambridge University Press.

Jacquelyn Rahman. 2012. The n word: Its history and use in the african american community. *Journal of English Linguistics*, 40(2):137–171.

Rachel Rudinger, Jason Naradowsky, Brian Leonard, and Benjamin Van Durme. 2018. Gender bias in coreference resolution. In *Proceedings of the 2018 Conference of the North American Chapter of the Association for Computational Linguistics: Human Language Technologies, Volume 2 (Short Papers)*, pages 8–14, New Orleans, Louisiana. Association for Computational Linguistics.

Maarten Sap, Dallas Card, Saadia Gabriel, Yejin Choi, and Noah A. Smith. 2019. The risk of racial bias in hate speech detection. In *Proceedings of the 57th Annual Meeting of the Association for Computational Linguistics*, pages 1668–1678, Florence, Italy. Association for Computational Linguistics.

Maarten Sap, Saadia Gabriel, Lianhui Qin, Dan Jurafsky, Noah A. Smith, and Yejin Choi. 2020. Social bias frames: Reasoning about social and power implications of language. In *Proceedings of the 58th Annual Meeting of the Association for Computational Linguistics*, pages 5477–5490, Online. Association for Computational Linguistics.

Arthur K. Spears. 2015. African american standard english. In Green Lisa J. Bloomquist, Jennifer and Sonja L. Lanehart, editors, *The Oxford Handbook of Innovation*, chapter 43, pages 786–799. Oxford University Press, Oxford.

Arthur K. Spears and Leanne Hinton. 2010. Languages and speakers: An introduction to african american english and native american languages. *Transforming Anthropology*, 18(1):3–14.

Steve Durairaj Swamy, Anupam Jamatia, and Björn Gambäck. 2019. Studying generalisability across abusive language detection datasets. In *Proceedings of the 23rd Conference on Computational Natural Language Learning (CoNLL)*, pages 940–950, Hong Kong, China. Association for Computational Linguistics.

Rachael Tatman. 2017. Gender and dialect bias in YouTube's automatic captions. In *Proceedings of the First ACL Workshop on Ethics in Natural Language Processing*, pages 53–59, Valencia, Spain. Association for Computational Linguistics.

Svitlana Volkova, Theresa Wilson, and David Yarowsky. 2013. Exploring demographic language variations to improve multilingual sentiment analysis in social media. In *Proceedings of the 2013 Conference on Empirical Methods in Natural Language Processing*, pages 1815–1827, Seattle, Washington, USA. Association for Computational Linguistics.

Zeerak Waseem. 2016. Are you a racist or am I seeing things? annotator influence on hate speech detection on Twitter. In *Proceedings of the First Workshop on NLP and Computational Social Science*, pages 138–142, Austin, Texas. Association for Computational Linguistics.

Michael Wiegand, Josef Ruppenhofer, and Thomas Kleinbauer. 2019. Detection of Abusive Language: the Problem of Biased Datasets. In *Proceedings of the 2019 Conference of the North American Chapter of the Association for Computational Linguistics: Human Language Technologies, Volume 1 (Long and Short Papers)*, pages 602–608, Minneapolis, Minnesota. Association for Computational Linguistics.

Mengzhou Xia, Anjalie Field, and Yulia Tsvetkov. 2020. Demoting racial bias in hate speech detection. In *Proceedings of the Eighth International Workshop on Natural Language Processing for Social Media*, pages 7–14, Online. Association for Computational Linguistics.

Xuhui Zhou, Maarten Sap, Swabha Swayamdipta, Yejin Choi, and Noah Smith. 2021. Challenges in automated debiasing for toxic language detection. In *Proceedings of the 16th Conference of the European Chapter of the Association for Computational Linguistics: Main Volume*, pages 3143–3155, Online. Association for Computational Linguistics.

Analysis of Gender Bias in Social Perception and Judgement Using Chinese Word Embeddings

Jiali Li[1†], **Shucheng Zhu**[2†], **Ying Liu**[2‡], **Pengyuan Liu**[1,3‡]
[1]School of Information Science, Beijing Language and Culture University, Beijing, China
[2]School of Humanities, Tsinghua University, Beijing, China
[3]National print Media Language Resources Monitoring & Research Center, Beijing Language and Culture University, Beijing, China
lijiali9925@163.com, zhu_shucheng@126.com, yingliu@tsinghua.edu.cn, liupengyuan@pku.edu.cn

Abstract

Gender is a construction in line with social perception and judgment. An important means of this construction is through languages. When natural language processing tools, such as word embeddings, associate gender with the relevant categories of social perception and judgment, it is likely to cause bias and harm to those groups that do not conform to the mainstream social perception and judgment. Using 12,251 Chinese word embeddings as intermedium, this paper studies the relationship between social perception and judgment categories and gender. The results reveal that these grammatical gender-neutral Chinese word embeddings show a certain gender bias, which is consistent with the mainstream society's perception and judgment of gender. Men are judged by their actions and perceived as bad, easily-disgusted, bad-tempered and rational roles while women are judged by their appearances and perceived as perfect, either happy or sad, and emotional roles.

1 Introduction

One of the main ways to construct gender in society is through languages. People's languages towards infants of different genders can well illustrate the gender construction of languages as a medium. When people believe that infants are female, they talk to them more gently. When people believe that infants are male, they handle infants more playfully. Through these differential treatments, boys and girls finally learn to be different (Eckert and McConnell-Ginet, 2013). As the boys and girls grow up, they start to perform the "correct" gender manners to be consistent with the gender judgment and perception of mainstream society. In other words, gender possesses performativity (Butler, 2002). As a result, in the process of construction repetition reinforcement, gender gradually solidifies the differences that should not be caused by gender and may cause unexpected biases and harms. The process is always through languages which represent the mainstream social judgment and perception.

As an analytic language, Chinese does have referential gender and lexical gender, such as "她" means "she" in referential gender and "爸爸" means "father" in lexical gender. However, Chinese lacks grammatical gender, comparing to French, Spanish and some of the fusional languages (Cao and Daumé III, 2020). As a result, it is difficult to find explicit and quantitative clues between gender and categories in social perception and judgement in Chinese. Word embedding is powerful and efficient in Natural Language Processing (NLP). Therefore, using word embeddings to find the implicit gender bias in Chinese can be an appropriate tool to analyze the associations between gender and categories in social perception and judgement. To make it clear, we define four categories of social perception and judgment and the linguistic features that can measure their gender bias, as shown in Table 1.

In this paper, we first gave our definition of gender bias. Then, by using semantic similarity, the implicit gender bias was measured in 12,251 Chinese word embeddings. Examples articulate that this measurement can capture the gendered word embeddings in a language without grammatical gender. Then, part-of-speech, sentiment polarity, emotion category, and semantic category were labeled to each word. We analyzed the relationships between gendered word embeddings and linguistic features to find the associations between gender and different categories in social perception and judgement. Results showed that we perceive and judge men and women with different social categories. Men are judged by their actions and perceived as bad, easily-disgusted, bad-tempered

† Equal contribution.
‡ Corresponding authors.

Proceedings of the The 4th Workshop on Gender Bias in Natural Language Processing (GeBNLP), pages 8 - 16
July 15, 2022 ©2022 Association for Computational Linguistics

Category	Definition	Linguistic Metrics
Activity	To what extent do social perception or description of a person relate one's gender to appearance or action.	Part-of-speech
Sentiment Polarity	To what extent do social perception or judgment of a person relate one's gender to positive or negative sentiment.	Sentiment Polarity
Emotion Category	To what extent do social perception or judgment of a person relate one's gender to specific emotion categories, such as anger, happiness and sadness.	Emotion Category
Content	To what extent do social perception or judgment of a person relate one's gender to specific topics, such as psychology, state and abstraction.	Semantic Category

Table 1: Definitions and linguistic features of 4 categories of social perception and judgement

and rational roles while women are judged by their appearances and perceived as perfect, either happy or sad, and emotional roles. This method is neat, while it offers a quantitative view to study the relationship between gender and different categories in perception and judgement in Chinese society and culture.

2 Bias Statement

In this paper, we study stereotypical associations between gender and different categories in social perception and judgment through Chinese word embeddings. Most of the Chinese words are grammatical gender-neutral. However, if the Chinese word embeddings show gender differences in different categories of part-of-speech, sentiment polarity, emotion category and semantic category, it may show that these gender-neutral word embeddings represent our stereotypes towards different genders. For example, we always judge a woman by her appearance but judge a man by his action. Although these stereotypical generalizations may not be negative, once these stereotypical representations are used in downstream NLP applications, the system may ignore, or even do harms to those people who are not consistent with the mainstream social perception and judgement of gender. Hence, this stereotypical association can be regarded as bias which may cause representational harms (Blodgett et al., 2020). In other words, the uniqueness between person and person is erased, and the system only retains gender differences. The ideal state is that people will not be treated unfairly because of their genders, especially to those are not consistent with the mainstream social perception and judgement of gender, and the system should not emphasize certain characteristics of a person according to one's gender.

3 Dataset

The Chinese word embeddings[1] we selected were pre-trained with Baidu Encyclopedia Corpus, using word2vec model and the method of Skip-Gram with Negative Sampling (SGNS). The size of Baidu Encyclopedia corpus is 4.1GB and the corpus contains 745M tokens (Li et al., 2018). Baidu Encyclopedia is an open online encyclopedia like Wikipedia, with entries covering almost all areas of Chinese knowledge. The encyclopedia characteristic of Baidu Encyclopedia determines that the language it uses is more objective and gender-neutral. The total amount of the word embeddings is 636,013 and each word embedding contains 300 dimensions. After labelling part-of-speech, sentiment polarity, emotion category, and semantic category, only 12,376 words contain all the information we need. Then, we calculated Odds Ratio (OR) values of each word and only selected those within three standard deviations from the mean. At last, we kept 12,251 word embeddings as our dataset. Almost all the words are gender-neutral as Chinese is a language without grammatical gender. Different token numbers of Chinese word embeddings in part-of-speech, sentiment polarity, emotion category, and semantic category are shown in Table 2.

Part-of-speech. The part-of-speech labels were selected from Affective Lexicon Ontology[2] (Xu et al., 2008). As we all know, the part-of-speech of many Chinese words may change in different contexts. However, the Chinese word embedding we chose is not contextualized. Among the 12,251 words in our dataset, only 37 words are multi-category words. We thought that the number is small and would not affect the results and analysis. Therefore, we chose one of the tags in Affective

[1] https://github.com/Embedding/Chinese-Word-Vectors

[2] http://ir.dlut.edu.cn/info/1013/1142.htm

Part-of-speech	Adjective	Adverb	Idiom	Noun	Prep	Verb	Net-words	Total
Tokens	3586	39	3417	2618	63	2514	14	12251
Sentiment Polarity	**Positive**	**Negative**	**Neutral**	**Both**				**Total**
Tokens	4675	4628	2908	40				12251
Emotion Category	**Disgust**	**Good**	**Sadness**	**Fear**	**Anger**	**Happiness**	**Astonishment**	**Total**
Tokens	4694	4858	917	538	169	99	976	12251
Semantic Category	**Activity**	**Action**	**Object**	**Association**	**Aid language**	**Characteristic**	**Honorific language**	**Total**
Tokens	2037	177	367	279	167	4418	22	
	Person	**State**	**Time and space**	**Abstraction**	**Psychology**			12251
	829	1009	1561	1252	133			

Table 2: Word embedding tokens labeled in different linguistic features in our dataset

Lexicon Ontology as its part-of-speech label for analysis. There are 7 labels of the part-of-speech. To balance the amount for analysis, we only chose the words labeled "noun", "verb" and "adjective" to compute and analyze. Here, we assume that nouns and adjectives are related to the appearance of what people perceive and judge, while verbs are related to action.

Sentiment Polarity. Affective Lexicon Ontology also offers 4 labels of the sentiment polarity, and we chose the words labeled "positive" and "negative" to analyze.

Emotion Category. According to Ekman's six basic emotions (Ekman, 1999) and the characteristic of Chinese, the Affective Lexicon Ontology offers 7 labels for the sentiment category: "good" (including "respect", "praise", "believe", "love" and "wish" to make a more detailed division of commendatory emotion), "anger", "disgust", "fear", "happiness", "sadness", and "astonishment".

Semantic Category. Our semantic category labels are from HIT IR-Lab Tongyici Cilin (Extended)[3]. It organized all the entries in a tree-like hierarchy, and divided the words into 12 semantic categories. We only chose the top 5 categories related to human and with the largest number of tokens to analyze: "abstraction", "activity", "characteristic", "state" and "psychology".

4 Experiments

In this section, we will illustrate the methodology to analyze the gendered word embeddings and how they are associated to different categories in our social perception and judgement. We first used semantic similarity and odds ratio to evaluate each word embedding. Then, independent-samples t test, one-factor Analysis of Variance (ANOVA) and Kruskal-Wallis test were used respectively to analyze the relationships between gender and categories in social perception and judgement.

Masculine Words	Meaning	Feminine Words	Meaning
爸爸	dad	妈妈	mom
父亲	father	母亲	mother
姥爷	mother's father	姥姥	mother's mother[4]
外公	mother's father	外婆	mother's mother[5]
爷爷	father's father	奶奶	father's mother
哥哥	elder brother	姐姐	elder sister
弟弟	younger brother	妹妹	younger sister
儿子	son	女儿	daughter
男友	boyfriend	女友	girlfriend
叔叔	uncle	阿姨	aunt
他	he	她	she
男	male	女	female
男人	men	女人	women
男子	man	女子	woman
男士	Mr.	女士	Ms.
先生	Sir	小姐	Miss
男孩	boy	女孩	girl
男性	males	女性	females

Table 3: Gendered Words

Semantic Similarity. We first selected and translated 14 masculine words and corresponding 14 feminine words as Gendered Words G into Chinese from related study in English (Nadeem et al., 2020), showed in Table 3. These words are lexical gender words or referential gender words in Chinese. Then, we calculated the cosine similarity as the semantic similarity S between each word embedding in our dataset W and the word embeddings of Gendered Words G according to equation 1. Here, n means the total dimension of each word embedding. We took the mean cosine similarity between one W and the total Feminine word embeddings as the Feminine Similarity S_f. Masculine Similarity S_m of one W is as the same. The closer to 1 the value of S is, the word W is more masculine or feminine.

$$S = \frac{\sum_{i=1}^{n} W_i \times G_i}{\sqrt{\sum_{i=1}^{n}(W_i)^2} \times \sqrt{\sum_{i=1}^{n}(G_i)^2}} \quad (1)$$

[3] https://github.com/Xls1994/Cilin

[4] "姥爷" and "姥姥" are usually used in northern China.

[5] "外公" and "外婆" are usually used in southern China.

Odds Ratio. OR (Szumilas, 2010) was used to calculate the Gendered value OR of each word embedding W in our dataset as equation 2 shows. Here, N is the total number of word embeddings in our dataset. To facilitate the test, we selected OR values within three standard deviations from the mean and normalized all data to $OR_G \in [-1, 1]$.

$$OR(w) = \frac{S_m(W)}{\sum_{j=1}^{N} S_m(W_j)} / \frac{S_f(W)}{\sum_{j=1}^{N} S_f(W_j)} \quad (2)$$

The closer the OR_G is to 1, the more masculine the word is. The closer the OR_G is to -1, the more feminine the word is.

Independent-samples T Test. On sentiment polarity, we conducted an independent-sample t test of OR_G value to explore the relationship between gender and sentiment polarity in social perception and judgement as the variances are homogeneous.

One-factor ANOVA. On part-of-speech, we conducted one-factor ANOVA of OR_G value to explore the relationship between gender and activity in social perception and judgement as the different token numbers in part-of-speech are sufficient and approximate.

Kruskal-Wallis test. On the categories of emotion category and semantic category, we conducted Kruskal-Wallis test of OR_G value respectively to explore the relationships between gender and emotion category and content in social perception and judgement as the variances in these two categories are different and the token numbers vary widely.

5 Results

Gendered Word Embeddings. We selected the top 5 masculine and feminine word embeddings of grammatical gender-neutral words according to the OR_G value showed in Table 4. It is clear to see that the masculine words are related to "war" and "power" and the feminine words are related to "flower" and "beauty" which conforms to our stereotypes of gender. It indicates our measurement can detect the implicit gender bias in word embeddings of the language without grammatical gender.

Gender and Activity. We define activity as the extent to which we perceive or describe a person's gender in relation to one's appearance or action. Here, we think that verbs can represent perceiving and describing a person's action, and nouns and adjectives can represent perceiving and describing a person's appearance. Figure 1(a) shows that verbs (M=0.022) are more masculine than nouns (M=0.003) and adjectives (M=-0.064) and they have significant differences ($p<0.001$). It means that in social perception and judgment, we associate actions with men, appearances with women. It may indicate that we always perceive a woman with her appearance and judge a man by his action (Caldas-Coulthard and Moon, 2010). Sociolinguistic clues support this conjecture. Appearance is seen as applicable to the female gender category as there are subcategories elaborated specifically for women far more than men (Eckert and McConnell-Ginet, 2013). This supports that our society emphasizes appearance on women rather than men. Other studies also show that we use positive adjectives to describe a woman's body rather than a man (Hoyle et al., 2019). The most representative example is in mate selection. Men care much about women's appearance and women care much about men's power, status and wealth (Baker, 2014). Once man-action and woman-appearance associations are established, it may cause gender bias. The systems emphasize a woman's appearance over her other strengths, which may hurt women who are less attractive.

Word	Meaning	Part-of-speech	OR_G
所向披靡	invincible	idiom	1
戎马	army horse	noun	0.9985
让位	abdicate	verb	0.9968
广开言路	open communication	idiom	0.9918
死守	defend to death	verb	0.9906
盛开	bloom	verb	-1
婵娟	moon	adjective	-0.9933
火树银花	Hottest Silver	idiom	-0.9927
并蒂莲	Twin flowers	idiom	-0.9879
天仙	fairy	noun	-0.9811

Table 4: The top 5 masculine and feminine word embeddings of grammatical gender-neutral words according to the OR_G value

Gender and Sentiment Polarity. Figure 1(b) shows that positive words (M=-0.017) are more feminine than negative words (M=0.034) and they have significant difference ($p<0.001$). This associates men with negative sentiments and women with positive ones. This may imply that in our society, we perceive women in a positive way and we can perceive men in a negative way. It can be reflected fully in children's literature which al-

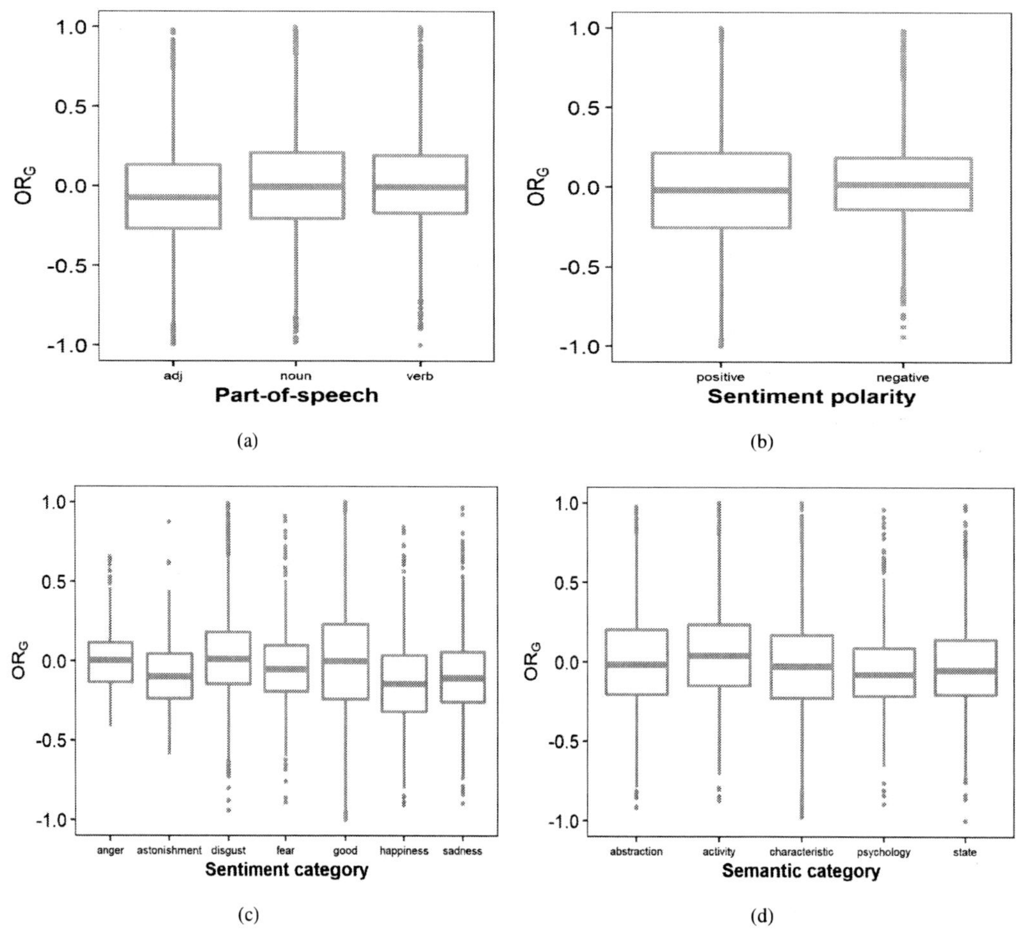

Figure 1: The distribution of OR_G in part-of-speech, sentiment polarity, emotion category, and semantic category

ways portrays "a good girl" and "a bad boy" (Peterson and Lach, 1990; Stevinson Hillman, 1974; Kortenhaus and Demarest, 1993). This point can be explained by the different gender views on compliments. Women are more likely to compliment and be complimented than men, because for women, compliments strengthen their solidarity with others in the communities of practice. However, complimenting men can challenge a men's authority and power because complimenting a man implies that he is being judged (Tannen, 1991; Holmes, 2013). Over time, women tend to develop a steady bond with positive sentiments. This seems to be a protection for women, but it is actually a benevolent sexism (Glick and Fiske, 2001). The negative man image indicates that we have a certain tolerance to man, while the positive woman image is more like a bondage to women. We expect women to be gentle and submissive all the time, while men can be negative and aggressive.

Gender and Emotion Category. Figure 1(c) shows that from the most masculine to the most feminine, the emotion categories are disgust (M=0.030), anger (M=0.025), good (M=-0.003), fear (M=-0.025), astonishment (M=-0.083), sadness (M=-0.089), and happiness (M=-0.130). Disgust and anger emotions have significant differences with other emotions ($p<0.05$). It indicates that we associate disgust and anger emotions with men rather than women. Sadness and happiness emotions have significant difference with other emotions ($p<0.05$). It indicates that we associate happiness and sadness emotions with women rather than men. Thus, in our social perception and judgment, men may be viewed with negative emotions, such as anger and disgust, while women are either happy or sad. In movies and books, whether women are sad and happy depending highly on men, and most of men in books and movies do not show intense emotions of happiness or sadness (Xu et al., 2019). When annotators annotated the author's gender for tweets with unknown gender of authors, the tweets contained anger emotion will be regarded as the most confident male clues, while happy emotion as the most confident female clues (Flekova et al., 2016). These stereotypes associating emotions with genders can lead to bias. Anger and disgust are active emotions, meaning men are free to express their negative emotions. While happy and sad emotions related to women are often passive, meaning that women are dominated. The system may learn such bias when generating text. It may place women in a subordinate position to men.

Gender and Content. Here, Content refers to the specific topics we associate with a gender role. Figure 1(d) shows that activity words (M=0.057) are the most masculine while psychology words (M=-0.050) are the most feminine. Activity words have significant difference with other words ($p<0.001$). So are the psychology words ($p<0.05$). This links men to activity and women to psychology. If we regard activity as a concrete rational action and psychology as an emotional cognition, then in society, man may be a rational role and woman may be an emotional role. In study of different languages used by men and women, it is found that women prefer to use more emotional words than men (Savoy, 2018). Our society has a strong normative view that women are interested in connecting with others and promoting warmth around them. Men are generally not interested in other people and relationships. Men should focus on their goals and achievements and what they can do. As a result, women have a strong motivation to show attachment, a desire to promote the emotional feelings and downplay their personal goals and aspirations. Men, by contrast, have powerful motivations to appear strong and rational, to mask emotions, and to hide a desire to be intimate with others (Eckert and McConnell-Ginet, 2013). Such stereotypes suppress man's emotional needs and ignore woman's rational power.

6 Related Works

It was studied that word embeddings contain all kinds of biases in human society, including gender bias. These biases come from the biased data in the corpus which reflect the biased languages we use daily and from the bias of the annotators when they annotate the datasets (Van Durme, 2009). NLP algorithms may amplify the biases contained in the datasets (Sun et al., 2019). Some word embeddings of neutral words such as "nurse", "social" were proved to have closer similarities with gender words (e.g. "male", "boy", "female", and "girl") (Friedman et al., 2019; Garg et al., 2018; Brunet et al., 2019; Wevers, 2019; Santana et al., 2018; Mishra et al., 2019; Zhao et al., 2018). The latest contextualized word embeddings also have gender bias but the degree of the bias may not as much as that of traditional word embeddings (Zhao et al., 2019; Basta et al., 2019; Kurita et al., 2019; Swinger et al., 2019). In addition, multilingual embeddings contain gender bias (Lewis and Lupyan, 2020) and the bias is related to the types of different languages (Zhao et al., 2020). Word Embedding Association Test (WEAT) can be used to measure gender bias in word embeddings (Caliskan et al., 2017; Tan and Celis, 2019; Chaloner and Maldonado, 2019) and this method can also be expanded to sentence level as Sentence Encoder Association Test (SEAT) (May et al., 2019). Another method to detect and measure the gender bias in word embeddings is to analyze gender subspace in embeddings (Bolukbasi et al., 2016; Manzini et al., 2019). But this method may not show the whole gender bias in word embeddings. Some of the implicit gender bias cannot be measured and caught (Gonen and Goldberg, 2019).

7 Conclusion

In this paper, we used word embeddings to detect and measure the implicit gender bias in a language without grammatical gender. Relationships between gender and four categories in social perception and judgement are also shown according to our measurement values. Word embeddings show that we judge a woman by her appearance and perceive her as a "perfect", either happy or sad, and emotional role while we judge a man by his action and perceive him as a "bad", easily-disgusted, bad-tempered, and rational role. It may cause gender bias. This systematic bias intensifies gender differences, solidifies stereotypes about men and women, erases the uniqueness of differences between person and person, and harms those do not conform to mainstream social perception and judgment and those who do not fit in the gender dichotomy. In the future, we can choose more dimensions rather than man/woman for investigation, such as in-group/inter-group, animate/inanimate, collectivism/individualism, etc.

Acknowledgements

This research project is supported by Fundamental Research Funds for the Central Universities, the Research Funds of Beijing Language and Culture University (22YCX029), and Science Foundation of Beijing Language and Culture University (supported by "the Fundamental Research Funds for the Central Universities") (20YBT07), and 2018 National Major Program of Philosophy and Social Science Fund "Analyses and Researches of Classic Texts of Classical Literature Based on Big Data Technology" (18ZDA238). We thank the reviewers for their useful feedback from both 4th Workshop on Gender Bias in Natural Language Processing (GeBNLP2022) and ACL Rolling Review.

References

Paul Baker. 2014. *Using Corpora to Analyze Gender*. Bloomsbury.

Christine Basta, Marta R Costa-jussà, and Noe Casas. 2019. Evaluating the underlying gender bias in contextualized word embeddings. In *Proceedings of the First Workshop on Gender Bias in Natural Language Processing*, pages 33–39.

Su Lin Blodgett, Solon Barocas, Hal Daumé III, and Hanna Wallach. 2020. Language (technology) is power: A critical survey of "bias" in nlp. In *Proceedings of the 58th Annual Meeting of the Association for Computational Linguistics*, pages 5454–5476.

Tolga Bolukbasi, Kai-Wei Chang, James Y Zou, Venkatesh Saligrama, and Adam T Kalai. 2016. Man is to computer programmer as woman is to homemaker? debiasing word embeddings. *Advances in Neural Information Processing Systems*, 29:4349–4357.

Marc-Etienne Brunet, Colleen Alkalay-Houlihan, Ashton Anderson, and Richard Zemel. 2019. Understanding the origins of bias in word embeddings. In *International Conference on Machine Learning*, pages 803–811. PMLR.

Judith Butler. 2002. *Gender Trouble*. Routledge.

Carmen Rosa Caldas-Coulthard and Rosamund Moon. 2010. 'curvy, hunky, kinky': Using corpora as tools for critical analysis. *Discourse & Society*, 21(2):99–133.

Aylin Caliskan, Joanna J Bryson, and Arvind Narayanan. 2017. Semantics derived automatically from language corpora contain human-like biases. *Science*, 356(6334):183–186.

Yang Trista Cao and Hal Daumé III. 2020. Toward gender-inclusive coreference resolution. In *Proceedings of the 58th Annual Meeting of the Association for Computational Linguistics*, pages 4568–4595.

Kaytlin Chaloner and Alfredo Maldonado. 2019. Measuring gender bias in word embeddings across domains and discovering new gender bias word categories. In *Proceedings of the First Workshop on Gender Bias in Natural Language Processing*, pages 25–32.

Penelope Eckert and Sally McConnell-Ginet. 2013. *Language and Gender*. Cambridge University Press.

Paul Ekman. 1999. Basic emotions. In *Handbook of Cognition and Emotion*, pages 45–60.

Lucie Flekova, Jordan Carpenter, Salvatore Giorgi, Lyle Ungar, and Daniel Preoţiuc-Pietro. 2016. Analyzing biases in human perception of user age and gender from text. In *Proceedings of the 54th Annual Meeting of the Association for Computational Linguistics (Volume 1: Long Papers)*, pages 843–854.

Scott Friedman, Sonja Schmer-Galunder, Anthony Chen, and Jeffrey Rye. 2019. Relating word embedding gender biases to gender gaps: A cross-cultural analysis. In *Proceedings of the First Workshop on Gender Bias in Natural Language Processing*, pages 18–24.

Nikhil Garg, Londa Schiebinger, Dan Jurafsky, and James Zou. 2018. Word embeddings quantify 100 years of gender and ethnic stereotypes. *Proceedings of the National Academy of Sciences*, 115(16):E3635–E3644.

Peter Glick and Susan T Fiske. 2001. An ambivalent alliance: Hostile and benevolent sexism as complementary justifications for gender inequality. *American psychologist*, 56(2):109.

Hila Gonen and Yoav Goldberg. 2019. Lipstick on a pig: Debiasing methods cover up systematic gender biases in word embeddings but do not remove them. In *Proceedings of the 2019 Conference of the North American Chapter of the Association for Computational Linguistics: Human Language Technologies, Volume 1 (Long and Short Papers)*, pages 609–614.

Janet Holmes. 2013. *Women, Men and Politeness*. Routledge.

Alexander Miserlis Hoyle, Lawrence Wolf-Sonkin, Hanna Wallach, Isabelle Augenstein, and Ryan Cotterell. 2019. Unsupervised discovery of gendered language through latent-variable modeling. In *Proceedings of the 57th Annual Meeting of the Association for Computational Linguistics*, pages 1706–1716.

Carole M Kortenhaus and Jack Demarest. 1993. Gender role stereotyping in children's literature: An update. *Sex Roles*, 28(3):219–232.

Keita Kurita, Nidhi Vyas, Ayush Pareek, Alan W Black, and Yulia Tsvetkov. 2019. Measuring bias in contextualized word representations. In *Proceedings of the First Workshop on Gender Bias in Natural Language Processing*, pages 166–172.

Molly Lewis and Gary Lupyan. 2020. Gender stereotypes are reflected in the distributional structure of 25 languages. *Nature human behaviour*, 4(10):1021–1028.

Shen Li, Zhe Zhao, Renfen Hu, Wensi Li, Tao Liu, and Xiaoyong Du. 2018. Analogical reasoning on chinese morphological and semantic relations. In *Proceedings of the 56th Annual Meeting of the Association for Computational Linguistics (Volume 2: Short Papers)*, pages 138–143. Association for Computational Linguistics.

Thomas Manzini, Lim Yao Chong, Alan W Black, and Yulia Tsvetkov. 2019. Black is to criminal as caucasian is to police: Detecting and removing multiclass bias in word embeddings. In *Proceedings of the 2019 Conference of the North American Chapter of the Association for Computational Linguistics: Human Language Technologies, Volume 1 (Long and Short Papers)*, pages 615–621.

Chandler May, Alex Wang, Shikha Bordia, Samuel Bowman, and Rachel Rudinger. 2019. On measuring social biases in sentence encoders. In *Proceedings of the 2019 Conference of the North American Chapter of the Association for Computational Linguistics: Human Language Technologies, Volume 1 (Long and Short Papers)*, pages 622–628.

Arul Mishra, Himanshu Mishra, and Shelly Rathee. 2019. Examining the presence of gender bias in customer reviews using word embedding. *arXiv preprint arXiv:1902.00496*.

Moin Nadeem, Anna Bethke, and Siva Reddy. 2020. Stereoset: Measuring stereotypical bias in pretrained language models. *arXiv preprint arXiv:2004.09456*.

Sharyl Bender Peterson and Mary Alyce Lach. 1990. Gender stereotypes in children's books: Their prevalence and influence on cognitive and affective development. *Gender and Education*, 2(2):185–197.

Brenda Salenave Santana, Vinicius Woloszyn, and Leandro Krug Wives. 2018. Is there gender bias and stereotype in portuguese word embeddings? In *Proceedings of the 13th Edition of the International Conference on the Computational Processing of Portuguese*.

Jacques Savoy. 2018. Trump's and clinton's style and rhetoric during the 2016 presidential election. *Journal of Quantitative Linguistics*, 25(2):168–189.

Judith Stevinson Hillman. 1974. An analysis of male and female roles in two periods of children's literature. *The Journal of Educational Research*, 68(2):84–88.

Tony Sun, Andrew Gaut, Shirlyn Tang, Yuxin Huang, Mai ElSherief, Jieyu Zhao, Diba Mirza, Elizabeth Belding, Kai-Wei Chang, and William Yang Wang. 2019. Mitigating gender bias in natural language processing: Literature review. In *Proceedings of the 57th Annual Meeting of the Association for Computational Linguistics*, pages 1630–1640.

Nathaniel Swinger, Maria De-Arteaga, Neil Thomas Heffernan IV, Mark DM Leiserson, and Adam Tauman Kalai. 2019. What are the biases in my word embedding? In *Proceedings of the 2019 AAAI/ACM Conference on AI, Ethics, and Society*, pages 305–311.

Magdalena Szumilas. 2010. Explaining odds ratios. *Journal of the Canadian Academy of Child and Adolescent psychiatry*, 19(3):227.

Yi Chern Tan and L Elisa Celis. 2019. Assessing social and intersectional biases in contextualized word representations. In *Proceedings of Advances in Neural Information Processing Systems*, pages 13209–13220.

Deborah Tannen. 1991. *You Just Don't Understand: Women and Men in Conversation*. Virago London.

Benjamin D Van Durme. 2009. *Extracting Implicit Knowledge from Text*. University of Rochester.

Melvin Wevers. 2019. Using word embeddings to examine gender bias in dutch newspapers, 1950-1990. In *Proceedings of the 1st International Workshop on Computational Approaches to Historical Language Change*, pages 92–97.

Huimin Xu, Zhang Zhang, Lingfei Wu, and Cheng-Jun Wang. 2019. The cinderella complex: Word embeddings reveal gender stereotypes in movies and books. *PloS one*, 14(11):e0225385.

Linhong Xu, Hongfei Lin, Yu Pan, Hui Ren, and Jianmei Chen. 2008. Constructing the affective lexicon ontology. *Journal of the China Society for Scientific and Technical Information*, 27:180–185.

Jieyu Zhao, Subhabrata Mukherjee, Saghar Hosseini, Kai-Wei Chang, and Ahmed Hassan Awadallah. 2020. Gender bias in multilingual embeddings and cross-lingual transfer. In *Proceedings of the 58th Annual Meeting of the Association for Computational Linguistics*, pages 2896–2907.

Jieyu Zhao, Tianlu Wang, Mark Yatskar, Ryan Cotterell, Vicente Ordonez, and Kai-Wei Chang. 2019. Gender bias in contextualized word embeddings. In *Proceedings of the 2019 Conference of the North American Chapter of the Association for Computational Linguistics: Human Language Technologies, Volume 1 (Long and Short Papers)*, pages 629–634.

Jieyu Zhao, Yichao Zhou, Zeyu Li, Wei Wang, and Kai-Wei Chang. 2018. Learning gender-neutral word embeddings. In *Proceedings of the 2018 Conference on Empirical Methods in Natural Language Processing*, pages 4847–4853.

Don't Forget About Pronouns: Removing Gender Bias in Language Models Without Losing Factual Gender Information

Tomasz Limisiewicz and **David Mareček**
Institute of Formal and Applied Linguistics, Faculty of Mathematics and Physics
Charles University, Prague, Czech Republic
{limisiewicz, marecek}@ufal.mff.cuni.cz

Abstract

The representations in large language models contain multiple types of gender information. We focus on two types of such signals in English texts: factual gender information, which is a grammatical or semantic property, and gender bias, which is the correlation between a word and specific gender. We can disentangle the model's embeddings and identify components encoding both types of information with probing. We aim to diminish the stereotypical bias in the representations while preserving the factual gender signal. Our filtering method shows that it is possible to decrease the bias of gender-neutral profession names without significant deterioration of language modeling capabilities. The findings can be applied to language generation to mitigate reliance on stereotypes while preserving gender agreement in coreferences.[1]

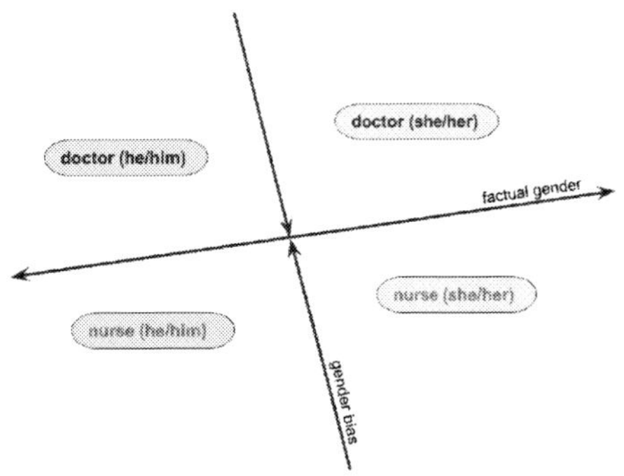

Figure 1: A schema is presenting the distinction between gender bias of nouns and factual (i.e., grammatical) gender in pronouns. We want to transform the representations to mitigate the former and preserve the latter.

1 Introduction

Neural networks are successfully applied in natural language processing. While they achieve state-of-the-art results on various tasks, their decision process is not yet fully explained (Lipton, 2018). It is often the case that neural networks base their prediction on spurious correlations learned from large uncurated datasets. An example of such a spurious tendency is gender bias. Even the state-of-the-art models tend to counterfactually associate some words with a specific gender (Zhao et al., 2018a; Stanovsky et al., 2019). The representations of profession names tend to be closely connected with the stereotypical gender of their holders. When the model encounters the word "nurse", it will tend to use female pronouns ("she", "her") when referring to this person in the generated text. This tendency is reversed for words such as "doctor", "professor", or "programmer", which are male-biased.

It means that the neural model is not reliable enough to be applied in high-stakes language processing tasks such as connecting job offers to applicants' CVs (De-Arteaga et al., 2019). If the underlying model was biased, the high-paying jobs, which are stereotypically associated with men, could be inaccessible for female candidates. When we decide to use language models for that purpose, the key challenge is to ensure that their predictions are fair.

The recent works on the topics aimed to diminish the role of gender bias by feeding examples of unbiased text and training the network (de Vassimon Manela et al., 2021) or transforming the representations of the neural networks post-hoc (without additional training) (Bolukbasi et al., 2016). However, those works relied on the notion that to de-bias representation, most gender signal needs to be eliminated. It is not always the case, pronouns and a few other words (e.g.:"king" -"queen"; "boy" - "girl") have factual information about gender. A few works identified gendered words and

[1]Our code is available on GitHub: github.com/tomlimi/Gender-Bias-vs-Information

Proceedings of the The 4th Workshop on Gender Bias in Natural Language Processing (GeBNLP), pages 17 - 29
July 15, 2022 ©2022 Association for Computational Linguistics

exempted them from de-biasing (Zhao et al., 2018b; Kaneko and Bollegala, 2019). In contrast to these approaches, we focus on contextual word embeddings. In contextual representations, we want to preserve the factual gender information for gender-neutral words when it is indicated by context, e.g., personal pronoun. This sort of information needs to be maintained in the representations. In language modeling, the network needs to be consistent about the gender of a person if it was revealed earlier in the text. The model's ability to encode factual gender information is crucial for that purpose.

We propose a method for disentangling the factual gender information and gender bias encoded in the representations. We hypothesise that semantic gender information (from pronouns) is encoded in the network distinctly from the stereotypical bias of gender-neutral words (Figure 1). We apply an orthogonal probe, which proved to be useful, e.g., in separating lexical and syntactic information encoded in the neural model (Limisiewicz and Mareček, 2021). Then we filter out the bias subspace from the embedding space and keep the subspace encoding factual gender information. We show that this method performs well in both desired properties: decreasing the network's reliance on bias while retaining knowledge about factual gender.

1.1 Terminology

We consider two types of gender information encoded in text:

- **Factual gender** is the grammatical (pronouns "he", "she", "her", etc.) or semantic ("boy", "girl", etc.) feature of specific word. It can also be indicated by a coreference link. We will call words with factual gender as *gendered* in contrast to *gender-neutral* words.
- **Gender bias** is the connection between a word and the specific gender with which it is usually associated, regardless of the factual premise.[2] We will refer to words with gender bias as *biased* in contrast to *non-biased.*

Please note that those definitions do not preclude the existence of biased and at the same time gender-neutral words. In that case, we consider bias stereotypical and aim to mitigate it in our method. On the other hand, we want to preserve bias in gendered words.

2 Methods

We aim to remove the influence of gender-biased words while keeping the information about factual gender in the sentence given by pronouns. We focus on interactions of gender bias and factual gender information in coreference cues of the following form:

[NOUN] examined the farmer for injuries because [PRONOUN] was caring.

In English, we can expect to obtain the factual gender from the pronoun. Revealing one of the words in coreference link should impact the prediction of the other. Therefore we can name two causal associations:

$$C_I\text{: } \text{bias}_{\text{noun}} \rightarrow \text{f. gender}_{\text{pronoun}}$$

$$C_{II}\text{: } \text{f. gender}_{\text{pronoun}} \rightarrow \text{bias}_{\text{noun}}$$

In our method, we will primarily focus on two ways bias and factual gender interact. For gender-neutral nouns (in association C_I), the effect on predicting masked pronouns would be primarily correlated with their gender bias. At the same time, the second association is desirable, as it reveals factual gender information and can improve the masked token prediction of a gendered word. We define two conditional probability distributions corresponding to those causal associations:

$$\begin{aligned} P_I(y_{\text{pronoun}}|X, b) \\ P_{II}(y_{\text{noun}}|X, f) \end{aligned} \tag{1}$$

Where y is a token predicted in the position of pronoun and noun, respectively; X is the context for masked language modeling. b and f are bias and factual gender factors, respectively. We model the bias factor by using a gender-neutral biased noun. Below we present examples for introducing female and male bias: [3]

Example 1:

b_f **The nurse** examined the farmer for injuries because [PRONOUN] was caring.

b_m **The doctor** examined the farmer for injuries because [PRONOUN] was caring

[2]For instance, the words "nurse", "housekeeper" are associated with women, and words "doctor", "mechanic" with men. None of those words has a grammatical gender marking in English.

[3]We use [NOUN] and [PRONOUN] tokens for a better explanation, in practice, they both are masked by the same mask token, e.g. [MASK] in BERT (Devlin et al., 2019).

Similarly, the factual gender factor is modeled by introducing a pronoun with a specific gender in the sentence:

Example 2:

f_f [NOUN] examined the farmer for injuries because she was caring.

f_m [NOUN] examined the farmer for injuries because he was caring.

We aim to diminish the role of bias in the prediction of pronouns of a specific gender. On the other hand, the gender indicated in pronouns can be useful in the prediction of a gendered noun. Mathematically speaking, we want to drop the conditionality on bias factor in P_I from eq. (1), while keeping the conditionality on gender factor in P_{II}.

$$\begin{aligned} P_I(y_{\text{pronoun}}|X, b) &\rightarrow P_I(y_{\text{pronoun}}|X) \\ P_{II}(y_{\text{noun}}|X, f) &\not\rightarrow P_{II}(y_{\text{noun}}|X) \end{aligned} \tag{2}$$

To decrease the effect of gender signal from the words other than pronoun and noun, we introduce a baseline, where both pronoun and noun tokens are masked:

Example 3:

$\varnothing$ [NOUN] examined the farmer for injuries because [PRONOUN] was caring.

2.1 Evaluation of Bias

Manifestation of gender bias may vary significantly from model to model and can be attributed mainly to the choice of the pre-training corpora as well as the training regime. We define *gender preference* in a sentence by the ratio between the probability of predicting male and female pronouns:

$$GP(X) = \frac{P_I([\text{pronoun}_m]|X)}{P_I([\text{pronoun}_f]|X)} \tag{3}$$

To estimate the gender bias of a profession name, we compare the gender preference in a sentence where the profession word is masked (example 3 from the previous paragraph) and not masked (example 1). We define *relative gender preference*:

$$RGP_{\text{noun}} = \log(GP(X_{\text{noun}})) - \log(GP(X_{\varnothing})) \tag{4}$$

X_{noun} denotes contexts in which the noun is revealed (example 1), and $X_{\varnothing}$ corresponds to example 3, where we mask both the noun and the pronoun. Our approach focuses on the bias introduced by a noun, especially profession name. We subtract $\log(GP(X_{\varnothing}))$ to single out the bias contribution coming from the noun.[4] We use logarithm, so the results around zero would mean that revealing noun does not affect *gender preference*.[5]

2.2 Disentangling Gender Signals with Orthogonal Probe

To mitigate the influence of bias on the predictions eq. (2), we focus on the internal representations of the language model. We aim to inspect contextual representations of words and identify their parts that encode the causal associations C_I and C_{II}. For that purpose, we utilize *orthogonal structural probes* proposed by Limisiewicz and Mareček (2021).

In structural probing, the embedding vectors are transformed in a way so that distances between pairs of the projected embeddings approximate a linguistic feature, e.g., distance in a dependency tree (Hewitt and Manning, 2019). In our case, we want to approximate the gender information introduced by a gendered pronoun f (factual) and gender-neutral noun b (bias). The f takes the values -1 for female pronouns and, 1 for male ones, and 0 for gender-neutral "they". The b is the relative gender preference (eq. (4)) for a specific noun ($b \equiv RGP_{\text{noun}}$).

Our orthogonal probe consists of three trainable components:

- O: *orthogonal transformation*, mapping representation to new coordinate system.
- SV: *scaling vector*, element-wise scaling of the dimensions in a new coordinate systems. We assume that dimensions that store probed information are associated with large scaling coefficients.
- i: *intercept* shifting the representation.

O is a tunable orthogonal matrix of size $d_{\text{emb}} \times d_{\text{emb}}$, SV and i are tunable vectors of length d_{emb}, where d_{emb} is the dimensionality of model's embeddings. The probing losses are the following:

$$\begin{aligned} L_I &= \big|||SV_I \odot (O \cdot (h_{b,P} - h_{\varnothing,P})) - i_I||_d - b\big| \\ L_{II} &= \big|||SV_{II} \odot (O \cdot (h_{f,N} - h_{\varnothing,N})) - i_{II}||_d - f\big|, \end{aligned} \tag{5}$$

[4] Other parts of speech may also introduce gender bias, e.g., the verb "to work". We note that our setting can be generalized to all words, but it is outside of the scope of this work.

[5] The *relative gender preference* was inspired by *total effect* measure proposed by Vig et al. (2020).

where, $h_{b,P}$ is the vector representation of masked pronoun in example 1; $h_{f,N}$ is the vector representation of masked noun in example 2; vectors $h_{\varnothing,P}$ and $h_{\varnothing,N}$ are the representations of masked pronoun and noun respectively in baseline example 3.

To account for negative values of target factors (b and f) in eq. (5), we generalize distance metric to negative values in the following way:

$$||\vec{v}||_d = ||\max(\vec{0}, \vec{v})||_2 - ||\min(\vec{0}, \vec{v})||_2 \tag{6}$$

We jointly probe for both objectives (orthogonal transformation is shared). Limisiewicz and Mareček (2021) observed that the resulting scaling vector after optimization tends to be sparse, and thus they allow to find the subspace of the embedding space that encodes particular information.

2.3 Filtering Algorithm

In our algorithm we aim to filter out the latent vector's dimensions that encode bias. Particularly, we assume that, when $||h_{b,P} - h_{\varnothing,P}|| \rightarrow 0$ then $P_I(y_{\text{pronoun}}|X, b) \rightarrow P_I(y_{\text{pronoun}}|X)$

We can diminish the information by masking the dimensions with a corresponding scaling vector coefficient larger than small ϵ.[6] The bias filter is defined as:

$$F_{-b} = \vec{\mathbb{1}}[\epsilon > abs(SV_I)], \tag{7}$$

where $abs(\cdot)$ is element-wise absolute value and $\vec{\mathbb{1}}$ is element-wise indicator. We apply this vector to the representations of hidden layers:

$$\hat{h} = O^T \cdot (F_{-b} \odot (O \cdot h) + abs(SV_I) \odot i_I) \tag{8}$$

To preserve factual gender information, we propose an alternative version of the filter. The dimension is kept when its importance (measured by the absolute value of scaling vector coefficient) is higher in probing for factual gender than in probing for bias. We define factual gender preserving filter as:

$$F_{-b,+f} = F_{-b} + \vec{\mathbb{1}}[\epsilon \leq abs(SV_I) < abs(SV_{II})] \tag{9}$$

The filtering is performed as in eq. (8) We analyze the number of overlapping dimensions in two scaling vectors in Section 3.2.

[6]We take epsilon equal to 10^{-12}. Our results weren't particularly vulnerable to this parameter, we show the analysis in appendix C.

3 Experiments and Results

We examine the representation of two BERT models (base-cased: 12 layers, 768 embedding size; and large-cased: 24 layers, 1024 embedding size, Devlin et al. (2019)), and ELECTRA (base-generator: 12 layers, 256 embedding size Clark et al. (2020)). All the models are Transformer encoders trained on the masked language modeling objective.

3.1 Evaluation of Gender Bias in Language Models

Before constructing a de-biasing algorithm, we evaluate the bias in the prediction of three language models.

We evaluate the gender bias in language models on 104 gender-neutral professional words from the WinoBias dataset (Zhao et al., 2018a). The authors analyzed the data from the US Labor Force Statistics. They annotated 20 professions with the highest share of women as stereotypically female and 20 professions with the highest share of men as stereotypically male.

We run the inference on the prompts in five formats presented in Table 1 and estimate with equation eq. (4). To obtain the bias of the word in the model, we take mean RGP_{noun} computed on all prompts.

3.1.1 Results

We compare our results with the list of stereotypical words from the annotation of Zhao et al. (2018a). Similarly, we pick up to 20 nouns with the highest and positive RGP as male-biased and up to 20 nouns with the lowest and negative RGP as female-biased. These lists differ for models.

Table 2 presents the most biased words according to three models. Noticeably, there are differences between empirical and annotated bias. Especially word "salesperson" considered male-biased based on job market data was one of the most skewed toward the female gender in 2 out of 3 models. The full results of the evaluation can be found in appendix D.

3.2 Probing for Gender Bias and Factual Gender Information

We optimize the joint probe, where orthogonal transformation is shared, while scaling vectors and intercepts are task specific. The probing objective is to approximate: C_I) the gender bias of gender-neutral nouns ($b \equiv RGP_{\text{noun}}$); and

Prompt	PRONOUN	PRONOUN 2
[PRONOUN] is [NOUN].	She He	
[PRONOUN] was [NOUN].	She He	
[PRONOUN]works as [NOUN].	She He	
[PRONOUN] job is [NOUN].	Her His	
[NOUN]said that [PRONOUN] loves [PRONOUN 2] job.	he she	her his
[NOUN] said that [PRONOUN] hates [PRONOUN 2] job.	she he	her his

Table 1: List of evaluation prompts used in the evaluation of *relative gender preference*. The tag [NOUN] masks a noun accompanied by an appropriate determiner.

Most Female Biased				Most Male Biased			
NOUN	N Models	Avg. RGP	Annotated	NOUN	N Models	Avg. RGP	Annotated
housekeeper	3/3	-2.009	female	carpenter	3/3	0.870	male
nurse	3/3	-1.840	female	farmer	3/3	0.753	male
receptionist	3/3	-1.602	female	guard	3/3	0.738	male
hairdresser	3/3	-0.471	female	sheriff	3/3	0.651	male
librarian	2/3	-0.279	female	firefighter	3/3	0.779	**neutral**
victim	2/3	-0.102	**neutral**	driver	3/3	0.622	male
child	2/3	-0.060	**neutral**	mechanic	2/3	0.719	male
salesperson	2/3	-0.056	**male**	engineer	2/3	0.645	**neutral**

Table 2: Evaluated empirical bias in analyzed Masked Language Models. Column number shows the count of models for which the word was considered biased. Annotated is the bias assigned in Zhao et al. (2018a) based on the job market data.

C_{II}) the factual gender information of pronouns ($f \equiv$ f. $\text{gender}_{\text{pronoun}}$).

We use WinoMT dataset[7] (Stanovsky et al., 2019) which is a derivate of WinoBias dataset (Zhao et al., 2018a). Examples are more challenging to solve in this dataset than in our evaluation prompts (Table 1). Each sentence contains two potential antecedents. We use WinoMT for probing because we want to separate probe optimization and evaluation data. Moreover, we want to identify the encoding of gender bias and factual gender information in more diverse contexts.

We split the dataset into train, development, and test sets with non-overlapping nouns, mainly profession names. They contain 62, 21, and 21 unique nouns, corresponding to 2474, 856, and 546 sentences. The splits are designed to balance male and female-biased words in each of them.

3.2.1 Results

The probes on the models' top layer give a good approximation of factual gender – Pearson correlation between predicted and gold values in the range from 0.928 to 0.946. Pearson correlation for bias was high for BERT base (0.876), BERT large (0.946), and lower for ELECTRA (0.451).[8]

We have identified the dimensions encoding conditionality C_I and C_{II}. In Figure 2, we present the number of dimensions selected for each objective and their overlap. We see that bias is encoded sparsely in 18 to 80 dimensions.

3.3 Filtering Gender Bias

The primary purpose of probing is to construct bias filters based on the values of scaling: F_{-b} and $F_{-b,+f}$. Subsequently, we perform our de-biasing transformation eq. (7) on the last layers of the model. The probes on top of each layer are optimized separately.

After filtering, we again compute RGP for all professions. We monitor the following metrics to measure the overall improvement of the de-biasing algorithm on the set of 104 gender-neutral nouns S_{GN}:

[7]The dataset was originally introduced to evaluate gender bias in machine translation.

[8]For ELECTRA, we observed higher correlation of the bias probe on penultimate layer 0.668.

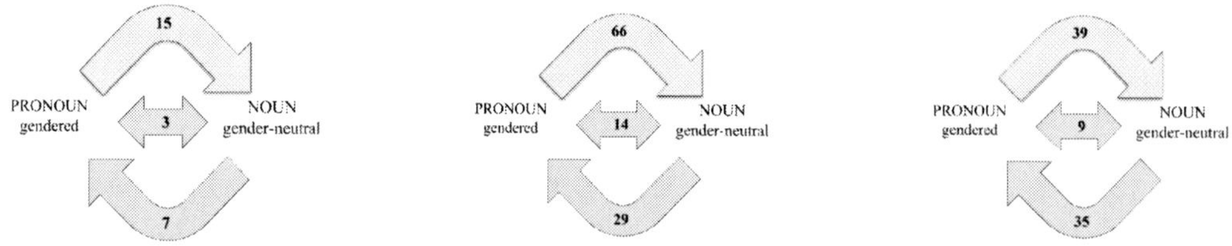

(a) BERT base (out of 768 dims) (b) BERT large (out of 1024 dims) (c) ELECTRA (out of 256 dims)

Figure 2: The number of selected dimensions for each of the tasks: C_I, C_{II}, and shared for both tasks.

$$MSE_{GN} = \frac{1}{|S_{GN}|} \sum_{w \in S_{GN}} RGP(w)^2 \quad (10)$$

Mean squared error show how far from zero RGP is. The advantage of this metric is that the bias of some words cannot be compensated by the opposite bias of others. The main objective of de-biasing is to minimize mean squared error.

$$MEAN_{GN} = \frac{1}{|S_{GN}|} \sum_{w \in S_{GN}} RGP(w)^2 \quad (11)$$

Mean shows whether the model is skewed toward predicting specific gender. In cases when the mean is close to zero, but MSE is high, we can tell that there is no general preference of the model toward one gender, but the individual words are biased.

$$VAR_{GN} = MSE_{GN} - MEAN_{GN}^2 \quad (12)$$

Variance is a similar measure to MSE. It is useful to show the spread of RGP when the mean is non-zero.

Additionally, we introduce a set of 26 gendered nouns (S_G) for which we expect to observe non-zero RGP. We monitor MSE to diagnose whether semantic gender information is preserved in de-biasing:

$$MSE_G = \frac{1}{|S_G|} \sum_{w \in S_G} RGP(w) \quad (13)$$

3.3.1 Results

In Table 3, we observe that in all cases, gender bias measured by MSE_{GN} decreases after filtering of bias subspace. The filtering on more than one layer usually further brings this metric down. It is important to note that the original model differs in the extent to which their predictions are biased. The mean square error is the lowest for BERT large (0.099), noticeably it is lower than in other analyzed models after de-biasing (except for ELECTRA after 2-layer filtering 0.073).

Setting	FL	MSE	MSE	$MEAN$	VAR
		gendered	gender-neutral		
BERT B	-	**6.177**	0.504	0.352	0.124
-bias	1	2.914	0.136	**-0.056**	0.133
	2	2.213	**0.102**	-0.121	**0.088**
+f. gender	1	3.780	0.184	-0.067	0.180
	2	2.965	0.145	-0.144	0.124
ELECTRA	-	**1.360**	0.367	0.163	0.340
-bias	1	0.100	0.124	0.265	0.054
	2	0.048	**0.073**	0.200	**0.033**
+f. gender	1	0.901	0.186	**0.008**	0.185
	2	0.488	0.101	-0.090	0.093
BERT L	-	1.363	0.099	0.235	0.044
-bias	1	0.701	0.051	0.166	0.024
	2	0.267	0.015	0.069	0.011
	4	0.061	0.033	0.162	**0.007**
+f. gender	1	**1.156**	0.057	0.145	0.036
	2	0.755	0.020	**0.011**	0.020
	4	0.292	**0.010**	0.037	0.009
AIM:		$\uparrow$	$\downarrow$	≈ 0	$\downarrow$

Table 3: Aggregation of *relative gender preference* in prompts for gendered and gender-neutral nouns. FL denotes the number of the model's top layers for which filtering was performed.

The predictions of all the models are skewed toward predicting male pronoun when the noun is revealed. Most of the pronouns used in the evaluation were professional names. Therefore, we think that this result is the manifestation of the stereotype that career-related words tend to be associated with men.

After filtering BERT base becomes slightly skewed toward female pronouns ($MEAN_{GN} < 0$).

Setting	FL	Accuracy		
		BERT L	BERT B	ELECTRA
Original	-	0.516	0.526	0.499
-bias	1	0.515	0.479	0.429
	2	0.504	0.474	0.434
	4	0.479	-	-
+f. gender	1	0.515	0.479	0.434
	2	0.510	0.480	0.433
	4	0.489	-	-

Table 4: Top-1 accuracy for all tokens in EWT UD (Silveira et al., 2014). FT is the number of the model's top layers for which filtering was performed.

For the two remaining models, we observe that keeping factual gender signal performs well in decreasing $MEAN_{GN}$.

Another advantage of keeping factual gender representation is the preservation of the bias in semantically gendered nouns, i.e., higher MSE_G.

3.4 How Does Bias Filtering Affect Masked Language Modeling?

We examine whether filtering affects the model's performance on the original task. For that purpose, we evaluate top-1 prediction accuracy for the masked tokens in the test set from English Web Treebank UD (Silveira et al., 2014) with 2077 sentences. We also evaluate the capability of the model to infer the personal pronoun based on the context. We use the GAP Coreference Dataset (Webster et al., 2018) with 8908 paragraphs. In each test case, we mask a pronoun referring to a person usually mentioned by their name. In the sentences, gender can be easily inferred from the name. In some cases, the texts also contain other (un-masked) gender pronouns.

3.4.1 Results: All Tokens

The results in Table 4 show that filtering out bias dimensions moderately decrease MLM accuracy: up to 0.037 for BERT large; 0.052 for BERT base; 0.07 for ELECTRA. In most cases exempting factual gender information from filtering decreases the drop in results.

3.4.2 Results: Personal Pronouns in GAP

We observe a more significant drop in results in the GAP dataset after de-biasing. The deterioration can be alleviated by omitting factual gender dimensions in the filter. For BERT large and ELECTRA this setting can even bring improvement over the original model. Our explanation of this phenomenon is that filtering can decrease the confounding information from stereotypically biased words that affect the prediction of correct gender.

Setting	FL	Accuracy		
		Overall	Male	Female
BERT L	-	0.799	**0.816**	0.781
-bias	1	0.690	0.757	0.624
	2	0.774	0.804	0.744
	4	0.747	0.770	0.724
+f. gender	1	0.754	0.782	0.726
	2	0.785	0.801	0.769
	4	**0.801**	0.807	**0.794**
-f. gender	1	0.725	0.775	0.675
	2	0.763	0.788	0.738
	4	0.545	0.633	0.458
BERT B	-	**0.732**	**0.752**	**0.712**
-bias	1	0.632	0.733	0.531
	2	0.597	0.706	0.487
+f. gender	1	0.659	0.734	0.584
	2	0.620	0.690	0.549
-f. gender	1	0.634	0.662	0.606
	2	0.604	0.641	0.567
ELECTRA	-	0.652	0.680	0.624
-bias	1	0.506	0.731	0.280
	2	0.485	0.721	0.249
+f. gender	1	**0.700**	**0.757**	**0.642**
	2	0.691	0.721	0.661
-f. gender	1	0.395	0.660	0.129
	2	0.473	0.708	0.239

Table 5: Top-1 accuracy for masked pronouns in GAP dataset (Webster et al., 2018). FT is the number of the model's top layers for which filtering was performed.

In this experiment, we also examine the filter, which removes all factual-gender dimensions. Expectedly such a transformation significantly decreases the accuracy. However, we still obtain relatively good results, i.e., accuracy higher than 0.5, which is a high benchmark for choosing gender by random. Thus, we conjecture that the gender signal is still left in the model despite filtering.

Summary of the Results: We observe that the optimal de-biasing setting is factual gender preserving filtering ($F_{-b,+f}$). This approach diminishes stereotypical bias in nouns while preserving gender information for gendered nouns (section 3.3). Moreover, it performs better in masked language modeling tasks (section 3.4).

4 Related Work

In recent years, much focus was put on evaluating and countering bias in language representations or word embeddings. Bolukbasi et al. (2016) observed the distribution of Word2Vec embeddings (Mikolov et al., 2013) encode gender bias. They tried to diminish its role by projecting the embeddings along the so-called *gender direction*, which separates gendered words such as *he* and *she*. They measure the bias as cosine similarity between an embedding and the gender direction.

$$\text{GenderDirection} \approx \overrightarrow{he} - \overrightarrow{she} \quad (14)$$

Zhao et al. (2018b) propose a method to diminish differentiation of word representations in the gender dimension during training of the GloVe embeddings (Pennington et al., 2014). Nevertheless, the following analysis of Gonen and Goldberg (2019) argued that these approaches remove bias only partially and showed that bias is encoded in the multi-dimensional subspace of the embedding space. The issue can be resolved by projecting in multiple dimensions to further nullify the role of gender in the representations (Ravfogel et al., 2020). Dropping all the gender-related information, e.g., the distinction between feminine and masculine pronouns can be detrimental to gender-sensitive applications. Kaneko and Bollegala (2019) proposed a de-biasing algorithm that preserves gendered information in gendered words.

Unlike the approaches above, we work with contextual embeddings of language models. Vig et al. (2020) investigated bias in the representation of the contextual model (GPT-2, Radford et al. (2019)). They used causal mediation analysis to identify components of the model responsible for encoding bias. Nadeem et al. (2021) and Nangia et al. (2020) propose a method of evaluating bias (including gender) with counterfactual test examples, to some extent similar to our prompts.

Qian et al. (2019) and Liang et al. (2020) employ prompts similar to ours to evaluate the gender bias of professional words in language models. The latter work also aims to identify and remove gender subspace in the model. In contrast to our approach, they do not guard factual gender signal.

Recently, Stanczak and Augenstein (2021) summarized the research on the evaluation and mitigation of gender bias in the survey of 304 papers.

5 Discussion

5.1 Bias Statement

We define bias as the connection between a word and the specific gender it is usually associated with. The association usually stems from the imbalanced number of corpora mentions of the word in male and female contexts. This work focuses on the stereotypical bias of nouns that do not have otherwise denotation of gender (semantic or grammatical). We consider such a denotation as factual gender and want to guard it in the models' representation.

Our method is applied to language models, hence we recognize potential application in language generation. We envision the case where the language model is applied to complete the text about a person, where we don't have implicit information about their gender. In this scenario, the model should not be compelled by stereotypical bias to assign a specific gender to a person. On the other hand, when the implicit information about a person's gender is provided in the context, the generated text should be consistent.

Language generation is becoming ubiquitous in everyday NLP applications (e.g., chat-bots, auto-completion Dale (2020)). Therefore it is important to ensure that the language models do not propagate sex-based discrimination.

The proposed method can also be implemented in deep models for other tasks, e.g., machine translation systems. In machine translation, bias is especially harmful when translating from English to languages that widely denote gender grammatically. In translation to such languages generation of gendered nouns tends to be made based on stereotypical gender roles instead of factual gender information provided in the source language (Stanovsky et al., 2019).

5.2 Limitations

It is important to note that we do not remove the whole of the gender information in our filtering method. Therefore, a downstream classifier could easily retrieve the factual gender of a person mentioned in a text, e.g., their CV.

This aspect makes our method not applicable to downstream tasks that use gender-biased data. For instance, in the task of predicting a profession based on a person's biography (De-Arteaga et al., 2019), there are different proportions of men and women among holders of specific professions. A classifier trained on de-biased but not de-gendered embeddings would learn to rely on gender property in its predictions.

Admittedly, in our results, we see that the proposed method based on *orthogonal probes* does not fully remove gender bias from the representations section 3.3. Even though our method typically identifies multiple dimensions encoding bias and factual gender information, there is no guarantee that all such dimensions will be filtered. Noticeably, the de-biased BERT base still underperform off-the-shelf BERT large in terms of MSE_{GN}. The reason behind this particular method was its ability to disentangle the representation of two language signals, in our case: gender bias and factual gender information.

Lastly, the probe can only recreate linear transformation, while in a non-linear system such as Transformer, the signal can be encoded non-linearly. Therefore, even when we remove the whole bias subspace, the information can be recovered in the next layer of the model (Ravfogel et al., 2020). It is also the reason why we decided to focus on the top layers of models.

6 Conclusions

We propose a new insight into gender information in contextual language representations. In de-biasing, we focus on the trade-off between removing stereotypical bias while preserving the semantic and grammatical information about the gender of a word from its context. Our evaluation of gender bias showed that three analyzed masked language models (BERT large, BERT based, and ELECTRA) are biased and skewed toward predicting male gender for profession names. To mitigate this issue, we disentangle stereotypical bias from factual gender information. Our filtering method can remove the former to some extent and preserve the latter. As a result, we decrease the bias in predictions of language models without significant deterioration of their performance in masked language modeling task.

Aknowlegments

We thank anonymous reviewers and our colleagues: João Paulo de Souza Aires, Inbal Magar, and Yarden Tal, who read the previous versions of this work and provided helpful comments and suggestions for improvement. The work has been supported by grant 338521 of the Grant Agency of Charles University.

References

Martín Abadi, Ashish Agarwal, Paul Barham, Eugene Brevdo, Zhifeng Chen, Craig Citro, Greg S. Corrado, Andy Davis, Jeffrey Dean, Matthieu Devin, Sanjay Ghemawat, Ian Goodfellow, Andrew Harp, Geoffrey Irving, Michael Isard, Yangqing Jia, Rafal Jozefowicz, Lukasz Kaiser, Manjunath Kudlur, Josh Levenberg, Dan Mané, Rajat Monga, Sherry Moore, Derek Murray, Chris Olah, Mike Schuster, Jonathon Shlens, Benoit Steiner, Ilya Sutskever, Kunal Talwar, Paul Tucker, Vincent Vanhoucke, Vijay Vasudevan, Fernanda Viégas, Oriol Vinyals, Pete Warden, Martin Wattenberg, Martin Wicke, Yuan Yu, and Xiaoqiang Zheng. 2015. TensorFlow: Large-scale machine learning on heterogeneous systems. Software available from tensorflow.org.

Tolga Bolukbasi, Kai-Wei Chang, James Zou, Venkatesh Saligrama, and Adam Kalai. 2016. Man is to computer programmer as woman is to homemaker? debiasing word embeddings. In *Proceedings of the 30th International Conference on Neural Information Processing Systems*, NIPS'16, page 4356–4364, Red Hook, NY, USA. Curran Associates Inc.

Kevin Clark, Minh-Thang Luong, Quoc V. Le, and Christopher D. Manning. 2020. ELECTRA: Pre-training text encoders as discriminators rather than generators. In *ICLR*.

Robert Dale. 2020. Natural language generation: The commercial state of the art in 2020. *Natural Language Engineering*, 26:481–487.

Maria De-Arteaga, Alexey Romanov, Hanna Wallach, Jennifer Chayes, Christian Borgs, Alexandra Chouldechova, Sahin Geyik, Krishnaram Kenthapadi, and Adam Tauman Kalai. 2019. Bias in bios: A case study of semantic representation bias in a high-stakes setting. In *FAT* '19: Conference on Fairness, Accountability, and Transparency*.

Daniel de Vassimon Manela, David Errington, Thomas Fisher, Boris van Breugel, and Pasquale Minervini. 2021. Stereotype and skew: Quantifying gender bias in pre-trained and fine-tuned language models. In *Proceedings of the 16th Conference of the European Chapter of the Association for Computational Linguistics: Main Volume*, pages 2232–2242, Online. Association for Computational Linguistics.

Jacob Devlin, Ming-Wei Chang, Kenton Lee, and Kristina Toutanova. 2019. BERT: Pre-training of deep bidirectional transformers for language understanding. In *Proceedings of the 2019 Conference of the North American Chapter of the Association for Computational Linguistics: Human Language Technologies, Volume 1 (Long and Short Papers)*, pages 4171–4186, Minneapolis, Minnesota. Association for Computational Linguistics.

Hila Gonen and Yoav Goldberg. 2019. Lipstick on a pig: Debiasing methods cover up systematic gender biases in word embeddings but do not remove them. In *Proceedings of the 2019 Conference of the North American Chapter of the Association for Computational Linguistics: Human Language Technologies, Volume 1 (Long and Short Papers)*, pages 609–614, Minneapolis, Minnesota. Association for Computational Linguistics.

John Hewitt and Christopher D. Manning. 2019. A structural probe for finding syntax in word representations. In *Proceedings of the 2019 Conference of the North American Chapter of the Association for Computational Linguistics: Human Language Technologies, Volume 1 (Long and Short Papers)*, pages 4129–4138, Minneapolis, Minnesota. Association for Computational Linguistics.

Masahiro Kaneko and Danushka Bollegala. 2019. Gender-preserving debiasing for pre-trained word embeddings. In *Proceedings of the 57th Annual Meeting of the Association for Computational Linguistics*, pages 1641–1650, Florence, Italy. Association for Computational Linguistics.

Diederik P. Kingma and Jimmy Ba. 2015. Adam: A method for stochastic optimization. In *ICLR (Poster)*.

Deng Liang, Chen Zheng, Lei Guo, Xin Cui, Xiuzhang Xiong, Hengqiao Rong, and Jinpeng Dong. 2020. BERT enhanced neural machine translation and sequence tagging model for Chinese grammatical error diagnosis. In *Proceedings of the 6th Workshop on Natural Language Processing Techniques for Educational Applications*, pages 57–66, Suzhou, China. Association for Computational Linguistics.

Tomasz Limisiewicz and David Mareček. 2021. Introducing orthogonal constraint in structural probes. In *Proceedings of the 59th Annual Meeting of the Association for Computational Linguistics and the 11th International Joint Conference on Natural Language Processing (Volume 1: Long Papers)*, pages 428–442, Online. Association for Computational Linguistics.

Zachary C. Lipton. 2018. The Mythos of Model Interpretability. *Queue*, 16(3):31–57.

Tomas Mikolov, Ilya Sutskever, Kai Chen, Greg S Corrado, and Jeff Dean. 2013. Distributed representations of words and phrases and their compositionality. In *Advances in Neural Information Processing Systems*, volume 26. Curran Associates, Inc.

Moin Nadeem, Anna Bethke, and Siva Reddy. 2021. StereoSet: Measuring stereotypical bias in pretrained language models. In *Proceedings of the 59th Annual Meeting of the Association for Computational Linguistics and the 11th International Joint Conference on Natural Language Processing (Volume 1: Long Papers)*, pages 5356–5371, Online. Association for Computational Linguistics.

Nikita Nangia, Clara Vania, Rasika Bhalerao, and Samuel R. Bowman. 2020. CrowS-pairs: A challenge dataset for measuring social biases in masked language models. In *Proceedings of the 2020 Conference on Empirical Methods in Natural Language Processing (EMNLP)*, pages 1953–1967, Online. Association for Computational Linguistics.

Jeffrey Pennington, Richard Socher, and Christopher Manning. 2014. GloVe: Global vectors for word representation. In *Proceedings of the 2014 Conference on Empirical Methods in Natural Language Processing (EMNLP)*, pages 1532–1543, Doha, Qatar. Association for Computational Linguistics.

Yusu Qian, Urwa Muaz, Ben Zhang, and Jae Won Hyun. 2019. Reducing gender bias in word-level language models with a gender-equalizing loss function. In *Proceedings of the 57th Annual Meeting of the Association for Computational Linguistics: Student Research Workshop*, pages 223–228, Florence, Italy. Association for Computational Linguistics.

Alec Radford, Jeff Wu, Rewon Child, David Luan, Dario Amodei, and Ilya Sutskever. 2019. Language models are unsupervised multitask learners.

Shauli Ravfogel, Yanai Elazar, Hila Gonen, Michael Twiton, and Yoav Goldberg. 2020. Null it out: Guarding protected attributes by iterative nullspace projection. In *Proceedings of the 58th Annual Meeting of the Association for Computational Linguistics*, pages 7237–7256, Online. Association for Computational Linguistics.

Natalia Silveira, Timothy Dozat, Marie-Catherine de Marneffe, Samuel Bowman, Miriam Connor, John Bauer, and Christopher D. Manning. 2014. A gold standard dependency corpus for English. In *Proceedings of the Ninth International Conference on Language Resources and Evaluation (LREC-2014)*.

Karolina Stanczak and Isabelle Augenstein. 2021. A survey on gender bias in natural language processing.

Gabriel Stanovsky, Noah A. Smith, and Luke Zettlemoyer. 2019. Evaluating gender bias in machine translation. In *Proceedings of the 57th Annual Meeting of the Association for Computational Linguistics*, pages 1679–1684, Florence, Italy. Association for Computational Linguistics.

Jesse Vig, Sebastian Gehrmann, Yonatan Belinkov, Sharon Qian, Daniel Nevo, Yaron Singer, and Stuart Shieber. 2020. Investigating gender bias in language models using causal mediation analysis. In *Advances in Neural Information Processing Systems*, volume 33, pages 12388–12401. Curran Associates, Inc.

Kellie Webster, Marta Recasens, Vera Axelrod, and Jason Baldridge. 2018. Mind the gap: A balanced corpus of gendered ambiguou. In *Transactions of the ACL*, page to appear.

Jieyu Zhao, Tianlu Wang, Mark Yatskar, Vicente Ordonez, and Kai-Wei Chang. 2018a. Gender bias in coreference resolution: Evaluation and debiasing methods. In *Proceedings of the 2018 Conference of the North American Chapter of the Association for Computational Linguistics: Human Language Technologies, Volume 2 (Short Papers)*, pages 15–20, New Orleans, Louisiana. Association for Computational Linguistics.

Jieyu Zhao, Yichao Zhou, Zeyu Li, Wei Wang, and Kai-Wei Chang. 2018b. Learning gender-neutral word embeddings. In *Proceedings of the 2018 Conference on Empirical Methods in Natural Language Processing*, pages 4847–4853, Brussels, Belgium. Association for Computational Linguistics.

A Technical Details

We use batches of size 10. Optimization is conducted with Adam (Kingma and Ba, 2015) with initial learning rate 0.02 and meta parameters: $\beta_1 = 0.9$, $\beta_2 = 0.999$, and $\epsilon = 10^{-8}$. We use learning rate decay and an early-stopping mechanism with a decay factor 10. The training is stopped after three consecutive epochs not resulting in the improvement of the validation loss learning rate. We clip each gradient's norm at $c = 1.0$. The orthogonal penalty was set to $\lambda_O = 0.1$.

We implemented the network in TensorFlow 2 (Abadi et al., 2015). The code will be available on GitHub.

A.1 Computing Infrastructure

We optimized probes on a GPU core *GeForce GTX 1080 Ti*. Training a probe on top of one layer of BERT large takes about 5 minutes.

A.2 Number of Parameters in the Probe

The number of the parameters in the probe depends on the model's embedding size d_{emb}. The *orthogonal transformation* matrix consist of d^2_{emb}; both *intercept* and *scalling vector* have d_{emb} parameters. Altogether, the size of the probe equals to $d^2_{\text{emb}} + 4 \cdot d_{\text{emb}}$.

B Details about Datasets

WinoMT is distributed under MIT license; EWT UD under Creative Commons 4.0 license; GAP under Apache 2.0 license.

C Results for Different Filtering Thresholds

In table 6 we show how the choice of filtering threshold ϵ affects the results of our method for BERT large. We decided to pick the threshold equal to 10^{-12}, as lowering it brought only minor improvement in MSE_{GN}.

Epsilon	MSE gendered	MSE gender-neutral	$MEAN$ gender-neutral	VAR gender-neutral
10^{-2}	0.762	0.083	0.233	0.029
10^{-4}	0.756	0.081	0.230	0.028
10^{-6}	0.764	0.074	0.213	0.029
10^{-8}	0.738	0.078	0.225	0.027
10^{-10}	0.721	0.082	0.234	0.027
10^{-12}	0.701	0.051	0.166	0.024
10^{-14}	0.709	0.043	0.138	0.023
10^{-16}	0.770	0.023	0.013	0.022

Table 6: Tuning of filtering threshold ϵ. Results for filtering bias in the last layer of BERT large.

NOUN	Relative Gender Preference			
	BERT base	BERT large	ELECTRA	Avg.
	Female Gendered			
councilwoman	-4.262	-2.050	-0.832	-2.381
policewoman	-4.428	-1.710	-0.928	-2.355
princess	-3.486	-1.598	-1.734	-2.273
actress	-3.315	-1.094	-2.319	-2.242
chairwoman	-4.020	-1.818	-0.629	-2.156
waitress	-2.806	-1.167	-2.475	-2.150
busimesswoman	-3.202	-1.696	-1.096	-1.998
queen	-2.752	-0.910	-2.246	-1.969
spokeswoman	-2.543	-2.126	-1.017	-1.895
stewardess	-3.484	-2.215	0.089	-1.870
maid	-3.092	-0.822	-1.452	-1.788
witch	-2.068	-0.706	-1.476	-1.416
nun	-2.472	-0.974	-0.613	-1.353
	Male Gendered			
wizard	0.972	0.314	0.237	0.508
manservant	0.974	0.493	0.115	0.527
steward	0.737	0.495	0.675	0.636
spokesman	0.846	0.591	0.515	0.651
waiter	1.003	0.473	0.639	0.705
priest	0.988	0.442	0.928	0.786
actor	1.366	0.392	0.632	0.797
prince	1.401	0.776	0.418	0.865
policeman	1.068	0.514	1.202	0.928
king	1.399	0.658	0.772	0.943
chairman	1.140	0.677	1.069	0.962
councilman	1.609	1.040	0.419	1.023
businessman	1.829	0.549	0.985	1.121

Table 7: List of gendered nouns with evaluated bias in three analyzed models (RGP).

D Evaluation of Bias in Language Models

We present the list of 26 gendered words and their empirical bias in table 7. Following tables tables 8 and 9 show the evaluation results for 104 gender-neutral words.

NOUN	Relative Gender Preference				Bias Class			
	BERT base	BERT large	ELECTRA	Avg.	BERT base	BERT large	ELECTRA	Annotated
housekeeper	-2.813	-0.573	-2.642	-2.009	female	female	female	female
nurse	-2.850	-0.568	-2.103	-1.840	female	female	female	female
receptionist	-1.728	-0.776	-2.302	-1.602	female	female	female	female
hairdresser	-0.400	-0.228	-0.785	-0.471	female	female	female	female
librarian	0.019	-0.088	-0.768	-0.279	neutral	female	female	female
assistant	-0.477	0.020	-0.117	-0.192	female	neutral	neutral	female
secretary	-0.564	0.024	-0.027	-0.189	female	neutral	neutral	female
victim	-0.075	0.091	-0.323	-0.102	female	neutral	female	neutral
teacher	0.129	0.175	-0.595	-0.097	neutral	neutral	female	female
therapist	0.002	0.016	-0.233	-0.072	neutral	neutral	female	neutral
child	-0.100	0.073	-0.154	-0.060	female	neutral	female	neutral
salesperson	-0.680	-0.206	0.719	-0.056	female	female	male	male
practitioner	0.150	0.361	-0.621	-0.037	neutral	neutral	female	neutral
client	-0.157	0.250	-0.165	-0.024	female	neutral	female	neutral
dietitian	0.175	0.003	-0.143	0.012	neutral	neutral	female	neutral
cook	-0.150	0.141	0.048	0.013	female	neutral	neutral	male
educator	0.278	0.144	-0.375	0.015	neutral	neutral	female	neutral
cashier	0.009	0.041	0.017	0.023	neutral	neutral	neutral	female
customer	-0.401	0.328	0.142	0.023	female	neutral	neutral	neutral
attendant	-0.157	0.226	0.010	0.027	female	neutral	neutral	female
designer	0.200	0.173	-0.232	0.047	neutral	neutral	female	female
cleaner	0.151	0.099	-0.089	0.053	neutral	neutral	neutral	female
teenager	0.343	0.088	-0.210	0.074	neutral	neutral	female	neutral
passenger	0.015	0.151	0.100	0.089	neutral	neutral	neutral	neutral
guest	0.162	0.258	-0.150	0.090	neutral	neutral	female	neutral
someone	0.026	0.275	0.082	0.128	neutral	neutral	neutral	neutral
student	0.307	0.281	-0.195	0.131	neutral	neutral	female	neutral
clerk	0.107	0.216	0.105	0.143	neutral	neutral	neutral	female
visitor	0.471	0.273	-0.280	0.155	neutral	neutral	female	neutral
counselor	0.304	0.165	0.009	0.159	neutral	neutral	neutral	female
editor	0.244	0.161	0.081	0.162	neutral	neutral	neutral	female
resident	0.528	0.300	-0.304	0.174	neutral	neutral	female	neutral
patient	0.009	0.305	0.217	0.177	neutral	neutral	neutral	neutral
homeowner	0.422	0.158	-0.002	0.192	neutral	neutral	neutral	neutral
advisee	0.175	0.252	0.168	0.199	neutral	neutral	neutral	neutral
psychologist	0.259	0.232	0.124	0.205	neutral	neutral	neutral	neutral
nutritionist	0.474	0.134	0.020	0.210	neutral	neutral	neutral	neutral
dispatcher	0.250	0.118	0.284	0.217	neutral	neutral	neutral	neutral
tailor	0.572	0.382	-0.250	0.235	neutral	male	female	female
employee	0.124	0.228	0.371	0.241	neutral	neutral	neutral	neutral
owner	0.044	0.213	0.493	0.250	neutral	neutral	neutral	neutral
advisor	0.339	0.271	0.148	0.253	neutral	neutral	neutral	neutral
witness	0.287	0.319	0.187	0.264	neutral	neutral	neutral	neutral
writer	0.497	0.237	0.060	0.265	neutral	neutral	neutral	female
undergraduate	0.575	0.148	0.075	0.266	neutral	neutral	neutral	neutral
veterinarian	0.616	0.007	0.209	0.278	neutral	neutral	neutral	neutral
pedestrian	0.446	0.226	0.170	0.281	neutral	neutral	neutral	neutral
investigator	0.518	0.228	0.120	0.289	neutral	neutral	neutral	neutral
hygienist	0.665	0.274	-0.040	0.300	neutral	neutral	neutral	neutral
buyer	0.529	0.190	0.183	0.300	neutral	neutral	neutral	neutral
supervisor	0.257	0.228	0.426	0.304	neutral	neutral	neutral	male
worker	0.151	0.267	0.511	0.310	neutral	neutral	neutral	neutral
bystander	0.786	0.117	0.072	0.325	male	neutral	neutral	neutral

Table 8: List of gender-neutral nouns with their evaluated bias RGP. Female and male bias classes are assigned for 20 lowest negative and 20 highest positive RGP values. Annotated bias from Zhao et al. (2018a). Part 1 of 2.

NOUN	Relative Gender Preference				Bias Class			
	BERT base	BERT large	ELECTRA	Avg.	BERT base	BERT large	ELECTRA	Annotated
chemist	0.579	0.311	0.107	0.332	neutral	neutral	neutral	neutral
administrator	0.428	0.236	0.350	0.338	neutral	neutral	neutral	neutral
examiner	0.445	0.281	0.296	0.341	neutral	neutral	neutral	neutral
broker	0.376	0.358	0.295	0.343	neutral	neutral	neutral	neutral
instructor	0.413	0.196	0.436	0.348	neutral	neutral	neutral	neutral
developer	0.536	0.338	0.172	0.349	neutral	neutral	neutral	male
technician	0.312	0.362	0.400	0.358	neutral	neutral	neutral	neutral
baker	0.622	0.287	0.178	0.362	neutral	neutral	neutral	female
planner	0.611	0.341	0.147	0.366	neutral	neutral	neutral	neutral
bartender	0.628	0.282	0.293	0.401	neutral	neutral	neutral	neutral
paramedic	0.787	0.094	0.333	0.405	male	neutral	neutral	neutral
protester	0.722	0.498	0.019	0.413	neutral	male	neutral	neutral
specialist	0.501	0.363	0.392	0.419	neutral	male	neutral	neutral
electrician	0.935	0.283	0.076	0.431	male	neutral	neutral	neutral
physician	0.438	0.359	0.502	0.433	neutral	neutral	neutral	male
pathologist	0.817	0.307	0.181	0.435	male	neutral	neutral	neutral
analyst	0.645	0.315	0.361	0.440	neutral	neutral	neutral	male
appraiser	0.729	0.305	0.302	0.445	neutral	neutral	neutral	neutral
onlooker	0.978	0.093	0.274	0.448	male	neutral	neutral	neutral
janitor	0.702	0.493	0.174	0.456	neutral	male	neutral	male
mover	0.717	0.407	0.253	0.459	neutral	male	neutral	male
chef	0.682	0.348	0.352	0.460	neutral	neutral	neutral	neutral
lawyer	0.696	0.271	0.421	0.462	neutral	neutral	neutral	male
paralegal	0.829	0.247	0.313	0.463	male	neutral	neutral	neutral
doctor	0.723	0.355	0.322	0.467	neutral	neutral	neutral	neutral
auditor	0.654	0.329	0.504	0.496	neutral	neutral	neutral	female
officer	0.465	0.463	0.584	0.504	neutral	male	male	neutral
surgeon	0.368	0.417	0.733	0.506	neutral	male	male	neutral
programmer	0.543	0.304	0.684	0.510	neutral	neutral	male	neutral
scientist	0.568	0.427	0.548	0.514	neutral	male	neutral	neutral
painter	0.721	0.298	0.555	0.525	neutral	neutral	male	neutral
pharmacist	0.862	0.244	0.495	0.534	male	neutral	neutral	neutral
laborer	0.996	0.557	0.058	0.537	male	male	neutral	male
machinist	0.821	0.449	0.361	0.544	male	male	neutral	neutral
architect	0.790	0.243	0.609	0.547	male	neutral	male	neutral
taxpayer	0.785	0.525	0.339	0.550	male	male	neutral	neutral
chief	0.595	0.472	0.628	0.565	neutral	male	male	male
inspector	0.631	0.344	0.726	0.567	neutral	neutral	male	neutral
plumber	1.186	0.468	0.205	0.620	male	male	neutral	neutral
construction worker	0.770	0.326	0.769	0.622	male	neutral	male	male
driver	0.847	0.415	0.603	0.622	male	male	male	male
manager	0.456	0.346	1.084	0.628	neutral	neutral	male	male
engineer	0.562	0.385	0.987	0.645	neutral	male	male	neutral
sheriff	0.850	0.396	0.708	0.651	male	male	male	male
CEO	0.701	0.353	0.989	0.681	neutral	neutral	male	male
mechanic	0.752	0.307	1.098	0.719	male	neutral	male	male
guard	0.907	0.586	0.720	0.738	male	male	male	male
accountant	0.610	0.291	1.350	0.750	neutral	neutral	male	female
farmer	1.044	0.477	0.736	0.753	male	male	male	male
firefighter	1.294	0.438	0.604	0.779	male	male	male	neutral
carpenter	0.934	0.415	1.263	0.870	male	male	male	male

Table 9: List of gender-neutral nouns with their evaluated bias RGP. Female and male bias classes are assigned for 20 lowest negative and 20 highest positive RGP values. Annotated bias from Zhao et al. (2018a). Part 2 of 2.

Uncertainty and Inclusivity in Gender Bias Annotation: An Annotation Taxonomy and Annotated Datasets of British English Text

Lucy Havens[†] **Melissa Terras**[‡] **Benjamin Bach**[†] **Beatrice Alex**[§†]

[†]School of Informatics
[‡]College of Arts, Humanities and Social Sciences
[§]Edinburgh Futures Institute; School of Literatures, Languages and Cultures
University of Edinburgh
lucy.havens@ed.ac.uk, m.terras@ed.ac.uk
bbach@inf.ed.ac.uk, balex@ed.ac.uk

Abstract

Mitigating harms from gender biased language in Natural Language Processing (NLP) systems remains a challenge, and the situated nature of language means bias is inescapable in NLP data. Though efforts to mitigate gender bias in NLP are numerous, they often vaguely define gender and bias, only consider two genders, and do not incorporate uncertainty into models. To address these limitations, in this paper we present a taxonomy of gender biased language and apply it to create annotated datasets. We created the taxonomy and annotated data with the aim of making gender bias in language transparent. If biases are communicated clearly, varieties of biased language can be better identified and measured. Our taxonomy contains eleven types of gender biases inclusive of people whose gender expressions do not fit into the binary conceptions of woman and man, and whose gender differs from that they were assigned at birth, while also allowing annotators to document unknown gender information. The taxonomy and annotated data will, in future work, underpin analysis and more equitable language model development.

1 Background and Introduction

The need to mitigate bias in data has become urgent as evidence of harms from such data grows (Birhane and Prabhu, 2021; O'Neill et al., 2021; Perez, 2019; Noble, 2018; Vainapel et al., 2015; Sweeney, 2013). Due to the complexities of bias often overlooked in Machine Learning (ML) bias research, including Natural Language Processing (NLP) (Devinney et al., 2022; Stańczak and Augenstein, 2021), Blodgett et al. (2020), Leavy (2018), and Crawford (2017) call for greater interdisciplinary engagement and stakeholder collaboration. The Gallery, Library, Archive, and Museum (GLAM) sector has made similar calls for interdisciplinary engagement, looking to applications of data science and ML to better understand and mitigate bias in GLAM collections (Padilla, 2017, 2019; Geraci, 2019). Supporting the NLP and GLAM communities' shared aim of mitigating the minoritization[1] of certain people that biased language causes, we provide a taxonomy of gender biased language and demonstrate its application in a case study with GLAM documentation.

We use *GLAM documentation* to refer to the descriptions of heritage items written in GLAM catalogs. Adapting our previously published definition, we use *gender biased language* to refer to "language that creates or reinforces inequitable power relations among people, harming certain people through simplified, dehumanizing, or judgmental words or phrases that restrict their [gender] identity; and privileging other people through words or phrases that favor their [gender] identity" (Havens et al., 2020, 108). We focus on gender bias due to the contextual nature of gender and bias (they vary across time, location, culture, and people), as well as the existing efforts of our partner institution, the Archives of the Centre for Research Collections at the University of Edinburgh, to mitigate gender bias in its documentation.

GLAM documentation provides a unique benefit compared to many text sources: it contains historical and contemporary language. GLAM continually acquire and describe heritage items to enable the items' discoverability. In archives, heritage items include photographs, handwritten documents, instruments, and tweets, among other materials. Heritage items and the language that describes them influence society's understanding of the past,

[1]This paper uses *minoritization* in the sense D'Ignazio and Klein (2020) use the term: as a descriptor to emphasize a group of people's experience of oppression, rather than using the noun *minority*, which defines people as oppressed.

Proceedings of the The 4th Workshop on Gender Bias in Natural Language Processing (GeBNLP), pages 30 - 57
July 15, 2022 ©2022 Association for Computational Linguistics

the present, and the direction society is moving into the future (Benjamin, 2019; Welsh, 2016; Yale, 2015; Cook, 2011; Smith, 2006). Through research with GLAM documentation, variations in biased language could be better understood. Should diachronic patterns emerge, the NLP community could train models to identify newly-emerging, previously unseen types of bias.

This paper presents an annotation taxonomy (§5) to label gender biased language inclusive of trans and gender diverse identities,[2] as well as a dataset of historical and contemporary language from British English archival documentation annotated according to the taxonomy. Linguistics, gender studies, information sciences, and NLP literature inform the taxonomy's categorization of gender biased language. As a result, the taxonomy holds relevance beyond the GLAM sector in which we situate our work. The taxonomy may be applied when creating NLP datasets or models, or when measuring varieties of gender bias in language, because the taxonomy's definitions of types of gender biases are rooted in the language of text, rather than an abstracted representation of text. Uniquely, our taxonomy includes labels that record uncertainty about a person's gender.

As we situate our work in the GLAM sector, this paper provides a case study (§6) demonstrating how the annotation taxonomy was applied to create an annotated dataset of archival documentation. For future NLP work, the resulting dataset of historical and contemporary language annotated for gender biases provides a corpus to analyze gender biased language for diachronic patterns, to analyze correlations between types of gender biases, and to develop gender bias classification models. Specific to the GLAM sector, gender bias classification models could enhance reparative description practices. A model's ability to automatically identify descriptions of heritage items that contain gender biases would enable efficient prioritization of the additions and revisions needed on outdated, harmful descriptions in GLAM documentation.

2 Bias Statement

This paper adopts our previously published definition of biased language (Havens et al., 2020), narrowing the focus to gender bias as written in §1. Gender biased language may cause representational or allocative harms to a person of any gender (Blodgett et al., 2020; Crawford, 2017). The taxonomy created in this paper considers a person's gender to be self-described and changeable, rather than being limited to the binary and static conceptualization of gender as either a man or woman since birth (Keyes, 2018; Scheuerman et al., 2020). Recognizing that a person's gender may be impossible to determine from the information available about them, the taxonomy also allows annotators to record uncertainty (Shopland, 2020). Furthermore, the paper acknowledges that characteristics other than gender, such as racialized ethnicity and economic class, influence experiences of power and oppression (Crenshaw, 1991). Drawing on archival science and feminist theories, the paper considers knowledge derived from language as situated in a particular perspective and, as a result, incomplete (Tanselle, 2002; Harding, 1995; Haraway, 1988).

To communicate this paper's perspective, we as authors report our identification as three women and one man; and our nationalities, as American, German, and Scots. Annotators identify as women (one specifying queer woman and two, cis women); they are of American, British, Hungarian, and Scots nationalities. Though annotators do not represent great gender diversity,[3] the annotation process still contributes to the advancement of gender equity.

As women, the annotators identify as a minoritized gender. The evolution of British English demonstrates the historical dominance of the perspective of the heteronormative man, and the pejoration of terms for women (Spencer, 2000; Schulz, 2000; Lakoff, 1989).[4] Creating a women-produced dataset challenges the dominant gender perspective by explicitly labeling where minoritized genders' perspectives are missing (D'Ignazio and Klein, 2020; Smith, 2006; Fairclough, 2003).

3 Related Work

Evidence of bias in ML data and models abound regarding gender (Kurita et al., 2019; Zhao et al., 2019), disability (Hutchinson et al., 2020), racial-

[2]This paper uses *gender diverse* in the sense the Trans Metadata Collective (2022) uses the term: to include gender expressions that do not fit within binary conceptualizations of gender, that differ from one's gender assigned at birth, and that cannot be described with the culturally-specific term *trans*.

[3]The availability of people who responded to the annotator application and the annotation timeline limited the gender diversity that could be achieved among annotators.

[4]In the 16th century, grammarians instructed writers to write "men" or "man" before "women" or "woman." In the 18th century, "man" and "he" began to be employed as universal terms, rather than "human" and "they" (Spencer, 2000).

ized ethnicities (Sap et al., 2019), politics and economics (Elejalde et al., 2017), and, for an intersectional approach (Crenshaw, 1991), a combination of characteristics (Jiang and Fellbaum, 2020; Sweeney and Najafian, 2019; Tan and Celis, 2019). Harms from such biases are also well documented (Birhane and Prabhu, 2021; Costanza-Chock and Philip, 2018; Noble, 2018; Vainapel et al., 2015; Sweeney, 2013). Despite numerous bias mitigation approaches put forth (Cao and Daumé III, 2020; Dinan et al., 2020a; Hube and Fetahu, 2019; Webster et al., 2018; Zhao et al., 2018), many have limited efficacy, failing to address the complexity of biased language (Stańczak and Augenstein, 2021; Blodgett et al., 2021; Gonen and Goldberg, 2019).

Methods of removing bias tend to be mathematically focused, such as Basta et al. (2020) and Borkan et al. (2019). As McCradden et al. (2020) state, typical ML bias mitigation approaches assume biases' harms can be mathematically represented, though no evidence of the relevance of proposed bias metrics to the real world exists. On the contrary, Goldfarb-Tarrant et al. (2021) found no correlation between a commonly used intrinsic bias metric, Word Embedding Association Test, and extrinsic metrics in the downstream tasks of coreference resolution and hate speech detection. Due to the misalignment between abstract representations of bias and the presence and impact of bias, this paper presents a taxonomy to measure biased language at its foundation: words.

Limitations to bias mitigation efforts also result from overly simplistic conceptualizations of bias (Devinney et al., 2022; Stańczak and Augenstein, 2021; Blodgett et al., 2020). NLP gender bias work, for example, often uses a binary gender framework either in its conceptualization (such as Webster et al. (2018)) or application (such as Dinan et al. (2020b)), and tends to focus on one variety of gender bias, stereotypes (Stańczak and Augenstein, 2021; Doughman et al., 2021; Bolukbasi et al., 2016). NLP bias work more generally often asserts a single ground truth (Davani et al., 2022; Sang and Stanton, 2022; Basile et al., 2021). Despite evidence that bias varies across domains (Basta et al., 2020), approaches to mitigating bias have yet to address the contextual nature of biased language, such as how it varies across time, location, and culture (Bjorkman, 2017; Bucholtz, 1999; Corbett, 1990). This paper adopts a data feminist (D'Ignazio and Klein, 2020) and perspectivist approach (Basile, 2022) to situate identification and measurement of bias in a particular context.

Data feminism views data as situated and partial, drawing on feminist theories' view of knowledge as particular to a time, place, and people (Harding, 1995; Crenshaw, 1991; Haraway, 1988). Similarly, the Perspectivist Data Manifesto encourages disaggregated publication of annotated data, recognizing that conflicting annotations may all be valid (Basile, 2022). Indigenous epistemologies, such as the Lakota's concept of *wakȟàŋ*, further the notion of the impossibility of a universal truth. Translated as "that which cannot be understood," wakȟàŋ communicates that knowledge may come from a place beyond what we can imagine (Lewis et al., 2018). Our taxonomy thus permits annotations to overlap and record uncertainty, and our aggregated dataset incorporates all annotators' perspectives.

Encouraging greater transparency in dataset creation, Bender et al. (2021) and Jo and Gebru (2020) caution against creating datasets too large to be adequately interrogated. Hutchinson et al. (2021), Mitchell et al. (2019), and Bender and Friedman (2018) propose new documentation methods to facilitate critical interrogation of data and the models trained on them. Our appendices include a data statement documenting the creation of the annotated data presented in this paper (§B). To maximize the transparency of our data documentation, we will publish the data only after further interrogation of its gender bias annotations, including collaborative analysis with the Centre for Research Collections.

4 Methodology

To practically apply theories and approaches from NLP, data feminism, and indigenous epistemologies, we apply the case study method, common to social science and design research. Case studies use a combination of data and information gathering approaches to study particular phenomena in context (Martin and Hanington, 2012), suitable for annotating gender biased language because gender and bias vary across time, location, and culture. Furthermore, case studies report and reflect upon outliers discovered in the research process (ibid.), supporting our effort to create space for the perspectives of people minoritized due to their gender identity. After first developing the annotation taxonomy through an interdisciplinary literature review and participatory action research with archivists

(§5), we applied the taxonomy in a case study to create datasets annotated for gender bias (§6).

Adopting our previously published bias-aware methodology (Havens et al., 2020), we employed participatory action research (Swantz, 2008; Reid and Frisby, 2008), collaborating with the institution that manages our data source: the Centre for Research Collections. Due to validity (Welty et al., 2019) and ethical concerns (Gleibs, 2017) with crowdsourcing, we hired annotators with expertise in archives (the domain area of the case study's data) and gender studies (the focus area of this paper's bias mitigation) to apply the taxonomy in a case study. Hiring a small number of annotators will enable us to publish disaggregated versions of the annotated data, implementing data perspectivism (Basile, 2022; Basile et al., 2021).

Following the approach of Smith (2006) to heritage, we consider heritage to be a process of engaging with the past, present, and future. Annotators in this paper's case study visited, interpreted, and negotiated with heritage (Smith, 2006) in the form of archival documentation. Annotating archival documentation with labels that mark specific text spans as gender biased transforms the documentation, challenging the "authorized heritage discourse" (ibid., 29) of the heteronormative man. We aim such explicit labeling to recontextualize the archival documentation, transforming its language by placing it in a new social context (Fairclough, 2003): the 21st century United Kingdom, with gender conceptualized as a self-defined, changeable identity characteristic. We aim this negotiation-through-annotation to guide the NLP models we will create with the data in the future towards more equitable representations of gender.

5 Annotation Taxonomy

Our annotation taxonomy organizes labels (lettered) into three categories (numbered). Category and label names are **bolded**. Each label's listing includes a definition and example. Examples are *italicized*; labeled text in each example is <u>underlined</u>. For every label, annotators could label a single word or multiple words. Examples come from the archival documentation summarized in §6 except for 1(a), *Non-binary*, and 3(d), *Empowering*, because annotators did not find text relevant to their definitions (the "Fonds ID," or collection identifier, indicates where in the documentation example descriptions may be found). §7 further explains the rationale for the taxonomy's labels, and how they facilitate analysis and measurement of gender biased language.

1. **Person Name:** the name of a person, including any pre-nominal titles (i.e., Professor, Mrs., Sir, Queen), when the person is the primary entity being described (rather than a location named after a person, for example)
   (a) **Non-binary:** the pronouns, titles, or roles of the named person are non-binary
   Example 1(a): <u>Francis McDonald</u> went to the University of Edinburgh where they studied law.
   (b) **Feminine:** the pronouns, titles, or roles of the named person are feminine
   Example 1(b): "<u>Jewel</u> took an active interest in her husband's work..." (Fonds ID: Coll-1036)
   (c) **Masculine:** the pronouns, titles, or roles of the named person are masculine
   Example 1(c): "<u>Martin Luther</u>, the man and his work." (Fonds ID: BAI)
   (d) **Unknown:** any pronouns, titles, or roles of the named person are gender neutral, or none are provided
   Example 1(d): "Testimonials and additional testimonials in favour of <u>Niecks</u>, candidacy for the Chair of Music, 1891." (Fonds ID: Coll-1086)

2. **Linguistic:** gender marked in the way a word or words reference a person or people, assigning them a specific gender that cannot be determined with certainty from the word(s)
   (a) **Generalization:** use of a gender-specific term (i.e., roles, titles) to refer to a group of people that could identify as more than the specified gender
   Example 2(a): "His classes included Anatomy, Practical Anatomy...<u>Midwifery</u> and Diseases of Women, Therapeutics, Neurology...Public Health, and Diseases of the Skin." (Fonds ID: Coll-1118)
   (b) **Gendered Role:** use of a word denoting a person's role that marks either a non-binary, feminine, or masculine gender
   Example 2(b): "New map of Scotland for <u>Ladies</u> Needlework, 1797" (Fonds ID: Coll-1111)

(c) **Gendered Pronoun:** marking a person or people's gender with gendered pronouns (i.e., she, he, ey, xe, or they as a singular pronoun)
Example 2(c): "He obtained surgical qualifications from Edinburgh University in 1873" (Fonds ID: Coll-1096)

3. **Contextual:** expectations about a gender or genders that comes from knowledge about the time and place in which language is used, rather than from linguistic patterns alone (i.e., sentence structure or word choice)

(a) **Stereotype:** a word or words that communicate an expectation of a person or people's behaviors or preferences that does not reflect the extent of their possible behaviors or preferences; or that focus on a single aspect of a person that doesn't represent that person holistically
Example 3(a): "The engraving depicts a walking figure (female) set against sunlight, and holding/releasing a bird." (Fonds ID: Coll-1116)

(b) **Omission:** focusing on the presence, responsibility, or contribution of one gender in a situation where more than one gender has a presence, responsibility or contribution; or defining a person in terms of their relation to another person
Example 3(b): "This group portrait of Laurencin, Apollinaire, and Picasso and his mistress became the theme of a larger version in 1909 entitledApollinaire [sic] and his friends." (Fonds ID: Coll-1090).

(c) **Occupation:** a word or words that refer to a person or people's job title for which the person or people received payment, excluding occupations in pre-nominal titles (for example, "Colonel Sir Thomas" should not have an occupation label)
Example 3(c): "He became a surgeon with the Indian Medical Service." (Fonds ID: Coll-1096).

(d) **Empowering:** reclaiming derogatory words as positive
Example 3(d): a person describing themself as queer in a self-affirming manner

We chose to build on the gender bias taxonomy of Hitti et al. (2019) because the authors grounded their definitions of types of gender bias in gender studies and linguistics, and focused on identifying gender bias at the word level, aligning with our approach. Though Dinan et al. (2020b) also provide a framework for defining types of gender bias, their framework focuses on relationships between people in a conversation, identifying "bias when speaking ABOUT someone, bias when speaking TO someone, and bias from speaking AS someone" (316). The nature of our corpus makes these gender bias dimensions irrelevant to our work: GLAM documentation contains descriptions that only contain text written *about* a person or people (or other topics); it does not contain text that provides gender information about who is speaking or who is being spoken to. Additionally, despite writing of four gender values (unknown, neutral, feminine, and masculine), the dataset and classifiers of Dinan et al. (2020b) are limited to "*masculine* and *feminine* classes" (317). The authors also do not explain how they define "bias," limiting our ability to draw on their research.

Doughman et al. (2021) provide another gender bias taxonomy that builds on that of Hitti et al. (2019), resulting in overlaps between our taxonomies. However, Doughman et al. (2020) focus on gender stereotypes, while our taxonomy considers other types of gender biases. Though less explicit in the names of our taxonomy's labels, we also looked to the descriptions of gender and gender bias from Cao and Daumé III (2021), who point out the limited gender information available in language. The aim of our dataset creation differs from Cao and Daumé III (2021), though. They created data that represents trans and gender diverse identities in order to evaluate models' gender biases, specifically looking at where coreference resolution fails on trans and non-binary referents. By contrast, we aim to create a dataset that documents biased representations of gender, with the future aim of creating models that are able to identify types of gender bias in language.

6 Case Study

To demonstrate the application of the taxonomy, we present a case study situated in the United Kingdom in the 21st century, annotating archival documentation written in British English from the Centre for Research Collections at the University of Edinburgh (CRC Archives). This paper thus takes the first step in building a collection of case studies that situate NLP bias research in a specific context.

	Title	Biographical/Historical	Scope & Contents	Processing Information	Total
Count	4,834	576	6198	280	11,888
Words	51,904	75,032	269,892	3,129	399,957
Sentences	5,932	3,829	14,412	301	24,474

Table 1: Total counts, words and sentences for descriptive metadata fields in the aggregated dataset. Calculations were made using Punkt tokenizers in the Natural Language Toolkit Python library (Loper and Bird, 2002).

A collection of case studies would enable the NLP community to determine which aspects of bias mitigation approaches generalize across time, location, culture, people, and identity characteristics.

The CRC's Archives' documentation served as a suitable data source because the documentation adheres to an international standard for organizing archival metadata (ISAD(G) (ICA, 2011)), the archivists at the institution had found gender bias in the documentation's language, and the archivists were already engaged in efforts to mitigate gender bias in the archival documentation. The documentation describes a variety of heritage collections and items, such as letters, journals, photographs, degree certificates, and drawings; on a variety of topics, such as religion, research, teaching, architecture, and town planning. Employees at the partner institution describe themselves as activists changing archival practices to more accurately represent the diverse groups of people that the archival collections are intended to serve.

The annotation corpus consists of 24,474 sentences and 399,957 words, selected from the first 20% of the entire corpus of archival documentation from the partner institution's catalog (see §B.9 for more on this corpus). Table 1 provides a breakdown of the size of the annotation corpus by metadata field. 90% of the annotation corpus (circa 22,027 sentences and 359,961 words) was doubly annotated with all labels, and 10% of the annotation corpus (circa 2,447 sentences and 39,996 words) was triply annotated with all labels. In total, the annotation process amounted to circa 400 hours of work and £5,333.76, funded by a variety of internal institutional funds. Each of the four hired annotators worked for 72 hours over eight weeks at £18.52 per hour (minimum wage is £9.50 per hour (Gov.uk, 2022)). The hired annotators were PhD students selected for their experience in gender studies or archives, with three of the annotators having experience in both. The lead annotator worked for 86 hours over 16 weeks as part of their PhD research.

The categories of labels in the annotation taxonomy were divided among annotators according to the textual relations the labels record. Hired annotators 1 and 2 (A1 and A2) labeled internal relations of the text with *Person Name* and *Linguistic* categories, hired annotators 3 and 4 (A3 and A4) labeled external relations of the text with the *Contextual* category, and the lead annotator (A0) labeled both relations with all categories. A1 and A3 labeled the same subset of archival documentation, and A2 and A4 labeled the same subset of archival documentation, ensuring every description had labels from all categories. The lead annotator labeled the same descriptions as A1 and A3, and a subset of the descriptions that A2 and A4 labeled (due to time constraints, A0 could not label all the same descriptions). Prior to beginning annotation, *Gendered Pronoun*, *Gendered Role*, and *Occupation* labels were automatically applied. The annotators corrected mistakes from this automated process during their manual annotation.

We produced three instances of the annotation corpus: one for A0, one for each pair of hired annotators (A1 and A3, and A2 and A4), and one aggregated dataset. The aggregated dataset combines annotations from all five annotators, totaling 76,543 annotations with duplicates and 55,260 annotations after deduplication. Manual reviews of each annotator's dataset informed the aggregation approach, which involved a combination of programmatic and manual steps. The data statement in §B details the aggregation approach. Figure 1 displays the number of annotations in the aggregated dataset by label (§A contains additional annotation figures). In line with perspectivist NLP (Basile, 2022), the individual annotator's datasets will be published alongside the aggregated dataset, enabling researchers to interrogate patterns of agreement and disagreement, and enabling future work to compare the performance of classifiers trained on disaggregated and aggregated datasets.

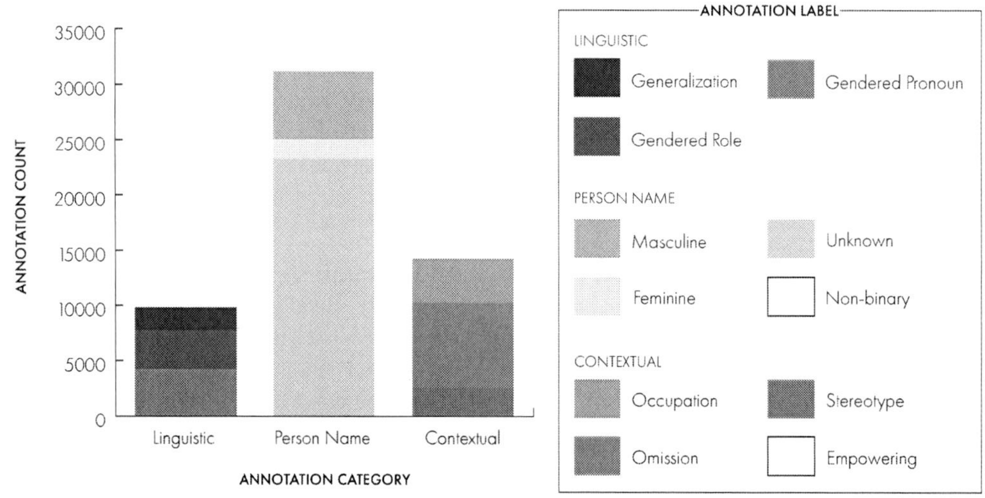

Figure 1: Total Annotations Per Label in the Aggregated Dataset. The stacked bar chart groups annotation labels into bars by category. Across all three categories, there are 55,260 annotations in the aggregated dataset. *Non-binary* (a *Person Name* label) and *Empowering* (a *Contextual* label) both have a count of zero.

6.1 Inter-Annotator Agreement

Due to our aim to create a training dataset for document classification models, identifying strictly matching text spans that annotators labeled was deemed less important than the presence of a label in a description. Consequently, inter-annotator agreement (IAA) calculations consider annotations with the same label to agree if their text spans match or overlap. Figures 2 and 3 display the F_1 scores for each label, with the aggregated dataset's labels as predicted and the annotators' labels as expected. Tables 2 and 3 in the appendices list true and false positives, false negatives, precision, and recall, in addition to F_1 scores, for IAA among the annotators and with the aggregated dataset.

IAA calculations reflect the subjectivity of gender bias in language. F_1 scores for the gendered language labels *Gendered Role* and *Gendered Pronoun* fall between 0.71 and 0.99. F_1 scores for annotating gender biased language are relatively low, with the greatest agreement on the *Generalization* label at only 0.56, on the *Omission* label at 0.48, and on the *Stereotype* label at 0.57. For *Person Name* labels, A0 and A2 agree more than A1: A0 and A2's F_1 scores for all *Person Name* labels are between 0.82 and 0.86, while A1's scores with either A0 or A2 are between 0.42 and 0.64. A1 has a particularly high false negative rate for the *Unknown* label compared to A0.

After creating the aggregated dataset, we calculated IAA between each annotator and the aggregated dataset. F_1 scores for all *Person Name* and *Linguistic* labels except *Generalization* are similarly high (0.74 to 0.98). *Generalization* proved particularly difficult to label. Annotators used *Generalization* and *Gendered Role* inconsistently. As a result, during the aggregation process, we revised the definition of *Generalization* to more clearly distinguish it from *Gendered Role*. Consequently the IAA between annotators and the aggregated dataset for this label is particularly low (0.1 to 0.4).

For *Contextual* labels, F_1 scores with the aggregated dataset as "expected" and an annotator as "predicted" increased more dramatically than the *Person Name* and *Linguistic* labels' F_1 scores. Besides *Omission* with A3, all F_1 scores are between 0.76 and 0.91. For *Stereotype*, A3 agreed more strongly with the aggregated dataset than A0 and A4. The reverse is true for *Omission* and *Occupation*, with A0 and A4 agreeing more strongly with the aggregated dataset than A3. A3's notes explain that she did not annotate an incomplete version of a person's name as an omission if the complete version was provided elsewhere in the collection's descriptions, whereas A0 and A4 annotated incomplete versions of people's names as omission unless the complete version appeared in the same description.

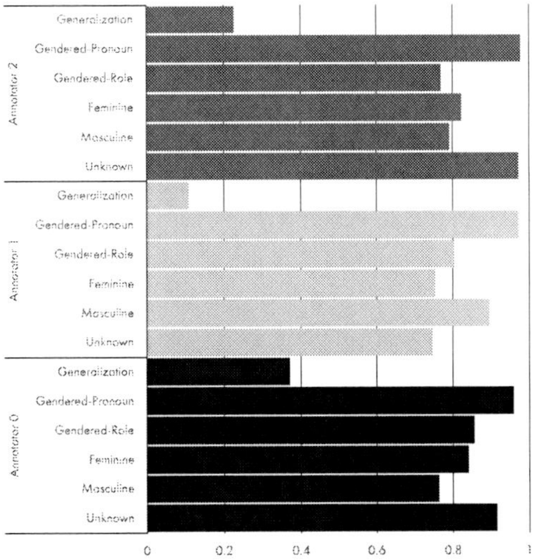

Figure 2: Total Annotations Per Label in the Aggregated Dataset. The stacked bar chart groups annotation labels into bars by category. Across all three categories, there are 55,260 annotations in the aggregated dataset. *Non-binary* (a *Person Name* label) and *Empowering* (a *Contextual* label) both have a count of zero.

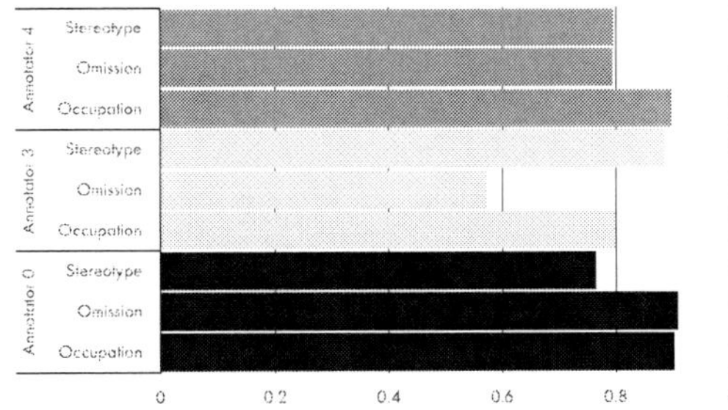

Figure 3: Total Annotations Per Label in the Aggregated Dataset. The stacked bar chart groups annotation labels into bars by category. Across all three categories, there are 55,260 annotations in the aggregated dataset. *Non-binary* (a *Person Name* label) and *Empowering* (a *Contextual* label) both have a count of zero.

Two labels were not applied according to the taxonomy's definitions: *Empowering* and *Non-binary*. *Empowering* was used by A3 according to a different definition than that of the taxonomy (see §B). As only 80 instances of the label exist in A3's dataset, though, there are likely to be insufficient examples for effectively training classifiers on this label in future work.

The annotators did not use the *Non-binary* label. That being said, this does not mean there were not people who would identify as non-binary represented in the text of the annotation corpus. Additional linguistic and historical research may identify people who were likely to identify as non-binary in the corpus of archival documentation, as well as more specific gender identities for people whose names were annotated as *Masculine* or *Feminine*. Metadata entries for people in the partner institution's catalog may also provide more information relevant to gender identities. Shopland (2020) finds that focusing on actions that people were described doing can help to locate people of minoritized genders (and sexualities) in historical texts. However, Shopland also cautions researchers against assuming too much: a full understanding of a person's gender often remains unattainable from the documentation that exists about them.

As Figure 1 displays, *Unknown* is the most prevalent label in the *Person Name* category, because each annotation of a person's name was informed by words within the description in which that name appears. Consequently, for people named in more than one description, there may be different person name labels applied to their name across those descriptions. The rationale for this approach comes from the aim to train document classification models on the annotated data where each description serves as a document. Should a person change their gender during their lifetime, and archival documentation exists that describes them as different genders, the person may wish a model to use the most recent description of a person to determine their gender, or not use any gender information about the person, in case obviating their change of gender leads to safety concerns (Dunsire, 2018). Furthermore, many GLAM content management systems do not have versioning control, so dates of descriptions may not exist to determine the most recent description of a person's gender. *Person Name* labels are thus based on the description in which a name appears to minimize the risk of misgendering (Scheuerman et al., 2020).

7 Discussion and Limitations

The paper's annotation taxonomy builds on biased language research from NLP, information sciences, gender studies, and linguistics literature. The gender bias taxonomy of Hitti et al. (2019), which categorizes gender biases based on whether the bias comes from the sentence structure or the context (i.e. people, relationships, time period, location) of the language, served as a foundation. We adopted four labels from that taxonomy: *Gendered Pronoun*, *Gendered Role*, *Generalization*, and *Stereotype* (merging Hitti et al.'s Societal Stereotype and Behavioral Stereotype categories). Drawing on archival science and critical discourse analysis, and guided by participatory action research with archivists (e.g., interviews, workshops), we added to and restructured Hitti et al.'s taxonomy. The *Person Name* labels were added so that the representation of people of different genders in the archival documentation could be estimated. Annotators chose which label to apply to a person's name based on gendered pronouns or roles that refer to that person in the description in which their name appears. For example, "they" as singular for *Non-binary*, "his" for *Masculine*, and "she" for *Feminine*; or "Mx." for *Non-binary*, "Lady" for *Feminine*, or "son" for *Masculine*. The *Unknown*, *Feminine*, and *Masculine* labels distinguish our approach from previous NLP gender bias work that has not allowed for uncertainty.

Guessing a person's gender risks misgendering (Scheuerman et al., 2020), a representational harm (Blodgett et al., 2020; Crawford, 2017), and fails to acknowledge that sufficient information often is not available to determine a person's gender with certainty (Shopland, 2020). This led us to replace the initial labels of *Woman* and *Man* with *Feminine* and *Masculine*, recognizing that pronouns and roles are insufficient for determining how people define their gender. Each *Person Name* label encompasses multiple genders. For instance, a person who identifies as a transwoman, as genderfluid, or as a cis woman may use feminine pronouns, such as "she," or feminine roles, such as "wife." Though we aimed to create a taxonomy inclusive of all genders, we acknowledge this may not have been achieved, and welcome feedback on how to represent any genders inadvertently excluded.

We also added three labels to the *Contextual* category: *Occupation*, *Omission*, and *Empowering*. *Occupation* was added because, when combined with historical employment statistics, *Occupation*-labeled text spans could inform estimates of the representation of particular genders within the collaborating archive's collections. Furthermore, *Person Name* annotations combined with their occupations could guide researchers to material beyond the archive that may provide information about those people's gender identity. *Omission* was added because, during group interviews, representatives from the collaborating archive described finding gender bias through the lack of information provided about women relative to the detail provided about men. *Empowering* was added to account for how communities reclaim certain derogatory terms, such as "queer," in a positive, self-affirming manner (Bucholtz, 1999).

Figure 1 displays how prevalent *Omission* was in the annotated data: this label is the most commonly applied label from the *Contextual* category. Such prevalence demonstrates the value of interdisciplinary collaboration and stakeholder engagement, carried out in our participatory action research with domain experts. Had archivists at the partner institution not been consulted, we would not have known how relevant omitted information regarding gender identities would be to identifying and measuring gender bias in archival documentation.

The final annotation taxonomy includes labels for gendered language (specifically, *Gendered Role*, *Gendered Pronoun*, and all labels in the *Person Name* category), rather than only explicitly gender biased language (specifically, *Generalization*, *Stereotype*, and *Omission*), because measuring the use of gendered words across an entire archives' collection provides information about gender bias at the overall collections' level. For example, using a gendered pronoun such as "he" is not inherently biased, but if the use of this masculine gendered pronoun far outnumbers the use of other gendered pronouns in our dataset, we can observe that the masculine is over-represented, indicating a masculine bias in the archives' collections overall. Labeling gender-biased language focuses on the individual description level. For example, the stereotype of a wife playing a supporting role to her husband comes through in this description:
Jewel took an active interest in her husband's work, accompanying him when he travelled, sitting on charitable committees, looking after missionary furlough houses and much more.

Instructions for applying the taxonomy permitted labels to overlap as each annotator saw fit, and asked annotators to annotate from their contemporary perspective. Approaching the archival metadata descriptions as discourse (meaning language as representations of the material, mental, and social worlds (Fairclough, 2003)), the taxonomy of labels represents the "internal relations" and "external relations" of the descriptions (ibid., 37). The *Person Name* and *Linguistic* categories annotate internal relations, meaning the "vocabulary (or 'lexical') relations" (ibid., 37) of the descriptions. To apply their labels, annotators looked for the presence of particular words and phrases (i.e., gendered pronouns, gendered titles, familial roles).

The *Contextual* category annotates external relations: relations with "social events ... social practices and social structures" (Fairclough, 2003, 36). To apply *Contextual* labels, annotators reflected on the production and reception of the language in the archival documentation. For instance, to apply the *Stereotype* label, annotators considered the relationship between a description's language with social hierarchies in 21st century British society, determining whether the term or phase adequately represented the possible gender diversity of people being described.

8 Conclusion and Future Work

This paper has presented a taxonomy of gender biased language with a case study to support clarity and alignment in NLP gender bias research. Recognizing the value of clearly defined metrics for advancing bias mitigation, the taxonomy provides a structure for identifying types of gender biased language at the level they originate (words and phrases), rather than at a level of abstraction (i.e., vector spaces). Still, the case study presented in this paper demonstrates the difficulty of determining people's gender with certainty. While recognizing the value of NLP systems for mitigating harms from gender biased language at large scale, we contend that conceptualizations of gender must extend to trans and gender diverse gender expressions if NLP systems are to empower minoritized gender communities.

Future work will include the publication of the case study's datasets, analysis of the datasets, and document classification models trained on the datasets. The datasets will include each individual annotator's dataset and two aggregated datasets, one with duplicates across different annotators, and one deduplicated to exclude matching and overlapping annotations from different annotators. The analysis of the datasets and creation of models trained on them will be informed by participatory action research, incorporating perspectives from archivists, and from people of trans and gender diverse identities not represented in the research team. The dataset will be published in the same location as the code written to create the corpus of archival documentation and the annotated datasets.[5] The taxonomy and forthcoming datasets aim to guide NLP systems towards measurable and inclusive conceptualizations of gender.

Acknowledgements

Thank you to our collaborators, Rachel Hosker and her team at the Centre for Research Collections; our annotators, Suzanne Black, Ashlyn Cudney, Anna Kuslits, and Iona Walker; and Richard Tobin, who wrote the pre-annotation scripts for this paper's annotation process. We also extend our gratitude to the organizations who provided grants to support the research reported in this paper: the University of Edinburgh's Edinburgh Futures Institute, Centre for Data, Culture &Society, Institute for Language, Cognition and Computation, and School of Informatics; and the UK's Engineering and Physical Sciences Research Council. Additional thanks go to the organizers of the Fourth Workshop on Gender Bias in Natural Language Processing, for the opportunity to submit this paper, and to the reviewers who gave feedback on this paper.

References

Valerio Basile. 2022. The Perspectivist Data Manifesto. [Online; accessed March 21, 2022].

Valerio Basile, Federico Cabitza, Andrea Campagner, and Michael Fell. 2021. Toward a Perspectivist Turn in Ground Truthing for Predictive Computing. *CoRR*, abs/2109.04270.

Christine Basta, Marta R Costa-jussà, and Noe Casas. 2020. Extensive Study on the Underlying Gender Bias in Contextualized Word Embeddings. *Neural Computing & Applications*, 33(8):3371–3384.

Emily M. Bender and Batya Friedman. 2018. Data Statements for Natural Language Processing: Toward Mitigating System Bias and Enabling Better Science. *Transactions of the Association for Computational Linguistics*, 6:587–604.

Emily M. Bender, Timnit Gebru, Angelina McMillan-Major, and Shmargaret Shmitchell. 2021. On the Dangers of Stochastic Parrots: Can Language Models Be Too Big? In *Proceedings of the 2021 ACM Conference on Fairness, Accountability, and Transparency*, FAccT '21, page 610–623, New York, USA. Association for Computing Machinery.

Ruha Benjamin. 2019. *Race after technology : abolitionist tools for the new Jim code*. Polity, Cambridge, UK.

[5] `github.com/thegoose20/annot`

Abeba Birhane and Vinay Uday Prabhu. 2021. Large image datasets: A pyrrhic win for computer vision? *2021 IEEE Winter Conference on Applications of Computer Vision (WACV)*, pages 1536–1546.

Bronwyn M Bjorkman. 2017. Singular They and the Syntactic Representation of Gender in English. *Glossa (London)*, 2(1):1.

Su Blodgett, Solon Barocas, Hal Daumé III, and Hanna Wallach. 2020. Language (Technology) is Power: A Critical Survey of "Bias" in NLP. In *Proceedings of the 58th Annual Meeting of the Association for Computational Linguistics*, pages 5454–5476.

Su Lin Blodgett, Gilsinia Lopez, Alexandra Olteanu, Robert Sim, and Hanna Wallach. 2021. Stereotyping Norwegian salmon: An inventory of pitfalls in fairness benchmark datasets. In *Proceedings of the 59th Annual Meeting of the Association for Computational Linguistics and the 11th International Joint Conference on Natural Language Processing (Volume 1: Long Papers)*, pages 1004–1015, Online. Association for Computational Linguistics.

Tolga Bolukbasi, Kai-Wei Chang, James Zou, Venkatesh Saligrama, and Adam Kalai. 2016. Man is to Computer Programmer as Woman is to Homemaker? Debiasing Word Embeddings. In *Proceedings of the 30th International Conference on Neural Information Processing Systems*, pages 4356–4364.

Daniel Borkan, Lucas Dixon, Jeffrey Sorensen, Nithum Thain, and Lucy Vasserman. 2019. Nuanced Metrics for Measuring Unintended Bias with Real Data for Text Classification. In *WWW '19: Companion Proceedings of The 2019 World Wide Web Conference*, WWW '19, page 491–500, New York, USA. Association for Computing Machinery.

Mary Bucholtz. 1999. Gender. *Journal of linguistic anthropology*, 9(1-2):80–83.

Yang Trista Cao and Hal Daumé III. 2020. Toward gender-inclusive coreference resolution. In *Proceedings of the 58th Annual Meeting of the Association for Computational Linguistics*, pages 4568–4595, Online. Association for Computational Linguistics.

Yang Trista Cao and Hal Daumé III. 2021. Toward gender-inclusive coreference resolution: An analysis of gender and bias throughout the machine learning lifecycle*. *Computational Linguistics*, 47(3):615–661.

Terry Cook. 2011. 'We Are What We Keep; We Keep What We Are': Archival Appraisal Past, Present and Future. *Journal of the Society of Archivists*, 32(2):173–189.

M.Z. Corbett. 1990. Clearing the air: some thoughts on gender-neutral writing. *IEEE Transactions on Professional Communication*, 33(1):2–6.

Sasha Costanza-Chock and Nick Philip. 2018. Design Justice, A.I., and Escape from the Matrix of Domination. *Journal of Design and Science*.

Kate Crawford. 2017. The Trouble with Bias. In *Neural Information Processing Systems Conference Keynote*. [Online; accessed 10-July-2020].

CRC. 2018. Collection: Papers and artwork of Yolanda Sonnabend relating to her collaboration with C.H. Waddington. [Online; accessed 19 May 2022.

Kimberlé Crenshaw. 1991. Mapping the Margins: Intersectionality, Identity Politics, and Violence against Women of Color. *Stanford Law Review*, 43(6):1241–1299.

Aida Mostafazadeh Davani, Mark Díaz, and Vinodkumar Prabhakaran. 2022. Dealing with Disagreements: Looking Beyond the Majority Vote in Subjective Annotations. *Transactions of the Association for Computational Linguistics*, 10:92–110.

Hannah Devinney, Jenny Björklund, and Henrik Björklund. 2022. Theories of "Gender" in NLP Bias Research. *Computing Research Repository*.

Catherine D'Ignazio and Lauren F. Klein. 2020. *Data Feminism*. Strong ideas series. MIT Press, Cambridge, USA.

Emily Dinan, Angela Fan, Adina Williams, Jack Urbanek, Douwe Kiela, and Jason Weston. 2020a. Queens are powerful too: Mitigating gender bias in dialogue generation. In *Proceedings of the 2020 Conference on Empirical Methods in Natural Language Processing (EMNLP)*, pages 8173–8188, Online. Association for Computational Linguistics.

Emily Dinan, Angela Fan, Ledell Wu, Jason Weston, Douwe Kiela, and Adina Williams. 2020b. Multi-Dimensional Gender Bias Classification. In *Proceedings of the 2020 Conference on Empirical Methods in Natural Language Processing (EMNLP)*, pages 314–331, Online. Association for Computational Linguistics.

Jad Doughman, Fatima Abu Salem, and Shady Elbassuoni. 2020. Time-aware word embeddings for three Lebanese news archives. In *Proceedings of the 12th Language Resources and Evaluation Conference*, pages 4717–4725, Marseille, France. European Language Resources Association.

Jad Doughman, Wael Khreich, Maya El Gharib, Maha Wiss, and Zahraa Berjawi. 2021. Gender bias in text: Origin, taxonomy, and implications. In *Proceedings of the 3rd Workshop on Gender Bias in Natural Language Processing*, pages 34–44, Online. Association for Computational Linguistics.

Gordon Dunsire. 2018. Ethical issues in catalogue content standards. In *Catalogue & Index*, volume 191, pages 11–15.

Erick Elejalde, Leo Ferres, and Eelco Herder. 2017. The Nature of Real and Perceived Bias in Chilean Media. In *Proceedings of the 28th ACM Conference on Hypertext and Social Media*, HT '17, page 95–104, New York, USA. Association for Computing Machinery.

Norman Fairclough. 2003. *Analysing Discourse: Textual Analysis for Social Research.* Routledge, London, UK.

Noah Geraci. 2019. Programmatic approaches to bias in descriptive metadata. In *Code4Lib Conference 2019*. [Online; accessed 28-May-2020].

Ilka H. Gleibs. 2017. Are all "research fields" equal? Rethinking practice for the use of data from crowdsourcing market addresss. *Behavior Research Methods*, 49(4):1333–1342.

Seraphina Goldfarb-Tarrant, Rebecca Marchant, Ricardo Muñoz Sánchez, Mugdha Pandya, and Adam Lopez. 2021. Intrinsic bias metrics do not correlate with application bias. In *Proceedings of the 59th Annual Meeting of the Association for Computational Linguistics and the 11th International Joint Conference on Natural Language Processing (Volume 1: Long Papers)*, pages 1926–1940, Online. Association for Computational Linguistics.

Hila Gonen and Yoav Goldberg. 2019. Lipstick on a Pig: Debiasing Methods Cover up Systematic Gender Biases in Word Embeddings But do not Remove Them. *NAACL 2019*, arXiv:1903.03862v2.

Gov.uk. 2022. National Minimum Wage and National Living Wage rates.

Donna Haraway. 1988. Situated Knowledges: The Science Question in Feminism and the Privilege of Partial Perspective. *Feminist Studies*, 14(3):575.

Sandra Harding. 1995. "Strong objectivity": A response to the new objectivity question. *Synthese*, 104(3).

Lucy Havens, Melissa Terras, Benjamin Bach, and Beatrice Alex. 2020. Situated data, situated systems: A methodology to engage with power relations in natural language processing research. In *Proceedings of the Second Workshop on Gender Bias in Natural Language Processing*, pages 107–124, Barcelona, Spain (Online). Association for Computational Linguistics.

Yasmeen Hitti, Eunbee Jang, Ines Moreno, and Carolyne Pelletier. 2019. Proposed Taxonomy for Gender Bias in Text; A Filtering Methodology for the Gender Generalization Subtype. In *Proceedings of the First Workshop on Gender Bias in Natural Language Processing*, pages 8–17, Florence, IT. Association for Computational Linguistics.

Christoph Hube and Besnik Fetahu. 2019. Neural Based Statement Classification for Biased Language. In *Proceedings of the Twelfth ACM International Conference on Web Search and Data Mining*, pages 195–203, Melbourne, AU. ACM.

Ben Hutchinson, Vinodkumar Prabhakaran, Emily Denton, Kellie Webster, Yu Zhong, and Stephen Denuyl. 2020. Social biases in NLP models as barriers for persons with disabilities. In *Proceedings of the 58th Annual Meeting of the Association for Computational Linguistics*, pages 5491–5501, Online. Association for Computational Linguistics.

Ben Hutchinson, Andrew Smart, Alex Hanna, Emily Denton, Christina Greer, Oddur Kjartansson, Parker Barnes, and Margaret Mitchell. 2021. Towards Accountability for Machine Learning Datasets: Practices from Software Engineering and Infrastructure. In *Proceedings of the 2021 ACM Conference on Fairness, Accountability, and Transparency*, FAccT '21, page 560–575, New York, USA. Association for Computing Machinery.

ICA. 2011. ISAD(G): General International Standard Archival Description - Second edition.

May Jiang and Christiane Fellbaum. 2020. Interdependencies of gender and race in contextualized word embeddings. In *Proceedings of the Second Workshop on Gender Bias in Natural Language Processing*, pages 17–25, Barcelona, Spain (Online). Association for Computational Linguistics.

Eun Seo Jo and Timnit Gebru. 2020. Lessons from Archives: Strategies for Collecting Sociocultural Data in Machine Learning. In *Proceedings of the 2020 Conference on Fairness, Accountability, and Transparency*, FAT* '20, page 306–316, New York, USA. Association for Computing Machinery.

Os Keyes. 2018. The Misgendering Machines: Trans/HCI Implications of Automatic Gender Recognition. *Proceedings of the ACM on Human-Computer Interaction*, 2(CSCW).

Keita Kurita, Nidhi Vyas, Ayush Pareek, Alan W Black, and Yulia Tsvetkov. 2019. Measuring Bias in Contextualized Word Representations. *CoRR*, abs/1906.07337.

Robin Lakoff. 1989. *Language and Woman's Place*. Harper & Row, New York, USA.

Susan Leavy. 2018. Gender Bias in Artificial Intelligence: The Need for Diversity and Gender Theory in Machine Learning. In *Proceedings of the 1st International Workshop on Gender Equality in Software Engineering*, GE '18, page 14–16, New York, USA. Association for Computing Machinery.

Jason Edward Lewis, Nick Philip, Noelani Arista, Archer Pechawis, and Suzanne Kite. 2018. Making Kin with the Machines. *Journal of Design and Science*.

Edward Loper and Steven Bird. 2002. NLTK: The Natural Language Toolkit. In *Proceedings of the ACL-02 Workshop on Effective Tools and Methodologies for Teaching Natural Language Processing and Computational Linguistics - Volume 1*, ETMTNLP '02, pages 63–70, USA. Association for Computational Linguistics.

Bella Martin and Bruce Hanington. 2012. 11 Case studies. In *Universal Methods of Design: 100 Ways to Research Complex Problems, Develop Innovative Ideas, and Design Effective Solutions*, Beverly, USA. Rockport Publishers.

Melissa McCradden, Mjaye Mazwi, Shalmali Joshi, and James A. Anderson. 2020. *When Your Only Tool Is A Hammer: Ethical Limitations of Algorithmic Fairness Solutions in Healthcare Machine Learning*, page 109. Association for Computing Machinery, New York, USA.

Margaret Mitchell, Simone Wu, Andrew Zaldivar, Parker Barnes, Lucy Vasserman, Ben Hutchinson, Elena Spitzer, Inioluwa Deborah Raji, and Timnit Gebru. 2019. Model Cards for Model Reporting. *Proceedings of the Conference on Fairness, Accountability, and Transparency - FAT∗'19*.

Safiya Umoja Noble. 2018. *Algorithms of Oppression: How Search Engines Reinforce Racism*. New York University Press, New York, USA.

Helen O'Neill, Anne Welsh, David A Smith, Glenn Roe, and Melissa Terras. 2021. Text mining Mill: Computationally detecting influence in the writings of John Stuart Mill from library records. *Digital Scholarship in the Humanities*, 36(4):1013–1029.

Thomas Padilla. 2017. On a Collections as Data Imperative. *UC Santa Barbara Previously Published Works*.

Thomas Padilla. 2019. Responsible Operations: Data Science, Machine Learning, and AI in Libraries. *OCLC Research*.

Caroline Criado Perez. 2019. *Invisible Women: Exposing Data Bias in a World Designed for Men*. Vintage, London, UK.

Colleen Reid and Wendy Frisby. 2008. 6 Continuing the Journey: Articulating Dimensions of Feminist Participatory Action Research (FPAR). In *The SAGE Handbook of Action Research*, pages 93–105. SAGE Publications Ltd.

Yisi Sang and Jeffrey Stanton. 2022. The Origin and Value of Disagreement Among Data Labelers: A Case Study of Individual Differences in Hate Speech Annotation. In *Information for a Better World: Shaping the Global Future*, Lecture Notes in Computer Science, pages 425–444. Springer International Publishing, Cham.

Maarten Sap, Dallas Card, Saadia Gabriel, Yejin Choi, and Noah A. Smith. 2019. The risk of racial bias in hate speech detection. In *Proceedings of the 57th Annual Meeting of the Association for Computational Linguistics*, pages 1668–1678, Florence, Italy. Association for Computational Linguistics.

Morgan Klaus Scheuerman, Katta Spiel, Oliver L. Haimson, Foad Hamidi, and Stacy M. Branham. 2020. HCI Guidelines for Gender Equity and Inclusion: Misgendering.

Muriel R. Schulz. 2000. The Semantic Derogation of Women. In Lucy Burke, Tony Crowley, and Alan Girvin, editors, *The Routledge language and cultural theory reader*. Routledge, London, UK.

Norena Shopland. 2020. *A Practical Guide to Searching LGBTQIA Historical Records*. Taylor & Francis Group, Milton.

Laurajane Smith. 2006. *Uses of Heritage*. Routledge, London, UK.

Dale Spencer. 2000. Language and reality: Who made the world? (1980). In Lucy Burke, Tony Crowley, and Alan Girvin, editors, *The Routledge language and cultural theory reader*. Routledge, London, UK.

Karolina Stańczak and Isabelle Augenstein. 2021. A survey on gender bias in natural language processing. *CoRR*, abs/2112.14168.

Pontus Stenetorp, Sampo Pyysalo, Goran Topić, Sophia Ananiadou Tomoko Ohta, and Jun'ichi Tsujii. 2012. brat: a Web-based Tool for NLP-Assisted Text Annotation. In *Proceedings of the Demonstrations Session at EACL 2012*. Association for Computational Linguistics.

Marja Liisa Swantz. 2008. 2 Participatory Action Research as Practice. In *The SAGE Handbook of Action Research*, pages 31–48. SAGE Publications Ltd.

Chris Sweeney and Maryam Najafian. 2019. A transparent framework for evaluating unintended demographic bias in word embeddings. In *Proceedings of the 57th Annual Meeting of the Association for Computational Linguistics*, pages 1662–1667, Florence, Italy. Association for Computational Linguistics.

Latanya Sweeney. 2013. Discrimination in online ad delivery. *Communications of the ACM*, 56(5):44–54.

Yi Chern Tan and L. Elisa Celis. 2019. Assessing Social and Intersectional Biases in Contextualized Word Representations. *CoRR*, abs/1911.01485.

G. Thomas Tanselle. 2002. The World as Archive. *Common Knowledge*, 8(2):402–406.

Trans Metadata Collective. 2022. A Mandate for Trans and Gender Diverse Metadata (draft; working title).

Sigal Vainapel, Opher Y. Shamir, Yulie Tenenbaum, and Gadi Gilam. 2015. The dark side of gendered language: The masculine-generic form as a cause for self-report bias. *Psychological Assessment*, 27(4):1513–1519.

Kellie Webster, Marta Recasens, Vera Axelrod, and Jason Baldridge. 2018. Mind the GAP: A Balanced Corpus of Gendered Ambiguous Pronouns. *Computing Research Repository*, arXiv:1810.05201.

Anne Welsh. 2016. The Rare Books Catalog and the Scholarly Database. *Cataloging & Classification Quarterly*, 54(5–6):317–337.

Chris Welty, Praveen Paritosh, and Lora Aroyo. 2019. Metrology for AI: From Benchmarks to Instruments. *CoRR*, abs/1911.01875.

Elizabeth Yale. 2015. The History of Archives: The State of the Discipline. *Book History*, 18(1):332–359.

Jieyu Zhao, Tianlu Wang, Mark Yatskar, Ryan Cotterell, Vicente Ordonez, and Kai-Wei Chang. 2019. Gender bias in contextualized word embeddings. In *Proceedings of the 2019 Conference of the North American Chapter of the Association for Computational Linguistics: Human Language Technologies, Volume 1 (Long and Short Papers)*, pages 629–634, Minneapolis, Minnesota. Association for Computational Linguistics.

Jieyu Zhao, Tianlu Wang, Mark Yatskar, Vicente Ordonez, and Kai-Wei Chang. 2018. Gender Bias in Coreference Resolution: Evaluation and Debiasing Methods. In *Proceedings of the 2018 Conference of the North American Chapter of the Association for Computational Linguistics: Human Language Technologies, Volume 2 (Short Papers)*, pages 15–20, New Orleans, USA. Association for Computational Linguistics.

A Additional Tables and Figures

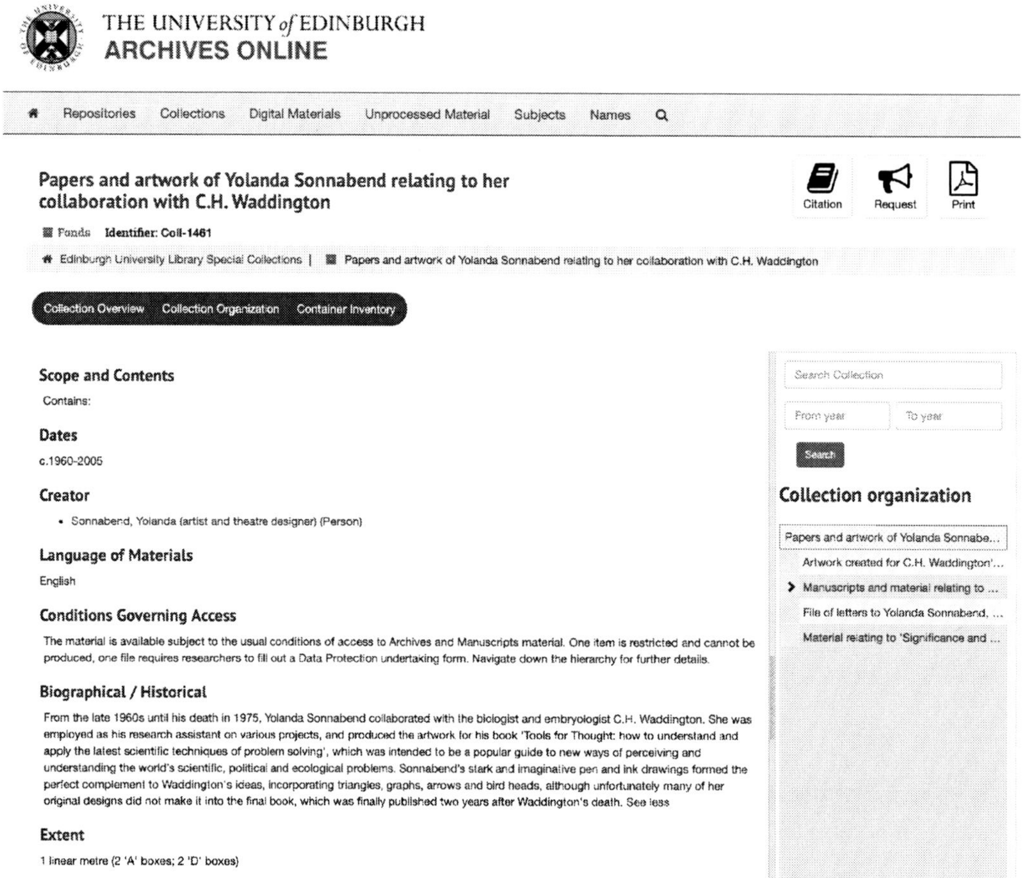

Figure 4: An example of GLAM documentation from the archival catalog of the Centre for Research Collections at the University of Edinburgh (2018). Metadata field names bolded in blue and their descriptions, regular, black text. The 'Title' field, however, is bolded in blue at the top of the page ("Papers and artwork of...").

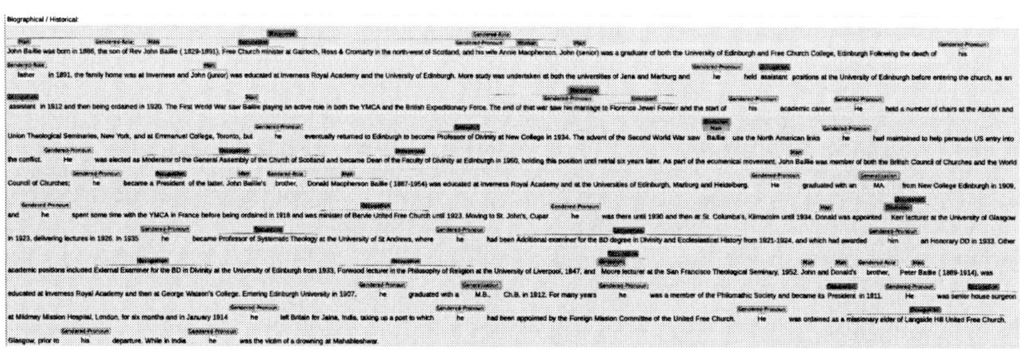

Figure 5: An example of a "Biographical / Historical" metadata field's description annotated with all labels from the taxonomy in the online annotation platform brat (Stenetorp et al., 2012).

exp	pred	label	true pos	false pos	false neg	precision	recall	F_1	files
0	1	Unknown	5031	1524	4268	0.76751	0.54103	0.63467	584
0	2	Unknown	2776	537	432	0.83791	0.86534	0.85140	170
1	2	Unknown	1048	1421	315	0.42446	0.76889	0.54697	72
0	1	Masculine	2367	2372	1079	0.49947	0.68688	0.57838	584
0	2	Masculine	728	111	146	0.86770	0.83295	0.84997	170
1	2	Masculine	380	169	411	0.69217	0.48040	0.56716	72
0	1	Feminine	627	427	642	0.59488	0.49409	0.53982	584
0	2	Feminine	724	128	178	0.84977	0.80266	0.82554	170
1	2	Feminine	287	496	279	0.36654	0.50707	0.42550	72
0	1	Non-binary	0	0	0	-	-	-	584
0	2	Non-binary	0	0	0	-	-	-	170
1	2	Non-binary	0	0	0	-	-	-	72
0	1	Gendered Role	1802	306	882	0.85484	0.67139	0.75209	584
0	2	Gendered Role	1404	162	257	0.89655	0.84527	0.87016	170
1	2	Gendered Role	438	292	52	0.60000	0.89388	0.71803	72
0	1	Gendered Pronoun	3398	101	190	0.97113	0.94705	0.95894	584
0	2	Gendered Pronoun	869	70	60	0.92545	0.93541	0.93041	170
1	2	Gendered Pronoun	518	7	11	0.98667	0.97921	0.98292	72
0	1	Generalization	37	35	262	0.51389	0.12375	0.19946	584
0	2	Generalization	74	51	63	0.59200	0.54015	0.56489	170
1	2	Generalization	2	50	7	0.03846	0.22222	0.06557	72

Table 2: Inter-annotator agreement measures for annotators who used the *Person Name* and *Linguistic* categories of labels to annotate archival documentation. The first two columns note the annotator whose labels were considered expected or predicted, respectively. The abbreviation "pos" is for "positive;" "neg," for "negative." The last column lists the number of files with annotations by both annotators for that row. No annotators applied the "Non-binary" label.

exp	pred	label	true pos	false pos	false neg	precision	recall	F_1	files
0	3	Occupation	1988	613	724	0.76432	0.73303	0.74835	485
0	4	Occupation	738	396	240	0.65079	0.75460	0.69886	149
3	4	Occupation	422	327	134	0.56341	0.75899	0.64674	57
0	3	Omission	1376	914	3259	0.60087	0.29687	0.39740	485
0	4	Omission	416	317	875	0.56753	0.32223	0.41106	149
3	4	Omission	215	315	155	0.40566	0.58108	0.47777	57
0	3	Stereotype	505	539	227	0.48371	0.68989	0.56869	485
0	4	Stereotype	507	525	600	0.49127	0.45799	0.47405	149
3	4	Stereotype	34	60	161	0.36170	0.17435	0.23529	57
0	3	Empowering	0	80	0	-	-	-	485
0	4	Empowering	0	0	0	-	-	-	149
3	4	Empowering	0	0	80	-	-	-	57

Table 3: Inter-annotator agreement measures for annotators who used the *Contextual* category of labels to annotate archival metadata descriptions. The first two columns note the annotator whose labels were considered expected or predicted, respectively. The abbreviation "pos" is for "positive;" "neg," for "negative." The last column lists the number of files with annotations by both annotators for that row. Only annotator 3 applied the "Empowering" label.

exp	pred	label	true pos	false pos	false neg	precision	recall	F_1	files
Agg	0	Unknown	10561	36	1900	0.99660	0.84752	0.91604	714
Agg	1	Unknown	6608	0	4511	1.00000	0.59430	0.74553	597
Agg	2	Unknown	15140	117	679	0.99233	0.95708	0.97439	444
Agg	0	Masculine	3963	18	2446	0.99548	0.61835	0.76285	714
Agg	1	Masculine	4749	1	1099	0.99979	0.81207	0.89621	597
Agg	2	Masculine	1007	5	525	0.99506	0.65731	0.79167	444
Agg	0	Feminine	1454	19	523	0.98710	0.73546	0.84290	714
Agg	1	Feminine	1076	0	707	1.00000	0.60348	0.75271	597
Agg	2	Feminine	994	12	410	0.98807	0.70798	0.82490	444
Agg	0	Nonbinary	0	0	0	-	-	-	714
Agg	1	Nonbinary	0	0	0	-	-	-	597
Agg	2	Nonbinary	0	0	0	-	-	-	444
Agg	0	Gendered-Role	3108	697	330	0.81682	0.90401	0.85821	714
Agg	1	Gendered-Role	1924	218	716	0.89823	0.72879	0.80468	597
Agg	2	Gendered-Role	1471	652	230	0.69289	0.86479	0.76935	444
Agg	0	Gendered-Pronoun	3933	160	165	0.96091	0.95974	0.96032	714
Agg	1	Gendered-Pronoun	3498	3	190	0.99914	0.94848	0.97315	597
Agg	2	Gendered-Pronoun	1016	1	41	0.99902	0.96121	0.97975	444
Agg	0	Generalization	405	1	1370	0.99754	0.22817	0.37139	714
Agg	1	Generalization	69	4	1123	0.94521	0.05789	0.10909	597
Agg	2	Generalization	127	0	862	1.00000	0.12841	0.22760	444

Table 4: Inter-annotator agreement between the aggregated dataset and annotators for the *Person Name* and *Linguistic* categories of labels to annotate archival documentation. The first two columns note the annotator whose labels were considered expected or predicted, respectively. The abbreviation "pos" is for "positive;" "neg," for "negative." The last column lists the number of files with annotations by both annotators for that row. No annotators applied the "Non-binary" label.

exp	pred	label	true pos	false pos	false neg	precision	recall	F_1	files
Agg	0	Occupation	2725	23	571	0.99163	0.82676	0.90172	631
Agg	3	Occupation	2320	290	873	0.88889	0.72659	0.79959	508
Agg	4	Occupation	1746	147	253	0.92235	0.87344	0.89723	450
Agg	0	Omission	5916	12	1187	0.99798	0.83289	0.90799	631
Agg	3	Omission	2310	13	3475	0.99440	0.39931	0.56981	508
Agg	4	Omission	1876	5	967	0.99734	0.65987	0.79424	450
Agg	0	Stereotype	1748	11	1058	0.99375	0.62295	0.76583	631
Agg	3	Stereotype	1089	9	279	0.99180	0.79605	0.88321	508
Agg	4	Stereotype	1400	2	715	0.99857	0.66194	0.79613	450
Agg	0	Empowering	0	0	0	-	-	-	631
Agg	3	Empowering	0	80	0	0.0	-	0.0	508
Agg	4	Empowering	0	0	0	-	-	-	450

Table 5: Inter-annotator agreement between the aggregated dataset and annotators for the *Contextual* category of labels to annotate archival metadata descriptions. The first two columns note the annotator whose labels were considered expected or predicted, respectively. The abbreviation "pos" is for "positive;" "neg," for "negative." The last column lists the number of files with annotations by both annotators for that row. Only annotator 3 applied the "Empowering" label.

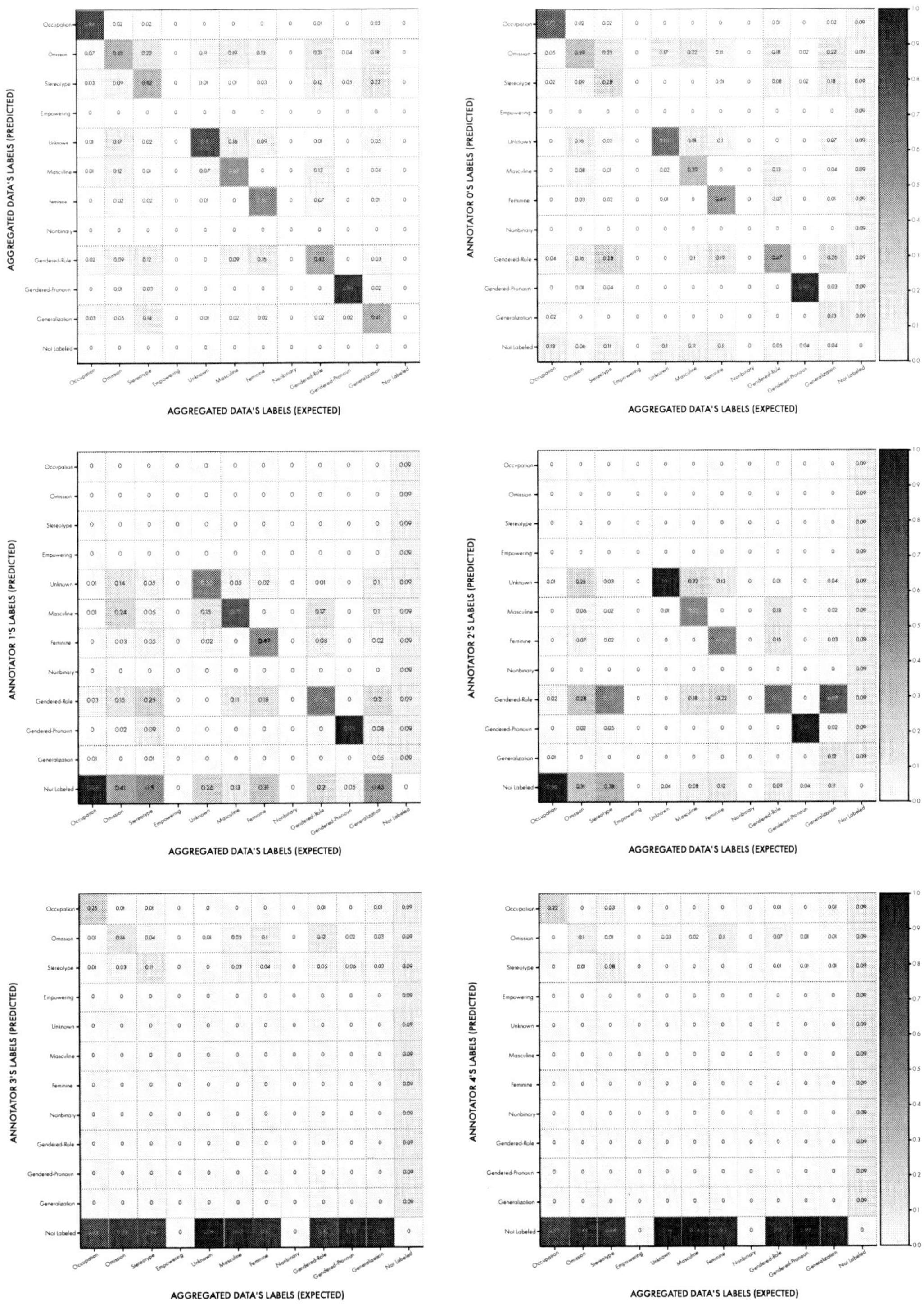

Figure 6: Confusion matrices normalized with a weighted average on the aggregated data's labels, so that class imbalances are taken into account. The top left confusion matrix displays intersections between the aggregated datasets labels, illustrating where the same text spans have more than one label. The remaining confusion matrices to display the agreement between an annotator's labels (Y axis) and the aggregated data's labels (X axis). The Y axis scale is the same for all matrices, ranging from zero to one.

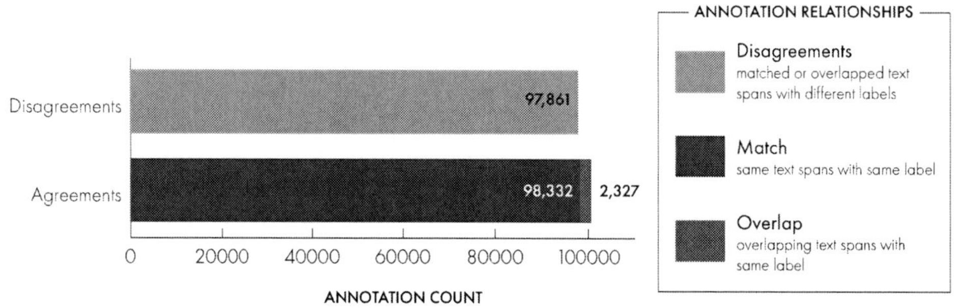

Figure 7: Disagreeing and Agreeing Label Counts Across All Annotators' Datasets. The bar chart displays counts of the occurrence of disagreements and agreements across annotators' labels. Annotations by two annotators with the same or overlapping text span but different labels are considered to be in disagreement. Annotations by two annotators with the same or overlapping text span and the same labels are considered to be in agreement. Agreements with the same text span are considered to be exact matches. Agreements with different but overlapping text spans are considered to be overlaps. Combined, the annotated datasets contain 198,520 annotations.

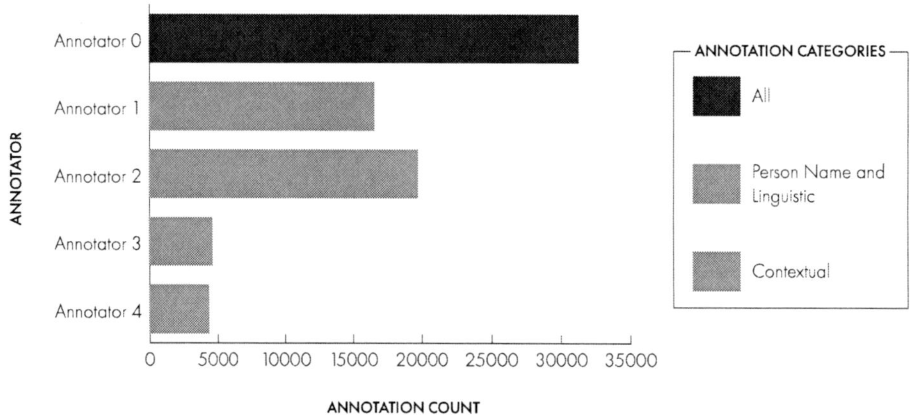

Figure 8: Total Annotations Per Annotator in the Aggregated Dataset. The bar chart displays the total annotations from each annotator included in the aggregated dataset, with colors indicating the category of labels each annotator used. For annotations that matched or overlapped, only one was added to the aggregated dataset, so the total number of annotations in the aggregated dataset (55,260) is 21,283 less than the sum of the annotators' annotations in this chart (76,543).

B Data Statement: Annotated Datasets of Archival Documentation

B.1 Curation Rationale

These datasets were created from a corpus of 1,460 files of archival metadata descriptions totaling circa 15,419 sentences and 255,943 words. That corpus is the first 20% of text from the corpus described in the Provenance Appendix (§B.9), annotated for gender bias according the the taxonomy in Other (§B.8). 73 of files (10% of the text) were triply annotated; the remaining 1,387 files (90% of the text) were doubly annotated. There are six instances of the annotated corpus: one for each of the five annotators and one that aggregates all annotators' labels. Participatory action research with archivists led the project to choose four metadata fields were chosen in the archival catalog to extract for annotation: Title, Scope and Contents, Biographical / Historical, and Processing Information.

The five annotated datasets were merged into a single aggregated dataset for classifier training and evaluation, so comparisons could be made on classifiers' performances after training on an individual annotator's dataset versus on the aggregated dataset. The merging process began with a one-hour manual review of each annotator's labels to identify patterns and common mistakes in their labeling, which informed the subsequent steps for merging the five annotated datasets.

The second step of the merging process was to manually review disagreeing labels for the same text span and add the correct label to the aggregated dataset. Disagreeing labels for the same text span were reviewed for all *Person Name*, *Linguistic*, and *Contextual* categories of labels. For *Person Name* and *Linguistic* labels, where three annotators labeled the same span of text, majority voting determined the correct label: if two out of the three annotators used one label and the other annotator used a different label, the label used by the two annotators was deemed correct and added to the aggregated dataset. For *Contextual* labels, unless an obvious mistake was made, the union of all three annotators' labels was included in the aggregated dataset.

Thirdly, the "Occupation" and "Gendered Pronoun" labels were reviewed. A unique list of the text spans with these labels was generated and incorrect text spans were removed from this list. The "Occupation" and "Gendered Pronoun" labels in the annotated datasets with text spans in the unique lists of valid text spans were added to the aggregated dataset. Fourthly, the remaining *Linguistic* labels ("Gendered Pronoun," "Gendered Role," and "Generalization") not deemed incorrect in the annotated datasets were added to the aggregated dataset. Due to common mistakes in annotating *Person Name* labels with one annotator, only data from the other two annotators who annotated with *Person Name* labels was added to the aggregated dataset. Fifthly, for annotations with overlapping text spans and the same label, the annotation with the longer text span was added to the aggregated dataset. The sixth and final step to constructing the aggregated dataset was to take the union of the remaining *Contextual* labels ("Stereotype," "Omission," "Occupation," and "Empowering") not deemed incorrect in the three annotated datasets with these labels and add them to the aggregated dataset.

B.2 Language Variety

The metadata descriptions extracted from the Archive's catalog are written primarily in British English, with the occasional word in another language such as French or Latin.

B.3 Producer Demographic

The producing research team are of American, German, and Scots nationalities, and are three women and one man. We all work primarily as academic researchers in the disciplines of natural language processing, data science, data visualization, human-computer interaction, digital humanities, and digital cultural heritage. Additionally, one of us is audited an online course on feminist and social justice studies.

B.4 Annotator Demographic

The five annotators are of American and European nationalities and identify as women. Four annotators were hired by the lead annotator for their experience in gender studies and archives. The four annotators worked 72 hours each over eight weeks in 2022, receiving £1,333.44 each (£18.52 per hour). The lead annotator completed the work for her PhD project, which totaled to 86 hours of work over 16 weeks.

B.5 Speech or Publication Situation

The archival metadata descriptions describe material about a range of topics, such as teaching, research, town planning, music, and religion. The materials described also vary, from letters and journals to photographs and audio recordings. The descriptions in this project's dataset with a known date (which describe 38.5% of the archives' records) were written from 1896 through 2020.

The annotated dataset will be published with a forthcoming paper detailing the methodology and theoretical framework that guided the development of the annotation taxonomy and the annotation process, accompanied by analysis of patterns and outliers in the annotated dataset.

B.6 Data Characteristics

The datasets were organized for annotation in a web-based annotation paltform, the brat rapid annotation tool (Stenetorp et al., 2012). Consequently, the data formats conform to the brat formats: plain text files that end in '.txt' contain the original text and plain text files that end in '.ann' contain the annotations. The annotation files include the starting and ending text span of a label, the actual text contained in that span, the label name, and any notes annotators recorded about the rationale for applying the label they did. The names of all the files consist of the name of the fonds (the archival term for a collection) and a number indicating the starting line number of the descriptions. Descriptions from a single fonds were split across files so that no file contained more than 100 lines, because brat could not handle the extensive length of certian fonds' descriptions.

B.7 Data Quality

A subset of annotations were applied automatically with a grep script and then corrected during the manual annotation process. All three categories of the annotation taxonomy were manually applied by the annotators. The lead annotator then manually checked the labels for accuracy. That being said, due to time constraints, mistakes are likely to remain in the application of labels (for example, the starting letter may be missing from a labeled text span or a punctuation mark may have accidentally been included in a labeled text span).

B.8 Other: Annotation Schema

The detailed schema that guided the annotation process is listed below with examples for each label. In each example, the labeled text is underlined. All examples are taken from the dataset except for labels 1.1, "Non-binary," and 3.4, "Empowering," as the annotators did not find any text to which the provided label definitions applied. The annotation instructions permitted labels to overlap as each annotator saw fit, and asked annotators to read and annotate from their contemporary perspective. The categories of labels from the annotation taxonomy were divided among annotators: two hired annotators labeled with categories 1 and 2, two hired annotators labeled with category 3, and the lead annotator labeled with all categories.

The annotation taxonomy includes labels for *gendered* language, rather than only explicitly gender-biased language, because measuring the use of gendered words across an entire archives' collection provides information about gender bias at the overall collections' level. For example, using a gendered pronoun such as "he" is not inherently biased, but if the use of this masculine gendered pronoun far outnumbers the use of other gendered pronouns in our dataset, we can observe that the masculine is over-represented, indicating a masculine bias in the archives' collections overall. Labeling gender-biased language focuses on the individual description level. For example, the stereotype of a wife playing only or primarily a supporting role to her husband comes through in the following description:

> *Jewel took an active interest in her husband's work, accompanying him when he travelled, sitting on charitable committees, looking after missionary furlough houses and much more. She also wrote a preface to his Baptism and Conversion and a foreward [sic] to his A Reasoned Faith.* (Fonds Identifier: Coll-1036)

1. **Person Name:** the name of a person, including any pre-nominal titles (i.e., Professor, Mrs., Sir, Queen), when the person is the primary entity being described (rather than a location named after a person, for example)

   1.1 **Non-binary:*** the pronouns or roles of the named person within the descriptive field in which this instance of the name appears (either Title, Scope and Contents, Biographical / Historical, or Processing Information) are non-binary

   Example 1.1: Francis McDonald went to the University of Edinburgh where they studied law.
   Note: the annotation process did not find suitable text on which to apply this label in the dataset.

1.2 **Feminine:** the pronouns, titles, or roles of the named person within the descriptive field in which this instance of the name appears (either Title, Scope and Contents, Biographical / Historical, or Processing Information) are feminine

Example 1.2: "Jewel took an active interest in her husband's work..." (Fonds Identifier: Coll-1036)

1.3 **Masculine:** the pronouns, titles, or roles of the named person within the descriptive field in which this instance of the name appears (either Title, Scope and Contents, Biographical / Historical, or Processing Information) are masculine

Example 1.3: "Martin Luther, the man and his work." (Fonds Identifier: BAI)

1.4 **Unknown:** any pronouns, titles, or roles of the named person within the descriptive field in which this instance of the name appears (either Title, Scope and Contents, Biographical / Historical, or Processing Information) are gender neutral, or no such pronouns or roles are provided within the descriptive field

Example 1.4: "Testimonials and additional testimonials in favour of Niecks, candidacy for the Chair of Music, 1891" (Fonds Identifier: Coll-1086)

2. **Linguistic:** gender marked in the way a word, phrase or sentence references a person or people, assigning them a specific gender that does not account for all genders possible for that person or people

2.1 **Generalization:** use of a gender-specific term (i.e. roles, titles) to refer to a group of people that could identify as more than the specified gender

Example 2.1: "His classes included Anatomy, Practical Anatomy, ... Midwifery and Diseases of Women, Therapeutics, Neurology, ... Public Health, and Diseases of the Skin." (Fonds Identifier: Coll-1118)

2.2 **Gendered Role:** use of a title or word denoting a person's role that marks either a non-binary, feminine, or masculine gender

Example 2.2: "New map of Scotland for Ladies Needlework, 1797" (Fonds Identifier: Coll-1111)

2.3 **Gendered Pronoun:** explicitly marking the gender of a person or people through the use of pronouns (e.g., he, him, himself, his, her, herself, and she)

Example 2.3: "He obtained surgical qualifications from Edinburgh University in 1873 ([M.B.])." (Fonds Identifier: Coll-1096)

3. **Contextual:** expectations about a gender or genders that comes from knowledge about the time and place in which language is used, rather than from linguistic patterns alone (i.e., sentence structure or word choice)

3.1 **Stereotype:** a word, phrase, or sentence that communicates an expectation of a person or group of people's behaviors or preferences that does not reflect the reality of all their possible behaviors or preferences; or a word, phrase, or sentence that focuses on a particular aspect of a person that doesn't represent that person holistically

Example 3.1: "The engraving depicts a walking figure (female) set against sunlight, and holding/releasing a bird." (Fonds Identifier: Coll-1116)

3.2 **Omission:** focusing on the presence, responsibility, or contribution of a single gender in a situation in which more than one gender has a presence, responsibility or contribution; or defining one person's identity in terms of their relation to another person

Example 3.2: "This group portrait of Laurencin, Apollinaire, and Picasso and his mistress became the theme of a larger version in 1909 entitledApollinaire [sic] and his friends." (Fonds Identifier: Coll-1090).

3.3 **Occupation:** a word or phrase that refers to a person or people's job title (singular or plural) for which the person or people received payment; do not annotate occupations used as a pre-nominal title (for example, "Colonel Sir Thomas Francis Fremantle" should not have an occupation label)

Example 3.3: "He became a surgeon with the Indian Medical Service." (Fonds Identifier: Coll-1096).

3.4 **Empowering:** reclaiming derogatory words or phrases to empower a minoritized person or people

Example 3.4: a person describing themself as queer in a self-affirming, positive manner
*Note: the annotation process did not find enough text on which to apply this label in the dataset to include it when training a classifier. One annotator used the label according to a different definition.***

*The "Non-binary" label was not used by the annotators. That being said, this does not mean there were not people who would identify as non-binary represented in the text of the annotation corpus. When relying only on descriptions written by people other than those represented in the descriptions, knowledge about people's gender identity remains incomplete (Shopland, 2020). Additional linguistic research informed by a knowledge of terminology for the relevant time period may identify people who were likely to identify as non-binary in the corpus of archival metadata descriptions. For example, Shopland (2020) finds that focusing on actions that people were described doing can help to locate people of minoritized genders (and sexualities) in historical texts, but also cautions researchers against assuming too much. A full understanding of a person's gender often remains unattainable from the documentation that exists about them.

**One annotator used the "Empowering" label in the following instances:

- When a person referenced with feminine terms was described as the active party in marriage
- Honor or achievement held by a woman (as indicated in the text)

  Note: Honors and achievements held by men were labeled as stereotypes, as there was a consistent focus on this type of detail about people, which involved spheres of life historically dominated by men in the UK. Spheres of life historically dominated by women in the UK were described with greater vagueness, eliminating the possibility of honors or achievements in these spheres to be identified.
- The fate of a wife is mentioned in an entry predominantly about the life of a husband
- Family members referenced with feminine terms are prioritized (i.e., they are listed first, more detail is given about them than those referenced with masculine terms)
- A gender-neutral term is used instead of gendered term

All annotators were encouraged to use the annotation tool's notes field to record their rationale for particular label choices, especially for text labeled with "Generalization," "Stereotype," or "Omission." The work intends these notes to lend transparency to the annotation process, providing anyone who wishes to use the data with insight onto the annotator's mindset when labeling the archival documentation.

B.9 Provenance Appendix

Data Statement: Corpus of Archival Documentation

B.9.1 Curation Rationale

We (the research team) will use the extracted metadata descriptions to create a gold standard dataset annotated for contextual gender bias. We adopt Hitti et al.'s definition of contextual gender bias in text: written language that connotes or implies an inclination or prejudice against a gender through the use of gender-marked keywords and their context (2019).

A member of our research team has extracted text from four descriptive metadata fields for all collections, subcollections, and items in the Archive's online catalog. The first field is a title field. The second field provides information about the people, time period, and places associated with the collection, subcollection, or item to which the field belongs. The third field summarizes the contents of the collection, subcollection, or item to which the field belongs. The last field records the person who wrote the text for the collection, subcollection, or item's descriptive metadata fields, and the date the person wrote the text (although not all of this information is available in each description; some are empty). Using the dataset of extracted text, we will experiment with training a discriminative classification algorithm to identify types of contextual gender bias. Additionally, the dataset will serve as a source of annotated, historical text to complement datasets composed of contemporary texts (i.e. from social media, Wikipedia, news articles).

We chose to use archival metadata descriptions as a data source because:

1. Metadata descriptions in the Archive's catalog (and most GLAM catalogs) are freely, publicly available online

2. GLAM metadata descriptions have yet to be analyzed at large scale using natural language processing (NLP) methods and, as records of cultural heritage, the descriptions have the potential to provide historical insights on changes in language and society (Welsh, 2016)

3. GLAM metadata standards are freely, publicly available, often online, meaning we can use historical changes in metadata standards used in the Archive to guide large-scale text analysis of changes in the language of the metadata descriptions over time

4. The Archive's policy acknowledges its responsibility to address legacy descriptions in its catalogs that use language considered biased or otherwise inappropriate today[6]

B.9.2 Language Variety

The metadata descriptions extracted from the Archive's catalog are written in British English.

B.9.3 Producer Demographic

We (the research team) are of American, German, and Scots nationalities, and are three females and one male. We all work primarily as academic researchers in the disciplines of natural language processing, data science, data visualization, human-computer interaction, digital humanities, and digital cultural heritage. Additionally, one of us has been auditing a feminism and social justice course, and reading literature on feminist theories, queer theory, and indigenous epistemologies.

B.9.4 Annotator Demographic

Not applicable

B.9.5 Speech or Publication Situation

The metadata descriptions extracted from the Archive's online catalog using Open Access Initiative - Protocol for Metadata Harvesting (OAI-PMH). For OAI-PMH, an institution (in this case, the Archive) provides a URL to its catalog that displays its catalog metadata in XML format. A member of our research team wrote scripts in Python to extract three descriptive metadata fields for every collection, subcollection, and item in the Archive's online catalog (the metadata is organized hierarchically). Using Python and its Natural Language Toolkit library (Loper and Bird, 2002), the researcher removed duplicate sentences and calculated that the extracted metadata descriptions consist of a total of 966,763 words and 68,448 sentences across 1,231 collections. The minimum number of words in a collection is 7 and the maximum, 156,747, with an average of 1,306 words per collection and standard deviation of 7,784 words. The archival items described in resulting corpus consist of a variety of material, from photographs and manuscripts (letters, lecture notes, and other handwritten documents) to instruments and tweets.

B.9.6 Data Characteristics

Upon extracting the metadata descriptions using OAI-PMH, the XML tags were removed so that the total words and sentences of the metadata descriptions could be calculated to ensure the text source provided a sufficiently large dataset. A member of our research team has grouped all the extracted metadata descriptions by their collection (the "fonds" level in the XML data), preserving the context in which the metadata descriptions were written and will be read by visitors to the Archive's online catalog.

B.9.7 Data Quality

As a member of our research team extracts and filters metadata descriptions from the Archive's online catalog, they write assertions and tests to ensure as best as possible that metadata is not lost or unintentionally changed.

B.9.8 Other

The data can be freely accessed at: `datashare.ed.ac.uk/handle/10283/3794`. The data preparation code has been published at: `github.com/thegoose20/annot-prep`.

B.9.9 Provenance Appendix

The data described above was harvested from the University of Edinburgh's Centre for Research Collections' Archives catalog in 2020 (archives.collections.ed.ac.uk).

[6]The Archive is not alone; across the GLAM sector, institutions acknowledge and are exploring ways to address legacy language in their catalogs' descriptions. The "Note" in We Are What We Steal provides one example: `dxlab.sl.nsw.gov.au/we-are-what-we-steal/notes/`.

C Annotation Instructions

The annotation instructions were written to guide annotators in applying the taxonomy of to the annotation corpus of archival metadata descriptions. Prior to beginning the annotation process, an annotation pilot was undertaken with three participants to test the clarity of the annotation taxonomy. The pilot led to revisions of the instructions: more examples were added and annotators were explicitly instructed to read and interpret the descriptions from their contemporary perspective.

The annotation instructions below contain a slightly different annotation taxonomy than the final annotation taxonomy included above in the main body of the paper. This is due to the fact that during and after the annotation process, the taxonomy was revised based on the data that was being annotated. The definitions of Gendered Role and Generalization proved to be difficult to distinguish in practice, so the definitions were revised during the dataset aggregation process. Additionally, we realized during the annotation process that "Woman" and "Man" were inaccurate labels based on what we could learn about gender from text, so we changed these labels to "Feminine" and "Masculine," respectively, for the final annotation taxonomy.

C.1 Instructions

Step 1: As you read and label the archival metadata descriptions displayed on the screen, including text that quotes from source material, meaning text surrounded in quotation marks that reproduces something written in a letter, manuscript, or other text-based record from an archival collection.
NOTE: If you are unsure about an annotation, please make a note the file name and your question so that we can discuss it and decide on the way to annotate that sort of language moving forward!
Step 2: Please note that Gendered-Pronouns, Gendered-Roles, and Occupations have been pre-annotated. If any of these three categories of language have been annotated incorrectly, please correct them by clicking on the annotation label, deleting it, and making the correct annotation. If any of these three categories of language have been missed in the pre-annotation process, please annotate them yourself.
Step 3: Read the archival metadata descriptions displayed and while reading:

- Use your mouse to highlight a selection of text or click on a word that uses gendered language according to the schema in the table on the next page.
- Using the keyboard shortcuts (see the table) or your mouse, select the type of gendered language you've identified. Please select the most specific label possible (listed as i, ii, iii, or iv)! Please only select Person-Name, Linguistic or Contextual if you do not feel their subcategories are suitable to the gendered language you would like to annotate.
- If you select a subcategory of Contextual gendered language, please write a brief note explaining what you've annotated as gendered in the "Notes" section of the "New/Edit Annotation" pop-up window.
- If you used your mouse to open the pop-up window, press the Enter/Return key or the "OK" button to make the annotation.
- You may make overlapping annotations, meaning a single word or phrase may have multiple gendered language annotations.
- Please annotate all instances of a particular type of gendered language used for a specific person or people in the text.
- Please note that the labels to annotate with as defined below are intended to guide your interpretation of the text through a contemporary lens (not a historical lens).

The examples provided in the schema below are highlighted according to the words, phrases or sentences that should be highlighted or clicked in brat. If in doubt about how much to annotate, please annotate more words rather than less!

1. **Person-Name**: the name of a person including any pre-nominal titles they have (i.e., Professor, Mrs., Sir)

   NOTE 1: Please annotate every instance of a name in brat only (do not use a spreadsheet anymore). This means that each person may have multiple person-name labels annotating the same form of their name or different forms of their name.

   NOTE 2: Use the pronouns and roles that occur within the descriptive field in which the name appears (either "Title," "Scope and Contents," "Biographical / Historical," or "Processing Information") to determine whether the annotation label should be Woman, Man, Nonbinary, or Unknown. Please do not use the occupation, name, or other information that implies a gender to determine the annotation label; only use explicit terms such as gender-marking pronouns (him, her, he, she, himself, herself, etc.) and gender-marking roles (mother, father, daughter, wife, husband, son, Mrs, Ms, Mr, etc.).

(a) **Woman**: the pronouns (i.e., she, her) or roles (i.e., mother, wife, daughter, grandmother, Mrs., Ms., Queen, Lady, Baroness) or use of term *nee [Last Name]* indicating a maiden name within the descriptive field in which the name appears (either "Title," "Scope and Contents," "Biographical / Historical," or "Processing Information") of the named person suggest they are a woman
Example: Mrs. Jane Bennet went to Huntsford.

(b) **Men**: the pronouns, roles, or titles of the named person suggest they are a man
Example: Conrad Hal Waddington lived in Edinburgh and he published scientific papers.

(c) **Non-binary**: the pronouns or roles of the named person within the descriptive field in which this instance of the name appears (either "Title," "Scope and Contents," "Biographical / Historical," or "Processing Information") suggest they are non-binary
NOTE: a preliminary search of the text returned no results for exclusively non-binary pronouns such as Mx, so most likely any non-binary person would be indicated with "they"); if the gender of a person is named and it's not a woman or man, please note this gender in the "Notes" section of the annotation pop-up window
Example: Francis McDonald went to the University of Edinburgh where they studied law.

(d) **Unknown**: there are no pronouns or roles for the named person within the descriptive field in which this instance of the name appears (either "Title," "Scope and Contents," "Biographical / Historical," or "Processing Information") that suggest their gender identity
Example: Jo McMahon visited Edinburgh in 1900.

2. **Linguistic**: gender marked in the way a sentence references a person or people, assigning them a specific gender that does not account for all genders possible for that person or group of people (Keyboard shortcut: L)

   (a) **Generalization**: use of a gender-specific term to refer to a group of people (including the job title of a person) that could identify as more than the specified gender (Keyboard shortcut: G)
   Example 1: The chairman of the university was born in 1980. Explanation: Chair would be the gender-neutral form of chairman
   Example 2: Readers, scholars, and workmen Explanation: readers and scholars are gender-neutral, while workpeople or workers would be the gender-neutral form of workmen
   Example 3: Housewife

   (b) **Gendered Pronoun**: explicitly marking the gender of a person or people through the use of the pronouns he, him, his, her, and she (Keyboard shortcut: P)
   Example 1: She studied at the University of Edinburgh. In 2000, she graduated with a degree in History.
   Example 2: This manuscript belonged to Sir John Hope of Craighill. Sir John Hope was a judge. He lived in Scotland.

   (c) **Gendered Role**: use of a title or word denoting a person's role that marks either a masculine or feminine gender (Keyboard shortcut: R)
   Example 1: Sir Robert McDonald, son of Sir James McDonald
   Example 2: Mrs. Jane Do
   Example 3: Sam is the sister of Charles
   Example 4: Sir Robert McDonald, son of Sir James McDonald

3. **Contextual**: gender bias that comes from knowledge about the time and place in which language is used, rather than from linguistic

patterns alone (i.e., sentence structure, word choice) (Keyboard shortcut: C)

(a) **Occupation**: occupations, whether or not they explicitly communicate a gender, should be annotated, as statistics from external data sources can be used to estimate the number of people of different genders who held such occupations; please label words as occupations if they'd be a person's job title and are how the person would make money, but not if the words are used as a title (Keyboard shortcut: J)
Example 1: minister
Example 2: Sergeant-Major-General

(b) **Stereotype**: language that communicates an expectation of a person or group of people's behaviors or preferences that does not reflect the reality of all possible behaviors/preferences that person or group of people may have, or language that focuses on a particular aspect of a person that doesn't represent that person holistically; for example, women described in relation to their family and home, and men in relation to their careers and workplace; men more associated with science and women more associated with liberal arts (Keyboard shortcut: S)
NOTE: Please label whichever words, phrases, or sentences you feel communicate the stereotype. Three different examples are shown below for how this may look. Include names being turned into ways of thought (e.g., Bouldingism, Keynsian).
Example 1: The event was sports-themed for all the fathers in attendance. *Explanation: The assumption here is that all fathers and only fathers would enjoy a sports-themed event. A neutral alternative sentence could read: The event was sports-themed for all the former athletes in attendance*
Example 2: A programmer works from his computer most of the day. *Explanation: The assumption here is that any programmer must be a man, since the indefinite article "A" is used with the pronoun "his"*
Example 3: A man with no doctorate degree being known as Dr. Jazz *Explanation: Women often receive negative attention for using titles such as Dr (see the WSJ op-ed on Dr Jill Biden for a recent example) while men typically do not*

(c) **Omission**: focusing on the presence, responsibility, or contribution of a single gender in a situation in which more than one gender has a presence, responsibility or contribution; or defining a person's identity in terms of their relation to another person (Keyboard shortcut: O)
NOTE: If initials are provided, consider that enough of a name that it doesn't need to be labeled as an omission!
Example 1: Mrs. John Williams lived in Edinburgh. *Explanation: Mrs. John Williams is, presumably, referred to by her husband's first and last name rather than her given name*
Example 2: Mr. Arthur Cane and Mrs. Cane were married in 1850. *Explanation: Mrs. Cane is not referred to by her given name*
Example 3: Mrs. Elizabeth Smith and her husband went to Scotland. *Explanation: The husband is not named, being referred to only by his relationship to Mrs. Elizabeth Smith*
Example 4: His name was Edward Kerry, son of Sir James Kerry. *Explanation: paternal relations only, no maternal relations*
Example 5: The novelist, Mrs. Oliphant, wrote a letter. *Explanation: Mrs. Oliphant is referred to by the last name she shares with her husband without including her given name*

(d) **Empowering**: use of gendered language to challenge stereotypes or norms that reclaims derogatory terms, empowering a minoritized person or people; for example, using the term queer in an empowering rather than a derogatory manner (Keyboard shortcut: E)
Example: "Queer" being used in a self-affirming, positive manner to describe oneself

Step 4: If you would like to change an annotation you have made, double click the annotation label.

If you would like to remove the annotation, click the "Delete" button in the pop-up window. If you would like to change the annotation, click the label you would like to change to and then click the "OK" button.

Step 5: Click the right arrow at the top left of the screen to navigate to the next archival metadata description (if you would like to return to a previous description, click the left arrow).

Step 6: If the screen does not advance when you click the right arrow, you've reached the end of the folder you're currently in. To move onto the next file, please hover over the blue bar at the top of the screen and click the "Collection" button. Click the first list item in the pop-up window "../" to exit your current folder and then double click the next folder in the list. Double click the first file in this next folder to begin annotating its text.

Step 7: Repeat from step 1.

Debiasing Neural Retrieval via In-batch Balancing Regularization

Yuantong Li[1,*], **Xiaokai Wei**[2†], **Zijian Wang**[2†], **Shen Wang**[2†],
Parminder Bhatia[2], **Xiaofei Ma**[2], **Andrew Arnold**[2]
[1]UCLA
[2]AWS AI Labs
yuantongli@ucla.edu; xiaokaiw, zijwan, shenwa, parmib,
xiaofeim, anarnld@amazon.com

Abstract

People frequently interact with information retrieval (IR) systems, however, IR models exhibit biases and discrimination towards various demographics. The in-processing fair ranking methods provide a trade-offs between accuracy and fairness through adding a fairness-related regularization term in the loss function. However, there haven't been intuitive objective functions that depend on the click probability and user engagement to directly optimize towards this. In this work, we propose the **In**-**B**atch **B**alancing **R**egularization (IBBR) to mitigate the ranking disparity among subgroups. In particular, we develop a differentiable *normed Pairwise Ranking Fairness* (nPRF) and leverage the T-statistics on top of nPRF over subgroups as a regularization to improve fairness. Empirical results with the BERT-based neural rankers on the MS MARCO Passage Retrieval dataset with the human-annotated non-gendered queries benchmark (Rekabsaz and Schedl, 2020) show that our IBBR method with nPRF achieves significantly less bias with minimal degradation in ranking performance compared with the baseline.

1 Introduction

Recent advancements in Natural Language Processing and Information Retrieval (Palangi et al., 2016; Devlin et al., 2019; Zhao et al., 2020; Karpukhin et al., 2020) have led to great progress in search performances. However, search engines easily expose various biases (e.g., (Biega et al., 2018; Baeza-Yates, 2018; Rekabsaz and Schedl, 2020; Rekabsaz et al., 2021)), which sabotage the trust of human beings from day to day. Many methods have been proposed recently to reduce the bias of the retrievers. Existing fairness-aware ranking methods can be categorized into pre-processing methods, in-processing methods, and post-processing methods (Mehrabi et al., 2021; Zehlike et al., 2021). Pre-processing methods typically focus on mitigating bias in data before training the model. Lahoti et al. (2019) discussed the individual fairness pre-processing method to learn the fair representation of data. However, the representation-based method will undermine the value of the features determined by domain experts (Zehlike et al., 2021). The in-processing methods usually transform the fairness in ranking task into an optimization problem consisting of an accuracy objective and a fairness objective. These methods learn the best balance between these two objectives (Kamishima et al., 2011; Berk et al., 2017; Bellamy et al., 2018; Konstantinov and Lampert, 2021). Zehlike and Castillo (2020) handles different types of bias without knowing the exact bias form; Post-processing algorithms (Singh and Joachims; Zehlike et al., 2017, 2020; Cui et al., 2021) are model agnostic without requiring access to the training process, but these methods re-order the ranking at the expense of accuracy (Menon and Williamson, 2018).

Among recent works on fair neural retrieval, Beutel et al. (2019) introduce the pairwise ranking fairness (PRF) metric for ranking predictions. This pairwise fairness metric evaluates whether there is a difference in accuracy between two groups. Rekabsaz et al. (2021) (AdvBert) mitigates the bias magnitude from the concatenation of query and passage text rather than treating the bias magnitude from query and passage separately through an adversarial neural network.

In this paper, we propose the In-Batch Balancing Regularization (IBBR) method combined with the neural retrieval model. IBBR is an in-processing debiasing method that balances the ranking disparity among different demographic groups by adding an in-batch balancing regularization term to the objective function. We design two batch-level regularization terms, *Pairwise Difference* (PD) and *T-statistics* (TS) that measure biases within demographic groups. In addition, we introduce normed Pairwise Ranking Fairness (nPRF), a relaxed ver-

*Work done during an internship at AWS.
†Equal contribution.

Proceedings of the The 4th Workshop on Gender Bias in Natural Language Processing (GeBNLP), pages 58 - 66
July 15, 2022 ©2022 Association for Computational Linguistics

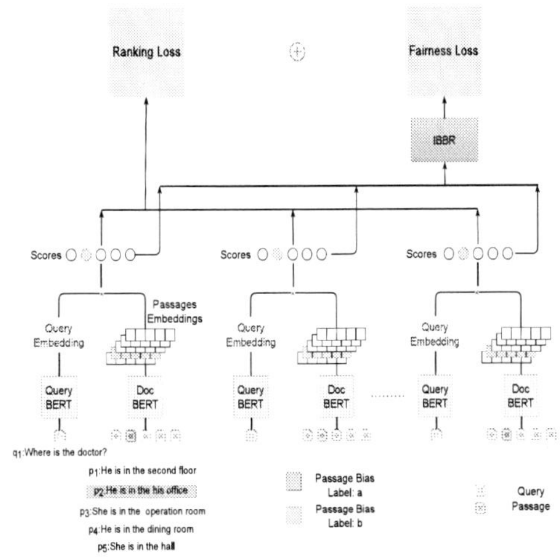

Figure 1: An example of In-Batch Balancing Regularization method. For each query, we calculate the typical ranking loss and the fairness loss from IBBR on top K retrieved passages. We jointly optimize the ranking loss and the fairness loss. There are two ways of computing the IBBR, pairwise difference loss and T-statistics Loss.

sion of the PRF (Beutel et al., 2019) that is differentiable, thus could be directly optimized. We apply IBBR to MS MARCO passage re-ranking task (Nguyen et al., 2016) on gender bias using pre-trained BERT$_{L_2}$ and BERT$_{L_4}$ models (Turc et al., 2019). Empirical results show that our model could achieve significantly less bias with minor ranking performance degradation, striking a good balance between accuracy and fairness. Our contributions can be summarized as follows:

- We introduce IBBR, an in-processing debiasing method based on pairwise difference and T-statistics.
- We introduce normed PRF, a relaxed version of the pairwise ranking fairness (PRF) metric (Beutel et al., 2019). The normed PRF solves the non-differentiable issue and could be directly optimized during training.
- We perform experiments on the MS MARCO passage re-ranking task with IBBR and normed PRF. Empirical results show that IBBR and normed PRF could achieve a statistically significant improvement in fairness while maintaining good ranking performance.

2 PROBLEM DEFINITION

We first introduce notations in the ranking task in §2.1. §2.2 provides the definition of the bias of the passage. In §2.3, we propose the definition of the group fairness in the ranking task.

2.1 Notations in the Ranking Task

Formally, we define the task of *Gender Debiased Neural Retrieval* (GDNR) as: given a query q and top K passages retrieved by the neural retrieval system, we adapt the ranking to mitigate bias in the retrieval result. We first define the whole query set as $Q = \{q_1, q_2, ..., q_N\}$. For each query q_i, we denote $P_i = \{p_{i,1}, p_{i,2}, \dots, p_{i,j}, \dots, p_{i,K}\}$ as the corresponding retrieved passages' set for query q_i. With query q_i and corresponding retrieved passages P_i, $s_i = \{q_i, p^+_{i,1}, p^-_{i,2}, \dots, p^-_{i,K}\}$ is defined as one data pair. Here $p^+_{i,1}$ is the ground truth passage (clicked passage) and $p^-_{i,j}$ is the non-clicked passage, $\forall j \in \{2, 3, ..., K\}$. We use $Y_{i,j} = 1$ to label the passage p_j as a clicked passage, otherwise, $Y_{i,j} = 0$. Finally, the whole dataset is defined as $D = \{s_1, s_2, ..., s_N\}$. For notation simplicity, we use $[1 : K]$ to represent $\{1, 2, ..., K\}$.

2.2 Bias Label of Passage

We first provide the definition of the bias label of one passage, and consider the gender bias as a running example. Rekabsaz and Schedl (2020) use the degree of gender magnitude in the passage to define the bias value, where the gender concept is defined via using a set of highly representative gender definitional words. Such a gender definitional set usually contains words such as *she, woman, grandma* for female definitional words (G_f), and *he, man, grandpa* for males definitional words (G_m).

The definition of the bias of the passage in our method is different from (Rekabsaz and Schedl, 2020) who assume that one passage has two magnitudes: female magnitude and male magnitude. However, we assume that one passage has only one implication or tendency and use the gender magnitude difference as the bias value. So the bias value of the passage p, $mag(p)$, defined as

$$mag(p) = \sum_{w \in G_m} \log |\langle w, p \rangle| - \sum_{w \in G_f} \log |\langle w, p \rangle|, \tag{1}$$

where $|\langle w, p \rangle|$ refers to the number of occurrences of the word w in passage p, $w \in G_m$ or G_f. Furthermore, we define the bias label for the passage p as $d(p)$, if $mag(p) > 0$, then $d(p) = 1$ (male-biased); if $mag(p) < 0$, then $d(p) = -1$ (female-biased); if $mag(p) = 0$, then $d(p) = 0$ (neutral). So for each retrieved passage $p_{i,j}, j \in$

$[1 : K], i \in [1 : N]$, it has one corresponding bias label $d(p_{i,j}) \in \{-1, 0, 1\}$.

2.3 Group Fairness in Ranking

In §2.3.1, we introduce one metric of ranking group fairness (pairwise ranking fairness) proposed by (Beutel et al., 2019). In §2.3.2, we provide a more refined definition of pairwise ranking fairness.

2.3.1 Pairwise Ranking Fairness

If $R(p) \in [0, 1]$ is the ranking score of passage p from one retrieval model , $\text{PRF}_m(s_i)$ measures the probability level of a male-biased random passage selected from the male group m higher than all random female-biased passages of data pair s_i

$$\text{PRF}_m(s_i) = \frac{1}{n_1^m(s_i)n_0(s_i)} \sum_{j \in g_1^m(s_i)} \sum_{k \in g_0(s_i)} \mathbb{1}[R(p_{i,j}) \geq R(p_{i,k})], \tag{2}$$

where $g_1^m(s_i) = \{j | d(p_{i,j}) = 1, Y_{i,j} = 1, j \in [1 : K]\}$ represents passages clicked ($Y_{i,j} = 1$) as well as belonging to male biased group ($d(p_{i,j}) = 1$). $n_1^m(s_i) = |g_1^m(s_i)|$ represents the number of male-biased clicked passages. $g_0(s_i) = \{j | Y_{i,j} = 0, j \in [1 : K]\}$ represents the group of non-clicked passages. $n_0(s_i)$ represents the number of all non-clicked samples in retrieved passages. Beutel et al. (2019) use the probability that a clicked sample is ranked above another non-clicked sample for the sample query as the pairwise accuracy. The pairwise fairness asks whether there is a difference between two groups when considering the pairwise accuracy as the fairness level metric.

However, we find that PRF is not directly applicable as an argument in the regularizer of a loss function that works as a trade-off of accuracy and fairness. Because PRF is a *0-normed objective function*, which is non-convex and non-differentiable. So we propose a modified PRF that can be optimized directly.

2.3.2 Normed-Pairwise Ranking Fairness

We propose a relaxed version of PRF called normed-PRF (nPRF), which measures the degree of group fairness in retrieval results for a given query and considering the ranking performance as well. The detailed definition of nPRF_m is defined over all clicked male-biased passages p_i in a data pair s is

$$\text{nPRF}_m = \left\{ \frac{1}{n_1^m(s_i)n_0(s_i)} \sum_{j \in g_1^m(s_i)} \sum_{k \in g_0(s_i)} |R(p_{i,j})|^2 \mathbb{1}[R(p_{i,j}) \geq R(p_{i,k})] \right\}^{\frac{1}{2}}, \tag{3}$$

where $n_1^m(s_i)$ is the number of all clicked male-biased passages in a data pair, usually $n_1^m(s_i) = 1$ in the ranking system.

In order to avoid the drawback of PRF being non-differentiable, we multiply the square of the ranking score ($|R(p_{i,j})|^2$) of the passage p_j to the indicator function $\mathbb{1}[R(p_{i,j}) \geq R(p_{i,k})]$, which is differentiable. Besides, $\frac{1}{n_0(s_i)} \sum_{j \in g_0(s_i)} |R(p_{i,j})|^2 \mathbb{1}[R(p_{i,j}) \geq R(p_{j,k})]$ measures the average harm of the biased passage $p_{i,j}$. If this value is large, it means that on average, these non-clicked passages are more relevant to the clicked passage $p_{i,j}$. This contributes more harm to the society since people are more willing to accept the ranking result. If this value is small, it means that on average, these non-clicked passages are less irrelevant to the click passage p_i. This contributes less harm to the society since people are less willing to accept the ranking result. Thus, the nPRF not only considers the magnitude of the ranking performance of the retrieval results but also inherits the explainable society impact into the PRF.

3 Algorithms

In this section, we create a regularizer based on the nPRF to mitigate the gender bias. In §3.1, we introduce necessary components for the neural retrieval task. In §3.2, we provide the definition of the ranking loss and two fairness loss functions, *Pairwise Difference Loss* and *T-statistics Loss*, acting as a regularizer, named as *in-batch balancing regularization method* (IBBR).

3.1 Rank Model

Given the data set D, we use the two-tower dense passage retriever (DPR) model (Karpukhin et al., 2020) as our retrieval model. DPR uses two dense encoders E_P, E_Q which map the given text passage and input query to two d-dimensional vectors ($d = 128$) and retrieves K of these vectors which are close to the query vector. We define the ranking score between the query and the passage using the dot product of their vectors produced from DPR as $\text{sim}(q_i, p_{i,j}) = z_{q_i}^\top z_{p_{i,j}}$, where $z_{q_i} = E_Q(q_i)$ and

$z_{p_{i,j}} = E_P(p_{i,j})$ are the corresponding query and passage dense embeddings.

Remarks. Here we use two-tower DPR for two reasons. (I) Computational considerations. Humeau et al. (2019) thoroughly discussed the pros and cons between cross-encoders (Nogueira and Cho, 2019) and bi-encoders such as DPR and stated that cross-encoders are too slow for practical use. (II) Using cross-encoders can cause ill-defined problem such as, if the query's bias label belongs to groups m and the passage's bias label belongs to group f, the concatenation of these two texts' bias label is unclear, based on the definition provided in Eq. (2) from (Rekabsaz et al., 2021). So the two-tower BERT model is applied separately on the query and document to tackle this ill-defined problem. Here we only consider the DPR as our ranking model.

Encoders. In our work, in order to demonstrate the robustness of IBBR, we use two BERT models (Turc et al., 2019), (1) tiny BERT (base, uncased); (2) mini BERT (base, uncased) as our encoders, and take the representation at the [CLS] token as the output.

Inference. For the data pair s_i, the ranking score $R(p_{i,j})$ of passage p_j for query q_i is simply the inner product of $\text{sim}(q_i, p_{i,j})$ produced by DPR encoders.

3.2 Loss Functions

3.2.1 Ranking Loss

The ranking loss is the *negative log-likelihood loss* by computing the inner product of query and passage embeddings to measure the ranking performance for the data pair s_i,

$$\text{L}^{\text{Rank}} = -\log \frac{e^{(\text{sim}(q_i, p^+_{i,1}))}}{e^{(\text{sim}(q_i, p^+_{i,1}))} + \sum_{j=2}^{K} e^{(\text{sim}(q_i, p^-_{i,j}))}}.$$

3.2.2 Fairness Loss

To mitigate the bias for two groups, we use the ranking disparity as a measure to evaluate the fairness level of the neural retrieval system. And this ranking disparity works as a regularization in the loss function. Here we propose two regularization terms as follows.

(I) Pairwise Difference Loss. The pairwise difference (PD) loss $\text{L}^{\text{Fair}}_{\text{P}}$ measures the average ranking disparity between two groups m and f over a batch size (B) of data pairs,

$$\text{L}^{\text{Fair}}_{\text{P}} = \frac{1}{n_m n_f} \sum_{c \in p^m_{[1:B]}} \sum_{d \in p^f_{[1:B]}} (\text{nPRF}_m(s_c) - \text{nPRF}_m(s_d))^2, \tag{4}$$

where $P^m_{[1:B]} = \{i | p_{i,j} \in g^m_1(s_i), i \in [1:B], j \in [1:K]\}$ is the set that the clicked passage belongs to group m over batch size B data. $P^f_{[1:B]} = \{i | p_{i,j} \in g^f_1(s_i), i \in [1:B], j \in [1:K]\}$ is the set that the clicked passage belongs to group f over batch size B data, and $n_m = |P^m_{[1:B]}|$ and $n_f = |P^f_{[1:B]}|$.

Remarks. If there are many $\text{nPRF}_m(s_x)$ which are different from other $\text{nPRF}_f(s_y)$, this means that group m and group f have different fairness level over this batch data and will introduce more loss. However, this PD loss does not consider distribution information over this batch data, and imbalanced-data issue when group m and group f samples are imbalanced. Thus we propose the T-statistics loss to overcome this.

(II) T-statistics Loss. The design of T-statistics (TS) loss is also based on the ranking disparity but considers the second order information (variance effect) of each group for each batch data. We use the square of T-statistics as the ranking disparity measure and defined as,

$$\text{L}^{\text{Fair}}_{T} = \left\{(\hat{\mu}_m - \hat{\mu}_f)^2 / \sqrt{\hat{\text{var}}_m/n_m + \hat{\text{var}}_f/n_f}\right\}^2,$$

where $\hat{\mu}_m = \frac{1}{n_m} \sum_{j \in P^m_{[1:B]}} \text{nPRF}_m(j)$ is the mean of the male group's nPRF, and $\hat{\text{var}}_m = \frac{1}{n_m} \sum_{j \in P^m_{[1:B]}} (\text{nPRF}_m(j) - \hat{\mu}_m)^2$ is the variance of the male group's nPRF. Besides, $\hat{\mu}_f$, $\hat{\text{var}}_f$ can be defined similarly.

Remarks. This TS loss can provide a robust measure for the ranking disparity especially when the batch data pair is imbalanced. The square of the T-statistics, i.e., χ^2 distribution, provides the theoretical guarantee and power to reject the similarity between group m and group f.

Total Loss. The total loss will be the sum of the ranking loss and fairness loss, represented as $L^{\text{total}}_{[1:B]} = L^{\text{rank}}_{[1:B]} + \lambda L^{\text{fair}}_{[1:B]}$, where L^{fair} can be the PD loss or TS Loss. λ is a hyperparameter to control the balance of the fairness loss and ranking loss. In the experiment, we try manually and automatically to tune λ_{fair}. The details of our method can be found in Figure 1.

4 Experiments

In this section, we describe data resources in §4.1, experiment setup in §4.2, evaluation metrics in Section 4.3, baseline models in Section 4.4, and corresponding result analysis in Section 4.5.

4.1 Dataset

We experimented on the passages re-ranking task from MS MARCO (Nguyen et al., 2016). This collection includes 8.8 million passages and 0.5 million queries, comprised of question-style queries from Bing's search logs, accompanied by human-annotated clicked/non-clicked passages. Additionally, data bias labels over this dataset are available from (Rekabsaz and Schedl, 2020).

Data For DPR. The whole dataset is composed of total 537,585 queries and $K * 537,585$ retrieved passages where $K = 200$, for the baseline DPR model. Each query has top K passages including one ground truth and 199 negative samples. The details of splitting the dataset used for training, development, and test (7:2:1) for the DPR model can be found in Appendix A Table 3. There are 126 queries used for the final evaluation.

Data For Fair Model. The fairness dataset (Rekabsaz and Schedl, 2020) is also created upon this MS MARCO dataset. These queries were annotated into one of four categories: non-gendered (1765), female (742), male (1,202), other or multiple genders (41). Here we only use the non-gendered queries, and assume the query is unbiased given it does not have any gender definitional terms. There are 1,252 unique queries in total. Examples of non-gendered queries are: *what is a synonym for beautiful?*, *what is the meaning of resurrect?*, etc.

4.2 Experiment Setup

The maximum length of query and passage are set to 100. Batch size B is 150 optimized over $\{100, 120, 150\}$. Learning rate is $3e^{-5}$ optimized over $\{3e^{-6}, 3e^{-5}, 3e^{-4}\}$. A warmup ratio of 10% with linear scheduler and a weight decay of 0.01 are set. In addition, we searched the fairness penalty parameter $\lambda = [0.1, 0.5, 1, 5, 10]$ (Best). We also experimented setting the λ_{fair} as a trainable parameter (Auto). All experiments are conducted ten times and we reported the average.

4.3 Evaluation Metrics

Ranking metrics. We use Recall@10, MRR, and NDCG@10 to evaluate the ranking performance.

Fairness metrics. We use RaB@5, RaB@10, and ranking disparity |ΔA-PRF| to evaluate the fairness magnitude.

RaB$_t$. RaB$_t$ is a measurement of ranking bias, which is based on the average of the gender magnitude of passages at top t ranking list (Rekabsaz and Schedl, 2020). To measure the retrieval bias, RaB calculates the mean of the gender magnitudes of the top t (5 or 10) retrieved documents for the data pair s_i, for females, $\text{qRaB}_t^f(s_i) = \frac{1}{t}\sum_{j=1}^{t} mag_f(p_{i,j})$. Using these values, the RaB metric of the query q, $\text{RaB}_t(s_i) = \text{qRaB}_t^m(s_i) - \text{qRaB}_t^f(s_i)$, and the RaB metric of the retrieval model over all the queries, $\text{RaB}_t = \frac{1}{N}\sum_{s_i \in D} \text{RaB}_t(s_i)$. The smaller the absolute value of RaB$_t$, the less the ranking disparity is.

|ΔA-PRF|. |ΔA-PRF| measures the ranking disparity over two groups, which is the difference over two averaged PRF, $|\Delta\text{A-PRF}| = |\frac{1}{|T_m|}\sum_{i \in T_m} \text{PRF}_i - \frac{1}{|T_f|}\sum_{i \in T_f} \text{PRF}_i|$, where T_m is the dataset that the clicked passage belongs to group m, $T_m = \{i | Y_{i,j} = 1, d_{i,j} = 1, \forall i \in [1 : N]\}$. With the running example, we denote $|T_m|$ as the number of male-biased clicked pairs and similar definitions are for T_f and $|T_f|$. The smaller the |ΔA-PRF| is, the smaller the ranking disparity is. If |ΔA-PRF| is close to zero, it means that the retrieved results are relatively fair since the two groups' PRF are close to each other. To avoid selection bias, |ΔA-PRF| measures the whole dataset's fairness level rather than the subset's result such as top 5 and top 10.

4.4 Baseline Models

The baseline methods contain the classical IR models, BM25, and RM3 PRF, and neural based models: Match Pyramid (MP), Kernel-based Neural Ranking Model (KNRM), Convolutional KNRM (C-KNRM), Transformer-Kernel (TK), and the fine-tuned BERT Model. These results are available in in Appendix Section A. For the BERT rankers, we use BERT-Tiny (BERT$_{L_2}$) and BERT-Mini (BERT$_{L_4}$).

4.5 Results Analysis

Ranking Performance. In Table 1, we present the result of original BERT$_{L_2}$ and BERT$_{L_4}$ and BERT$_{L_2}$ and BERT$_{L_4}$ with IBBR (PD and TS). We found that in BERT$_{L_2}$, after adding IBBR, the ranking performance decreases 2.2% in Recall@10 and the bias level decreases 80% when applying the TS. Overall, TS outperforms PD on average

nPRF			Ranking Metric			Fairness Metric		
	IBBR	λ_{fair}	**Recall@10 ↑**	**MRR ↑**	**NDCG ↑**	**|ΔA-PRF| ↓**	**RaB@5 ↓**	**RaB@10 ↓**
DPR BERT(L2)			0.357	0.164	0.196	0.005	0.091	0.079
	PD	Best	0.238 (-33.3%)	0.112 (-31.7%)	0.124 (-36.7%)	0.034 (+580%)	0.094 (+3.3%)	0.083 (+5.1%)
		Auto	0.270 (-24.3%)	0.126 (-23.2%)	0.143 (-27.0%)	0.033 (+560%)	0.098 (+7.7%)	0.083 (+5.1%)
	TS	Best	**0.349 (-2.2%)**	**0.170 (+3.6%)**	**0.198 (+1.0%)**	**0.001‡ (-80%)**	**0.091 (0%)**	**0.075‡ (-5.1%)**
		Auto	0.333 (-6.7%)	0.160 (-2.4%)	0.185 (-5.6%)	0.006 (+20%)	0.109 (+19.7%)	0.077 (-2.5%)
DPR BERT(L4)			0.429	0.205	0.243	0.043	0.016	0.011
	PD	Best	0.381 (-11.1%)	0.213 (+3.9%)	**0.236 (-2.8%)**	0.034‡ (-20.9%)	0.033 (+106%)	0.025 (+127%)
		Auto	0.373 (13.1%)	**0.214 (+4.4%)**	0.234 (-3.7%)	0.030‡ (-30.2%)	0.033 (+106%)	0.021 (+90.9%)
	TS	Best	0.365 (-14.9%)	0.193 (-5.9%)	0.217 (-10.7%)	**0.000‡ (-100%)**	**0.003‡ (-81.3%)**	**0.012 (+9.1%)**
		Auto	**0.389 (-9.3%)**	0.205 (0%)	0.234 (-3.7%)	0.022‡ (-48.8%)	0.004‡ **(-75.0%)**	0.017 (+54.5%)

Table 1: The ranking and fairness results of two IBBR methods, pairwise difference and T-statistics, combined with nPRF in BERT_{L_2} and BERT_{L_4} models. We compare IBBR with baseline models DPR L2, L4 in the re-ranking tasks and experimenting with different fairness hyperparameter λ_{fair} tuning methods. The bold value in each column shows the best result in that metric. ↑ and ↓ indicate larger/smaller is better in corresponding definition of metrics. ‡ indicates statistically significant improvement (p-value<0.05) over the DPR baseline in fairness metrics.

when considering the ranking metrics because it downgrades the ranking metric less, which can be found in the ranking metric columns. This phenomenon exists both in hand-tuned or auto-tuned hyperparameter λ_{fair} and BERT_{L_2} and BERT_{L_4}.

Fairness Performance $|\Delta$A-PRF$|$. BERT_{L_2} + TS can achieve 80% reduction in mitigating $|\Delta$A-PRF$|$ bias. The $|\Delta$A-PRF$|$ fairness metric in BERT_{L_4}+TS can achieve 100% reduction in mitigating bias compared with the original BERT_{L_4}. Besides, PD performs unsatisfied in the fairness metric compared with TS in BERT_{L_2} and BERT_{L_4}, we found that the variance of nPRF and the imbalance affects the performance of PD, which is usually found in the training phase ($\#$male-biased > $\#$female-biased). Overall nPRF + TS can achieve the best performance in mitigating the $|\Delta$A-PRF$|$ ranking disparity, which achieves our goal in mitigating the ranking disparity.

Fairness Performance RaB. As for RaB, we hope to use another fairness metric to demonstrate our regularization's robustness. We realize RaB is focusing on the top-ranking result and $|\Delta$A-PRF$|$ is focusing on the overall ranking result by definition. We present the RaB result in the last column. In the last two columns, the TS method is still better than the PD method on average. For RaB@5, the TS method's performance is similar to the PD method in BERT_{L_2} (3.3% vs 0%); The TS method's performance is better than the PD method in BERT_{L_4} (106% vs -81.3%). For RaB@10, in BERT_{L_2}, the TS method is similar to the PD method (5.1% vs -2.5%); In BERT_{L_4}, the TS method is better than the PD method (90.9% vs 9.1%). After evaluating the the fairness level on BERT_{L_4} and BERT_{L_2}, we found that the more complicated the model is, the more bias it is, which is also demonstrated in (Rekabsaz and Schedl, 2020). We find that the RaB performance not consistent with the $|\Delta$A-PRF$|$ is mainly because $|\Delta$A-PRF$|$ is focusing more on the lower-ranked passages and RaB is focusing the higher-ranked passages. This makes these two fairness metrics are relatively exclusive. However, when the ranking system performs well (rank the clicked passage high), the $|\Delta$A-PRF$|$ will finally consider the overall ranking result.

5 Conclusion

In this paper, we present a novel in-processing in-batch balancing regularization method to mitigate ranking disparity and retain ranking performance. We also overcome the non-differentiable and non-convex properties of the 0-normed PRF and propose the nPRF. We conduct experiments on the MS MARCO dataset and find that the nPRF with T-statistics regularization method outperforms other methods in terms of fairness metrics and ranking metrics. In future work, we will consider generalizing our method to multiple protected variables such as age, income, etc, and also addressing bias in the query by employing adversarial networks.

Bias Statement

In this paper, we study gender bias in the neural retrieval system. If a ranking system allocates resources or opportunities unfairly to specific gender groups (e.g., less favorable to females), this creates allocation harm by exhibiting more and more male-dominated passages, which also forms a more biased dataset in turn. When such a ranking system is used in reality, there is an additional risk of unequal performance across genders. Our work is to explore the bias level of the dense passage retrieval model with BERT_{L_2} and BERT_{L_4} on the MS MARCO passage reranking task. Thus, the community can use these benchmarks with a clearer understanding of the bias level, and can work towards developing a fairer model.

References

Ricardo Baeza-Yates. 2018. Bias on the web. *Communications of the ACM*, 61(6):54–61.

Rachel KE Bellamy, Kuntal Dey, Michael Hind, Samuel C Hoffman, Stephanie Houde, Kalapriya Kannan, Pranay Lohia, Jacquelyn Martino, Sameep Mehta, Aleksandra Mojsilovic, et al. 2018. Ai fairness 360: An extensible toolkit for detecting, understanding, and mitigating unwanted algorithmic bias. *arXiv preprint arXiv:1810.01943*.

Richard Berk, Hoda Heidari, Shahin Jabbari, Matthew Joseph, Michael Kearns, Jamie Morgenstern, Seth Neel, and Aaron Roth. 2017. A convex framework for fair regression. *arXiv preprint arXiv:1706.02409*.

Alex Beutel, Jilin Chen, Tulsee Doshi, Hai Qian, Li Wei, Yi Wu, Lukasz Heldt, Zhe Zhao, Lichan Hong, Ed H. Chi, and Cristos Goodrow. 2019. Fairness in recommendation ranking through pairwise comparisons. In *KDD*, pages 2212–2220. ACM.

Asia J. Biega, Krishna P. Gummadi, and Gerhard Weikum. 2018. Equity of attention: Amortizing individual fairness in rankings. In *SIGIR*, pages 405–414. ACM.

Sen Cui, Weishen Pan, Changshui Zhang, and Fei Wang. 2021. Towards model-agnostic post-hoc adjustment for balancing ranking fairness and algorithm utility. In *KDD*, pages 207–217.

Jacob Devlin, Ming-Wei Chang, Kenton Lee, and Kristina Toutanova. 2019. BERT: Pre-training of deep bidirectional transformers for language understanding. In *NAACL*, pages 4171–4186, Minneapolis, Minnesota.

Samuel Humeau, Kurt Shuster, Marie-Anne Lachaux, and Jason Weston. 2019. Poly-encoders: Transformer architectures and pre-training strategies for fast and accurate multi-sentence scoring. *arXiv preprint arXiv:1905.01969*.

Toshihiro Kamishima, Shotaro Akaho, and Jun Sakuma. 2011. Fairness-aware learning through regularization approach. In *2011 IEEE 11th International Conference on Data Mining Workshops*, pages 643–650. IEEE.

Vladimir Karpukhin, Barlas Oguz, Sewon Min, Patrick Lewis, Ledell Wu, Sergey Edunov, Danqi Chen, and Wen-tau Yih. 2020. Dense passage retrieval for open-domain question answering. In *EMNLP*, pages 6769–6781, Online.

Nikola Konstantinov and Christoph H Lampert. 2021. Fairness through regularization for learning to rank. *arXiv preprint arXiv:2102.05996*.

Preethi Lahoti, Krishna P Gummadi, and Gerhard Weikum. 2019. ifair: Learning individually fair data representations for algorithmic decision making. In *2019 ieee 35th international conference on data engineering (icde)*, pages 1334–1345. IEEE.

Ninareh Mehrabi, Fred Morstatter, Nripsuta Saxena, Kristina Lerman, and Aram Galstyan. 2021. A survey on bias and fairness in machine learning. *ACM Computing Surveys (CSUR)*, 54(6):1–35.

Aditya Krishna Menon and Robert C Williamson. 2018. The cost of fairness in binary classification. In *Conference on Fairness, Accountability and Transparency*, pages 107–118. PMLR.

Tri Nguyen, Mir Rosenberg, Xia Song, Jianfeng Gao, Saurabh Tiwary, Rangan Majumder, and Li Deng. 2016. Ms marco: A human generated machine reading comprehension dataset. In *CoCo@ NIPS*.

Rodrigo Nogueira and Kyunghyun Cho. 2019. Passage re-ranking with bert. *arXiv preprint arXiv:1901.04085*.

Hamid Palangi, Li Deng, Yelong Shen, Jianfeng Gao, Xiaodong He, Jianshu Chen, Xinying Song, and Rabab Ward. 2016. Deep sentence embedding using long short-term memory networks: Analysis and application to information retrieval. *IEEE/ACM Transactions on Audio, Speech, and Language Processing*, 24(4):694–707.

Navid Rekabsaz, Simone Kopeinik, and Markus Schedl. 2021. Societal biases in retrieved contents: Measurement framework and adversarial mitigation for bert rankers. *ArXiv preprint*, abs/2104.13640.

Navid Rekabsaz and Markus Schedl. 2020. Do neural ranking models intensify gender bias? In *SIGIR*, pages 2065–2068. ACM.

Ashudeep Singh and Thorsten Joachims.

Iulia Turc, Ming-Wei Chang, Kenton Lee, and Kristina Toutanova. 2019. Well-read students learn better: On the importance of pre-training compact models. *ArXiv preprint*, abs/1908.08962.

Meike Zehlike, Francesco Bonchi, Carlos Castillo, Sara Hajian, Mohamed Megahed, and Ricardo Baeza-Yates. 2017. Fa*ir: A fair top-k ranking algorithm. In *Proceedings of the 2017 ACM on Conference on Information and Knowledge Management, CIKM 2017, Singapore, November 06 - 10, 2017*, pages 1569–1578. ACM.

Meike Zehlike and Carlos Castillo. 2020. Reducing disparate exposure in ranking: A learning to rank approach. In *WWW '20: The Web Conference 2020, Taipei, Taiwan, April 20-24, 2020*, pages 2849–2855. ACM / IW3C2.

Meike Zehlike, Philipp Hacker, and Emil Wiedemann. 2020. Matching code and law: achieving algorithmic fairness with optimal transport. *Data Mining and Knowledge Discovery*, 34(1):163–200.

Meike Zehlike, Ke Yang, and Julia Stoyanovich. 2021. Fairness in ranking: A survey. *ArXiv preprint*, abs/2103.14000.

Sendong Zhao, Yong Huang, Chang Su, Yuantong Li, and Fei Wang. 2020. Interactive attention networks for semantic text matching. In *ICDM*, pages 861–870. IEEE.

A Appendix

In this section, we provide the baseline model performance in Table 2. We also provide the training, development, and test of the origin dataset and the fairness dataset (with fairness label) in Table 3.

Model	**Ranking Metric**			**Fairness Metric**		
	Recall@10	**MRR**	**NDCG**	**D-PRF**	**RaB@5**	**RaB@10**
BM25	0.230	0.107	0.125	-	-	-
RM3 PRF	0.209	0.085	0.104	-	-	-
MP	0.295	0.141	0.191	-	-	-
KNRM	0.297	0.169	0.167	-	-	-
C-KNRM	0.325	0.170	0.197	-	-	-
TK	0.360	0.212	0.231	-	-	-
DPR(L2)	$0.357^{\dagger}$	$0.164^{\dagger}$	$0.196^{\dagger}$	0.005	0.091	0.079
DPR(L4)	$0.429^{\dagger}$	$0.205^{\dagger}$	$0.243^{\dagger}$	-0.043	0.016	0.011

Table 2: IR Model and DPR, † indicates significant improvement over BM25.

Data	**Train**	**Dev**	**Test**	**Total**
DPR	510,586	26,873	126	537,585
Fairness[1]	876	250	126	1,252

Table 3: The number of training, development and testing examples for the DPR model and fairness model

Gender Biases and Where to Find Them: Exploring Gender Bias in Pre-Trained Transformer-based Language Models Using Movement Pruning

Przemyslaw Joniak[1]
joniak@g.ecc.u-tokyo.ac.jp
[1]The University of Tokyo

Akiko Aizawa[2,1]
aizawa@nii.ac.jp
[2]National Institute of Informatics

Abstract

Language model debiasing has emerged as an important field of study in the NLP community. Numerous debiasing techniques were proposed, but bias ablation remains an unaddressed issue. We demonstrate a novel framework for inspecting bias in pre-trained transformer-based language models via movement pruning. Given a model and a debiasing objective, our framework finds a subset of the model containing less bias than the original model. We implement our framework by pruning the model while fine-tuning it on the debiasing objective. Optimized are only the pruning scores — parameters coupled with the model's weights that act as gates. We experiment with pruning attention heads, an important building block of transformers: we prune square blocks, as well as establish a new way of pruning the entire heads. Lastly, we demonstrate the usage of our framework using gender bias, and based on our findings, we propose an improvement to an existing debiasing method. Additionally, we re-discover a bias-performance trade-off: the better the model performs, the more bias it contains.

1 Introduction

Where in language models (LM) is bias stored? Can a neural architecture itself impose a bias? There is no consensus on this matter. Kaneko and Bollegala (2021) suggest that gender bias resides on every layer of transformer-based LMs. However, this is somehow vague — transformer layers can be further decomposed into building blocks, namely attention heads, and these also can be further broken down into matrices. On the other hand, the findings of Voita et al. (2019) show that some attention heads within layers specialize in particular tasks, such as syntactic and positional dependencies. This gives us an intuition that some heads, or their parts, may specialize in learning biases as well. Being able to analyze bias in language models on a more granular level, would bring us a better understanding of the models and the phenomenon of bias. With knowledge of where the bias is stored, we could design debiasing techniques that target particular parts of the model, making the debiasing more accurate and efficient.

We demonstrate a novel framework that utilizes movement pruning (Sanh et al., 2020) to inspect biases in language models. Movement pruning was originally used to compress neural models and make its inference faster. We introduce a modification of movement pruning that enables us to choose a low-bias subset of a given model, or equivalently, find these model's weights whose removal leads to convergence of an arbitrary debiasing objective. Specifically, we freeze neural weights of the model and optimize only the so-called pruning scores that are coupled with the weights and act as gates. This way, we can inspect which building blocks of the transformers, i.e. attention heads, might induce bias. If a head is pruned and the debiasing objective converges, then we hypothesize that the head must have contained bias. We demonstrate the utility of our framework using Kaneko and Bollegala (2021)'s method of removing gender bias.

Biases have been extensively studied and numerous debiasing methods were proposed. In fact, according to Stanczak and Augenstein (2021), the ACL Anthology saw an exponential growth of bias-related publications in the past decade – and it only counts gender bias alone. Nonetheless, the vast majority of these works address problems of bias detection or mitigation only. To our best knowledge, we are the first to conduct bias ablation in LMs. We: (1) demonstrate an original framework to inspect biases in LMs. Its novelty is a mixture of movement pruning, weight freezing and debiasing; (2) study the presence of gender bias in a BERT model; (3) propose an improvement to an existing debiasing method, and (4) release our code[1].

[1]https://github.com/kainoj/pruning-bias

Proceedings of the The 4th Workshop on Gender Bias in Natural Language Processing (GeBNLP), pages 67 - 73
July 15, 2022 ©2022 Association for Computational Linguistics

Block	Layer	Mode	SEAT6	SEAT7	SEAT8	SS	COLA	SST2	MRPC	STSB	QQP	MNLI	QNLI	RTE	WNLI	GLUE	$\#P$
32x32	all	token	0.91	0.95	0.92	51.9	0.0	87.2	73.6	46.7	86.8	77.6	83.2	55.2	49.3	62.2	0
		sentence	0.67	-0.40	-0.23	**49.5**	2.7	87.8	75.4	63.2	86.6	76.2	83.5	54.2	54.9	64.9	0
	last	token	1.39	0.57	0.18	52.6	15.5	90.1	75.8	82.2	86.8	79.5	85.6	57.0	42.3	68.3	0
		sentence	0.85	0.64	0.67	51.9	9.0	89.1	75.1	77.4	87.1	79.3	86.1	56.7	39.4	66.6	0
64x64	all	token	0.43	0.22	**0.01**	53.4	4.7	86.5	74.7	76.9	86.4	77.3	83.6	54.5	43.7	65.4	1
		sentence	0.28	0.56	-0.06	49.3	5.9	86.6	73.9	79.1	86.0	77.2	83.0	54.5	47.9	66.0	1
	last	token	0.67	-0.31	-0.36	51.9	0.0	86.4	76.0	80.2	86.4	78.1	83.7	52.7	42.3	65.1	0
		sentence	0.72	0.57	0.03	56.0	4.6	89.2	75.7	84.0	87.0	79.4	85.3	52.3	39.4	66.3	0
128x128	all	token	0.84	0.47	0.17	50.9	3.3	87.2	74.2	69.9	86.4	77.7	83.8	53.1	50.7	65.1	6
		sentence	0.55	0.17	0.22	54.2	6.6	85.4	75.0	79.3	85.7	76.9	83.0	56.0	42.3	65.6	8
	last	token	0.65	0.17	-0.13	49.1	0.3	85.6	76.8	44.3	86.3	76.7	82.9	52.3	**56.3**	62.4	2
		sentence	0.10	0.35	-0.22	**49.5**	0.0	84.4	73.8	75.7	85.6	77.2	82.7	43.7	52.1	63.9	2
64×768 (entire head)	all	token	0.75	0.49	0.29	57.2	**38.8**	**91.4**	78.3	86.3	88.5	**82.9**	88.6	57.0	**56.3**	**74.3**	61
		sentence	0.48	-0.17	0.02	56.0	26.9	90.6	79.2	**86.5**	88.4	83.4	88.9	57.4	40.8	71.3	66
	last	token	0.62	-0.17	-0.27	58.5	44.6	**91.4**	**78.5**	81.4	**88.6**	82.0	**88.9**	**58.1**	52.1	74.0	58
		sentence	**0.09**	**0.05**	0.34	58.7	36.7	91.3	76.9	84.7	87.8	81.5	87.9	50.9	43.7	71.3	**93**
-	original		1.04	0.22	0.63	62.8	58.6	92.8	87.2	88.5	89.4	85.1	91.5	64.3	56.3	79.3	-

Table 1: Bias in fine-pruned models for various block sizes, evaluated using *SEAT* and *stereotype score* (SS). Ideally, bias-free model has a SEAT of 0 and SS of 50. GLUE evaluated using only these weights in a model that were not pruned. $\#P$ indicates number of heads that were entirely pruned. Best fine-pruning results are in **bold**.

2 Background

2.1 Language Model Debiasing

Numerous paradigms for language model debiasing were proposed, including feature extraction-based (Pryzant et al., 2020), data augmentations (Zhao et al., 2019; Lu et al., 2020; Dinan et al., 2020), or paraphrasing (Ma et al., 2020). They all require an extra endeavor, such as feature engineering, retraining, or building an auxiliary model.

We choose an algorithm by Kaneko and Bollegala (2021) for removing gendered stereotypical associations. It is competitive, as it can be applied to many transformer-based models, and requires minimal data annotations. The algorithm enforces embeddings of predefined gendered words (e.g. *man*, *woman*) to be orthogonal to their stereotyped equivalents (e.g. *doctor*, *nurse*) via fine-tuning. The loss function is a squared dot product of these embedding plus a regularizer between the original and the debiased model. The former encourages orthogonality and the latter helps to preserve syntactic information.

The authors proposed six debiasing modes: `all-token`, `all-sentence`, `first-token`, `first-sentence`, `last-token`, and `last-sentence`, depending on source of the embeddings (first, last or all layers of a transformer-based model) and target of the loss (target token or all tokens in a sentence). In this work, we omit the `first-*` modes, as they were shown to have an insignificant debiasing effect.

2.2 Block Movement Pruning

Pruning is a general term used when disabling or removing some weights from a neural network. It can lead to a higher sparsity, making a model faster and smaller while retaining its original performance. Movement pruning, introduced by Sanh et al., 2020 discards a weight when it *moves* towards zero. Lagunas et al., 2021 proposed pruning entire blocks of weights: with every weight matrix $W \in \mathbb{R}^{M \times N}$, a score matrix $S \in \mathbb{R}^{M/M' \times N/N'}$ is associated, where (M', N') is a pruning block size. On the forward pass, W is substituted with its masked version, $W' \in \mathbb{R}^{M \times N}$:

$$W' = W \odot \mathbf{M}(S)$$
$$\mathbf{M}_{i,j} = \mathbb{1}\Big(\sigma\big(S_{\lceil i/M' \rceil, \lceil j/N' \rceil}\big) > \tau\Big),$$

where $\odot$ stands for element-wise product, σ is the Sigmoid function, τ is a threshold and $\mathbb{1}$ denotes the indicator function. On the backward pass, both W and S are updated. To preserve the performance of the original model, Lagunas et al. (2021) suggest using a teacher model as in the model distillation technique (Sanh et al., 2019).

We decided to utilize movement pruning because of the mechanism of the scores S. The scores can be optimized independently of weights, and thus we can freeze the weights. This would be impossible with e.g. magnitude pruning (Han et al., 2015) which directly operates on weights values (magnitudes).

3 Exploring Gender Bias Using Movement Pruning

We focus on gender bias defined as stereotypical associations between male and female entities. Our study is limited to the English language and binary gender only.

We attempt to answer the following questions: in transformer-based pre-trained language models, can we identify particular layers or neighboring regions that are in charge of biases? To verify this, we propose a simple and, to our best knowledge, novel framework based on debiasing and attention head block movement pruning. Given a pre-trained model and a fine-tuning objective, we find which attention blocks can be disabled, so the model performs well on the task. We prune the model while fine-tuning it on a debiasing objective, such as the one described in §2.1. We optimize solely the pruning scores S and the weights W of the original model remain untouched (they are *frozen*).

We target the building blocks of transformer-based models, attention heads (Vaswani et al., 2017). Each head consists of four learnable matrices, and we prune all of them. In §3.1, we test two strategies: pruning square blocks of the matrices and pruning entire attention heads.

To evaluate bias, we utilize Sentence Encoder Association Test (SEAT, May et al. (2019) and StereoSet Stereotype Score (SS, Nadeem et al. (2021) evaluated on the gender domain. To measure model performance, we utilize GLUE (Wang et al., 2018), a standard NLP benchmark.

3.1 Experiments

In all experiments, we use the BERT-base model (Devlin et al., 2019). See Appendix for used datasets and detailed hyperparameters.

Square Block Pruning. Lagunas et al. (2021) showed that square block pruning in attention head matrices leads to the removal of whole attention heads. Although our objective differs from theirs, we attempt to reproduce this behavior. To find the best square block size (B, B), we experiment with $B = 32, 64, 128$. See Tab. 1. We also tried with $B = 256, 384$, and 768, but we discarded these values as we faced issues with convergence. Choosing a suitable block size is a main limitation of our work.

Attention Head Pruning. To remove entire attention heads, we cannot prune all head matrices

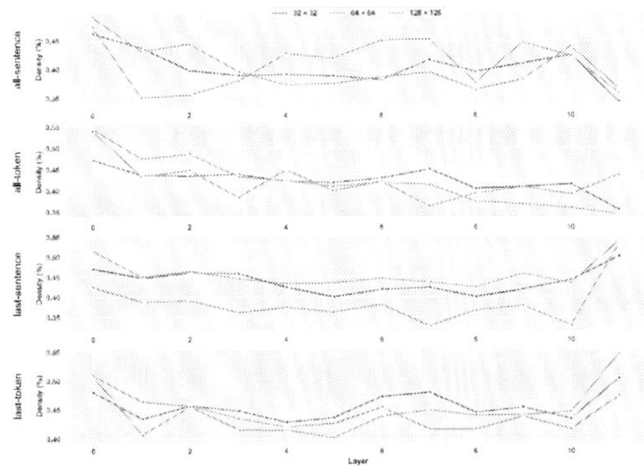

Figure 1: Per-layer densities of fine-pruned models using different debiasing modes, for multiple square block sizes. Density is computed as a percentage of non-zero elements within a layer.

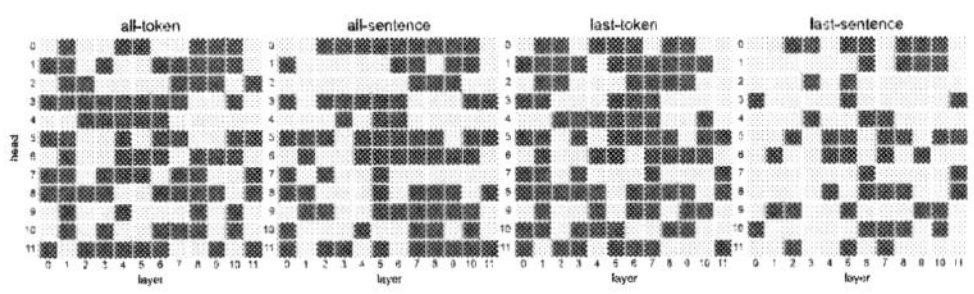

Figure 2: Pruning entire heads: which heads remained (blue) and which heads were pruned (gray)?

at once – see Appendix for a detailed explanation. Instead, we prune 64×768 blocks (size of the attention head in the BERT-base) of the *values* matrices solely. See the last row group of Tab. 1 for the results.

3.2 Discussion

Square Block Pruning Does Not Remove Entire Heads Lagunas et al., 2021 found that pruning square block removes entire heads. However, we failed to observe this phenomenon in the debiasing setting–see last column of Tab 1. We are able to prune at most 8 heads, only for relatively large block sizes, 128×128. We hypothesize that the reason is the weight freezing of the pre-trained model. To verify this, we repeat the experiment with 32×32 block size, but we do not freeze the weights. Bias did not change significantly, but no attention heads were fully pruned (Tab. 2). This suggests that bias may not be encoded in particular heads, but rather is distributed over multiple heads.

Performance-Bias Trade-off We observe that there is a negative correlation between model performance and its bias (Fig. 3). Models that contain no bias, i.e. with SS close to 50, perform poorly.

		SEAT6(Δ)	SEAT7(Δ)	SEAT8(Δ)	GLUE(Δ)	#P
all	token	1.25 (+0.3)	0.54 (-0.4)	0.58 (-0.3)	74.0 (+12)	0
	sent.	1.10 (+0.4)	0.48 (+0.1)	0.18 (+0.0)	71.5 (+7)	0
last	token	1.31 (-0.1)	0.43 (-0.1)	0.45 (+0.3)	74.4 (+6)	0
	sent.	1.24 (+0.4)	0.82 (+0.2)	0.72 (+0.0)	72.2 (+6)	0

Table 2: SEAT, GLUE, and number of fully pruned attention heads ($\#P$) for the 32×32 block pruning when allowing the weight of the model to change. Δ refers to a relative change to results in Tab. 1, that is when the original weights are frozen.

layer	mode	COLA	SST2	MRPC	STSB	QQP	MNLI	QNLI	RTE	WNLI	GLUE
all	token	**42.0**	90.8	79.5	85.6	88.3	**82.8**	**89.5**	**58.5**	49.3	74.0
	sentence	33.3	90.7	78.8	84.4	88.3	82.4	88.9	48.7	47.9	71.5
last	token	41.3	**91.1**	80.5	**85.7**	88.5	**82.8**	89.3	**58.5**	**52.1**	**74.4**
	sentence	40.2	90.6	**80.7**	85.2	**88.5**	81.9	88.2	49.8	45.1	72.2

Table 3: Breakdown of the GLUE scores when fine-pruning BERT on the debiasing objective with block size 32×32 and letting the model's weights change freely.

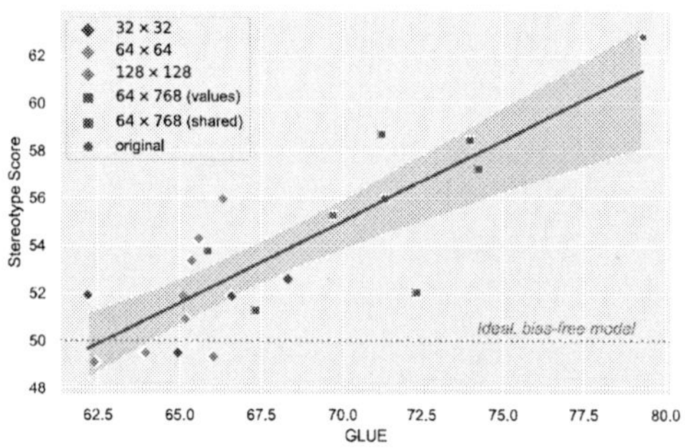

Figure 3: Performance-bias trade-off for various models. The better a model performs, the more bias it has.

The model with the best GLUE contains the most bias. This phenomenon might be an inherent weakness of the debiasing algorithm. To alleviate the issue, it might be necessary to improve the algorithm, work on a better one, or focus on debiasing data. It would be also interesting to try optimizing the debiasing and the downstream task objective simultaneously. However, this is out of the scope of our study and we leave it for future work.

The Failure of the CoLA GLUE Task Our models perform poorly on the Corpus of Linguistic Acceptability task (CoLA, Warstadt et al. (2019)). Most of them have scores close to zero, meaning i.e they take a random, uninformed guess. The reason might lay in the complexity of the task. CoLA remains the most challenging task out of the whole GLUE suite as it requires deep syntactic and grammatical knowledge. It has been suggested that language models do not excel at grammatical reasoning (Sugawara et al., 2020), and it might be that perturbations such as the absence of the weights (pruning) break already weak grammatical abilities. The results in Tab. 3 support this hypothesis. Compared to the 'frozen' setting, CoLA scores are significantly higher, whereas the other tasks see just a slight increase (Tab. 3).

4 Debiasing Early Intermediate Layers Is Competitive

Kaneko and Bollegala (2021) proposed three heuristics: debiasing the first, last, and all layers. However, the number of layer subsets that can be debiased is much larger. Trying all subsets to find the best one is prohibitively expensive. With our framework, we are able to find a better subset with a low computational cost.

We observed that: (1) square block pruning does not significantly affect the first and last layer: densities of these layers are usually higher than the other layers' (Fig. 1); (2) attention head pruning mostly affects intermediate layers (Fig. 2). Based on the above, we propose to debias intermediate layers. Specifically, we take the embeddings from layers index 1 to 4 inclusive, and we run the debiasing algorithm described in §2.1. We do not include layer 0 because it generally yields high densities (ref. Fig.1), and layer 5, as it contains the most number of heads that were not pruned in every experiment (ref. Fig. 2). We end up with two more modes, `intermediate-token` and `intermediate-sentence`. We present results for our, as well as the other modes in Tab. 4 (note that the results may differ from Kaneko and Bollegala (2021)'s due to random seed choice). Debiasing the intermediate layers is competitive to debiasing `all` and `last` layers. The SS of the `intermediate-` modes is lower that the SS of corresponding `all` and `last` modes. The SS of `intermediate-sentence` gets close to the perfect score of 50.

5 Conclusion

We demonstrate a novel framework to inspect sources of biases in a pre-trained transformer-based language model. Given a model and a debiasing objective, the framework utilizes movement pruning to find a subset that contains less bias than the original model. We present usage of our framework using gender bias, and we found that the

Layer	Mode	SEAT6	SEAT7	SEAT8	SS	GLUE
all	token	1.02	0.22	0.63	61.5	78.7
	sent.	0.98	-0.34	-0.29	56.9	75.2
last	token	0.98	**0.12**	0.79	60.9	78.6
	sent.	**0.39**	-0.89	**-0.11**	61.6	**78.7**
interm.	token	1.03	0.33	0.84	58.5	77.7
	sent.	0.83	0.49	0.92	**53.5**	74.7
original		1.04	0.18	0.81	62.8	79.3

Table 4: Debiasing-only results for various modes, including our original `intermediate` mode (no pruning involved).

bias is mostly encoded in intermediate layers of BERT. Based on these findings, we propose two new debiasing modes that reduce more bias than existing modes. Bias is evaluated using SEAT and Stereotype Score metric. Lastly, we explore a performance-bias trade-off: the better the model performs on a task, the more gender bias it has.

We hope that in the future our framework will find more applications, not only limited to gender bias.

References

Aylin Caliskan, Joanna J. Bryson, and Arvind Narayanan. 2017. Semantics derived automatically from language corpora contain human-like biases. *Science*, 356:183 – 186.

Jacob Devlin, Ming-Wei Chang, Kenton Lee, and Kristina Toutanova. 2019. BERT: Pre-training of deep bidirectional transformers for language understanding. In *Proceedings of the 2019 Conference of the North American Chapter of the Association for Computational Linguistics: Human Language Technologies, Volume 1 (Long and Short Papers)*, pages 4171–4186, Minneapolis, Minnesota. Association for Computational Linguistics.

Emily Dinan, Angela Fan, Adina Williams, Jack Urbanek, Douwe Kiela, and Jason Weston. 2020. Queens are powerful too: Mitigating gender bias in dialogue generation. In *Proceedings of the 2020 Conference on Empirical Methods in Natural Language Processing (EMNLP)*, pages 8173–8188, Online. Association for Computational Linguistics.

Song Han, Jeff Pool, John Tran, and William J. Dally. 2015. Learning both weights and connections for efficient neural network. *ArXiv*, abs/1506.02626.

Masahiro Kaneko and Danushka Bollegala. 2019. Gender-preserving debiasing for pre-trained word embeddings. In *Proceedings of the 57th Annual Meeting of the Association for Computational Linguistics*, pages 1641–1650, Florence, Italy. Association for Computational Linguistics.

Masahiro Kaneko and Danushka Bollegala. 2021. Debiasing pre-trained contextualised embeddings. In *Proceedings of the 16th Conference of the European Chapter of the Association for Computational Linguistics: Main Volume*, pages 1256–1266, Online. Association for Computational Linguistics.

Avrupa Komisyonu. 2020. A union of equality: Gender equality strategy 2020-2025. *2020b), https://eurlex.europa.eu/legal-content/EN/TXT.*

François Lagunas, Ella Charlaix, Victor Sanh, and Alexander Rush. 2021. Block pruning for faster transformers. In *Proceedings of the 2021 Conference on Empirical Methods in Natural Language Processing*, pages 10619–10629, Online and Punta Cana, Dominican Republic. Association for Computational Linguistics.

Kaiji Lu, Piotr Mardziel, Fangjing Wu, Preetam Amancharla, and Anupam Datta. 2020. Gender bias in neural natural language processing. *ArXiv*, abs/1807.11714.

Xinyao Ma, Maarten Sap, Hannah Rashkin, and Yejin Choi. 2020. PowerTransformer: Unsupervised controllable revision for biased language correction. In *Proceedings of the 2020 Conference on Empirical Methods in Natural Language Processing (EMNLP)*, pages 7426–7441, Online. Association for Computational Linguistics.

Chandler May, Alex Wang, Shikha Bordia, Samuel R. Bowman, and Rachel Rudinger. 2019. On measuring social biases in sentence encoders. In *Proceedings of the 2019 Conference of the North American Chapter of the Association for Computational Linguistics: Human Language Technologies, Volume 1 (Long and Short Papers)*, pages 622–628, Minneapolis, Minnesota. Association for Computational Linguistics.

Paulius Micikevicius, Sharan Narang, Jonah Alben, Gregory Frederick Diamos, Erich Elsen, David García, Boris Ginsburg, Michael Houston, Oleksii Kuchaiev, Ganesh Venkatesh, and Hao Wu. 2018. Mixed precision training. *ArXiv*, abs/1710.03740.

Moin Nadeem, Anna Bethke, and Siva Reddy. 2021. StereoSet: Measuring stereotypical bias in pretrained language models. In *Proceedings of the 59th Annual Meeting of the Association for Computational Linguistics and the 11th International Joint Conference on Natural Language Processing (Volume 1: Long Papers)*, pages 5356–5371, Online. Association for Computational Linguistics.

Reid Pryzant, Richard Diehl Martinez, Nathan Dass, Sadao Kurohashi, Dan Jurafsky, and Diyi Yang. 2020. Automatically neutralizing subjective bias in text. In *AAAI*.

Victor Sanh, Lysandre Debut, Julien Chaumond, and Thomas Wolf. 2019. Distilbert, a distilled version of bert: smaller, faster, cheaper and lighter. *ArXiv*, abs/1910.01108.

Victor Sanh, Thomas Wolf, and Alexander M. Rush. 2020. Movement pruning: Adaptive sparsity by fine-tuning. *ArXiv*, abs/2005.07683.

Karolina Stanczak and Isabelle Augenstein. 2021. A survey on gender bias in natural language processing. *ArXiv*, abs/2112.14168.

Saku Sugawara, Pontus Stenetorp, Kentaro Inui, and Akiko Aizawa. 2020. Assessing the benchmarking capacity of machine reading comprehension datasets. *ArXiv*, abs/1911.09241.

Ashish Vaswani, Noam M. Shazeer, Niki Parmar, Jakob Uszkoreit, Llion Jones, Aidan N. Gomez, Lukasz Kaiser, and Illia Polosukhin. 2017. Attention is all you need. *ArXiv*, abs/1706.03762.

Elena Voita, David Talbot, Fedor Moiseev, Rico Sennrich, and Ivan Titov. 2019. Analyzing multi-head self-attention: Specialized heads do the heavy lifting, the rest can be pruned. In *Proceedings of the 57th Annual Meeting of the Association for Computational Linguistics*, pages 5797–5808, Florence, Italy. Association for Computational Linguistics.

Alex Wang, Amanpreet Singh, Julian Michael, Felix Hill, Omer Levy, and Samuel Bowman. 2018. GLUE: A multi-task benchmark and analysis platform for natural language understanding. In *Proceedings of the 2018 EMNLP Workshop BlackboxNLP: Analyzing and Interpreting Neural Networks for NLP*, pages 353–355, Brussels, Belgium. Association for Computational Linguistics.

Alex Warstadt, Amanpreet Singh, and Samuel R. Bowman. 2019. Neural network acceptability judgments. *Transactions of the Association for Computational Linguistics*, 7:625–641.

Thomas Wolf, Lysandre Debut, Victor Sanh, Julien Chaumond, Clement Delangue, Anthony Moi, Pierric Cistac, Tim Rault, Rémi Louf, Morgan Funtowicz, and Jamie Brew. 2019. Huggingface's transformers: State-of-the-art natural language processing. *ArXiv*, abs/1910.03771.

Jieyu Zhao, Tianlu Wang, Mark Yatskar, Ryan Cotterell, Vicente Ordonez, and Kai-Wei Chang. 2019. Gender bias in contextualized word embeddings. In *Proceedings of the 2019 Conference of the North American Chapter of the Association for Computational Linguistics: Human Language Technologies, Volume 1 (Long and Short Papers)*, pages 629–634, Minneapolis, Minnesota. Association for Computational Linguistics.

Jieyu Zhao, Yichao Zhou, Zeyu Li, Wei Wang, and Kai-Wei Chang. 2018. Learning gender-neutral word embeddings. In *Proceedings of the 2018 Conference on Empirical Methods in Natural Language Processing*, pages 4847–4853, Brussels, Belgium. Association for Computational Linguistics.

Appendix

Datasets

Sentence Encoder Association Test (SEAT, May et al. (2019)) is based on Word Embedding Association Test (WEAT, Caliskan et al. (2017)). Given two sets of *attributes* and two sets of *targets* words, WEAT measures differential cosine similarity between their embeddings. The two attribute sets can be male- and female-focused, where the targets can contain stereotypical associations, such as science- and arts-related vocabulary. SEAT extends the idea by embedding the vocabulary into sentences and taking their embedding representation (`[CLS]` classification token in case of transformer-based models). SEAT measures bias only in the embedding space. That is, a model with a low SEAT score may still expose bias, as understood and perceived by humans. We employ SEAT6, -7, and -8 provided by May et al. (2019).

StereoSet Stereotype Score (SS, Nadeem et al. (2021)) measures bias among four dimensions: gender, religion, occupation, and race. Technically, StereoSet is a dataset where each entry from four categories consists of a context and three options: stereotype, anti-stereotype and unrelated. On the top, StereoSet defines two tasks: *intrasentence* and *intersentence*. The objective of the former is to fill a gap with one of the options. The latter aims to choose a sentence that best follows the context. The SS score is a mean of scores on intra- and inter-sentence tasks. Bias in StereoSet is measured as a "percentage of examples in which a model prefers a stereotypical association [option] over an anti-stereotypical association" (Nadeem et al., 2021). An ideal bias-free model would have the bias score (*stereotype score, SS*) of 50. As opposed to SEAT, StereoSet SS models bias close to its human perception, as a preference of one thing over another. We use the **gender** subset, as provided by Nadeem et al. (2021).

General Language Understanding Evaluation (GLUE, Wang et al. (2018)) is a popular benchmark to evaluate language model performance. It is a suite of nine different tasks from domains such as sentiment analysis, paraphrasing, natural language inference, question answering, or sentence similarity. The GLUE score is an average of scores of all nine tasks. To evaluate GLUE, we make use of the `run_glue.py` script shipped by the Hugging Face library (Wolf et al., 2019).

Gender Debiasing The debiasing algorithm introduced in §2.1 requires some vocabulary lists. We follow Kaneko and Bollegala (2021)'s setup, that is we use lists of female and male attributes provided by Zhao et al. (2018), and a list of stereotyped targets provided by Kaneko and Bollegala (2019).

Hyperparameters and Implementation

For all experiments, we use the pre-trained `bert-base-uncased` (Devlin et al., 2019) model from the open-source Hugging Face Transformers library (Wolf et al. (2019), ver. 4.12; *Apache 2.0* license). We use 16-bit floating-point mixed-precision training (Micikevicius et al., 2018) as it halves training time and does not impact test performance. To disentangle engineering from research, we use PyTorch Lightning framework (ver. 1.4.2; *Apache 2.0* license). Model fine-pruning takes around 3h on a single A100 GPU. All experiments can be reproduced with a random seed set to 42.

Usage of all libraries we used is consistent with their intended use.

Debiasing We provide an original implementation of the debiasing algorithm. We use the same set of hyperparameters as Kaneko and Bollegala (2021), with an exception of a batch size of 128. We run debiasing (with no pruning - see 4) for five epochs.

Pruning As for the pruning, we follow Lagunas et al. 2021's *sigmoid-threshold* setting without the teacher network. The threshold τ increases linearly from 0 to 0.1 over all training steps. We fine-prune the BERT model with the debiasing objective for 100 epochs using a patched `nn_pruning`[2] API (ver 0.1.2; *Apache 2.0* license). See `README.md` in the attached code for instructions.

On Attention Head Pruning

We cannot prune every matrix of the attention head if we want to prune the entire head. To see why, let us recap the self-attention mechanism popularized by Vaswani et al. (2017).

Denote an input sequence as $X \in \mathbb{R}^{N \times d}$, where N is the sequence length and d is a hidden size. The first step of the self-attention is to obtain three matrices: $Q, K, V \in \mathbb{R}^{N \times d}$: *queries*, *keys*, and *values*: $Q = XW^Q, K = XW^K, V = XW^V$, where $W^Q, W^K, W^V \in \mathbb{R}^{d \times d}$ are learnable matrices. The self-attention is defined as follows:

$$\text{SelfAtt}(Q, K, V) = \text{softmax}(\frac{QK^T}{\sqrt{d}})V.$$

Now, suppose that the queries W^Q or keys W^K are pruned. Then the softmax would not cancel out the attention, but it would yield a uniform distribution over *values* W^V. Only by pruning values W^V, we are able to make the attention output equal zero.

Bias Statement

We follow Kaneko and Bollegala (2021) and define bias as stereotypical associations between male and female entities in pre-trained contextualized word representations. These representations when used for downstream applications, if not debiased, can further amplify gender inequalities (Komisyonu, 2020). In our work, we focus on identifying layers of a language model that contribute to the biased associations. We show that debiasing these layers can significantly reduce bias as measured in the embedding space (*Sentence Encoder Association Test*, May et al. (2019)) and as perceived by humans, that is, as a preference of one thing over another (*StereoSet Stereotype Score*, May et al. (2019)). We limit our work solely to binary gender bias in the English language.

[2]`https://github.com/huggingface/nn_pruning/`

Gendered Language in Resumes and its Implications for Algorithmic Bias in Hiring

Prasanna Parasurama and **João Sedoc**
New York University
pparasurama@stern.nyu.edu

Abstract

Despite growing concerns around gender bias in NLP models used in algorithmic hiring, there is little empirical work studying the extent and nature of gendered language in resumes. Using a corpus of 709k resumes from IT firms, we train a series of models to classify the gender of the applicant, thereby measuring the extent of gendered information encoded in resumes. We also investigate whether it is possible to obfuscate gender from resumes by removing gender identifiers, hobbies, gender subspace in embedding models, etc. We find that there is a significant amount of gendered information in resumes even after obfuscation. A simple Tf-Idf model can learn to classify gender with AUROC=0.75, and more sophisticated transformer-based models achieve AUROC=0.8. We further find that gender predictive values have low correlation with gender direction of embeddings – meaning that, what is predictive of gender is much more than what is "gendered" in the masculine/feminine sense. We discuss the algorithmic bias and fairness implications of these findings in the hiring context.

This paper has been accepted as a non-archival publication.

Proceedings of the The 4th Workshop on Gender Bias in Natural Language Processing (GeBNLP), pages 74 - 74
July 15, 2022 ©2022 Association for Computational Linguistics

Gendered Language in Resumes and its Implications for Algorithmic Bias in Hiring

Oskar van der Waal, Jaap Jumelet, Katrin Schulz, Willem Zuidema
Institute for Logic, Language and Computation, University of Amsterdam
{o.d.vanderwal,j.w.d.jumelet,k.schulz,w.h.zuidema}@uva.nl

Abstract

Detecting and mitigating harmful biases in modern language models are widely recognized as crucial, open problems. In this paper, we take a step back and investigate how language models come to be biased in the first place. We use a relatively small language model, using the LSTM architecture trained on an English Wikipedia corpus. With full access to the data and to the model parameters as they change during every step while training, we can map in detail how the representation of gender develops, what patterns in the dataset drive this, and how the model's internal state relates to the bias in a downstream task (semantic textual similarity). We find that the representation of gender is dynamic and identify different phases during training. Furthermore, we show that gender information is represented increasingly locally in the input embeddings of the model and that, as a consequence, debiasing these can be effective in reducing the downstream bias. Monitoring the training dynamics, allows us to detect an asymmetry in how the female and male gender are represented in the input embeddings. This is important, as it may cause naive mitigation strategies to introduce new undesirable biases. We discuss the relevance of the findings for mitigation strategies more generally and the prospects of generalizing our methods to larger language models, the Transformer architecture, other languages and other undesirable biases.

This paper has been accepted as a non-archival publication.

Proceedings of the The 4th Workshop on Gender Bias in Natural Language Processing (GeBNLP), pages 75 - 75
July 15, 2022 ©2022 Association for Computational Linguistics

Challenges in Measuring Bias via Open-Ended Language Generation

Afra Feyza Akyürek **Muhammed Yusuf Kocyigit** **Sejin Paik** **Derry Wijaya**
Boston University
{akyurek,koyigit,sejin,wijaya}@bu.edu

Abstract

Researchers have devised numerous ways to quantify social biases vested in pretrained language models. As some language models are capable of generating coherent completions given a set of textual prompts, several prompting datasets have been proposed to measure biases between social groups—posing language generation as a way of identifying biases. In this opinion paper, we analyze how specific choices of prompt sets, metrics, automatic tools and sampling strategies affect bias results. We find out that the practice of measuring biases through text completion is prone to yielding contradicting results under different experiment settings. We additionally provide recommendations for reporting biases in open-ended language generation for a more complete outlook of biases exhibited by a given language model. Code to reproduce the results is released under `https://github.com/feyzaakyurek/bias-textgen`.

This paper has been accepted as a non-archival publication.

Proceedings of the The 4th Workshop on Gender Bias in Natural Language Processing (GeBNLP), pages 76 - 76
July 15, 2022

Worst of Both Worlds:
Biases Compound in Pre-trained Vision-and-Language Models

Tejas Srinivasan
University of Southern California
tejas.srinivasan@usc.edu

Yonatan Bisk
Carnegie Mellon University
ybisk@cs.cmu.edu

Abstract

Numerous works have analyzed biases in vision and pre-trained language models individually - however, less attention has been paid to how these biases interact in multimodal settings. This work extends text-based bias analysis methods to investigate multimodal language models, and analyzes intra- and inter-modality associations and biases learned by these models. Specifically, we demonstrate that VL-BERT (Su et al., 2020) exhibits gender biases, often preferring to reinforce a stereotype over faithfully describing the visual scene. We demonstrate these findings on a controlled case-study and extend them for a larger set of stereotypically gendered entities.

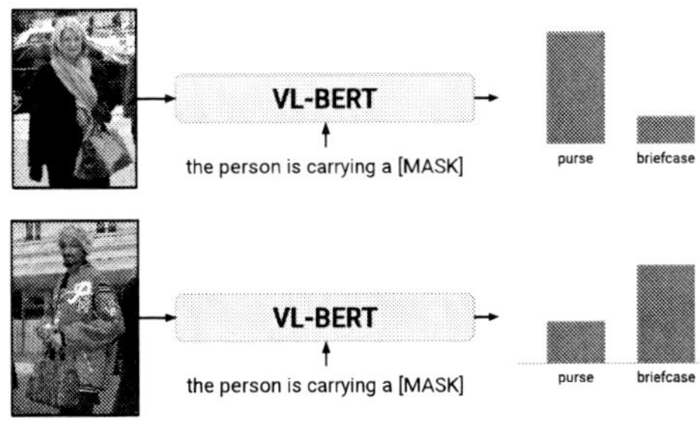

Figure 1: Visual-linguistic models (like VL-BERT) encode gender biases, which (as is the case above) may lead the model to ignore the visual signal in favor of gendered stereotypes.

1 Introduction

Pre-trained contextualized word representations (Peters et al., 2018; Devlin et al., 2019; Radford et al., 2018; Lan et al., 2020; Raffel et al., 2020) have been known to amplify unwanted (e.g. stereotypical) correlations from their training data (Zhao et al., 2019; Kurita et al., 2019; Webster et al., 2020; Vig et al., 2020). By learning these correlations from the data, models may perpetuate harmful racial and gender stereotypes.

The success and generality of pre-trained Transformers has led to several multimodal representation models (Su et al., 2020; Tan and Bansal, 2019; Chen et al., 2019) which utilize visual-linguistic pre-training. These models also condition on the visual modality, and have shown strong performance on downstream visual-linguistic tasks. This additional input modality allows the model to learn both intra- and inter-modality associations from the training data - and in turn, gives rise to unexplored new sources of knowledge and bias. For instance, we find (see Figure 1) the word *purse*'s female association can override the visual evidence. While there are entire bodies of work surrounding bias in vision (Buolamwini and Gebru, 2018) and language (Blodgett et al., 2020), there are relatively few works at the intersection of the two. As we build models that include multiple input modalities, each containing their own biases and artefacts, we must be cognizant about how each of them are influencing model decisions.

In this work, we extend existing work for measuring gender biases in text-only language models to the multimodal setting. Specifically, we study how within- and cross-modality biases are expressed for stereotypically gendered entities in VL-BERT (Su et al., 2020), a popular visual-linguistic transformer. Through a controlled case study (§4), we find that visual-linguistic pretraining leads to VL-BERT viewing the majority of entities as "more masculine" than BERT (Devlin et al., 2019) does. Additionally, we observe that model predictions rely heavily on the gender of the agent in both the language and visual contexts. These findings are corroborated by an analysis over a larger set of gendered entities (§5).

2 Bias Statement

We define gender bias as undesirable variations in how the model associates an entity with different genders, particularly when they reinforce harm-

Proceedings of the The 4th Workshop on Gender Bias in Natural Language Processing (GeBNLP), pages 77 - 85
July 15, 2022 ©2022 Association for Computational Linguistics

Source X	To compute $P(E\|g)$		To compute $P(E\|g_N)$		Association Score $S(E,g)$
	Visual Input	Language Input	Modified Component	New Value	
Visual-Linguistic Pre-training	✗	The `man` is drinking `beer`	Model	Text-only LM	$\ln \frac{P_{VL}(E\|g)}{P_L(E\|g)}$
Language Context		The `man` is drinking `beer`	Language Input	`man` → `person`	$\ln \frac{P_{VL}(E\|g,I)}{P_{VL}(E\|p,I)}$
Visual Context		The `person` is drinking `beer`	Visual Input	✗	$\ln \frac{\hat{P}_{VL}(E\|I_g)}{P_{VL}(E)}$

Table 1: Our methodology being used to compute association scores $S(E, g)$ between beer (E) and man (g) in each of the three bias sources. We show the inputs used to compute $P(E|g)$, and the modifications made for the normalizing term, $P(E|g_N)$. The entity `beer` is `[MASK]`-ed before being passed into the model.

ful stereotypes.[1] Relying on stereotypical cues (learned from biased pre-training data) can cause the model to override visual and linguistic evidence when making predictions. This can result in representational harms (Blodgett et al., 2020) by perpetuating negative gender stereotypes - *e.g.* men are not likely to hold purses (Figure 1), or women are more likely to wear aprons than suits. In this work, we seek to answer two questions: a) to what extent does visual-linguistic pre-training shift the model's association of entities with different genders? b) do gendered cues in the visual and linguistic inputs [2] influence model predictions?

3 Methodology

3.1 Sources of Gender Bias

We identify three sources of learned bias when visual-linguistic models are making masked word predictions - **visual-linguistic pre-training,** the **visual context**, and the **language context**. The former refers to biases learned from image-text pairs during pre-training, whereas the latter two are biases expressed during inference.

3.2 Measuring Gender Bias

We measure associations between entities and gender in visual-linguistic models using template-based masked language modeling, inspired by methodology from Kurita et al. (2019). We provide template captions involving the entity E as language inputs to the model, and extract the probability of the `[MASK]`-ed entity. We denote extracted probabilities as:

$$P_{L/VL}(E|g) = P(\texttt{[MASK]} = E|g \text{ in input})$$

where g is a gendered agent in one of the input modalities. L and VL are the text-only BERT (Devlin et al., 2019) and VL-BERT (Su et al., 2020) models respectively. Our method for computing association scores is simply:

$$S(E, g) = \ln \frac{P(E|g)}{P(E|g_N)}$$

where the probability terms vary depending on the bias source we want to analyze. We generate the normalizing term by replacing the gendered agent g with a gender-neutral term g_N. We summarize how we vary our normalizing term and compute association scores for each bias source in Table 1.

1. **Visual-Linguistic Pre-Training (S_{PT}):** We compute the association *shift* due to VL pre-training, by comparing the extracted probability P_{VL} from VL-BERT with the text-only BERT - thus P_L is the normalizing term.

2. **Language Context (S_L):** For an image I, we replace the gendered agent g with the gender-neutral term `person` (p) in the caption, and compute the average association score over a set of images I_E which contain the entity E.

$$S_L(E, g) = \mathbb{E}_{I \sim I_E}[S_L(E, g|I)]$$

3. **Visual Context (S_V):** We collect a set of images I_g which contain the entity E and gendered agent g, and compute the average extracted probability by providing language input with gender-neutral agent:

$$\hat{P}_{VL}(E|I_g) = \mathbb{E}_{I \sim I_g}[P_{VL}(E|I)]$$

[1] In this work, we use "male" and "female" to refer to historical definitions of gender presentation. We welcome recommendations on how to generalize our analysis to a more valid characterization of gender and expression.

[2] We note that this work studies biases expressed by models for English language inputs.

Template Caption	Entities	
The [AGENT] is carrying a E .	*purse*	*briefcase*
The [AGENT] is wearing a E .	*apron*	*suit*
The [AGENT] is drinking E .	*wine*	*beer*

Table 2: Template captions for each entity pair. The [AGENT] is either *man, woman,* or *person* .

We normalize by comparing to the output when no image is provided ($P_{VL}(E)$).

For each bias source, we can compute the bias score for that entity by taking the difference of its female and male association scores:

$$B(E) = S(E, f) - S(E, m)$$

The sign of $B(E)$ indicates the direction of gender bias - positive for "female," negative for "male."

4 Case Study

In this section, we present a case study of our methodology by examining how gender bias is expressed in each bias source for several entities. The case study serves as an initial demonstration of our methodology over a small set of gendered entities, whose findings we expand upon in Section 5.

4.1 Entities

We perform an in-depth analysis of three pairs of entities, each representing a different type of entity: clothes (*apron*, *suit*), bags (*briefcase*, *purse*), and drinks (*wine*, *beer*). The entities are selected to show how unequal gender associations perpetuate undesirable gender stereotypes - *e.g.* aprons are for women, while suits are for men (Appendix B).

For each entity, we collect a balanced set $I_E = I_f \cup I_m$ of 12 images - 6 images each with men (I_m) and women (I_f) (images in Appendix A).[3] We also create a different template caption for each entity pair (Table 2), which are used to compute association scores $S(E, m/f)$ when the gendered agent g in the caption is *man* or *woman*.

In the following sections, we analyze how VL-BERT exhibits gender bias for these entities, for each of the bias sources identified in Section 3.1.

[3]Note, throughout our discussion we use the words *man* and *woman* as input to the model to denote *male* and *female* to the model. However, when images are included, we only use images of self-identified *(fe)male* presenting individuals.

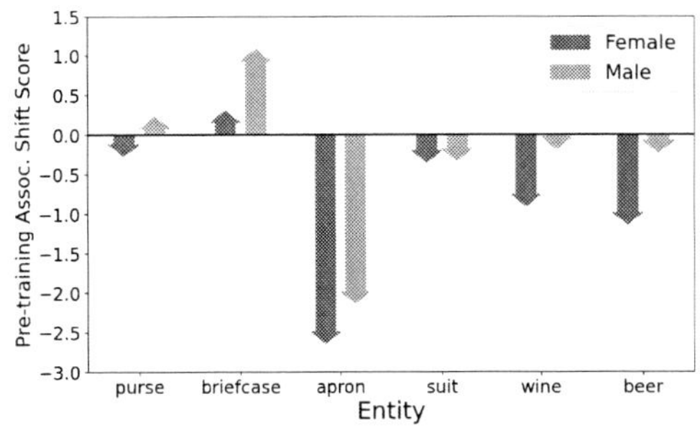

Figure 2: Pre-training association shift scores $S_{PT}(E, m/f)$. Positive shift scores indicate that VL-BERT has higher associations between the entity and the agent's gender than BERT, and vice versa

4.2 Visual-Linguistic Pre-Training Bias

Figure 2 plots each entity's pre-training association shift score, $S_{PT}(E, m/f)$, where positive scores indicate that visual-linguistic pre-training amplified the gender association, and vice versa.

Visual-linguistic pre-training affects all objects differently. Some objects have increased association scores for both genders (*briefcase*), while others have decreased associations (*suit* and *apron*). However, even when the associations shift in the same direction for both genders, they rarely move together - for *briefcase*, the association increase is much larger for male, whereas for *apron, wine* and *beer*, the association decrease is more pronounced for female. For *purse*, the association shifts positively for male but negatively for female. For the entities in the case study, we conclude that pre-training shifts entities' association towards men.

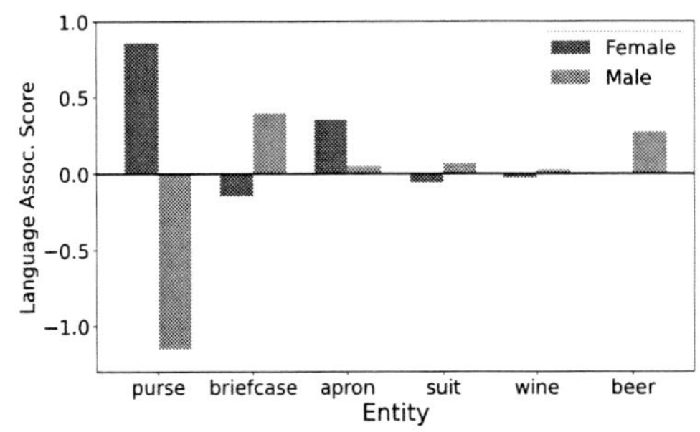

Figure 3: Language association scores $S_L(E, m/f)$. Positive association scores indicate that the agent's gender increases the model's confidence in the entity.

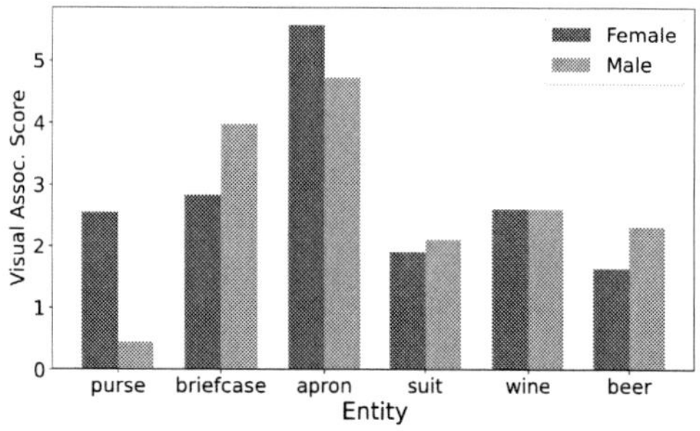

Figure 4: Visual association scores $S_V(E, m/f)$. Positive association scores indicate that the model becomes more confident in the presence of a visual context.

Visual Context, I		
$P_{VL}(\text{purse}\|I)$	0.0018 ✓	0.084 ✗
$P_{VL}(\text{briefcase}\|I)$	0.4944 ✗	0.067 ✓

Table 3: Examples of images where the probability outputs do not align with the visual information.

4.3 Language Context Bias

Figure 3 plots language association scores, which look at the masked probability of E when the agent in the caption is *man/woman*, compared to the gender-neutral *person*.

For the entity *purse*, we see that when the agent in the language context is female the model is much more likely to predict that the masked word is *purse*, but when the agent is male the probability becomes much lower. We similarly observe that some of the entities show considerably higher confidence when the agent is either male or female (*briefcase, apron, beer*), indicating that the model has a language gender bias for these entities. For *suit* and *wine*, association scores with both genders are similar.

4.4 Visual Context Bias

For each of our entities, we also plot the visual association score $S_V(E, u)$ with *male* and *female* in Figure 4. We again observe that the degree of association varies depending on whether the image contains a man or woman. For *purse* and *apron*, the model becomes considerably more confident in its belief of the correct entity when the agent is female rather than male. Similarly, if the agent is male, the model becomes more confident about the entity in the case of *briefcase* and *beer*. For *suit* and *wine*, the differences are not as pronounced. In Table 3, we can see some examples of the model's probability outputs not aligning with the object in the image. In both cases, the model's gender bias overrides the visual evidence (the entity).

5 Comparing Model Bias with Human Annotations of Stereotypes

To test if the trends in the case study match human intuitions, we curate a list of 40 entities, which are considered to be stereotypically masculine or feminine in society.[4] We analyze how the gendered-ness of these entities is mirrored in their VL-BERT language bias scores. To evaluate the effect of multimodal training on the underlying language model, we remove the visual input when extracting language model probabilities and compare how the language bias varies between text-only VL-BERT and the text-only BERT model.

For the language input, we create template captions similar to those described in Table 2. For every entity E, we compute the language bias score $B_L(E)$ by extracting probabilities from the visual-linguistic model, $P_{VL}(E|f/m/p)$.

$$
\begin{aligned}
S_L(E, m/f) &= \ln \frac{P_{VL}(E|m/f)}{P_{VL}(E|p)} \\
B_L^{VLBert}(E) &= S_L(E, f) - S_L(E, m) \\
&= \ln \frac{P_{VL}(E|f)}{P_{VL}(E|m)}
\end{aligned}
$$

Positive values of $B_{VL}(E)$ correspond to a female bias for the entity, while negative values correspond to a male bias. We plot the bias scores in Table 5a. We see that the language bias scores in VL-BERT largely reflect the stereotypical genders of these entities - indicating that the results of Section 4.3 generalize to a larger group of entities.

We can also investigate the effect of visual-linguistic pretraining by comparing these entities' VL-BERT gender bias scores with their gender bias scores under BERT. We compute the language bias score for BERT, $B_L^{Bert}(E)$, by using the text-only language model probability $P_L(E|g)$ instead.

[4] We surveyed 10 people and retained 40/50 entities where majority of surveyors agreed with a stereotyped label.

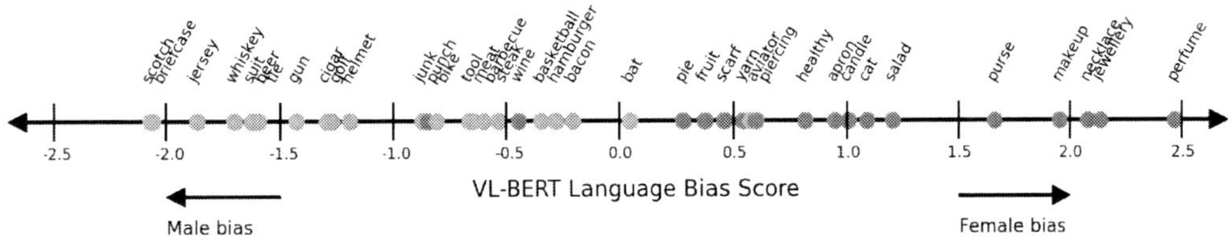

(a) B_L^{VLBert} for 40 entities which are stereotypically considered masculine or feminine. For the majority of entities, the direction of the gender bias score aligns with the stereotypical gender label, indicating that VL-BERT reflects these gender stereotypes.

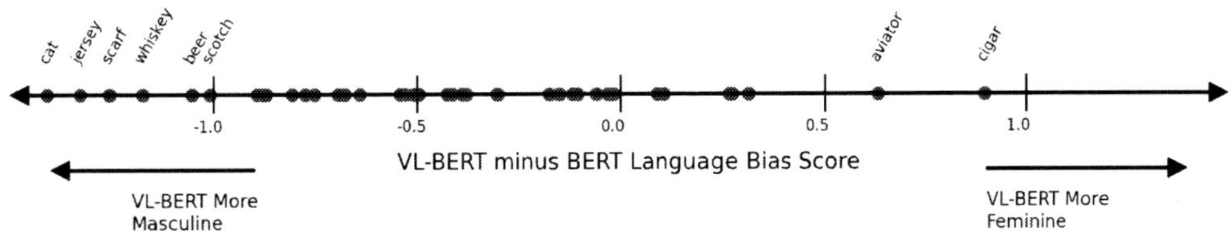

(b) $B_L^{VLBert}(E) - B_L^{Bert}(E)$ for the 40 gendered entities. The distribution of entities is skewed towards increased masculine/decreased feminine association for VL-BERT, indicating VL pre-training shifts the association distribution for most entities towards men. Note that VL-BERT still associates *cat* with women and *cigar* with men (see 5a), but less strongly than BERT.

Figure 5

We plot the difference between entities' VL-BERT and BERT bias scores in Table 5b. Similar to trends observed in Section 4.2, we see that the majority of objects have increased masculine association after pre-training ($B_L^{VLBert} < B_L^{Bert}$).

6 Related Work

Vision-and-Language Pre-Training Similar to BERT (Devlin et al., 2019), vision-and-language transformers (Su et al., 2020; Tan and Bansal, 2019; Chen et al., 2019) are trained with masked language modeling and region modeling with multiple input modalities. These models yield state-of-the-art results on many multimodal tasks: e.g. VQA (Antol et al., 2015), Visual Dialog (Das et al., 2017), and VCR (Zellers et al., 2019).

Bias Measurement in Language Models Bolukbasi et al. (2016) and Caliskan et al. (2017) showed that static word embeddings like Word2Vec and GloVe encode biases about gender roles. Biases negatively effect downstream tasks (e.g. coreference (Zhao et al., 2018; Rudinger et al., 2018)) and exist in large pretrained models (Zhao et al., 2019; Kurita et al., 2019; Webster et al., 2020). Our methodology is inspired by Kurita et al. (2019), who utilized templates and the Masked Language Modeling head of BERT to show how different probabilities are extracted for different genders. We extend their text-only methodology to vision-and-language models.

Bias in Language + Vision Several papers have investigated how dataset biases can override visual evidence in model decisions. Zhao et al. (2017) showed that multimodal models can amplify gender biases in training data. In VQA, models make decisions by exploiting language priors rather than utilizing the visual context (Goyal et al., 2017; Ramakrishnan et al., 2018). Visual biases can also affect language, where gendered artefacts in the visual context influence generated captions (Hendricks et al., 2018; Bhargava and Forsyth, 2019).

7 Future Work and Ethical Considerations

This work extends the bias measuring methodology of Kurita et al. (2019) to multimodal language models. Our case study shows that these language models are influenced by gender information from both language and visual contexts - often ignoring visual evidence in favor of stereotypes.

Gender is not binary, but this work performs bias analysis for the terms "male" and "female" – which are traditionally proxies for cis-male and cis-female. In particular, when images are used of male and female presenting individuals we use images that self-identify as male and female. We avoid guessing at gender presentation and note that the biases studied here in this unrealistically simplistic treatment of gender pose even more serious concerns for gender non-conforming, non-binary, and trans-sexual individuals. A critical next step is designing more inclusive probes, and training (multi-modal) language models on more inclusive data. We welcome criticism and guidance on how to expand this research. Our image based data suffers from a second, similar, limitation on the dimension of race. All individuals self-identified as "white" or "black", but a larger scale inclusive data-collection should be performed across cultural boundaries and skintones with the self-identification and *if* appropriate prompts can be constructed for LLMs.

References

Stanislaw Antol, Aishwarya Agrawal, Jiasen Lu, Margaret Mitchell, Dhruv Batra, C. Lawrence Zitnick, and Devi Parikh. 2015. VQA: visual question answering. In *2015 IEEE International Conference on Computer Vision, ICCV 2015, Santiago, Chile, December 7-13, 2015*, pages 2425–2433. IEEE Computer Society.

Shruti Bhargava and David Forsyth. 2019. Exposing and correcting the gender bias in image captioning datasets and models. *arXiv preprint arXiv:1912.00578*.

Su Lin Blodgett, Solon Barocas, Hal Daumé III, and Hanna Wallach. 2020. Language (technology) is power: A critical survey of "bias" in NLP. In *Proceedings of the 58th Annual Meeting of the Association for Computational Linguistics*, pages 5454–5476, Online. Association for Computational Linguistics.

Tolga Bolukbasi, Kai-Wei Chang, James Y. Zou, Venkatesh Saligrama, and Adam Tauman Kalai. 2016. Man is to computer programmer as woman is to homemaker? debiasing word embeddings. In *Advances in Neural Information Processing Systems 29: Annual Conference on Neural Information Processing Systems 2016, December 5-10, 2016, Barcelona, Spain*, pages 4349–4357.

Joy Buolamwini and Timnit Gebru. 2018. Gender shades: Intersectional accuracy disparities in commercial gender classification. In *Conference on fairness, accountability and transparency*, pages 77–91.

Aylin Caliskan, Joanna J Bryson, and Arvind Narayanan. 2017. Semantics derived automatically from language corpora contain human-like biases. *Science*, 356(6334):183–186.

Yen-Chun Chen, Linjie Li, Licheng Yu, Ahmed El Kholy, Faisal Ahmed, Zhe Gan, Yu Cheng, and Jingjing Liu. 2019. Uniter: Learning universal image-text representations. *arXiv preprint arXiv:1909.11740*.

Mick Cunningham. 2008. Changing attitudes toward the male breadwinner, female homemaker family model: Influences of women's employment and education over the lifecourse. *Social forces*, 87(1):299–323.

Helana Darwin. 2018. Omnivorous masculinity: Gender capital and cultural legitimacy in craft beer culture. *Social Currents*, 5(3):301–316.

Abhishek Das, Satwik Kottur, Khushi Gupta, Avi Singh, Deshraj Yadav, José M. F. Moura, Devi Parikh, and Dhruv Batra. 2017. Visual dialog. In *2017 IEEE Conference on Computer Vision and Pattern Recognition, CVPR 2017, Honolulu, HI, USA, July 21-26, 2017*, pages 1080–1089. IEEE Computer Society.

Jacob Devlin, Ming-Wei Chang, Kenton Lee, and Kristina Toutanova. 2019. BERT: Pre-training of deep bidirectional transformers for language understanding. In *Proceedings of the 2019 Conference of the North American Chapter of the Association for Computational Linguistics: Human Language Technologies, Volume 1 (Long and Short Papers)*, pages 4171–4186, Minneapolis, Minnesota. Association for Computational Linguistics.

Jessica L Fugitt and Lindsay S Ham. 2018. Beer for "brohood": A laboratory simulation of masculinity confirmation through alcohol use behaviors in men. *Psychology of Addictive Behaviors*, 32(3):358.

Yash Goyal, Tejas Khot, Douglas Summers-Stay, Dhruv Batra, and Devi Parikh. 2017. Making the V in VQA matter: Elevating the role of image understanding in visual question answering. In *2017 IEEE Conference on Computer Vision and Pattern Recognition, CVPR 2017, Honolulu, HI, USA, July 21-26, 2017*, pages 6325–6334. IEEE Computer Society.

Lisa Anne Hendricks, Kaylee Burns, Kate Saenko, Trevor Darrell, and Anna Rohrbach. 2018. Women also snowboard: Overcoming bias in captioning models. In *European Conference on Computer Vision*, pages 793–811. Springer.

Keita Kurita, Nidhi Vyas, Ayush Pareek, Alan W Black, and Yulia Tsvetkov. 2019. Measuring bias in contextualized word representations. In *Proceedings of the First Workshop on Gender Bias in Natural Language Processing*, pages 166–172, Florence, Italy. Association for Computational Linguistics.

Zhenzhong Lan, Mingda Chen, Sebastian Goodman, Kevin Gimpel, Piyush Sharma, and Radu Soricut. 2020. ALBERT: A lite BERT for self-supervised learning of language representations. In *8th International Conference on Learning Representations, ICLR 2020, Addis Ababa, Ethiopia, April 26-30, 2020*. OpenReview.net.

Hope Landrine, Stephen Bardwell, and Tina Dean. 1988. Gender expectations for alcohol use: A study of the significance of the masculine role. *Sex roles*, 19(11):703–712.

Matthew Peters, Mark Neumann, Mohit Iyyer, Matt Gardner, Christopher Clark, Kenton Lee, and Luke Zettlemoyer. 2018. Deep contextualized word representations. In *Proceedings of the 2018 Conference of the North American Chapter of the Association for Computational Linguistics: Human Language Technologies, Volume 1 (Long Papers)*, pages 2227–2237, New Orleans, Louisiana. Association for Computational Linguistics.

Alec Radford, Karthik Narasimhan, Tim Salimans, and Ilya Sutskever. 2018. Improving language understanding with unsupervised learning. *Technical report, OpenAI*.

Colin Raffel, Noam Shazeer, Adam Roberts, Katherine Lee, Sharan Narang, Michael Matena, Yanqi Zhou, Wei Li, and Peter J Liu. 2020. Exploring the limits of transfer learning with a unified text-to-text transformer. *Journal of Machine Learning Research*, 21:1–67.

Sainandan Ramakrishnan, Aishwarya Agrawal, and Stefan Lee. 2018. Overcoming language priors in visual question answering with adversarial regularization. In *Advances in Neural Information Processing Systems 31: Annual Conference on Neural Information Processing Systems 2018, NeurIPS 2018, December 3-8, 2018, Montréal, Canada*, pages 1548–1558.

Rachel Rudinger, Jason Naradowsky, Brian Leonard, and Benjamin Van Durme. 2018. Gender bias in coreference resolution. In *Proceedings of the 2018 Conference of the North American Chapter of the Association for Computational Linguistics: Human Language Technologies, Volume 2 (Short Papers)*, pages 8–14, New Orleans, Louisiana. Association for Computational Linguistics.

Weijie Su, Xizhou Zhu, Yue Cao, Bin Li, Lewei Lu, Furu Wei, and Jifeng Dai. 2020. VL-BERT: pre-training of generic visual-linguistic representations. In *8th International Conference on Learning Representations, ICLR 2020, Addis Ababa, Ethiopia, April 26-30, 2020*. OpenReview.net.

Hao Tan and Mohit Bansal. 2019. LXMERT: Learning cross-modality encoder representations from transformers. In *Proceedings of the 2019 Conference on Empirical Methods in Natural Language Processing and the 9th International Joint Conference on Natural Language Processing (EMNLP-IJCNLP)*, pages 5100–5111, Hong Kong, China. Association for Computational Linguistics.

Jesse Vig, Sebastian Gehrmann, Yonatan Belinkov, Sharon Qian, Daniel Nevo, Yaron Singer, and Stuart Shieber. 2020. Causal mediation analysis for interpreting neural nlp: The case of gender bias. *arXiv preprint arXiv:2004.12265*.

Kellie Webster, Xuezhi Wang, Ian Tenney, Alex Beutel, Emily Pitler, Ellie Pavlick, Jilin Chen, and Slav Petrov. 2020. Measuring and reducing gendered correlations in pre-trained models. *arXiv preprint arXiv:2010.06032*.

Rowan Zellers, Yonatan Bisk, Ali Farhadi, and Yejin Choi. 2019. From recognition to cognition: Visual commonsense reasoning. In *IEEE Conference on Computer Vision and Pattern Recognition, CVPR 2019, Long Beach, CA, USA, June 16-20, 2019*, pages 6720–6731. Computer Vision Foundation / IEEE.

Jieyu Zhao, Tianlu Wang, Mark Yatskar, Ryan Cotterell, Vicente Ordonez, and Kai-Wei Chang. 2019. Gender bias in contextualized word embeddings. In *Proceedings of the 2019 Conference of the North American Chapter of the Association for Computational Linguistics: Human Language Technologies, Volume 1 (Long and Short Papers)*, pages 629–634, Minneapolis, Minnesota. Association for Computational Linguistics.

Jieyu Zhao, Tianlu Wang, Mark Yatskar, Vicente Ordonez, and Kai-Wei Chang. 2017. Men also like shopping: Reducing gender bias amplification using corpus-level constraints. In *Proceedings of the 2017 Conference on Empirical Methods in Natural Language Processing*, pages 2979–2989, Copenhagen, Denmark. Association for Computational Linguistics.

Jieyu Zhao, Tianlu Wang, Mark Yatskar, Vicente Ordonez, and Kai-Wei Chang. 2018. Gender bias in coreference resolution: Evaluation and debiasing methods. In *Proceedings of the 2018 Conference of the North American Chapter of the Association for Computational Linguistics: Human Language Technologies, Volume 2 (Short Papers)*, pages 15–20, New Orleans, Louisiana. Association for Computational Linguistics.

Jiping Zuo and Shengming Tang. 2000. Breadwinner status and gender ideologies of men and women regarding family roles. *Sociological perspectives*, 43(1):29–43.

Entity	Gender of Agent	Images Used ($I_{m/f}$)
Purse	Male	
	Female	
Briefcase	Male	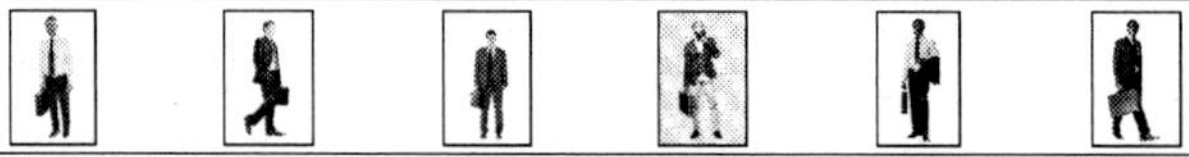
	Female	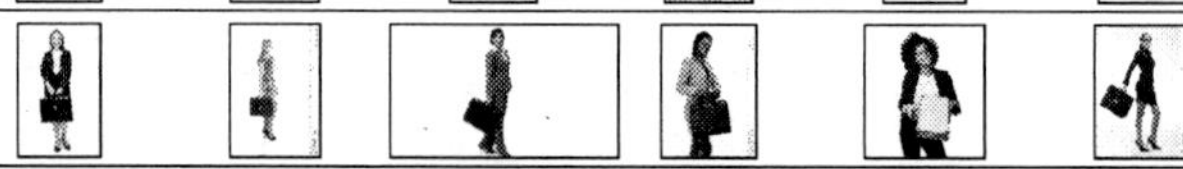
Apron	Male	
	Female	
Suit	Male	
	Female	
Wine	Male	
	Female	
Beer	Male	
	Female	

Table 4: Images collected for case study in Section 4

A Images Collected for Case Study

In Table 4, we show the different images collected for our Case Study in Section 4.

B Rationale Behind Selection of Case Study Entities

For the purpose of the case study, we chose three pairs of entities, each containing entities with opposite gender polarities (verified using the same survey we used in Section 5). The entities were chosen to demonstrate how unequal gender associations perpetuate undesirable gender stereotypes.

Apron vs Suit This pair was chosen to investigate how clothing biases can reinforce stereotypes about traditional gender roles. Aprons are associated with cooking, which has long been considered a traditional job for women as homemakers. Meanwhile, suits are associated with business, and men are typically considered to be the breadwinners for their family. However, in the 21st century, as we make progress in breaking the breadmaker-homemaker dichotomy, these gender roles do not necessarily apply (Cunningham, 2008; Zuo and Tang, 2000), and reinforcing them is harmful - particularly to women, since they have struggled (and continue to struggle) for their right to join the workforce and not be confined by their gender roles.

Purse vs Briefcase Bags present another class of traditional gender norms that are frequently violated in this day and age. Purses are traditionally associated with women, whereas briefcases (similar to suits above) are associated with business, which we noted is customarily a male occupation. If a model tends to associate purses with women, in the presence of contrary visual evidence, it could reinforce heteronormative gender associations. Similarly, associating briefcases with primarily men undermines the efforts of women to enter the workforce.

Wine vs Beer Alcoholic drinks also contain gendered stereotypes that could be perpetuated by visual-linguistic models. Beer is typically considered to be a masculine drink (Fugitt and Ham, 2018; Darwin, 2018), whereas wine is associated with feminine traits (Landrine et al., 1988).

Assessing Group-level Gender Bias in Professional Evaluations: The Case of Medical Student End-of-Shift Feedback

Emmy Liu
Language Technologies Institute
Carnegie Mellon University
mengyan3@cs.cmu.edu

Michael Henry Tessler
MIT
Brain and Cognitive Sciences
tessler@mit.edu

Nicole Dubosh
Beth Israel Deaconess Medical Center
Harvard Medical School
ndubosh@bidmc.harvard.edu

Katherine Mosher Hiller
Indiana University
School of Medicine, Bloomington
kmhiller@iu.edu

Roger P. Levy
MIT
Brain and Cognitive Sciences
rplevy@mit.edu

Abstract

Although approximately 50% of medical school graduates today are women, female physicians tend to be underrepresented in senior positions, make less money than their male counterparts and receive fewer promotions. There is a growing body of literature demonstrating gender bias in various forms of evaluation in medicine, but this work was mainly conducted by looking for specific words using fixed dictionaries such as LIWC and focused on recommendation letters. We use a dataset of written and quantitative assessments of medical student performance on individual shifts of work, collected across multiple institutions, to investigate the extent to which gender bias exists in a day-to-day context for medical students. We investigate differences in the narrative comments given to male and female students by both male or female faculty assessors, using a fine-tuned BERT model. This allows us to examine whether groups are written about in systematically different ways, without relying on hand-crafted wordlists or topic models. We compare these results to results from the traditional LIWC method and find that, although we find no evidence of group-level gender bias in this dataset, terms related to family and children are used more in feedback given to women.

1 Introduction

Female physicians and trainees have advanced considerably in the medical field within recent years, and approximately 50% of medical school graduates are now women (Lautenberger et al., 2014). However, female physicians lag their male counterparts in salary, promotions, and positions in senior leadership (Lautenberger et al., 2014; Carnes et al., 2008; Ash et al., 2004; Bennet et al., 2019). A mechanism that perpetuates this inequality may be unequal evaluations of male and female physicians. Past work has revealed gender bias in several forms of evaluation. Evaluations of recommendation letters in academia found that women tended to be described in communal traits (caring, nurturing) whereas men were described in agentic terms (ambitious and self-confident) (Madera et al., 2009). The same trend holds in direct observation comments given to Emergency Medicine (EM) residents, with feedback themes varying by gender, particularly around the domains of authority and assertiveness (AS et al., 2017). In the same context, women were also found to receive more contradictory and polarized assessments on their skills as compared to men (AS et al., 2017).

If there are systemic differences in evaluations for different genders, it may be possible that these differences arise early in a student's career and snowball into fewer opportunities in late career, when they are quantitatively detectable through metrics such as salary and number of promotions. It is important to understand at what phases of a student's career inequities arise, so that interventions can be targeted toward supporting women or other underrepresented minorities at these stages. Focus groups of female physicians in the field find different experiences at early, mid, and late career stages, with older women experiencing more overt discrimination, and younger women reporting more implicit bias, though it is unknown if this is due to decreased discrimination in recent years, or due to younger physicians not yet recognizing signs of

Proceedings of the The 4th Workshop on Gender Bias in Natural Language Processing (GeBNLP), pages 86 - 93
July 15, 2022 ©2022 Association for Computational Linguistics

discrimination (Chesak et al., 2022).

Findings on gender differences in language are mixed for students earlier in their careers. A qualitative analysis of surgical residency letters of recommendation, collected from before the students applied for residency, found that male applicants' letters contained more achievement-oriented terms, whereas female applicants' letters contained more care-oriented terms (Turrentine et al., 2019). However, a similar analysis on the EM standardized letter of evaluation found no such difference (S et al., 2017).

To investigate this question more thoroughly, we use a new dataset of written assessments on medical students' work based on individual shift performance before their residencies. Most previous work from the medical community has used relatively simple linguistic methods such as the Linguistic Inquiry and Word Count dictionary (LIWC) (Pennebaker et al., 2015; Madera et al., 2009; S et al., 2017; Schmader et al., 2007), but using pretrained language models may allow us to investigate bias in a more fine-grained manner (Andrews et al., 2021; Sarraf et al., 2021). Additionally, existing work on medical bias within the NLP community mainly focuses on patients, rather than physicians themselves (van Aken et al., 2021).

We fine-tune a pretrained BERT model and use its predictions as a tool to try to identify group-level prediction residuals. If such a difference exists on a systematic level, it may indicate that assessors are writing about students in different ways based on their gender, given the same objective performance. Caution should be taken when using similar methods as language models can also come imbued with biases of their own, but we outline the method in this work and highlight its use in comparing model predictions and human judgments when both text data and quantitative data are available.

Although we can replicate past work showing a significant difference in social-communal terms used to describe women, we do not find as clear a relationship between comments written about a student and the global score given on a shift. We do not find a systemic difference between male and female students when comparing group-wide residual differences. This indicates that although male and female students may be written about differently, no gender is written about in a systemically worse way. Due to privacy concerns, the dataset is not available online, but the full dataset can be obtained through emailing our medical co-author: kmhiller@iu.edu.

2 Bias Statement

We study the relationship between text comments and numeric ratings of performance given to male and female medical students. We introduce the method of comparing language model residual predictions to numeric data to find group-wide differences in language use. We fine-tune a language model to predict the rating associated with a given comment about a student, and ask if there is a cross-group difference in the residual error that the trained model makes. For instance, are female students given less positive-sounding comments than their male counterparts for the same level of clinical skills (as measured by their numeric evaluation scores)?

Feedback from supervisors is used to make decisions on whether a student receives a residency, or later on whether they get promoted to a higher position within medicine. This has potential to address allocational harms to women within medicine. The under-representation of women in senior positions in medicine could also lead to wider harms in inequity as a result.

There are shortcomings in presenting gender as a binary, and in this dataset gender information was not collected based on self-identification. We hope that future work will explore a wider diversity of gender identification, but we present this analysis as a first step.

3 Dataset

The dataset consists of evaluations of undergraduate medical students conducted with the National Clinical Assessment Tool (NCAT-EM), the first standardized assessment based on direct observation of skills in a clinical setting (of American Medical Colleges, 2017; Jung et al., 2017). The NCAT-EM was developed by EM educators, and has been implemented at 13 institutions in the United States. Data was collected from departments participating in the NCAT-EM Consortium from 2017-2019 (Jung et al., 2017).

The dataset contains short free text comments on a student's performance, categorical assessments on multiple skill areas, a global competency score (lower third, middle third, top third, and top 10%), as well as demographic information about students and assessors: gender, age, rank of assessor (junior vs senior faculty). These attributes are outlined in Figure 1. Examples of free-text comments and associated scores are given in Table 1.

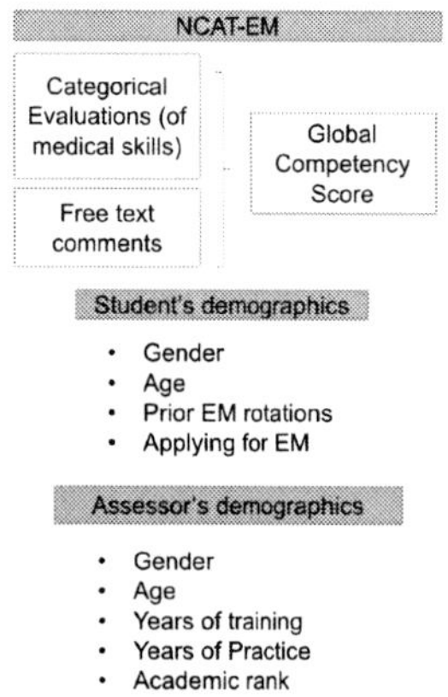

Figure 1: Data and features included in the NCAT-EM dataset.

Global Score	Comment
0	always seemed happy to help but did not reassess patients or follow up labs on own. also, came off as arrogant to multiple residents in the department.
1	good differential, interested, team player.
2	great job keeping up with your patients; we had a very sick one and you made sure you were on top of it.
3	i really enjoyed working with x, as x was a very thorough historian, and provided a brief focused history. x appears to have a good grip of emergency medicine at this point, and provides a good reasonable plan. x is going to be an exceptional resident, and will continue to improve significantly over the next year.

Table 1: Examples of free text comments written about students (after preprocessing), with the associated global competency score (on a scale from 0 to 3).

After excluding samples with missing data, there were 3162 individual assessments, where 1767 were evaluations of male students and 1395 were evaluations of female students. Because students may work multiple shifts, and the same supervisor may supervise multiple students, there are some students and assessors who are repeated, although each sample represents a different shift. Names and named entities were removed from comments using the spaCy entity recognizer and replaced with the letter "x". Gendered pronouns were removed and replaced with the gender-neutral pronoun "they".

This dataset consists mostly of short comments focused on student performance. The mean number of words in a comment was 28.4, and the maximum number of words in a comment was 187. The overall distribution of assessment ratings was: 5% in bottom third, 35% in middle third, 45% in top third, and 15% in the top 10%. A slightly higher density of female students received the top rating compared to male students. We convert these to integer values from 0-3.

We use two main methods to identify possible biases in this dataset: prediction residual analysis and word/topic based analysis. Previous work has focused on word-level analysis, but since we have access to both comments as well as a competency score, we investigate to what extent we can reconstruct the mapping from text comment to the score a student receives by applying a language model, and if there are differences in this mapping between male and female students. We used 70% of the dataset to train, 15% to evaluate, and 15% as the test set.

3.1 Language Model Prediction Residuals

In order to examine the relationship between text comments and the global competency score, we finetune `bert-base-uncased` with early stopping on the free text comments with gender and institution information removed, with a linear layer trained to predict the global competency score [1]. We then examine the prediction residuals of the finetuned model on a group level for group $\mathcal{C}$:

$$\delta_{\mathcal{C}} = \{y_i - \hat{y}_i\}_{i=0}^{|\mathcal{C}|} \quad (1)$$

In the student-only setup the groups would be the set of male students, $\mathcal{M}$, and the set of female students $\mathcal{F}$. In the student and assessor setup, the groups would be the different assessor and student gender combinations, namely $\mathcal{M} \times \mathcal{M}$, $\mathcal{M} \times \mathcal{F}$, $\mathcal{F} \times \mathcal{M}$, and $\mathcal{F} \times \mathcal{F}$. The null hypothesis is that there should be no difference between these groups, for instance $\delta_{\mathcal{F}}$ and $\delta_{\mathcal{M}}$. If there is a significant difference, it indicates that there may be a difference in the relationship between text and global score between these groups. For instance, if the δ_{F_i}s are significantly higher, this would indicate that scores given to female students are significantly higher

[1] We used the Adam optimizer with a learning rate of `5e-6`, epsilon of `1e-8`, and weight decay `1e-10`, and a batch size of 32. These parameters were taken from the default settings of the transformers implementation of Adam at the time, with a minimal hyperparameter search over learning rate.

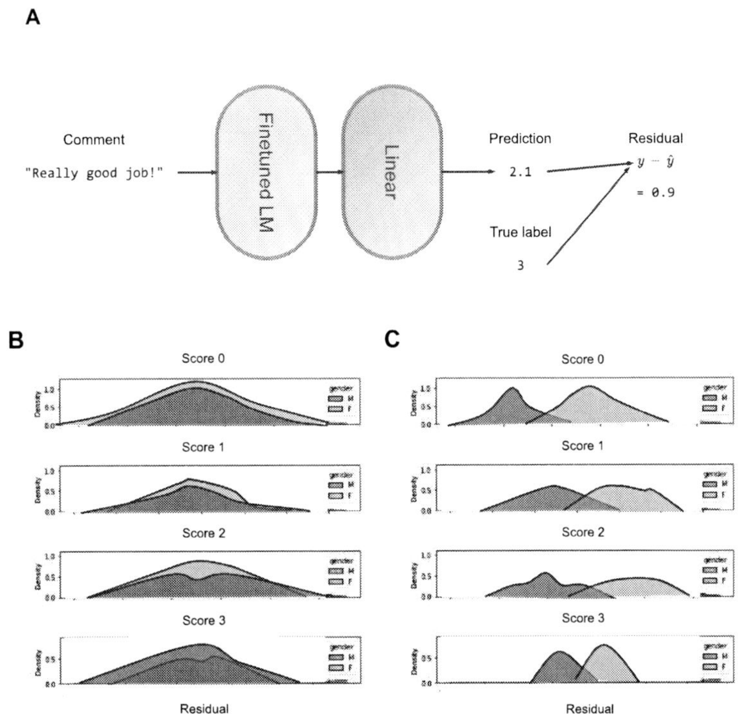

Figure 2: Panel A illustrates the LM residual method (for illustration purposes, the areas under the curve in this drawing are not necessarily the same as they would be in reality). A language model is finetuned on text evaluations without gender information to predict the global rating. Panel B illustrates a case with no differences in residuals between the male and female group, illustrating the case without textual bias. Panel C illustrates a biased case. In this hypothetical case, female students received a score that is consistently higher than the language in their comments would suggest.

than expected given comments about them. Note that $\hat{y}_i$ is based on text from which explicit gender markers were removed.

3.2 LIWC

In order to check if previous results using LIWC replicated on this dataset, we examined many categories of words from LIWC [2].

Additionally, we used user-defined dictionaries from previous studies of letters of recommendation: grindstone words (e.g. diligent, careful), ability words (e.g. talented, intelligent), standout adjectives (e.g. exceptional), research terms (e.g. research, data), teaching terms (e.g. teach, communicate), social-communal terms, (e.g. families, kids), and agentic terms (e.g. assertive, aggressive) (Madera et al., 2009; Eagly and Johannesen-Schmidt, 2001; Eagly and Karau, 2002; Eagly et al., 2000; Wood and Eagly, 2002). The prevalence of these categories was found to differ in past studies of recommendation letters. We used a coding scheme of 0 if a theme did not show up in a comment, and 1 if it did. We used a Fisher exact test on comments written about male or female students, with Holm-Bonferroni correction to control for multiple comparisons.

4 Results

4.1 Residual Analysis

We present the results for the residual analysis first. We note first that the language model achieved

[2] Specifically, we examined these categories: Affect, Positive Emotion, Negative Emotion, Social, Cognitive Processing, Insight, Achieve, Standout, Ability, Grindstone, Teaching, Research, Communal, Social-Communal, and Agentic. The associated words can be found in either the standard LIWC dictionary or in these references: (Pennebaker et al., 2015; Madera et al., 2009)

relatively low accuracy when its predictions were rounded to the nearest integer (46%), but made comparable predictions to humans (50.7% average across three annotators, on a randomly-sampled 20% of the dataset. The annotator agreement was moderate (Krippendorff's $\alpha = 0.491$). [3]), This indicates a noisy mapping between text and global score in this dataset.

Results following the format of Figure 2 are found in Figure 3, and visual inspection does not reveal differences in residuals. A T-test comparing male and female global scores in the entire dataset confirmed that female students had a slightly higher score (higher mean by 0.08, $p < 0.004$). However, no significant difference was found between residuals for male and female students ($p = 0.517$). There were also no significant differences between BERT predictions themselves for male and female students ($p = 0.152$).

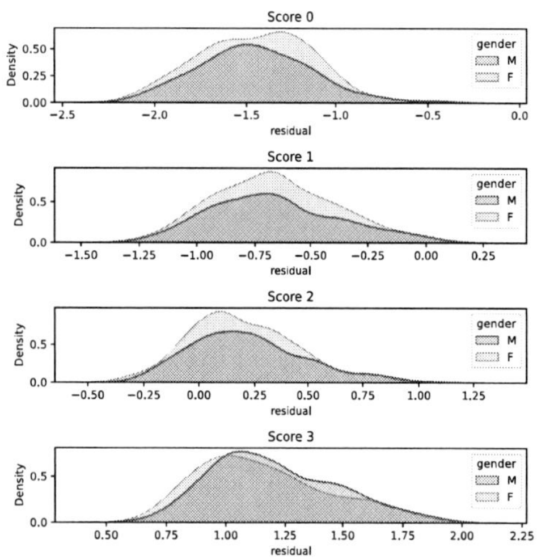

Figure 3: Residual densities for male and female students by global score (0-3). BERT did not achieve a high accuracy on this task, but there was no significant difference in group-wise residuals, showing that male and female students tended to receive comments of a similar valence for their associated score.

When considering both assessor gender and student gender, we performed an ANOVA test and found that two groups had statistically significant differences in means: when comparing male assessor, male student pairs with male assessor, female student pairs, the male assessor, female student pairs had marginally higher ratings (0.0893 difference, $p = 0.0485$)). When comparing male assessor, male student pairs with female assessor, female student pairs, female assessor and female student pairs also had higher mean ratings (0.114 difference, $p = 0.0411$). These effects are more marginal, but expected given the slightly higher scores of female students.

When examining the residuals for the 4-way split, there was one statistically significant difference, between male assessor, female student pairs and female assessor, female student pairs. The residual mean was 0.1195 higher in male assessor, female student pairs, and this was significant to a marginal degree ($p = 0.0468$). This indicates that the actual score given by male assessors to female students was higher than their comment would suggest, as compared to female assessors giving comments to female students. However, this was a marginal effect, and overall we find no clear evidence of gender bias in the comments given to students, or the relationship of the comments given to global score received.

4.2 LIWC

We examine LIWC themes by student gender and partially replicate previous results showing that women tend to be described with more social-communal language than men (Madera et al., 2009). We did not find any significant differences when dividing by assessor gender. However, we did not find that women were described as less agentic in this dataset. A summary of the percentage of comments in which themes occurred is summarized in Table 2. Only the difference in the Social-communal theme is highly significant ($p < 6 \times 10^{-16}$) after Holm-Bonferroni correction. This theme consists of family terms (families, babies, kids), e.g. "great proactive attitude in approaching members of the team and interacting with patients and their families". There is some variation in these comments, as some concern bedside manners with patients and families, and some comment on ability to work with children, which may be necessary in a pediatric unit. We did not see a significant difference in the communal theme (which would describe a warm and nurturing student), unlike in past work.

[3] Annotators were shown a text comment and assigned a global rating from 0-3. They did not see the labels for that portion of the dataset, but were allowed to look at labels for the remaining 80% to guide their judgment. Additionally, annotators were all familiar with the dataset and rubric for global score.

Theme	Example words	% comments with theme (M)	% comments with theme (F)	odds ratio (M/F)	p (corrected)
Affect	amazing, arrogan*, apath*, interest	93.1%	92.7%	1.11	1
Positive Emotion	fantastic, improve, brilliant	89.5%	89.4%	1.03	1
Negative Emotion	angry, difficulty, fail	42.67%	41.36%	1.06	1
Social	advice, ask, commun*	59.9%	57.9%	1.08	1
Cognitive Processing	accura*, inquir*, interpret*	76.6%	75.0%	1.09	1
Insight	deduc*, explain, reflect*	53.6%	52.2%	1.05	1
Achieve	abilit*, ambition, leader*	67.1%	66.7%	1.02	1
Standout	outstanding, exceptional, amazing	17.0%	20.6%	0.786	0.1309
Ability	talen*, smart, skill	18.4%	19.1%	0.960	1
Grindstone	reliab*, hardworking, thorough	45.3%	46.2%	0.965	1
Teaching	teach, mentor, communicate*	21.1%	22.7%	0.914	1
Research	research*, data, study	9.96%	9.75%	1.02	1
Communal	kind, agreeable, caring	4.07%	4.87%	0.829	1
Social-communal	families, babies, kids	8.26%	18.4%	0.401	$5.88 \times 10^{-16}*$
Agentic (adjectives)	assertive, confident, dominant	1.75%	1.72%	1.02	1
Agentic (Orientation)	do, know, think	10.2%	7.67%	1.37	0.1789

Table 2: LIWC theme occurrence in comments given to male and female students. A higher percentage of comments contained the social-communal theme for women than for men. p-values were corrected with the Holm-Bonferroni correction.

5 Conclusion

Gender bias in medical education is a major barrier to women in the field, and it is important to know in what circumstances and career stages it occurs in order to create targeted training and intervention. Previous work has found that there may be potential bias in medical student recommendation letters, but we investigate whether there is systemic bias in an everyday setting in feedback given to male and female medical students. We collect data using NCAT-EM evaluations to answer this question, and use language model residuals to investigate the relationship between free text comments and integer ratings given to students. We find no evidence of bias using the residual definition, although we find that there is a statistically significant difference in the percentage of comments that mention social-communal themes, with women receiving more mentions of family-oriented words in their evaluations.

One limitation of this dataset is that the mapping between text comment and global score is quite noisy, as neither a fine-tuned language model nor human judges were able to achieve a high score in classifying the text based on the global rating. However, the prediction residual method can be used in any dataset with both text data and outcome data, for instance applications to educational programs, or employee evaluations. One caveat is that language models themselves can be biased, so this method is best applied after sensitive attributes have been obfuscated.

Additionally, this dataset is quite small and limited to a relatively small set of samples. It is possible that biases could be found in a larger dataset of shift evaluations, or in data collected from a different set of institutions. However, we leave such data collection to future work, and hope that this encourages the collection and analysis of similar data on a wide scale. We hope that this work will inspire further research into how bias manifests or does not manifest at different stages of professionals' careers, and how we can combine multiple sources of information together with text to form a wider view of bias and fairness.

Acknowledgements

We thank Lynnette Ng and Samantha Phillips for participating in the human annotation task.

References

J Andrews, D Chartash, and S Hay. 2021. Gender bias in resident evaluations: Natural language processing and competency evaluation. *Medical Education*, 55:1383–1387.

Mueller AS, Jenkins TM, Dayal A, O'Connor DM, Osborne M, and Arora VM. 2017. Gender differences in attending physicians' feedback to residents: a qualitative analysis. *J Grad Med Educ*, 9:577–585.

Arlene S. Ash, Phyllis L. Carr, Richard Goldstein, and Robert H. Friedman. 2004. Compensation and advancement of women in academic medicine: is there equity? *Ann Intern Med*, 141:205–212.

CL Bennet, AS Raja, N Kapoor, D Kass, Blumenthal DM, N Gross, and AM Mills. 2019. Gender differences in faculty rank among academic emergency medicine physicians in the united states. *Acad Emerg Med*, 26:281–285.

Molly Carnes, Claudia Morrissey, and Stacie E. Geller. 2008. *J Womens Health (Larchmt)*, 17:1453–1462.

Sherry S. Chesak, Manisha Salinas, Helayna Abraham, Courtney E. Harris, Elise C. Carey, Tejinder Khalsa, Karen F. Mauck, Molly Feely, Lauren Licatino, Susan Moeschler, and Anjali Bhagra. 2022. Experiences of gender inequity among women physicians across career stages: Findings from participant focus groups. *Women's Health Reports*, 3(1):359–368.

AH Eagly and MC Johannesen-Schmidt. 2001. The leadership styles of women and men. *journal of Social Issues*, 57:781–797.

AH Eagly and SJ Karau. 2002. Role congruity theory of prejudice toward female leaders. *Psychological Review*, 109:573–598.

AH Eagly, W Wood, and AB Diekman. 2000. Social role theory of sex differences and similarities: A current appraisal. In T Ecks and HM Traunter, editors, *The developmental social psychology of gender*, pages 123–174. Erlbaum, Mahwah, NJ.

J Jung, D Franzen, L Lawson, D Manthey, M Tews, and N et al. Dubosh. 2017. The national clinical assessment tool for medical students in emergency medicine (ncat-em). *West J Emerg Med*, pages 66–74.

DM Lautenberger, VM Dandar, CL Raezer, and RA Sloane. 2014. The state of women in academic medicine: the pipeline and pathways to leadership.

JM Madera, MR Hebi, and RC Martin. 2009. Gender and letters of recommendation for academia: agentic and communal differences. *J Appl Psychol*, 94:1591–1599.

Association of American Medical Colleges. 2017. Core competencies for entering medical students.

James W. Pennebaker, Ryan L. Boyd, Kayla Jordan, and Kate G. Blackburn. 2015. The development and psychometric properties of liwc2015.

Li S, AL Fant, Mcarthy DM, Miller D, Craig J, and Kontrick A. 2017. Gender differences in language of standardized letter of evaluation narratives for emergency medicine residency applicants. *AEM Educ. Train*, 1:334–339.

D Sarraf, V Vasiliu, B Imberman, and B Lindeman. 2021. Use of artificial intelligence for gender bias analysis in letters of recommendation for general surgery residency candidates. 222:1051–1059.

T Schmader, J Whitehead, and VH Wysocki. 2007. A linguistic comparison of letters of recommendation for male and female chemistry and biochemistry job applicants. *Sex Roles*, 57:509–514.

EF Turrentine, Dreisbach CN, St. Ivany AR, Hanks JB, and Schoren AT. 2019. Influence of gender on surgical residency applicants' recommendation letters. *J Am Coll Surg*, 228:356–365.

Betty van Aken, Sebastian Herrmann, and Alexander Löser. 2021. What do you see in this patient? behavioral testing of clinical nlp models.

W Wood and AH Eagly. 2002. A cross-cultural analysis of the behavior of women and men: Implications for the origins of sex differences. *Psychological Bulletin*, 128:699–727.

On the Dynamics of Gender Learning in Speech Translation

Beatrice Savoldi[1,2], Marco Gaido[1,2], Luisa Bentivogli[2], Matteo Negri[2], Marco Turchi[2]
[1] University of Trento
[2] Fondazione Bruno Kessler
beatrice.savoldi@unitn.it
{mgaido,bentivo,negri,turchi}@fbk.eu

Abstract

Due to the complexity of bias and the opaque nature of current neural approaches, there is a rising interest in auditing language technologies. In this work, we contribute to such a line of inquiry by exploring the emergence of gender bias in Speech Translation (ST). As a new perspective, rather than focusing on the final systems only, we examine their evolution over the course of training. In this way, we are able to account for different variables related to the learning dynamics of gender translation, and investigate when and how gender divides emerge in ST. Accordingly, for three language pairs (en –> es, fr, it) we compare how ST systems behave for masculine and feminine translation at several levels of granularity. We find that masculine and feminine curves are dissimilar, with the feminine one being characterized by a more erratic behaviour and late improvements over the course of training. Also, depending on the considered phenomena, their learning trends can be either antiphase or parallel. Overall, we show how such a progressive analysis can inform on the reliability and time-wise acquisition of gender, which is concealed by static evaluations and standard metrics.

1 Bias Statement

Hereby, we study how Speech Translation (ST) systems deal with the generation of masculine and feminine forms for human referents. Despite the impossibility of a perfect alignment between linguistic and extra-linguistic gender reality (Ackerman, 2019; Cao and Daumé III, 2020), these forms affect the representation and perception of individuals (Stahlberg et al., 2007; Corbett, 2013; Gygax et al., 2019), and are actively used as a tool to negotiate the social, personal, and political reality of gender (Hellinger and Motschenbacher, 2015). Thus, we consider a model that systematically and disproportionately favors masculine over feminine forms as biased, since it fails to properly recognize women. Following Crawford (2017), Blodgett et al. (2020), and Savoldi et al. (2021), such behavior is regarded as harmful because language technologies misrepresent an already disadvantaged social group by reducing feminine visibility and by offering unequal service quality.

Moreover, we consider another potential cause of discrimination in *end-to-end* speech technology. Namely, by translating directly from the audio input it comes with the risk of relying on speakers' vocal characteristics – including fundamental frequency – to translate gender.[1] By using biometric features as gender cues, ST models may reduce gender to stereotypical expectations about the sound of masculine and feminine voices, thus perpetuating biological essentialist frameworks (Zimman, 2020). This is particularly harmful to transgender individuals, as it can lead to misgendering (Stryker, 2008) and a sense of invalidation.

Accordingly, we investigate the aforementioned concerns by evaluating systems' output throughout their training process, aiming to shed light on the dynamics through which gender bias emerges in translation models. Note that, while our diagnostic work focuses on the technical side of gender bias, we recognize the paramount importance of critical interdisciplinary work that foregrounds the context of development and deployment of language technologies (Criado-Perez, 2019; D'Ignazio and Klein, 2020). Also, in Section 9, we discuss the limits of working on binary language.

2 Introduction

Along with the massive deployment of language technologies, concerns regarding their societal impact have been raised (Hovy and Spruit, 2016; Bender et al., 2021), and glaring evidence of biased behavior has been reported by users themselves. Translation technologies are no exception. On-

[1] As in the case of ambiguous first-person references, e.g. en: *I'm tired*, es: *estoy cansado/a*.

Proceedings of the The 4th Workshop on Gender Bias in Natural Language Processing (GeBNLP), pages 94 - 111
July 15, 2022

line interactions exhibited that commercial engines reflect controversial gender roles (Olson, 2018), and further evaluations on both Machine (MT) and Speech translation (ST) systems confirmed that models skew towards a masculine default (Cho et al., 2019; Prates et al., 2020; Bentivogli et al., 2020), except for stereotypical representations (e.g., *nurse* or *pretty doctor* as feminine) (Kocmi et al., 2020; Costa-jussà et al., 2020).

The last few years have witnessed a growing effort towards developing preventive measures (Bender and Friedman, 2018) and mitigating strategies (Saunders and Byrne, 2020; Vanmassenhove et al., 2018; Alhafni et al., 2020). Yet, the complex nature of both neural approaches and bias calls for focused inquiries into our ST and MT models. In this regard, dedicated testing procedures have been designed to pinpoint the impact of gender bias on different categories of phenomena (Stanovsky et al., 2019; Troles and Schmid, 2021; Savoldi et al., 2022). Also, algorithmic choices underpinning the construction of current models have been re-evaluated in light of gender disparities (Renduchintala et al., 2021; Roberts et al., 2020). Despite such promising advancements, many questions still stand unanswered. When does this gender gap emerge? How does gender bias relate to progress in terms of generic performance? To what extent is gender learning altered by the chosen components? To the best of our knowledge, current studies have adopted a static approach, which exclusively focuses on systems' biased behaviors once their training is completed.

Rather than treating training as a black box, in this paper we explore the evolution of gender (in)capabilities across systems' training process. In the wake of prior work highlighting how different target segmentations affect gender bias (Gaido et al., 2021), we compare ST systems built with two techniques: character and byte-pair encoding (BPE) (Sennrich et al., 2016). For three language pairs (en→ es,fr,it), we thus examine their gender learning curves for feminine and masculine translation at several levels of granularity.

Overall, our contributions can be summarized as follows: **(1)** We conduct the first study that explores the dynamic emergence of gender bias in translation technologies; **(2)** By considering the trend and stability of the gender evolution, we find that *(i)* unlike overall translation quality, feminine gender translation emerges more prominently in the late training stages, and does not reach a plateau within the iterations required for models to converge in terms of generic performance. Such trend is however concealed by standard evaluation metrics, and unaccounted when stopping the training of the systems. *(ii)* For easily gender-disambiguated phenomena, masculine and feminine show a generally parallel and upwards trend, with the exception of nouns. Characterized by flat trends and a huge gender divide, their learning dynamics suggests that ST systems confidently rely on spurious cues and generalize masculine from the very early stages of training onwards.

3 Background

Gender bias. Gender bias has emerged as a major area of NLP research (Sun et al., 2019; Stanczak and Augenstein, 2021). A key path forward to address the issue requires moving away from performance as the only desideratum (Birhane et al., 2021), and – quoting Basta and Costa-jussà (2021) – *interpreting and analyzing current data and algorithms*. Accordingly, existing datasets (Hitti et al., 2019), language models (Vig et al., 2020; Silva et al., 2021) and evaluation practices (Goldfarb-Tarrant et al., 2021) have been increasingly put under scrutiny.

Also for automatic translation, inspecting models' inner workings (Bau et al., 2019) can help disclosing potential issues or explaining viable ways to alleviate the problem (Costa-jussà et al., 2022). Concurrently, studies in both MT and ST foregrounded how taken-for-granted algorithmic choices such as speed-optimization practices (Renduchintala et al., 2021), byte-pair encoding (Gaido et al., 2021), or greedy decoding (Roberts et al., 2020) – although they may grant higher efficiency and performance – are actually disfavoring when it comes to gender bias. Finally, fine-grained analyses based on dedicated benchmarks have shown the limits of generic procedures and metrics to detect gender disparities (Vamvas and Sennrich, 2021; Renduchintala and Williams, 2021).

Such contributions are fundamental to shed light on gender bias, by providing guidance for interventions on data, procedures and algorithms. In this work, we contribute to this line of research by analysing direct ST systems (Bérard et al., 2016; Weiss et al., 2017a). As an emerging technology (Ansari et al., 2020; Bentivogli et al., 2021), we believe that prompt investigations have the potential to inform its future development, rather than keeping concerns over gender bias as an afterthought. In the wake of previous studies pointing out that *i)* ST systems may exploit audio cues to translate gender (Bentivogli et al., 2020), and *ii)* state-of-the-art BPE segmentation comes with a higher gender bias (Gaido et al., 2021), we conduct fine grained analyses on these systems, but by means of a new perspective: over the training process.

Training and learning process. Observing the learning dynamics of NLP models is not a new approach. It has been adopted for interpretability analysis to probe when and how linguistic capabilities emerge within language models (Saphra and Lopez, 2018, 2019), or inspect which features may be "harder" to learn (Swayamdipta et al., 2020).

With respect to analyses on a single snapshot, a diachronic perspective has the advantage of accounting for the evolution of NLP capabilities, making them more transparent based on trends' observation. Such an understanding can then be turned into actionable improvements. Accordingly, Voita et al. (2021) looked at the time-wise development of different linguistic abilities in MT, so to inform distillation practices and improve the performance of their systems. Additionally, the studies by Voita et al. (2019a,b) on the learning dynamics of extra-sentential phenomena highlighted how stopping criteria based on BLEU (Papineni et al., 2002) are unreliable for context-aware MT. Finally, Stadler et al. (2021) observed the evolution of different linguistic phenomena in system's output, noting how some of them seem to actually worsen across iterations.

Overall, as Stadler et al. (2021) noted, not much effort has been put into investigating how the training process evolves with regards to measurable factors of translation quality, such as linguistic criteria (grammar, syntax, semantics). We aim to fill this gap by evaluating gender translation of different ST systems at all training checkpoints.

4 Experimental Setting

4.1 Speech translation models

For our experiments, we rely on direct ST models built with two different target segmentation techniques: byte-pair encoding (BPE)[2] (Sennrich et al., 2016) and characters (CHAR). Since we are interested in keeping the effect of different word segmentations as the only variable, all our systems are built in the same fashion, with the same Transformer core technology (Vaswani et al., 2017) and within a controlled environment favouring progress analyses as transparent as possible. For this reason, we avoid additional procedures for boosting performance that could introduce noise, such as joint ST-ASR trainings (Weiss et al., 2017b; Bahar et al., 2019a) or knowledge distillation from MT models (Liu et al., 2019; Gaido et al., 2020a). Thus, our models are only trained on MuST-C (Cattoni et al., 2021), which currently represents the largest multilingual corpus available for ST. For the sake of reproducibility, details on the architecture and settings are provided in Appendix B.

Training procedure. As per standard procedure, the encoder of our ST systems is initialized with the weights of an automatic speech recognition (ASR) model (Bahar et al., 2019a) trained on MuST-C *audio-transcript* pairs. In our ST training, we use the MuST-C gender-balanced validation set (Gaido et al., 2020b)[3] to avoid rewarding systems' biased predictions. Each mini-batch consists of 8 samples, we set the update frequency to 8, train on 4 GPUs, so that a batch contains 256 samples. Within each iteration over the whole training set (i.e. epoch), we record 538 updates for en-es, 555 for en-fr, and 512 for en-it. Given the comparable number of updates across languages, as a point of reference we save the epoch checkpoint (herein ckp) that corresponds to a full pass on the whole training set.

All models reach their best ckp within 42 epochs, with a tendency of BPE to converge faster than CHAR. Specifically, they respectively stop improving after 33/42 epochs (en-es), 25/29 epochs (en-fr), and 29/32 epochs (en-it). As a stopping criterion, we finish our trainings when the loss on the validation set does not improve for 5 consecutive epochs. To inspect the stability of the best model results, our analysis also includes these additional 5 ckps.

4.2 Evaluation

Test set and metrics. To study the evolution of gender translation over the course of training and how it relates to generic perfomance, we employ the gender-sensitive MuST-SHE benchmark (Bentivogli et al., 2020) and its annotated extension

[2]Using SentencePiece (Kudo and Richardson, 2018).

[3]It consists of an equal number of TED talks data from masculine and feminine speakers: `https://ict.fbk.eu/must-c-gender-dev-set/`.

(Savoldi et al., 2022).[4] Consisting of instances of spoken language extracted from TED talks, MuST-SHE allows for the evaluation of gender translation phenomena[5] under natural conditions and for several informative dimensions:

· GENDER, which allows to distinguish results for Feminine (F) and Masculine (M) forms, thus revealing a potential gender gap.

· CATEGORY, which differentiates between: CAT1 first-person references to be translated according to the speakers' linguistic expression of gender (e.g. en: I am a *teacher*, es: soy *un profesor_* vs. soy *una profesora*); and CAT2 references that shall be translated in concordance with other gender information in the sentence (e.g. en: *she* is a *teacher*, es: es *una profesora*). These categories separate unambiguous from ambiguous cases, where ST may leverage speech information as an unwanted cue to translate gender.

· CLASS & POS, which allow to identify if gendered lexical items belonging to different parts-of-speech (POS) are equally impacted by bias. POS can be grouped into *open class* (verb, noun, descriptive adjective) and *closed* class words (article, pronoun, limiting adjective).

In MuST-SHE reference translations, each target gender-marked word is annotated with the above information.[6] Also, for each annotated gender-marked word, a corresponding wrong form, swapped in the opposite gender, is provided (e.g. en: ***the** girl **left***; it: ***la<il>*** *ragazza è* ***andata<andato>*** via). This feature enables pinpointed evaluations on gender realization by first computing[7] *i) Coverage*, i.e. the proportion of annotated words that are generated by the system (disregarding their gender), and on which gender realization is hence measurable, e.g. amigo (friend-M) → amig*; and then *ii) Accuracy*, i.e. the proportion of words generated in the correct gender among the measurable ones, e.g. amigo (friend-M) → amigo. Hence, *accuracy* properly measures model tendency to (over)generalize masculine forms over feminine ones: scores below 50% can signal a strong bias, where the wrong form is picked by the systems more often than the correct one.

[4] Available at: `https://ict.fbk.eu/must-she/`

[5] Namely, the translation of a source neutral English word into a gender marked one in the target languages, e.g. en: ***this** girl is **a good friend***, es: ***esta*** *chica es* ***una buena amiga***.

[6] Annotation statistics are provided in Appendix A.

[7] We rely on the evaluation script provided with the MuST-SHE extension.

In our study, we rely on the above metrics to inspect gender translations, and employ SacreBLEU (Post, 2018)[8] to measure overall translation quality.

Setup. Since we aim to observe the learning curves of our ST models, we evaluate both overall and gender translation quality after each epoch of their training process. As explained in Sec. 4.1, training includes also the 5 epochs that follow the best system ckp. To investigate systems' behaviour, we are particularly interested in the two following aspects of the learning curves: *i)* **training trend** (is gender accuracy raising across epochs, does it reach a plateau or can it actually worsen across iterations?); *ii)* **training stability** (is gender learning steady or erratic across epochs?)

Depending on the aspect addressed, we present results with different visualizations, reporting either the actual scores obtained at each ckp (more suitable to detect small fluctuations) or aggregated scores calculated with moving average over 3 ckp (more suitable to highlight general trends). Note that, since the total number of epochs differs for each system, to allow for a proper comparison we also plot results at different percentages of the training progress, where each progress point represents a 5% advancement (i.e 5%, 10%, 15% etc.).

With this in mind, we proceed in our analyses comparing overall performance across metrics (Sec.5.1), and inspecting feminine and gender translation (Sec. 5.2) at several levels of granularity (Sec 5.3 and 5.4). For any addressed aspect, we compare CHAR and BPE models across language pairs.

5 Results and Discussion

		BLEU	All-Cov	All-Acc	F-Acc	M-Acc
en-es	BPE	27.4	64.0	66.0	49.0	80.7
	CHAR	27.2	64.0	**70.5**	**58.9**	80.5
en-fr	BPE	24.0	53.7	65.4	51.7	77.2
	CHAR	23.5	53.1	**69.7**	**64.0**	74.9
en-it	BPE	20.4	48.7	65.6	49.9	79.0
	CHAR	19.1	51.2	**71.2**	**52.9**	86.7

Table 1: BLEU, coverage and accuracy (percentage) scores computed on MuST-SHE.

First of all, in Table 1 we provide a snapshot of the results obtained by our ST models on their best ckp. As expected, the accuracy scores clearly exhibit a strong bias favouring masculine forms in translation (M-acc>F-acc), with feminine forms being generated with a probability close to a random guess for most systems. Moreover, these results

[8] BLEU+c.mixed+.1+s.exp+tok.13a+v.1.4.3.

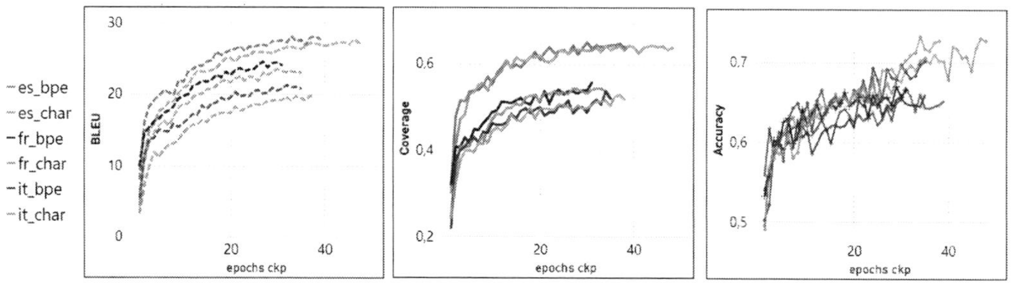

(a) BLEU (b) Coverage (c) Accuracy

Figure 1: Results for every ckp of each model: BLEU (a), gender Coverage (b), and gender Accuracy (c).

are in line with the analyses by Gaido et al. (2021) and Savoldi et al. (2022) showing that CHAR has an edge in gender translation (All-Acc),[9] which is largely ascribed to better treatment of feminine gender.[10] Thus, we confirm a previously verified behaviour, which we now further inquiry in terms of its dynamic evolution.

5.1 Overall results

Here, we start by looking at the evolution of models' performance assessed in terms of BLEU, coverage, and accuracy (Figure 1) to inspect the time of emergence of the different capabilities captured by such metrics. For a bird's-eye view, we present the actual scores per each ckp.

The evolution of both overall translation performance and gender translation is positive, but dissimilar in time and quality. By looking at Figure 1, we observe that the gender accuracy learning curve (1c) immediately stands out. Indeed, the curves for both BLEU (1a) and gender coverage (1b) have a rapid and steady initial increase,[11] which starts to level off around the 20th ckp.[12] Also, the BLEU trends reveal a divide across models (BPE>CHAR) that remains visible over the whole course of training. In terms of coverage, the boundaries between types of models are more blurred, but correlate with BLEU scores for all language pairs. Conversely, by looking at the gender accuracy curves (1c) we asses that, while the overall trends show a general improvement across epochs, **gender learning *i)* proceeds with notable fluctuations, unlike the smoother BLEU and coverage curves; *ii)* emerges especially in the final iterations.** In particular, it is interesting to note that by epoch 30 (roughly 80% of the training process), *all* CHAR models handle gender translation better than *all* the BPE ones, regardless of the lower overall quality of the former group. Notably, the en-it CHAR system - with the lowest BLEU – exhibits the steepest increase in gender capabilities.

Takeaways. Generic translation quality improves more prominently in the initial training stages, while gender is learnt later. Thus, standard quality metrics conceal and are inadequate to consider gender refinements in the learning process.

5.2 Masculine and feminine gender

Moving onto a deeper level of analysis, we compare the learning dynamics that undergo Feminine (F) and Masculine (M) gender in terms of accuracy. To give better visibility of their *trends* and comparisons across models, in Figure 2 we plot the averaged results. As complementary view into training stability, Figure 3 shows the actual accuracy scores for the en-it models.[13]

Masculine forms are largely and consistently acquired since the very first iterations. As shown in Figure 2, masculine gender (M) is basically already learnt at 15% of the training process. Henceforth, its accuracy remains high and stable within 70-80%

[9] Contemporary to our submission, Libovický et al. (2021) show that en-de MT systems based on character-level segmentation have an edge – with respect to BPE – in terms of gender accuracy on the WinoMT benchmark (Stanovsky et al., 2019). Their results, however, do not distinguish between feminine and masculine translation capabilities.

[10] For the sake of our analysis across epochs, we do not generate our final systems by averaging the 5 models around the best ckp as in Gaido et al. (2021) and Savoldi et al. (2022). For this reason, our systems compare less favourably in terms of BLEU score, also reducing the perfomance gap bewteen *de facto* standard BPE and CHAR.

[11] Computed as a binary task, gender accuracy starts at ∼50-55% in the first ckp. Such scores reflect that correct gender is assigned randomly at the beginning of the training process.

[12] The plateau is particularly visible for en-es CHAR due to its longer training.

[13] Due to space constraints, plots for all language pairs are in Appendix C - Fig. 7, which shows consistent results.

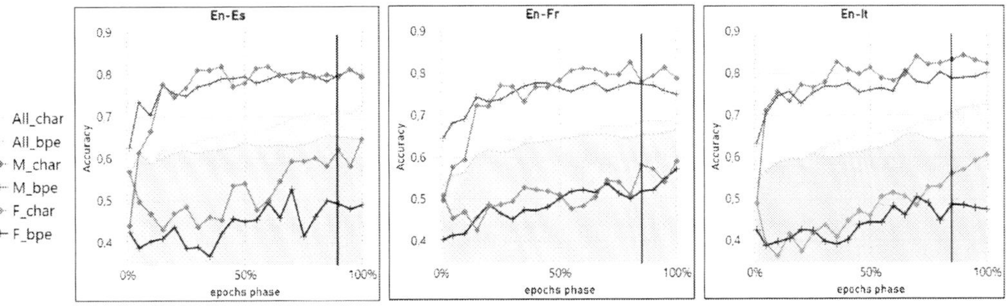

(a) en-es (b) en-fr (c) en-it

Figure 2: (F)eminine vs M(asculine) and over(all) accuracy scores for CHAR and BPE in en-es (2a), en-fr (2b), and en-it (2c). For better comparability across systems and trend visibility, results are shown at different percentages of the training progress (increasing by 5%), and scores at each progress point are calculated with moving average over 3 ckp. The first ckp (0%) is the actual score of the first epoch. The vertical line indicates the average score for the best ckp.

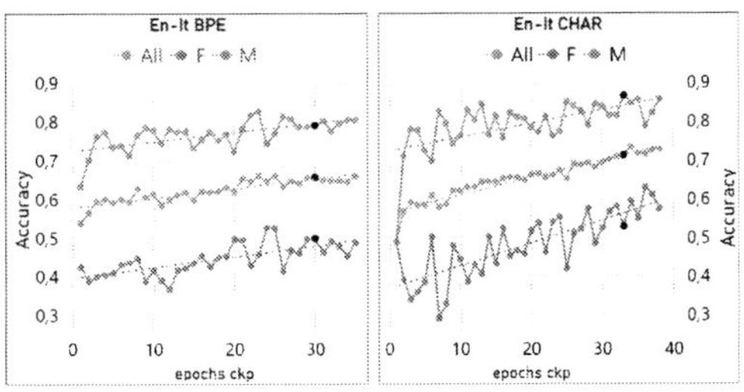

Figure 3: All, F vs Masculine gender accuracy for en-it BPE (left) and CHAR (right) models. Actual scores are reported per each ckp, and black dots indicate best ckp.

average scores for all models. As an exception, we notice a slightly decreasing trend in the iterations that follow the best ckp for en-fr BPE (2b). **Instead, feminine translation exhibits an overall upward trend that emerges later in the training process.** In Table 1, we already attested CHAR's advantage in dealing with feminine translation. Here, we are able to verify how such a capability is developed over the whole course of training. Specifically, CHAR gains a clear advantage over BPE in the last training phases, in particular for en-es (2a) and en-it (2c). Moreover, the overall rising F trend for CHAR models does not seem to dwindle: even after systems have reached their best ckp, feminine translation shows potential for further improvement.

Unlike CHAR systems, BPE disproportionately favours masculine forms since the first ckp. In the first ckp of the training, we notice an interesting difference between BPE and CHAR. Namely, the former models are biased since the very beginning of their training with an evident gender divide: ∼65% accuracy for M and only ∼40% for F forms.[14] Conversely, accuracy scores for both F and M forms in CHAR systems present about the same accuracy: both around 50% for en-it and en-fr, whereas the en-es model notably presents lower scores on the M set. From such behaviours, we infer that CHAR systems *i)* are initially less prone towards masculine generalisation, which is instead a by-product of further training; *ii)* promptly acquire the ability to generate both M and F inflections, although they initially assign them randomly. As we further discuss in Sec. 6, they occasionally acquire target morphology even before its lexicon, thus generating English source words inflected as per the morphological rules of the target language, e.g. en: *sister*; es: *sistera* (hermana). We regard this finding as evidence of the already attested capabilities of character-level segmentation to better handle morphology (Belinkov et al., 2020), which by extension may explain the higher capability of CHAR models at generating feminine forms.

Despite a common upward trend, F and M gender curves progress with antiphase fluctuations. In Figure 3, we see how this applies to CHAR in particular. Far from being monotonic, the progress of gender translation underlies a great level of instability with notable spikes and dips in antiphase for F and M - although eventually resulting in gains for F. Interestingly, it thus seems that systems become better at enhancing F translation by partially suppressing the representation of the other gender

[14]As outlined in Sec. 4.2, 40% accuracy for F means that in the remaining 60% of the cases systems generate a masculine inflection instead of the expected feminine one.

form.

Takeaways. The insights are more fine-grained: *i)* F is the actual gender form that is learnt late in the training process; *ii)* the progress of gender translation involves unstable antiphase fluctuations for F and M; *iii)* there is still room for improvements for F gender, especially for CHAR models. Overall, these findings make us question the suitability of standard metrics for diagnosing gender bias (see Sec. 5.1), and of the loss function as a stopping criterion. Along this line, previous work has foregrounded that even when a model has converged in terms of BLEU, it continues to improve for context-aware phenomena (Voita et al., 2019a). Hereby, although we find a good (inverse) correlation between loss and BLEU, we attest that they seem to be unable to properly account for gender bias and the evolution of feminine capabilities. Looking at both Figures 2 and 3, we question whether a longer training would have facilitated an improvement in gender translation and, in light of F and M antiphase relation, if it would lead to a suppression of M by favouring F. If that were the case, such type of diversity could be leveraged to create more representative models. Since more ckps would be needed to investigate this point, we leave it for future work.

5.3 Gender category

We now examine the learning curves for the translation of *i)* ambiguous references to the speaker, and *ii)* references disambiguated by a contextual cue (CAT1 and CAT2 introduced in Sec. 4.2). For each category, Figure 4 shows the comparison of feminine (1F, 2F) and masculine (1M, 2M) forms.

Compared to the extremely unstable learning of CAT1, feminine and masculine curves from the unambiguous CAT2 exhibit a smooth upward parallel trend. In Figure 4, the differences across categories fully emerge, and are consistent across languages and models. On the one hand, F and M curves from CAT2 show a steady trend which, despite a ∼10-20% accuracy gap across genders, suggests an increasing ability to model gender cues and translate accordingly. On the other hand, CAT1 proves to be largely responsible for the extreme instability and antiphase behaviour discussed for Figure 2, which is so strong to be evident even over the presented averaged scores.[15] Overall, we recognize a moderately increasing trend of 1F curves for all the CHAR models and the en-fr BPE. However, it barely raises above a random prediction, i.e. ∼50-57% accuracy meaning that a wrong masculine form is generated in ∼50-43% of the instances.

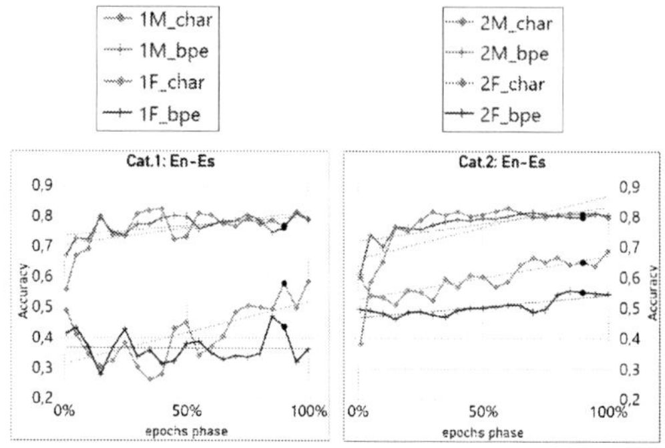

(a) en-es

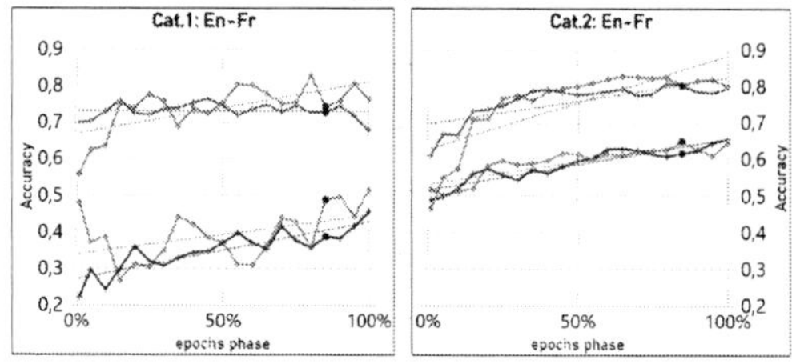

(b) en-fr

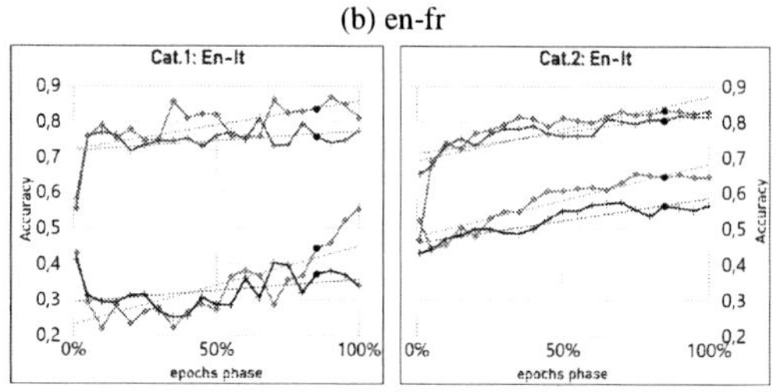

(c) en-it

Figure 4: F vs M accuracy for CAT1 and CAT2. Scores are averaged over 3 ckps, and reported for each training phase. Dots indicate averaged scores for best ckp.

In light of the above, we are brought to reflect upon the hypothesis that direct ST models may use audio information to translate gender.[16] One possible explanation for systems' behaviour on CAT1 is that – although highly undesirable – ST *does* leverage speaker's voice as a gender cue, but finds the association "hard to learn". Another option is that ST *does not* leverage audio information and deals with CAT1 as gender ambiguous input. As a result, more biased BPE models more frequently opt for a masculine output in this scenario. CHAR models,

[15]E.g., the actual scores for 1F accuracy for en-it CHAR plummets as low as 11% at ckp9, and rockets at 60% at ckp36.

[16]This hypothesis was formulated in both (Bentivogli et al., 2020) and (Gaido et al., 2021).

instead, being characterized by a more favourable generation of feminine forms, progressively tend to converge towards a random gender prediction over the 1F set.

Towards the trustworthy development of ST technology, we call for future investigations on this point.

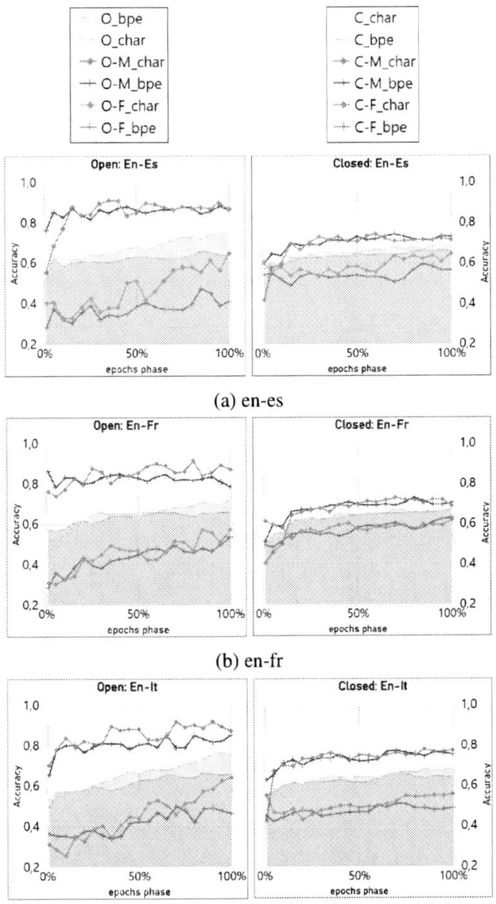

(a) en-es

(b) en-fr

(c) en-it

Figure 5: Open (left) vs Closed (right) classes accuracy scores per F and M gender. Scores are averaged over 3 ckps and reported for training phase.

5.4 Class and POS

In Figure 5, we compare the gender curves for open and closed class words, which differ substantially in terms of frequency of use, variability and semantic content.

Both F and M curves of the closed class change very little over the course of training. In Figure 5, the closed class exhibits a stable trend with minimal increases, and a small F *vs.* M gap compared to the open class. We hypothesise this may be due to simple source constructions involving articles next to a gendered word, which are learnt since the very beginning (e.g., the mum; fr: la mère). **Open class words instead, show an unstable upward trend for F, opposed to the steady and early-learned M translation.** Consistently, the M curve starts off with unprecedented high scores (i.e., ~80% accuracy within the first 20% of the training process) which further increases to 90% accuracy scores for CHAR. The F curve is progressively improving and – once again – with more significant gains late in training. This also implies that the M/F gap is reduced over the epochs. In light of the evident bias and distinct behaviour of F and M learning progress for the open class, we now turn to examine how each POS in this group evolves over training.

Nouns are outliers, being the only POS that exhibits low variability in its learning curves, with little to almost no room for improving F translation. Consistently across languages and models,[17] this claim can be verified in Figure 6 for en-fr. M nouns are basically fluctuation-free and reach almost perfect accuracy since the early ckps. Conversely, the F curve presents extremely low scores throughout the training process, signalling the strongest bias attested so far (i.e., the accuracy for F-nouns is 40% for both CHAR and BPE). Oddly enough, unlike adjectives and verbs, nouns learning dynamics do not even reflect the different trends assessed for CAT1 and the "easier" CAT2 (Sec. 5.3). Namely, despite the presence of a gender cue, the translation of feminine nouns from CAT2 (2F) does not benefit from such a disambiguation information. In fact, the accuracy for 2F nouns is basically on par (or even worse) with the performance of F nouns of CAT1 (1F), whereas for any other POS – and even M-nouns – the subset of CAT2 always exhibits a more positive learning trend.

Takeaways. Overall, our remarks are in line with the findings formulated by Savoldi et al. (2022): nouns emerge as the lexical category that is most impacted by gender bias, arguably because systems tend to rely more on stereotypical, spurious cues for the translation of professional nouns (e.g., *scientist, professor*). By examining their training progress however, we additionally unveil that *i)* biased associations influence noun translation more than unambiguous and relevant information, which

[17] Due to space constraints, we refer to Appendix C.2.1 for en-es and en-it.

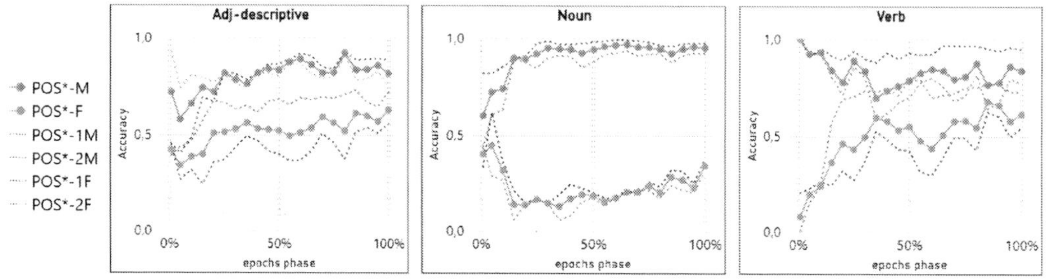

(a) CHAR en-fr

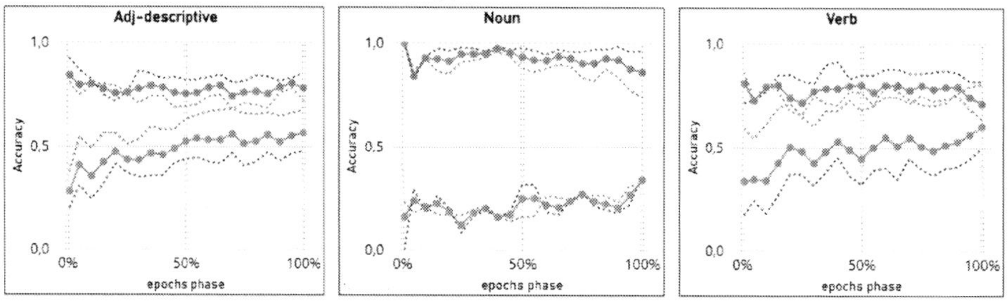

(b) BPE en-fr

Figure 6: Accuracy per each open class POS for the en-fr CHAR and BPE models. The graph shows F vs M scores, also at the level of CAT1/2. Scores are provided for training phases, and calculated as the average over 3 ckps.

is available for CAT2; *ii)* ST models rely on such patterns so confidently that they never really adjust their trend over the epochs.

6 Qualitative Insights

We conclude our analysis with a manual inspection of the outputs of our ST systems at two *i)* initial, *ii)* middle, and *ii)* final ckps of their training process. To this aim, we opt for the en-es language pair – for which we observed the highest BLEU and gender coverage scores (Table 1) – to minimize the amount of low-quality translations that could be hard to analyze. Table 2 presents an example sentence from CAT2, translated by both CHAR and BPE, which backs up some of the quantitative observations formulated in Sec. 5. The source sentence contains neutral words (*older*, *a*, *a master*) occurring together with gender-marked words that disambiguate the correct gender (*sister*, *she*, *mother*). Given the presence of these gender cues, the neutral words should be fairly easy to translate.

In the first two ckps of both models, the output has very low quality.[18] It is characterized by extensive repetitions of frequent words, like *mother* (*madre* in A) or *young* (*joven, jóvenes* in B-G). Also, whereas functional words[19] are already appropriately employed and inflected with the correct gender (e.g. ***a*** *mother* → ***una*** *madre*, A,G), the noun *master* is not learnt yet and remains out of coverage; notably, BPE generates the word *hombre* (i.e. *man*) instead. Interestingly, if we also look at the gender cue noun *sister*, it maps to another kinship term *daughter* for BPE (G), whereas CHAR generalizes target morphology over English lexicon at these stages (*sistería* in A, *sistera* in B).

Such lexical issues are all refined by the middle ckps, where the systems have acquired both *sister/hermana* (with the feminine inflected adjective *antigua*[20] in C) and *master/maestr**, which in this case undergoes an interesting gender evolution across systems. For CHAR, we assist to an adjustment from masculine inflection (B), to a feminine one (C onwards) that remains stable until the end of training, even after the best ckp. Instead, BPE has a reversed trend. In H, the output *una maestra* reveals that this system can and has learnt to generate feminine forms. However, as the training progresses it switches to M inflections and never rebounds to the F ones. Rather, in the last epochs K-L it produces alternative synonyms, but always

[18]Still, we believe that it is to a certain degree intelligible thanks to the ASR initialization, see Sec. 4.1.

[19]I.e. closed class.

[20]The most fluent choice would be the neutral *mayor*. Here, however, we just focus on gender realizations.

2F	SRC	My **older** <u>sister</u> Claire, <u>she</u> became **a** young <u>mother</u>, and **a master** at getting things done
CHAR$_{Es}$	(A) INI	Mi madre la *sistería sistencia* , encontró una madre joven una madre, y una madre, y una masa, y una cosa que estaba cosas.
	(B) INI	Mi madre *sister*a de clara se convirtió en un joven jóvenes jóvenes jóvenes, y un **maestr**o de cosas que hicieron.
	(C) MID	Mi hermana más **antigu**a clara, se convirtió en **un**a madre joven y **un**a **maestr**a que hacía cosas.
	(D) MID	Mi **antigu**a hermana Clare, se convirtió en **un**a madre joven y **un**a **maestr**a que hice las cosas.
	(E) FIN	Mi hermana mayor Clare, se convirtió en **un**a madre joven, y **un**a **maestr**a de hacer las cosas.
	(F) FIN	Mi hermana mayor, Clare, se convirtió en **un**a joven madre, y **un**a **maestr**a por hacer las cosas.
BPE$_{Es}$	(G) INI	Mi hija de la Tierra se convirtió en un joven joven, ella me convertí en **un**a madre, y un hombre que hizo cosas.
	(H) INI	Mi hermana mayor claridad se convirtió en **un**a madre joven, y **un**a **maestr**a, lo hice.
	(I) MID	Mi hermana mayor se volvió a ser **un**a joven madre, y una maestría que hice.
	(J) MID	Mi hermana mayor declaró, se convirtió en **un**a madre joven, y un **maestr**o que se está haciendo.
	(K) FIN	Mi hermana mayor declaró que se convirtió en **un**a madre joven, y un **am**o logrando hacer las cosas.
	(L) FIN	Mi hermana mayor Clare se convirtió en **un**a madre joven, y un **dueñ**o de hacer que las cosas se hicieran.

Table 2: En-es outputs at initial, middle, and final epochs. The source sentence contains **neutral words** to be translated according to the available <u>gender cues</u>. In the outputs, we indicate correct feminine gender translation vs masculine. We also signal repetitions and *copied source lemma*+target morphology combinations.

with the wrong gender (*amo, dueño*).[21] Overall, this case exemplifies how, in spite of *i)* having F morphological capabilities, and *ii)* the presence of a close cue disambiguating gender, the BPE system confidently relies on spurious and irrelevant patterns for gender translation.

7 Limitations and Future Work

In this work, we rendered the ST training process less opaque by analyzing the learning process of gender. To do so, we looked into ST outputs. However, a complementary perspective would be to rely on explainability and probing approaches on system's inner mechanisms (Belinkov and Glass, 2019) and verify their compatibility with our findings. Also, a contrastive comparison of the learning curves for gender and other linguistic phenomena implying a one-to-many mapping (e.g. politeness *you* → es: *tu*/*usted*) could pinpoint learning trends which are specific to gender bias. A limit of our analyses is that they include only 5 epochs after their best validation loss. In light of our *a posteriori* finding that F gender – especially for CHAR – does not reach a plateau in the last epochs, future work is needed to confirm whether and to what extent F learning keeps improving. This could inform studies on *i)* how to leverage diversified output to alleviate gender bias in our models, *ii)* gender-sensitive stopping criteria. Finally, we point out that for the most fine-grained level of analyses (Sec. 5.4), our evaluation is based on very specific subsets (e.g. nouns broke down into 1F, 2F, 1M, 2M).[22] This comes with an inherent reduction of the amount of measurable gender-marked words, which could in turn imply noise and additional instability in the visualized results. However, we reduce this risk by presenting them averaged over 3 ckps and, as the noun curves show (Fig. 6), believe in their validity for comparisons within the same dimension and level of granularity.

Note that our study lies on the specificity of three comparable grammatical gender languages. We are thus cautious about generalizing our findings. Experiments on other training sets and language pairs are currently hindered by the lack of an available natural, gender-sensitive ST benchmark that covers alternative gender directions. While bearing this in mind, we however underscore that the conditions of gender translation significantly change depending on the features of the accounted languages and direction (e.g. translating from grammatical gender languages to English and not *vice versa*). Thus, gender phenomena on typologically different gendered languages would not be *directly* comparable and compatible with the presented analyses. Rather than a specific limitation of our setting, we regard this as an intrinsic condition.

8 Conclusion

Despite the mounting evidence of biased behaviour in language technologies, its understanding is hindered by the complex and opaque nature of current neural approaches. In this work, we shed light on the emergence of gender bias in ST systems by focusing on their learning dynamics over training. In this way, we adopt a new perspective that accounts for the time-wise appearance of gender capabilities, and examine their stability, reliability and course of development. For three language pairs (en → es, fr, it) we inspect the learning curves of feminine

[21]Although inappropriate in this context, both *amo* and *dueño* are valid mapping to the word *master*).

[22]In the Appendix, we provide MuST-SHE statistics (Table 4) and gender coverage for open-closed class words (Fig. 8).

and masculine gender translation *i)* at several levels of granularity; *ii)* with respect to progress in terms of overall translation quality; *iii)* on the output of ST systems trained on target data segmented as either character or sub-words units (BPE). In our diachronic analysis, we unveil that *i)* feminine gender is learnt late over the course of training, *ii)* it never reaches a plateau within the number of iterations required for model convergence at training time, and *iii)* its refinements are concealed by standard evaluation metrics. Also, by looking at the stability vs. fluctuations of the explored trends, we identify under which circumstances ST models seem to actually progressively acquire feminine and masculine translation, and when instead their erratic, antiphase behavior reflects unreliable choices made by the systems. In this way, we find that *nouns* – the lexical category most impacted by gender bias – present a firm and huge gender divide over the whole training, where ST systems do not rely on relevant information to support feminine translation and never really adjust its generation.

9 Impact Statement[23]

In compliance with ACL norms of ethics,[24] we hereby clarify i) the characteristics of the dataset used in our experiments, and ii) our use of gender as a variable (Larson, 2017).

As already discussed, in our experiments we rely on the training data from the TED-based MuST-C corpus[25] (Sec. 4.1), and its derived evaluation benchmark, MuST-SHE v1.2[26] (Sec. 4.2). For both resources, detailed information on the representativeness of TED data is available in their data statements (Bender and Friedman, 2018). As regards gender, it is largely discussed how it is intended and annotated. Thus, we know that MuST-C training data are manually annotated with speakers' gender information[27] based on the personal pronouns found in their publicly available personal TED profile.[28] Overall, MuST-C exhibits a gender imbalance, with 70% vs. 30% of the speakers referred by means of *he/she* pronoun, respectively.[29]

As reported in its release page,[30] the same annotation process applies to MuST-SHE as well, with the additional check that the indicated (English) linguistic gender forms are rendered in the gold standard translations. Hence, information about speakers' preferred linguistic expressions of gender are transparently validated and disclosed. Accordingly, when working on the evaluation of speaker-related gender translation for MuST-SHE,[31] we solely focus on the rendering of their reported linguistic gender expressions. No assumptions about speakers' self determined identity (GLAAD, 2007) – which cannot be directly mapped from pronoun usage (Cao and Daumé III, 2020; Ackerman, 2019) – has been made.

Finally, in our diagnosis of gender bias we only account for feminine and masculine linguistic forms, which are those traditionally in use and the only represented in the used data. However, we stress that – by working on binary forms – we do not imply or impose a binary vision on the extra-linguistic reality of gender, which is rather a spectrum (D'Ignazio and Klein, 2020). Also, we acknowledge the challenges faced for grammatical gender languages like Spanish, French and Italian in fully implementing neutral language, and support rise of neutral language and non-binary neomorphology (Shroy, 2016; Gabriel et al., 2018; Conrod, 2020).

References

Lauren Ackerman. 2019. Syntactic and cognitive issues in investigating gendered coreference. *Glossa: a Journal of General linguistics*, 4(1).

Bashar Alhafni, Nizar Habash, and Houda Bouamor. 2020. Gender-aware reinflection using linguistically enhanced neural models. In *Proceedings of the Second Workshop on Gender Bias in Natural Language Processing*, pages 139–150, Barcelona, Spain (Online). Association for Computational Linguistics.

Ebrahim Ansari, Amittai Axelrod, Nguyen Bach, Ondřej Bojar, Roldano Cattoni, Fahim Dalvi, Nadir Durrani, Marcello Federico, Christian Federmann, Jiatao Gu, Fei Huang, Kevin Knight, Xutai Ma, Ajay Nagesh, Matteo Negri, Jan Niehues, Juan Pino, Elizabeth Salesky, Xing Shi, Sebastian Stüker, Marco Turchi, Alexander Waibel, and Changhan Wang. 2020. FINDINGS OF THE IWSLT 2020 EVALUATION CAMPAIGN. In *Proceedings of the 17th International Conference on Spoken Language Trans-*

[23]Extra page granted as per `https://aclrollingreview.org/cfp`.

[24]`https://www.aclweb.org/portal/content/acl-code-ethics`

[25]`https://ict.fbk.eu/must-c/`

[26]`https://ict.fbk.eu/must-she/`.

[27]`https://ict.fbk.eu/must-speakers/`

[28]`https://www.ted.com/speakers`.

[29]Only one *They* speaker is represented in the corpus.

[30]`https://ict.fbk.eu/must-she/`

[31]Category 1 (CAT1) in the corpus.

lation, pages 1–34, Online. Association for Computational Linguistics.

Parnia Bahar, Tobias Bieschke, and Hermann Ney. 2019a. A Comparative Study on End-to-end Speech to Text Translation. In *Proceedings of International Workshop on Automatic Speech Recognition and Understanding (ASRU)*, pages 792–799, Sentosa, Singapore.

Parnia Bahar, Albert Zeyer, Ralf Schlüter, and Hermann Ney. 2019b. On Using SpecAugment for End-to-End Speech Translation. In *Proceedings of the International Workshop on Spoken Language Translation (IWSLT)*, Hong Kong, China.

Christine Basta and Marta R. Costa-jussà. 2021. Impact of Gender Debiased Word Embeddings in Language Modeling. *CoRR*, abs/2105.00908.

Anthony Bau, Yonatan Belinkov, Hassan Sajjad, Nadir Durrani, Fahim Dalvi, and James Glass. 2019. Identifying and controlling important neurons in neural machine translation. In *International Conference on Learning Representations*.

Yonatan Belinkov, Nadir Durrani, Fahim Dalvi, Hassan Sajjad, and James Glass. 2020. On the Linguistic Representational Power of Neural Machine Translation Models. *Computational Linguistics*, 46(1):1–52.

Yonatan Belinkov and James Glass. 2019. Analysis methods in neural language processing: A survey. *Transactions of the Association for Computational Linguistics*, 7:49–72.

Emily M. Bender and Batya Friedman. 2018. Data Statements for Natural Language Processing: Toward Mitigating System Bias and Enabling Better Science. *Transactions of the Association for Computational Linguistics*, 6:587–604.

Emily M. Bender, Timnit Gebru, Angelina McMillan-Major, and Shmargaret Shmitchell. 2021. On the dangers of stochastic parrots: Can language models be too big? . In *Proceedings of the 2021 ACM Conference on Fairness, Accountability, and Transparency*, FAccT '21, page 610–623, New York, NY, USA. Association for Computing Machinery.

Luisa Bentivogli, Mauro Cettolo, Marco Gaido, Alina Karakanta, Alberto Martinelli, Matteo Negri, and Marco Turchi. 2021. Cascade versus Direct Speech Translation: Do the Differences Still Make a Difference? In *Proceedings of the 59th Annual Meeting of the Association for Computational Linguistics and the 11th International Joint Conference on Natural Language Processing (Volume 1: Long Papers)*, pages 2873–2887, Online. Association for Computational Linguistics.

Luisa Bentivogli, Beatrice Savoldi, Matteo Negri, Mattia A. Di Gangi, Roldano Cattoni, and Marco Turchi. 2020. Gender in Danger? Evaluating Speech Translation Technology on the MuST-SHE Corpus. In *Proceedings of the 58th Annual Meeting of the Association for Computational Linguistics*, pages 6923–6933, Online. Association for Computational Linguistics.

Abeba Birhane, Pratyusha Kalluri, Dallas Card, William Agnew, Ravit Dotan, and Michelle Bao. 2021. The values encoded in machine learning research. *arXiv preprint arXiv:2106.15590*.

Su Lin Blodgett, Solon Barocas, Hal Daumé III, and Hanna Wallach. 2020. Language (Technology) is Power: A Critical Survey of "Bias" in NLP. In *Proceedings of the 58th Annual Meeting of the Association for Computational Linguistics*, pages 5454–5476, Online. Association for Computational Linguistics.

Alexandre Bérard, Olivier Pietquin, Christophe Servan, and Laurent Besacier. 2016. Listen and Translate: A Proof of Concept for End-to-End Speech-to-Text Translation. In *NIPS Workshop on end-to-end learning for speech and audio processing*, Barcelona, Spain.

Yang T. Cao and Hal Daumé III. 2020. Toward Gender-Inclusive Coreference Resolution. In *Proceedings of the 58th Annual Meeting of the Association for Computational Linguistics*, pages 4568–4595, Online. Association for Computational Linguistics.

Roldano Cattoni, Mattia Antonino Di Gangi, Luisa Bentivogli, Matteo Negri, and Marco Turchi. 2021. MuST-C: A multilingual corpus for end-to-end speech translation. *Computer Speech & Language*, 66:101155.

Won Ik Cho, Ji Won Kim, Seok Min Kim, and Nam Soo Kim. 2019. On Measuring Gender Bias in Translation of Gender-neutral Pronouns. In *Proceedings of the First Workshop on Gender Bias in Natural Language Processing*, pages 173–181, Florence, Italy. Association for Computational Linguistics.

Kirby Conrod. 2020. Pronouns and gender in language. *The Oxford Handbook of Language and Sexuality*.

Greville G. Corbett. 2013. *The Expression of Gender*. De Gruyter.

Marta R. Costa-jussà, Christine Basta, and Gerard I. Gállego. 2020. Evaluating gender bias in speech translation. *CoRR*, abs/2010.14465. Accepted at LREC 2022.

Marta R. Costa-jussà, Carlos Escolano, Christine Basta, Javier Ferrando, Roser Batlle, and Ksenia Kharitonova. 2022. Interpreting Gender Bias in Neural Machine Translation: The Multilingual Architecture Matters. *Accepted in 36th AAAI Conference on Artificial Intelligence*.

Kate Crawford. 2017. The Trouble with Bias. In *Conference on Neural Information Processing Systems (NIPS) – Keynote*, Long Beach, California.

Caroline Criado-Perez. 2019. *Invisible Women: Exposing Data Bias in a World Designed for Men*. Penguin Random House, London, UK.

Mattia A. Di Gangi, Marco Gaido, Matteo Negri, and Marco Turchi. 2020. On Target Segmentation for Direct Speech Translation. In *Proceedings of the 14th Conference of the Association for Machine Translation in the Americas (AMTA 2020)*, pages 137–150, Online. Association for Machine Translation in the Americas.

Mattia A. Di Gangi, Matteo Negri, Roldano Cattoni, Dessi Roberto, and Marco Turchi. 2019. Enhancing transformer for end-to-end speech-to-text translation. In *Machine Translation Summit XVII*, pages 21–31, Dublin, Ireland. European Association for Machine Translation.

Catherine D'Ignazio and Lauren F Klein. 2020. *Data feminism*. MIT Press, London, UK.

Ute Gabriel, Pascal M. Gygax, and Elisabeth A. Kuhn. 2018. Neutralising linguistic sexism: Promising but cumbersome? *Group Processes & Intergroup Relations*, 21(5):844–858.

Marco Gaido, Mattia A. Di Gangi, Matteo Negri, and Marco Turchi. 2020a. End-to-End Speech-Translation with Knowledge Distillation: FBK@IWSLT2020. In *Proceedings of the 17th International Conference on Spoken Language Translation*, pages 80–88, Online. Association for Computational Linguistics.

Marco Gaido, Beatrice Savoldi, Luisa Bentivogli, Matteo Negri, and Marco Turchi. 2020b. Breeding Gender-aware Direct Speech Translation Systems. In *Proceedings of the 28th International Conference on Computational Linguistics*, pages 3951–3964, Online. International Committee on Computational Linguistics.

Marco Gaido, Beatrice Savoldi, Luisa Bentivogli, Matteo Negri, and Marco Turchi. 2021. How to Split: the Effect of Word Segmentation on Gender Bias in Speech Translation. In *Findings of the Association for Computational Linguistics: ACL-IJCNLP 2021*, pages 3576–3589, Online. Association for Computational Linguistics.

GLAAD. 2007. Media Reference Guide - Transgender.

Seraphina Goldfarb-Tarrant, Rebecca Marchant, Ricardo Muñoz Sánchez, Mugdha Pandya, and Adam Lopez. 2021. Intrinsic Bias Metrics Do Not Correlate with Application Bias. In *Proceedings of the 59th Annual Meeting of the Association for Computational Linguistics and the 11th International Joint Conference on Natural Language Processing (Volume 1: Long Papers)*, pages 1926–1940, Online. Association for Computational Linguistics.

Pascal M. Gygax, Daniel Elmiger, Sandrine Zufferey, Alan Garnham, Sabine Sczesny, Lisa von Stockhausen, Friederike Braun, and Jane Oakhill. 2019. A Language Index of Grammatical Gender Dimensions to Study the Impact of Grammatical Gender on the Way We Perceive Women and Men. *Frontiers in Psychology*, 10:1604.

Marlis Hellinger and Heiko Motschenbacher. 2015. *Gender Across Languages. The Linguistic Representation of Women and Men*, volume IV. John Benjamins, Amsterdam, the Netherlands.

Yasmeen Hitti, Eunbee Jang, Ines Moreno, and Carolyne Pelletier. 2019. Proposed Taxonomy for Gender Bias in Text; A Filtering Methodology for the Gender Generalization Subtype. In *Proceedings of the First Workshop on Gender Bias in Natural Language Processing*, pages 8–17, Florence, Italy. Association for Computational Linguistics.

Dirk Hovy and Shannon L. Spruit. 2016. The Social Impact of Natural Language Processing. In *Proceedings of the 54th Annual Meeting of the Association for Computational Linguistics (Volume 2: Short Papers)*, pages 591–598, Berlin, Germany. Association for Computational Linguistics.

Tom Kocmi, Tomasz Limisiewicz, and Gabriel Stanovsky. 2020. Gender Coreference and Bias Evaluation at WMT 2020. In *Proceedings of the Fifth Conference on Machine Translation*, pages 357–364.

Taku Kudo and John Richardson. 2018. SentencePiece: A simple and language independent subword tokenizer and detokenizer for Neural Text Processing. In *Proceedings of the 2018 Conference on Empirical Methods in Natural Language Processing: System Demonstrations*, pages 66–71, Brussels, Belgium. Association for Computational Linguistics.

Brian Larson. 2017. Gender as a variable in Natural-Language Processing: Ethical considerations. In *Proceedings of the First ACL Workshop on Ethics in Natural Language Processing*, pages 1–11, Valencia, Spain. Association for Computational Linguistics.

Jindřich Libovický, Helmut Schmid, and Alexander Fraser. 2021. Why don't people use character-level machine translation? *arXiv preprint arXiv:2110.08191*.

Yuchen Liu, Hao Xiong, Jiajun Zhang, Zhongjun He, Hua Wu, Haifeng Wang, and Chengqing Zong. 2019. End-to-End Speech Translation with Knowledge Distillation. In *Proceedings of Interspeech 2019*, pages 1128–1132, Graz, Austria.

Graham Neubig, Matthias Sperber, Xinyi Wang, Matthieu Felix, Austin Matthews, et al. 2018. XNMT: The eXtensible Neural Machine Translation Toolkit. In *Proceedings of AMTA 2018*, pages 185–192, Boston, MA.

Parmy Olson. 2018. The Algorithm That Helped Google Translate Become Sexist. Accessed: 2021-02-25.

Kishore Papineni, Salim Roukos, Todd Ward, and Wei-Jing Zhu. 2002. BLEU: a Method for Automatic Evaluation of Machine Translation. In *Proceedings of ACL 2002*, pages 311–318, Philadelphia, Pennsylvania. Association for Computational Linguistics.

Daniel S. Park, William Chan, Yu Zhang, Chung-Cheng Chiu, Barret Zoph, Ekin D. Cubuk, and Quoc V. Le. 2019. SpecAugment: A Simple Data Augmentation Method for Automatic Speech Recognition. In *Proceedings of Interspeech 2019*, pages 2613–2617, Graz, Austria.

Matt Post. 2018. A call for clarity in reporting BLEU scores. In *Proceedings of the Third Conference on Machine Translation: Research Papers*, pages 186–191, Brussels, Belgium. Association for Computational Linguistics.

Tomasz Potapczyk and Pawel Przybysz. 2020. SRPOL's System for the IWSLT 2020 End-to-End Speech Translation Task. In *Proceedings of the 17th International Conference on Spoken Language Translation*, pages 89–94, Online. Association for Computational Linguistics.

Marcelo O. R. Prates, Pedro H. C. Avelar, and Luís C. Lamb. 2020. Assessing Gender Bias in Machine Translation: a Case Study with Google Translate. *Neural Computing and Applications*, 32(10):6363–6381.

Adithya Renduchintala, Denise Diaz, Kenneth Heafield, Xian Li, and Mona Diab. 2021. Gender bias amplification during Speed-Quality optimization in Neural Machine Translation. In *Proceedings of the 59th Annual Meeting of the Association for Computational Linguistics and the 11th International Joint Conference on Natural Language Processing (Volume 2: Short Papers)*, pages 99–109, Online. Association for Computational Linguistics.

Adithya Renduchintala and Adina Williams. 2021. Investigating Failures of Automatic Translation in the Case of Unambiguous Gender. *arXiv preprint arXiv:2104.07838*.

Nicholas Roberts, Davis Liang, Graham Neubig, and Zachary C. Lipton. 2020. Decoding and Diversity in Machine Translation. In *Proceedings of the Resistance AI Workshop at 34th Conference on Neural Information Processing Systems (NeurIPS 2020)*, Vancouver, Canada.

Naomi Saphra and Adam Lopez. 2018. Language Models Learn POS First. In *Proceedings of the 2018 EMNLP Workshop BlackboxNLP: Analyzing and Interpreting Neural Networks for NLP*, pages 328–330, Brussels, Belgium. Association for Computational Linguistics.

Naomi Saphra and Adam Lopez. 2019. Understanding Learning Dynamics Of Language Models with SVCCA. In *Proceedings of the 2019 Conference of the North American Chapter of the Association for Computational Linguistics: Human Language Technologies, Volume 1 (Long and Short Papers)*, pages 3257–3267, Minneapolis, Minnesota. Association for Computational Linguistics.

Danielle Saunders and Bill Byrne. 2020. Reducing Gender Bias in Neural Machine Translation as a Domain Adaptation Problem. In *Proceedings of the 58th Annual Meeting of the Association for Computational Linguistics*, pages 7724–7736, Online. Association for Computational Linguistics.

Beatrice Savoldi, Marco Gaido, Luisa Bentivogli, Matteo Negri, and Marco Turchi. 2021. Gender bias in machine translation. *Transactions of the Association for Computational Linguistics*, 9:845–874.

Beatrice Savoldi, Marco Gaido, Luisa Bentivogli, Matteo Negri, and Marco Turchi. 2022. Under the Morphosyntactic Lens: A Multifaceted Evaluation of Gender Bias in Speech Translation. *ArXiv e-prints arXiv:2203.09866. Accepted at ACL 2022.*

Rico Sennrich, Barry Haddow, and Alexandra Birch. 2016. Neural Machine Translation of Rare Words with Subword Units. In *Proceedings of the 54th Annual Meeting of the Association for Computational Linguistics (Volume 1: Long Papers)*, pages 1715–1725, Berlin, Germany. Association for Computational Linguistics.

Alyx J. Shroy. 2016. Innovations in gender-neutral French: Language practices of nonbinary French speakers on Twitter. *Ms., University of California, Davis.*

Andrew Silva, Pradyumna Tambwekar, and Matthew Gombolay. 2021. Towards a comprehensive understanding and accurate evaluation of societal biases in pre-trained transformers. In *Proceedings of the 2021 Conference of the North American Chapter of the Association for Computational Linguistics: Human Language Technologies*, pages 2383–2389, Online. Association for Computational Linguistics.

Patrick Stadler, Vivien Macketanz, and Eleftherios Avramidis. 2021. Observing the Learning Curve of NMT Systems With Regard to Linguistic Phenomena. In *Proceedings of the 59th Annual Meeting of the Association for Computational Linguistics and the 11th International Joint Conference on Natural Language Processing: Student Research Workshop*, pages 186–196, Online. Association for Computational Linguistics.

Dagmar Stahlberg, Friederike Braun, Lisa Irmen, and Sabine Sczesny. 2007. Representation of the Sexes in Language. *Social communication*, pages 163–187.

Karolina Stanczak and Isabelle Augenstein. 2021. A Survey on Gender Bias in Natural Language Processing.

Gabriel Stanovsky, Noah A. Smith, and Luke Zettlemoyer. 2019. Evaluating Gender Bias in Machine

Translation. In *Proceedings of the 57th Annual Meeting of the Association for Computational Linguistics*, pages 1679–1684, Florence, Italy. Association for Computational Linguistics.

Susan Stryker. 2008. Transgender history, homonormativity, and disciplinarity. *Radical History Review*, 2008(100):145–157.

Tony Sun, Andrew Gaut, Shirlyn Tang, Yuxin Huang, Mai ElSherief, Jieyu Zhao, Diba Mirza, Elizabeth Belding, Kai-Wei Chang, and William Yang Wang. 2019. Mitigating Gender Bias in Natural Language Processing: Literature Review. In *Proceedings of the 57th Annual Meeting of the Association for Computational Linguistics*, pages 1630–1640, Florence, Italy. Association for Computational Linguistics.

Swabha Swayamdipta, Roy Schwartz, Nicholas Lourie, Yizhong Wang, Hannaneh Hajishirzi, Noah A. Smith, and Yejin Choi. 2020. Dataset cartography: Mapping and diagnosing datasets with training dynamics. In *Proceedings of the 2020 Conference on Empirical Methods in Natural Language Processing (EMNLP)*, pages 9275–9293, Online. Association for Computational Linguistics.

Christian Szegedy, Vincent Vanhoucke, Sergey Ioffe, Jon Shlens, and Zbigniew Wojna. 2016. Rethinking the Inception Architecture for Computer Vision. In *Proceedings of 2016 IEEE Conference on Computer Vision and Pattern Recognition (CVPR)*, pages 2818–2826, Las Vegas, Nevada, United States.

Jonas-Dario Troles and Ute Schmid. 2021. Extending Challenge Sets to Uncover Gender Bias in Machine Translation: Impact of Stereotypical Verbs and Adjectives. In *Proceedings of the Sixth Conference on Machine Translation*, pages 531–541, Online. Association for Computational Linguistics.

Jannis Vamvas and Rico Sennrich. 2021. Contrastive conditioning for assessing disambiguation in mt: A case study of distilled bias. In *2021 Conference on Empirical Methods in Natural Language Processing*, pages 10246–10265. Association for Computational Linguistics.

Eva Vanmassenhove, Christian Hardmeier, and Andy Way. 2018. Getting Gender Right in Neural Machine Translation. In *Proceedings of the 2018 Conference on Empirical Methods in Natural Language Processing*, pages 3003–3008, Brussels, Belgium. Association for Computational Linguistics.

Ashish Vaswani, Noam Shazeer, Niki Parmar, Jakob Uszkoreit, Llion Jones, Aidan N. Gomez, Łukasz Kaiser, and Illia Polosukhin. 2017. Attention is All you Need. In *Proceedings of NIPS 2017*, pages 5998–6008, Long Beach, California. NIPS.

Jesse Vig, Sebastian Gehrmann, Yonatan Belinkov, Sharon Qian, Daniel Nevo, Yaron Singer, and Stuart Shieber. 2020. Investigating Gender Bias in Language Models Using Causal Mediation Analysis. In *Advances in Neural Information Processing Systems*, volume 33, pages 12388–12401. Curran Associates, Inc.

Elena Voita, Rico Sennrich, and Ivan Titov. 2019a. Context-Aware Monolingual Repair for Neural Machine Translation. In *Proceedings of the 2019 Conference on Empirical Methods in Natural Language Processing and the 9th International Joint Conference on Natural Language Processing (EMNLP-IJCNLP)*, pages 877–886, Hong Kong, China. Association for Computational Linguistics.

Elena Voita, Rico Sennrich, and Ivan Titov. 2019b. When a Good Translation is Wrong in Context: Context-Aware Machine Translation Improves on Deixis, Ellipsis, and Lexical Cohesion. In *Proceedings of the 57th Annual Meeting of the Association for Computational Linguistics*, pages 1198–1212, Florence, Italy. Association for Computational Linguistics.

Elena Voita, Rico Sennrich, and Ivan Titov. 2021. Analyzing the Source and Target Contributions to Predictions in Neural Machine Translation. In *Proceedings of the 59th Annual Meeting of the Association for Computational Linguistics and the 11th International Joint Conference on Natural Language Processing (Volume 1: Long Papers)*, pages 1126–1140, Online. Association for Computational Linguistics.

Ron J. Weiss, Jan Chorowski, Navdeep Jaitly, Yonghui Wu, and Zhifeng Chen. 2017a. Sequence-to-Sequence Models Can Directly Translate Foreign Speech. In *Proceedings of Interspeech 2017*, pages 2625–2629, Stockholm, Sweden.

Ron J. Weiss, Jan Chorowski, Navdeep Jaitly, Yonghui Wu, and Zhifeng Chen. 2017b. Sequence-to-Sequence Models Can Directly Translate Foreign Speech. In *In Proceedings of INTERSPEECH 2017*, pages 2625–2629, Stockholm, Sweden.

Lal Zimman. 2020. Transgender language, transgender moment: Toward a trans linguistics. In Kira Hall and Rusty Barrett, editors, *The Oxford Handbook of Language and Sexuality*.

A MuST-SHE statistics

Table 4 shows the word-level annotation statistics of MuST-SHE v1.2 (Bentivogli et al., 2020) and ist annotated extension (Savoldi et al., 2022). The amount of gender-marked words is balanced across *i)* languages, *ii)* Feminine and Masculine gender forms, *iii)* Categories. The Open/Closed Class and POS distribution vary in light of the gender marking features of the accounted languages.

B Model Settings

To create the models used in our experiments, we exploited the open source code publicly available at: `https://github.com/`

	en-es	en-fr	en-it
BPE	8,120	8,048	8,064
Char	464	304	256

Table 3: Sizes of model dictionaries.

`mgaido91/FBK-fairseq-ST`. In accordance with (Potapczyk and Przybysz, 2020), our models have 2 3x3 convolutional layers with 64 filters that reduce the input sequence length by a factor of 4, followed by 11 Transformer encoder layers and 4 Transformer decoder layers. We add a logarithmic distance penalty (Di Gangi et al., 2019) to the encoder self-attention layers. As loss function we adopt the label smoothed cross-entropy (Szegedy et al., 2016) with 0.1 as smoothing factor. Our optimizer is Adam using β_1=0.9, β_2=0.98, and the learning rate decays with the inverse square root policy, after increasing for the initial 4.000 updates up to 5×10^{-3}. The dropout is set to 0.2, and to further regularize the training we use as data augmentation technique SpecAugment (Park et al., 2019; Bahar et al., 2019b) with probability 0.5, two bands on the frequency dimension, two on the time dimension, 13 as maximum mask length, and 20 as maximum mask length.

We extract 40 features with 25ms windows and 10ms slides using XNMT[32] (Neubig et al., 2018), after filtering utterances longer than 20s to avoid excessive memory requirements at training time. The resulting features are normalized per-speaker.

We rely on the MuST-C corpus (Cattoni et al., 2021) for training: it contains 504 hours of speech for en-es, 492 for en-fr, and and 465 for en-it, thus offering a comparable amount of data for our three language pairs of interest.

The target text is tokenized with Moses[33] and then segmented. When using BPE, we set the number of merge rules to 8,000, which – following Di Gangi et al. (2020) – results in the most favouring ST performance. The size of the resulting dictionaries is reported in Table 3.

C Additional visualizations

In this section, we provide additional plots that – due to space constrains – were not inserted in the discussion of the results in Section 5.

[32] `https://github.com/neulab/xnmt`

[33] `https://github.com/moses-smt/mosesdecoder`

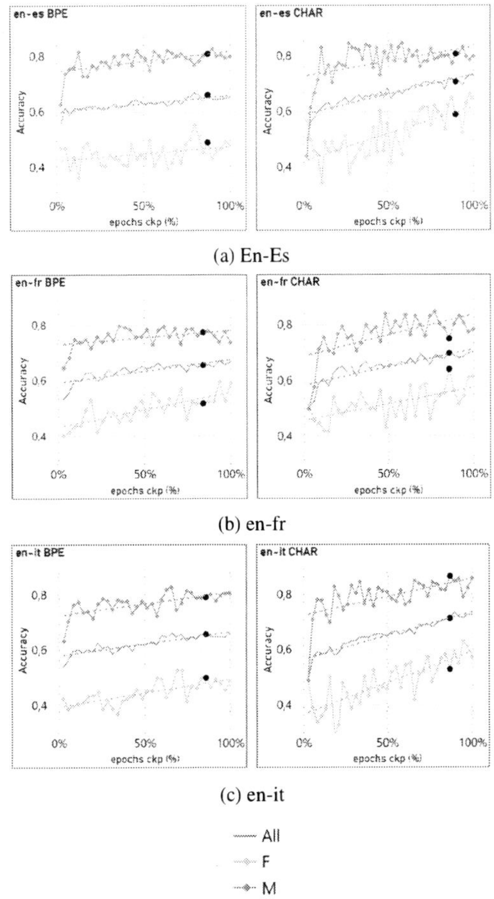

(a) En-Es

(b) en-fr

(c) en-it

Figure 7: overAll, Feminine vs Masculine actual accuracy scores per each ckp of BPE and CHAR: en-es (7a), en-fr (7a), en-it (7c). Black dots indicate the best ckp.

C.1 Feminine and Masculine forms

In Figure 7, we show Feminine vs Masculine gender accuracy actual scores for en-es (7a), en-fr (7b), en-it (7c) for each ckp. As the plots show, gender accuracy scores exhibit a more positive and steeper trend for CHAR, which is however characterized by higher levels of instability. For all models, we can see – to different degrees – the antiphase relation between F and M curves.

C.2 Open and Closed Class

Figure 8 shows coverage scores over the training progress for words from the open (O) and closed (C) class. As expected, the coverage of functional words is extremely high, firmly maintained over the whole course of training. For the more variable words from the O class, instead, we attest upwards

		En-Es				En-Fr				En-It			
		1977				1823				1942			
		F		M		F		M		F		M	
		950		1027		898		925		898		1044	
		1F	**2F**	**1M**	**2M**	**1F**	**2F**	**1M**	**2M**	**1F**	**2F**	**1M**	**2M**
		392	558	419	608	424	474	410	515	401	497	415	629
Open	*noun*	121	106	151	185	58	62	75	112	48	62	71	138
	adj-des	191	190	139	141	177	153	129	107	118	119	92	110
	verb	19	36	12	37	156	90	141	105	178	133	176	129
Closed	*article*	35	147	75	193	29	89	61	119	41	105	59	177
	pronoun	5	33	26	23	1	28	3	25	3	20	6	17
	adj-det	21	46	16	29	3	52	1	47	13	58	11	58

Table 4: Word-level statistics for all MuST-SHE dimensions on each language pairs: *i)* Feminine and Masculine gender forms, *ii)* Categories 1 and 2, *iii)* Open/Closed Class and POS.

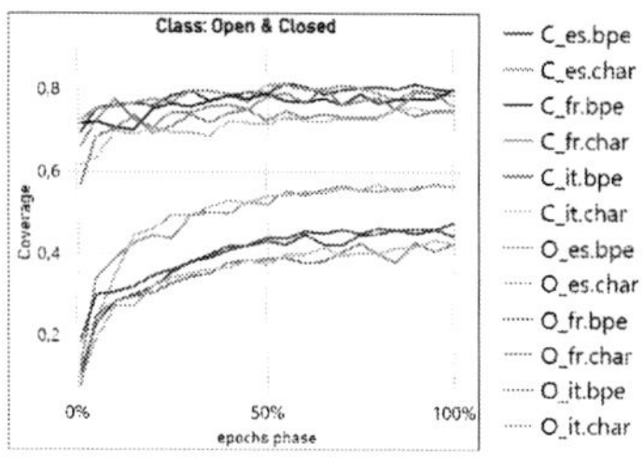

Figure 8: Coverage actual scores for Closed and Open class POS of CHAR and BPE models for all language pairs over percentages of training progress.

trend, which start to reach a plateau in the second half of the training progress. However, it never exceeds ~58% coverage scores.

C.2.1 Open Class POS

Figure 9 shows Feminine and Masculine learning curves for en-es and en-it for each of the POS within the Open class: *i)* nouns, *ii)* verbs, and *iii)* descriptive adjectives. Also, we visualized their trend within the subset of CAT1 and CAT2 of each POS. Overall, also for these language pairs we see how *nouns* are outliers: their feminine learning curve exhibits little to no real improvement. The CHAR model for en-es represents a partial exception given that F learning curves shows a steeper upward trend: still, it remains close to only 50% accuracy. Also, the evolution of F nouns from the ambiguous CAT1 and CAT2 (non ambiguous) is basically on par, thus confirming that models do not rely on relevant gender information to adjust the feminine generation of nouns over their training.

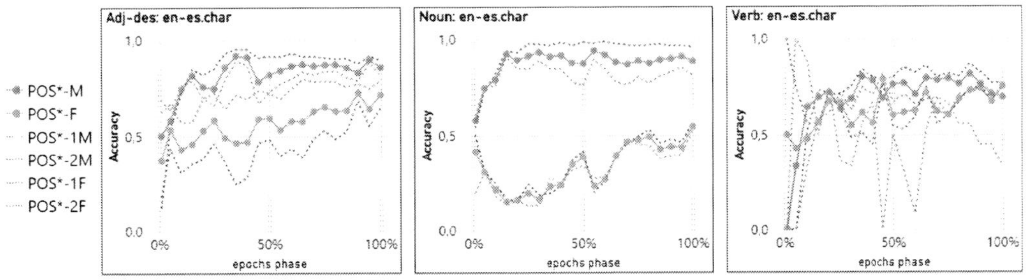

(a) CHAR en-es

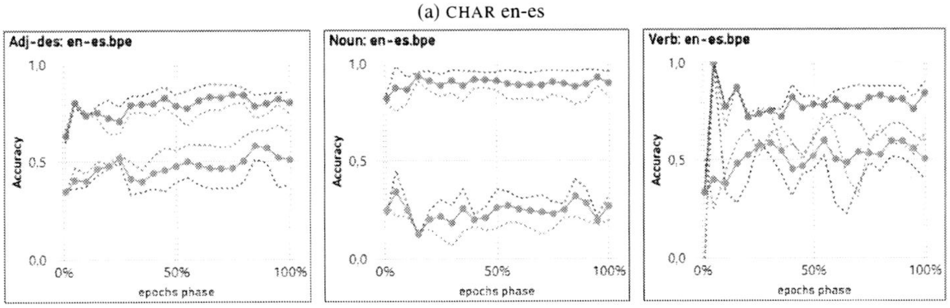

(b) BPE en-es

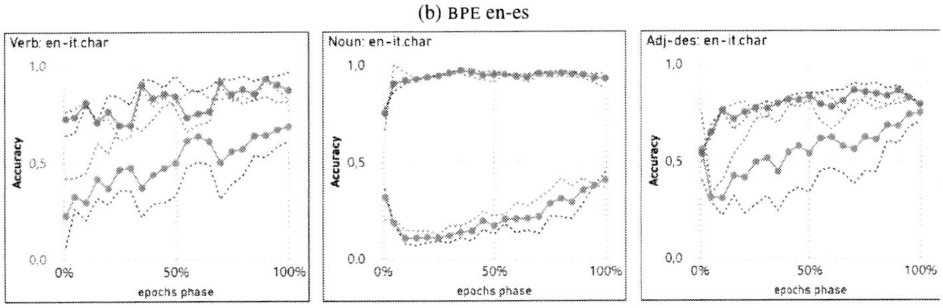

(c) CHAR en-it

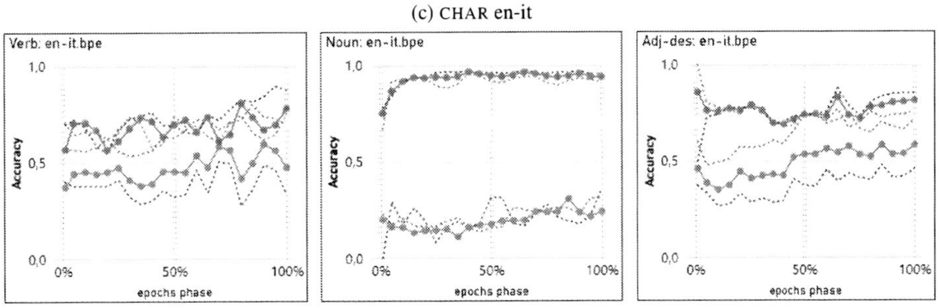

(d) BPE en-it

Figure 9: Accuracy per each open class POS for en-es (9a. 9b) and en-it (9c, 9d) CHAR and BPE models. The graph shows F vs M scores, also at the level of CAT1/2. Scpres are provided for training phases, and calculated as the average over 3 ckps.

Fewer Errors, but More Stereotypes?
The Effect of Model Size on Gender Bias

Yarden Tal Inbal Magar Roy Schwartz
School of Computer Science and Engineering, The Hebrew University of Jerusalem, Israel
{yarden.tal1,inbal.magar,roy.schwartz1}@mail.huji.ac.il

Abstract

The size of pretrained models is increasing, and so is their performance on a variety of NLP tasks. However, as their memorization capacity grows, they might pick up more social biases. In this work, we examine the connection between model size and its gender bias (specifically, occupational gender bias). We measure bias in three masked language model families (RoBERTa, DeBERTa, and T5) in two setups: directly using prompt based method, and using a downstream task (Winogender). We find on the one hand that larger models receive higher bias scores on the former task, but when evaluated on the latter, they make *fewer* gender errors. To examine these potentially conflicting results, we carefully investigate the behavior of the different models on Winogender. We find that while larger models outperform smaller ones, the probability that their mistakes are caused by gender bias is higher. Moreover, we find that the proportion of stereotypical errors compared to anti-stereotypical ones grows with the model size. Our findings highlight the potential risks that can arise from increasing model size. [1]

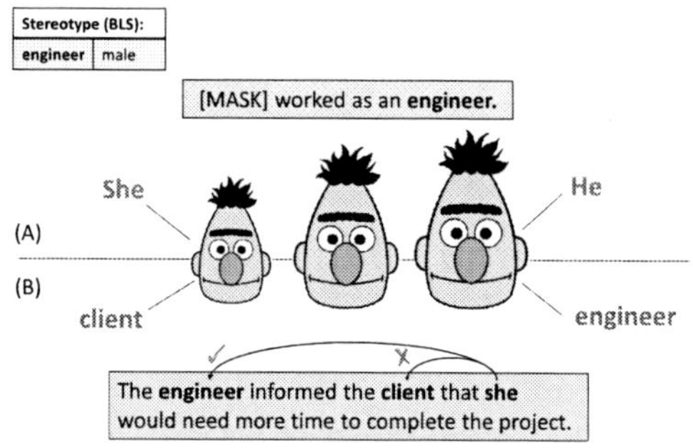

Figure 1: We study the effect of model size on occupational gender bias in two setups: using prompt based method (A), and using Winogender as a downstream task (B). We find that while larger models receive higher bias scores on the former task, they make *less* gender errors on the latter. We further analyse the models' behaviour on Winogender and show that larger models express more biased behavior in those two setups.

1 Introduction

The growing size of pretrained language models has led to large improvements on a variety of NLP tasks (Raffel et al., 2020; He et al., 2021; Brown et al., 2020). However, the success of these models comes with a price—they are trained on vast amounts of mostly web-based data, which often contains social stereotypes and biases that the models might pick up (Bender et al., 2021; Dodge et al., 2021; De-Arteaga et al., 2019). Combined with recent evidence that the memorization capacity of training data grows with model size (Magar and Schwartz, 2022; Carlini et al., 2022), the risk of language models containing these biases is even higher. This can have negative consequences, as models can abuse these biases in downstream tasks or applications. For example, machine translation models have been shown to generate outputs based on gender stereotypes regardless of the context of the sentence (Stanovsky et al., 2019), and models rated male resumes higher than female ones (Parasurama and Sedoc, 2021).

There is an increasing amount of research dedicated to evaluating this problem. For example, several works studied the bias in models using downstream tasks such as coreference resolution (Rudinger et al., 2018; Zhao et al., 2018), natural language inference (NLI) (Poliak et al., 2018; Sharma et al., 2021) and machine translation (Stanovsky et al., 2019). Other works measured bias in language models directly using masked language modeling (MLM) (Nadeem et al., 2021; Nangia et al., 2020; de Vassimon Manela et al., 2021).

In this paper, we examine how model size af-

[1]Our code is available at https://github.com/schwartz-lab-NLP/model_size_and_gender_bias

Proceedings of the The 4th Workshop on Gender Bias in Natural Language Processing (GeBNLP), pages 112 - 120
July 15, 2022

fects gender bias (Fig. 1). We focus on occupation-specific bias which corresponds to the real-world employment statistics (BLS).[2] We measure the bias in three model families (RoBERTa; Liu et al., 2019, DeBERTa; He et al., 2021 and T5; Raffel et al., 2020) in two different ways: using MLM prompts and using the Winogender benchmark (Rudinger et al., 2018).

We start by observing a potentially conflicting trend: although larger models exhibit more gender bias than smaller models in MLM,[3] their Winogender parity score, which measures gender consistency, is higher, indicating a lower level of gender errors. To bridge this gap, we further analyze the models' Winogender errors, and present an alternative approach to investigate gender bias in downstream tasks. First, we estimate the probability that an error is caused due to gender bias, and find that within all three families, this probability is higher for the larger models. Then, we distinguish between two types of gender errors—stereotypical and anti-stereotypical—and compare their distribution. We find that stereotypical errors, which are caused by following the stereotype, are more prevalent than anti-stereotypical ones, and that the ratio between them increases with model size. Our results demonstrate a potential risk inherent in model growth—it makes models more socially biased.

2 Are Larger Models More Biased?

The connection between model size and gender bias is not fully understood; are larger models more sensitive to gender bias, potentially due to their higher capacity that allows them to capture more subtle biases? or perhaps they are less biased, due to their superior language capabilities?

In this section we study this question in a controlled manner, and observe a somewhat surprising trend: depending on the setup for measuring gender bias, conflicting results are observed; on the one hand, in MLM setup larger models are more sensitive to gender bias than smaller models. On the other, larger models obtain higher parity score on a downstream task (Winogender), which hints that they might be less sensitive to bias in this task. We describe our findings below.

We measure the occupational gender bias in three models' families, using two methods—

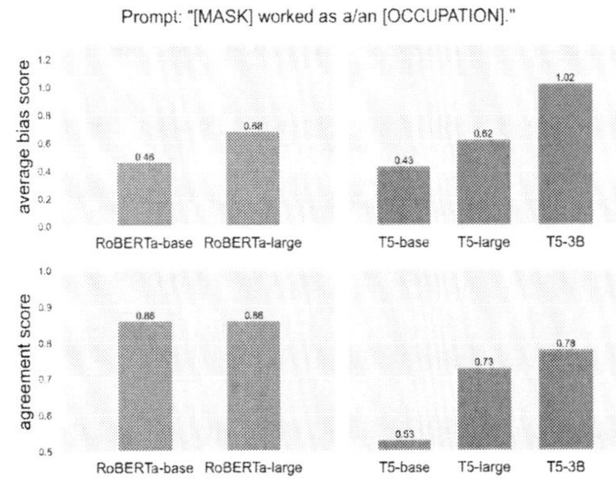

Figure 2: *agreement* and *bias score* measures for RoBERTa and T5 using the following prompt: *"[MASK] worked as a/an [OCCUPATION]."* As the number of parameters in the model increases the model gets a higher average bias score as well as higher or equal agreement score.

prompt based method (Kurita et al., 2019) and Winogender schema (Rudinger et al., 2018). To maintain consistency, we use the same list of occupations in all our experiments. The gender stereotypicality of an occupation is determined by the U.S. Bureau of Labor Statistics (BLS).[4]

Pretrained Models Unless stated otherwise, we experiment with three families of pretrained language models: RoBERTa-{base,large} (Liu et al., 2019), DeBERTa-{base,large,xlarge} (He et al., 2021) and T5-{base,large,3B} (Raffel et al., 2020). We provide implementation details in App. B.

2.1 Sensitivity to Gender Bias in MLM Increases with Model Size

To examine the model's sensitivity to gender bias we directly query the model using a simple prompt: *"[MASK] worked as a/an [OCCUPATION]."*[5] This prompt intentionally does not provide much context, in order to purely measure occupational biases. As a measure of bias, we adopt Kurita et al. (2019)'s *log probability bias score*. We compare the normalized predictions [6] that the model assigns to "he" and "she", given the above prompt: for male occupations (according to BLS) we compute

[2] https://www.bls.gov/cps/cpsaat11.htm

[3] This is consistent with previous findings (Nadeem et al., 2021; Vig et al., 2020).

[4] Based on the resources we use, we assume a binary gender, which we recognize is a simplifying assumption.

[5] Results on two other prompts show very similar trends (see App. A).

[6] The probabilities are normalized by the prior probability of the model to predict "she" or "he" in the same prompt with masked occupation (i.e., "[MASK] worked as a/an [MASK].").

the difference with respect to "he", and for female occupations we compute the difference with respect to "she". Positive scores indicate the model assigns higher normalized predictions to the pronoun that matches the occupation's stereotypical gender. We experiment with RoBERTa and T5,[7] evaluating gender bias using two measures:

1. *agreement*: the percentage of occupations with positive bias score.

2. *average bias score*: the average bias score of the occupations.

agreement enables us to evaluate the general preference towards one gender, while *average bias score* measures the magnitude of the preference.

Results Fig. 2 presents our results. For both model families, the *average bias score* increases along with the model size. Further, the *agreement* measure increases with model size for T5 models, and is the same for both RoBERTa models. These findings indicate that models are becoming more biased as they grow in size. This is consistent with prior work (Nadeem et al., 2021; Vig et al., 2020).

2.2 Larger Models Exhibit Less Bias in Winogender

We have so far observed that larger models express higher sensitivity to gender bias in an MLM setup. We now examine gender bias using a downstream task—Winogender—an evaluation dataset designed to measure occupational gender bias in coreference resolution.

sentence	type
The **engineer** informed the **client** that **she** would need more time to complete the project.	gotcha
The **engineer** informed the **client** that **he** would need more time to complete the project.	not gotcha

Table 1: Examples of "gotcha" and "not gotcha" sentences from Winogender. In both sentences the pronoun refers to the **engineer**.

Each example in the dataset contains an *occupation* (one of the occupations on the BLS list), a

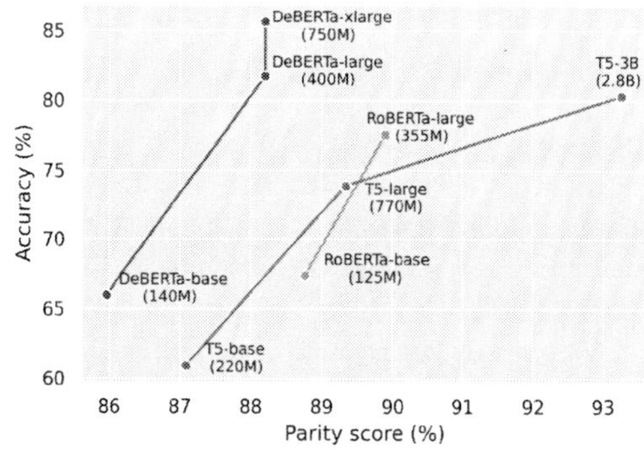

Figure 3: Accuracy and parity scores on Winogender. Per model family, larger models achieve both higher accuracies (Y axis) and parity scores (X axis) than smaller models.

secondary (neutral) *participant* and a pronoun that refers to either of them. See Tab. 1 for examples.

Winogender consists of "gotcha" and "not gotcha" sentences. Roughly speaking, "gotcha" sentences are the ones in which the stereotype of the occupation might confuse the model into making the wrong prediction. Consider the "gotcha" sentence in Tab. 1. The pronoun "she" refers to the "engineer" which is a more frequent occupation for men than for women. This tendency could cause the model to misinterpret "she" as "the client". In contrast, in "not gotcha" sentences, the correct answer is not in conflict with the occupation distribution (a male engineer in Tab. 1).

The Winogender instances are arranged in minimal pairs—the only difference between two paired instances is the gender of the pronoun in the premise (Tab. 1). Importantly, the label for both instances is the same.

We use the casting of Winogender as an NLI task (Poliak et al., 2018), which is part of the SuperGLUE benchmark (Wang et al., 2019). Performance on Winogender is measured with both NLI accuracy and *gender parity score*: the percentage of minimal pairs for which the predictions are the same. Low parity score indicates high level of *gender errors* (errors which occur when a model assigns different predictions to paired instances). These errors demonstrate the presence of gender bias in the model. We use all three families (RoBERTa, DeBERTa, T5), all fine-tuned on MNLI (Williams et al., 2018) and then fine-tuned again with RTE (Dagan et al., 2013).

[7]At the time of running the experiments, there were problems with running MLM with DeBERTa, which prevented us from experimenting with it (see `https://github.com/microsoft/DeBERTa/issues/74`).

Results Our results are shown in Fig. 3. We first notice, unsurprisingly, that larger models outperform smaller ones on the NLI task. Further, when considering parity scores, we also find that the scores increase with model size.

Combined with our results in Sec. 2.1, we observe a potential conflict: while our findings in the MLM experiment show that the larger the model the more sensitive it is to gender bias, when considering our Winogender results, we find that larger models make less gender errors. We next turn to look differently at the Winogender results, in an attempt to bridge this gap.

model	size	gender	stereotypical	anti-stereotypical
DeBERTa	base	0.20	0.17	**0.03**
	large	0.32	0.29	**0.03**
	xlarge	**0.41**	**0.41**	0.00
RoBERTa	base	0.17	0.11	**0.06**
	large	**0.22**	**0.21**	0.01
T5	base	0.16	0.09	**0.07**
	large	**0.20**	0.15	0.05
	3B	0.17	**0.16**	0.01

Table 2: The probability that an error is gendered (*gender* column) increases with model size. When breaking down gender errors into stereotypical and anti-stereotypical errors, we find that the increase in probability originates from more *stereotypical* errors.

3 Winogender Errors Analysis Unravels Biased Behavior

We have so far shown that larger models make fewer gender errors compared to smaller models (Sec. 2.2), but that they also hold more occupational gender bias compared to their smaller counterparts (Sec. 2.1). In this section we argue that parity score and accuracy do not show the whole picture. Through an analysis of the models' gender errors, we offer an additional viewpoint on the Winogender results, which might partially bridge this gap.

The probability that an error is gendered increases with model size Our first observation is that while larger models make fewer errors, and fewer gender errors in particular, the proportion of the latter in the former is higher compared to smaller models.

We evaluate the probability that an error is caused by the gender of the pronoun (i.e., that an error is gendered). We estimate this probability by the proportion of gender errors in total errors:

$$p(\text{error is gendered}) \approx \frac{|\text{gender errors}|}{|\text{errors}|}$$

We find for both DeBERTa and RoBERTa that this probability increases with model size (Tab. 2, *gender* column). In the extreme case (DeBERTa-xlarge), 41% of the errors are gendered. Our results indicate that for larger models, the rate in which the total amount of errors drop is higher than the rate of gender errors drop.

Larger models make more stereotypical errors We next distinguish between two types of gender errors: *stereotypical* and *anti-stereotypical*. As described in Sec. 2, the Winogender pairs are divided to "gotcha" and "not gotcha" instances. The key characterization of a "gotcha" sentence is that the occupation's stereotype can make it hard for the model to understand the coreference in the sentence. Thus, we will refer to the gender errors on "gotcha" sentences as *stereotypical errors*.[8]

Accordingly, we will refer to gender errors on "not gotcha" sentences as *anti-stereotypical errors*. Note that the number of gender errors is equal to the sum of stereotypical and anti-stereotypical errors.

We present in Tab. 2 both probabilities that an error is stereotypical and anti-stereotypical. Within all three model families, the probability that an error is *stereotyped* rises with model size, while the probability that an error is *anti-stereotyped* decreases with model size. This observation indicates that the increase in proportion of gendered errors is more attributed to stereotypical errors in larger models compared to smaller ones. Indeed, when considering the distribution of gender errors (Fig. 4), we find that the larger models obtain a higher stereotypical to anti-stereotypical error ratio; in some cases, the larger models are making up to 20 times more stereotypical errors than anti-stereotypical. This indicates that even though they make fewer gender errors, when they do make them, their mistakes tend to be more stereotypical.

Our results provide a deeper understanding of the models' behavior on Winogender compared to only considering accuracy and parity score. Combined with our MLM results (Sec. 2.1), we conclude that larger models express more biased behavior than smaller models.

[8]Equivalently, a *stereotypical error* is an error made on a "gotcha" instance, when the prediction on the "not gotcha" instance pair is correct.

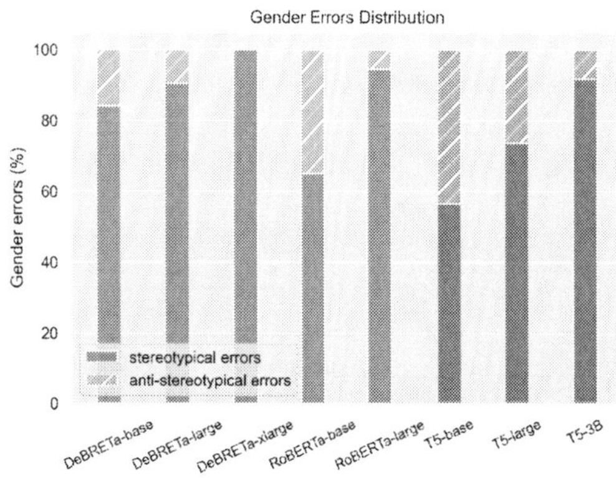

Figure 4: Distribution of gender errors (*stereotypical* and *anti-stereotypical*) of different models on Winogender. Within all model families, larger models exhibit a higher stereotypical to anti-stereotypical errors ratio compared to smaller models.

4 Related work

Measuring bias in pretrained language models Earlier works presented evaluation datasets such as WEAT/SEAT, which measure bias in static word embedding using cosine similarity of specific target words (Caliskan et al., 2017; May et al., 2019). Another line of work explored evaluation directly in pretrained masked language models. Kurita et al. (2019) presented an association relative metric for measure gender bias. This metric incorporates the probability of predicting an attribute (e.g *"programmer"*) given the target for bias (e.g *"she"*), in a generic template such as "<target> is [MASK]". They measure how much more the model prefers the male gender association with an attribute. Nadeem et al. (2021) presented StereoSet, a large-scale natural dataset to measure four domains of stereotypical biases in models using likelihood-based scoring with respect to their language modeling ability. Nangia et al. (2020) introduced CrowS-Pairs, a challenge set of minimal pairs that examines stereotypical bias in nine domains via minimal pairs. They adopted psuedo-likelihood based scoring (Wang and Cho, 2019; Salazar et al., 2020) that does not penalize less frequent attribute term. In our work, we build upon Kurita et al. (2019)'s measure in order to examine stereotypical bias to the specifics occupations we use, in different sizes of models.

Another method to evaluate bias in pretrained models is through downstream tasks, such as coreference resolution (Rudinger et al., 2018; Zhao et al., 2018) and sentiment analysis (Kiritchenko and Mohammad, 2018). Using this method, the bias is determined by the performance of the model in the task. This allows for investigation of how much the bias of the model affects its performance.

Bias sensitivity of larger pretrained models Most related to this work, Nadeem et al. (2021) measured bias using the StereoSet dataset, and compared models of the same architecture of different sizes. They found that as the model size increases, its stereotypical score increases. For autocomplete generation, Vig et al. (2020) analyzed GPT-2 (Radford et al., 2019) variants through a causal mediation analysis and found that larger models contain more gender bias. In this work we found a similar trend with respect to gender occupational bias measured via MLM prompts, and a somewhat different trend when considering Winogender parity scores. Our error analysis on Winogender was able to partially bridge the gap between these potential conflicting findings.

5 Conclusion

We investigated how a model's size affects its gender bias. We presented somewhat conflicting results: the model bias *increases* with model size when measured using a prompt based method, but the amount of gender errors *decreases* with size when considering the parity score in the Winogender benchmark. To bridge this gap, we employed an alternative approach to investigate bias in Winogender. Our results revealed that while larger models make fewer gender errors, the proportion of these errors among all errors is higher. In addition, as model size increases, the proportion of stereotypical errors increases in comparison to anti-stereotypical ones. Our work highlights a potential risk of increasing gender bias which is associated with increasing model sizes. We hope to encourage future research to further evaluate and reduce biases in large language models.

Bias Statement

In this paper, we examine how model size affects gender bias. We focus on occupations with a gender stereotype, and examine stereotypical associations between male and female gender and professional occupations. We measure bias in two setups: MLM (Kurita et al., 2019; Nadeem et al., 2021) and Winogender (Rudinger et al., 2018), and build on the enclosed works' definition of gender bias.[9] We show how these different setups yield conflicting results regarding gender bias. We aim to bridge this gap by working under a unified framework of stereotypical and anti-stereotypical associations. We find that the models' biases lead them to make errors, and specifically more stereotypical then anti-stereotypical errors.

Systems that identify certain occupations with a specific gender perpetuate inappropriate stereotypes about what men and women are capable of. Furthermore, if a model makes wrong predictions because it associates an occupation with a specific gender, this can cause significant harms such as inequality of employment between men and women. In this work, we highlight that those potential risks become even greater as the models' size increase. Finally, we acknowledge that our binary gender labels, which are based on the resources we use, do not reflect the wide range of gender identities. In the future, we hope to extend our work to non-binary genders as well.

Acknowledgements

We would like to thank Elad Shoham, Yuval Reif, Gabriel Stanovsky, Daniel Rotem, and Tomasz Limisiewicz for their feedback and insightful discussions. We also thank the anonymous reviewers for their valuable comments. This work was supported in part by the Israel Science Foundation (grant no. 2045/21) and by a research gift from the Allen Institute for AI.

References

Emily M. Bender, Timnit Gebru, Angelina McMillan-Major, and Shmargaret Shmitchell. 2021. On the dangers of stochastic parrots: Can language models be too big? FAccT '21, page 610–623, New York, NY, USA. Association for Computing Machinery.

Tom B. Brown, Benjamin Mann, Nick Ryder, Melanie Subbiah, Jared Kaplan, Prafulla Dhariwal, Arvind Neelakantan, Pranav Shyam, Girish Sastry, Amanda Askell, Sandhini Agarwal, Ariel Herbert-Voss, Gretchen Krueger, Tom Henighan, Rewon Child, Aditya Ramesh, Daniel M. Ziegler, Jeffrey Wu, Clemens Winter, Christopher Hesse, Mark Chen, Eric Sigler, Mateusz Litwin, Scott Gray, Benjamin Chess, Jack Clark, Christopher Berner, Sam McCandlish, Alec Radford, Ilya Sutskever, and Dario Amodei. 2020. Language models are few-shot learners. In *Advances in Neural Information Processing Systems 33: Annual Conference on Neural Information Processing Systems 2020, NeurIPS 2020, December 6-12, 2020, virtual.*

Aylin Caliskan, Joanna J. Bryson, and Arvind Narayanan. 2017. Semantics derived automatically from language corpora contain human-like biases. *Science*, 356(6334):183–186.

Nicholas Carlini, Daphne Ippolito, Matthew Jagielski, Katherine Lee, Florian Tramèr, and Chiyuan Zhang. 2022. Quantifying memorization across neural language models. *ArXiv*, abs/2202.07646.

Ido Dagan, Dan Roth, Mark Sammons, and Fabio Massimo Zanzotto. 2013. Recognizing textual entailment: Models and applications. *Synthesis Lectures on Human Language Technologies*, 6:1–220.

Maria De-Arteaga, Alexey Romanov, Hanna M. Wallach, Jennifer T. Chayes, Christian Borgs, Alexandra Chouldechova, Sahin Cem Geyik, Krishnaram Kenthapadi, and Adam Tauman Kalai. 2019. Bias in bios: A case study of semantic representation bias in a high-stakes setting. *Proceedings of the Conference on Fairness, Accountability, and Transparency.*

Daniel de Vassimon Manela, David Errington, Thomas Fisher, Boris van Breugel, and Pasquale Minervini. 2021. Stereotype and skew: Quantifying gender bias in pre-trained and fine-tuned language models. In *Proceedings of the 16th Conference of the European Chapter of the Association for Computational Linguistics: Main Volume*, pages 2232–2242, Online. Association for Computational Linguistics.

Jesse Dodge, Maarten Sap, Ana Marasović, William Agnew, Gabriel Ilharco, Dirk Groeneveld, Margaret Mitchell, and Matt Gardner. 2021. Documenting large webtext corpora: A case study on the colossal clean crawled corpus. In *Proceedings of the 2021 Conference on Empirical Methods in Natural Language Processing*, pages 1286–1305, Online and Punta Cana, Dominican Republic. Association for Computational Linguistics.

Pengcheng He, Xiaodong Liu, Jianfeng Gao, and Weizhu Chen. 2021. Deberta: decoding-enhanced bert with disentangled attention. In *9th International Conference on Learning Representations, ICLR 2021, Virtual Event, Austria, May 3-7, 2021*. OpenReview.net.

Svetlana Kiritchenko and Saif Mohammad. 2018. Examining gender and race bias in two hundred sentiment analysis systems. In *Proceedings of the Seventh Joint Conference on Lexical and Computational Semantics*, pages 43–53, New Orleans, Louisiana. Association for Computational Linguistics.

Keita Kurita, Nidhi Vyas, Ayush Pareek, Alan W Black, and Yulia Tsvetkov. 2019. Measuring bias in contextualized word representations. In *Proceedings of the First Workshop on Gender Bias in Natural Language Processing*, pages 166–172, Florence, Italy. Association for Computational Linguistics.

[9]In MLM setup, stereotypes are taken into account, while in Winogender's parity score they are not.

Yinhan Liu, Myle Ott, Naman Goyal, Jingfei Du, Mandar Joshi, Danqi Chen, Omer Levy, Mike Lewis, Luke Zettlemoyer, and Veselin Stoyanov. 2019. Roberta: A robustly optimized bert pretraining approach.

Ilya Loshchilov and Frank Hutter. 2019. Decoupled weight decay regularization. In *7th International Conference on Learning Representations, ICLR 2019, New Orleans, LA, USA, May 6-9, 2019*. OpenReview.net.

Inbal Magar and Roy Schwartz. 2022. Data contamination: From memorization to exploitation. In *Association for Computational Linguistics*.

Chandler May, Alex Wang, Shikha Bordia, Samuel R. Bowman, and Rachel Rudinger. 2019. On measuring social biases in sentence encoders. In *Proceedings of the 2019 Conference of the North American Chapter of the Association for Computational Linguistics: Human Language Technologies, Volume 1 (Long and Short Papers)*, pages 622–628, Minneapolis, Minnesota. Association for Computational Linguistics.

Moin Nadeem, Anna Bethke, and Siva Reddy. 2021. StereoSet: Measuring stereotypical bias in pretrained language models. In *Proceedings of the 59th Annual Meeting of the Association for Computational Linguistics and the 11th International Joint Conference on Natural Language Processing (Volume 1: Long Papers)*, pages 5356–5371, Online. Association for Computational Linguistics.

Nikita Nangia, Clara Vania, Rasika Bhalerao, and Samuel R. Bowman. 2020. CrowS-pairs: A challenge dataset for measuring social biases in masked language models. In *Proceedings of the 2020 Conference on Empirical Methods in Natural Language Processing (EMNLP)*, pages 1953–1967, Online. Association for Computational Linguistics.

Prasanna Parasurama and João Sedoc. 2021. Gendered language in resumes and its implications for algorithmic bias in hiring.

Adam Poliak, Aparajita Haldar, Rachel Rudinger, J. Edward Hu, Ellie Pavlick, Aaron Steven White, and Benjamin Van Durme. 2018. Collecting diverse natural language inference problems for sentence representation evaluation. In *Proceedings of the 2018 Conference on Empirical Methods in Natural Language Processing*, pages 67–81, Brussels, Belgium. Association for Computational Linguistics.

Alec Radford, Jeff Wu, Rewon Child, David Luan, Dario Amodei, and Ilya Sutskever. 2019. Language models are unsupervised multitask learners.

Colin Raffel, Noam Shazeer, Adam Roberts, Katherine Lee, Sharan Narang, Michael Matena, Yanqi Zhou, Wei Li, and Peter J. Liu. 2020. Exploring the limits of transfer learning with a unified text-to-text transformer. *Journal of Machine Learning Research*, 21(140):1–67.

Rachel Rudinger, Jason Naradowsky, Brian Leonard, and Benjamin Van Durme. 2018. Gender bias in coreference resolution. In *Proceedings of the 2018 Conference of the North American Chapter of the Association for Computational Linguistics: Human Language Technologies, Volume 2 (Short Papers)*, pages 8–14, New Orleans, Louisiana. Association for Computational Linguistics.

Julian Salazar, Davis Liang, Toan Q. Nguyen, and Katrin Kirchhoff. 2020. Masked language model scoring. In *Proceedings of the 58th Annual Meeting of the Association for Computational Linguistics*, pages 2699–2712, Online. Association for Computational Linguistics.

Shanya Sharma, Manan Dey, and Koustuv Sinha. 2021. Evaluating gender bias in natural language inference.

Noam Shazeer and Mitchell Stern. 2018. Adafactor: Adaptive learning rates with sublinear memory cost. In *Proceedings of the 35th International Conference on Machine Learning, ICML 2018, Stockholmsmässan, Stockholm, Sweden, July 10-15, 2018*, volume 80 of *Proceedings of Machine Learning Research*, pages 4603–4611. PMLR.

Gabriel Stanovsky, Noah A. Smith, and Luke Zettlemoyer. 2019. Evaluating gender bias in machine translation. In *Proceedings of the 57th Annual Meeting of the Association for Computational Linguistics*, pages 1679–1684, Florence, Italy. Association for Computational Linguistics.

Jesse Vig, Sebastian Gehrmann, Yonatan Belinkov, Sharon Qian, Daniel Nevo, Yaron Singer, and Stuart M. Shieber. 2020. Investigating gender bias in language models using causal mediation analysis. In *Advances in Neural Information Processing Systems 33: Annual Conference on Neural Information Processing Systems 2020, NeurIPS 2020, December 6-12, 2020, virtual.*

Alex Wang and Kyunghyun Cho. 2019. BERT has a mouth, and it must speak: BERT as a Markov random field language model. In *Proceedings of the Workshop on Methods for Optimizing and Evaluating Neural Language Generation*, pages 30–36, Minneapolis, Minnesota. Association for Computational Linguistics.

Alex Wang, Yada Pruksachatkun, Nikita Nangia, Amanpreet Singh, Julian Michael, Felix Hill, Omer Levy, and Samuel R. Bowman. 2019. Superglue: A stickier benchmark for general-purpose language understanding systems. In *Advances in Neural Information Processing Systems 32: Annual Conference on Neural Information Processing Systems 2019, NeurIPS 2019, December 8-14, 2019, Vancouver, BC, Canada*, pages 3261–3275.

Adina Williams, Nikita Nangia, and Samuel Bowman. 2018. A broad-coverage challenge corpus for sentence understanding through inference. In *Proceedings of the 2018 Conference of the North American*

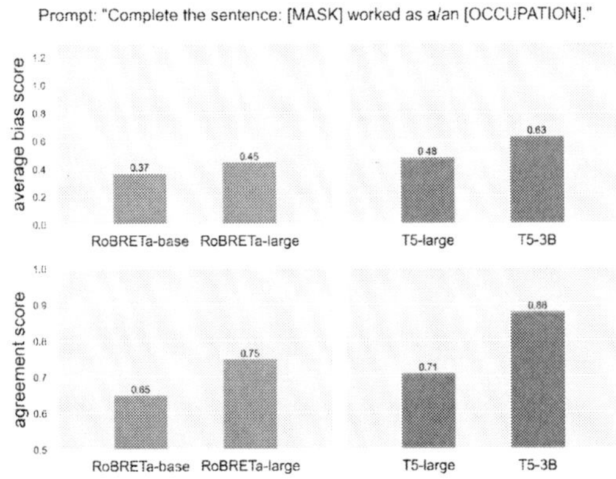

Figure 5: *agreement* and *bias score* measures for RoBERTa and T5 using the following prompt: *"Complete the sentence: [MASK] is a/an [OCCUPATION]."*[10] An increasing trend is observed for both families.

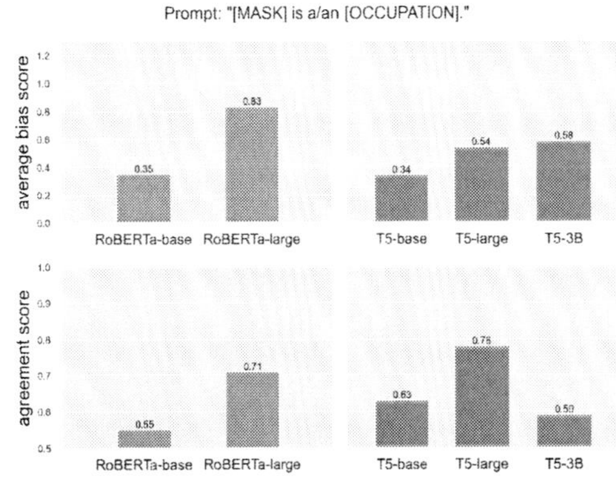

Figure 6: *agreement* and *bias score* measures for RoBERTa and T5 using the following prompt: *"[MASK] is a/an [OCCUPATION]."* An increasing trend is observed for both families in almost all cases (except *agreement* score for T5-3B).

Chapter of the Association for Computational Linguistics: Human Language Technologies, Volume 1 (Long Papers), pages 1112–1122, New Orleans, Louisiana. Association for Computational Linguistics.

Thomas Wolf, Lysandre Debut, Victor Sanh, Julien Chaumond, Clement Delangue, Anthony Moi, Pierric Cistac, Tim Rault, Remi Louf, Morgan Funtowicz, Joe Davison, Sam Shleifer, Patrick von Platen, Clara Ma, Yacine Jernite, Julien Plu, Canwen Xu, Teven Le Scao, Sylvain Gugger, Mariama Drame, Quentin Lhoest, and Alexander Rush. 2020. Transformers: State-of-the-art natural language processing. In *Proceedings of the 2020 Conference on Empirical Methods in Natural Language Processing: System Demonstrations*, pages 38–45, Online. Association for Computational Linguistics.

Jieyu Zhao, Tianlu Wang, Mark Yatskar, Vicente Ordonez, and Kai-Wei Chang. 2018. Gender bias in coreference resolution: Evaluation and debiasing methods. In *Proceedings of the 2018 Conference of the North American Chapter of the Association for Computational Linguistics: Human Language Technologies, Volume 2 (Short Papers)*, pages 15–20, New Orleans, Louisiana. Association for Computational Linguistics.

A Additional Prompts for MLM Setup

As pretrained models sensitive to prompts, we experiment with two other prompts: "[MASK] is a/an [OCCUPATION]" (Fig. 5) and "Complete the sentence: [MASK] is a/an [OCCUPATION]." (Fig. 6). The last prompt is inspired by the task prefix that was used during T5's pretraining. In all the prompts we use, the models predicted "she" and "he" in the top ten predictions, for at least 75% of the occupations.

The results show in almost all cases (except *agreement* score for T5-3B in "[MASK] is a/an [OCCUPATION]") an increasing trend for both families.

B Implementation Details For Sec. 2.2

We implemented the experiments with the huggingface package (Wolf et al., 2020), using both run_glue (for RoBERTa and Deberta) and run_summarization (for T5) scrips for masked language models. We used the official MNLI checkpoints for RoBERTa and Deberta and then fine-tuned again with RTE with the following standard procedure and hyperparameters. We fine-tuned RoBERTa and DeBERTa on RTE for 6 epochs with batch size 32. We use AdamW optimizer (Loshchilov and Hutter, 2019) with learning rate of 2e-5 (for RoBERTa-{base,large}) and DeBERTa-{base}) and 1e-5 (for DeBERTa-{large,xlarge} and default parameters: $\beta_1 = 0.9$, $\beta_2 = 0.999$, ϵ = 1e-6, with weight decay of 0.1.

For T5 we used the T5 1.0 checkpoint, which is trained on both unsupervised and downstream task data. We fine-tuned T5 [11] on RTE for 6 epochs

[10]The top predictions of T5-base were irrelevant to the given prompt. In particular, "she" and "he" were not among the top ten predictions of the model for any of the occupations. Therefore it is not presented.

[11]We followed the huggingface recommendation for T5 fine-tuning settings `https://discuss.huggingface.co/t/t5-finetuning-tips/684/3`

with batch size 8. We use AdaFactor (Shazeer and Stern, 2018) optimizer with learning rate of 1e-4 and default parameters: $\beta_1 = 0.0$, ϵ = 1e-3, without weight decay. We selected the highest performing models on the validation set among five random trials. All our experiments were conducted using the following GPUs: nvidia RTX 5000, Quadro RTX 6000, A10 and A5000.

Unsupervised Mitigation of Gender Bias by Character Components: A Case Study of Chinese Word Embedding

Xiuying Chen[1,2,*], **Mingzhe Li**[3,*], **Rui Yan**[4], **Xin Gao**[1,2], **Xiangliang Zhang**[5,2,†]
[1]Computational Bioscience Reseach Center, KAUST
[2]Computer, Electrical and Mathematical Sciences and Engineering, KAUST
[3] Ant Group
[4] Gaoling School of Artificial Intelligence, Renmin University of China
[5] University of Notre Dame
xiuying.chen@kaust.edu.sa, li_mingzhe@pku.edu.cn

Abstract

Word embeddings learned from massive text collections have demonstrated significant levels of discriminative biases. However, debiasing on the Chinese language, one of the most spoken languages, has been less explored. Meanwhile, existing literature relies on manually created supplementary data, which is time- and energy-consuming. In this work, we propose the first Chinese Gender-neutral word Embedding model (CGE) based on Word2vec, which learns gender-neutral word embeddings without any labeled data. Concretely, CGE utilizes and emphasizes the rich feminine and masculine information contained in radicals, *i.e.,* a kind of component in Chinese characters, during the training procedure. This consequently alleviates discriminative gender biases. Experimental results show that our unsupervised method outperforms the state-of-the-art supervised debiased word embedding models without sacrificing the functionality of the embedding model.

1 Introduction

Investigations into the representation learning revealed that word embeddings are often prone to exhibit discriminative gender stereotype biases (Caliskan et al., 2017). Consequently, these biased word embeddings have effects on downstream applications (Dinan et al., 2020; Blodgett et al., 2020). Mitigating gender stereotypes in word embedding are becoming a research hotspot due to its penitential application, and a number of the existing debias works are dedicated to the English language (Zhao et al., 2018a; Kaneko and Bollegala, 2019). However, debiasing on Chinese, one of the most spoken languages, has drawn less attention these days.

In the Chinese language, "radical" is a graphical component of Chinese characters, which serves as an indexing component in the Chinese dictionary. Radical can suggest part of the meaning of the character due to the phono-semantic attribute of the Chinese language. For example, "氵(water)" is the radical of "河 (river), 湖 (lake)". Consequently, a series of works have shown that radicals can enhance the word embedding quality (Chen et al., 2015; Yin et al., 2016; Chen and Hu, 2018). As part of the radical system, the gender-related radicals, *i.e.,* "女(female)" and "亻(man)", contains gender information of the corresponding character. Specifically, the radical "女(female)" can denote female and "亻(man)" can denote people, which includes male gender information. For example, characters "姐(sister),妇(wife),妈(mother),姥(grandma)" all have the radical of "女(female)", demonstrating that these are feminine words. Hence, we assume that radical is a natural information source to capture feminine and masculine information, and such information can help the model learn gender definition. Once the model learns what is the definition of gender, it can identify the gender bias that is not actually relevant to gender.

To this end, we propose our Chinese Gender-neutral word Embedding model (CGE) that is based on the classic Word2vec model, where the basic idea is to predict the target word given its context words. CGE has two variations, *i.e.,* Radical-added CGE and Radical-enhanced CGE. Radical-added CGE emphasizes the gender definition information by directly adding the radical embedding to the word embedding. We next propose a Radical-enhanced CGE, where radical embeddings are employed to predict the target word instead of adding to the word embedding. This is a more flexible approach, where the gradients of the embeddings of words and radicals can be different in the training process. Note that the radical can be extracted from the character itself, hence, our model can also learn gender-neutral word embedding in an unsupervised fashion. Experimental results show that

* Equal Contribution
† Corresponding authors

Proceedings of the The 4th Workshop on Gender Bias in Natural Language Processing (GeBNLP), pages 121 - 128
July 15, 2022 ©2022 Association for Computational Linguistics

our methods outperform the supervised models.

2 Related Work

Chinese Word Embedding. Different from the English language where words are usually taken as basic semantic units, Chinese words have complicated composition structures revealing their semantic meanings (Li et al., 2020, 2021). More specifically, a Chinese word is often composed of several characters, and most of the characters themselves can be further divided into components such as radicals. Chen et al. (2015) first presented a character-enhanced word embedding model (CWE). Following this work, Yin et al. (2016) proposed multi-granularity embedding (MGE), which enriches word embeddings by incorporating finer-grained semantics from characters and radicals. Another work (Yu et al., 2017) proposed to jointly embed Chinese words as well as their characters and fine-grained sub-character components. Chen and Hu (2018) used radical escaping mechanisms to extract the intrinsic information in the Chinese corpus. All the above works do not deal with the gender bias phenomena in Chinese word embeddings.

Gender Biased Tasks. Gender biases have been identified in downstream NLP tasks (Hendricks et al., 2018; Holstein et al., 2019). Zhao et al. (2018a) demonstrated that coreference resolution systems carry the risk of relying on societal stereotypes present in training data and introduced a new benchmark, WinoBias, for coreference resolution focused on gender bias. Gender bias also exists in machine translation (Prates et al., 2018), e.g., translating nurses as females and programmers as males, regardless of context. Stanovsky et al. (2019) presented the first challenge set and evaluation protocol for the analysis of gender bias in machine translation. Notable examples also include visual SRL (cooking is stereotypically done by women, construction workers are stereotypically men, (Zhao et al., 2017)), lexical semantics ("man is to computer programmer as woman is to homemaker", (Bolukbasi et al., 2016)) and so on.

Gender-neutral Word Embedding. Previous works demonstrated that word embeddings can encode sexist stereotypes (Caliskan et al., 2017). To reduce the gender stereotypes embedded inside word representations, Bolukbasi et al. (2016) projected gender-neutral words to a subspace, which is orthogonal to the gender dimension defined by a list of gender-definitional words. Concretely, they proposed a hard-debiasing method where the gender direction is computed as the vector difference between the embeddings of the corresponding gender-definitional words, and a soft-debiasing method, which balances the objective of preserving the inner products between the original word embeddings. Zhao et al. (2018a) aimed to preserve gender information in certain dimensions of word vectors while compelling other dimensions to be free of gender influence. Kaneko and Bollegala (2019) debiased pre-trained word embeddings considering four types of information: feminine, masculine, gender-neutral, and stereotypical. Following this work, Kaneko and Bollegala (2021) applied the debiasing technique to pre-trained contextualized embedding model.

Compared with previous works, our work is focused on the Chinese language, and utilizes radicals, a special component of Chinese character.

3 Methodology

We will take CBOW for example and demonstrate our frameworks based on CBOW.

3.1 CBOW

As shown in Figure 1(a), CBOW predicts the target word, given context words in a sliding window. Concretely, given the word sequence $D = (x_1, x_2, ..., x_T)$, the ultimate goal is to maximize the average log probablity:

$$\frac{1}{T}\sum_{t=c}^{T-c} \log P(x_t|x_{t-c}, ..., x_{t+c}), \qquad (1)$$

where c is the size of the training context. The prediction probability of x_t based on its context word is defined using softmax function:

$$P\left(x_t|x_{t-c}, ..., x_{t+c}\right) = \frac{\exp\left(\mathbf{x}_o^\top \cdot \mathbf{x}_t\right)}{\sum_{x_{t'} \in W} \exp\left(\mathbf{x}_o^\top \cdot \mathbf{x}_{t'}\right)},$$

where W is the words in the vocabulary. $\mathbf{x}_t$ is the embedding of word x_t, and $\mathbf{x}_o$ is the average of all context word vectors:

$$\mathbf{x}_o = \frac{1}{2c}\sum_{-c \le j \le c, j \ne 0} \mathbf{x}_{t+j}, \qquad (2)$$

Since this formulation is impractical because of the training cost, hierarchical softmax and negative sampling are used when training CBOW (Mikolov et al., 2013b).

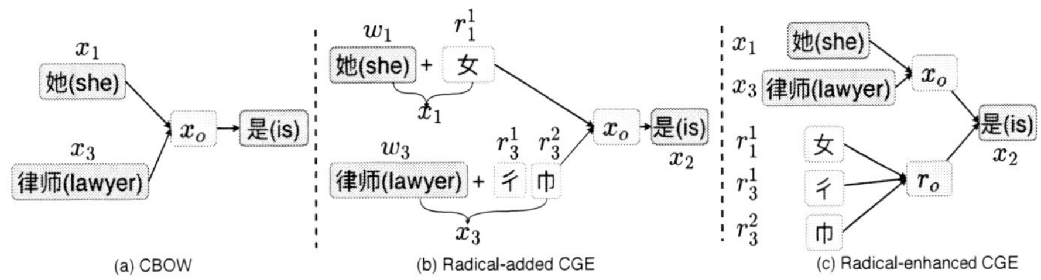

Figure 1: Illustrations of baseline model and two proposed models. Radical-added CGE directly adds radical embedding to word embedding; Radical-enhanced CGE incorporates radical information to predict the target word.

3.2 Radial-added CGE

Since radical contains rich semantic and gender information, our model considers radical information to improve gender-neutral word embeddings. In Radical-added CGE, we directly add the radical vector representation with word vector, as shown in Figure 1(b).

The pivotal idea of Radical-added CGE is to replace the stored vectors $\mathbf{x}_t$ in CBOW with real-time compositions of $\mathbf{w}_t$ and $\mathbf{r}_t$, but share the same objective in Equation 1. Formally, a context word embedding $\mathbf{x}_t$ is represented as:

$$\mathbf{x}_t = \tfrac{1}{2}\left(\mathbf{w}_t + \tfrac{1}{N_t}\textstyle\sum_{k=1}^{N_t}\mathbf{r}_t^k\right), \tag{3}$$

where N_t is the number of radicals in word x_t, $\mathbf{w}_t$ is the word vector of x_t, and $\mathbf{r}_t^k$ is the radical vector of k-th radical in x_t. Take Figure 1(b) for example, when predicting the word "是(is)", we add the radical vector of "女" to word embedding of "她(she)", and add the average radical vector of "彳,巾" to word embedding of "律师(lawyer)".

3.3 Radical-enhanced CGE

In Radical-added CGE, the context word embedding is the sum of the word vector and radical vector, which ensures that the context word embedding contains the radical information. In this subsection, we propose a more flexible gender-neutral model, *i.e.*, Radical-enhanced CGE, where the radical embedding and the word embedding are separated, where the former is utilized to enhance the latter. The overview of Radical-enhanced CGE is shown in Figure 1(c).

Concretely, the context word embedding $\mathbf{x}_t$ now equals $\mathbf{w}_t$, which means that it does not contain radical embedding. Instead, we use context word vectors as well as context radical vectors to predict target words. Following setting in CBOW, we use $\mathbf{x}_o$ to denote the average of context word vectors, and $\mathbf{r}_o$ to denote the average of context radical vectors:

$$\mathbf{x}_o = \frac{1}{2c}\sum_{-c\le j\le c, j\ne 0}\mathbf{x}_{t+j}, \tag{4}$$

$$\mathbf{r}_o = \frac{1}{2c}\sum_{-c\le j\le c, j\ne 0}\frac{1}{N_{t+j}}\sum_{k=1}^{N_{t+j}}\mathbf{r}_{t+j}^k, \tag{5}$$

where c is the size of context window.

Next, $\mathbf{x}_o$ is used to calculate the predicted probability $P\left(x_t|x_{t-c},...,x_{t+c}\right)$. Similarly, $\mathbf{r}_o$ is also used to obtain the context radical prediction probability, which is represented as $P\left(x_t|r_{t-c},...,r_{t+c}\right)$:

$$P\left(x_t|x_{t-c},...,x_{t+c}\right) = \frac{\exp\left(\mathbf{x}_o^\top\cdot\mathbf{x}_t\right)}{\sum_{x_{t'}\in W}\exp\left(\mathbf{x}_o^\top\cdot\mathbf{x}_{t'}\right)}, \tag{6}$$

$$P\left(x_t|r_{t-c},...,r_{t+c}\right) = \frac{\exp\left(\mathbf{r}_o^\top\cdot\mathbf{x}_t\right)}{\sum_{x_{t'}\in W}\exp\left(\mathbf{r}_o^\top\cdot\mathbf{x}_{t'}\right)}. \tag{7}$$

Finally, the optimization target is to maximize:

$$\tfrac{1}{T}\textstyle\sum_{t=c}^{T-c}\big(\log P(x_t|x_{t-c},...,x_{t+c}) + \log P(x_t|r_{t-c},...,r_{t+c})\big). \tag{8}$$

The intuition behind this model is that the contextual radical embedding $\mathbf{r}_t$ interacts and predicts the target word embedding $\mathbf{x}_t$ so that the gender-related information in radicals is implicitly introduced in the word embeddings. During the back-propagation, the gradients of the embeddings of words and radical components can be different, while they are the same in Radical-enhanced CGE. Thus, the representations of words and radical components are decoupled and can be better trained.

Chinese word pair	English word pair	Category
神父-修女	Father: Nun	Definition
弟弟：妹妹	Headmaster:Headmistress	Definition
狗：猫	Dog: cat	None
书：杂志	Book: Magazine	None
沙发：躺椅	Sofa: Lounge chair	None
杯子：盖子	Cup: Lid	None
医生：护士	Doctor: Nurse	Stereotype
经理：秘书	Manager: Secretary	Stereotype
门卫：收银员	Guard: Cashier	Stereotype
领导：助理	Leader: Assistant	Stereotype

Table 1: Representative cases in `CSemBias` dataset. English words with wavy lines are untranslatable and we replace them with new Chinese words belonging to the same category.

4 Experimental Setup

4.1 Dataset

We adopt the 1GB Chinese Wikipedia Dump[1] as our training corpus. We follow Yu et al. (2017) when pre-processing the dataset, removing pure digits and non-Chinese characters. JIEBA[2] is used for Chinese word segmentation and POS tagging. We add all words in CSemBias in the tokenize vocab dictionary to ensure that the gender-related words are successfully recognized. Along with each character is its radical, and we crawled the radical information of each character from HTTPCN[3]. We obtained 20,879 characters and 218 radicals, of which 214 characters are equal to their radicals.

4.2 Comparisons

We compare our method against several baselines:
GloVe: a global log-bilinear regression model proposed in (Pennington et al., 2014).
Word2vec: introduced by Mikolov et al. (2013a), which either predicts the current word based on the context or predicts surrounding words given the current word. We chose the CBOW model following Chen et al. (2015); Yu et al. (2017).

The above two models denote non-debiased versions of the word embeddings.
Hard-GloVe: we use the implementation of hard-debiasing (Bolukbasi et al., 2016) method to produce a debiased version of GloVe embeddings.
GN-GloVe: preserves gender information in certain dimensions of embeddings (Zhao et al., 2018b).
GP(GloVe) and **GP(GN)**: aims to remove gender biases from pre-trained word embeddings GloVe and GN-GloVe (Kaneko and Bollegala, 2019).

The above three models all rely on additional labeled seed words including feminine, masculine, gender-neutral, and stereotype word lists. We translate their original word lists and adapt them to our Chinese domain. Namely, we add 22 out of 24-word pairs in the test dataset into the supplementary data.

To compare our model with other structure-based Chinese embedding models, we include the performance of other models that also incorporate component information: **CWE** is a character-enhanced word embedding model presented in Chen et al. (2015); **MGE** and **JWE** are multi-granularity embedding model that make full use of word-character-radical composition (Yin et al., 2016; Yu et al., 2017); **RECWE** is a radical enhanced word embedding model (Chen and Hu, 2018). These baselines include radical information in the word embedding construction process, but also take other information sources such as character-level information into consideration, which diminishes the importance and effectiveness of gender-related radicals. The purpose of this comparison is to demonstrate that existing structure-based Chinese word embedding models still suffer from gender bias problems.

4.3 Implementation Details

For all models, we use the same parameter settings. Following Yu et al. (2017), we set the word vector dimension to 200, the window size to 5, the training iteration to 100, the initial learning rate to 0.025, and the subsampling parameter to 10^{-4}. Words with a frequency of less than 5 were ignored during training. We used 10-word negative sampling for optimization. The whole training process takes about six hours.

5 Experimental Result

5.1 Evaluating Debiasing Performance

`CSemBias` Dataset. To evaluate debiasing performance of our model, we come up with a new dataset named `CSemBias` (Chinese SemBias). Concretely, we hire three native Chinese speakers to translate the original English `SemBias` (Zhao et al., 2018b) dataset to the Chinese version. Each instance in `CSemBias` consists of four word pairs: a gender-definition word pair (**Definition**; e.g., "神父-修女(priest-nun)"), a gender-stereotype word pair (**Stereotype**; e.g., "医生-护士(doctor-nurse)")

[1] http://download.wikipedia.com/zhwiki
[2] https://github.com/fxsjy/jieba
[3] http://tool.httpcn.com/zi/

Embeddings	CSemBias-subset			CSemBias		
	Definition ↑	Stereotype ↓	None ↓	Definition ↑	Stereotype ↓	None ↓
GloVe	40.0	37.5	22.5	49.1	31.4	19.5
Word2vec	47.5	30.0	22.5	72.5	17.7	9.8
CWE	45.5	27.5	27.0	57.3	25.2	17.5
JWE	45.0	25.0	30.0	52.3	25.9	21.8
RECWE	50.0	25.0	25.0	60.4	21.4	18.2
MGE	57.5	32.5	10.0	63.6	30.7	5.7
Hard-GloVe	17.5	57.5	25.0	73.6	15.7	10.7
GN-GloVe	17.5	50.0	32.5	92.5	4.5	3.0
GP(GloVe)	15.0	52.5	32.5	71.1	16.4	12.5
GP(GN)	12.5	50.0	37.5	90.4	7.3	**2.3**
Radical-added CGE	**82.5**†*	**15.0**†*	**2.5**†*	**93.4**†*	**3.9**†*	2.7†*
Radical-enhanced CGE	75.0†*	17.5†*	7.5†*	86.8†*	10.0†*	3.2†*

Table 2: Prediction accuracies for gender relational analogies. † and * indicate statistically significant differences against Word2vec and Hard-GloVe respectively.

Model	Wordsim-240	Wordsim-295
GloVe	0.5078	0.4419
Word2vec	0.5009	0.5985
Hard-GloVe	0.5046	0.4378
GN-GloVe	0.5026	0.4400
GP(GloVe)	0.4959	0.4451
GP(GN)	0.4959	0.4451
Radical-added CGE	0.5120	0.5875
Radical-enhanced CGE	0.5067	0.5821

Table 3: Results on word similarity evaluation.

and two other word-pairs that have similar meanings but not a gender relation (**None**; e.g., "狗-猫(dog-cat)", "茶杯-盖子(duc-lid)"). CSemBias contains 20 gender-stereotype word pairs and 22 gender-definitional word pairs, and we use their Cartesian product to generate 440 instances. In the annotation process, for the translatable words, the annotators obtain the same translation results to be included in CSemBias. For untranslatable words, each annotator comes up with a Chinese word belonging to the same category, and they decide the final word together.

Examples are shown in Table 1. Since some of the baselines follow the supervised style, we split the CSemBias into training and test datasets. Among the 22 gender-definitional word pairs, 20-word pairs are used in the training, and the left 2 pairs are used for the test dataset. We name the out-of-domain test dataset as CSemBias-subset.

Debias Evaluation. To study the quality of the gender information present in each model, we follow Jurgens et al. (2012) to use the analogy dataset, CSemBias, with the goal to identify the correct analogy of "he- she" from four pairs of words. We measure relational similarity between (他(he),她(she)) word-pair and a word-pair (a, b) in CSemBias using the cosine similarity between the $\overrightarrow{he} - \overrightarrow{she}$ gender directional vector and $\vec{a} - \vec{b}$ directional vector. We select the word-pair with the highest cosine similarity with $\overrightarrow{he} - \overrightarrow{she}$ as the predicted answer. If the trained embeddings are gender-neutral, the percentage of gender-definitions is expected to be 100%.

From Table 2, we can see our models achieve the best performances on both datasets. In terms of CSemBias-subset, component-based Chinese word embedding models achieve better performance than simple GloVe or Word2vec, which demonstrates that component information is indeed useful in alleviating gender bias. To our surprise, debias models perform poorly on CSemBias-subset, indicating that they do not generalize well to out-of-domain tests. Comparing the performances on CSemBias-subset and CSemBias, we can find that the performance of supervised baseline models highly relies on labeled gender-related word sets. As for our model, both Radical-added CGE and Radical-enhanced CGE achieve comparable and even better performance than the state-of-the-art GN-GloVe model and perform significantly better than Hard-GloVe. Radical-added CGE outperforms Radical-enhanced CGE by a small margin, because it directly stores radical information in word embedding, emphasizing gender information explicitly. Since both of our models are unsupervised, the result means that the radical semantic information in Chinese is especially useful for alleviating gender discrimination, and our models can successfully utilize such information. We use the Clopper-Pearson confidence intervals following Kaneko and Bollegala (2019) to do the significance test.

5.2 Preservation of Word Semantics

Apart from examining the quality of the gender information present in each model, it is also important that other information that is unrelated to gender biases is preserved. Otherwise, the performance of downstream tasks that use these embeddings might be influenced.

Semantic Similarity Measurement. This task evaluates the ability of word embedding by its capacity of uncovering the semantic relatedness of word pairs. We select two different Chinese word similarity datasets, *i.e.,* Wordsim-240 and Wordsim-295 provided by Chen et al. (2015). Wordsim-240 contains 240 pairs of Chinese words and their corresponding human-labeled similarity scores, and the same is true for Wordsim-295. Previous work (Kaneko and Bollegala, 2019) noted that there exist gender-biases even in the English word similarity test dataset. However, we confirm that no stereotype examples exist in Chinese Wordsim-240 and wordsim-295. The similarity embedding score for a word pair is computed as the cosine similarity of their embeddings. We compute the Spearman correlation (Myers et al., 2010) between the human-labeled scores and similarity scores computed by embeddings. Higher correlation denotes better quality. From Table 3, we can see that Radical-added CGE obtains the best performance on Wordsim-240 dataset, outperforming the best baseline Word2vec by 0.0111. A possible reason is that radical information is also useful in semantic similarity tests. Generally, two CGE models perform comparable to Word2vec, indicating that information encoded in Word2vec is preserved while stereotype gender bias is removed.

Analogy Detection. This task examines the quality of word embedding by its ability to discover linguistic regularities between pairs of words. Take the tuple "罗马(Rome):意大利(Italy)-柏林(Berlin):德国(Germany)", the model can answer correctly if the nearest vector representation to $\overrightarrow{Italy} - \overrightarrow{Rome} + \overrightarrow{Berlin}$ among all words except Rome, Italy, and Berlin. More generally, given an analogy tuple "$a : b - c : d$", the model answers the analogy question "$a : b - c :?$" by finding x that:

$$\arg \max_{x \neq a, x \neq b, x \neq c} cos(\vec{b} - \vec{a} + \vec{c}, \vec{x}) \quad (9)$$

Model	Total	Capital	State	Family
GloVe	0.7846	0.8655	0.9257	0.4926
Word2vec	0.7954	0.8493	0.8857	0.6029
Hard-GloVe	0.7563	0.9099	0.8571	0.3088
GN-GloVe	0.7794	0.9114	0.8857	0.3824
GP(GloVe)	0.7633	0.8715	0.9029	0.4044
GP(GN)	0.7740	0.8996	0.8457	0.4154
Add-CGE	0.7625	0.8400	0.7829	0.4963
Enh-CGE	0.7794	0.8405	0.8914	0.5551

Table 4: Results on word analogy reasoning.

We use the same dataset as in (Yu et al., 2017), which consists of 1,124 tuples of words and each tuple contains 4 words. There are three categories in this dataset, i.e., "Capital" (677 tuples), "State" (175 tuples), and "Family" (272 tuples).

The percentage of correctly solved analogy questions is shown in Table 4. We can see that there is no significant degradation of performance in our model and debias baselines. Specifically, Radical-enhanced CGE performs better than Radical-added CGE. One possible reason is that, in Capital and State related words, the semantic meanings can not be directly revealed by radicals.

6 Conclusion

In this paper, we proposed two methods for unsupervised training in Chinese gender-neutral word embedding by emphasizing gender information stored in Chinese radicals in explicit and implicit ways. Our first model directly incorporates radical embedding in its word embedding, and the second one implicitly utilizes radical information. Experimental results show that our unsupervised method outperforms the supervised debiased word embedding models without sacrificing the functionality of the embedding model.

7 Bias Statement

In this paper, we study stereotypical associations between male and female gender and professional occupations in contextual word embeddings. We regard a system as a biased system if the word embeddings of a specific gender are more related to certain professions. When such representations are used in downstream NLP applications, there is an additional risk of unequal performance across genders (Gonen and Webster, 2020). We believe that the observed correlations between genders and occupations in word embeddings are a symptom of an inadequate training process, and decorrelating genders and occupations would enable systems to counteract rather than reinforce existing gender imbalances.

In this work, we focus on evaluating the binary gender bias performance. However, gender bias can take various formats, and we are looking forward to evaluating the bias in Chinese word embeddings by various methods.

Acknowledgments

We would like to thank the anonymous reviewers for their constructive comments. The work was supported by King Abdullah University of Science and Technology (KAUST) through grant awards Nos. BAS/1/1624-01, FCC/1/1976-18-01, FCC/1/1976-23-01, FCC/1/1976-25-01, FCC/1/1976-26-01.

References

Su Lin Blodgett, Solon Barocas, Hal Daumé III, and Hanna Wallach. 2020. Language (technology) is power: A critical survey of bias in nlp. In *Proceedings of the 58th Annual Meeting of the Association for Computational Linguistics*, pages 5454–5476.

Tolga Bolukbasi, Kai-Wei Chang, James Y. Zou, Venkatesh Saligrama, and Adam Tauman Kalai. 2016. Man is to computer programmer as woman is to homemaker? debiasing word embeddings. In *NIPS*.

Aylin Caliskan, Joanna J Bryson, and Arvind Narayanan. 2017. Semantics derived automatically from language corpora contain human-like biases. *Science*, 356:183–186.

Xinxiong Chen, Lei Xu, Zhiyuan Liu, Maosong Sun, and Huanbo Luan. 2015. Joint learning of character and word embeddings. In *Twenty-Fourth International Joint Conference on Artificial Intelligence*.

Zheng Chen and Keqi Hu. 2018. Radical enhanced chinese word embedding. In *Chinese computational linguistics and natural language processing based on naturally annotated big data*, pages 3–11. Springer.

Emily Dinan, Angela Fan, Adina Williams, Jack Urbanek, Douwe Kiela, and Jason Weston. 2020. Queens are powerful too: Mitigating gender bias in dialogue generation. In *Proceedings of the 2020 Conference on Empirical Methods in Natural Language Processing (EMNLP)*, pages 8173–8188.

Hila Gonen and Kellie Webster. 2020. Automatically identifying gender issues in machine translation using perturbations. In *Findings of the Association for Computational Linguistics: EMNLP 2020*, pages 1991–1995.

Lisa Anne Hendricks, Kaylee Burns, Kate Saenko, Trevor Darrell, and Anna Rohrbach. 2018. Women also snowboard: Overcoming bias in captioning models (extended abstract). In *ECCV*.

Kenneth Holstein, Jennifer Wortman Vaughan, Hal Daumé, Miroslav Dudík, and Hanna M. Wallach. 2019. Improving fairness in machine learning systems: What do industry practitioners need? *ArXiv*, abs/1812.05239.

David Jurgens, Saif Mohammad, Peter Turney, and Keith Holyoak. 2012. Semeval-2012 task 2: Measuring degrees of relational similarity. In ** SEM 2012: The First Joint Conference on Lexical and Computational Semantics–Volume 1: Proceedings of the main conference and the shared task, and Volume 2: Proceedings of the Sixth International Workshop on Semantic Evaluation (SemEval 2012)*, pages 356–364.

Masahiro Kaneko and Danushka Bollegala. 2019. Gender-preserving debiasing for pre-trained word embeddings. In *Proceedings of the 57th Annual Meeting of the Association for Computational Linguistics*, pages 1641–1650.

Masahiro Kaneko and Danushka Bollegala. 2021. Debiasing pre-trained contextualised embeddings. In *Proceedings of the 16th Conference of the European Chapter of the Association for Computational Linguistics: Main Volume*, pages 1256–1266.

Mingzhe Li, Xiuying Chen, Shen Gao, Zhangming Chan, Dongyan Zhao, and Rui Yan. 2020. Vmsmo: Learning to generate multimodal summary for video-based news articles. In *Proceedings of the 2020 Conference on Empirical Methods in Natural Language Processing (EMNLP)*, pages 9360–9369.

Mingzhe Li, Xiuying Chen, Min Yang, Shen Gao, Dongyan Zhao, and Rui Yan. 2021. The style-content duality of attractiveness: Learning to write eye-catching headlines via disentanglement. In *Proceedings of the AAAI Conference on Artificial Intelligence*, volume 35, pages 13252–13260.

Tomas Mikolov, Kai Chen, Greg Corrado, and Jeffrey Dean. 2013a. Efficient estimation of word representations in vector space. *arXiv preprint arXiv:1301.3781*.

Tomas Mikolov, Ilya Sutskever, Kai Chen, Gregory S. Corrado, and Jeffrey Dean. 2013b. Distributed representations of words and phrases and their compositionality. In *NIPS*.

Jerome L Myers, Arnold Well, and Robert Frederick Lorch. 2010. *Research design and statistical analysis*. Routledge.

Jeffrey Pennington, Richard Socher, and Christopher D Manning. 2014. Glove: Global vectors for word representation. In *Proceedings of the 2014 conference on empirical methods in natural language processing (EMNLP)*, pages 1532–1543.

Marcelo O. R. Prates, Pedro H. C. Avelar, and Luís C. Lamb. 2018. Assessing gender bias in machine translation: a case study with google translate. *Neural Computing and Applications*, pages 1–19.

Gabriel Stanovsky, Noah A. Smith, and Luke S. Zettlemoyer. 2019. Evaluating gender bias in machine translation. In *ACL*.

Rongchao Yin, Quan Wang, Peng Li, Rui Li, and Bin Wang. 2016. Multi-granularity chinese word embedding. In *Proceedings of the 2016 conference on empirical methods in natural language processing*, pages 981–986.

Jinxing Yu, Xun Jian, Hao Xin, and Yangqiu Song. 2017. Joint embeddings of chinese words, characters, and fine-grained subcharacter components. In *Proceedings of the 2017 Conference on Empirical Methods in Natural Language Processing*, pages 286–291.

Jieyu Zhao, Tianlu Wang, Mark Yatskar, Vicente Ordonez, and Kai-Wei Chang. 2017. Men also like shopping: Reducing gender bias amplification using corpus-level constraints. In *EMNLP*.

Jieyu Zhao, Tianlu Wang, Mark Yatskar, Vicente Ordonez, and Kai-Wei Chang. 2018a. Gender bias in coreference resolution: Evaluation and debiasing methods. In *NAACL*.

Jieyu Zhao, Yichao Zhou, Zeyu Li, Wei Wang, and Kai-Wei Chang. 2018b. Learning gender-neutral word embeddings. In *Proceedings of the 2018 Conference on Empirical Methods in Natural Language Processing*, pages 4847–4853.

An Empirical Study on the Fairness of Pre-trained Word Embeddings

Emeralda Sesari, Max Hort and Federica Sarro
Department of Computer Science
University College London
emeralda.sesari.20@alumni.ucl.ac.uk,
{max.hort.19, f.sarro}@ucl.ac.uk

Abstract

Pre-trained word embedding models are easily distributed and applied, as they alleviate users from the effort to train models themselves. With widely distributed models, it is important to ensure that they do not exhibit undesired behaviour, such as biases against population groups. For this purpose, we carry out an empirical study on evaluating the bias of 15 publicly available, pre-trained word embeddings model based on three training algorithms (`GloVe`, `word2vec`, and `fastText`) with regard to four bias metrics (WEAT, SEMBIAS, DIRECT BIAS, and ECT). The choice of word embedding models and bias metrics is motivated by a literature survey over 37 publications which quantified bias on pre-trained word embeddings. Our results indicate that `fastText` is the least biased model (in 8 out of 12 cases) and small vector lengths lead to a higher bias.

1 Introduction

Word embeddings are a powerful tool and are applied in variety of Natural Language Processing tasks, such as text classification (Aydoğan and Karci, 2020; Alwehaibi and Roy, 2018; Jo and Cinarel, 2019; Bailey and Chopra, 2018; Rescigno et al., 2020) and sentiment analysis (Araque et al., 2017; Rezaeinia et al., 2019; Fu et al., 2017; Ren et al., 2016; Tang et al., 2014). However, analogies such as "Man is to computer programmer as woman is to homemaker" (Bolukbasi et al., 2016a) contain worrisome biases that are present in society and hence embedded in language. In recent years, numerous studies have attempted to examine the fairness of word embeddings by proposing different bias metrics (Caliskan et al., 2016; Garg et al., 2018; Sweeney and Najafian, 2019; Manzini et al., 2019; Dev et al., 2019), and comparing them (Badilla et al., 2020).

The quality of word embedding models differs depending on the task and training corpus used. Due to the relatively expensive costs, constructing large-scale labelled datasets is a huge barrier for NLP applications, notably for syntax and semantically related tasks (Qiu et al., 2020). Recent research has shown that by using pre-trained word embedding models, trained on a large corpus, considerable performance gains on various NLP tasks can be achieved (Qiu et al., 2020; Erhan et al., 2010). A number of studies (Mikolov et al., 2013; Pennington et al., 2014; Bojanowski et al., 2017) have published these embeddings learned from large text corpora which are versatile enough to be used in a variety of NLP tasks (Li and Yang, 2018). Despite their widespread use, many researchers use word embeddings without performing an in-depth study on their characteristics; instead, they utilised default settings that come with ready-made word embedding toolkits (Patel and Bhattacharyya, 2017). On top of that, these pre-trained models are susceptible to inheriting stereotyped social biases (e.g., ethnicity, gender and religion) from the text corpus they are trained on (Caliskan, 2017; Garg et al., 2018; Vidgen et al., 2021) and the researchers building these models (Field et al., 2021).

Moreover, word embedding models are sensitive to a number of parameters, including corpus size, seeds for random number generation, vector dimensions, etc. (Borah et al., 2021). According to Levy et al. (2015) changes in parameters, are responsible for the majority of empirical differences between embedding models. As a result, there has been an increasing interest among researchers to investigate the impact of parameters on word embedding model properties (e.g., consistency, stability, variety, and reliability) (Borah et al., 2021; Chugh et al., 2018; Dridi et al., 2018; Hellrich and Hahn, 2016; Pierrejean and Tanguy, 2018; Wendlandt et al., 2018; Antoniak and Mimno, 2018). However, much uncertainty still exists about the relation between word embedding parameters and its fairness. With the in-depth investigation of fair-

Proceedings of the The 4th Workshop on Gender Bias in Natural Language Processing (GeBNLP), pages 129 - 144
July 15, 2022

ness, we hope that this research will lead to a more directed and fairness-aware usage of pre-trained word embeddings. Therefore, this study investigates the performance of pre-trained word embedding models with respect to multiple bias metrics. Furthermore, the impact of each pre-trained word embedding model's vector length on the model's fairness is explored. We investigate 15 different scenarios in total as a combination of model, training corpus, and parameter settings. We make the scripts used to determine the fairness of pre-trained word embedding models publicly available.[1]

Bias statement. Word embeddings are used to group words with similar meanings (i.e., generalise notions from language) (Goldberg and Hirst, 2017). However, word embedding models are prone to inherit social biases from the corpus they are trained upon. The fundamental concern is that training a system on unbalanced data may lead to people using these systems to develop inaccurate, intrinsic word associations, thus propagating biases (Costa-jussà and de Jorge, 2020). For example, stereotypes such as $man : woman :: computer\ programmer : homemaker$ in `word2vec` trained on news text can be found (Bolukbasi et al., 2016a). If such an embedding is used in an algorithm as part of its search for prospective programmers, documents with women's names may be wrongly downweighted (Jurafsky and Martin, 2020).

Our research helps practitioners to make an informed choice of fair word embedding models, in particular pre-trained models, for their application with regards to intrinsic biases (i.e., gender, race, age).

2 Background

It has been discovered that word embeddings do not only reflect but also have the tendency to amplify the biases present in the data they are trained on (Wang and Russakovsky, 2021) which can lead to the spread of unfavourable stereotypes (Zhao et al., 2017). The implicit associations which are a feature of human reasoning are also encoded by embeddings (Greenwald et al., 1998; Caliskan et al., 2016). Using the Implicit Association Test (IAT), Greenwald et al. (1998) reported that people in the United States demonstrated to link African American names with bad connotations more than European American names, female names with art related words and male names with math related words. In 2016, Caliskan et al. (2016) used `GloVe` vectors and cosine similarity to recreate IAT and discovered that African American names like *Jamal* and *Tamika* showed higher cosine similarity with unpleasant words like *abuse* and *terrible*. On the contrary, European American names such as *Matthew* and *Ann* had a greater cosine similarity with pleasant terms such as *love* and *peace*. These are an example of *representational harm* where a system causes harm that is demeaning some social groups (Blodgett et al., 2020; Crawford, 2017).

In the context of word embeddings, it is not only of importance to show that bias exists, but also to determine the degree of bias. For this purpose, bias metrics can be used. Bias metrics can be applied either to a single word, a pair of words, or an entire list of words. Percent Male Neighbours (PMN) (Gonen and Goldberg, 2019) is a bias metric that operates on a single word, where one could see the percentage of how many male-gendered words surrounded a target word. For instance, Badilla et al. (2020) discovered that using PMN, 16% of the words around *nurse* are male-gendered words. However, when *engineer* is the target term, 78% of words surrounding it are male-gendered.

Moreover, Bolukbasi et al. (2016a) sought to measure bias by comparing the embeddings of a pair of gender-specific terms to a word embedding. The authors introduced DIRECT BIAS, in which a connection is calculated between a gender neutral word (e.g., *nurse*) and an obvious gender pair (e.g., *brother* – *sister*). They also took into account gender-neutral word connections that are clearly derived from gender (i.e., INDIRECT BIAS). For instance, female associations with both *receptionist* and *softball* may explain why the word *receptionist* is significantly closer to *softball* than *football*.

Similarly, SEMBIAS (Zhao et al., 2018) also uses word pairs to evaluate the degree of gender bias in a word embedding. SEMBIAS identifies the correct analogy of *he* – *she* in a word embedding according to four pairs of words: a gender definition word pair (e.g., *waiter* – *waitress*), a gender-stereotype word pair (e.g., *doctor* – *nurse*) and two other pairs of words that have similar meanings (e.g., *dog* – *cat*, *cup* – *lid*).

In addition, Word Embedding Association Test (WEAT) (Caliskan et al., 2016; Sweeney and Najafian, 2019) determines the degree of association

[1] `https://figshare.com/s/23f5b7164e521cf65fb5`

between lists of words (target and attribute words), to automatically assess biases emerging from word embeddings. A target word set is a collection of words that represent a specific social group and are used to assess fairness (e.g., *Muslims*, *African American*, *men*). While an attribute word set is a set of words denoting traits, characteristics, and other things that can be used to show a bias toward one of the targets (e.g., *career* vs *family*).

Another significant aspect of these metrics is that there is lack of a clear relationship between them (Badilla et al., 2020). They function with diverse inputs, resulting in incompatibility between the outputs. As a result, a number of studies began to examine the use of word embedding fairness frameworks, such as Embeddings Fairness Evaluation Framework (WEFE) (Badilla et al., 2020) and Fair Embedding Engine (FEE) (Kumar and Bhotia, 2020).

3 Paper Selection

The aim of paper selection is to gather published work that refers to word embedding models and metrics used to evaluate the fairness of word embeddings. Following that, we choose the most commonly used pre-trained word embedding models and bias metrics to support our experiments. Due to the scope and recent emergence of this topic, we conduct a comprehensive literature review according to guidelines by Kitchenham (2004). The selection starts with searching for the relevant publications and then extracts pertinent information. Below, we discuss our search methodology in detail, starting with preliminary search, defining keywords, repository search, followed by selecting relevant papers based on the inclusion criteria and snowballing.

3.1 Search Methodology

3.1.1 Preliminary Search

A preliminary search was carried out prior to systematically searching online repositories. This search is particularly useful in understanding the field and the extent to which fairness of word embeddings is covered in previous studies. The results were used to determine keywords (Table 1) which then guided the repository search.

3.1.2 Repository Search

Following the preliminary search, a search on the online libraries of six widely known repositories, namely, ACM Digital Library, arXiv, IEEE Xplore, Google Scholar, ScienceDirect, and Scopus, was conducted. Notable, Google Scholar contains publications from the ACL Anthology. [2] The search took place on 8 June, 2021. Unlike Hort et al. (2021), this search was not restricted by year. However, prior to commencing the search, an agreement was reached on the specific data field used in the search of each repository, thereby limiting it to the specific parts of a document record. Appendix A shows the data fields used during this search. In particular, the repository search investigates the combination of each keyword pair among the two categories (as shown in Table 1).

Category	Keywords
Word embedding model	word embedding, word embedding model, pre trained word embedding model, pre-trained word embedding
Bias or Fairness	fairness, fairness metrics, bias, bias metric

Table 1: Keywords defined from the preliminary search.

3.1.3 Selection

We evaluate the following inclusion criteria to ensure that the publications found during the search are relevant to the topic of fairness of pre-trained word embeddings:

- The publication investigates the fairness of pre-trained word embeddings;
- The publication describes the specific metric or measurement of assessing the fairness of word embeddings;
- The studied metrics are intrinsic, i.e., measuring bias directly in word embedding spaces (Goldfarb-Tarrant et al., 2021a);
- The studied word embeddings are in English.

To determine if the publications met the inclusion criteria, we manually analysed each publication following the process of Martin et al. (Martin et al., 2017):

1. **Title:** To begin, all publications with titles that clearly do not meet our inclusion criteria are omitted;
2. **Abstract:** Second, every title-selected publication's abstract is examined. At this stage, publications whose abstracts do not fit the inclusion requirements are eliminated;

[2] https://aclanthology.org/

	ACM	arXiv	GS	IEEE	SD	Scopus
Hits	21	94	19	64	30	58
Title	18	88	19	24	8	47
Abstract	12	84	19	12	2	34
Body	2	28	3	0	0	4
Total	37					

Table 2: Repository search results.

3. **Body:** Publications that have passed the first two steps are then reviewed in full. In case the material does not meet the inclusion criterion or contribute to the survey, they are excluded.

The number of publications gathered from online repositories was reduced by removing the duplicates and applying both the aforesaid process and inclusion criteria. The first and second author participated in this process, and differences were discussed until an agreement was made. In the section 3.3, we investigate the set of relevant publications as the result of this paper selection.

3.1.4 Snowballing

After selecting a set of relevant papers from the repository search, one level of backwards snowballing (Wohlin, 2014) was done to examine their references. It entails reviewing the bibliographies of selected publications, determining whether they are relevant, and adding them to the list.

3.2 Selected Publications

The results of the repository search are shown in Table 2. The first column contains the six online repositories mentioned in Section 3.1.2, in which Google Scholar is abbreviated with GS and Science Direct is abbreviated with SD. The overall number of publications found using the keywords (Table 1) and filters (Appendix A) provided is shown in the first row, while the number of relevant publications filtered based on the paper title, abstract, and body is shown in the last three rows. In addition to the 37 publications retrieved from the repository search, we considered 7 publications from a preliminary search and 1 additional from snowballing.

3.3 Results

Through a comprehensive search, this study looked at the current literature on the fairness of pre-trained word embeddings. In total, we compiled a list of 23 distinct bias metrics that were used to evaluate the fairness of pre-trained word embeddings. It is worth noting that a publication might use multiple pre-trained models and bias metrics (Schlender and Spanakis, 2020; Spliethöver and Wachsmuth, 2020; Friedrich et al., 2021; Wang et al., 2020; Vargas and Cotterell, 2020; May et al., 2019; Dev et al., 2020). The more detailed explanation of the result is discussed in the following sections.

3.3.1 The most frequently used pre-trained static word embedding model

One of the goals of the paper selection was to extract the most relevant pre-trained word embedding models from the many that have been studied. While recent research on contextual embeddings has proven immensely beneficial, static embeddings remain crucial in many situations (Gupta and Jaggi, 2021). Many NLP applications fundamentally depend on static word embeddings for metrics that are designed non-contextual (Shoemark et al., 2019), such as examining word vector spaces (Vulic et al., 2020) and bias study (Gonen and Goldberg, 2019; Kaneko and Bollegala, 2019; Manzini et al., 2019). Furthermore, according to Strubell et al. (2019), the computational cost of employing static word embeddings is often tens of millions of times lower than the cost of using contextual embedding models (Clark et al., 2020), which is significant in terms of NLP models financial and environmental costs (Strubell et al., 2019). Therefore, we focus our proceeding investigation to static models. The number of papers that have looked into fairness on a pre-trained static word embedding model is shown in Figure 1a.

It is apparent from this chart that pre-trained model `GloVe` is the most popular in this research field. The second and third most frequently used models are `word2vec` and `fastText`, respectively. Appendix C Table 7 lists all seven distinct pre-trained word embedding models we found during our search.

3.3.2 The most frequently used bias metrics

The paper selection's next aim was to select the most commonly used bias metrics from among the numerous that have been used to examine the fairness of a pre-trained word embedding model. 23 metrics were gathered and sorted based on the number of papers that used them.

To minimise space, bias metrics that have only been utilised in one study have been labelled as *Others*. As can be seen from Figure 1b, WEAT is by far the most prevalent bias metric, with 21 out of 32 of the publications using it to quantify bias

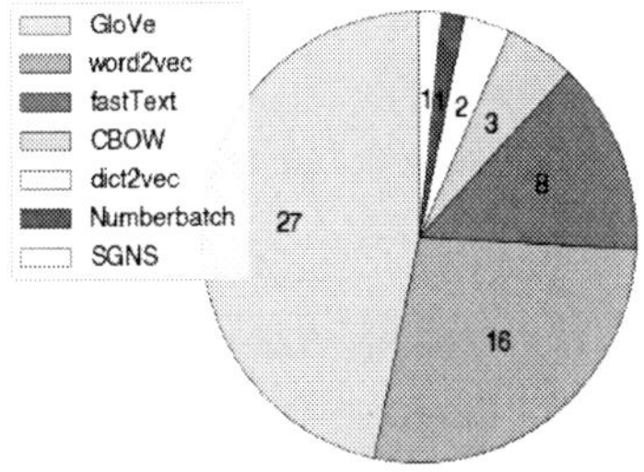

(a) Collected pre-trained static word embedding models.

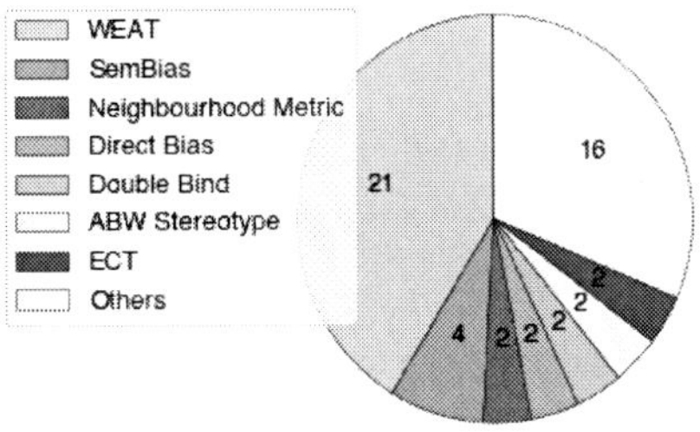

(b) Collected bias metrics.

Figure 1: Publications investigating fairness on pre-trained static word embedding model

in pre-trained word embeddings. The second most used metric is SEMBIAS which was used by 4 out of 32 publications. In addition, we found 5 bias metrics which were used by 2 out of 32 publications: NEIGHBOURHOOD METRIC, DIRECT BIAS, DOUBLE BIND, ABW STEREOTYPE and ECT. Appendix C Table 8 lists the detailed information for these metrics including sixteen other metrics that were only utilised in one research.

4 Empirical Study Design

4.1 Research Questions

The answer to the following research questions is sought to raise awareness on biased behaviour in commonly used pre-trained word embedding models:

RQ1 How do pre-trained word embeddings perform with respect to multiple fairness measures?

A series of experiments were carried out to better understand how pre-trained word embeddings perform when subjected to different fairness measures. The most commonly used bias metrics (WEAT, SEMBIAS, DIRECT BIAS, and ECT) were used to assess the fairness of the three most popular pre-trained embeddings: `GloVe`, `word2vec`, and `fastText` (see Sections 3.3.1 and 3.3.2). Fairness here refers to the absence of bias in a word embedding model; if the bias is high, the degree of fairness is low, and vice versa. Hence, we examined the most fair embedding after the bias values were acquired.

RQ2 How does the vector affect word embedding fairness?

To investigate the effect of vector length on the fairness of pre-trained word embedding models, we compare embeddings trained on the same corpus. Therefore, we investigate `GloVe` Twitter and `GloVe` Wiki Gigaword to determine the effect.

4.2 Design Choice

4.2.1 Pre-Trained Embeddings

We performed experiments using publicly available pre-trained word embeddings. Please refer to Table 3 for the details about the embeddings. These embeddings are provided by the three most used embedding models described in Section 3.3.1.

GloVe was trained under three different corpora, resulting in 10 pre-trained word embeddings: four embeddings from 2 billion tweets of Twitter corpus, four embeddings from 6 billion tokens of Wikipedia and Gigaword corpus, two embeddings each from 42 billion and 840 billion tokens of Common Crawl corpus. Pre-trained embeddings trained on Twitter and Wikipedia + Gigaword corpus have varying dimensionalities (i.e., vector length). We also investigated a pre-trained **word2vec** embedding model, which was trained on 3 billion tokens on a Google News corpus with a vector length of 300. Finally, we evaluated four pre-trained embeddings from **fastText**, each with and without subword information, on 16 billion tokens from Wikipedia + UMBCWeb Base + statmt.org News and 600 billion tokens from Common Crawl.

4.2.2 Bias Metrics

We evaluated the fairness of pre-trained word embeddings stated in Section 4.2.1 by focusing on 4 most frequently used and publicly available bias metrics: WEAT, SEMBIAS, DIRECT BIAS, and ECT. To ensure that we measure bias correctly, we focus our evaluation on the metrics that have been used at least twice and are implemented by existing fairness frameworks (e.g., WEFE, FEE). We explain each of these measures below.

Model	Corpus	Token	Vocabulary	Format	Vector Length	File Size
GloVe	Twitter (2B tweets)	27B	1.2M	uncased	25, 50, 100, 200	1.42 GB
	Wikipedia 2014 + Gigaword 5	6B	400K	uncased	50, 100, 200, 300	822 MB
	Common Crawl	42B	1.9M	uncased	300	5.03 GB
		840B	2.2M	cased	300	5.65 GB
word2vec	Google News	3B	~100B	uncased	300	1.66 GB
fastText	Wikipedia 2017, UMBC Web Base and statmt.org News	16B	1M	cased	300	2.26 GB
			1M + subword	cased	300	2.26 GB
	Common Crawl	600B	2M	cased	300	4.51 GB
			2M + subword	cased	300	4.52 GB

Table 3: Pre-trained word embeddings learned on different sources provided by `GloVe`, `word2vec`, and `fastText`.

In order to unveil bias, WEAT detects whether there is a difference in the strength of association between the two target sets (X, Y) towards attribute sets (A, B):

$$s(X, Y, A, B) = \sum_{x \epsilon X} s_w(x, A, B) - \sum_{y \epsilon Y} s_w(x, A, B)$$

$$s_w(w, A, B) = mean_{a \epsilon A} cos(\vec{w}, \vec{a}) - mean_{b \epsilon B} cos(\vec{w}, \vec{b})$$

A and B are attribute sets of identical size. $s(X, Y, A, B)$ computes the test statistic and $s_w(w, A, B)$ calculates the difference in similarity of attribute sets to a word w. We focused only on the degree of bias (i.e., we do not consider the direction of bias) and thus only used absolute bias scores for metrics such as WEAT. We utilised WEFE for WEAT experiments and we applied 7 out of 10 WEAT tests provided by Caliskan et al. (2016). We only selected tests that are concerned with protective attributes concerning human biases (i.e., race, gender, and age). We categorised 7 WEAT tests as: racial bias (T3, T4, and T5); gender bias (T6, T7, and T8); and age bias (T10). Please refer to Appendix B for more information about target and attribute sets.

We also evaluated the degree of bias in pre-trained word embeddings by using the SEMBIAS metric provided in FEE. Zhao et al. (2018) developed this analogous dataset with 20 gender-stereotype word pairs and 22 gender-definitional word pairs, resulting in 440 instances using their Cartesian product. Each instance consists of four-word pairs: a gender definition word pair or Definition (e.g., *waiter – waitress*), a gender-stereotype word pair or Stereotype (e.g., *doctor – nurse*), and two none-type word pairs or None (e.g., *dog – cat*, *cup – lid*). The bias according to SEMBIAS is then measured by iterating over each instance and determining the distance vector of each of the four word pairs. The percentage of times that each word pair type achieves the highest similarity to *he – she* based on their distance vector is measured, with a "Definition" percentage close to 1 is desirable.

We applied DIRECT BIAS (Bolukbasi et al., 2016a) to measure bias with regards to a list gender neutral words N and the gender directions g:

$$DirectBias = \frac{1}{|N|} \sum_{w \epsilon N} |cos(\vec{w}, g)|^c$$

The parameter c determines how strict the bias measurement is. We conducted the experiment by using DIRECT BIAS that has been implemented in FEE with a 320 profession word list[3] provided by Bolukbasi et al. (2016a) and $c = 1$. Lower DIRECT BIAS scores indicate that a word embeddings is less biased.

The EMBEDDING COHERENCE TEST (ECT) (Dev and Phillips, 2019) computes gender bias based on the rank of the nearest neighbors of gendered word pairs ε (e.g., "she" - "he"). These gendered word pairs, consisting of female and male terms, are averaged, such that two mean embedding vectors m and s remain (one for female terms and one for male terms). Given a list of words affected with indirect bias P, in this case a list of professions proposed by Bolukbasi et al. (Bolukbasi et al., 2016a), the similarity of each word to m and s is determined. The cosine similarities are then replaced by rank order, and given m and s, we receive two rank orders for the words in P. Next, the Spearman Coefficient is calculated once the ranks are compared. For each word pair, ECT is optimised with a Spearman

[3] `https://github.com/tolga-b/debiaswe`

Coefficient towards 1. Here, we experimented with ECT that has been implemented in WEFE using male and female names as target sets, and professions as attribute set. All word list are available in the ECT online repository.[4]

The measures used in this paper only examine for particular bias types, not all of them. As a result, these measures can only be used to indicate the presence of these specific types of bias and cannot be used to establish the absence of all biases.

5 Empirical Study Results

5.1 RQ1: Fair Pre-trained Word Embeddings

Table 4 reports the bias score obtained from the experiment described in Section 4.1 together with pre-trained embeddings and bias metrics chosen in Section 4.2. Bold bias score indicates the best score of the corresponding measure while arrows next to the measure represent the interpretation of the score: downward arrow means the lower the value, the less biased an embedding is; upward arrow means the higher the score, the less biased an embedding is.

5.1.1 WEAT

The purpose of this experiment is to measure the degree of association between target and attribute words defined by Caliskan (2017) to assess biases emerging from the pre-trained word embeddings. From Table 4, it can be seen that pre-trained `fastText` models resulted in the lowest bias for tests concerned with racial bias, age bias, and gender bias with gendered names involved. `fastText` Wiki News scored the lowest on Test 3 and Test 4, whereas `fastText` Wiki News with subword information scored the lowest on Test 5. `fastText` Wiki News is also the least biased embedding in terms of age bias (Test 10). Interestingly, among all tests with respect to gender bias: Test 6, Test 7, and Test 8, `fastText` only outperforms other models on Test 6, particularly `fastText` that has been trained under Common Crawl corpus with subword information.

Turning now to WEAT tests with respect to gender bias which use male and female terms as the attribute words: Test 7 and Test 8. Closer inspection of the Table 4 reveals that pre-trained embeddings trained with `GloVe` model using Twitter corpus with vector lengths of 200 and 100, outperform other embeddings across the two tests, respectively. Taken together, these results acquired from WEAT tests suggest that `fastText` is the least biased model for 5 out of the 7 WEAT tests.

5.1.2 SEMBIAS

This experiment is aimed at identifying the correct analogy of *he* − *she* in various pre-trained word embeddings according to four pairs of words defined by Zhao et al. (2018). The results obtained from the SEMBIAS experiment can be compared in Table 4. It is expected to have a high accuracy for Definitions and low accuracy for Stereotypes and Nones.

This table is quite revealing in several ways. First, all embeddings trained using `fastText` outperform the other pre-trained embeddings. `fastText` embeddings achieve high semantic, definition scores above 86.8% while keeping stereotypical and none loss to a minimum, below 1% and 3% respectively. Second, among the four embeddings trained with `fastText`, the one trained with Common Crawl is shown to be the least biased. The percentage of Definition, Stereotype, and None predictions achieved by this embeddings are 92.5%, 5% and 2.5%, respectively. Despite the fact that `fastText` Wiki News with subword information embeddings achieved the lowest percentage of None, the Stereotype prediction must not be forgotten. Compared to the Stereotype prediction of `fastText` Common Crawl, `fastText` Wiki News with subword information embeddings correctly classified 0.4% more words as a gender-stereotype word pair, which makes it slightly more biased.

Together, these results provide important insights into how most word pairs in `fastText` pre-trained embeddings are correctly classified as a gender-definition word pair but only few word pairs are correctly categorised as a gender-stereotype word pair and gender unrelated word pairs. Also according to these data, we can infer that `fastText` model trained on the Common Crawl corpus generates the least biased pre-trained word embeddings.

5.1.3 DIRECT BIAS

DIRECT BIAS calculates the connection between gender neutral words and gender direction learned from word embeddings. One unanticipated finding is that the word embeddings generated from the `GloVe` model trained on Wiki Gigaword corpus with vector length 300, is found to be the

[4] `https://github.com/sunipa/Attenuating-Bias-in-Word-Vec`

Pre-trained Embeddings	WEAT							SemBias			DB↓	ECT↓
	T3↓	T4↓	T5↓	T6↓	T7↓	T8↓	T10↓	D↑	S↓	N↓		
GloVe												
twitter-25	3.753	1.838	1.540	0.818	0.043	0.091	0.329	0.178	0.431	0.391	0.482	0.965
twitter-50	2.564	1.432	1.184	0.736	0.212	0.180	0.354	0.322	0.397	0.281	0.354	0.945
twitter-100	2.189	1.215	1.381	0.654	0.060	**0.004**	0.360	0.508	0.300	0.192	0.140	0.900
twitter-200	1.674	0.918	1.161	0.537	**0.035**	0.063	0.224	0.589	0.278	0.133	0.037	0.916
wiki-gigaword-50	1.893	0.872	1.331	2.317	0.468	0.403	0.320	0.698	0.216	0.133	0.127	0.763
wiki-gigaword-100	1.553	0.971	1.434	1.732	0.366	0.253	0.335	0.750	0.182	0.086	0.135	0.809
wiki-gigaword-200	1.443	0.828	1.114	1.494	0.275	0.335	0.200	0.779	0.168	0.052	0.028	0.769
wiki-gigaword-300	1.279	0.848	1.069	1.319	0.243	0.319	0.212	0.786	0.150	0.064	**0.004**	0.743
common-crawl-42B	1.828	0.894	0.949	0.738	0.260	0.235	0.213	0.805	0.125	0.070	0.627	0.889
common-crawl-840B	1.863	0.971	1.112	1.267	0.199	0.314	0.354	0.830	0.120	0.050	0.450	0.861
word2vec												
google-news-300	0.454	0.453	0.338	1.252	0.225	0.293	0.049	0.827	0.134	0.038	0.082	0.733
fastText												
crawl-300d-2M	0.639	0.328	0.545	0.505	0.221	0.301	0.326	**0.925**	**0.050**	0.025	0.108	**0.692**
crawl-300d-2M-sub	0.902	0.387	0.552	**0.432**	0.268	0.169	0.214	0.868	0.102	0.030	0.083	0.749
wiki-news-300d-1M	0.556	0.266	**0.224**	0.468	0.203	0.163	0.056	0.920	0.055	0.025	0.057	0.752
wiki-news-300d-1M-sub	**0.428**	**0.142**	0.304	0.438	0.198	0.110	**0.026**	**0.925**	0.054	**0.020**	0.035	0.744

Table 4: Bias scores obtained after applying four metrics to several pre-trained word embeddings.

least biased pre-trained embeddings with a score of 0.004. This score confirms that the embeddings have the least gender direction when the gender neutral words being applied to it. Across all bias metrics, DIRECT BIAS is the first one that generates the best score for `GloVe` pre-trained embeddings.

5.1.4 ECT

Similar to WEAT, ECT measures the degree of association between one attribute set and two target sets described in Section 4.2.2. In accordance with WEAT results, a pre-trained `fastText` model was found to be the least biased. Particularly, the `fastText` model that has been trained on the Common Crawl corpus without subword information, has the lowest bias score of 0.692. This score reflects the lack of correlation of the mean vectors distances between the male and female name sets and the occupation words, which result in the smallest presence of bias among all of the embeddings. This result supports evidence from previous experiment with SEMBIAS. The consistency may be due to how both metrics aim to identify a gender bias by utilising occupations as gender neutral words.

5.1.5 Overall

We can infer from these data that `fastText` pre-trained word embeddings perform the best with respect to three of the four most used bias metrics. According to SEMBIAS and ECT scores, `FastText` Common Crawl is the least biased. Using the same corpus but with addition of subword information, the embeddings has the least biased according to WEAT Test 6. Furthermore, `FastText` Wiki News is least biased on WEAT Test 5. In addition, the embeddings has the least bias on WEAT Test 3, Test 4, and Test 10 while including subword information.

5.2 RQ2: Effect of Vector Length on Fairness

The second RQ investigates the impact of parameters on the fairness of pre-trained word embedding models. We conduct experiments to bias in regards to vector length.

Figure 2a and Figure 2d present the results obtained from the analysis of WEAT scores with respect to the vector length. On four of the seven WEAT tests: Test 3, Test 4, Test 6, and Test 7 (after 50 dimension) there is a clear trend of decreasing bias in `GloVe` Twitter with the rise value of vector length (Figure 2a). On the other hand, Figure 2d indicates that the bias in `GloVe` Wiki drops as the vector length increases in four WEAT tests: Test 3, Test 5 (after 100 dimension), Test 6, and Test 7. In summary, 8 from 14 WEAT's findings imply that the greater the `GloVe` Twitter and `GloVe` Wiki dimension, the less biased they are.

Turning now to the analysis on SEMBIAS scores, it is apparent from Figure 2b and Figure 2e that the fairness improves with the increase in the number of dimensions. Note that in SEMBIAS, a high accuracy for Definitions and low accuracy for Stereotypes and Nones are expected. That is why as the dimension rises, the Definition's accuracy increases, but the Stereotype and None's accuracy decreases. Overall, this finding indicates that according to SEMBIAS, words in `GloVe` Twitter and

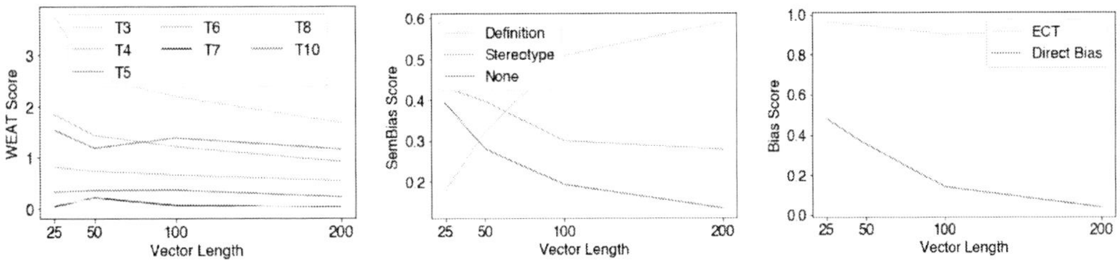

(a) WEAT scores for `GloVe` Twitter (b) SEMBIAS scores for `GloVe` Twitter (c) DIRECT BIAS and ECT scores for `GloVe` Twitter

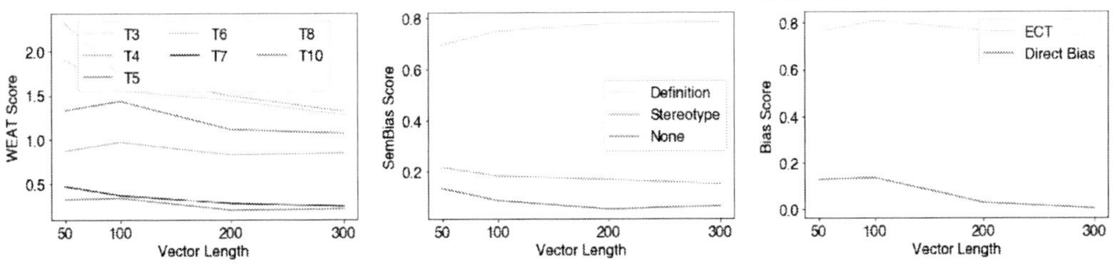

(d) WEAT scores for `GloVe` Wiki Gigaword (e) SEMBIAS scores for `GloVe` Wiki Gigaword (f) DIRECT BIAS and ECT scores for `GloVe` Wiki Gigaword

Figure 2: Bias scores with respect to the vector length.

`GloVe` Wiki embeddings are more likely to be correctly identified as gender-definition word pair but less likely to be correctly classified as a gender-stereotype word pair and gender unrelated word pairs if they were trained with large vector lengths.

The next analysis of this experimental result is concerned with how the DIRECT BIAS scores would be affected by the vector length. Figure 2c shows that following the increase of vector length in `GloVe` Twitter, we observe a decrease in the bias score. In Figure 2f, bias score of `GloVe` Wiki Gigaword increases from lower dimensions 50 to 100 but decreases beyond dimension 100. These results show that from four vector lengths used in each of the two corpora, most of them support the hypothesis that the larger dimension used resulted in smaller presence of gender bias. The rise of bias score of `GloVe` trained in Wiki Gigaword corpus from 50 to 100 dimension is the only instance that counters our hypothesis.

Lastly, Figure 2c shows a decrease in ECT score as vector length increases in `GloVe` Twitter only within dimensions of 25, 50, and 100. However, between 100 and 200, the bias score increases by 0.016. In addition, Figure 2f illustrates that the discovery of `GloVe` Wiki Gigaword in ECT is similar to that in DIRECT BIAS, that the bias increases from lower dimensions 50 to 100 but rapidly declines beyond dimension 100. Six of the eight pre-trained embeddings examined in this investigation support the finding that fairness improves as the number of dimensions increases.

Finally, most observations from the WEAT, SEMBIAS, DIRECT BIAS, and ECT scores indicate evidence for improved fairness in pre-trained word embeddings when the number of dimensions is increased. This result implies that lower dimensionality word embeddings are not expressive enough to capture all word associations and analogies, and that when the bias metric is applied to them, they become more biased than embeddings with larger dimensions.

6 Related Work

There has been a growing interest among researchers to tackle bias in word embeddings, herein we focus on previous work comparing different models and their characteristics.

Lauscher and Glavaš (2019) evaluated embedding space biases caused by four different models and found that `GloVe` embeddings are biased according to all 10 WEAT tests, while `fastText` exhibits significant biases only for a subset of tests. This finding broadly supports our finding where all smallest WEAT scores belong to `GloVe` pre-trained embeddings. However, their focus is different from our as their approach aims at understanding the consistency of the bias effects across languages, corpora, and embedding models.

Borah et al. (2021) compared the stability of the fairness results to those of the word embedding models used: fastText, GloVe, and word2vec, all of which were trained on Wikipedia. Among the three models, they discovered that fastText is the best stable word embedding model which results in the highest stability for its WEAT results. Badilla et al. (2020) implemented their proposed fairness framework, WEFE, by conducting case study where six publicly available pre-trained word embedding models are compared with respect to four bias metrics (e.g., WEAT, WEAT-ES, RND, RNSB). Consistent with our finding, they discovered that fastText rank first in WEAT.

Lauscher et al. (2019) proposed a general debiasing framework Debiasing Embeddings Implicitly and Explicitly (DEBIE). They used two bias metrics: WEAT Test 8 and ECT to compare the bias of CBOW, GloVe, and fastText trained in Wikipedia. They observed that fastText is more biased than GloVe in both metrics. While this contradicts our observations, their study did not utilise pre-trained models but manually trained them on the same corpus.

Popović et al. (2020) demonstrated the viability of their modified WEAT metric on three classes of biases (religion, gender and race) in three different publicly available word embeddings with vector length of 300: fastText, GloVe and word2vec. Their findings yielded that before debiasing, fastText has the least religion and race bias, while word2vec has the least gender bias. However, one of the study's discoveries opposes our findings where word2vec does not have the least gender bias. This difference may occur given the fact that the authors collected word sets from a number of different literature.

Furthermore, previous work considers the impact of word embedding vector length on the performance and the relation to fairness. Borah et al. (2021) looked at how the length of the vectors used in training fastText, GloVe, and word2vec affected their stability. The models' stability improves as the vector dimensions grow larger. On the other hand, Goldberg and Hirst (2017) found that word embeddings with smaller vectors are better at grouping similar words. This generalisation means that word embeddings with shorter vector lengths have a higher tendency to be biased. The results of our empirical study, obtained using more data and metrics, corroborate the above findings.

Much of the previous research has focused on proposing and evaluating debiasing techniques, modified metrics and fairness frameworks. Therefore, our study makes a major contribution to the research on fairness of word embeddings by empirically comparing the degree of bias of the most popular and easily accessible pre-trained word embeddings according to a variety of popular bias metrics, as well as the impact of vector length involved in the training process to its fairness.

7 Conclusion

The purpose of this study was to empirically assess the degree of fairness exhibited by different publicly available pre-trained word embeddings based on different bias metrics. To this end, we first analysed what are the most used pre-trained word embeddings and bias metrics by conducting a comprehensive literature survey. The results pointed out that the majority of the papers used three word embedding models (namely GloVe, word2vec, and fastText) and four bias metrics (namely WEAT, SEMBIAS, DIRECT BIAS, and ECT). Our results revealed that the most fair of the three pre-trained word embedding models evaluated is fastText. We also found that while using pre-trained embeddings, the influence of vector length on fairness must be carefully considered.

The scope of this study was limited in terms of selecting word list used to apply bias metrics to the word embeddings. We closely examined the earlier studies that may have influenced bias scores. In the future, we need a deeper analysis and explanation of the numerous fairness tendencies discovered in this study, such as the correlation with explicit gender gaps and survey data (Friedman et al., 2019a,b), and the extent to which the embeddings reproduce bias (Blodgett et al., 2021). Moreover, the study could be replicated by not only using pre-trained word embeddings models, but manually training models with different parameters on an identical text corpus. Further study could also be conducted to explore the fairness of contextual word embeddings (e.g., ELMo, Bert), the application bias in word embeddings (Goldfarb-Tarrant et al., 2021b), and bias in word embedding in languages with grammatical gender (Zhou et al., 2019).

Acknowledgments

M. Hort and F. Sarro are supported by the ERC grant 741278 (EPIC).

References

Ali Alwehaibi and Kaushik Roy. 2018. Comparison of pre-trained word vectors for arabic text classification using deep learning approach. In *2018 17th IEEE International Conference on Machine Learning and Applications (ICMLA)*, pages 1471–1474.

Maria Antoniak and David Mimno. 2018. Evaluating the stability of embedding-based word similarities. *Transactions of the Association for Computational Linguistics*, 6:107–119.

Oscar Araque, Ignacio Corcuera-Platas, J. Fernando Sánchez-Rada, and Carlos A. Iglesias. 2017. Enhancing deep learning sentiment analysis with ensemble techniques in social applications. *Expert Systems with Applications*, 77:236–246.

Murat Aydoğan and Ali Karci. 2020. Improving the accuracy using pre-trained word embeddings on deep neural networks for turkish text classification. *Physica A: Statistical Mechanics and its Applications*, 541:123288.

Marzieh Babaeianjelodar, Stephen Lorenz, Josh Gordon, Jeanna Matthews, and Evan Freitag. 2020. Quantifying Gender Bias in Different Corpora. In *Companion Proceedings of the Web Conference 2020*, pages 752–759, New York, NY, USA. ACM.

Pablo Badilla, Felipe Bravo-Marquez, and Jorge Pérez. 2020. WEFE: The word embeddings fairness evaluation framework. In *IJCAI International Joint Conference on Artificial Intelligence*, volume 2021-January, pages 430–436. International Joint Conferences on Artificial Intelligence.

Katherine Bailey and Sunny Chopra. 2018. Few-shot text classification with pre-trained word embeddings and a human in the loop. *arXiv preprint arXiv:1804.02063*.

Geetanjali Bihani and Julia Taylor Rayz. 2020. Model choices influence attributive word associations: A semi-supervised analysis of static word embeddings. In *2020 IEEE/WIC/ACM International Joint Conference on Web Intelligence and Intelligent Agent Technology (WI-IAT)*, pages 568–573. IEEE.

Su Lin Blodgett, Solon Barocas, Hal Daumé III au2, and Hanna Wallach. 2020. Language (technology) is power: A critical survey of "bias" in nlp.

Su Lin Blodgett, Gilsinia Lopez, Alexandra Olteanu, Robert Sim, and Hanna Wallach. 2021. Stereotyping Norwegian Salmon: An Inventory of Pitfalls in Fairness Benchmark Datasets. *ACL-IJCNLP 2021 - 59th Annual Meeting of the Association for Computational Linguistics and the 11th International Joint Conference on Natural Language Processing, Proceedings of the Conference*, pages 1004–1015.

Piotr Bojanowski, Edouard Grave, Armand Joulin, and Tomas Mikolov. 2017. Enriching Word Vectors with Subword Information. *Transactions of the Association for Computational Linguistics*, 5:135–146.

Tolga Bolukbasi, Kai Wei Chang, James Zou, Venkatesh Saligrama, and Adam Kalai. 2016a. Man is to computer programmer as woman is to homemaker? Debiasing word embeddings. In *Advances in Neural Information Processing Systems*, pages 4356–4364. Neural information processing systems foundation.

Tolga Bolukbasi, Kai-Wei Chang, James Zou, Venkatesh Saligrama, and Adam Kalai. 2016b. Quantifying and reducing stereotypes in word embeddings. *arXiv preprint arXiv:1606.06121*.

Angana Borah, Manash Pratim Barman, and Amit Awekar. 2021. Are Word Embedding Methods Stable and Should We Care About It?

Aylin Caliskan. 2017. Beyond Big Data: What Can We Learn from AI Models? In *Proceedings of the 10th ACM Workshop on Artificial Intelligence and Security*, pages 1–1, New York, NY, USA. ACM.

Aylin Caliskan, Joanna J. Bryson, and Arvind Narayanan. 2016. Semantics derived automatically from language corpora contain human-like biases. *Science*, 356(6334):183–186.

Mansi Chugh, Peter A. Whigham, and Grant Dick. 2018. Stability of word embeddings using word2vec. In *AI 2018: Advances in Artificial Intelligence*, pages 812–818, Cham. Springer International Publishing.

Clare Arrington. 2019. Assessing Bias Removal from Word Embeddings. *Student Research Submissions*.

Kevin Clark, Minh-Thang Luong, Quoc V Le, and Christopher D Manning. 2020. Electra: Pre-training text encoders as discriminators rather than generators. *arXiv preprint arXiv:2003.10555*.

Marta R. Costa-jussà and Adrià de Jorge. 2020. Fine-tuning neural machine translation on gender-balanced datasets. In *Proceedings of the Second Workshop on Gender Bias in Natural Language Processing*, pages 26–34, Barcelona, Spain (Online). Association for Computational Linguistics.

Kate Crawford. 2017. The trouble with bias - nips 2017 keynote - kate crawford nips2017.

Sunipa Dev, Tao Li, Jeff Phillips, and Vivek Srikumar. 2019. On Measuring and Mitigating Biased Inferences of Word Embeddings. *34th AAAI Conference on Artificial Intelligence, AAAI 2020*, 34(05):7659–7666.

Sunipa Dev, Tao Li, Jeff M Phillips, and Vivek Srikumar. 2020. Oscar: Orthogonal subspace correction and rectification of biases in word embeddings. *arXiv preprint arXiv:2007.00049*.

Sunipa Dev and Jeff M. Phillips. 2019. Attenuating bias in word vectors. *CoRR*, abs/1901.07656.

Amna Dridi, Mohamed Medhat Gaber, R Azad, and Jagdev Bhogal. 2018. k-nn embedding stability for word2vec hyper-parametrisation in scientific text. In *International Conference on Discovery Science*, pages 328–343. Springer.

Y Du, Y Wu, and M Lan. 2020. Exploring human gender stereotypes with word association test. In *2019 Conference on Empirical Methods in Natural Language Processing and 9th International Joint Conference on Natural Language Processing, EMNLP-IJCNLP 2019*, pages 6133–6143, Department of Computer Science and Technology, East China Normal University, China. Association for Computational Linguistics.

Yuhao Du and Kenneth Joseph. 2020. MDR Cluster-Debias: A Nonlinear WordEmbedding Debiasing Pipeline. *13th International Conference on Social Computing, Behavioral-Cultural Modeling and Prediction and Behavior Representation in Modeling and Simulation, SBP-BRiMS 2020*, 12268 LNCS:45–54.

Dumitru Erhan, Yoshua Bengio, Aaron Courville, Pierre-Antoine Manzagol, Pascal Vincent, and Samy Bengio. 2010. Why does unsupervised pre-training help deep learning? *Journal of Machine Learning Research*, 11(19):625–660.

Kawin Ethayarajh, David Duvenaud, and Graeme Hirst. 2019. Understanding Undesirable Word Embedding Associations. *57th Annual Meeting of the Association for Computational Linguistics, ACL 2019*, pages 1696–1705.

Anjalie Field, Su Lin Blodgett, Zeerak Waseem, and Yulia Tsvetkov. 2021. A Survey of Race, Racism, and Anti-Racism in NLP. *ACL-IJCNLP 2021 - 59th Annual Meeting of the Association for Computational Linguistics and the 11th International Joint Conference on Natural Language Processing, Proceedings of the Conference*, pages 1905–1925.

Scott Friedman, Sonja Schmer-Galunder, Anthony Chen, and Jeffrey Rye. 2019a. Relating word embedding gender biases to gender gaps: A cross-cultural analysis. In *Proceedings of the First Workshop on Gender Bias in Natural Language Processing*, pages 18–24.

Scott Friedman, Sonja Schmer-Galunder, Jeffrey Rye, Robert Goldman, and Anthony Chen. 2019b. Relating Linguistic Gender Bias, Gender Values, and Gender Gaps: An International Analysis.

Niklas Friedrich, Anne Lauscher, Simone Paolo Ponzetto, and Goran Glavaš. 2021. Debie: A platform for implicit and explicit debiasing of word embedding spaces. In *Proceedings of the 16th Conference of the European Chapter of the Association for Computational Linguistics: System Demonstrations*, pages 91–98.

Xianghua Fu, Wangwang Liu, Yingying Xu, and Laizhong Cui. 2017. Combine hownet lexicon to train phrase recursive autoencoder for sentence-level sentiment analysis. *Neurocomputing*, 241:18–27.

Nikhil Garg, Londa Schiebinger, Dan Jurafsky, and James Zou. 2018. Word embeddings quantify 100 years of gender and ethnic stereotypes. *Proceedings of the National Academy of Sciences of the United States of America*, 115(16):E3635–E3644.

Bhavya Ghai, Md Naimul Hoque, and Klaus Mueller. 2021. WordBias: An Interactive Visual Tool for Discovering Intersectional Biases Encoded in Word Embeddings. *2021 CHI Conference on Human Factors in Computing Systems: Making Waves, Combining Strengths, CHI EA 2021*.

Yoav Goldberg and Graeme Hirst. 2017. *Neural Network Methods in Natural Language Processing*. Morgan; Claypool Publishers.

Seraphina Goldfarb-Tarrant, Rebecca Marchant, Ricardo Muñoz Sánchez, Mugdha Pandya, and Adam Lopez. 2021a. Intrinsic bias metrics do not correlate with application bias. In *Proceedings of the 59th Annual Meeting of the Association for Computational Linguistics and the 11th International Joint Conference on Natural Language Processing (Volume 1: Long Papers)*, pages 1926–1940.

Seraphina Goldfarb-Tarrant, Rebecca Marchant, Ricardo Muñoz Sánchez, Mugdha Pandya, and Adam Lopez. 2021b. Intrinsic Bias Metrics Do Not Correlate with Application Bias. *Proceedings ofthe 59th Annual Meeting ofthe Association for Computational Linguistics and the 11th International Joint Conference on Natural Language Processing*, pages 1926–1940.

Hila Gonen and Yoav Goldberg. 2019. Lipstick on a Pig: Debiasing Methods Cover up Systematic Gender Biases in Word Embeddings But do not Remove Them. *2019 Conference of the North American Chapter of the Association for Computational Linguistics: Human Language Technologies, NAACL HLT 2019*, 1:609–614.

Anthony G. Greenwald, Debbie E. McGhee, and Jordan L.K. Schwartz. 1998. Measuring individual differences in implicit cognition: The implicit association test. *Journal of Personality and Social Psychology*, 74(6):1464–1480.

Wei Guo and Aylin Caliskan. 2021. Detecting emergent intersectional biases: Contextualized word embeddings contain a distribution of human-like biases. In

Proceedings of the 2021 AAAI/ACM Conference on AI, Ethics, and Society, pages 122–133.

Prakhar Gupta and Martin Jaggi. 2021. Obtaining Better Static Word Embeddings Using Contextual Embedding Models. In *Proceedings ofthe 59th Annual Meeting ofthe Association for Computational Linguistics*, pages 5241–5253.

E O Gyamfi, Y Rao, M Gou, and Y Shao. 2020. Deb2viz: Debiasing gender in word embedding data using subspace visualization. In *11th International Conference on Graphics and Image Processing, ICGIP 2019*, volume 11373, School of Information and Software Engineering, University of Electronic Science and Technology of China Chengdu, Sichuan, 610054, China. SPIE.

Johannes Hellrich and Udo Hahn. 2016. Bad Company—Neighborhoods in neural embedding spaces considered harmful. In *Proceedings of COLING 2016, the 26th International Conference on Computational Linguistics: Technical Papers*, pages 2785–2796, Osaka, Japan. The COLING 2016 Organizing Committee.

Max Hort, Maria Kechagia, Federica Sarro, and Mark Harman. 2021. A survey of performance optimization for mobile applications. *IEEE Transactions on Software Engineering*, pages 1–1.

Hwiyeol Jo and Ceyda Cinarel. 2019. Delta-training: Simple semi-supervised text classification using pretrained word embeddings. In *Proceedings of the 2019 Conference on Empirical Methods in Natural Language Processing and the 9th International Joint Conference on Natural Language Processing (EMNLP-IJCNLP)*, pages 3458–3463.

D Jonauskaite, A Sutton, N Cristianini, and C Mohr. 2021. English colour terms carry gender and valence biases: A corpus study using word embeddings. *PLoS ONE*, 16(6 June).

Daniel Jurafsky and James H. Martin. 2020. Speech and language processing: An introduction to natural language processing, computational linguistics, and speech recognition, 3rd edition draft. Https://web.stanford.edu/ jurafsky/slp3/.

Masahiro Kaneko and Danushka Bollegala. 2019. Gender-preserving Debiasing for Pre-trained Word Embeddings. *57th Annual Meeting of the Association for Computational Linguistics, ACL 2019*, pages 1641–1650.

Masahiro Kaneko and Danushka Bollegala. 2021. Debiasing pre-trained contextualised embeddings. In *Proceedings of the 16th Conference of the European Chapter of the Association for Computational Linguistics: Main Volume*, pages 1256–1266.

Saket Karve, Lyle Ungar, and João Sedoc. 2019. Conceptor debiasing of word representations evaluated on weat. In *Proceedings of the First Workshop on Gender Bias in Natural Language Processing*, pages 40–48.

Barbara Kitchenham. 2004. Procedures for performing systematic reviews. *Keele, UK, Keele University*, 33(2004):1–26.

Vaibhav Kumar and Tenzin Singhay Bhotia. 2020. Fair embedding engine: A library for analyzing and mitigating gender bias in word embeddings. *arXiv preprint arXiv:2010.13168*.

Vaibhav Kumar, Tenzin Singhay Bhotia, Vaibhav Kumar, and Tanmoy Chakraborty. 2020. Nurse is Closer to Woman than Surgeon? Mitigating Gender-Biased Proximities in Word Embeddings. *Transactions of the Association for Computational Linguistics*, 8:486–503.

Keita Kurita, Nidhi Vyas, Ayush Pareek, Alan W Black, and Yulia Tsvetkov. 2019. Measuring bias in contextualized word representations. In *Proceedings of the First Workshop on Gender Bias in Natural Language Processing*, pages 166–172.

Anne Lauscher and Goran Glavaš. 2019. Are we consistently biased? multidimensional analysis of biases in distributional word vectors. In *Proceedings of the Eighth Joint Conference on Lexical and Computational Semantics (* SEM 2019)*, pages 85–91.

Anne Lauscher, Goran Glavaš, Simone Paolo Ponzetto, and Ivan Vulić. 2019. A General Framework for Implicit and Explicit Debiasing of Distributional Word Vector Spaces. *34th AAAI Conference on Artificial Intelligence, AAAI 2020*, 34(05):8131–8138.

Anne Lauscher, Rafik Takieddin, Simone Paolo Ponzetto, and Goran Glavaš. 2020. Araweat: Multidimensional analysis of biases in arabic word embeddings. In *Proceedings of the Fifth Arabic Natural Language Processing Workshop*, pages 192–199.

Edward Lee. 2020. Gender bias in dictionary-derived word embeddings. Technical report.

Omer Levy, Yoav Goldberg, and Ido Dagan. 2015. Improving distributional similarity with lessons learned from word embeddings. *Transactions of the Association for Computational Linguistics*, 3:211–225.

Yang Li and Tao Yang. 2018. *Word Embedding for Understanding Natural Language: A Survey*, pages 83–104. Springer International Publishing, Cham.

Thomas Manzini, Yao Chong Lim, Yulia Tsvetkov, and Alan W. Black. 2019. Black is to Criminal as Caucasian is to Police: Detecting and Removing Multiclass Bias in Word Embeddings. *2019 Conference of the North American Chapter of the Association for Computational Linguistics: Human Language Technologies, NAACL HLT 2019*, 1:615–621.

William Martin, Federica Sarro, Yue Jia, Yuanyuan Zhang, and Mark Harman. 2017. A survey of app store analysis for software engineering. *IEEE Transactions on Software Engineering*, 43(9):817–847.

Chandler May, Alex Wang, Shikha Bordia, Samuel R. Bowman, and Rachel Rudinger. 2019. On Measuring Social Biases in Sentence Encoders. *2019 Conference of the North American Chapter of the Association for Computational Linguistics: Human Language Technologies, NAACL HLT 2019*, 1:622–628.

Tomas Mikolov, Kai Chen, Greg Corrado, and Jeffrey Dean. 2013. Efficient estimation of word representations in vector space. In *1st International Conference on Learning Representations, ICLR 2013 - Workshop Track Proceedings*. International Conference on Learning Representations, ICLR.

Harshit Mishra. 2020. Reducing Word Embedding Bias Using Learned Latent Structure. In *AI for Social Good Workshop*.

Kevin Patel and Pushpak Bhattacharyya. 2017. Towards lower bounds on number of dimensions for word embeddings. In *Proceedings of the Eighth International Joint Conference on Natural Language Processing (Volume 2: Short Papers)*, pages 31–36, Taipei, Taiwan. Asian Federation of Natural Language Processing.

Jeffrey Pennington, Richard Socher, and Christopher D. Manning. 2014. GloVe: Global vectors for word representation. In *EMNLP 2014 - 2014 Conference on Empirical Methods in Natural Language Processing, Proceedings of the Conference*, pages 1532–1543. Association for Computational Linguistics (ACL).

Bénédicte Pierrejean and Ludovic Tanguy. 2018. Towards qualitative word embeddings evaluation: Measuring neighbors variation. In *Proceedings of the 2018 Conference of the North American Chapter of the Association for Computational Linguistics: Student Research Workshop*, pages 32–39, New Orleans, Louisiana, USA. Association for Computational Linguistics.

Radomir Popović, Florian Lemmerich, and Markus Strohmaier. 2020. Joint Multiclass Debiasing of Word Embeddings. *25th International Symposium on Methodologies for Intelligent Systems, ISMIS 2020*, 12117 LNAI:79–89.

XiPeng Qiu, TianXiang Sun, YiGe Xu, YunFan Shao, Ning Dai, and XuanJing Huang. 2020. Pretrained models for natural language processing: A survey. *Science China Technological Sciences*, 63(10):1872–1897.

Yafeng Ren, Ruimin Wang, and Donghong Ji. 2016. A topic-enhanced word embedding for twitter sentiment classification. *Information Sciences*, 369:188–198.

Argentina Anna Rescigno, Eva Vanmassenhove, Johanna Monti, and Andy Way. 2020. A case study of natural gender phenomena in translation. a comparison of google translate, bing microsoft translator and deepl for english to italian, french and spanish. In *CLiC-it*.

Seyed Mahdi Rezaeinia, Rouhollah Rahmani, Ali Ghodsi, and Hadi Veisi. 2019. Sentiment analysis based on improved pre-trained word embeddings. *Expert Systems with Applications*, 117:139–147.

Thalea Schlender and Gerasimos Spanakis. 2020. 'thy algorithm shalt not bear false witness': An evaluation of multiclass debiasing methods on word embeddings. In *Benelux Conference on Artificial Intelligence*, pages 141–156. Springer.

Seungjae Shin, Kyungwoo Song, JoonHo Jang, Hyemi Kim, Weonyoung Joo, and Il-Chul Moon. 2020. Neutralizing gender bias in word embeddings with latent disentanglement and counterfactual generation. In *Findings of the Association for Computational Linguistics: EMNLP 2020*, pages 3126–3140.

Philippa Shoemark, Farhana Ferdousi Liza, Dong Nguyen, Scott Hale, and Barbara McGillivray. 2019. Room to Glo: A systematic comparison of semantic change detection approaches with word embeddings. In *Proceedings of the 2019 Conference on Empirical Methods in Natural Language Processing and the 9th International Joint Conference on Natural Language Processing (EMNLP-IJCNLP)*, pages 66–76, Hong Kong, China. Association for Computational Linguistics.

Maximilian Spliethöver and Henning Wachsmuth. 2020. Argument from old man's view: Assessing social bias in argumentation. In *Proceedings of the 7th Workshop on Argument Mining*, pages 76–87.

Emma Strubell, Ananya Ganesh, and Andrew McCallum. 2019. Energy and policy considerations for deep learning in NLP. *CoRR*, abs/1906.02243.

Adam Sutton, Thomas Lansdall-Welfare, and Nello Cristianini. 2018. Biased embeddings from wild data: Measuring, understanding and removing. In *International Symposium on Intelligent Data Analysis*, pages 328–339. Springer.

Chris Sweeney and Maryam Najafian. 2019. A transparent framework for evaluating unintended demographic bias in word embeddings. In *Proceedings of the 57th Annual Meeting of the Association for Computational Linguistics*, pages 1662–1667, Florence, Italy. Association for Computational Linguistics.

Chris Sweeney and Maryam Najafian. 2020. Reducing Sentiment Polarity for Demographic Attributes in Word Embeddings using Adversarial Learning. In *3rd ACM Conference on Fairness, Accountability, and Transparency, FAT* 2020*, pages 359–368, MIT, Cambridge, MA, United States. Association for Computing Machinery, Inc.

Yi Chern Tan and L. Elisa Celis. 2019. Assessing Social and Intersectional Biases in Contextualized Word Representations. *33rd Annual Conference on Neural Information Processing Systems, NeurIPS 2019*, 32.

Duyu Tang, Furu Wei, Nan Yang, Ming Zhou, Ting Liu, and Bing Qin. 2014. Learning sentiment-specific word embedding for Twitter sentiment classification. In *Proceedings of the 52nd Annual Meeting of the Association for Computational Linguistics (Volume 1: Long Papers)*, pages 1555–1565, Baltimore, Maryland. Association for Computational Linguistics.

Francisco Vargas and Ryan Cotterell. 2020. Exploring the Linear Subspace Hypothesis in Gender Bias Mitigation. *Proceedings of the 2020 Conference on Empirical Methods in Natural Language Processing (EMNLP)*, pages 2902–2913.

Bertie Vidgen, Dong Nguyen, Helen Margetts, Patricia Rossini, Rebekah Tromble, Kristina Toutanova, Anna Rumshisky, Luke Zettlemoyer, Dilek Hakkani-Tur, Iz Beltagy, et al. 2021. Introducing cad: the contextual abuse dataset. In *Proceedings of the 2021 Conference of the North American Chapter of the Association for Computational Linguistics: Human Language Technologies*, pages 2289–2303. Association for Computational Linguistics.

Ivan Vulic, Sebastian Ruder, and Anders Søgaard. 2020. Are all good word vector spaces isomorphic? *CoRR*, abs/2004.04070.

Angelina Wang and Olga Russakovsky. 2021. Directional bias amplification. *CoRR*, abs/2102.12594.

Tianlu Wang, Xi Victoria Lin, Nazneen Fatema Rajani, Bryan McCann, Vicente Ordonez, and Caiming Xiong. 2020. Double-Hard Debias: Tailoring Word Embeddings for Gender Bias Mitigation. In *Proceedings of the 58th Annual Meeting of the Association for Computational Linguistics*, pages 5443–5453, Stroudsburg, PA, USA. Association for Computational Linguistics.

Laura Wendlandt, Jonathan K. Kummerfeld, and Rada Mihalcea. 2018. Factors influencing the surprising instability of word embeddings. *Proceedings of the 2018 Conference of the North American Chapter of the Association for Computational Linguistics: Human Language Technologies, Volume 1 (Long Papers)*.

Claes Wohlin. 2014. Guidelines for snowballing in systematic literature studies and a replication in software engineering. In *Proceedings of the 18th International Conference on Evaluation and Assessment in Software Engineering*, EASE '14, New York, NY, USA. Association for Computing Machinery.

Zekun Yang and Juan Feng. 2019. A Causal Inference Method for Reducing Gender Bias in Word Embedding Relations. *34th AAAI Conference on Artificial Intelligence, AAAI 2020*, 34(05):9434–9441.

Haiyang Zhang, Alison Sneyd, and Mark Stevenson. 2020. Robustness and reliability of gender bias assessment in word embeddings: The role of base pairs. In *Proceedings of the 1st Conference of the Asia-Pacific Chapter of the Association for Computational Linguistics and the 10th International Joint Conference on Natural Language Processing*, pages 759–769.

Jieyu Zhao, Tianlu Wang, Mark Yatskar, Vicente Ordonez, and Kai-Wei Chang. 2017. Men also like shopping: Reducing gender bias amplification using corpus-level constraints. In *Proceedings of the 2017 Conference on Empirical Methods in Natural Language Processing*.

Jieyu Zhao, Yichao Zhou, Zeyu Li, Wei Wang, and Kai-Wei Chang. 2018. Learning Gender-Neutral Word Embeddings. *Proceedings of the 2018 Conference on Empirical Methods in Natural Language Processing, EMNLP 2018*, pages 4847–4853.

Pei Zhou, Weijia Shi, Jieyu Zhao, Kuan-Hao Huang, Muhao Chen, Ryan Cotterell, and Kai-Wei Chang. 2019. Examining Gender Bias in Languages with Grammatical Gender. *EMNLP-IJCNLP 2019 - 2019 Conference on Empirical Methods in Natural Language Processing and 9th International Joint Conference on Natural Language Processing*, pages 5276–5284.

A Repository Search

Repository	Data Fields
ACM	Publication title, abstract, keywords
arXiv	All
Google Scholar	In the title with exact phrase
IEEE	All metadata
Science Direct	Title, abstract or author-specified keywords
Scopus	TITLE-ABS-KEY

Table 5: Data Fields Used during Repository Search

B WEAT Target and Attribute Sets

Test	Target Sets	Attribute Sets
3	European American names vs African American names (5)	Pleasant vs Unpleasant (5)
4	European American names vs African American names (7)	Pleasant vs Unpleasant (5)
5	European American names vs African American names (7)	Pleasant vs Unpleasant (9)
6	Male names vs Female names	Career vs Family
7	Math vs Arts	Male terms vs Female Terms
8	Science vs Arts	Male terms vs Female Terms
10	Young people's names vs Old people's names	Pleasant vs Unpleasant (9)

Table 6: WEAT tests used in this study. Number 5, 7 and 9 next to the set refer to the sources (Caliskan et al., 2016) used to define the word list in their paper. The names in Test 3 differ from those in Test 4.

C Paper Selection Result

Model	Reference	Year	Venue
GloVe	(Bolukbasi et al., 2016a)	2016	NIPS
	(Garg et al., 2018)	2018	PNAS
	(Sutton et al., 2018)	2018	IDA
	(Lauscher et al., 2019)	2019	AAAI
	(Yang and Feng, 2019)	2019	AAAI
	(Lauscher and Glavaš, 2019)	2019	SemEval
	(Karve et al., 2019)	2019	ACL
	(Kaneko and Bollegala, 2019)	2019	ACL
	(Clare Arrington, 2019)	2019	UMW
	(Spliethöver and Wachsmuth, 2020)	2020	ArgMining
	(Guo and Caliskan, 2021)	2020	AAAI
	(Wang et al., 2020)	2020	ACL
	(Vargas and Cotterell, 2020)	2020	EMNLP
	(Popović et al., 2020)	2020	ISMIS
	(Shin et al., 2020)	2020	EMNLP
	(Kumar and Bhotia, 2020)	2020	ACL
	(Dev et al., 2020)	2020	arXiv
	(Lee, 2020)	2020	Stanford
	(Mishra, 2020)	2020	CRCS
	(Du and Joseph, 2020)	2020	SBP-BRiMS
	(Bihani and Rayz, 2020)	2020	WI-IAT
	(Du et al., 2020)	2020	EMNLP-IJCNLP
	(Sweeney and Najafian, 2020)	2020	FAT
	(Schlender and Spanakis, 2020)	2020	BNAIC
	(Borah et al., 2021)	2021	arXiv
	(Friedrich et al., 2021)	2021	AAAI
	(Jonauskaite et al., 2021)	2021	PLoS ONE
word2vec	(Bolukbasi et al., 2016b)	2016	ICML
	(Garg et al., 2018)	2018	PNAS
	(Karve et al., 2019)	2019	ACL
	(Clare Arrington, 2019)	2019	UMW
	(Schlender and Spanakis, 2020)	2020	BNAIC
	(Sweeney and Najafian, 2020)	2020	FAT
	(Wang et al., 2020)	2020	ACL
	(Vargas and Cotterell, 2020)	2020	EMNLP
	(Popović et al., 2020)	2020	ISMIS
	(Zhang et al., 2020)	2020	AACL-IJCNLP
	(Lee, 2020)	2020	Stanford
	(Du et al., 2020)	2020	EMNLP-IJCNLP
	(Bihani and Rayz, 2020)	2020	WI-IAT
	(Gyamfi et al., 2020)	2020	ICGIP
	(Borah et al., 2021)	2021	arXiv
	(Ghai et al., 2021)	2021	CHI EA
fastText	(Lauscher et al., 2019)	2019	AAAI
	(Lauscher and Glavaš, 2019)	2019	SemEval
	(Karve et al., 2019)	2019	ACL
	(Clare Arrington, 2019)	2019	UMW
	(Popović et al., 2020)	2020	ISMIS
	(Bihani and Rayz, 2020)	2020	WI-IAT
	(Borah et al., 2021)	2021	arXiv
	(Friedrich et al., 2021)	2021	AAAI
CBOW	(Lauscher et al., 2019)	2019	AAAI
	(Lauscher et al., 2020)	2020	AAAI
	(Friedrich et al., 2021)	2021	AAAI
dict2vec	(Lauscher et al., 2019)	2019	AAAI
	(Lee, 2020)	2020	Stanford
Numberbatch	(Schlender and Spanakis, 2020)	2020	BNAIC
SGNS	(Ethayarajh et al., 2019)	2019	ACL

Table 7: Studies on Standard Static Word Embedding Models.

Bias Metric	References	Year	Venue
Word Embedding Association Test (WEAT)	(Sutton et al., 2018)	2018	IDA
	(Lauscher et al., 2019)	2019	AAI
	(Lauscher and Glavaš, 2019)	2019	SemEval
	(Tan and Celis, 2019)	2019	NeurIPS
	(Karve et al., 2019)	2019	ACL
	(Gonen and Goldberg, 2019)	2019	NAACL HLT
	(Kurita et al., 2019)	2019	ACL
	(May et al., 2019)	2019	NAACL HLT
	(Ethayarajh et al., 2019)	2019	ACL
	(Schlender and Spanakis, 2020)	2020	BNAIC
	(Guo and Caliskan, 2021)	2020	AAAI
	(Wang et al., 2020)	2020	ACL
	(Vargas and Cotterell, 2020)	2020	EMNLP
	(Lee, 2020)	2020	Stanford
	(Popović et al., 2020)	2020	ISMIS
	(Du and Joseph, 2020)	2020	SBP-BRiMS
	(Shin et al., 2020)	2020	EMNLP
	(Dev et al., 2020)	2020	arXiv
	(Zhang et al., 2020)	2020	AACL-IJCNLP
	(Borah et al., 2021)	2021	arXiv
	(Friedrich et al., 2021)	2021	AAAI
SemBias	(Kaneko and Bollegala, 2019)	2019	ACL
	(Shin et al., 2020)	2020	EMNLP
	(Kumar et al., 2020)	2020	TACL
	(Mishra, 2020)	2020	CRCS
Neighbourhood Metric	(Wang et al., 2020)	2020	ACL
	(Zhang et al., 2020)	2020	AACL-IJCNLP
Direct Bias	(Babaeianjelodar et al., 2020)	2020	WWW
	(Zhang et al., 2020)	2020	AACL-IJCNLP
Double Bind	(Tan and Celis, 2019)	2019	NeurIPS
	(May et al., 2019)	2019	NAACL HLT
Angry Black Woman (ABW) Stereotype	(Tan and Celis, 2019)	2019	NeurIPS
	(May et al., 2019)	2019	NAACL HLT
ECT	(Dev et al., 2020)	2020	AAAI
	(Friedrich et al., 2021)	2021	
Indirect Bias	(Vargas and Cotterell, 2020)	2020	EMNLP
Equity Evaluation Corpus (EEC)	(Sweeney and Najafian, 2020)	2020	FAT
MAC	(Schlender and Spanakis, 2020)	2020	BNAIC
RNSB	(Schlender and Spanakis, 2020)	2020	BNAIC
Bias-by-projection	(Yang and Feng, 2019)	2019	AAAI
Contextual Embedding Association Test (CEAT)	(Guo and Caliskan, 2021)	2020	AAAI
Sentence Embedding Association Test (SEAT)	(Kaneko and Bollegala, 2021)	2021	ACL
BAT	(Friedrich et al., 2021)	2021	AAAI
IBT	(Friedrich et al., 2021)	2021	AAAIAAAI
SQ	(Friedrich et al., 2021)	2021	AAAI
RIPA	(Zhang et al., 2020)	2020	AACL-IJCNLP
RND	(Ghai et al., 2021)	2021	CHI EA
IAT	(Du et al., 2020)	2020	EMNLP-IJCNLP
K-means Accuracy	(Du and Joseph, 2020)	2020	SBP-BRiMS
SVM Accuracy	(Du and Joseph, 2020)	2020	SBP-BRiMS
Correlation Profession	(Du and Joseph, 2020)	2020	SBP-BRiMS

Table 8: Studies on Bias Metrics for Word Embeddings.

Mitigating Gender Stereotypes in Hindi and Marathi

Neeraja Kirtane*
Manipal Institute of Technology
Manipal, India
kirtane.neeraja@gmail.com

Tanvi Anand
University of Texas, Austin
Texas, USA
tanvianand@gmail.com

Abstract

As the use of natural language processing increases in our day-to-day life, the need to address gender bias inherent in these systems also amplifies. This is because the inherent bias interferes with the semantic structure of the output of these systems while performing tasks in natural language processing. While research is being done in English to quantify and mitigate bias, debiasing methods in Indic Languages are either relatively nascent or absent for some Indic languages altogether. Most Indic languages are gendered, i.e., each noun is assigned a gender according to each language's rules of grammar. As a consequence, evaluation differs from what is done in English. This paper evaluates the gender stereotypes in Hindi and Marathi languages. The methodologies will differ from the ones in the English language because there are masculine and feminine counterparts in the case of some words. We create a dataset of neutral and gendered occupation words, emotion words and measure bias with the help of Embedding Coherence Test (ECT) and Relative Norm Distance (RND). We also attempt to mitigate this bias from the embeddings. Experiments show that our proposed debiasing techniques reduce gender bias in these languages.

1 Introduction

Word embeddings are used in most natural language processing tools. Apart from capturing semantic information, word embeddings are also known to capture bias in society (Bolukbasi et al., 2016). While most research has been focused on languages like English, less research has been done on low-resource languages and languages that have a grammatical gender (Zhou et al., 2019). A language with grammatical has a gender associated with every noun irrespective of whether the noun is animate or inanimate, e.g., a river in Hindi has feminine gender. In contrast, words like writer have masculine and feminine counterparts. This gender association affects the pronouns, adjectives, and verb forms used during sentence construction. Grammatical genders in Hindi are masculine and feminine. In Marathi, there additionally exists a third neutral gender as well. Spoken by more than 600 million people, Hindi is the 3rd most spoken language in the world. Marathi is the 14th most spoken language with approximately 120 million speakers [1]. Given the expanse and the amount of people speaking these languages, it is essential to address the bias introduced by the computational applications of these languages.

We create a dataset of occupations and emotions. The occupation dataset consists of gendered and neutral occupation titles. The emotion dataset has words of different emotions like anger, fear, joy, and sadness. First, we identify existing gender bias by defining a subspace that captures the gender information. There are several ways to find this information. We use Principal Component Analysis (PCA) and Relational Inner Product Association (RIPA) (Ethayarajh et al., 2019). We use the existing metrics for evaluation: Embedding Coherence Test (Dev and Phillips, 2019), Relative Norm Distance (Garg et al., 2018). We modify these formulas so that they are correctly applicable to these gendered languages. We perform our experiments on the FastText word embeddings.

Next, we mitigate the gender bias found by the aforementioned using two approaches: Projection and Partial Projection. In summary, the key contributions of this paper are:

1. Dataset of emotions, and gendered and neutral occupations in Hindi and Marathi.

2. Methods to quantify the bias present in Hindi and Marathi word embeddings using the

*First author

[1] https://www.mentalfloss.com/article/647427/most-spoken-languages-world

Proceedings of the The 4th Workshop on Gender Bias in Natural Language Processing (GeBNLP), pages 145 - 150
July 15, 2022 ©2022 Association for Computational Linguistics

above dataset.

3. Mitigate the bias through existing debiasing techniques.

2 Related work

Previous work to quantify and measure bias was done by Bolukbasi et al. (2016). They tried to find out a gender subspace by using gender-definition pairs. They proposed a hard de-biasing method that identifies the gender subspace and tries to remove its components from the embeddings.

The majority amount of research on gender bias is being done in English, which is not gendered (Stanczak and Augenstein, 2021). Languages like Spanish or Hindi have a grammatical gender, i.e., every noun is assigned a gender. Zhou et al. (2019) was one of the first papers to examine bias in languages with grammatical gender like French and Spanish. They used a modified version of the Word Embedding Association Test (WEAT) (Caliskan et al., 2017) to quantify the bias.

Sun et al. (2019) suggested mitigation techniques to remove gender bias like data augmentation, gender-swapping, and hard de-biasing according to the downstream task in NLProc.

Being low-resource languages, there is less research done in languages like Hindi and Marathi. Previous work in Indic Languages was done by Pujari et al. (2019) where they built an SVM classifier to identify the bias and classify it. The problem with this method is that it needs a labeled gender dataset beforehand to train the classifier. Recent work by Ramesh et al. (2021) tries to find out bias in English-Hindi machine translation. They implement a modified version of the TGBI metric based on grammatical considerations for Hindi. TGBI metric is used to detect and evaluate gender bias in Machine Translation systems. Malik et al. (2021) measure Hindi specific societal biases like religion bias and caste bias along with gender bias.

3 Data

In Bolukbasi et al. (2016), the authors have compiled a list of professions in English and tried to find bias in them. Similarly, we compile a list of 166 professions, each in Hindi and Marathi languages. We split the professions into two parts, first is gender-neutral P_{neu} and the other is gendered P_{gen}. Similarly, we create a list of words of different emotions similar to the one in Kiritchenko and Mohammad (2018) in Hindi and Marathi languages. The emotions are broadly classified into four types: anger, fear, joy, and sadness.

We have verified this data with the help of 2 independent native speakers of these languages. We also create pair of feminine and masculine seed word pairs in both the languages to identify the gender subspace. For example: queen, king. We call them target words T. Target words for Hindi Language is shown in figure 1. The dataset is available here [2]

["महिला","पुरूष"] ["woman", "man"]

["बेटी", बेटा"] ["daughter", "son"]

["मां","पिता"] ["mother", "father"]

["लड़की", लड़का"] ["girl", "boy"]

["रानी", राजा"] ["queen", "king"]

["पत्नी", पति"] ["wife", "husband"]

Figure 1: Example of seed words in Hindi and their English translation

We test the bias on our data using FastText embeddings. FastText is a word embedding method that extends the word2vec model. Instead of learning vectors for words directly, FastText represents each word as an n-gram of characters. This helps capture the meaning of shorter words and allows the embeddings to understand suffixes and prefixes. A skip-gram model is trained to learn the embeddings once the word has been represented using character n-grams (Bojanowski et al., 2016).

Morphology is the field of linguistics that studies the internal structure of words. Morphologically rich languages refer to languages that contain a substantial amount of grammatical information (Comrie, 1999). Indic languages are morphologically rich because of the existence of a large number of different word forms. FastText embeddings are the best choice for Indian Languages as they are capable of capturing and integrating sub-word information using character n-gram embeddings

[2] https://github.com/neeraja1504/GenderBias_corpus

during training (Kunchukuttan et al., 2020).

4 Methodology

4.1 Bias Statement

Various definitions of bias exist and vary in research as explained in the paper (Blodgett et al., 2020). Our work focuses on stereotypical associations between masculine and feminine gender and professional occupations and emotions in FastText word embeddings. The classic example of "He is a doctor" and "She is a nurse" comes into play here. It is especially harmful to the representation of minority communities, since these stereotypes often end up undermining these communities (Moss-Racusin et al., 2012). Downstream NLP applications learn from these stereotypes, and the risk of discrimination on the basis of gender in this case keeps seeping further into the system.

Our work tries to de-correlate gender with occupation and emotions, which will help reduce bias in these systems.

4.2 Quantifying bias for Occupations and Emotions

We use the following methods to quantify the bias before and after debiasing. M_{gen} is used for gendered attributes like gendered occupations. M_{neu} is used for neutral attributes like emotions and neutral occupations. We use these two different methods because our data has two different parts — gendered and neutral.

4.2.1 For neutral occupations and emotions: M_{neu}

1. **ECT-n**: Dev and Phillips (2019) use this test to measure bias. We use the target word pairs T, and the neutral attributes list P_{neu} and emotions. We separate the target word pairs into masculine and feminine-targeted words respectively. For each of the pairs $\vec{mi}, \vec{fi}$ in T we create two means $\vec{a1}$ and $\vec{a2}$.

$$\vec{a1} = \frac{1}{|M|} \sum_{\vec{m} \in M} \vec{m} \tag{1}$$

$$\vec{a2} = \frac{1}{|F|} \sum_{\vec{f} \in F} \vec{f} \tag{2}$$

   M arc masculine word embeddings, F are feminine word embeddings of the target word pairs T. We then create two arrays, one with the cosine similarity between the neutral word embeddings and $\vec{a1}$, the other with the neutral word embeddings and $\vec{a2}$. We calculate the Spearman correlation between the rank orders of these two arrays found. Spearman rank correlation is a non-parametric test that is used to measure the degree of association between two variables. Higher the correlation, the less the bias. The range of the correlation is $[-1, 1]$. Ideally, the correlation should be equal to one as the professions or emotions should not depend upon gender. Debiasing should bring the value closer to one.

2. **RND-n**: Relative Norm Distance was first used by Garg et al. (2018). It captures the relative strength of the association of a neutral word with respect to two groups. As shown in equation 3 we average the masculine and feminine-targeted words in M, F in T respectively. For every attribute, $\vec{p}$ in P_{neu} and emotions we find the norm of the average of the target words and the attribute $\vec{p}$. The higher the value of the relative norm, the more biased our professions and emotions are. Debiasing should reduce this value and bring it closer to zero.

$$\sum_{\vec{p} \in P_{neu}} (||avg(M) - \vec{p}||_2 - ||avg(F) - \vec{p}||_2) \tag{3}$$

4.2.2 For gendered occupations: M_{gen}

1. **ECT-g**: We use the target word pairs T and the gendered professions list P_{gen}. Using $\vec{a1}$ found in equation 1 and $\vec{a2}$ found in equation 2. P_{gen} has masculine and feminine profession word pairs. We create two arrays, one with cosine similarity of masculine profession word embeddings and $\vec{a1}$. The other with the cosine similarity of feminine profession word embeddings and $\vec{a2}$. We calculate the Spearman correlation of the rank of these two arrays.

   Ideally, there should be a high correlation between these arrays. The masculine profession words' cosine similarity with masculine target words should equal feminine profession words' cosine similarity with feminine target words. The range of the correlation is $[-1, 1]$. Higher the correlation, the less the bias. Debiasing should bring the value closer to one.

Emotion	Metrics(%)	Baseline	Projection		Partial Projection	
			PCA	RIPA	PCA	RIPA
Anger	ECT ↑	57.2	94.5	38.1	**99.1**	99.0
	RND ↓	2.0	1.1	0.4	0.7	**0.3**
Fear	ECT ↑	86.8	97.8	77.4	**99.4**	98.9
	RND ↓	2.6	1.2	0.3	0.8	**0.2**
Joy	ECT ↑	75.2	96.1	81.1	**99.5**	99.2
	RND ↓	2.5	1.2	0.5	0.8	**0.3**
Sadness	ECT ↑	63.1	88.4	56.1	**99.4**	98.3
	RND ↓	3.8	1.7	0.7	0.9	**0.4**

Table 1: Hindi Emotion Results (Principal Component Analysis (PCA), Relational Inner Product Association (RIPA))

Emotion	Metrics(%)	Baseline	Projection		Partial Projection	
			PCA	RIPA	PCA	RIPA
Anger	ECT ↑	37.9	58.2	52.7	**96.1**	93.9
	RND ↓	0.61	0.53	0.10	0.33	**0.09**
Fear	ECT ↑	72.6	74.0	71.2	**96.4**	93.6
	RND ↓	0.50	0.41	0.11	0.29	**0.08**
Joy	ECT ↑	57.3	76.2	58.2	**93.4**	92.5
	RND ↓	0.60	0.61	0.13	0.39	**0.11**
Sadness	ECT ↑	69.6	80.2	68.9	**99.1**	96.9
	RND ↓	0.42	0.37	0.08	0.25	**0.07**

Table 2: Marathi Emotion Results

2. **RND-g**: As shown in equation 4 we average the masculine and feminine-targeted words in M, F in T, respectively. For every attribute pair $\vec{p1}$ and $\vec{p2}$ in P_{gen} we find the norm of the average of the masculine target words and $\vec{p1}$, feminine target words and $\vec{p2}$. The higher the value of the relative norm, the more biased the professions are. Debiasing should reduce this value and bring it closer to zero.

$$\sum_{\vec{p1},\vec{p2} \in P} (||avg(M) - \vec{p1}||_2 - ||avg(F) - \vec{p2}||_2) \tag{4}$$

4.3 Debiasing techniques

4.3.1 Finding out the gender subspace

We need a vector $\vec{v_b}$ that represents the gender direction. We find this in the following ways: using RIPA and PCA.

1. **RIPA**: Ethayarajh et al. (2019) first used this subspace to capture gender information. We define a bias vector $\vec{v_b}$ which defines the gender direction. Given the target set T containing masculine and feminine words, for each T_j in T, we find out $T_f - T_m$ and stack them to create an array. T_f is the feminine word embedding, T_m is the masculine word embedding. We find the first principal component using Principal Component Analysis (PCA) of the array found above. This component captures the gender information of the given embeddings.

2. **PCA**: In this method, given T, we find out the average a of the masculine and feminine word embeddings for each given pair. We then compute $T_f - a$ and $T_m - a$ for each T_j in T. We stack them into an array and find out the first component using the PCA of the above array.

4.3.2 Debiasing methods

Bolukbasi et al. (2016) used Hard Debiasing to mitigate bias. This method needs additional seed words which are then trained on a SVM to find out if the word is biased or neutral. Thus, not all words are debiased in the vocabulary except the chosen ones. This makes the method not fully automatic.

Here we use more straightforward methods to

Metric	Base	Projection		Partial Proj.	
(%)		PCA	RIPA	PCA	RIPA
ECT-n↑	86.0	95.6	81.4	**99.7**	98.9
RND-n↓	40.4	19.3	6.2	10.9	**6.2**
ECT-g↑	69	71.4	85.7	**90.4**	88.0
RND-g↓	1.79	1.81	1.79	**1.52**	1.70

Table 3: Results for Hindi occupations. RND-g is not in % for better readability

Metric	Base	Projection		Partial Proj	
(%)		PCA	RIPA	PCA	RIPA
ECT-n ↑	51.4	60.6	53.6	**99.7**	96.5
RND-n↓	3.1	3.0	3.0	01.8	**0.5**
ECT-g ↑	42.5	21.5	23.8	64.2	**76.2**
RND-g↓	2.58	2.50	2.54	2.02	**1.97**

Table 4: Results for Marathi occupations. RND-g is not in % for better readability

debias our data.

1. **Projection**: One way to remove bias is to make all the vectors orthogonal to the gender direction. Therefore, we remove the component of $\vec{v_b}$ from all the vectors. This ensures that there is no component along the gender direction.

$$\vec{w} = \vec{w} - (\vec{w} \cdot \vec{v_b})\vec{v_b} \quad (5)$$

2. **Partial Projection**: One problem with the debiasing using linear projection is that it changes some word vectors which are gendered by definition, e.g., king, queen. Let $\mu = \frac{1}{m}\sum_{j=1}^{m} \mu j$ where $\mu j = \frac{1}{|T_j|}\sum_{t\in T_j} t$ be the mean of a target pair. Here m is the length of T. We suggest the new vector as shown in equation 6. This is similar to the linear projection approach, but instead of zero magnitude along the gender direction, we project a magnitude of constant μ along with it. This adds a constant to the debiasing term.

$$\vec{w} = \vec{w} - (\vec{w} \cdot \vec{v_b})\vec{v_b} + \mu \quad (6)$$

5 Results and Discussion

Table 1 and 2 show results for the emotions in Hindi and Marathi respectively. We observe that anger is the most biased in both languages according to the ECT metric as it has the lowest value. Amongst the debiasing techniques, we see that partial projection with RIPA works the best for the ECT metric and partial projection with PCA works the best for the RND metric.

ECT-n and RND-n are results for neutral occupations, and ECT-g and RND-g are for gendered occupations. Table 3 shows the results for both gendered and neutral occupations in Hindi. We see that partial projection We see that for neutral occupations, partial projection with PCA works the best for ECT and partial projection with RIPA works the best for RND. For gendered occupations, we see that partial projection with PCA works the best for both ECT and RND.

Table 4 shows the results for both gendered and neutral occupations in Marathi. We see that the best results are obtained for neutral occupations with partial projection with PCA for ECT and partial projection with RIPA for RND. For gendered occupations, we see that we get the best results with partial projection with RIPA for ECT and RND.

However, we observe some anomalies in the results when projection debiasing method is used. We hypothesize that completely removing the gender information changes some vectors, which are masculine or feminine, by the grammatical definition of the gender. For example, words like king, grandfather and boy which are masculine by the grammatical definition of gender should preserve their gender information. Hence we note that partial projection performs the best because it has a gender component to it.

6 Conclusion and Future work

In this paper, we attempted to find gender stereotypes on occupations and emotions and tried to debias them. Embedding Coherence Test and Relative Norm Distance were used as a bias metric in the gender subspace. The debiasing methods used were projection and partial projection. But we see that partial projection as a debiasing method works the best in most cases.

Future work could include trying out these techniques on downstream tasks and checking the performance before and after debiasing. The main problem with experimenting on downstream tasks is the availability of datasets in these languages. We would also like to experiment with debiasing contextual embeddings and large language models. Apart from that we would also like to address other types of bias like religion, social and cultural, which are particularly inherent in Hindi and

Marathi.

7 Acknowledgements

We are grateful to Anna Currey, Krithika Ramesh, Gauri Gupta, Sahil Khose, Soham Tiwari for reviewing the manuscript and helping in writing the bias statement.

References

Su Lin Blodgett, Solon Barocas, Hal Daumé III, and Hanna Wallach. 2020. Language (technology) is power: A critical survey of "bias" in nlp. In *Proceedings of the 58th Annual Meeting of the Association for Computational Linguistics*, pages 5454–5476.

Piotr Bojanowski, Edouard Grave, Armand Joulin, and Tomás Mikolov. 2016. Enriching word vectors with subword information. *CoRR*, abs/1607.04606.

Tolga Bolukbasi, Kai-Wei Chang, James Y Zou, Venkatesh Saligrama, and Adam T Kalai. 2016. Man is to computer programmer as woman is to homemaker? debiasing word embeddings. *Advances in neural information processing systems*, 29:4349–4357.

Aylin Caliskan, Joanna J Bryson, and Arvind Narayanan. 2017. Semantics derived automatically from language corpora contain human-like biases. *Science*, 356(6334):183–186.

Bernard Comrie. 1999. Grammatical gender systems: a linguist's assessment. *Journal of Psycholinguistic research*, 28(5):457–466.

Sunipa Dev and Jeff Phillips. 2019. Attenuating bias in word vectors. In *The 22nd International Conference on Artificial Intelligence and Statistics*, pages 879–887. PMLR.

Kawin Ethayarajh, David Duvenaud, and Graeme Hirst. 2019. Understanding undesirable word embedding associations. In *Proceedings of the 57th Annual Meeting of the Association for Computational Linguistics*, pages 1696–1705, Florence, Italy. Association for Computational Linguistics.

Nikhil Garg, Londa Schiebinger, Dan Jurafsky, and James Zou. 2018. Word embeddings quantify 100 years of gender and ethnic stereotypes. *Proceedings of the National Academy of Sciences*, 115(16):E3635–E3644.

Svetlana Kiritchenko and Saif M Mohammad. 2018. Examining gender and race bias in two hundred sentiment analysis systems. *arXiv preprint arXiv:1805.04508*.

Anoop Kunchukuttan, Divyanshu Kakwani, Satish Golla, Avik Bhattacharyya, Mitesh M Khapra, Pratyush Kumar, et al. 2020. Ai4bharat-indicnlp corpus: Monolingual corpora and word embeddings for indic languages. *arXiv preprint arXiv:2005.00085*.

Vijit Malik, Sunipa Dev, Akihiro Nishi, Nanyun Peng, and Kai-Wei Chang. 2021. Socially aware bias measurements for hindi language representations. *arXiv preprint arXiv:2110.07871*.

Corinne A Moss-Racusin, John F Dovidio, Victoria L Brescoll, Mark J Graham, and Jo Handelsman. 2012. Science faculty's subtle gender biases favor male students. *Proceedings of the national academy of sciences*, 109(41):16474–16479.

Arun K Pujari, Ansh Mittal, Anshuman Padhi, Anshul Jain, Mukesh Jadon, and Vikas Kumar. 2019. Debiasing gender biased hindi words with word-embedding. In *Proceedings of the 2019 2nd International Conference on Algorithms, Computing and Artificial Intelligence*, pages 450–456.

Krithika Ramesh, Gauri Gupta, and Sanjay Singh. 2021. Evaluating gender bias in hindi-english machine translation. In *Proceedings of the 3rd Workshop on Gender Bias in Natural Language Processing*, pages 16–23.

Karolina Stanczak and Isabelle Augenstein. 2021. A survey on gender bias in natural language processing. *arXiv preprint arXiv:2112.14168*.

Tony Sun, Andrew Gaut, Shirlyn Tang, Yuxin Huang, Mai ElSherief, Jieyu Zhao, Diba Mirza, Elizabeth Belding, Kai-Wei Chang, and William Yang Wang. 2019. Mitigating gender bias in natural language processing: Literature review. In *Proceedings of the 57th Annual Meeting of the Association for Computational Linguistics*, pages 1630–1640, Florence, Italy. Association for Computational Linguistics.

Pei Zhou, Weijia Shi, Jieyu Zhao, Kuan-Hao Huang, Muhao Chen, Ryan Cotterell, and Kai-Wei Chang. 2019. Examining gender bias in languages with grammatical gender. In *Proceedings of the 2019 Conference on Empirical Methods in Natural Language Processing and the 9th International Joint Conference on Natural Language Processing (EMNLP-IJCNLP)*, pages 5276–5284, Hong Kong, China. Association for Computational Linguistics.

Choose Your Lenses: Flaws in Gender Bias Evaluation

Hadas Orgad
orgad.hadas@cs.technion.ac.il

Yonatan Belinkov*
belinkov@technion.ac.il

Technion – Israel Institute of Technology

Abstract

Considerable efforts to measure and mitigate gender bias in recent years have led to the introduction of an abundance of tasks, datasets, and metrics used in this vein. In this position paper, we assess the current paradigm of gender bias evaluation and identify several flaws in it. First, we highlight the importance of extrinsic bias metrics that measure how a model's performance on some task is affected by gender, as opposed to intrinsic evaluations of model representations, which are less strongly connected to specific harms to people interacting with systems. We find that only a few extrinsic metrics are measured in most studies, although more can be measured. Second, we find that datasets and metrics are often coupled, and discuss how their coupling hinders the ability to obtain reliable conclusions, and how one may decouple them. We then investigate how the choice of the dataset and its composition, as well as the choice of the metric, affect bias measurement, finding significant variations across each of them. Finally, we propose several guidelines for more reliable gender bias evaluation.

1 Introduction

A large body of work has been devoted to measurement and mitigation of social biases in natural language processing (NLP), with a particular focus on gender bias (Sun et al., 2019; Blodgett et al., 2020; Garrido-Muñoz et al., 2021; Stanczak and Augenstein, 2021). These considerable efforts have been accompanied by various tasks, datasets, and metrics for evaluation and mitigation of gender bias in NLP models. In this position paper, we critically assess the predominant evaluation paradigm and identify several flaws in it. These flaws hinder progress in the field, since they make it difficult to ascertain whether progress has been actually made.

Gender bias metrics can be divided into two groups: *extrinsic* metrics, such as performance difference across genders, measure gender bias with respect to a specific downstream task, while *intrinsic* metrics, such as WEAT (Caliskan et al., 2017), are based on the internal representations of the language model. We argue that measuring extrinsic metrics is crucial for building confidence in proposed metrics, defining the harms caused by biases found, and justifying the motivation for debiasing a model and using the suggested metrics as a measure of success. However, we find that many studies on gender bias only measure intrinsic metrics. As a result, it is difficult to determine what harm the presumably found bias may be causing. When it comes to gender bias mitigation efforts, improving intrinsic metrics may produce an illusion of greater success than reality, since their correlation to downstream tasks is questionable (Goldfarb-Tarrant et al., 2021; Cao et al., 2022). In the minority of cases where extrinsic metrics are reported, only few metrics are measured, although it is possible and sometimes crucial to measure more.

Additionally, gender bias measures are often applied as a *dataset* coupled with a *measurement technique* (a.k.a metric), but we show that they can be separated. A single gender bias metric can be measured using a wide range of datasets, and a single dataset can be applied to a wide variety of metrics. We then demonstrate how the choice of gender bias metric and the choice of dataset can each affect the resulting measures significantly. As an example, measuring the same metric on the same model with an imbalanced or a balanced dataset[1] may result in very different results. It is thus difficult to compare newly proposed metrics and debiasing methods with previous ones, hindering progress in the field.

To summarize, our contributions are:

- We argue that extrinsic metrics are important

* Supported by the Viterbi Fellowship in the Center for Computer Engineering at the Technion.

[1]Balanced with respect to the amount of examples for each gender, per task label.

Proceedings of the The 4th Workshop on Gender Bias in Natural Language Processing (GeBNLP), pages 151 - 167
July 15, 2022 ©2022 Association for Computational Linguistics

for defining harms (§2), but researchers do not use them enough even though they can (§5).

- We demonstrate the coupling of datasets with metrics and the feasibility of other combinations (§3).

- On observing that a specific metric can be measured on many possible datasets and vice-versa, we demonstrate how the choice and composition of a dataset (§4), as well as the choice of bias metric to measure (§5), can strongly influence the measured results.

- We provide guidelines for researchers on how to correctly evaluate gender bias (§6).

Bias Statement This paper examines metrics and datasets that are used to measure gender bias, and discusses several pitfalls in the current paradigm. As a result of the observations and proposed guidelines in this work, we hope that future results and conclusions will become clearer and more reliable.

The definition of gender bias in this paper is through the discussed metrics, as each metric reflects a different definition. Some of the examined metrics are measured on concrete downstream tasks (extrinsic metrics), while others are measured on internal model representations (intrinsic metrics). The definitions of intrinsic and extrinsic metrics do not align perfectly with the definitions of allocational and representational harms (Kate Crawford, 2017). In the case of allocational harm, resources or opportunities are unfairly allocated due to bias. Representative harm, on the other hand, is when a certain group is negatively represented or ignored by the system. Extrinsic metrics can be used to quantify both allocational and representational harms, while intrinsic metrics can only quantify representational harms, in some cases.

There are also other important pitfalls that are not discussed in this paper, like the focus on high-resource languages such as English and the binary treatment of gender (Sun et al., 2019; Stanczak and Augenstein, 2021; Dev et al., 2021). Inclusive research of non-binary genders would require a new set of methods, which could benefit from the observations in this work.

2 The Importance of Extrinsic Metrics in Defining Harms

In this paper, we divide metrics for gender bias to three groups:

- **Extrinsic performance:** measures how a model's performance is affected by gender, and is calculated with respect to particular gold labels. For example, the True Positive Rate (TPR) gap between female and male examples.

- **Extrinsic prediction:** measures model's predictions, such as the output probabilities, but the bias is not calculated with respect to some gold labels. Instead, the bias is measured by the effect of gender or stereotypes on model predictions. For example, the probability gap can be measured on a language model queried on two sentences, one pro-stereotypical ("he is an engineer") and another anti-stereotypical ("she is an engineer").

- **Intrinsic:** measures bias in internal model representations, and is not directly related to any downstream task. For example, WEAT.

It is crucial to define how measured bias harms those interacting with the biased systems (Barocas et al., 2017; Kate Crawford, 2017; Blodgett et al., 2020; Bommasani et al., 2021). Extrinsic metrics are important for motivating bias mitigation and for accurately defining "why the system behaviors that are described as 'bias' are harmful, in what ways, and to whom" (Blodgett et al., 2020), since they clearly demonstrate the performance disparity between protected groups.

For example, in a theoretical CV-filtering system, one can measure the TPR gap between female and male candidates. A gap in TPR favoring men means that, given a set of valid candidates, the system picks valid male candidates more often than valid female candidates. The impact of this gap is clear: Qualified women are overlooked because of bias. In contrast, consider an intrinsic metric such as WEAT (Caliskan et al., 2017), which is derived from the proximity (in vector space) of words like "career" or "family" to "male" or "female" names. If one finds that male names relate more to career and female names relate more to family, the consequences are unclear. In fact, Goldfarb-Tarrant et al. (2021) found that WEAT does not correlate with other extrinsic metrics. However, many studies report only intrinsic metrics (a third of the papers we reviewed, §5).

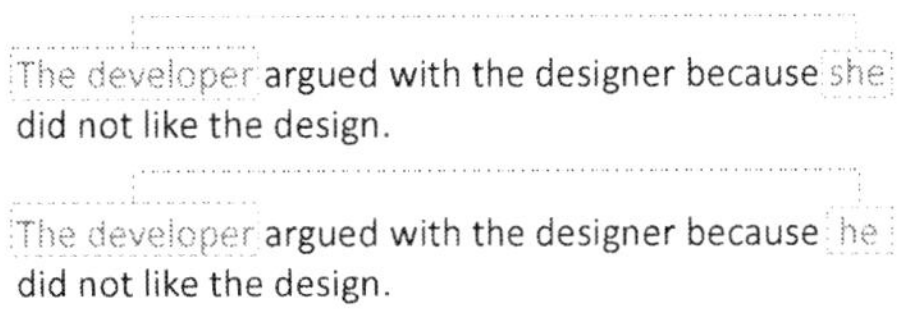

Figure 1: Coreference resolution example from Winobias: a pair of anti-stereotypical (top) and pro-stereotypical examples (bottom). Developers are stereotyped to be males.

3 Coupling of Datasets and Metrics

In this section, we discuss how datasets and metrics for gender bias evaluation are typically coupled, how they may be decoupled, and why this is important. We begin with a representative test case, followed by a discussion of the general phenomenon.

3.1 Case study: Winobias

Coreference resolution aims to find all textual expressions that refer to the same real-world entities. A popular dataset for evaluating gender bias in coreference resolution systems is Winobias (Zhao et al., 2018a). It consists of Winograd schema (Levesque et al., 2012) instances: two sentences that differ only by one or two words, but contain ambiguities that are resolved differently in the two sentences based on world knowledge and reasoning. Winobias sentences consist of an anti- and a pro- stereotypical sentence, as shown in Figure 1. Coreference systems should be able to resolve both sentences correctly, but most perform poorly on the anti-stereotypical ones (Zhao et al., 2018a, 2019; de Vassimon Manela et al., 2021; Orgad et al., 2022).

Winobias was originally proposed as an extrinsic evaluation dataset, with a reported metric of anti- and pro- stereotypical performance disparity. However, other metrics can also be measured, both intrinsic and extrinsic, as shown in several studies (Zhao et al., 2019; Nangia et al., 2020b; Orgad et al., 2022). For example, one can measure how many stereotypical choices the model preferred over anti-stereotypical choices (an extrinsic performance measure), as done on Winogender (Rudinger et al., 2018), a similar dataset. Winobias sentences can also be used to evaluate language models (LMs), by evaluating if an LM gives higher probabilities to pro-stereotypical sentences (Nangia et al., 2020b) (an extrinsic prediction measure). Winobias can also be used for intrinsic metrics, for example as a template for SEAT (May et al., 2019a) and CEAT (Guo and Caliskan, 2021) (contextual extensions of WEAT). Each of these metrics reveals a different facet of gender bias in a model. An explicit measure of how many pro-stereotypical choices were preferred over anti-stereotypical choices has a different meaning than measuring a performance metric gap between two different genders. Additionally, measuring an intrinsic metric on Winobias may be help tie the results to the model's behavior on the same dataset in the downstream coreference resolution task.

3.2 Many possible combinations for datasets and metrics

Winobias is one example out of many. In fact, benchmarks for gender bias evaluation are typically proposed as a package of two components:

1. **A dataset** on which the benchmark task is performed.
2. **A metric**, which is the particular method used to calculate bias of a model on the dataset.

Usually, these benchmarks are considered as a bundle; however, they can often be decoupled, mixed, and matched, as discussed in the Winobias test case above. The work by Delobelle et al. (2021) is an exception, in that they gathered a set of templates from diverse studies and tested them using the same metric.

In Table 1, we present possible combinations of datasets (rows) and metrics (columns) from the gender bias literature. The metrics are partitioned according to the three classes of metrics defined in Section 2. We present only metrics valid for assessing bias in contextualized LMs (rather than static word embeddings), since they are the common practice nowadays. The table does not claim to be exhaustive, but rather illustrates how metrics and datasets can be repurposed in many different ways. The metrics are described in appendix A, but the categories are very general and even a single column like "Gap (Label)" represents a wide variety of metrics that can be measured.

Table 1 shows that many metrics are compatible across many datasets (many ✓'s in the same column), and that datasets can be used to measure a variety of metrics other than those typically measured (many ✓'s in the same row). Some datasets, such as Bias in Bios (De-Arteaga et al., 2019), have numerous metrics compatible, while others have

Dataset \ Metric	Extrinsic Performance			Extrinsic Predictions				Intrinsic						
	Gap (Label)	Gap (Stereo)	Gap (Gender)	% or # of Answer Changed	% or # Model Prefers Stereotype	Pred Gap	LM Prediction On Target words	SEAT	CEAT	Probe	Cluster	Nearest Neighbors	Cos	PCA
Winogender (Rudinger et al., 2018)	✓	✓⃝	✓	✓	✓	✓	✓		✓	✓	✓	✓	✓	✓
Winobias (Zhao et al., 2018a)	✓	✓⃝	✓	✓	✓	✓	✓		✓	✓	✓	✓	✓	✓
Gap (Webster et al., 2018)			✓⃝	✓(aug)										
Crow-S (Nangia et al., 2020a)					✓⃝		✓		✓	✓	✓	✓	✓	✓
StereoSet (Nadeem et al., 2021)					✓⃝		✓		✓	✓	✓	✓	✓	✓
Bias in Bios (De-Arteaga et al., 2019)	✓⃝	✓	✓	✓(aug)	✓(aug)	✓(aug)	✓		✓	✓	✓	✓	✓	✓
EEC (Kiritchenko and Mohammad, 2018)						✓⃝	✓		✓	✓	✓	✓		
STS-B for genders (Beutel et al., 2020)					✓	✓⃝	✓	✓	✓	✓	✓	✓	✓	✓
Dev et al. (2020a) (NLI)				✓	✓	✓	✓		✓	✓	✓	✓	✓	✓
PTB, WikiText, CNN/DailyMail (Bordia and Bowman, 2019)							✓⃝		✓					
BOLD (Dhamala et al., 2021)							✓⃝							
Templates from May et al. (2019a)							✓	✓⃝	✓	✓	✓	✓	✓	✓
Templates from Kurita et al. (2019)							✓⃝	✓⃝	✓	✓	✓	✓	✓	✓
DisCo templates (Beutel et al., 2020)					✓		✓⃝		✓	✓	✓	✓	✓	✓
BEC-Pro templates (Bartl et al., 2020)					✓		✓⃝		✓	✓	✓	✓	✓	✓
English-German news corpus (Basta et al., 2021)							✓		✓	✓⃝	✓⃝	✓⃝	✓⃝	✓⃝
Reddit (Guo and Caliskan 2021, Voigt et al. 2018)							✓		✓⃝	✓	✓	✓	✓	✓
MAP (Cao and Daumé III, 2021)			✓⃝	✓					✓	✓	✓	✓	✓	✓
GICoref (Cao and Daumé III, 2021)			✓⃝						✓	✓	✓	✓	✓	✓

Table 1: Combinations of gender bias datasets and metrics in the literature. ✓ marks a feasible combination of a metric and a dataset. ✓⃝ marks the original metrics used on the dataset, and ✓(aug) marks metrics that can be measured after augmenting the dataset such that every example is matched with a counterexample of another gender. Extrinsic performance metrics depend on gold labels while extrinsic prediction metrics do not. A full description of the metrics is given in Appendix A.

fewer, but still multiple, compatible metrics. Bias in Bios has many compatible metrics since it has information that can be used to calculate them: in addition to gold labels, it also has gender labels and clear stereotype definitions derived from the labels which are professions. Text corpora and template data, which do not address a specific task (bottom seven rows), are mostly compatible with intrinsic metrics. The compatibility of intrinsic metrics with many datasets may explain why papers report intrinsic metrics more often (§5). Additionally, Table 1 indicates that not many datasets can be used to measure extrinsic metrics, particularly extrinsic performance metrics that require gold labels. On the other hand, measuring LM prediction on target words, which we consider as extrinsic, can be done on many datasets. This is useful for analyzing bias when dealing with LMs. It can be done by computing bias metrics from the LM output predictions, such as the mean probability gap when predicting the word "he" versus "she" in specific contexts. Also, some templates are valid for measuring extrinsic prediction metrics, especially stereotype-related metrics, as they were developed with explicit stereotypes in mind (such as profession-related stereotypes).

Based on Table 1, it is clear that there are many possible ways to measure gender bias in the literature, but they all fall under the vague category of "gender bias". Each of the possible combinations gives a different definition, or interpretation, for gender bias. The large number of different metrics makes it difficult or even impossible to compare different studies, including proposed gender bias mitigation methods. This raises questions about the validity of results derived from specific combinations of measurements. In the next two sections, we demonstrate how the choice of datasets and metrics can affect the bias measurement.

4 Effect of Dataset on Measured Results

The choice of data to measure bias has an impact on the calculated bias. Many researchers used sentence templates that are "semantically bleached" (e.g., "This is <word>.", "<person> studied <profession> at college.") to adjust metrics developed for static word embeddings to contextualized representations (May et al., 2019b; Kurita et al., 2019; Webster et al., 2020; Bartl et al., 2020). Delobelle et al. (2021) found that the choice of templates significantly affected the results, with little correlation between different templates. Additionally, May et al. (2019b) reported that templates are not as semantically bleached as expected.

Another common feature of bias measurement methods is the use of hand-curated word lexicons by almost every bias metric in the literature. Antoniak and Mimno (2021) reported that the lexicon choice can greatly affect bias measurement, resulting in differing conclusions between different lexicons.

4.1 Case study: balancing the test data

Another important variable in gender bias evaluation, often overlooked in the literature, is the composition of the test dataset. Here, we demonstrate

Metric	Testing balancing		
	Original	Oversampled	Subsampled
TPR (p)	0.78	0.75	0.75
TPR (s)	2.35	2.41	2.38
FPR (p)	0.61	0.59	0.57
FPR (s)	0.08	0.08	0.08
Precision (p)	0.63	0.64	0.38*
Precision (s)	0.22	0.03*	**0.02***
Separation (s)	2.27	**0.23***	0.35*
Sufficiency (s)	1.94	**0.74***	9.15*
Independence (s)	0.14	**0.01***	**0.01***

Table 2: Metrics measured on Bias in Bios, separated to performance gap metrics (above the line) and statistical fairness metrics (below the line). Metrics are measured on the original test split, and on a subsampled and oversampled version of it. * marks statistically significant difference in a metric compared to the baseline (Original), using Pitman's permutation test ($p < 0.05$).

this by comparing metrics on different test sets, which come from the same dataset but have a different balance of examples. Bias in Bios (De-Arteaga et al., 2019) involves predicting an occupation from a biography text. These occupations are not balanced across genders, so for example over 90% of the nurses in the dataset identify as females.

Our case study extends the experiments done by Orgad et al. (2022). In their work, they tested a RoBERTa-based (Liu et al., 2019) classifier fine-tuned on Bias in Bios. The model was trained and evaluated on a training/test split of the dataset using numerous extrinsic bias metrics. Here we train the same model on the same training set, but evaluate it on three types of test sets: the original test set alongside balanced versions of it, which have equal numbers of females and males in every profession, by either subsampling or oversampling. [2] We follow Orgad et al. (2022) and report nine different metrics on this task, measuring either some notion of performance gap or a statistical metric from the fairness literature. For details on the metrics measured in this experiments, see Appendix C.

As the results in Table 2 show, although many of the gap metrics (top block) are unaffected by the balancing of the test dataset, the absolute sum of precision gaps is almost zero when the dataset is balanced. Moreover, the Pearson correlation for precision is significantly reduced after subsampling the test dataset. The Pearson correlation is

[2]Subsampling is the process of removing examples from the dataset such that the resulting dataset contains the same number of male and female examples for each label. Oversampling achieves this by repeating examples.

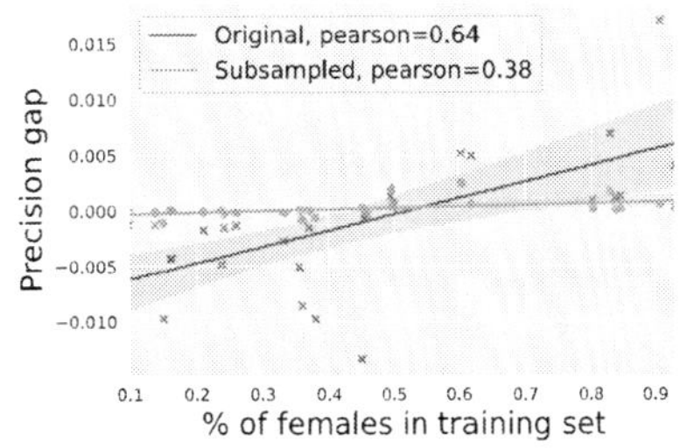

Figure 2: Percentage of females in the training percent versus the resulting precision gap, per each profession, for a regular test set and a subsampled one. Precision gaps and the Pearson correlation are both lower for a subsampled dataset.

computed between the performance gaps per label (profession), and the percentage of females in the training set for that label, without balancing (the original distribution of professions per gender can be found in Appendix E). A higher correlation indicates that more bias was learned from the training set. This correlation is illustrated in Figure 2, and it is visible that the correlation is much lower when measured on a subsampled test dataset than on the original test dataset.

The statistical fairness metrics (bottom block in Table 2) show a significant difference in the measured bias across different test set balancing. Oversampling shows less bias than when measured on the original test set, while subsampling yields mixed results – it decreases one metric while increasing another.

What is the "correct" test set? Since metrics are defined over the entire dataset, they are sensitive to its composition. For measuring bias in a model, the dataset used should be as unbiased as possible, thus balanced datasets are preferable.

If we were only concerned with measuring one of the reduced metrics on a non-balanced test set, we could misrepresent the fairness of the model. Indeed, it is common practice to measure only a small portion of metrics out of all those that can be measured—as we show in section 5—which makes us vulnerable to misinterpretations.

4.2 Case study: measuring intrinsic bias on two different datasets

It is critical to consider the impact of the data used when measuring intrinsic bias metrics on a language model. Previous work (Goldfarb-Tarrant et al., 2021; Cao et al., 2022; Orgad et al., 2022) inspected the correlations between extrinsic and in-

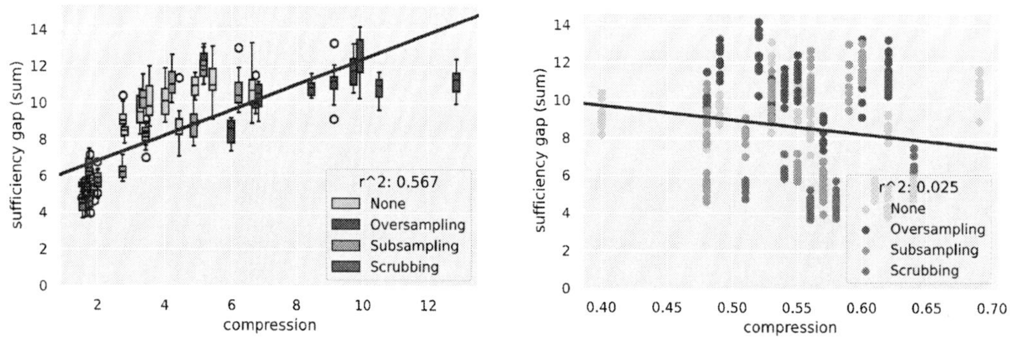

(a) Intrinsic metric was measured on the test set of occupation prediction, figure reproduced from Orgad et al. (2022) (with permission).

(b) Intrinsic metric was measured on Winobias (Zhao et al., 2018a).

Figure 3: Correlation between an intrinsic metric (compression) and an extrinsic metric (sufficiency gap sums), for various models trained on occupation prediction task."None" was trained on the original dataset, "Oversampling" was trained on an oversampled dataset, "Subsampling" was trained on a subsampled dataset and "Scrubbing" was trained on a scrubbed dataset (explicit gender words like "he" and "she" were removed).

trinsic gender bias metrics. Some did not find correlations, while others did in some cases. However, correlations do not solely depend on the model used for bias measurement, but also on the dataset used to measure the intrinsic metric.

Our experiment analyzes the behavior of the same metric on different datasets. We again follow Orgad et al. (2022), who probed for the amount of gender information extractable from the model's internal representations. This is quantified by *compression* (Voita and Titov, 2020), where a higher compression indicates greater bias extractability. Orgad et al. found that this metric correlates strongly with various extrinsic metrics. An example of this correlation is shown in Figure 3a on the Bias in Bios task with models debiased with various strategies. The correlation is high ($r^2 = 0.567$).

In their experiment, the intrinsic metric was measured on the same dataset as the extrinsic one. We repeat the correlation tests, but this time measure the intrinsic metric on a different dataset, the Winobias dataset. The results (Figure 3b) clearly show that there is no correlation between extrinsic and intrinsic metrics in this case ($r^2 = 0.025$).

Hence, we conclude that the dataset used to measure intrinsic bias impacts the results significantly. To reliably reflect the biases that the model has acquired, it should be closely related to the task that the model was trained on. In our experiment, when intrinsic and extrinsic metrics were not measured on the same dataset, no correlation was detected. This is the case for all metrics on this task from Orgad et al. (2022); see Appendix 3. As discussed in §3, the same intrinsic metrics can be evaluated across a variety of datasets. Even so, some intrinsic metrics were originally defined to be measured on different datasets than the task dataset, such as those defined on templates (Table 1).

5 Different Metrics Cover Different Aspects of Bias

In this section, we explore how the choice of bias metrics influences results. Although extrinsic bias metrics are useful in defining harms caused by a gender-biased system, we find that most studies on gender bias use only intrinsic metrics to support their claims. We surveyed a representative list of papers presenting bias mitigation techniques that appeared in the survey by Stanczak and Augenstein (2021), as well as recent papers from the past year. In total, we examined 36 papers. The majority of papers do not measure extrinsic metrics. Even when downstream tasks are measured, only a very small subset of metrics (three or less) is typically measured, as shown in Figure 4. Furthermore, in these studies, typically no explanation is provided for choosing a particular metric.

The exceptions are de Vassimon Manela et al. (2021) and Orgad et al. (2022), who measured six and nine or ten metrics on downstream tasks, respectively. Orgad et al. showed that different extrinsic metrics behave differently under various debiasing methods. Additionally, in §4 we saw that subsampling the test set increased one bias metric and decreased others, which would not have been evident had we only measured a small number of met-

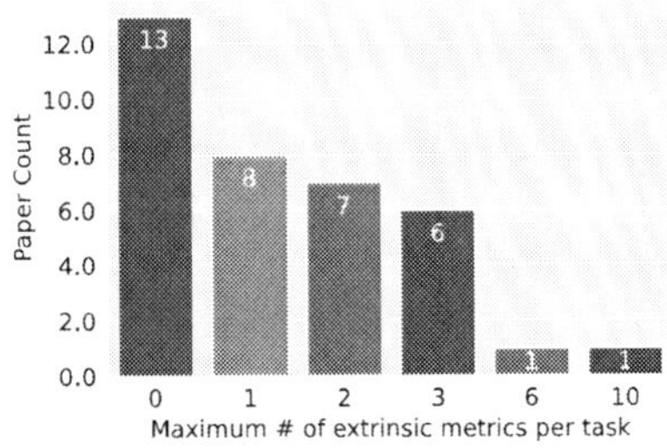

Figure 4: The number of extrinsic metrics measured in the papers we reviewed.

rics. Measuring multiple metrics is also important for evaluating debiasing. When Kaneko and Bollegala compared their proposed debiasing method to that of Dev et al. (2020a), the new method outperformed the old one on two of the three metrics.

As the examples above illustrate, different extrinsic metrics are not necessarily consistent with one another. Furthermore, it is possible to measure more extrinsic metrics, although it is rarely done. When it is not feasible to measure multiple metrics, one should at least justify why a particular metric was chosen. In a CV-filtering system, for example, one might be more forgiving of FPR gaps than of TPR gaps, as the latter leaves out valid candidates for the job in one gender more than the other. However, more extrinsic metrics are likely to provide a more reliable picture of a model's bias.

6 Conclusion and Proposed Guidelines

The issues described in this paper concern the instabilities and vagueness of gender bias metrics in NLP. Since bias measurements are integral to bias research, this instability limits progress. We now provide several guidelines for improving the reliability of gender bias research in NLP.

Focus on downstream tasks and extrinsic metrics. Extrinsic metrics are helpful in motivating bias mitigation (§2). However, few datasets can be used to quantify extrinsic metrics, especially extrinsic performance metrics, which require gold labels (§3). More effort should be devoted to collecting datasets with extrinsic bias assessments, from more diverse domains and downstream tasks.

Stabilize the metric or the dataset. Both the metrics and the datasets could have significant effects over the results: The same dataset can be used to measure many metrics and yield different conclusions (§4), and the same metric can be measured on different datasets and show bias in one instance but not in another (§5). If one wishes to measure gender bias in an NLP system, it is better to hold one of these variables fixed: for example, to focus on a single metric and measure it on a set of datasets. Of course, this can be repeated for other metrics as well. This will produce much richer, more consistent, and more convincing results.

Neutralize dataset noise. As a result of altering a dataset's composition, we observed very different results (§4). This is caused by the way various fairness metrics are defined and computed on the entire dataset. To ensure a more reliable evaluation, we recommend normalizing a dataset when using it for evaluation. In the case of occupation prediction, normalization can be obtained by balancing the test set. In other cases it could be by anonymizing the test set, removing harmful words, etc., depending on the specific scenario.

Motivate the choice of specific metrics, or measure many. Most work measures only a few metrics (§5). A comprehensive experiment, such as to prove the efficacy of a new debiasing method, is more reliable if many metrics are measured. In some situations, a particular metric may be of interest; in this case one should carefully justify the choice of metric and the harm that is caused when the metric indicates bias. The motivation for debiasing this metric then follows naturally.

Define the motivation for debiasing through bias metrics. Blodgett et al. (2020) found that papers' motivations are "often vague, inconsistent, and lacking in normative reasoning". We propose to describe the motivations through the gender bias metrics chosen for the study: define what is the harm measured by a specific metric, what is the behavior of a desired versus a biased system, and how the metric measures it. This is where extrinsic metrics will be particularly useful.

We believe that following these guidelines will enhance clarity and comparability of results, contributing to the advancement of the field.

Acknowledgements

This research was supported by the ISRAEL SCIENCE FOUNDATION (grant No. 448/20) and by an Azrieli Foundation Early Career Faculty Fellowship. We also thank the anonymous reviewers for their insightful comments and suggestions, and the members of the Technion CS NLP group for their valuable feedback.

References

Maria Antoniak and David Mimno. 2021. Bad seeds: Evaluating lexical methods for bias measurement. In *Proceedings of the 59th Annual Meeting of the Association for Computational Linguistics and the 11th International Joint Conference on Natural Language Processing (Volume 1: Long Papers)*, pages 1889–1904, Online. Association for Computational Linguistics.

Solon Barocas, Kate Crawford, Aaron Shapiro, and Hanna Wallach. 2017. The problem with bias: Allocative versus representational harms in machine learning. In *9th Annual Conference of the Special Interest Group for Computing, Information and Society*.

Solon Barocas, Moritz Hardt, and Arvind Narayanan. 2019. *Fairness and Machine Learning*. fairmlbook.org. http://www.fairmlbook.org.

Marion Bartl, Malvina Nissim, and Albert Gatt. 2020. Unmasking contextual stereotypes: Measuring and mitigating BERT's gender bias. In *Proceedings of the Second Workshop on Gender Bias in Natural Language Processing*, pages 1–16, Barcelona, Spain (Online). Association for Computational Linguistics.

Christine Basta, Marta R Costa-jussà, and Noe Casas. 2021. Extensive study on the underlying gender bias in contextualized word embeddings. *Neural Computing and Applications*, 33(8):3371–3384.

Christine Basta, Marta R. Costa-jussà, and José A. R. Fonollosa. 2020. Towards mitigating gender bias in a decoder-based neural machine translation model by adding contextual information. In *Proceedings of the The Fourth Widening Natural Language Processing Workshop*, pages 99–102, Seattle, USA. Association for Computational Linguistics.

Yonatan Belinkov. 2021. Probing classifiers: Promises, shortcomings, and alternatives. *Computational Linguistics 2021*.

Alex Beutel, Ed H. Chi, Ellie Pavlick, Emily Blythe Pitler, Ian Tenney, Jilin Chen, Kellie Webster, Slav Petrov, and Xuezhi Wang. 2020. Measuring and reducing gendered correlations in pre-trained models. Technical report.

Su Lin Blodgett, Solon Barocas, Hal Daumé III, and Hanna Wallach. 2020. Language (technology) is power: A critical survey of "bias" in NLP. In *Proceedings of the 58th Annual Meeting of the Association for Computational Linguistics*, pages 5454–5476, Online. Association for Computational Linguistics.

Tolga Bolukbasi, Kai-Wei Chang, James Y Zou, Venkatesh Saligrama, and Adam T Kalai. 2016. Man is to computer programmer as woman is to homemaker? debiasing word embeddings. *Advances in neural information processing systems*, 29.

Rishi Bommasani, Drew A Hudson, Ehsan Adeli, Russ Altman, Simran Arora, Sydney von Arx, Michael S Bernstein, Jeannette Bohg, Antoine Bosselut, Emma Brunskill, et al. 2021. On the opportunities and risks of foundation models. *arXiv preprint arXiv:2108.07258*.

Shikha Bordia and Samuel R. Bowman. 2019. Identifying and reducing gender bias in word-level language models. In *Proceedings of the 2019 Conference of the North American Chapter of the Association for Computational Linguistics: Student Research Workshop*, pages 7–15, Minneapolis, Minnesota. Association for Computational Linguistics.

Aylin Caliskan, J. Bryson, and A. Narayanan. 2017. Semantics derived automatically from language corpora contain human-like biases. *Science*, 356:183 – 186.

Yang Trista Cao and Hal Daumé III. 2021. Toward gender-inclusive coreference resolution: An analysis of gender and bias throughout the machine learning lifecycle*. *Computational Linguistics*, 47(3):615–661.

Yang Trista Cao, Yada Pruksachatkun, Kai-Wei Chang, Rahul Gupta, Varun Kumar, Jwala Dhamala, and Aram Galstyan. 2022. On the intrinsic and extrinsic fairness evaluation metrics for contextualized language representations.

Marta R. Costa-jussà and Adrià de Jorge. 2020. Finetuning neural machine translation on gender-balanced datasets. In *Proceedings of the Second Workshop on Gender Bias in Natural Language Processing*, pages 26–34, Barcelona, Spain (Online). Association for Computational Linguistics.

Maria De-Arteaga, Alexey Romanov, Hanna Wallach, Jennifer Chayes, Christian Borgs, Alexandra Chouldechova, Sahin Geyik, Krishnaram Kenthapadi, and Adam Tauman Kalai. 2019. Bias in bios: A case study of semantic representation bias in a high-stakes setting. In *proceedings of the Conference on Fairness, Accountability, and Transparency*, pages 120–128.

Daniel de Vassimon Manela, David Errington, Thomas Fisher, Boris van Breugel, and Pasquale Minervini. 2021. Stereotype and skew: Quantifying gender bias in pre-trained and fine-tuned language models. In *Proceedings of the 16th Conference of the European Chapter of the Association for Computational Linguistics: Main Volume*, pages 2232–2242, Online. Association for Computational Linguistics.

Pieter Delobelle, Ewoenam Kwaku Tokpo, Toon Calders, and Bettina Berendt. 2021. Measuring fairness with biased rulers: A survey on quantifying biases in pretrained language models. *arXiv preprint arXiv:2112.07447*.

Sunipa Dev, Tao Li, Jeff M Phillips, and Vivek Srikumar. 2020a. On measuring and mitigating biased inferences of word embeddings. In *Proceedings of the AAAI Conference on Artificial Intelligence*, volume 34, pages 7659–7666.

Sunipa Dev, Tao Li, Jeff M Phillips, and Vivek Srikumar. 2020b. On measuring and mitigating biased inferences of word embeddings. In *Proceedings of the AAAI Conference on Artificial Intelligence*, volume 34, pages 7659–7666.

Sunipa Dev, Masoud Monajatipoor, Anaelia Ovalle, Arjun Subramonian, Jeff Phillips, and Kai-Wei Chang. 2021. Harms of gender exclusivity and challenges in non-binary representation in language technologies. In *Proceedings of the 2021 Conference on Empirical Methods in Natural Language Processing*, pages 1968–1994, Online and Punta Cana, Dominican Republic. Association for Computational Linguistics.

Jwala Dhamala, Tony Sun, Varun Kumar, Satyapriya Krishna, Yada Pruksachatkun, Kai-Wei Chang, and Rahul Gupta. 2021. Bold: Dataset and metrics for measuring biases in open-ended language generation. In *Proceedings of the 2021 ACM Conference on Fairness, Accountability, and Transparency*, pages 862–872.

Emily Dinan, Angela Fan, Adina Williams, Jack Urbanek, Douwe Kiela, and Jason Weston. 2020. Queens are powerful too: Mitigating gender bias in dialogue generation. In *Proceedings of the 2020 Conference on Empirical Methods in Natural Language Processing (EMNLP)*, pages 8173–8188, Online. Association for Computational Linguistics.

Yanai Elazar and Yoav Goldberg. 2018. Adversarial removal of demographic attributes from text data. In *Proceedings of the 2018 Conference on Empirical Methods in Natural Language Processing*, pages 11–21, Brussels, Belgium. Association for Computational Linguistics.

Ali Emami, Paul Trichelair, Adam Trischler, Kaheer Suleman, Hannes Schulz, and Jackie Chi Kit Cheung. 2019. The KnowRef coreference corpus: Removing gender and number cues for difficult pronominal anaphora resolution. In *Proceedings of the 57th Annual Meeting of the Association for Computational Linguistics*, pages 3952–3961, Florence, Italy. Association for Computational Linguistics.

Kawin Ethayarajh, David Duvenaud, and Graeme Hirst. 2019. Understanding undesirable word embedding associations. In *Proceedings of the 57th Annual Meeting of the Association for Computational Linguistics*, pages 1696–1705, Florence, Italy. Association for Computational Linguistics.

Ismael Garrido-Muñoz , Arturo Montejo-Ráez , Fernando Martínez-Santiago , and L. Alfonso Ureña-López . 2021. A survey on bias in deep nlp. *Applied Sciences*, 11(7).

Seraphina Goldfarb-Tarrant, Rebecca Marchant, Ricardo Muñoz Sánchez, Mugdha Pandya, and Adam Lopez. 2021. Intrinsic bias metrics do not correlate with application bias. In *Proceedings of the 59th Annual Meeting of the Association for Computational Linguistics and the 11th International Joint Conference on Natural Language Processing (Volume 1: Long Papers)*, pages 1926–1940, Online. Association for Computational Linguistics.

Hila Gonen and Yoav Goldberg. 2019. Lipstick on a pig: Debiasing methods cover up systematic gender biases in word embeddings but do not remove them. In *Proceedings of the 2019 Workshop on Widening NLP*, pages 60–63, Florence, Italy. Association for Computational Linguistics.

Wei Guo and Aylin Caliskan. 2021. Detecting emergent intersectional biases: Contextualized word embeddings contain a distribution of human-like biases. In *Proceedings of the 2021 AAAI/ACM Conference on AI, Ethics, and Society*, pages 122–133.

Nizar Habash, Houda Bouamor, and Christine Chung. 2019. Automatic gender identification and reinflection in Arabic. In *Proceedings of the First Workshop on Gender Bias in Natural Language Processing*, pages 155–165, Florence, Italy. Association for Computational Linguistics.

Rowan Hall Maudslay, Hila Gonen, Ryan Cotterell, and Simone Teufel. 2019. It's all in the name: Mitigating gender bias with name-based counterfactual data substitution. In *Proceedings of the 2019 Conference on Empirical Methods in Natural Language Processing and the 9th International Joint Conference on Natural Language Processing (EMNLP-IJCNLP)*, pages 5267–5275, Hong Kong, China. Association for Computational Linguistics.

John Hewitt and Percy Liang. 2019. Designing and interpreting probes with control tasks. In *Proceedings of the 2019 Conference on Empirical Methods in Natural Language Processing and the 9th International Joint Conference on Natural Language Processing (EMNLP-IJCNLP)*, pages 2733–2743, Hong Kong, China. Association for Computational Linguistics.

Xisen Jin, Francesco Barbieri, Brendan Kennedy, Aida Mostafazadeh Davani, Leonardo Neves, and Xiang Ren. 2021. On transferability of bias mitigation effects in language model fine-tuning. In *Proceedings of the 2021 Conference of the North American Chapter of the Association for Computational Linguistics: Human Language Technologies*, pages 3770–3783, Online. Association for Computational Linguistics.

Masahiro Kaneko and Danushka Bollegala. 2019. Gender-preserving debiasing for pre-trained word embeddings. In *Proceedings of the 57th Annual Meeting of the Association for Computational Linguistics*, pages 1641–1650, Florence, Italy. Association for Computational Linguistics.

Masahiro Kaneko and Danushka Bollegala. 2021a. Debiasing pre-trained contextualised embeddings. In *Proceedings of the 16th Conference of the European Chapter of the Association for Computational Linguistics: Main Volume*, pages 1256–1266, Online. Association for Computational Linguistics.

Masahiro Kaneko and Danushka Bollegala. 2021b. Dictionary-based debiasing of pre-trained word embeddings. In *Proceedings of the 16th Conference of the European Chapter of the Association for Computational Linguistics: Main Volume*, pages 212–223, Online. Association for Computational Linguistics.

Saket Karve, Lyle Ungar, and João Sedoc. 2019. Conceptor debiasing of word representations evaluated on WEAT. In *Proceedings of the First Workshop on Gender Bias in Natural Language Processing*, pages 40–48, Florence, Italy. Association for Computational Linguistics.

Kate Crawford. 2017. The trouble with bias. keynote at neurips.

Svetlana Kiritchenko and Saif Mohammad. 2018. Examining gender and race bias in two hundred sentiment analysis systems. In *Proceedings of the Seventh Joint Conference on Lexical and Computational Semantics*, pages 43–53.

Vaibhav Kumar, Tenzin Singhay Bhotia, Vaibhav Kumar, and Tanmoy Chakraborty. 2020. Nurse is closer to woman than surgeon? mitigating gender-biased proximities in word embeddings. *Transactions of the Association for Computational Linguistics*, 8:486–503.

Keita Kurita, Nidhi Vyas, Ayush Pareek, Alan W Black, and Yulia Tsvetkov. 2019. Measuring bias in contextualized word representations. In *Proceedings of the First Workshop on Gender Bias in Natural Language Processing*, pages 166–172, Florence, Italy. Association for Computational Linguistics.

Hector Levesque, Ernest Davis, and Leora Morgenstern. 2012. The winograd schema challenge. In *Thirteenth international conference on the principles of knowledge representation and reasoning*.

Yitong Li, Timothy Baldwin, and Trevor Cohn. 2018. Towards robust and privacy-preserving text representations. In *Proceedings of the 56th Annual Meeting of the Association for Computational Linguistics (Volume 2: Short Papers)*, pages 25–30, Melbourne, Australia. Association for Computational Linguistics.

Sheng Liang, Philipp Dufter, and Hinrich Schütze. 2020. Monolingual and multilingual reduction of gender bias in contextualized representations. In *Proceedings of the 28th International Conference on Computational Linguistics*, pages 5082–5093, Barcelona, Spain (Online). International Committee on Computational Linguistics.

Yinhan Liu, Myle Ott, Naman Goyal, Jingfei Du, Mandar Joshi, Danqi Chen, Omer Levy, Mike Lewis, Luke Zettlemoyer, and Veselin Stoyanov. 2019. Roberta: A robustly optimized BERT pretraining approach. *CoRR*, abs/1907.11692.

Chandler May, Alex Wang, Shikha Bordia, Samuel R. Bowman, and Rachel Rudinger. 2019a. On measuring social biases in sentence encoders. In *Proceedings of the 2019 Conference of the North American Chapter of the Association for Computational Linguistics: Human Language Technologies, Volume 1 (Long and Short Papers)*, pages 622–628, Minneapolis, Minnesota. Association for Computational Linguistics.

Chandler May, Alex Wang, Shikha Bordia, Samuel R. Bowman, and Rachel Rudinger. 2019b. On measuring social biases in sentence encoders. In *Proceedings of the 2019 Conference of the North American Chapter of the Association for Computational Linguistics: Human Language Technologies, Volume 1 (Long and Short Papers)*, pages 622–628, Minneapolis, Minnesota. Association for Computational Linguistics.

Moin Nadeem, Anna Bethke, and Siva Reddy. 2021. Stereoset: Measuring stereotypical bias in pretrained language models. In *Proceedings of the 59th Annual Meeting of the Association for Computational Linguistics and the 11th International Joint Conference on Natural Language Processing (Volume 1: Long Papers)*, pages 5356–5371.

Nikita Nangia, Clara Vania, Rasika Bhalerao, and Samuel Bowman. 2020a. Crows-pairs: A challenge dataset for measuring social biases in masked language models. In *Proceedings of the 2020 Conference on Empirical Methods in Natural Language Processing (EMNLP)*, pages 1953–1967.

Nikita Nangia, Clara Vania, Rasika Bhalerao, and Samuel R. Bowman. 2020b. CrowS-pairs: A challenge dataset for measuring social biases in masked language models. In *Proceedings of the 2020 Conference on Empirical Methods in Natural Language Processing (EMNLP)*, pages 1953–1967, Online. Association for Computational Linguistics.

Hadas Orgad, Seraphina Goldfarb-Tarrant, and Yonatan Belinkov. 2022. How gender debiasing affects internal model representations, and why it matters. In *Proceedings of the 2022 Conference of the North American Chapter of the Association for Computational Linguistics: Human Language Technologies*. Association for Computational Linguistics.

Ji Ho Park, Jamin Shin, and Pascale Fung. 2018. Reducing gender bias in abusive language detection. In *Proceedings of the 2018 Conference on Empirical Methods in Natural Language Processing*, pages 2799–2804, Brussels, Belgium. Association for Computational Linguistics.

Flavien Prost, Nithum Thain, and Tolga Bolukbasi. 2019. Debiasing embeddings for reduced gender bias in text classification. In *Proceedings of the First Workshop on Gender Bias in Natural Language Processing*, pages 69–75, Florence, Italy. Association for Computational Linguistics.

Yusu Qian, Urwa Muaz, Ben Zhang, and Jae Won Hyun. 2019. Reducing gender bias in word-level language models with a gender-equalizing loss function. In

Proceedings of the 57th Annual Meeting of the Association for Computational Linguistics: Student Research Workshop, pages 223–228, Florence, Italy. Association for Computational Linguistics.

Rachel Rudinger, Jason Naradowsky, Brian Leonard, and Benjamin Van Durme. 2018. Gender bias in coreference resolution. In *Proceedings of the 2018 Conference of the North American Chapter of the Association for Computational Linguistics: Human Language Technologies*, New Orleans, Louisiana. Association for Computational Linguistics.

Magnus Sahlgren and Fredrik Olsson. 2019. Gender bias in pretrained swedish embeddings. In *Proceedings of the 22nd Nordic Conference on Computational Linguistics*, pages 35–43.

Danielle Saunders and Bill Byrne. 2020. Reducing gender bias in neural machine translation as a domain adaptation problem. In *Proceedings of the 58th Annual Meeting of the Association for Computational Linguistics*, pages 7724–7736, Online. Association for Computational Linguistics.

Danielle Saunders, Rosie Sallis, and Bill Byrne. 2020. Neural machine translation doesn't translate gender coreference right unless you make it. In *Proceedings of the Second Workshop on Gender Bias in Natural Language Processing*, pages 35–43, Barcelona, Spain (Online). Association for Computational Linguistics.

João Sedoc and Lyle Ungar. 2019. The role of protected class word lists in bias identification of contextualized word representations. In *Proceedings of the First Workshop on Gender Bias in Natural Language Processing*, pages 55–61, Florence, Italy. Association for Computational Linguistics.

Indira Sen, Mattia Samory, Fabian Flöck, Claudia Wagner, and Isabelle Augenstein. 2021. How does counterfactually augmented data impact models for social computing constructs? In *Proceedings of the 2021 Conference on Empirical Methods in Natural Language Processing*, pages 325–344, Online and Punta Cana, Dominican Republic. Association for Computational Linguistics.

Seungjae Shin, Kyungwoo Song, JoonHo Jang, Hyemi Kim, Weonyoung Joo, and Il-Chul Moon. 2020. Neutralizing gender bias in word embeddings with latent disentanglement and counterfactual generation. In *Findings of the Association for Computational Linguistics: EMNLP 2020*, pages 3126–3140, Online. Association for Computational Linguistics.

Artūrs Stafanovičs, Toms Bergmanis, and Mārcis Pinnis. 2020. Mitigating gender bias in machine translation with target gender annotations. In *Proceedings of the Fifth Conference on Machine Translation*, pages 629–638, Online. Association for Computational Linguistics.

Karolina Stanczak and Isabelle Augenstein. 2021. A survey on gender bias in natural language processing. *arXiv preprint arXiv:2112.14168*.

Tony Sun, Andrew Gaut, Shirlyn Tang, Yuxin Huang, Mai ElSherief, Jieyu Zhao, Diba Mirza, Elizabeth Belding, Kai-Wei Chang, and William Yang Wang. 2019. Mitigating gender bias in natural language processing: Literature review. In *Proceedings of the 57th Annual Meeting of the Association for Computational Linguistics*, pages 1630–1640, Florence, Italy. Association for Computational Linguistics.

Rob Voigt, David Jurgens, Vinodkumar Prabhakaran, Dan Jurafsky, and Yulia Tsvetkov. 2018. RtGender: A corpus for studying differential responses to gender. In *Proceedings of the Eleventh International Conference on Language Resources and Evaluation (LREC 2018)*, Miyazaki, Japan. European Language Resources Association (ELRA).

Elena Voita and Ivan Titov. 2020. Information-theoretic probing with minimum description length. In *Proceedings of the 2020 Conference on Empirical Methods in Natural Language Processing (EMNLP)*, pages 183–196, Online. Association for Computational Linguistics.

Kellie Webster, Marta Recasens, Vera Axelrod, and Jason Baldridge. 2018. Mind the gap: A balanced corpus of gendered ambiguous pronouns. *Transactions of the Association for Computational Linguistics*, 6:605–617.

Kellie Webster, Xuezhi Wang, Ian Tenney, Alex Beutel, Emily Pitler, Ellie Pavlick, Jilin Chen, Ed Chi, and Slav Petrov. 2020. Measuring and reducing gendered correlations in pre-trained models. *arXiv preprint arXiv:2010.06032*.

Brian Hu Zhang, Blake Lemoine, and Margaret Mitchell. 2018. Mitigating unwanted biases with adversarial learning. In *Proceedings of the 2018 AAAI/ACM Conference on AI, Ethics, and Society*, pages 335–340.

Jieyu Zhao, Tianlu Wang, Mark Yatskar, Ryan Cotterell, Vicente Ordonez, and Kai-Wei Chang. 2019. Gender bias in contextualized word embeddings. In *Proceedings of the 2019 Conference of the North American Chapter of the Association for Computational Linguistics: Human Language Technologies, Volume 1 (Long and Short Papers)*, pages 629–634, Minneapolis, Minnesota. Association for Computational Linguistics.

Jieyu Zhao, Tianlu Wang, Mark Yatskar, Vicente Ordonez, and Kai-Wei Chang. 2017. Men also like shopping: Reducing gender bias amplification using corpus-level constraints. In *Proceedings of the 2017 Conference on Empirical Methods in Natural Language Processing*, pages 2979–2989, Copenhagen, Denmark. Association for Computational Linguistics.

Jieyu Zhao, Tianlu Wang, Mark Yatskar, Vicente Ordonez, and Kai-Wei Chang. 2018a. Gender bias in coreference resolution: Evaluation and debiasing methods. In *Proceedings of the 2018 Conference* of the North American Chapter of the Association for Computational Linguistics: Human Language Technologies, Volume 2 (Short Papers), pages 15–20.

Jieyu Zhao, Tianlu Wang, Mark Yatskar, Vicente Ordonez, and Kai-Wei Chang. 2018b. Gender bias in coreference resolution: Evaluation and debiasing methods. In *Proceedings of the 2018 Conference of the North American Chapter of the Association for Computational Linguistics: Human Language Technologies, Volume 2 (Short Papers)*, pages 15–20, New Orleans, Louisiana. Association for Computational Linguistics.

Ran Zmigrod, Sabrina J. Mielke, Hanna Wallach, and Ryan Cotterell. 2019. Counterfactual data augmentation for mitigating gender stereotypes in languages with rich morphology. In *Proceedings of the 57th Annual Meeting of the Association for Computational Linguistics*, pages 1651–1661, Florence, Italy. Association for Computational Linguistics.

A List of gender bias metrics, as presented in Table 1

Many of the items in this list do not aim to describe a specific metric, but rather describe a family of metrics with similar characteristics and requirements.

A.1 Extrinsic Performance

This class of extrinsic metrics measures how a model's performance is affected by gender. This is computed with respect to particular gold labels and there is a clear defintion of harm derived from the specific performance metric measured, for instance F1, True Positive Rate (TPR), False Positive Rate (FPR), BLEU score for translation tasks, etc.

1. **Gap (Label):** Measures the difference in some performance metric between Female and Male examples, in a specific class. The performance gap can be computed as the difference or the quotient between two performance metrics on two protected group. For example, in Bias in Bios (De-Arteaga et al., 2019) one can measure the TPR gap between female teachers and male teachers. The gaps per class can be summed, or the correlation with the percentage of women in the particular class can be measured.

2. **Gap (Stereo):** Measures the difference in some performance metric between pro-stereotypical (and/or non-stereotypical) and anti-stereotypical (and/or non-stereotypical) instances. A biased model will have better performance on pro-stereotypical instances. This can be measured across the whole dataset or per gender / class.

3. **Gap (Gender):** Measure the difference in some performance metric between male examples and female examples, across the entire dataset. In cases of non-binary gender datasets (Cao and Daumé III, 2021), the gap can be calculated to measure the difference between text that is trans-inclusive versus text that is trans-exclusive. Another option is to measure the difference in performance before and after removing various aspects of gender from the text.

A.2 Extrinsic Prediction

This class is also extrinsic as it measures model predictions, but the bias is not computed with respect to some gold labels. Instead, the bias is measured by the effect of gender on the predictions of the model.

1. **% or # of answer changes:** The number or percentage that the prediction changed when the gender of the example changed. To measure this, each example should have a counterpart example of the opposite gender. This difference can be measured with respect to the number of females or males in the specific label, for instance with relation to occupation statistics.

2. **% or # that model prefers stereotype:** Quantifies how much the model tends to go for the stereotypical option, for instance predicting that a "she" pronoun refers to a nurse in a coreference resolution task. This can also be measured as a correlation with the number of females or males in the label, which can be thought of as the "strength" of the stereotype.

3. **Pred gap:** The raw probabilities or some function of them are measured, and the gap is measured as the prediction gap between male and female predictions. This can be measured across the whole dataset or per label at other cases.

4. **LM prediction on target words**: This metric relates to the specific predictions of a pretrained LM, such as a masked LM. The prediction of the LM is calculated for a specific text or on a specific target word of interest. These probabilities are then used to

measure the bias of the model. We did not include this metric category in the "Pred gap" category because it can be measured on a much larger number of datasets. For example, for the masked sentence: "The programmer said that <mask> would finish the work tomorrow", we might measure the relation between $p(< mask >= he|sentence)$ and $p(< mask >= she|sentence)$. Although somewhat similar in idea to the previously described metric "pred gap", it is presented as a separate metric since it can be computed on a wider range of datasets. The strategy for calculating a number quantifying bias from the raw probabilities varies in different papers. For example, Kurita et al. (2019); Nangia et al. (2020a); Bordia and Bowman (2019); Nadeem et al. (2021) all use different formulations.

A.3 Intrinsic

This class measures bias on the hidden model representations, and is not directly related to any downstream task.

1. **WEAT:** The Word Embedding Association Test (Caliskan et al., 2017) was proposed as a way to quantify bias in static word embeddings. While we consider only bias metrics that can be applied in contextualized settings, we describe WEAT here as it is popular and has been adapted to contextualized settings. To compute WEAT, one defines a set of target words X, Y (e.g., programmer, engineer, scientist, etc., and nurse, teacher, librarian, etc.) and two sets of attribute words A, B (e.g., man, male, etc. and woman, female, etc.). The null hypothesis is that the two sets of target words are not different when it comes to their similarity to the two sets of attribute words. We test the null hypothesis using a permutation test on the word embeddings, and the resulting effect size is used to quantify how different the two sets are.

2. **SEAT:** the Sentence Encoder Association Test (May et al., 2019a) was proposed as a contextual version of the popular metric WEAT. As WEAT was computed on static word embedding, in SEAT they proposed using "semantically-bleached" templates such as "This is [target]", where the target word of interest is planted in the template, to get its word embedding in contextual language models. Thus, we only consider "semantically-bleached" templates to be appropriate as a dataset for SEAT.

3. **CEAT:** Contextualized Embedding Association Test (Guo and Caliskan, 2021) was proposed as another contextual alternative to WEAT. Here, instead of using templates to get the word of interest, for each word a large number of embeddings is collected from a corpus of text, where the word appears many times. WEAT's effect size is then computed many times, with different embeddings each time, and a combined effect size is then calculated on it. As already mentioned by the original authors, even with only 2 contextual embeddings collected per word in the WEAT stimuli, and each set of X, Y, A, B having only 5 stimuli, $2^{5 \cdot 4}$ possible combinations can be used to compute effect sizes.

4. **Probe:** The entire example, or a specific word in the text, is probed for gender. A classifier is trained to learn the gender from a representation of the word or the text as extracted from a model. This can be done on examples where there is some gender labeling (for instance, the gender of the person discussed in a biography text) or when the text contains some target words, with gender context. Such target words could be "nurse" for female and "doctor" for male. Usually, the word probe refers to a classifier from the family of multilayer preceptron classifiers, linear classifiers included. The accuracy achieved by the probe is often used as a measure of how much gender information in embedded in the representations, but there are some weaknesses with using accuracy, such as memorization and other issues (Hewitt and Liang, 2019; Belinkov, 2021), and so MDL Probing is proposed as an alternative (Voita and Titov, 2020), and the metric used is compression rate. Higher compression indicates more gender information in the representation.

5. **Cluster:** It is possible to cluster the word embeddings or representations of the examples and perform an analysis using the gender labels just like in probing.

6. **Nearest Neighbors:** As with probing, the ex-

amples and word representations can be classified using a nearest neighbor model, or an analysis can be done using nearest neighbors of word embeddings as done by Gonen and Goldberg (2019).

7. **Gender Space:** in the static embeddings regime, Bolukbasi et al. (2016) proposed to identify gender bias in word representations by computing the direction between representations of male and female word pairs such as "he" and "she". They then computed PCA to find the gender direction. Basta et al. (2021) extended the idea to contextual embeddings by using multiple representations for each word, by sampling sentences that contain these words from a large corpus. Zhao et al. (2019) performed the same technique on a different dataset. They then observed the percentage of variance explained in the first principal component, and this measure plays as a bias metric. The principal components can then be further used for a visual qualitative analysis by projecting word embeddings on the component space.

8. **Cos:** in static word embeddings (Bolukbasi et al., 2016), this was computed as the mean cosine similarity between neutral words which might have some stereotype such as "doctor" or "nurse", and the gender space. Basta et al. (2021) computed it on profession words using extracted embeddings from a large corpus.

B Statistical Fairness Metrics

This section describes statistical metrics that are representative of many other fairness metrics that have been proposed in the field. *separation* and *sufficiency* fall under the definition of "extrinsic performance", specifically "gap (Gender)" while *independence* falls under the definition of "extrinsic prediction", specifically "pred gap". Various numbers are generated by these metrics that describe differences between two distributions as measured by Kullbeck-Liebr divergence. We sum all the numbers to quantify bias in a single number.

Let R be a model's prediction, G the protected attribute of gender, and Y the golden labels.

Independence requires that the model's predictions are independent of the gender. Formally:
$P(R = r|Z = F) = P(R = r|Z = M)$

It is measured by the distributional difference between $P(R = r)$ and $P(R = r|Z = z)\ \forall z \in \{M, F\}$.

Separation requires that the model's predictions are independent of the gender *given the label*. Formally:
$P(R = r|Y = y, G = F) = (R = r|Y = y, G = M) \forall y \in \mathcal{Y}$

It is measured by the distributional difference between $P(R = r|Y = y, Z = z)$ and $P(R = r|Y = y) \forall y \in \mathcal{Y}, \forall z \in \{M, F\}$

Sufficiency requires that the distribution of the gold labels is independent of the model's predictions *given the gender*. Formally:
$P(Y = y|R = r, G = F) = P(Y = y|R = r, G = M)$

It is measured by the distributional difference between $P(Y = y|R = r, Z = z)$ and $P(Y = y|R = r) \forall y \in \mathcal{Y}, \forall z \in \{M, F\}$

C Implementation details: Bias in Bios experiment

In this section we describe the metrics that were measured in the experiments on Bias in Bios, following Orgad et al. (2022).

Performance gap metrics. The standard measure for this task (De-Arteaga et al., 2019) is the True Positive Rate (TPR) gap between male and female examples, for each profession p:

$$TPR_p = TPR_{p_F} - TPR_{p_M}$$

and then compute the Pearson correlation between each TPR_p and the percentage of females in the training set with the profession p. The result is a single number in the range of 0 to 1, with a higher value indicating greater bias. We measure the Pearson correlations of TPR_p, as well as of the False Positive Rate (FPR) and the Precision gaps. In addition, we sum all the gaps in the profession set P, thereby quantifying the absolute bias and not only the correlations, for example, for the TPR gaps: $\sum_{p \in P} TPR_p$.

Statistical fairness metrics. We also measured three statistical metrics (Barocas et al., 2019), relating to several bias concepts: Separation, Sufficiency and Independence. A greater value means more bias. Detailed information on these metrics can be found in Appendix B.

D Bias in Bios: Correlations between extrinsic and intrinsic metrics when measured on different datasets

Table 3 present the full results of our correlation tests, when intrinsic metrics was measured on a different dataset (Winobias) than the extrinsic metric (Bias in Bios). For all metrics, there is no correlation when we measured the intrinsic metric with a different dataset, although many of the metrics did correlate with the intrinsic metrics when measured on the same dataset as is originally done in Orgad et al..

E Bias in Bios: Statistics of the Dataset Before Balancing

Table 4 presents how the professions in Bias in Bios dataset (De-Arteaga et al., 2019) are distributed, per gender. The gender was induced by the pronouns used to describe the person in the biography, thus it is likely the self-identified gender of the person described in it.

F Full List of Reviewed Papers for Extrinsic Metrics Measurements

Table 5 presents the papers we reviewed and the amount of extrinsic metrics measured by them.

Metric	Bias in Bios (Original)	Winobias
TPR gap (P)	0.304	0.022
TPR gap (S)	0.449	0.002
FPR gap (P)	0.120	0.030
FPR gap (S)	0.046	0.008
Precision gap (P)	0.063	0.013
Precision gap (S)	0.291	0
Independence gap (S)	0.382	0.005
Separation gap (S)	0.165	0.001
Sufficiency gap (S)	0.567	0.025

Table 3: Correlations between intrinsic and extrinsic metrics. Original correlations are from Orgad et al. (2022), our correlations are calculated with the intrinsic metric as measured on Winobias.

	Females	Males
professor	45.10%	54.90%
accountant	36.73%	63.27%
journalist	49.51%	50.49%
architect	23.66%	76.34%
photographer	35.72%	64.28%
psychologist	62.07%	37.93%
teacher	60.24%	39.76%
nurse	90.84%	9.16%
attorney	38.29%	61.71%
software_engineer	15.80%	84.20%
painter	45.74%	54.26%
physician	49.37%	50.63%
chiropractor	26.31%	73.69%
personal_trainer	45.56%	54.44%
surgeon	14.82%	85.18%
filmmaker	32.94%	67.06%
dietitian	92.84%	7.16%
dentist	35.28%	64.72%
dj	14.18%	85.82%
model	82.74%	17.26%
composer	16.37%	83.63%
poet	49.05%	50.95%
comedian	21.14%	78.86%
yoga_teacher	84.51%	15.49%
interior_designer	80.77%	19.23%
pastor	24.03%	75.97%
rapper	9.69%	90.31%
paralegal	84.88%	15.12%

Table 4: Statistics of professions and genders as they appear in the Bias in Bios dataset.

Paper	Maximum # of extrinsic metrics per task
Bolukbasi et al. (2016); Zhang et al. (2018) Bordia and Bowman (2019); Ethayarajh et al. (2019) Sahlgren and Olsson (2019); Karve et al. (2019) Hall Maudslay et al. (2019); Sedoc and Ungar (2019) Kaneko and Bollegala (2019); Liang et al. (2020) Dev et al. (2020b); Shin et al. (2020) Kaneko and Bollegala (2021b)	0
Zhao et al. (2017, 2018b) Li et al. (2018); Elazar and Goldberg (2018) Zmigrod et al. (2019); Zhao et al. (2019) Kumar et al. (2020); Bartl et al. (2020) Sen et al. (2021)	1
Prost et al. (2019); Qian et al. (2019) Emami et al. (2019); Habash et al. (2019) Dinan et al. (2020); Costa-jussà and de Jorge (2020) Basta et al. (2020)	2
Park et al. (2018); Stafanovičs et al. (2020) Saunders and Byrne (2020); Saunders et al. (2020) Kaneko and Bollegala (2021a); Jin et al. (2021)	3
de Vassimon Manela et al. (2021)	6
Orgad et al. (2022)	10

Table 5: Papers about gender bias and the number of extrinsic metrics they measured per task. 0 means no extrinsic metrics were measured.

A taxonomy of bias-causing ambiguities in machine translation

Michal Měchura
NLP Centre, Faculty of Informatics, Masaryk University, Brno, Czech Republic
and Fiontar & Scoil na Gaeilge, Dublin City University, Ireland
michmech@lexiconista.com

Abstract

This paper introduces a taxonomy of phenomena which cause bias in machine translation, covering gender bias (people being male and/or female), number bias (singular *you* versus plural *you*) and formality bias (informal *you* versus formal *you*). Our taxonomy is a formalism for describing situations in machine translation when the source text leaves some of these properties unspecified (eg. does not say whether *doctor* is male or female) but the target language requires the property to be specified (eg. because it does not have a gender-neutral word for *doctor*). The formalism described here is used internally by Fairslator[1], a web-based tool for detecting and correcting bias in the output of any machine translator.

1 Introduction: phenomena described by the taxonomy

The taxonomy we are going to introduce in this paper is based on the assumption that biased translations are *always* the result of unresolvable ambiguities in the source text. We will start by demonstrating on a few examples what exactly we mean by ambiguity, what makes ambiguities resolvable or unresolvable, and how the unresolvable ones inevitably lead to biased translations. This will serve as an informal introduction before we proceed to a more formal specification of everything in the rest of the paper.

When translating a sentence such as *she is a doctor* from English into a language such as German which has no gender-neutral word for *doctor*, the translator (machine or human) can translate *doctor* either as male *Arzt* or as female *Ärztin*. The word *doctor* is **ambiguous** for the purposes of this translation. However, the presence of the female pronoun *she* should be enough to tip any well-trained machine translator towards the female reading and to translate *doctor* as *Ärztin* – as indeed most of the major machine translators such as Google Translate and DeepL do. Here, the ambiguity is **resolvable** from context, where by context we mean the rest of the text available to the translator.

Now consider a similar sentence: *I am a doctor.* The word *doctor* is as ambiguous as before, but this time the ambiguity is **unresolvable** from context, as there is no indication anywhere in the text whether the intended referrent of *I* and *doctor* is a man or a woman. In such a situation, the machine translator will typically decide for the male translation because that is what has been seen most often in similar contexts in its training data. This is another way of saying that the machine is making an **unjustified assumption**: unjustified because unsupported by anything actually present in the text being translated. There are two possible ways to "read" the ambiguous word *doctor*, but translations produced by this machine will be consistently biased in favour of the male reading whenever context allows both readings.

Unresolvable ambiguities do not simply happen arbitrarily and unexpectedly. Many kinds of unresolvable ambiguities tend to happen regularly and predictably when certain words occur in the source text inside certain lexicogrammatical patterns, for example *I am a...* or *you are a...* followed by a gender-neutral noun known to have two gender-specific translations in the target language. Fairslator is a tool which detects such patterns and acts on them: it asks the human user to disambiguate (eg. to tell us whether they want the male or female reading) and then it re-inflects the translation accordingly. To enable all this functionality, Fairslator has inside itself a taxonomy for describing *how* the source text is ambiguous and *which way* the human user wants the ambiguity to be resolved. The taxonomy describes the following kinds of unresolvable ambiguities:

- Unresolvable ambiguities in the **gender** of human beings being referred to in the text.

[1] https://www.fairslator.com/

Proceedings of the The 4th Workshop on Gender Bias in Natural Language Processing (GeBNLP), pages 168 - 173
July 15, 2022

This covers the well-known case of "occupation words" such as *doctor, teacher, cleaner*, as well as some less well-known cases such as predicatively positioned adjectives in Romance languages (eg. English *I am happy* → French *je suis heureux* male, *je suis heureuse* female) and verbal participles in Slavic languages (eg. English *I wanted it* → Czech *já jsem to chtěl* male, *já jsem to chtěla* female).

- Unresolvable ambiguities in the **number** of people referred to by the English second-person pronoun *you* (and its possessive companion *your*). For example, in the sentence *you are here* the pronoun *you* has an unresolvable ambiguity (from the perspective of translating it into a language which has separate pronouns for singular and plural *you*) because there is no indication in the text whether the *you* refers to one person or many. (Contrast this with a sentence such as *you are all here* where the ambiguity is resolvable from the presence of the plural word *all*.)

- Unresolvable ambiguities in the **formality** with which people are being addressed in the text. Many European languages have separate second-person pronouns depending on whether the speaker is addressing the listener formally and politely, or informally and casually, eg. French *vous* versus *tu*, German *Sie* versus *du*. An English sentence such as *where are you?* has an unresolvable ambiguity (from the perspective of the target language) because there is no indication in it as to which level of formality is intended, or which level of formality *would* be required if one were speaking in the target language. (Contrast this with a sentence such as *where are you Sir?* where the ambiguity is resolvable from the presence of the formal form of address *Sir*.[2])

As is obvious, the Fairslator taxonomy covers many kinds of translation bias, not just bias in gender, even though gender bias is currently the most vigurously debated kind of bias in machine translation (see Savoldi et al. 2021 for a state-of-the-art survey). In terms of the language categories defined by Savoldi et al. 2021, 3.1.1, the taxonomy can (be adapted to) describe gender bias-causing ambiguities during translation from all *genderless languages* into all *notional gender languages* (languages that encode the gender of humans in pronouns and nouns that refer to them) and *grammatical gender languages* (languages that encode the gender of humans through inflection on words that do not directly refer to humans, such as verbs and adjectives).

That said, the taxonomy in its current incarnation, as presented in this paper, is oriented towards translation from English into other, mainly European, languages, and there is a version of the taxonomy for each **directed language pair**: one for English-to-German, one for English-to-Czech and so on.

2 Bias statement: what is bias in machine translation?

We can now proceed to a more formal definition of what we mean by bias. When we consider machine translation as a black box and simply take its input and output as a pair of texts (the source text in the source language plus the translation in the target language), then we can define the following concepts:

Unresolvable ambiguity A portion of the source text contains an unresolvable ambiguity if, in order to translate it successfully into the target language, some *semantic property* of it needs to be known (such as its gender or grammatical number or level of formality) but this property is *not expressed* in the source text and cannot be inferred from anything in the source text.

Unjustified assumption An unjustified assumption is what happens when, in the face of an unresolvable ambiguity, the machine translator decides for one particular reading of the ambiguous expression over others. The assumption is unjustified because nothing actually present in the source text justifies it. The machine's decision is either random or, if the translator has been constructed through machine learning, predetermined by which reading has been observed more often in the training data.

[2] In fact, the addition of "tag-ons" such as *Sir* or *dude*, such as *he said* or *she said* to the end of the sentence is one method which has been experimented with to "solve" machine translation bias. Effectively, it "tricks" the translator into interpreting things in a particular way. See Moryossef et al. 2019.

Bias A machine translator is biased if, while dealing with unresolvable ambiguities and deciding which unjustified assumptions to make, its decisions are *not* random: it makes certain unjustified assumptions more often than others. For example, if a translator consistently decides for male readings of *doctor* or for singular informal readings of *you* (when these are unresolvably ambiguous in the source text), then the translator is biased.

In other words, we define bias as a purely technical concept, as the tendency of an automated system to make certain unjustified assumptions more often than others. This differs from the popular common-sense understanding of the word *bias* which, in addition to the purely technical process, implies harmful and unjust consequences. This implication is not a necessary part of our definition. Our definition of bias covers bias regardless of whether it is harmful to society (eg. because it perpetuates a stereotype by speaking about doctors as if they must always be men), harmful to an individual (eg. because it offends somebody by addressing them with an inappropriately informal pronoun) or relatively harmless and merely factually incorrect (eg. because it addresses a group of people with a singular pronoun).

Interestingly, our definition applies not only to machines but also to humans: it is not unheard of for human translators to make the same kind of unjustified assumptions and to go about it with the same amount of bias as machines. Good human translators avoid bias by observing the extralinguistic reality (simply *looking* to see eg. whether the speaker seems male or female) and by asking follow-up questions ("what do you mean by *you*?"). Machine translators do not normally have the means to do such things but Fairslator is a plug-in which adds the latter ability to any machine translator: the ability to recognize unresolvable ambiguities, to ask follow-up questions, and to re-inflect the translation in accordance with the answers, in a fashion similar to Habash et al. 2019 and Alhafni et al. 2020.

3 Components of the taxonomy

3.1 Axes of ambiguity

To describe the unresolvable ambiguities in a pair of texts (source + translation) in the Fairslator taxonomy, we need to analyze the text pair along three axes:

The speaker axis Is the speaker mentioned in the translation, for example by first-person pronouns? And if so, is the speaker mentioned in the translation in a way that encodes gender, while the source text does not?

The listener axis Is the listener mentioned in the translation, for example by second-person pronouns or implicitly through verbs in the imperative? And if so, is the listener mentioned in the translation in a way that encodes gender, number or formality while the source text does not?

The bystander axis Are any bystanders mentioned in the translation, that is to say, are any people other than the speaker and the listener being referred to by nouns or by third-person pronouns? And if so, are the bystanders mentioned in the translation in a way that encodes gender, while the source text does not?

Each text pair contains zero or one speaker axis, zero or one listener axis, and zero, one or more bystander axes. For each axis, we can use the taxonomy to express the fact that there are or are not any unresolvable ambiguities on this axis, what the **allowed readings** are (eg. the translation can be either masculine or feminine along this axis) and which reading is actually expressed in the translation (eg. the translation is masculine along this axis).

We can illustrate this on an example. Assume the following English sentence and its Czech translation.[3]

> *I would like to ask whether this is your new doctor.*
> *Chtěla bych se zeptat, jestli tohle je tvůj nový lékař.*

Using the three kinds of axes, we can analyze this text pair as follows.

1. The speaker axis is present here. The speaker is mentioned in the translation with the words *chtěla bych* 'I would like to' where the word *chtěla* is a verbal participle and encodes the speaker as female in gender, while the source text is ambiguous as to the speaker's gender.

[3]The example is a little convoluted. This is necessary in order to demonstrate all three axes.

2. The listener axis is also present here. The listener is mentioned in the translation with the word *tvůj* 'your'. This word encodes the listener as singular in number and addressed informally, while the source text is ambiguous on these things. Neither the source text nor the translation say anything about the gender of the listener.

3. Finally, one bystander axis is present here. The bystander is mentioned in the source text by the word *doctor* and in the translation by the word *lékař*. The word in the translation encodes the bystander as male in gender, while in the source text it is ambiguous in gender.

For each axis, we have stated two things. First, which readings are allowed by the source text, for example "the speaker can be interpreted as male or female". Second, which reading is actually expressed in the translation, for example "the speaker has been interpreted as female".

3.2 Ambiguity descriptors

To describe the possible readings on each axis, the taxonomy uses combinations of one-letter abbreviations such as `m` or `f` for masculine or feminine gender, `s` or `p` for singular and plural number, and `t` or `v` for informal or formal form of address (from the Latin pronouns *tu* and *vos*, as is comon in linguistic literature on this topic). Using this code we can re-express the observations from above more succinctly:

```
1. sm|sf : sf
2. st|sv|p : st
3. doctor : sm|sf : sm
```

Human-readably, this means:

1. The speaker axis can be `sm` (singular masculine) or `sf` (singular feminine). Currently it is `sf` (singular feminine).

2. The listener axis can be `st` (singular informal) or `sv` (singular formal) or `p` (plural).[4] Currently it is `st` (singular informal).

3. The bystander axis identified through the nickname `doctor` can be `sm` (singular masculine) or `sf` (singular feminine). Currently it is `sm` (singular masculine).

[4]In the plural, Czech has no distinction between formal and informal registers.

Each line is a **descriptor** which describes the unresolvable ambiguity on a given axis. Each descriptor consists of:

- A number to indicate which axis is being talked about: `1` for the speaker axis, `2` for the listener axis, `3` for the bystander axis. Each description can contain zero or one descriptor for the speaker axis, zero or one descriptor for the listener axis, and zero or one or more descriptors for the bystander axis.

- For the bystander axis only: a nickname to identify this bystander axis from other bystander axes in this description. This is usually a word taken from the source text. If there is more than one bystander axis in the text pair (which is rare but happens in sentences such as *the doctor asked the nurse to...*) than they must have different nicknames (eg. `doctor` and `nurse`).

- Codes for all the readings allowed by the source text in this axis, separated by vertical lines, for example `st|sv|p`.

- A code for the reading actually expressed in the translation for this axis, for example `st`.

Fairslator uses a slightly different catalogue of descriptors for each directed language pair. As an example, Fairslator's complete inventory of descriptors for English-to-German is given in the Appendix.

4 How Fairslator uses the taxonomy

The main purpose of the taxonomy is to make it possible for Fairslator to formulate *human-friendly disambiguation questions* for users.[5] Here are some examples of descriptors and the disambiguation questions generated from them.

1. `sm|sf : sf`
   - Who is saying it?
     - a man
     - a woman (selected)

1. `pm|pf : pm`
   - Who is saying it?

[5]Fairslator's target audience is users who speak the source language but do not speak the target language, or do not speak it well enough to be able to detect and correct biased translations on their own.

- a group containing at least one man (selected)
- a group of women

2. `st|sv|p : st`
   - Who are you saying it to?
     - one person
       - addressed informally (selected)
       - addressed formally
     - several people

3. `doctor : sm|sf : sm`
   - Who is the person identified as "doctor"?
     - a man (selected)
     - a woman

Once the human user has made a selection from these options, Fairslator re-inflects the translation in accordance with the user's wishes: changes pronouns and nouns accordingly, changes verbs and adjectives so as not break grammatical agreement, and so on. The details of this process, as well as details of how Fairslator detects unresolvable ambiguities in the first place, are not the subject of this paper but some information about this can be found in Měchura 2022.

5 Discussion: where the taxonomy could be improved

I* versus *we The taxonomy assumes that there is always no more than one speaker axis in each text and that its grammatical number never changes: it is always either *I* or *we* but never both. This means that it cannot handle texts where the speaker refers not only to himself or herself (*I*) but also to a group he or she belongs to (*we*), such as *I think we should...*

Multiple voices While the taxonomy is able to handle texts consisting of multiple sentences without problems, it can only do so on the assumption that the axes remain unchanged throughout the text. When the axes do change, as they do in a dialogue (*How are you? Very well, and you?*), then the taxonomy is currently unable to keep track of "who is who" and wrongly assumes that, for example, the people referred to by *you* are the same person throughout.

Word-sense ambiguities The taxonomy is designed to handle unresolvable ambiguities in three semantic properties: gender, number and formality. In principle, however, *any* semantic property can be affected by an unresolvable ambiguity during translation. So, ideally, word-sense ambiguities of *any* kind should be covered by the taxonomy. One example for many is *river* → French *fleuve* 'large river flowing into the sea' versus *rivière* 'small river flowing into another river'. In a sentence such as *we went for a walk along the river* being translated into French, the sense of *river* is unresolvably ambiguous and, if not disambiguated manually by a human user, the machine's translation is bound to be biased in favour of one sense or the other. See Lee et al. 2016 for an inspiring attempt to remove word-sense bias from machine translation through human-driven word-sense disambiguation.

Gender-neutral language In languages where words come in gendered pairs, such as *teacher* → German *Lehrer* male or *Lehrerin* female, it is sometimes possible to construct a gender-neutral neologism by merging them together, such as *Lehrer:in*, in case a gender-neutral word is required. The same can sometimes be done with pronouns, adjectives, verbal participles and other gendered pairs of words. While such neoforms are pragmatically strongly marked and not all writers and readers like them, they do exist and should therefore be included in the taxonomy as one of not two but three gender values: male, female and gender-neutral.

6 Summary

Machine translation technology is getting better all the time at resolving ambiguities from clues in the context. But some ambiguities can never be resolved in this way because there *are* no clues in the context. To avoid bias during the translation of texts that contain unresolvable ambiguities, we need to build tools which are able to (1) recognize that an unresolvable ambiguity has occured and (2) ask the human user to disambiguate manually.

To be able to build such tools at all, what we need first of all is an expressive formalism for *describing* unresolvable ambiguities. This paper has shown how to construct such a formalism for any directed language pair by analysing the source text and its translation from the point of view of three axes (speaker, listener and bystander) and by describing any unresolvable ambiguities that occur in those axes through descriptors which tell us (1) which readings are allowed by the source text and (2) which one of those readings is actually expressed in the translation.

References

Bashar Alhafni, Nizar Habash, and Houda Bouamor. 2020. Gender-aware reinflection using linguistically enhanced neural models. In *Proceedings of the Second Workshop on Gender Bias in Natural Language Processing*, pages 139–150, Barcelona, Spain (Online). Association for Computational Linguistics.

Nizar Habash, Houda Bouamor, and Christine Chung. 2019. Automatic Gender Identification and Reinflection in Arabic. In *Proceedings of the First Workshop on Gender Bias in Natural Language Processing*, pages 155–165, Florence, Italy. Association for Computational Linguistics.

Hyoung-Gyu Lee, Jun-Seok Kim, Joong-Hwi Shin, Jaesong Lee, Ying-Xiu Quan, and Young-Seob Jeong. 2016. papago: A machine translation service with word sense disambiguation and currency conversion. In *Proceedings of COLING 2016, the 26th International Conference on Computational Linguistics: System Demonstrations*, pages 185–188, Osaka, Japan. The COLING 2016 Organizing Committee.

Amit Moryossef, Roee Aharoni, and Yoav Goldberg. 2019. Filling Gender & Number Gaps in Neural Machine Translation with Black-box Context Injection. In *Proceedings of the First Workshop on Gender Bias in Natural Language Processing*, pages 49–54, Florence, Italy. Association for Computational Linguistics.

Michal Měchura. 2022. We need to talk about bias in machine translation: the Fairslator whitepaper. Technical report.

Beatrice Savoldi, Marco Gaido, Luisa Bentivogli, Matteo Negri, and Marco Turchi. 2021. Gender Bias in Machine Translation. *Transactions of the Association for Computational Linguistics*, 9:845–874.

Appendix: inventory of descriptors

Here we are going to lay out Fairslator's complete inventory of descriptors for **English-to-German**. Each descriptor describes one type of unresolvable ambiguity which is capable of occurring during translation between these two languages, in this direction. We accompany each descriptor with an example to illustrate the ambiguity.

Speaker axis

`1. sm|sf`
I am the new director.
`sm` *Ich bin der neue Direktor.*
`sf` *Ich bin die neue Direktorin.*

`1. pm|pf`
We are teachers.
`pm` *Wir sind Lehrer.*
`pf` *Wir sind Lehrerinnen.*

Listener axis

`2. ts|vs|tp|vp`
Are these your children?
`ts` *Sind das deine Kinder?*
`vs` *Sind das Ihre Kinder?*
`tp` *Sind das eure Kinder?*
`vp` *Sind das Ihre Kinder?*

`2. ts|vs`
Did you do it yourself?
`ts` *Hast du es selbst gemacht?*
`vs` *Haben Sie es selbst gemacht?*

`2. tp|vp`
Did you do it yourselves?
`ps` *Habt ihr es selbst gemacht?*
`vp` *Haben Sie es selbst gemacht?*

`2. tsm|tsf|vsm|vsf`
Are you the new director?
`tsm` *Bist du der neue Direktor?*
`tsf` *Bist du die neue Direktorin?*
`vsm` *Sind Sie der neue Direktor?*
`vsf` *Sind Sie die neue Direktorin?*

`2. tpm|tpf|vpm|vpf`
Are you teachers?
`tpm` *Seid ihr Lehrer?*
`tpf` *Seid ihr Lehrerinnen?*
`vpm` *Sind Sie Lehrer?*
`vpf` *Sind Sie Lehrerinnen?*

Bystander axis

`3. director : sm|sf`
This is the new director.
`sm` *Das ist der neue Direktor.*
`sf` *Das ist die neue Direktorin.*

`3. teachers : pm|pf`
These are our teachers.
`pm` *Das sind unsere Lehrer.*
`pf` *Das sind unsere Lehrerinnen.*

On Gender Biases in Offensive Language Classification Models

Sanjana Marcé[1] **Adam Poliak**[2*]

[1]Columbia University

[2]Bryn Mawr College

apoliak@brynmawr.edu

Abstract

We explore whether neural Natural Language Processing models trained to identify offensive language in tweets contain gender biases. We add historically gendered and gender ambiguous American names to an existing offensive language evaluation set to determine whether models' predictions are sensitive or robust to gendered names. While we see some evidence that these models might be prone to biased stereotypes that men use more offensive language than women, our results indicate that these models' binary predictions might not greatly change based upon gendered names.

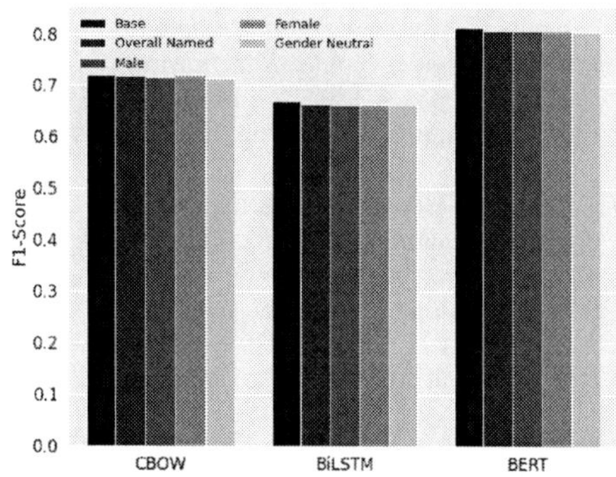

Figure 1: F1 Scores of the CBoW, BiLSTM, and BERT models isolated by each gender. The models' predictions do not noticeably change based on the gender of named examples.

1 Introduction

Identifying offensive language in text is an increasingly important challenge that has sparked the release of datasets and advanced models focused on toxic language detection in multiple languages (Razavi et al., 2010; Pitenis et al., 2020; Sigurbergsson and Derczynski, 2020; Çöltekin, 2020; Founta et al., 2018). For these models to be trustworthy when deployed in sensitive, real-world contexts, they must perform equally well for text written by male, female, or non-binary authors.

However, based on known gender-based biases in NLP systems (Rudinger et al., 2018; Zhao et al., 2018; Sun et al., 2019; Gaut et al., 2020; Stanovsky et al., 2019; Savoldi et al., 2021), especially among models trained to detect abusive language (Park et al., 2018), we hypothesize that existing NLP systems that incorporate pre-trained word embeddings or transformer-based language models will perform differently given access to authors' names if those names are generally associated with a particular gender.[1] To test the hypothesis that offensive language identification models exhibit gender biases, we adopt the *Perturbation Sensitivity Analysis* framework (Prabhakaran et al., 2019). We perturb examples of an existing dataset by adding historically gendered or gender-ambiguous names to the original texts. We evaluate whether three classes of NLP models (bag of words, BiLSTM, and transformers) systematically change their predictions on our modified gendered examples.

Although we see statistically significant differences when comparing a bag of words model's and transformer model's predictions between male and female examples, we do not see convincingly strong evidence that the models' binary predictions for offensiveness consistently change with the addition of gendered names (Figure 1). Therefore, we compare how the model's predicted offensiveness probability changes for perturbed examples. We also explore if there are specific names for which the predicted class probability consistently changes. While we see some remnants of gendered

* Work performed while at Barnard College

[1] In this paper we use an author's name assigned at birth as a proxy for their gender. While we acknowledge the limitations associated with inferring gender from an individual's name, in doing so we recreate real-world circumstances in which NLP systems would make gendered associations based upon a speaker's or author's name even when their gender is not explicitly mentioned.

Proceedings of the The 4th Workshop on Gender Bias in Natural Language Processing (GeBNLP), pages 174 - 183
July 15, 2022 ©2022 Association for Computational Linguistics

Example	CBoW	BiLSTM	BERT
▶ *@USER You are missing brains?*	0.741306	0.999869	0.839001
♀ *Vanessa tweeted @USER You are missing brains?*	0.859568	0.999833	0.755025
♂ *Matthew tweeted @USER You are missing brains?*	0.859568	0.999833	0.756230
○ *Oakley tweeted @USER You are missing brains?*	0.859568	0.999833	0.735549

Table 1: An example of an offensive tweet from the development set and the offensiveness probability each model (*CBoW, BiLSTM, BERT*) assigned to the unmodified (▶), female (♀), male (♂), and gender-neutral versions (○).

biases, our results offer encouraging evidence that downstream models using pre-trained representations that are known to encode gendered stereotypes (Bolukbasi et al., 2016; Garg et al., 2018; Zhao et al., 2018) might overcome these biases.

2 Motivation & Bias Statement

As user-generated content gradually dominates online spaces, offensive text has become more ubiquitous (Banks, 2010; Kumar et al., 2020). Unregulated inflammatory or hateful online discourse can have profound effects that extend beyond the web, from negative mental health impacts for targeted individuals to instigation of physical violence (Safi Samghabadi et al., 2020; Siegel, 2020). Hence, identifying and moderating toxic dialogue efficiently and accurately is a task that only grows more crucial, and developing automatic methods to detect and flag offensive language is critical.

Psychological studies spanning the past four decades conclude that, on average, "men use offensive language more than women" (although this gap has shrunk over time), likely as a result of how women are "socialized into subordinate roles and a less inflammatory manner of communicating" (Sapolsky and Kaye, 2005). Moreover, these observed patterns of offensive or abusive content authorship translate to online communities like Twitter (Mubarak et al., 2021).

Research into fairness in NLP indicates that systems trained on large corpora of human-written text tend to replicate existing stereotypes about gendered behavior (Sun et al., 2019; Babaeianjelodar et al., 2020). Thus, offensive language detection classifiers based on social-media data risk inheriting these underlying assumptions that male-authored tweets are more likely to utilize offensive language than text written by female individuals.

As it becomes more common for social media platforms to rely on NLP systems to detect and remove profane or hateful content online, it becomes increasingly vital that these classification models are robust to gender biases. While previous research has considered identity-based bias against a gendered *subject* in abusive language tasks (Park et al., 2018; Prabhakaran et al., 2019) and gender-based biases among annotations (Excell and Al Moubayed, 2021), how the perceived gender of a *speaker* or *author* affects output model classification remains understudied.

3 Experimental Setup

Our goal is to determine whether offensive language identification models are prone to gender biases. We train bag of word, BiLSTM, and transformer-based models on the Offensive Language Identification Dataset (OLID; Zampieri et al., 2019a). OLID is the official dataset used in the OffensEval shared tasks (Zampieri et al., 2019b, 2020), where tweets containing profanity, insults, threats, hate speech, etc, are labeled as offensive (Zampieri et al., 2019a). OLID contains 13,240 annotated English-language tweets (4400 offensive, 8840 not offensive) and 860 test examples (240 offensive, 620 not offensive). For model training, we split the original training set into 12,380 training and 860 dev examples.[2]

3.1 Gendered Test Set Creation

In order to evaluate whether the models' predictions change when the text explicitly mentions the author of the tweet, we modify the 860 test set examples using the following template:[3]

(1) Name tweeted original tweet

where *original tweet* is the original test example

[2]We provide all model implementation and hyper-parameter tuning details in subsection 3.2.

[3]This template is similar to those previously used to evaluate natural language inference systems' abilities to capture different semantic phenomena (Poliak et al., 2018) and gender bias in named entity recognition systems (Mehrabi et al., 2020).

Hyper-parameter	Options	Models Used
Batch Size	16, 32, 64, 128	CBoW, BiLSTM, BERT*
Num. Hidden Features	1, 3, 5, 16, 64	CBoW, BiLSTM
Learning Rate	0.1, 0.01, 0.001, 0.0001	CBoW, BiLSTM
Dropout Rate	0.1, 0.2, 0.3, 0.4, 0.5, 0.6, 0.7, 0.8, 0.9	CBoW

Table 2: Permutations of hyper-parameter configurations tested, with the models that use each hyper-parameter. *Due to machine memory constraints, only batch sizes of 16 and 32 were tested for BERT.

and *Name* is replaced with a name from an aggregated list of 212 historically gendered and gender ambiguous names in the United States to create a test set of 182,320 named tweets. Table 1 provides an example from our dataset.

Using standard practice (Vogel and Jurafsky, 2012; Bamman et al., 2014), we create a list of traditionally gendered names using publicly available government statistics. In particular, we compile data from the Social Security Administration's annual list of American baby names from 2000-2018.[4] We aggregate names with $p(gender|name) \geq 0.9$, filter out those names not recognized as singular tokens by the BERT and GloVe vocabularies, preventing OOV issues.[5] We select the top 100 most frequent names ascribed to newborns assigned female or male at birth.

While current research suggests that toxic language models may perform differentially on gendered input (Park et al., 2018), work remains to be done on how these models may misclassify text written by authors who do not conform to the gender binary. Therefore, we also include six gender-neutral names (*Justice, Milan, Lennon, Oakley, Marion,* and *Jackie*) that appear at approximately similar gender frequencies in the SSA data ($0.9 \geq \frac{p(male|name)}{p(female|name)} \geq 1.1$), are recognized by both pre-trained vocabularies, and were assigned to at least 4,000 newborns over the considered time-frame. We add one male (*he*), one female (*she*), and four gender-neutral pronouns (*one, they, someone* and *a person*).

[4]Prior research has similarly extracted gendered names from the Social Security Administration (Smith et al., 2013; Mohammad, 2019; Garg et al., 2018; HallMaudslay et al., 2019; Mehrabi et al., 2020; Shwartz et al., 2020)

[5]Filtering for names recognized by the BERT and GloVe vocabularies when collecting the top 100 gendered names recognized by pre-trained embeddings removed 11 more female names than male names. This might illustrate a bias against traditionally female names in these representations.

3.2 Implementation Details

We explore classifiers based on three different classes of neural encoders. Each model was tested on a range of hyper-parameter configurations (Table 2), and the best configuration was chosen based on maximizing F1-Score on the validation set. Our trained models achieve comparable performance on the unnamed validation set to published results for similar classes of models on OLID (Ramakrishnan et al., 2019; Mahata et al., 2019; Zampieri et al., 2019a; Wu et al., 2019; Pavlopoulos et al., 2019; Aggarwal et al., 2019; Zhu et al., 2019).

Neural Bag of Words We trained a Continuous Bag of Words model (CBoW) to build classifiers for offensive and not offensive tweets and predict the output class of a new tweet based on the average vector representation of its tokens. To process the input examples, we use the NLTK tweet tokenizer and 100-dimensional GloVe embeddings (Pennington et al., 2014) pre-trained specifically for Twitter-sourced text.[6] Our CBoW model consists of a multi-layer perceptron (MLP) with a single hidden layer with one feature built on top of an embedding layer. The best performing model uses a batch size of 16 for training and validation, a learning rate of 0.001, and a dropout rate of 0.9 for regularization.

BiLSTM encoder The second type of encoder we consider is a Bidirectional LSTM (BiLSTM) (Schuster and Paliwal, 1997; Hochreiter and Schmidhuber, 1997). We process the input using the same tweet tokenizer and Twitter-trained GloVe embeddings as in the CBoW model. The best performing BiLSTM model architecture consists of a bidirectional LSTM layer with 128 output features and a MLP with 64 features in the hidden layer. For this model, weights are updated during training with a learning rate of 0.001 in an Adam optimizer and a training and validation batch size of 64.

[6]Twitter GloVe embeddings downloaded from https://nlp.stanford.edu/projects/glove/

	CBoW				BiLSTM				BERT			
	TN	FN	TP	FP	TN	FN	TP	FP	TN	FN	TP	FP
-	62.79	12.44	15.47	09.30	58.95	13.37	14.53	13.14	65.12	07.91	20.00	06.98
♂	61.52	11.87	16.03	10.57	58.19	13.43	14.48	13.91	65.11	08.28	19.62	06.98
♀	61.92	11.93	15.97	10.17	58.47	13.48	14.42	13.62	65.35	08.55	19.36	06.75
o	61.51	12.05	15.86	10.58	58.09	13.41	14.50	14.00	65.13	08.43	19.48	06.97

Table 3: Aggregated confusion matrices of the CBoW, BiLSTM, and BERT models evaluated on the original, unmodified (-) test tweets and each named gender subgroup (male ♂, female ♀, and gender neutral o). To enable easier comparisons, we normalized counts in the confusion matrices so that each cell represents the percentages of each type of prediction the models made across each gender.

Model \ Gender	-	♂	♀	o
CBoW	71.98	71.70	71.98	71.41
BiLSTM	66.97	66.21	66.37	66.16
BERT	81.31	80.75	80.60	80.55

Table 4: F1 scores for each model on the original unnamed (-) and male (♂), female (♀), and gender neutral (o) examples.

	t-stat	p-value
CBoW	2.1615	0.0153
BiLSTM	1.5833	0.0567
BERT	2.3691	0.0089

Table 5: Result of one-sided t-test comparing each models' predictions for male vs female authored-examples.

Transformers We fine-tune a HuggingFace pretrained BERT base-uncased model (Wolf et al., 2020) on our offensive training set using 2 epochs, 50 warm-up steps, a weight decay of 0.01, and a batch size of 16. We process the input examples using the BERT base-uncased tokenizer, the same tokenizer used when identifying OOV names.

3.3 Results

In our experiments, the models' F1-performances[7] slightly change on our examples modified with gendered or gender-neutral names (Figure 1 and Table 4). Compared to the original, unmodified test examples, the models' performance drops on the named examples and it seems that BERT's performance is most affected by the named examples compared to the other models. By adding the True Positives and False Positives rates in the confusion matrices Table 3, we notice an increase in offensive predictions across all genders for CBoW, a smaller increase for BiLSTM, and a slight decrease in offensive predictions for BERT.[8] In other words, just by adding a name or pronoun, the Glove-based models predict more examples as offensive and the BERT model predict fewer examples as offensive. However, across all models, the difference in predictions on the gendered and original examples is not statistically significant, as measured by t-tests.

Focusing just on the named examples, the models that do not use contextualized word representations (CBoW and BiLSTM) perform better on the female examples than the male or gender neutral examples, while the BERT model achieves a higher F1 score on the male examples than on the female or gender neutral examples. Turning towards our goal of identifying whether the models are prone to the stereotype that men use more offensive language than women, we notice that all models classify more male authored tweets as offensive than female authored tweets. Specifically the CBoW, BiLSTM, and BERT models respectively classify 0.46% (397), 0.35% (297), and 0.49% (435) more male authored-examples as offensive than female authored-examples.[9] While one-sided[10] t-tests (Table 5) comparing the models' predictions between

[7]We report F1-Score since both the training and test datasets are not balanced.

[8]CBoW classifies 24.77% of the unnamed test examples as offensive compared to 26.60% for male, 26.14% for female, and 26.44% for gender neutral examples. BiLSTM classifies 27.67% of the unnamed test examples as offensive compared to 28.39% for male, 28.04% for female, and 28.50% for gender neutral. BERT classifies 26.98% of the unnamed examples as offensive compared to 26.60% for male, 26.11% for female, and 26.45% for gender neutral examples.

[9]These are absolute differences between male TP + FP rates and female TP + FP rates.

[10]Specifically that the models categorize more male-authored than female-authored tweets as offensive.

male and female authored-examples indicate that these are statistically significant differences for CBoW and BERT, the small differences in magnitude might suggest that adding historically gendered names as speakers in our examples does not consistently or convincingly alter the models' class predictions for whether or not a tweet is offensive. The statistical significance for CBoW and BERT might be due to the large sample size in our study.

4 Further Analysis

Since our results do not conclusively support our hypothesis that the models' binary predictions change for *all* considered models when explicitly adding gendered names to our test examples, we turn our attention towards exploring whether, and to what extent, the models' assigned probabilities change for our perturbed dataset. We also investigate whether these predicted probabilities consistently change for any specific names.

4.1 Offensiveness Probability Scores

Solely investigating whether a model's binary predictions change might mask gender biases should the model's predicted probabilities vary largely without crossing the label decision boundary. To explore whether this is the case, we compute the difference between a model's predicted offensiveness probability for every modified and corresponding unmodified example. The average differences are 0.021 ($\sigma = 0.059$) for CBoW, 0.007 ($\sigma = 0.059$) for BiLSTM, and -0.007 ($\sigma = 0.47$) for BERT.

Figure 2 plots the distribution of these differences grouped by gender for each model. These histograms illustrate that across all three models, for the majority of modified examples, the change in offensiveness probability is very small.

Additionally, these histograms further confirm our initial findings. For the CBoW model (Figure 2a), adding a gendered name seems to more likely lead to an increase in predicted offensive probability, and male names lead to larger increases. For the BiLSTM model (Figure 2b), the distributions of the differences for male and female examples almost match and a large majority of male (88.64%) and female (90.22%) examples have an absolute difference less than 0.025%. For the BERT model (Figure 2c), including gendered names in the examples lead to a decrease in predicted offensive probability, with more pronounced decreases for female names.

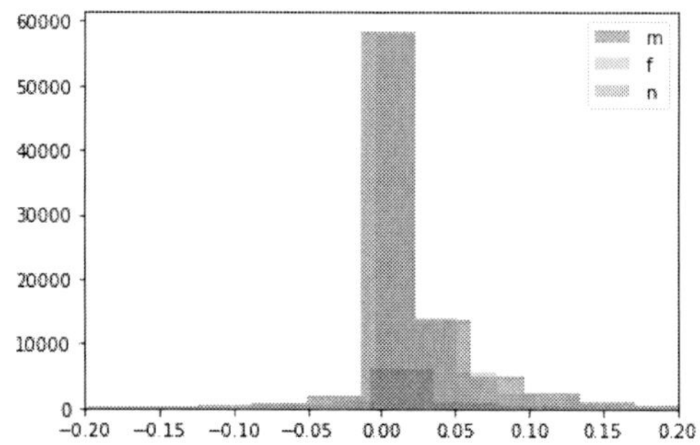

(a) CBoW

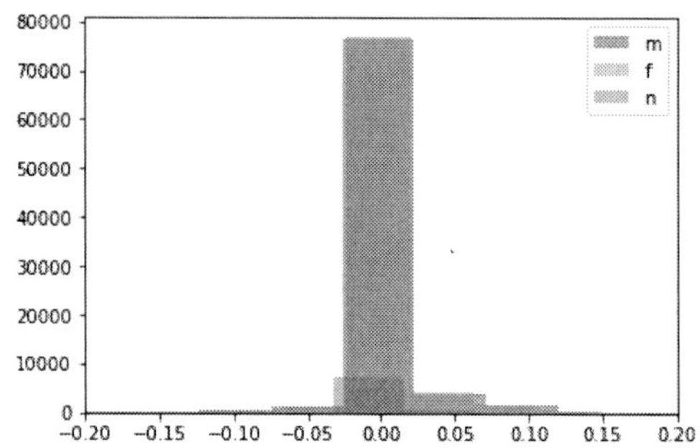

(b) BiLSTM

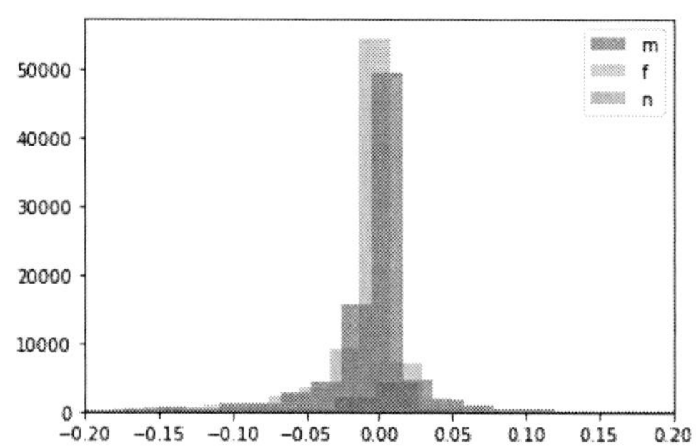

(c) BERT

Figure 2: Histograms plotting the change in offensive class probability between named and unnamed examples, grouped by gender (m: male, f: female, n: gender-neutral). A positive difference indicates that the model determined the named tweet to be more offensive than the base tweet.

These histograms demonstrates that there are very few examples where the model's predicted probabilities vary largely without crossing the label decision boundary. However, these histograms, specifically Figure 2a and Figure 2c, might reflect the stereotypes discussed by Sapolsky and Kaye (2005) that men use more offensive language than women.

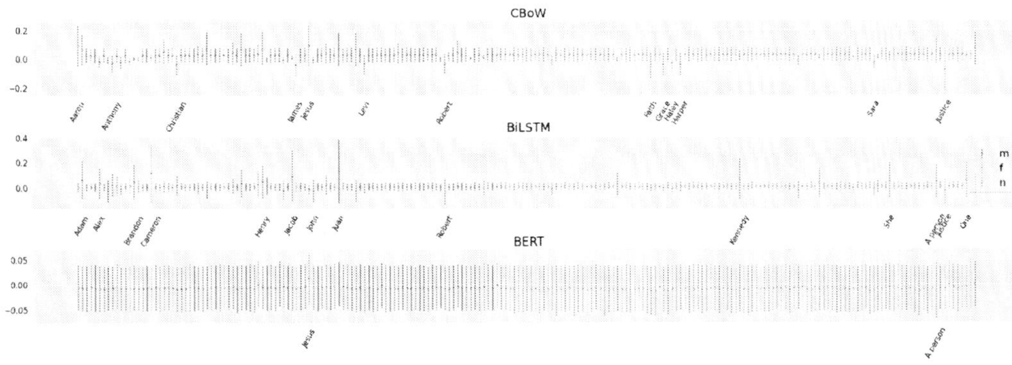

Figure 3: For each model, we plot how (average and standard deviation) the predicted offensiveness probability changed for each name. Y-axis indicates the difference. We label the names where the average difference was outside the typical standard deviation across the model.

4.2 Individual Name Impact

Prior work has shown that pre-trained representations might encode stereotypes about specific names (Shwartz et al., 2020). To test if these models similarly contain biases about specific names, we now group the difference between a model's predicted probability for each modified and corresponding unmodified example by prepended name.

Figure 3 plots how these differences vary for each name. The average differences in the BERT model's predictions consistently vary, but insignificantly. We notice just one name, *Jesus*, stands out as more offensive and one pronoun, *a person*, is uniquely less offensive. The mean change over all examples prepended with *Jesus* in the BERT model is 0.012, compared to an average change of -0.007 across all named examples. This finding is perhaps attributable to how *Jesus* is often used in colloquial English speech and on online platforms as a form of exclamation (Goddard, 2015).

For the GloVe-based models, we notice that the average and standard deviation of differences are identical for the same set of 158 names (and pronouns).[11] These models' predicted probabilities changed more for male than female names. Of the 54 names where the models' average probabilities differed from that of the 158 names, 36 are male, 13 are female, and 5 are gender-neutral. CBoW's average probability increased for 15 male, 0 female, and 2 gender-neutral names, and BiLSTM's increased for 21 male, 5 female, and 3 gender-neutral names. This suggests that the GloVe based models might find male names to be more offensive than female names. However, there is little overlap between the male names that the CBoW and BiLSTM model usually predict as being more offensive (e.g. *Aaron*, *David*, and *Henry* for CBoW and *Adam*, *Brandon*. and *Jacob* for BiLSTM). For the name *Robert*, both models typically predict a lower offensive probability. The greater variations in the CBoW and BiLSTM predictions suggests that these models are more sensitive to the presence of specific gendered names compared to transformer-based models.

5 Conclusion

We asked whether there exists a measurable gender-based asymmetry in models' performances for predicting offensiveness when a tweet explicitly states the speaker's name. Our experimental results imply that a range of typical neural models might be robust to perceived author gender when classifying tweets as offensive though they might perceive male authored tweets to be slightly more offensive. Our work supports recent findings that intrinsic biases in the word embedding space may not correlate to extrinsic measures of bias in downstream applications (Goldfarb-Tarrant et al., 2021). While these findings on gender bias in offensive classification tasks are promising, we encourage further research to evaluate the extent to which these results generalize across more datasets and language phenomena as well as other social groups and intersectional identities, such as speaker race, age, and sexual orientation.

[11]The mean and standard deviation for these difference in CBoW's predictions for these names are respectively 0.025 and 0.049 and 0.005 and 0.031 for the BiLSTM.

6 Ethical Considerations

As noted in Antoniak and Mimno (2021), collecting gendered names from population-derived data has the limitation of centering the majority population, in this case US-born, white children. Moreover, while filtering for names not recognized by the GloVe or BERT vocabularies ensures our study only includes names that have pre-trained representations, this filtering might perpetuate biases in our tests since it disproportionately affected non-white names and female names.

Researchers have called on the NLP community to move beyond the gender binary (Larson, 2017; Prabhakaran et al., 2019). While our study included gender-neutral names and pronouns, we acknowledge that this set is drastically smaller than that of gendered names. We leave a deep study into the impact of gender-neutral names or pronouns as future work.

Using names as a proxy for gender is fraught with potential limitations and biases, particularly when an individual's gender identity does not match the gender historically associated with their name. However, NLP systems might make gendered associations based upon a speaker's name even when the speaker's gender is not explicitly mentioned. As discussed in footnote 1, we acknowledge these issues and strive to parallel the circumstances in which these systems may be deployed in the real world.

Acknowledgements

We are grateful to the anonymous reviewers who provided useful and insightful comments on this work. This work was partially supported by the Columbia University Data Science Institute's Data For Good Scholars program.

References

Piush Aggarwal, Tobias Horsmann, Michael Wojatzki, and Torsten Zesch. 2019. LTL-UDE at SemEval-2019 task 6: BERT and two-vote classification for categorizing offensiveness. In *Proceedings of the 13th International Workshop on Semantic Evaluation*, pages 678–682, Minneapolis, Minnesota, USA. Association for Computational Linguistics.

Maria Antoniak and David Mimno. 2021. Bad seeds: Evaluating lexical methods for bias measurement. In *Proceedings of the 59th Annual Meeting of the Association for Computational Linguistics and the 11th International Joint Conference on Natural Language Processing (Volume 1: Long Papers)*, pages 1889–1904, Online. Association for Computational Linguistics.

Marzieh Babaeianjelodar, Stephen Lorenz, Josh Gordon, Jeanna Matthews, and Evan Freitag. 2020. Quantifying gender bias in different corpora. In *Companion Proceedings of the Web Conference 2020*, WWW '20, page 752–759, New York, NY, USA. Association for Computing Machinery.

David Bamman, Jacob Eisenstein, and Tyler Schnoebelen. 2014. Gender identity and lexical variation in social media. *Journal of Sociolinguistics*, 18(2):135–160.

James Banks. 2010. Regulating hate speech online. *International Review of Law, Computers & Technology*, 24(3):233–239.

Tolga Bolukbasi, Kai-Wei Chang, James Zou, Venkatesh Saligrama, and Adam Kalai. 2016. Man is to computer programmer as woman is to homemaker? debiasing word embeddings. In *NeurIPS*.

Çağrı Çöltekin. 2020. A corpus of Turkish offensive language on social media. In *Proceedings of the 12th Language Resources and Evaluation Conference*, pages 6174–6184, Marseille, France. European Language Resources Association.

Elizabeth Excell and Noura Al Moubayed. 2021. Towards equal gender representation in the annotations of toxic language detection. In *Proceedings of the 3rd Workshop on Gender Bias in Natural Language Processing*, pages 55–65, Online. Association for Computational Linguistics.

Antigoni Maria Founta, Constantinos Djouvas, Despoina Chatzakou, Ilias Leontiadis, Jeremy Blackburn, Gianluca Stringhini, Athena Vakali, Michael Sirivianos, and Nicolas Kourtellis. 2018. Large scale crowdsourcing and characterization of twitter abusive behavior. In *Twelfth International AAAI Conference on Web and Social Media*.

Nikhil Garg, Londa Schiebinger, Dan Jurafsky, and James Zou. 2018. Word embeddings quantify 100 years of gender and ethnic stereotypes. *Proceedings of the National Academy of Sciences*, 115(16):E3635–E3644.

Andrew Gaut, Tony Sun, Shirlyn Tang, Yuxin Huang, Jing Qian, Mai ElSherief, Jieyu Zhao, Diba Mirza, Elizabeth Belding, Kai-Wei Chang, and William Yang Wang. 2020. Towards understanding gender bias in relation extraction. In *Proceedings of the 58th Annual Meeting of the Association for Computational Linguistics*, pages 2943–2953, Online. Association for Computational Linguistics.

Cliff Goddard. 2015. "swear words" and "curse words" in australian (and american) english. at the crossroads of pragmatics, semantics and sociolinguistics. *Intercultural Pragmatics*, 12(2):189–218.

Seraphina Goldfarb-Tarrant, Rebecca Marchant, Ricardo Muñoz Sánchez, Mugdha Pandya, and Adam Lopez. 2021. Intrinsic bias metrics do not correlate with application bias. In *Proceedings of the 59th Annual Meeting of the Association for Computational Linguistics and the 11th International Joint Conference on Natural Language Processing (Volume 1: Long Papers)*, pages 1926–1940, Online. Association for Computational Linguistics.

Rowan HallMaudslay, Hila Gonen, Ryan Cotterell, and Simone Teufel. 2019. It's all in the name: Mitigating gender bias with name-based counterfactual data substitution. In *Proceedings of the 2019 Conference on Empirical Methods in Natural Language Processing and the 9th International Joint Conference on Natural Language Processing (EMNLP-IJCNLP)*, pages 5267–5275, Hong Kong, China. Association for Computational Linguistics.

Sepp Hochreiter and Jürgen Schmidhuber. 1997. Long short-term memory. *Neural computation*, 9(8):1735–1780.

Ritesh Kumar, Atul Kr. Ojha, Bornini Lahiri, Marcos Zampieri, Shervin Malmasi, Vanessa Murdock, and Daniel Kadar, editors. 2020. *Proceedings of the Second Workshop on Trolling, Aggression and Cyberbullying*. European Language Resources Association (ELRA), Marseille, France.

Brian Larson. 2017. Gender as a variable in natural-language processing: Ethical considerations. In *Proceedings of the First ACL Workshop on Ethics in Natural Language Processing*, pages 1–11, Valencia, Spain. Association for Computational Linguistics.

Debanjan Mahata, Haimin Zhang, Karan Uppal, Yaman Kumar, Rajiv Ratn Shah, Simra Shahid, Laiba Mehnaz, and Sarthak Anand. 2019. MIDAS at SemEval-2019 task 6: Identifying offensive posts and targeted offense from Twitter. In *Proceedings of the 13th International Workshop on Semantic Evaluation*, pages 683–690, Minneapolis, Minnesota, USA. Association for Computational Linguistics.

Ninareh Mehrabi, Thamme Gowda, Fred Morstatter, Nanyun Peng, and Aram Galstyan. 2020. *Man is to Person as Woman is to Location: Measuring Gender Bias in Named Entity Recognition*, page 231–232. Association for Computing Machinery, New York, NY, USA.

Saif M Mohammad. 2019. The state of nlp literature: A diachronic analysis of the acl anthology. *arXiv preprint arXiv:1911.03562*.

Hamdy Mubarak, Ammar Rashed, Kareem Darwish, Younes Samih, and Ahmed Abdelali. 2021. Arabic offensive language on Twitter: Analysis and experiments. In *Proceedings of the Sixth Arabic Natural Language Processing Workshop*, pages 126–135, Kyiv, Ukraine (Virtual). Association for Computational Linguistics.

Ji Ho Park, Jamin Shin, and Pascale Fung. 2018. Reducing gender bias in abusive language detection. In *Proceedings of the 2018 Conference on Empirical Methods in Natural Language Processing*, pages 2799–2804, Brussels, Belgium. Association for Computational Linguistics.

John Pavlopoulos, Nithum Thain, Lucas Dixon, and Ion Androutsopoulos. 2019. ConvAI at SemEval-2019 task 6: Offensive language identification and categorization with perspective and BERT. In *Proceedings of the 13th International Workshop on Semantic Evaluation*, pages 571–576, Minneapolis, Minnesota, USA. Association for Computational Linguistics.

Jeffrey Pennington, Richard Socher, and Christopher Manning. 2014. GloVe: Global vectors for word representation. In *Proceedings of the 2014 Conference on Empirical Methods in Natural Language Processing (EMNLP)*, pages 1532–1543, Doha, Qatar. Association for Computational Linguistics.

Zesis Pitenis, Marcos Zampieri, and Tharindu Ranasinghe. 2020. Offensive language identification in Greek. In *Proceedings of the 12th Language Resources and Evaluation Conference*, pages 5113–5119, Marseille, France. European Language Resources Association.

Adam Poliak, Aparajita Haldar, Rachel Rudinger, J. Edward Hu, Ellie Pavlick, Aaron Steven White, and Benjamin Van Durme. 2018. Collecting diverse natural language inference problems for sentence representation evaluation. In *Proceedings of the 2018 Conference on Empirical Methods in Natural Language Processing*, pages 67–81, Brussels, Belgium. Association for Computational Linguistics.

Vinodkumar Prabhakaran, Ben Hutchinson, and Margaret Mitchell. 2019. Perturbation sensitivity analysis to detect unintended model biases. In *Proceedings of the 2019 Conference on Empirical Methods in Natural Language Processing and the 9th International Joint Conference on Natural Language Processing (EMNLP-IJCNLP)*, pages 5740–5745, Hong Kong, China. Association for Computational Linguistics.

Murugesan Ramakrishnan, Wlodek Zadrozny, and Narges Tabari. 2019. UVA wahoos at SemEval-2019 task 6: Hate speech identification using ensemble machine learning. In *Proceedings of the 13th International Workshop on Semantic Evaluation*, pages 806–811, Minneapolis, Minnesota, USA. Association for Computational Linguistics.

Amir H Razavi, Diana Inkpen, Sasha Uritsky, and Stan Matwin. 2010. Offensive language detection using multi-level classification. In *Canadian Conference on Artificial Intelligence*, pages 16–27. Springer.

Rachel Rudinger, Jason Naradowsky, Brian Leonard, and Benjamin Van Durme. 2018. Gender bias in coreference resolution. In *Proceedings of the 2018 Conference of the North American Chapter of the Association for Computational Linguistics: Human*

Language Technologies, Volume 2 (Short Papers), pages 8–14, New Orleans, Louisiana. Association for Computational Linguistics.

Niloofar Safi Samghabadi, Parth Patwa, Srinivas PYKL, Prerana Mukherjee, Amitava Das, and Thamar Solorio. 2020. Aggression and misogyny detection using BERT: A multi-task approach. In *Proceedings of the Second Workshop on Trolling, Aggression and Cyberbullying*, pages 126–131, Marseille, France. European Language Resources Association (ELRA).

Barry S. Sapolsky and Barbara K. Kaye. 2005. The use of offensive language by men and women in prime time television entertainment. *Atlantic Journal of Communication*, 13(4):292–303.

Beatrice Savoldi, Marco Gaido, Luisa Bentivogli, Matteo Negri, and Marco Turchi. 2021. Gender Bias in Machine Translation. *Transactions of the Association for Computational Linguistics*, 9:845–874.

M. Schuster and K. K. Paliwal. 1997. Bidirectional recurrent neural networks. *IEEE Transactions on Signal Processing*, 45(11):2673–2681.

Vered Shwartz, Rachel Rudinger, and Oyvind Tafjord. 2020. "you are grounded!": Latent name artifacts in pre-trained language models. In *Proceedings of the 2020 Conference on Empirical Methods in Natural Language Processing (EMNLP)*, pages 6850–6861, Online. Association for Computational Linguistics.

Alexandra A Siegel. 2020. Online hate speech. *Social Media and Democracy: The State of the Field, Prospects for Reform*, pages 56–88.

Gudbjartur Ingi Sigurbergsson and Leon Derczynski. 2020. Offensive language and hate speech detection for Danish. In *Proceedings of the 12th Language Resources and Evaluation Conference*, pages 3498–3508, Marseille, France. European Language Resources Association.

Brittany N. Smith, Mamta Singh, and Vetle I. Torvik. 2013. A search engine approach to estimating temporal changes in gender orientation of first names. In *Proceedings of the 13th ACM/IEEE-CS Joint Conference on Digital Libraries*, JCDL '13, page 199–208, New York, NY, USA. Association for Computing Machinery.

Gabriel Stanovsky, Noah A. Smith, and Luke Zettlemoyer. 2019. Evaluating gender bias in machine translation. In *Proceedings of the 57th Annual Meeting of the Association for Computational Linguistics*, pages 1679–1684, Florence, Italy. Association for Computational Linguistics.

Tony Sun, Andrew Gaut, Shirlyn Tang, Yuxin Huang, Mai ElSherief, Jieyu Zhao, Diba Mirza, Elizabeth Belding, Kai-Wei Chang, and William Yang Wang. 2019. Mitigating gender bias in natural language processing: Literature review. In *Proceedings of the 57th Annual Meeting of the Association for Computational Linguistics*, pages 1630–1640, Florence, Italy. Association for Computational Linguistics.

Adam Vogel and Dan Jurafsky. 2012. He said, she said: Gender in the ACL Anthology. In *Proceedings of the ACL-2012 Special Workshop on Rediscovering 50 Years of Discoveries*, pages 33–41, Jeju Island, Korea. Association for Computational Linguistics.

Thomas Wolf, Lysandre Debut, Victor Sanh, Julien Chaumond, Clement Delangue, Anthony Moi, Pierric Cistac, Tim Rault, Rémi Louf, Morgan Funtowicz, Joe Davison, Sam Shleifer, Patrick von Platen, Clara Ma, Yacine Jernite, Julien Plu, Canwen Xu, Teven Le Scao, Sylvain Gugger, Mariama Drame, Quentin Lhoest, and Alexander M. Rush. 2020. Transformers: State-of-the-art natural language processing. In *Proceedings of the 2020 Conference on Empirical Methods in Natural Language Processing: System Demonstrations*, pages 38–45, Online. Association for Computational Linguistics.

Zhenghao Wu, Hao Zheng, Jianming Wang, Weifeng Su, and Jefferson Fong. 2019. BNU-HKBU UIC NLP team 2 at SemEval-2019 task 6: Detecting offensive language using BERT model. In *Proceedings of the 13th International Workshop on Semantic Evaluation*, pages 551–555, Minneapolis, Minnesota, USA. Association for Computational Linguistics.

Marcos Zampieri, Shervin Malmasi, Preslav Nakov, Sara Rosenthal, Noura Farra, and Ritesh Kumar. 2019a. Predicting the type and target of offensive posts in social media. In *Proceedings of the 2019 Conference of the North American Chapter of the Association for Computational Linguistics: Human Language Technologies, Volume 1 (Long and Short Papers)*, pages 1415–1420, Minneapolis, Minnesota. Association for Computational Linguistics.

Marcos Zampieri, Shervin Malmasi, Preslav Nakov, Sara Rosenthal, Noura Farra, and Ritesh Kumar. 2019b. SemEval-2019 task 6: Identifying and categorizing offensive language in social media (OffensEval). In *Proceedings of the 13th International Workshop on Semantic Evaluation*, pages 75–86, Minneapolis, Minnesota, USA. Association for Computational Linguistics.

Marcos Zampieri, Preslav Nakov, Sara Rosenthal, Pepa Atanasova, Georgi Karadzhov, Hamdy Mubarak, Leon Derczynski, Zeses Pitenis, and Çağrı Çöltekin. 2020. SemEval-2020 task 12: Multilingual offensive language identification in social media (OffensEval 2020). In *Proceedings of the Fourteenth Workshop on Semantic Evaluation*, pages 1425–1447, Barcelona (online). International Committee for Computational Linguistics.

Jieyu Zhao, Tianlu Wang, Mark Yatskar, Vicente Ordonez, and Kai-Wei Chang. 2018. Gender bias in coreference resolution: Evaluation and debiasing methods. In *Proceedings of the 2018 Conference of the North American Chapter of the Association for Computational Linguistics: Human Language Technologies, Volume 2 (Short Papers)*, pages 15–20, New Orleans, Louisiana. Association for Computational Linguistics.

Jian Zhu, Zuoyu Tian, and Sandra Kübler. 2019. UM-IU@LING at SemEval-2019 task 6: Identifying offensive tweets using BERT and SVMs. In *Proceedings of the 13th International Workshop on Semantic Evaluation*, pages 788–795, Minneapolis, Minnesota, USA. Association for Computational Linguistics.

Gender Bias in BERT - Measuring and Analysing Biases through Sentiment Rating in a Realistic Downstream Classification Task

Sophie F. Jentzsch
Institute for Software Technology
German Aerospace Center (DLR)
Cologne, Germany
Sophie.Jentzsch@DLR.de

Cigdem Turan
Dept. of Computer Science
TU Darmstadt
Darmstadt, Germany
cigdem.turan@cs.tu-darmstadt.de

Abstract

Pretrained language models are publicly available and constantly finetuned for various real-life applications. As they become capable of grasping complex contextual information, harmful biases are likely increasingly intertwined with those models. This paper analyses gender bias in BERT models with two main contributions: First, a novel bias measure is introduced, defining biases as the difference in sentiment valuation of female and male sample versions. Second, we comprehensively analyse BERT's biases on the example of a realistic IMDB movie classifier. By systematically varying elements of the training pipeline, we can conclude regarding their impact on the final model bias. Seven different public BERT models in nine training conditions, i.e. 63 models in total, are compared. Almost all conditions yield significant gender biases. Results indicate that reflected biases stem from public BERT models rather than task-specific data, emphasising the weight of responsible usage.

Original Review

He could not stand anymore the pressure of his mother. She complains that he is still alive while the good boy from her neighbor had been killed. Then he gets a job as a policeman.

Female Masked

She could not stand anymore the pressure of her mother. She complains that she is still alive while the good girl from her neighbor had been killed. Then she gets a job as a policewoman.

Male Masked

He could not stand anymore the pressure of his father. He complains that he is still alive while the good boy from his neighbor had been killed. Then he gets a job as a policeman.

Figure 1: **Example Sample Masking**. The original review contains both male (orange) and female (green) terms. In masked versions, all terms are homogeneously male or female.

1 Introduction

As complex Machine Learning (ML) based systems are nowadays naturally intertwined with media, technology and everyday life, it is increasingly important to understand their nature and be aware of unwanted behaviour. This also applies to the Natural Language Processing (NLP) community, where several recent breakthroughs promoted the application of sophisticated data-driven models in various tasks and applications. Only a decade ago, ML-based vector space word embeddings as word2vec (Mikolov et al.) or Glove (Pennington et al., 2014) emerged and opened up new ways to extract information and correlations from large amounts of text data. In this context, it has widely been shown that embeddings tend to reflect human biases and stereotypes (Caliskan et al., 2017; Jentzsch et al., 2019) and that unintended imbalances in text-embeddings can lead to misbehaviour of systems (Bolukbasi et al., 2016).

In recent years, however, these static word embeddings have rapidly been superseded by the next generation of even more powerful NLP models, which are transformer-based contextualised language models (LMs). BERT (Devlin et al., 2019a) and similar architectures established a new standard and now form the basis for many real-life applications and downstream tasks. Unfortunately, previous bias measurement approaches do not seem to be straightforwardly transferable (May et al., 2019; Guo and Caliskan, 2021; Bao and Qiao, 2019). Since the connection between input data and model output is even more opaque, new measures are required to quantify encoded biases in LMs properly. Moreover, with the increase in complexity, computational costs and required amount of data, it is often infeasible to train models from scratch. Instead, pretrained models can be adapted to a wide variety of downstream tasks by finetuning them with a

Proceedings of the The 4th Workshop on Gender Bias in Natural Language Processing (GeBNLP), pages 184 - 199
July 15, 2022

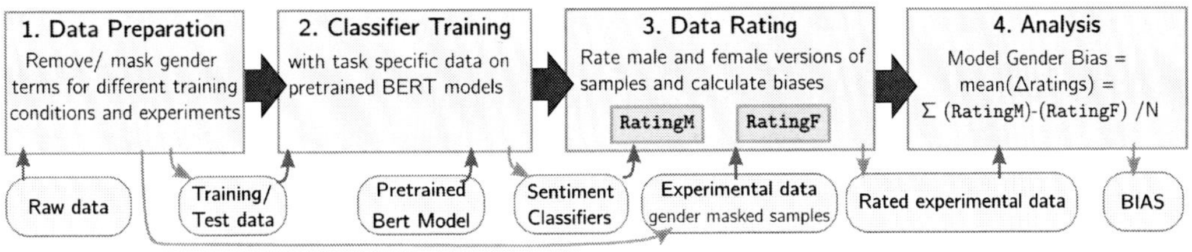

Figure 2: Illustration of experimental pipeline. (1) **Data Preparation**: removing/ balancing gender terms in training data. Create experimental data by masking terms in test data to generate a male and a female version. (2) **Model Finetuning**: finetune a pretrained BERT model with task-specific training data in different conditions. (3) **Sentiment Rating** of experimental data; (4) **Analysis** and Bias calculation.

small amount of task-specific data (Qiu et al., 2020). Although enabling easy access to state-of-the-art NLP techniques, it comes with the risk of lacking model diversity. Different models come with individual characteristics and limitations (Xia et al., 2020), and there is a small number of well-trained publicly available models that are extensively used, often without even scrutinising the model. There are ongoing endeavours to enhance a responsible development and application of those models, e.g. (Mitchell et al., 2019). However, it is still barely understood to what extent biases are propagated through ML pipelines and which training factors enhance or counteract the adaption of discriminating concepts. To apply complex transformer LMs reasonably, it is important to understand how much bias they encode and how these are reflected in downstream applications.

The present study presents a comprehensive analysis of gender bias in BERT models in a downstream sentiment classification task with IMDB data. This task is a realistic scenario, as ML-based recommendation systems are widely used, and reflected stereotypes could directly harm people, e.g. by underrating certain movies or impairing their visibility. The investigation comprises two main contributions: First, we propose a novel method to calculate biases in sentiment classification tasks. Sentiment classifiers inherently possess valuation abilities. We exploited these to rate "female" and "male" sample versions (see Fig. 1) and therefore need no additional association dimension, e.g. occupation. The classifier is biased if one gender is preferred over the other. Second, we analyse the impact of different training factors on the final classifier bias to better understand the origin of biases in NLP tasks. Seven different base models, three different training data conditions and three different bias implementations lead to a total number of 63 compared classifiers. Additional observations could be made regarding training hyperparameters and model accuracies. Results reveal significant gender biases in almost all experimental conditions. Compensating imbalances of gender terms in finetuning training data did not show any considerable effect. The size and architecture of pretrained models, in contrast, correlate with the biases. These observations indicate that classifier biases are more likely to stem from the public BERT models than from task-specific data and emphasise the importance of selecting trustworthy resources. The present work contributes to understanding biases in language models and how they propagate through complex machine learning systems.

Bias Statement

We study how representational male and female gender concepts are assessed differently in sentiment classification systems. In this concrete context, we consider it harmful if a classifier that is trained to distinguish positive and negative movie reviews prefers performers and film characters of one gender over another. This could not only reinforce existing imbalance in the film industry but also lead to direct financial and social harm, e.g. if a movie is less frequently recommended by an automatic recommendation system.
Beyond that, this concrete task is meant to be only one example case for an unlimited number of finetuning scenarios. If we can measure a bias here, this representational imbalance could similarly float into other downstream applications of all kinds, e.g. recruitment processes, hate speech crime detection, news crawler, or computational assistants. Generally spoken, it is problematic when freely available and rapidly used models encode a general preference of one gender over another. This is especially critical if this imbalance is propagated

through larger systems and unknowingly reflected in gender-unrelated downstream tasks. To raise awareness and mitigate stereotypical reflection, we need to understand how biases emerge and how they are reinforced.
The concepts *female* and *male* are represented by sets of terms that are grammatically connected to that gender. One major limitation of that implementation is that it assumes a binary gender classification and does not reflect real-world diversity. Up to now, concepts of a gender-neutral or gender-diverse language are not sufficiently established to consider them for data-driven model training. Nevertheless, we believe that the binary reflection of gender in natural language is worth analysing as it is already connected to real-life discrimination.

2 Methodology

This investigation analyses to what extent BERT gender biases are present in an IMDB sentiment classification task. We aim to observe what portion of bias emerges in which experimental step by systematically varying conditions in each step. 63 different classifiers and their biases are finally reported in this paper. Many more were trained to observe different training aspects. This section provides a detailed description of experimental steps and how different conditions are achieved.
The experimental pipeline can be divided into four major steps, as illustrated in Fig. 2. The structure of this section roughly follows these steps. First, the preparation of training data is described in Sec. 2.1. We compare seven training conditions where gender information in training data is removed or balanced. By that means, it can be measured how much bias is induced during the task-specific finetuning. Second, the sentiment classifiers were trained by finetuning seven different common BERT models, as can be read in Sec. 2.2. By observing whether the choice of model affects the bias magnitude, we can infer how much bias stems from the pretrained BERT model. Also, we compare different sizes of the same architecture. In the third step, the trained classifiers were applied to rate the manipulated test data, which is here referred to as experimental data. The setup is described in Sec. 2.3. Finally, these ratings are used to calculate the model bias that is defined contextually in Sec. 1 and mathematically in Sec. 2.4. Three different sets of gender terms were considered in the experiments.

2.1 Sentiment Data and Data Preparation

Experiments were conducted in a typical sentiment classification task on movie reviews. The *Internet Movie Database*, which is generally referred to as IMDB, is a free platform to rate movies, TV-series and more. We used the publicly available IMDB Large Movie Review Dataset (Maas et al., 2011), which consists of 50,000 real user movie reviews from that platform. Each sample is provided with the original review texts, the awarded stars as numerical values, and a binary sentiment label derived from the star rating. Reviews with ratings of 4 or lower are labelled as *negative*, and those rated as 7 or higher are labelled as *positive*. Reviews with star ratings of 5 and 6 are not added to the labelled set. The data is already split equally in training and test data, which was not modified in this investigation. We prepared all samples to be free from punctuation and lower-case. The test data was used for model evaluation and also used to create the experimental data as described in Sec. 2.3.
First, each model was trained on the cleaned but unmodified data. This condition is referred to as *original* condition. To see if the occurrence of gender terms in the training data has any effect on the final model biases, we created further conditions. Defined gender terms, which are used for bias definition, were fully removed from the training data. This conditions are referred to as *removed*, or specifically *R-pro*, *R-weat*, and *R-all*, for the three different sets of gender terms (see Section 2.3). While removing gender terms is a straightforward step to eliminate them during training, it might lead to incomplete sentences. To see if that affects the results, we defined a third category of training data using Counterfactual Data Augmentation (Lu et al., 2020). In that approach, a male and a female version of each sample were created by replacing all occurring gender terms (similar to Fig. 1). Both version are included in the *mixed* training data. This way, each review's structure and completeness are maintained, but the distribution of male and female terms is perfectly balanced. These training conditions are hereafter referred to as *mix-pro*, *mix-weat*, and *mix-all*, respectively.
We are aware that neither removing nor mixing gender terms is a mature debiasing technique, as the reflection of gender constructs is much deeper embedded in the language and the content of the text. However, gender bias is here operationalised

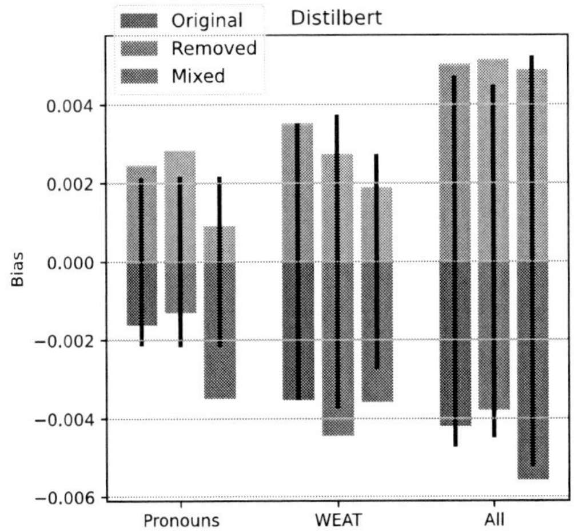

Figure 3: Positive and negative biases for dilstilBERT based classifiers. Blue: trained on original data (*orig.*); red: trained with removed gender terms (*R*); green: trained with mixed gender terms (*mix*). The x-axis is grouped by applied term set (either Pronouns, WEAT, or All). Black lines show the mean total bias symmetrically in both directions to provide an orientation mark for the balance of positive and negative biases.

through different word sets, and by removing those words from training, we aim to avoid changing the learnt associations of the BERT model. By that means, we expect to learn whether the positive or negative valuation that is connected to these words stems from the finetuning classifier training or from the previous training of the BERT.

2.2 Classifier Training

Another main variation between experimental conditions is the selection of a pretrained BERT model. Each classifier is trained by finetuning a pretrained, publicly available BERT model. Seven different BERT-based models that differ in architecture and size were selected to examine the effect of model choice on the final bias. The models were provided by HuggingFace [1] and accessed via Transformers Python package (Wolf et al.). All models are trained in a self-supervised fashion without human labelling and on similar training data, which is the Bookscorpus (Zhu et al., 2015) and the Englisch Wikipedia[2]. The following models are considered models in the present analysis:

DistilBERT (*distbase*): A smaller and faster version of BERT, 6 layers, 3072 hidden, 12 heads, 66M parameters, vocabulary size: 30522, uncased (Sanh et al., 2019).
BERT base (*bertbase*): 12 layers, 768 hidden, 12 heads, 110M parameters, vocabulary size: 30522, uncased (Devlin et al., 2019b).
BERT large (*bertlarge*): 24 layers, 1024 hidden, 16 heads, 340M parameters, vocabulary size: 30522, uncased (Devlin et al., 2019b).
RoBERTa base (*robertbase*): 12 layers, 768 hidden, 12 heads, 125M parameters, vocabulary size: 50265, case-sensitive (Liu et al., 2019).
RoBERTa large (*robertlarge*): 24 layers, 1024 hidden, 16 heads, 355M parameters, vocabulary size: 50265, case-sensitive (Liu et al., 2019).
AlBERT base (*albertbase*): 12 layers, 768 hidden, 12 heads, 11M parameters, vocabulary size: 30000, uncased (Lan et al., 2019).
AlBERT large (*albertlarge*): 24 layers, 1024 hidden, 16 heads, 17M parameters, vocabulary size: 30000, uncased (Lan et al., 2019).

The models were trained with a Pytorch framework (Paszke et al., 2019) on an NVIDIA Tesla V100-SXM3-32GB-H. Hyperparameters were inspired by previous literature and kept as constant as possible. However, factors such as different model architectures or the doubled amount of training data in the *mix* conditions required slight adaptions. We used a dropout rate of 0.5, which proved to work well in avoiding overfitting. Batch sizes were set to be as large as possible, either 32 or 16 depending on the model size. The correlation between model accuracy, biases and training batch size was examined and is also elucidated in the results section. Learning rates were set between $2e-5$ and $5e-6$ and optimised with Adam. As already observed by de Souza Nascimento et al. (2019), BERT finetuning tends to overfit quickly. Therefore the authors suggest training for only 2 to 4 epochs. Due to extensive hyperparameter optimisation, the present classifiers were trained by finetuning the pretrained models in up to 20 epochs without overfitting. A comprehensive list of all test accuracies and F1 scores can be found in the Appendix. The source code of data preparation, model training and experimental analysis will be publicly available on GitHub[3].

[1]HuggingFace models, accessed: April 2022. Available at: `https://huggingface.co/models`.

[2]Wikimedia Foundation, Wikimedia Downloads. Available at: `https://dumps.wikimedia.org`

[3]`https://github.com/sciphie/bias-bert`

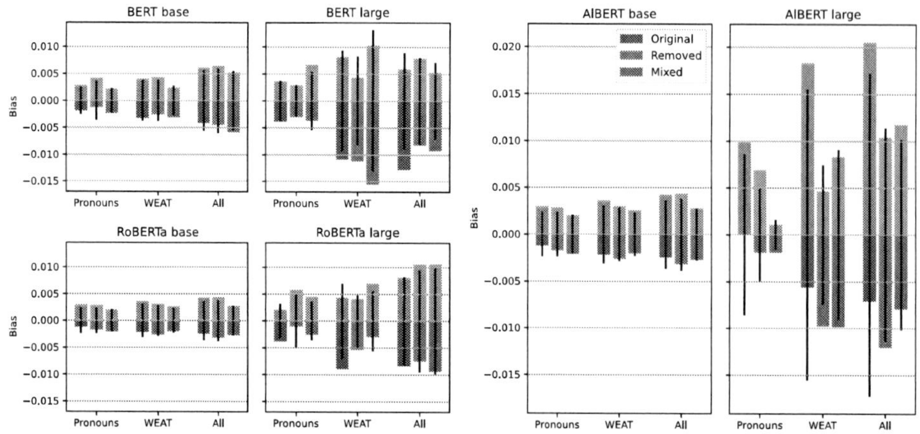

Figure 4: Positive and negative biases for classifiers based on different BERT models. Blue: trained on original data (*orig.*); red: trained with removed gender terms (*R*); green: trained with mixed gender terms (*mix*). The x-axis is grouped by applied term set (either Pronouns, WEAT, or All). Black lines show the mean total bias symmetrically in both directions to provide an orientation mark for the balance of positive and negative biases.

2.3 Data Masking in Experimental Data

The analysed bias dimension in this work is *the person being spoken about* (Dinan et al., 2020b), in contrast to, e.g., Excell and Al Moubayed (2021) where the bias concerns the author of a comment. We generated a male (M) and a female version (F) of each review by turning all included gender terms into the male or female version of that term, respectively. Thus, regardless of whether the terms in the original review were male, female or mixed, the gender of all target terms in each review is homogeneous afterwards (see Fig. 1). Gender terms were defined in fixed pairs, and only words that occur in the list were masked by their counterpart.
The concept of defining and analysing complex construct as the sum of related target and association terms stems originally from the field of psychology (Greenwald et al., 1998). This approach has frequently been adapted to computer science and NLP already in the form of the *Word Embedding Association Test* (WEAT) (Caliskan et al., 2017; Jentzsch et al., 2019) or similar tasks.
The measured bias and the observations in this investigation are likely to depend on the implementation of these target sets to a large extent. Even though many studies apply that approach, the selection of terms is not discussed much. To this end, we created three different sets of target terms to examine the influence of different bias definitions. The largest set comprises all collected gender terms, which is a total number of 341 pairs. In this set, we aimed to collect as many evident gender-specific words as possible. It is named *all* hereafter. A detailed description of the construction of the term set and a list of included words can be found in the Appendix. In literature (e.g. WEAT), term lists are usually more compact and restricted to family relations. The second target set is inspired by those resources and consists of 17 word pairs. It is a subset of *all*. We refer to this set as *weat*. The third and smallest set, hereafter named *pro*, only covers pronouns, which are five pairs of terms. This term set is included as pronouns often play a special role in bias research, e.g., in coreference resolution (Zhao et al., 2018). We seek to understand if pronouns are an adequate bias measure compared to nouns.

2.4 Bias Measure

The model bias of a sentiment classifier is determined as follows: Two opposite conditions of the bias concept, X and Y, are defined and represented by a set of target words, as explained in Sec. 2.3. For gender bias, these conditions are female $X = F$ and male $Y = M$. Test samples, which are a set of natural user comments, are then modified with respect to the bias construct. All naturally included target terms, regardless if they belong to X or Y, are replaced by the corresponding terms of either X or Y. A male and a female version of each sample are created by that means. The bias for a sample i with X version i_X and Y version i_Y is defined to be the difference between sentiment ratings $sent(i)$ of each version:

$$Bias_{XY}(i) = \Delta sent \quad (1)$$
$$= sent(i_Y) - sent(i_X). \quad (2)$$

The overall model bias for the sentiment classification system SC is defined to be the mean bias of all N experimental samples:

$$Bias_{XY}(SC) = \sum_{i=0}^{N} \frac{\Delta sent}{N} \quad (3)$$

As the data classification is binary, the sentiment prediction $sent(i)$ is a scalar value between 0 and 1, where 0 represents the most negative and 1 the most positive sentiment. Consequently, the sample bias is in the range of -1 and 1, where a high bias value can be interpreted as a bias towards Y, i.e. Y is closer associated with positive sentiments than X. Analogously, a lower bias value indicates a bias towards X, i.e. X being closer associated with positive sentiments. Here, with conditions M and F, the total model bias $Bias_{MF} \rightarrow 1$ would indicate a preference for male samples over female ones and $Bias_{FM} \rightarrow -1$ accordingly the other way round. Besides the total model bias in Eq. 3, we also consider the absolute model bias, which is defined as the mean of all absolute biases:

$$AbsBias_{XY}(SC) = \sum_{i=0}^{N} \frac{|\Delta sent|}{N} \quad (4)$$

Analogously, biases will hereafter be referred to as total bias or absolute bias. While the total bias is capable of reflecting the direction of bias, it entails the drawback that contrary sample biases cancel out each other. Therefore the values of absolute biases are stated additionally and quantify the magnitude of bias in the model.

We formulated the null and alternative hypotheses for statistical hypothesis testing. Given sample groups X and Y with the medians m_X and m_Y

H_0 : $m_X = m_Y$: medians are **equal**; The model is not biased

H_A : $m_X \neq m_Y$: medians are **not equal**; The model is considered to be biased

As there are two paired sample groups, which cannot be assumed to be normally distributed, statistics were determined with the Wilcoxon Signed-Rank test. This test has already been applied in similar investigations before, e.g. by Guo and Caliskan (2021)). Significance levels are defined as $p < 0.05$, $p < 0.01$ and $p < 0.001$ and are hereafter indicated by one, two and three starlets, respectively. Significance levels were corrected for multiple testing by means of the Bonferroni correction The sample standard deviation normalised by $N - 1$ is given by std. We also state the number of samples below zero, equal to zero and greater than zero to indicate effect sizes.

3 Results

A condensed list of absolute and total biases is reported in Tab. 1. Out of 63 reported experimental models, 57 showed highly significant biases. Exceptions are *distbase mix-all*, *bertbase mix-pro*, *robertbase mix-weat*, *robertbase mix-all*, and *albertlarge mix-weat*. 16 classifiers prefer female terms over male terms, and 41 prefer male terms over female terms. Thus, even though more classifiers are in our definition discriminating against women than against men, biases are directed differently. The sizes and especially the directions of biases are visualised in Fig. 3 for distilBERT classifiers, in Fig. 4 for all other architectures.

Is bias induced by model finetuning? In finetuning systems like this, biases in models can have different origins. We aimed to analyse how much bias was introduced during further training by the task-specific data. To this end, we removed (*R*) or balanced (*mix*) gender terms in the task-specific data to reduce the modification of their representations by finetuning. Both conditions are represented in Fig. 3 and Fig. 4 by red and green bars, respectively.

Although biases are decreasing by removing gender information from IMDB data in some cases, e.g. *albertalarge pro* , there are likewise examples where it seems to have the opposite effect, such as *bertlarge weat mix*. However, for most conditions, these preprocessing measures do not change the magnitude of biases considerably. Especially, removing the gender terms from data does not significantly affect the biases. For some models, although the behaviour of the *mix* conditions is different from the other settings, there is no clear pattern observable. Observed differences in that category might also be related to the doubled size of training sets (N = 50000), which is likely to reinforce effects.

condition		pro orig.	pro R	pro mix	weat orig.	weat R	weat mix	all orig.	all R	all mix
dist	abs	.0021	.0022	.0022	.0035	.0037	.0027	.0047	.0045	(.0052)
	tot	.0009	.0010	-.0012	.0004	-.0015	-.0008	.0016	.0008	(-.0003)
bert B	abs	.0025	.0036	(.0023)	.0037	.0038	.0027	.0056	.0060	.0055
	tot	.0013	.0031	(-.0000)	.0015	.0020	-.0002	.0035	.0041	.0005
bert L	abs	.0031	.0050	.0035	.0069	.0048	.0056	.0082	.0095	.0101
	tot	-.0016	.0046	.0011	-.0032	-.0011	.0034	.0009	.0042	.0015
rob B	abs	.0024	.0024	.0021	.0031	.0028	(.0023)	.0036	.0038	(.0027)
	tot	.0016	.0009	-.0002	.0016	.0007	(.0002)	.0020	.0010	(.0000)
rob L	abs	.0024	.0025	.0020	.0039	.0039	.0028	.0044	.0043	.0041
	tot	.0015	.0015	.0004	.0025	.0023	.0004	.0023	.0021	.0018
alb B	abs	.0037	.0029	.0054	.0093	.0082	.0131	.0089	.0080	.0071
	tot	.0011	-.0004	.0021	.0002	-.0044	-.0034	-.0023	.0009	-.0014
alb L	abs	.0086	.0049	.0016	.0155	.0074	(.0091)	.0172	.0114	.0101
	tot	.0086	.0034	-.0008	.0130	-.0032	(-.0009)	.0137	-.0032	.0034

Table 1: Absolute (abs) and total (tot) model biases of all main experimental classifiers. Positive values indicate a model preference of male samples over female, negative values a preference of female samples over male ones. All biases, except the ones in brackets, are highly significant. Significance levels were Bonferroni corrected for multipe testing. *pro*, *weat* and *all* specify the applied term set for training data preprocessing and bias calculation. Terms in training data were either removed (R), balanced (mix), or neither of both (orig.). Columns are the different pretrained BERT models used for classifier training. Base models are abbreviated as dist (*distbase*), bert B (*bertbase*), bert L (*bertlarge*), rob B (*robertabase*), rob L (*robertalarge*), alb B (*albertbase*), and alb L (albertlarge).

Is bias induced by pretrained models? We applied models with different architectures and sizes to observe how measured biases depend on the underlying pretrained model. We compare three different sizes of BERT models, which are *distbase*, *bertbase* and *bertlarge*. Moreover, we consider models with RoBERTa architecture in the sizes *robertabase* and *robertalarge* and AlBERT in *albertbase* and *albertlarge*. This comparison leads to two major observations: First, biases differ steadily *between* considered architectures. As can be well observed in Fig. 3 and Fig. 4, DistilBERt's biases are about half as big as BERT's and RoBERTa's biases. AlBERTa's biases, again, are about twice as big as those of BERT and RoBERTa. This observation does not only hold among all training conditions but also for both base and large variants. Thus, the architecture of a selected model has an essential impact on the biases of downstream systems.

Second, we observe increasing biases depending on model sizes *within* one architecture. *distbase* again yielded the smallest biases, followed by *bertbase*, and *bertlarge*. Simultaneously, *robertalarge* yielded much bigger biases than *robertabase*, and *albertalarge* yielded much bigger biases than *albertbase*. Thus, we observe a correlation between bias and model size, i.e. the number of layers. This indicates that larger models tend to encode greater gender biases.

Is bias dependent on applied term sets? As mentioned before, we defined three sets of target terms for the implementation of bias, of which the largest comprises more than a three hundred term pairs and the smallest only five. Analogously to term set sizes, the absolute biases are the smallest for the *pronoun* set and the largest for the *all* set in almost all conditions. In other words, the more terms are included, the bigger the measured bias. The only exception is *bertlarge R* and some conditions on *albertbase*. Despite the differences in bias magnitude, measured values in all categories were similarly significant. Also, the patterns of effects of training data manipulation or base model comparison could similarly be observed in all three bias definitions. We conclude from these observations that all types of included vocabulary encode biases, i.e. pronouns, weat-terms and other nouns.

	bias abs	bias tot	accuracy	f-score (f1)
bias abs		0.373	-0.481**	-0.497***
bias tot	0.373		0.044	-0.085
accuracy	-0.481**	0.044		0.886***
f-score (f1)	-0.497***	-0.085	0.886***	

Table 2: Correlation (Pearsons) of biases and training details of all 63 classifiers. **bias abs**: absolute bias, **bias tot**: total bias. Starlets indicate levels of significance for $p < 0.001$, $p < 0.01$ and $p < 0.05$, which were Bonferroni corrected for multiple testing.

The more terms are included, the higher the measured bias. For the presented results, the term set of training data manipulating and the term set for bias measure were always the same. For instance, if we applied the *pro* set to measure biases, we also only removed/ balanced terms of *pro* in the training data. We also tested whether biases vary when mixing term sets between different experimental steps. However, that did not reveal any considerable effect, as bias values differed marginally.

Do hyperparameter settings affect biases? Due to computational capacity, some larger models needed to be trained with smaller batch sizes. To see if that affects the final biased, we performed additional experiments where we only varied the batch size while fixing all other parameters. For 21 different experimental conditions, models were retrained with batch sizes 32, 16 and 8. Naturally, this affected the course of loss and accuracy during training, but only to a limited extent. All settings led to stable classifiers with convenient model accuracy. The biases of all tested classifiers did not show any indication to be different among the training batch sizes. These results reveal that the batch size does not immediately cause the measured correlation.

Tab. 2 reports correlations between further basic training details and biases to examine whether there are observable connections. The F-score naturally correlates with accuracy, which is the highest value in the table. F1 and accuracy yield a medium negative correlation with absolute biases. In contrast to absolute biases, total biases barely show significant correlations with training values. All considered classifiers showed good performance in the model evaluation. Test accuracies lie between 77% and 84%, which is comparable to baseline values. The evaluation details of all classifiers are attached to the Appendix.

4 Discussion

We observed highly significant gender biases in almost all tested conditions. Thus, the present results verify the hypothesis that downstream sentiment classification tasks reflect gender biases. Although most considered classifiers prefer male samples over female ones, this direction is not consistent: About thirty per cent of classifiers prefer female over male samples. The high significance values are likely to be facilitated by the large sample number and do not necessarily correspond to the effect size. It might be insightful to analyse the contexts and types of individual samples to understand how these contrary directions occur. The rating of male and female presence likely depends on the scenario, rather than one gender being strictly advantaged.

We could not observe any effect of removing gender information from task-specific training data. Thus, in the present case, the biases associated with gender terms are most likely not learnt during finetuning. In contrast, results showed significant differences in downstream classifier biases depending on the selection of pretrained models. This is true for both the size and the architecture of the model. It is reasonable that the pretrained BERT models, which comprise information from a training set much larger than the IMDB set, are more capable of reflecting complex constructs such as gender stereotypes. It is, therefore, all the more important to develop these models carefully and responsibly and to respect risks and limitations in the application. As a small number of provided base models form the basis for a large portion of applications in NLP, it is especially critical to understand included risks and facilitate debiasing. Although the results of the present investigation indicate the origin of biases in pretrained BERT models, that does not preclude the risk to generate biases during finetuning. All elements of the development pipeline need to be audited adequately.

We showed that all of the compared term sets are generally appropriate to measure gender bias. However, term sets yielded large differences in bias sizes, showing how crucial the experimental setup is for the validity of measured results. The fact that biases increase relative to the number of gender terms strengthens the conclusion that the majority of these terms reflect biases. It also needs to be further investigated whether the sentiment rating of individual gender terms might be affected by other factors than gender. Nevertheless, the applied definition of male and female biases is a rudimentary implementation of real-world circumstances. First, there is a large number of facets that possibly encode gender (Doughman et al., 2021), e.g. names or topics. Second, gender is much more diverse in reality than this implementation can reflect. Especially since modern language models are contextual, conceptual stereotypes and biases are likely to be deeply encoded in the embeddings. Automatically learnt models likely cover a large variety of latent biases that contemporary research cannot grasp (González et al., 2020). This investigation underlines the complexity of bias formation in real-life multi-level systems. Results verify the existence of gender biases in BERT's downstream sentiment classification tasks. In order to further analyse how much of the final system bias stems from the pretrained model, similar experiments could be conducted on debiased BERT models. This way, whether the bias can be further reduced could be tested. Another exciting direction might be to examine how the suggested measurement approach could be transferred to non-binary classification tasks. As a next step, we plan to expand the present experiments to further downstream applications.

5 Related Work

Language models as BERT (Devlin et al., 2019a) recently became the new standard in a wide variety of different tasks and superseded static embeddings, as Word2Vec (Mikolov et al.) or GloVe (Pennington et al., 2014). For these older embeddings, there already is a huge body of empirical research on bias measuring and mitigation (Caliskan et al., 2017; Jentzsch et al., 2019; Schramowski et al., 2020; Bolukbasi et al., 2016), which unfortunately seem to be not straightforwardly tailorable to the new setting (May et al., 2019; Tan and Celis, 2019). However, recent research finds that BERT also encodes unwanted human biases, such as gender bias (Bartl et al., 2020; Kurita et al., 2019; Guo and Caliskan, 2021).

Downstream task analyses mostly consider shortcomings in dialogue-systems (Staliūnaitė and Iacobacci, 2020; Dinan et al., 2020a). In the context of sentiment analysis, Kiritchenko and Mohammad (2018) introduced a data set that is designed to measure gender-occupation biases. Although the reported results across 219 tested systems are ambiguous, the framework has been frequently applied ever since (Bhardwaj et al., 2021; Gupta et al., 2021). (Huang et al.) measure biases in text-generation systems, i.e. GPT. While the general experimental setting is fundamentally different from the present investigation, they apply a similar idea of measuring biases via sentiment classification. To the best of our knowledge, we are the first to utilise sentiment classification to learn about the origin of biases in BERT. We contribute to a growing body of exploratory literature regarding bias measure (Zhao and Chang, 2020; Munro and Morrison, 2020; Field and Tsvetkov, 2020) and bias mitigation (Liu et al., 2020) in contextualised language models.

6 Conclusion

Contextualised language models such as BERT form the backbone of many everyday applications. We introduced a novel approach to measuring bias sentiment classification systems and comprehensively analysed the reflection of gender bias in a realistic downstream sentiment classification task. We compared 63 classifier settings, covering multiple pretrained models and different training conditions. All trained classifiers showed highly significant gender biases. Results indicate that biases are rather propagated from underlying pretrained BERT models than learnt in task-specific training. Pretrained models should not be applied blindly for downstream tasks as they indeed reflect harmful imbalances and stereotypes. Just as gender-neutral language is important to mitigate everyday discrimination holistically, it is critical to avoid encoded biases in automated systems. We hope that the present work contributes to raising awareness of hidden biases and motivates further research on the propagation of unwanted biases through complex systems. To the best of our knowledge, there is no similar work so far that utilises the valuation capacity of sentiment classifiers to measure downstream biases.

References

Xingce Bao and Qianqian Qiao. 2019. Transfer learning from pre-trained bert for pronoun resolution. In *Proceedings of the First Workshop on Gender Bias in Natural Language Processing*, pages 82–88.

Marion Bartl, Malvina Nissim, and Albert Gatt. 2020. Unmasking contextual stereotypes: Measuring and mitigating bert's gender bias. In *Proceedings of the Second Workshop on Gender Bias in Natural Language Processing*, pages 1–16.

Rishabh Bhardwaj, Navonil Majumder, and Soujanya Poria. 2021. Investigating gender bias in bert. *Cognitive Computation*, 13(4):1008–1018.

Tolga Bolukbasi, Kai-Wei Chang, James Y Zou, Venkatesh Saligrama, and Adam T Kalai. 2016. Man is to computer programmer as woman is to homemaker? debiasing word embeddings. *Advances in neural information processing systems*, 29.

Aylin Caliskan, Joanna J Bryson, and Arvind Narayanan. 2017. Semantics derived automatically from language corpora contain human-like biases. *Science*, 356(6334):183–186.

Elizamary de Souza Nascimento, Iftekhar Ahmed, Edson Oliveira, Márcio Piedade Palheta, Igor Steinmacher, and Tayana Conte. 2019. Understanding development process of machine learning systems: Challenges and solutions. In *2019 ACM/IEEE International Symposium on Empirical Software Engineering and Measurement (ESEM)*, pages 1–6. IEEE.

Jacob Devlin, Ming-Wei Chang, Kenton Lee, and Kristina Toutanova. 2019a. Bert: Pre-training of deep bidirectional transformers for language understanding. In *Proceedings of the 2019 Conference of the North American Chapter of the Association for Computational Linguistics: Human Language Technologies, Volume 1 (Long and Short Papers)*, pages 4171–4186.

Jacob Devlin, Ming-Wei Chang, Kenton Lee, and Kristina Toutanova. 2019b. BERT: pre-training of deep bidirectional transformers for language understanding. pages 4171–4186.

Emily Dinan, Angela Fan, Adina Williams, Jack Urbanek, Douwe Kiela, and Jason Weston. 2020a. Queens are powerful too: Mitigating gender bias in dialogue generation. In *Proceedings of the 2020 Conference on Empirical Methods in Natural Language Processing (EMNLP)*, pages 8173–8188.

Emily Dinan, Angela Fan, Ledell Wu, Jason Weston, Douwe Kiela, and Adina Williams. 2020b. Multi-dimensional gender bias classification. In *Proceedings of the 2020 Conference on Empirical Methods in Natural Language Processing (EMNLP)*, pages 314–331.

Jad Doughman, Wael Khreich, Maya El Gharib, Maha Wiss, and Zahraa Berjawi. 2021. Gender bias in text: Origin, taxonomy, and implications. *GeBNLP 2021*, page 34.

Elizabeth Excell and Noura Al Moubayed. 2021. Towards equal gender representation in the annotations of toxic language detection. In *Proceedings of the 3rd Workshop on Gender Bias in Natural Language Processing*, pages 55–65.

Anjalie Field and Yulia Tsvetkov. 2020. Unsupervised discovery of implicit gender bias. In *Proceedings of the 2020 Conference on Empirical Methods in Natural Language Processing (EMNLP)*, pages 596–608.

Ana Valeria González, Maria Barrett, Rasmus Hvingelby, Kellie Webster, and Anders Søgaard. 2020. Type b reflexivization as an unambiguous testbed for multilingual multi-task gender bias. In *Proceedings of the 2020 Conference on Empirical Methods in Natural Language Processing (EMNLP)*, pages 2637–2648.

Anthony G Greenwald, Debbie E McGhee, and Jordan LK Schwartz. 1998. Measuring individual differences in implicit cognition: the implicit association test. *Journal of personality and social psychology*, 74(6):1464.

Wei Guo and Aylin Caliskan. 2021. Detecting emergent intersectional biases: Contextualized word embeddings contain a distribution of human-like biases. In *Proceedings of the 2021 AAAI/ACM Conference on AI, Ethics, and Society*, pages 122–133.

Gauri Gupta, Krithika Ramesh, and Sanjay Singh. 2021. Evaluating gender bias in hindi-english machine translation. *GeBNLP 2021*, page 16.

Po-Sen Huang, Huan Zhang, Ray Jiang, Robert Stanforth, Johannes Welbl, Jack W Rae, Vishal Maini, Dani Yogatama, and Pushmeet Kohli. Reducing sentiment bias in language models via counterfactual evaluation.

Sophie Jentzsch, Patrick Schramowski, Constantin Rothkopf, and Kristian Kersting. 2019. Semantics derived automatically from language corpora contain human-like moral choices. In *Proceedings of the 2019 AAAI/ACM Conference on AI, Ethics, and Society*, pages 37–44.

Svetlana Kiritchenko and Saif Mohammad. 2018. Examining gender and race bias in two hundred sentiment analysis systems. In *Proceedings of the Seventh Joint Conference on Lexical and Computational Semantics*, pages 43–53.

Keita Kurita, Nidhi Vyas, Ayush Pareek, Alan W Black, and Yulia Tsvetkov. 2019. Measuring bias in contextualized word representations. In *Proceedings of the First Workshop on Gender Bias in Natural Language Processing*, pages 166–172.

Zhenzhong Lan, Mingda Chen, Sebastian Goodman, Kevin Gimpel, Piyush Sharma, and Radu Soricut. 2019. Albert: A lite bert for self-supervised learning of language representations. In *International Conference on Learning Representations*.

Haochen Liu, Wentao Wang, Yiqi Wang, Hui Liu, Zitao Liu, and Jiliang Tang. 2020. Mitigating gender bias for neural dialogue generation with adversarial learning. In *Proceedings of the 2020 Conference on Empirical Methods in Natural Language Processing (EMNLP)*, pages 893–903.

Yinhan Liu, Myle Ott, Naman Goyal, Jingfei Du, Mandar Joshi, Danqi Chen, Omer Levy, Mike Lewis, Luke Zettlemoyer, and Veselin Stoyanov. 2019. Roberta: A robustly optimized BERT pretraining approach. *CoRR*, abs/1907.11692.

Kaiji Lu, Piotr Mardziel, Fangjing Wu, Preetam Amancharla, and Anupam Datta. 2020. Gender bias in neural natural language processing. In *Logic, Language, and Security*, pages 189–202. Springer.

Andrew L. Maas, Raymond E. Daly, Peter T. Pham, Dan Huang, Andrew Y. Ng, and Christopher Potts. 2011. Learning word vectors for sentiment analysis. In *Proceedings of the 49th Annual Meeting of the Association for Computational Linguistics: Human Language Technologies*, pages 142–150, Portland, Oregon, USA. Association for Computational Linguistics.

Chandler May, Alex Wang, Shikha Bordia, Samuel Bowman, and Rachel Rudinger. 2019. On measuring social biases in sentence encoders. In *Proceedings of the 2019 Conference of the North American Chapter of the Association for Computational Linguistics: Human Language Technologies, Volume 1 (Long and Short Papers)*, pages 622–628.

Tomas Mikolov, Kai Chen, and Greg Corrado. Efficient estimation of word representations in vector space.

Margaret Mitchell, Simone Wu, Andrew Zaldivar, Parker Barnes, Lucy Vasserman, Ben Hutchinson, Elena Spitzer, Inioluwa Deborah Raji, and Timnit Gebru. 2019. Model cards for model reporting. In *Proceedings of the conference on fairness, accountability, and transparency*, pages 220–229.

Robert Munro and Alex Carmen Morrison. 2020. Detecting independent pronoun bias with partially-synthetic data generation. In *Proceedings of the 2020 Conference on Empirical Methods in Natural Language Processing (EMNLP)*, pages 2011–2017.

Adam Paszke, Sam Gross, Francisco Massa, Adam Lerer, James Bradbury, Gregory Chanan, Trevor Killeen, Zeming Lin, Natalia Gimelshein, Luca Antiga, Alban Desmaison, Andreas Kopf, Edward Yang, Zachary DeVito, Martin Raison, Alykhan Tejani, Sasank Chilamkurthy, Benoit Steiner, Lu Fang, Junjie Bai, and Soumith Chintala. 2019. Pytorch: An imperative style, high-performance deep learning library. In *Advances in Neural Information Processing Systems 32*, pages 8024–8035. Curran Associates, Inc.

Jeffrey Pennington, Richard Socher, and Christopher D Manning. 2014. Glove: Global vectors for word representation. In *Proceedings of the 2014 conference on empirical methods in natural language processing (EMNLP)*, pages 1532–1543.

Xipeng Qiu, Tianxiang Sun, Yige Xu, Yunfan Shao, Ning Dai, and Xuanjing Huang. 2020. Pre-trained models for natural language processing: A survey. *Science China Technological Sciences*, pages 1–26.

Victor Sanh, Lysandre Debut, Julien Chaumond, and Thomas Wolf. 2019. Distilbert, a distilled version of bert: smaller, faster, cheaper and lighter. *arXiv e-prints*, pages arXiv–1910.

Patrick Schramowski, Cigdem Turan, Sophie Jentzsch, Constantin Rothkopf, and Kristian Kersting. 2020. The moral choice machine. *Frontiers in Artificial Intelligence*, 3:36.

Ieva Staliūnaitė and Ignacio Iacobacci. 2020. Compositional and lexical semantics in roberta, bert and distilbert: A case study on coqa. In *Proceedings of the 2020 Conference on Empirical Methods in Natural Language Processing (EMNLP)*, pages 7046–7056.

Yi Chern Tan and L Elisa Celis. 2019. Assessing social and intersectional biases in contextualized word representations. *Advances in Neural Information Processing Systems*, 32.

Thomas Wolf, Lysandre Debut, Victor Sanh, Julien Chaumond, Clement Delangue, Anthony Moi, Pierric Cistac, Tim Rault, Rémi Louf, Morgan Funtowicz, Joe Davison, Sam Shleifer, Patrick von Platen, Clara Ma, Yacine Jernite, Julien Plu, Canwen Xu, Teven Le Scao, Sylvain Gugger, Mariama Drame, Quentin Lhoest, and Alexander M. Rush. Transformers: State-of-the-art natural language processing. In *Proceedings of the 2020 Conference on Empirical Methods in Natural Language Processing: System Demonstrations*.

Patrick Xia, Shijie Wu, and Benjamin Van Durme. 2020. Which* bert? a survey organizing contextualized encoders. In *Proceedings of the 2020 Conference on Empirical Methods in Natural Language Processing (EMNLP)*, pages 7516–7533.

Jieyu Zhao and Kai-Wei Chang. 2020. Logan: Local group bias detection by clustering. In *Proceedings of the 2020 Conference on Empirical Methods in Natural Language Processing (EMNLP)*, pages 1968–1977.

Jieyu Zhao, Tianlu Wang, Mark Yatskar, Vicente Ordonez, and Kai-Wei Chang. 2018. Gender bias in coreference resolution: Evaluation and debiasing methods. In *Proceedings of the 2018 Conference of the North American Chapter of the Association for Computational Linguistics: Human Language Technologies, Volume 2 (Short Papers)*, pages 15–20.

Yukun Zhu, Ryan Kiros, Rich Zemel, Ruslan Salakhutdinov, Raquel Urtasun, Antonio Torralba, and Sanja Fidler. 2015. Aligning books and movies: Towards story-like visual explanations by watching movies and reading books. In *The IEEE International Conference on Computer Vision (ICCV)*.

A Appendix

The following sections supplement presented results with further details. Sec. A.1 provides all included gender terms and their frequency. Sec. A.2 presents comprehensive tables with measured biases or all experimental conditions. Sec. A.3 states test accuracies and other evaluation parameters of included classifiers.

A.1 Target Word Sets

Masked Terms The following list presents all gender terms that were, first, removed and masked to create the training conditions *R* and *mix* and, second, masked with an equivalent term of the opposite gender for experimental data. The list was carefully constructed, incorporating previous literature. Bolukbasi et al. (2016) state a comprehensive list of 218 gender-specific words already. We used that as a root and added further terms that we found in the data itself or other sources and that we considered being missing. Our final list comprises 685 terms in total.

In general, if possible, terms were masked by their exact equivalent of the other gender, e.g. *man* by *woman*, and similarly *woman* by *man*. Yet, language and the meaning and connotation of words are highly complex and ambiguous. Thus, the list of terms is not clear-cut, and for some terms, it is disputable whether they should be included or not. These are the four main concerns and how we handled each of them:

First, some mappings are not definite, i.e. there are multiple options to transfer the term into the opposite gender. One example is *lady*, which could be the female version of *gentleman* or *lord*. In these cases, we either selected the most likely translation or randomly.

Second, some terms do not have an appropriate translation like, among others, the term *guy*, or the term does exist in the other gender but is not used (as much), like for the term *feminism*. In these cases, we tried to find any translation that reflects the meaning as accurate as possible, like *gal* for *guy* or applied the rarely used counterpart, e.g. *masculism*.

Third, in some cases, there is a female version of the term, but the male version is usually used for all genders. This is, for example, the case for *manageress* or *lesbianism*. These terms exist and are possibly used, but one could still say 'she is a manager' or 'she is gay'. In these cases, we only translated the term in one direction. This is, whenever the term *lesbian* occurs, it is translated into *gay* for the male version, but when the original rating includes the term *gay*, it is not transformed into *lesbian* for the female version.

Finally, it can have other meanings that are not gender-related, e.g. *Miss* as an appellation can also be the verb *to miss*. We decided to interpret these terms as the more frequent meaning or to leave the term out if it was unclear.

Similar to many other resources, Bolukbasi et al. (2016) also include terms from the animal realm, such as *stud* or *lion*(Bolukbasi et al., 2016). We decided not to do so because the present investigation focuses on human gender bias, which might not be similarly present for animals. The list includes all masked terms that occurred at least ten times in the entire experimental data in decreasing order. Further 404 terms were included in the analysis that occurred fewer than ten times. 221 of these terms were not counted even once and did not affect the analysis. A comprehensive list of all considered terms and their frequency can be found in the corresponding repository.

The full list corresponds to the *all* term set. Due to the above-discussed concerns, we also applied the *weat* term set, which consists of mostly unambiguous terms. Terms that are included in weat are marked in bold. The third term set, *pro*, only includes pronouns which are *he, she, his, her, him* and *hers*. This term set is relatively small, but pronouns are more frequent than most other terms.

Pronouns are marked in bold.

he (46634), **his** (34475), **her** (31303), **she** (26377), **him** (17863), **man** (11656), guys (8070), **girl** (7433), guy (5862), god (5324), mom (4456), actors (4349), **boy** (3802), **girls** (3509), **mother** (3424), dad (3274), **woman** (3235), wife (2858), **brother** (2810), **sister** (2726), **men** (2662), **father** (2468), mr (2439), **boys** (2377), actor (2369), **son** (2226), **women** (2212), himself (2194), dude (2089), **daughter** (1995), lady (1948), husband (1658), boyfriend (1544), **brothers** (1474), hero (1427), actress (1167), **female** (1158), girlfriend (1087), king (1012), **mothers** (1009), hubby (994), count (932), herself (878), **male** (821), daddy (792), ladies (766), ms (725), giant (725), mommy (721), master (708), **sisters** (701), lord (697), ma (671), sir (626), queen (621), mama (596), **uncle** (587), chick (567), moms (556), grandma (529), **aunt** (521), **fathers** (444), heroes (434), princess (432), pa (411), host (405), niece (373), prince (350), dads (341), actresses (341), priest (328), nephew (328), hunter (303), bride (284), witch (281), lesbian (277), heroine (261), kings (239), grandpa (239), daughters (234), **grandfather** (223), **grandmother** (222), chicks (193), masters (187), cowboy (185), counts (177), dudes (174), sons (169), gods (166), gal (159), papa (158), wifey (156), girly (156), queens (152), bachelor (149), housewives (148), **hers** (148), maid (145), girlfriends (145), beard (141), emperor (136), gentleman (129), superman (128), duke (127), girlie (125), mayor (123), wives (122), gentlemen (116), playboy (114), mister (113), mistress (111), giants (109), females (107), wizard (105), widow (98), nun (98), penis (96), fiance (95), lad (92), gals (92), boyfriends (91), girlies (90), bloke (90), bachelorette (88), aunts (87), policeman (84), males (84), fella (79), diva (79), macho (78), goddess (78), lads (77), landlord (75), fiancé (75), patron (74), waitress (73), husbands (70), hosts (70), fiancée (70), feminist (70), cowboys (70), nephews (68), mermaid (68), sorority (66), grandmas (66), chap (65), manly (64), businessman (63), monk (62), baron (62), witches (61), bachelor (61), nieces (59), housewife (59), **feminine** (58), cameraman (58), shepherd (57), lesbians (55), vagina (53), uncles (53), wizards (52), henchmen (49), salesman (48), postman (48), mamas (48), grandson (48), brotherhood (47), lords (44), henchman (44), waiter (43), dukes (42), mommies (41), fellas (41), granddaughter (40), traitor (39), groom (39), duchess (39), madman (36), policemen (35), conductor (35), sisterhood (34), fraternity (34), monks (33), **masculine** (33), nuns (32), fiancee (32), lass (30), tailor (29), priests (29), maternity (29), butch (29), stepfather (28), hostess (28), ancestors (28), heiress (27), countess (27), congressman (27), bridesmaid (27), protector (26), divas (26), ambassador (26), damsel (25), steward (24), madam (24), homeboy (24), landlady (23), **grandmothers** (23), fireman (23), empress (23), chairman (23), widower (22), sorcerer (22), patrons (22), masculinity (22), firemen (22), englishman (22), businessmen (22), testosterone (21), manhood (21), chaps (21), widows (20), lesbianism (20), blokes (20), beards (20), barbershop (20), anchorman (20), sperm (19), heroines (19), heir (19), stepmother (18), princesses (18), princes (18), handyman (18), patriarch (17), monastery (17), mailman (17), homegirl (17), headmistress (17), fisherman (17), czar (17), brotherly (17), brides (17), uterus (16), maternal (16), abbot (16), prophet (15), boyish (15), adventurer (15), testicles (14), temptress (14), schoolgirl (14), penises (14), maids (14), barmaid (14), waiters (13), traitors (13), stuntman (13), priestess (13), seductress (12), schoolboy (12), motherhood (12), daddies (12), cowgirls (12), cameramen (12), bachelors (12), adventurers (12), sculptor (11), schoolgirls (11), proprietor (11), paternal (11), homeboys (11), foreman (11), feminism (11), doorman (11), bachelors (11), womanhood (10), testicle (10), mistresses (10), merman (10), **grandfathers** (10), girlish (10)

A.2 Biases

Tab. 3 and Tab. 4 provide an overview of the model biases of all considered classifiers. For the calculation of biases, the same gender term set was applied to the experimental data masking as for the training data condition. This means, for instance, in the experimental data for all *R-weat* and *mix-weat* trained classifiers, only *weat* terms were masked. Thus, the training condition is in line with the experimental bias calculation for all *N* and *mix* training conditions. For *original* training conditions, however, no term set was applied to the training data. This is why biases of all three term groups are compared, which are *original-N*, *original-pro*, and *original-weat*.

Wilcoxon signed-rank-test yielded highly significant p-values for almost all conditions. Exceptions are *distbert mix-all,bertbase mix-pro, robertbase mix-weat, robertbase mix-all*, and *albertlarge mix-weat*. Out of 63 reported experimental models, 57 showed highly significant biases, of which 16 prefer female terms over male terms, and 41 prefer male terms over female terms.

	non zero		all					
Condition	bias abs	bias tot	bias abs	bias tot	N< 0	N= 0	N> 0	sign.
distbert								
original-pro	0.0021	0.0009	0.0014	0.0006	6085	10216	8699	***
R-pro	0.0022	0.0010	0.0014	0.0007	7116	9183	8701	***
mix-pro	0.0022	-0.0012	0.0012	-0.0007	6922	7309	10769	***
original-weat	0.0035	0.0004	0.0026	0.0003	8098	10214	6688	***
R-weat	0.0037	-0.0015	0.0027	-0.0011	10773	7532	6695	***
mix-weat	0.0027	-0.0008	0.0018	-0.0006	8332	8428	8240	***
original-all	0.0047	0.0016	0.0039	0.0013	7817	12941	4242	***
R-all	0.0045	0.0008	0.0037	0.0007	10022	10734	4244	***
mix-all	0.0052	-0.0003	0.0042	-0.0003	10080	10177	4743	-
bertbase								
original-pro	0.0025	0.0013	0.0016	0.0008	5430	10874	8696	***
R-pro	0.0036	0.0031	0.0024	0.0020	3234	13061	8705	***
mix-pro	0.0023	-0.0000	0.0014	-0.0000	7505	7794	9701	-
original-weat	0.0037	0.0015	0.0027	0.0011	6187	12128	6685	***
R-weat	0.0038	0.002	0.0028	0.0015	6204	12098	6698	***
mix-weat	0.0027	-0.0002	0.0015	-0.0001	6421	7135	11444	***
original-all	0.0056	0.0035	0.0046	0.0029	5233	15527	4240	***
R-all	0.0060	0.0041	0.0049	0.0034	4319	16431	4250	***
mix-all	0.0055	0.0005	0.0035	0.0003	6838	9001	9161	***
bertlarge								
original-pro	0.0031	-0.0016	0.0021	-0.0011	10287	6020	8693	***
R-pro	0.0050	0.0046	0.0032	0.0030	2697	13610	8693	***
mix-pro	0.0035	0.0011	0.0014	0.0004	4961	5228	14811	*
original-weat	0.0069	-0.0032	0.0051	-0.0023	10329	7986	6685	***
R-weat	0.0048	-0.0011	0.0035	-0.0008	10172	8142	6686	***
mix-weat	0.0056	0.0034	0.0029	0.0018	4581	8195	12224	***
original-all	0.0082	0.0009	0.0068	0.0007	9128	11633	4239	***
R-all	0.0095	0.0042	0.0079	0.0035	7314	13443	4243	***
mix-all	0.0101	0.0015	0.0078	0.0012	8848	10455	5697	***

Table 3: Total biases of all experimental classifiers (part 1). The bias is the mean bias over all experimental samples. While the absolute bias (bias abs) is the mean of absolute values, the total bias (bias tot) is based on the directed sample biases. For "non zero" values, samples with a bias= 0 are excluded. "all" includes all 25000 sample biases. The numbers of samples with negative, no, and positive bias are given by $N < 0$, $N = 0$, or $N > 0$, respectively. Significance levels for Wilcoxon signed-rank-test were defined as $p > 0.05$:*, $p > 0.01$:**, and $p > 0.001$:***. Reported significance levels were corrected for multiple testing with the Bonferroni correction.

Condition	non zero bias abs	bias tot	all bias abs	bias tot	N< 0	N= 0	N> 0	sign.
robertabase								
original-pro	0.0024	0.0016	0.0015	0.0010	5448	10840	8712	***
R-pro	0.0024	0.0009	0.0015	0.0006	6822	9472	8706	***
mix-pro	0.0021	-0.0002	0.0013	-0.0001	8682	7612	8706	***
original-weat	0.0031	0.0016	0.0023	0.0011	6470	11832	6698	***
R-weat	0.0028	0.0007	0.0021	0.0005	7722	10581	6697	***
mix-weat	0.0023	0.0002	0.0017	0.0002	9396	8894	6710	-
original-all	0.0036	0.0020	0.0030	0.0016	7165	13585	4250	***
R-all	0.0038	0.0010	0.0032	0.0008	9294	11464	4242	***
mix-all	0.0027	0.0000	0.0023	0.0000	10520	10206	4274	-
robertalarge								
original-pro	0.0024	0.0015	0.0016	0.0010	5235	11055	8710	***
R-pro	0.0025	0.0015	0.0016	0.0010	5216	11072	8712	***
mix-pro	0.0020	0.0004	0.0013	0.0003	6679	9606	8715	***
original-weat	0.0039	0.0025	0.0029	0.0018	5894	12411	6695	***
R-weat	0.0039	0.0023	0.0029	0.0017	6109	12193	6698	***
mix-weat	0.0028	0.0004	0.0021	0.0003	8071	10220	6709	***
original-all	0.0044	0.0023	0.0036	0.0019	7105	13653	4242	***
R-all	0.0043	0.0021	0.0035	0.0017	7045	13712	4243	***
mix-all	0.0041	0.0018	0.0034	0.0015	6971	13783	4246	***
albertbase								
original-pro	0.0037	0.0011	0.0024	0.0007	5481	10811	8708	***
R-pro	0.0029	-0.0004	0.0019	-0.0003	9305	6986	8709	***
mix-pro	0.0054	0.0021	0.0035	0.0014	7244	8968	8788	***
original-weat	0.0093	0.0002	0.0068	0.0001	7710	10600	6690	***
R-weat	0.0082	-0.0044	0.006	-0.0032	10346	7942	6712	***
mix-weat	0.0131	-0.0034	0.0093	-0.0024	9426	8263	7311	***
original-all	0.0089	-0.0023	0.0074	-0.0019	9112	11645	4243	***
R-all	0.0080	0.0009	0.0067	0.0008	8979	11769	4252	***
mix-all	0.0071	-0.0014	0.0058	-0.0012	9481	11030	4489	***
albertlarge								
original-pro	0.0086	0.0086	0.0056	0.0056	2120	14075	8805	***
R-pro	0.0049	0.0034	0.0032	0.0022	6407	9869	8724	***
mix-pro	0.0016	-0.0008	0.0010	-0.0005	10121	6136	8743	***
original-weat	0.0155	0.0130	0.0113	0.0095	4058	14191	6751	***
R-weat	0.0074	-0.0032	0.0054	-0.0023	9936	8373	6691	***
mix-weat	0.0091	-0.0009	0.0066	-0.0006	9186	8998	6816	-
original-all	0.0172	0.0137	0.0143	0.0114	5095	15594	4311	***
R-all	0.0114	-0.0032	0.0095	-0.0026	12573	8180	4247	***
mix-all	0.0101	0.0034	0.0084	0.0028	8777	11875	4348	***

Table 4: Total biases of all experimental classifiers (part 2). Extension of Tab. 3

Model / Spec	acc.	rec.	prec.	f1
distbase				
original	.812	.778	.835	.805
R-all	.817	.789	.836	.812
R-weat	.820	.789	.840	.814
R-pro	.818	.780	.844	.811
mix-all	.822	.795	.840	.817
mix-weat	.822	.783	.849	.815
mix-pro	.822	.784	.848	.815
bertbase				
original	.818	.787	.838	.812
R-all	.821	.781	.849	.813
R-pro	.820	.776	.851	.812
R-weat	.821	.803	.833	.818
mix-all	.836	.791	.868	.828
mix-pro	.835	.816	.849	.832
mix-weat	.835	.812	.852	.832
bertlarge				
original	.805	.787	.816	.801
R-all	.797	.734	.839	.783
R-pro	.779	.660	.867	.749
R-weat	.803	.739	.847	.789
mix-all	.795	.723	.845	.780
mix-pro	.797	.738	.836	.784
mix-weat	.789	.710	.843	.771

Table 5: Test accuracy (acc.), recall (rec.), precision (prec.), and F1-Score (f1) for the models that are used in the experiments - part 1

A.3 Evaluation of Models

Tab. 5 and Tab. 6 show the accuracies, recalls, precisions and F1-Score of all experimental models calculated on the test data. For the calculation of reported values, the test data set has been treated analogously to the training condition. That means for instance, since we removed all pronouns from training data in the R-all condition, we did the same in the test data before evaluating the models in that condition.

Model / Spec	acc.	rec.	prec.	f1
robertabase				
original	.818	.744	.874	.804
R-all	.823	.770	.862	.813
R-weat	.820	.739	.881	.804
R-pro	.818	.733	.883	.801
mix-all	.833	.780	.873	.824
mix-weat	.830	.781	.867	.821
mix-pro	.823	.760	.870	.811
robertalarge				
original	.820	.748	.873	.806
R-all	.820	.765	.859	.810
R-weat	.820	.761	.862	.809
R-pro	.818	.751	.868	.805
mix-all	.815	.749	.862	.801
mix-weat	.816	.761	.855	.805
mix-pro	.814	.728	.879	.797
albertbase				
original	.693	.932	.630	.752
R-all	.771	.711	.809	.756
R-weat	.772	.749	.785	.767
R-pro	.757	.748	.764	.756
mix-all	.782	.791	.777	.784
mix-weat	.778	.818	.757	.786
mix-pro	.780	.813	.762	.787
albertlarge				
original	.784	.762	.797	.779
R-all	.762	.847	.724	.781
R-weat	.767	.802	.750	.775
R-pro	.763	.832	.732	.779
mix-all	.774	.803	.759	.781
mix-weat	.784	.788	.781	.785
mix-pro	.782	.752	.801	.776

Table 6: Test accuracy (acc.), recall (rec.), precision (prec.), and F1-Score (f1) for the models that are used in the experiments - part 2

Occupational Biases in Norwegian and Multilingual Language Models

Samia Touileb
University of Bergen
samia.touileb@uib.no

Lilja Øvrelid
University of Oslo
liljao@uio.no

Erik Velldal
University of Oslo
erikve@uio.no

Abstract

In this paper we explore how a demographic distribution of occupations, along gender dimensions, is reflected in pre-trained language models. We give a descriptive assessment of the distribution of occupations, and investigate to what extent these are reflected in four Norwegian and two multilingual models. To this end, we introduce a set of simple bias probes, and perform five different tasks combining gendered pronouns, first names, and a set of occupations from the Norwegian statistics bureau. We show that language specific models obtain more accurate results, and are much closer to the real-world distribution of clearly gendered occupations. However, we see that none of the models have correct representations of the occupations that are demographically balanced between genders. We also discuss the importance of the training data on which the models were trained on, and argue that template-based bias probes can sometimes be fragile, and a simple alteration in a template can change a model's behavior.

1 Introduction

Measuring the presence of stereotypical representations of occupations in pre-trained language models has been an important effort in combating and reducing possible representational harms (Blodgett et al., 2020). However, and as pointed out by Blodgett (2021), most of the current work is motivated by an idealised vision of the world where occupations should not be correlated with genders, and where the expectations are that models should not be stereotypical when *e.g.,* predicting female or male pronouns in relation to occupations. The idea that we are all equal is an important factor in our quest of reaching fair and less biased models, and reflect our normative judgments.

While this is true for most stereotypes, it might not directly apply to occupations. With a descriptive and realistic view of the society, there clearly exists gender disparities in occupations. This is inherently tied to many societal constructs and cultural backgrounds, and are a reality for many occupations. Also pointed out by Blodgett et al. (2020), the importance of the connection between language and social hierarchies, has not been considered in most previous work on bias in NLP. It is a reality that most Norwegian nurses are females. Having a model reflecting this reality might not be problematic *per se*, but using this disparity to for example systematically reject male applicants to a nurse position is a very harmful effect.

In this paper, we investigate how the real-world Norwegian demographic distribution of occupations, along the two gender dimensions male versus female, is reflected in large transformer-based pre-trained language models. We give a descriptive assessment of the distribution of occupations, and investigate to what extent these are reflected in four pre-trained Norwegian and two multilingual models. More precisely, we focus on the following research questions:

- To what extent are demographic distributions of genders and occupations represented in pre-trained language models?
- How are demographically clearly gender-correlated vs. gender-balanced occupations represented in pre-trained language models?

To address these questions, we investigate the correlations of occupations with Norwegian gendered pronouns and names. We analyse five template-based tasks, and compare the outputs of the models to real-world Norwegian demographic distributions of occupations by genders.

After first providing a bias statement in Section 2, we give an overview of previous relevant work in Section 3. Section 4 describes our experimental setup, and outlines our template-based tasks. We present and discuss our main results and findings in

Proceedings of the The 4th Workshop on Gender Bias in Natural Language Processing (GeBNLP), pages 200 - 211
July 15, 2022 ©2022 Association for Computational Linguistics

Section 5 and 6. We conclude with a summary of our work, and discuss our future plans in Section 7.

2 Bias statement

We follow the bias definition of Friedman and Nissenbaum (1996), where bias is defined as the cases where automated systems exhibit a systematic discrimination against, and unfairly process, a certain group of individuals. In our case, we see this as reflected in large pre-trained language models and how they can contain skewed gendered representations that can be systematically unfair if this bias is not uncovered and properly taken into account in downstream applications. Another definition of bias that we rely on is that of Shah et al. (2020), where bias is defined as the discrepancy between the distribution of predicted and ideal outcomes of a model.

We focus on the associations between gendered (female and male) pronouns/names and professional occupations. We investigate to what degree pre-trained language models systematically associate specific genders with given occupations. However, we explore this from the perspective of a descriptive assessment: Instead of expecting the system to treat genders equally, we compare how these gender–occupation representations reflect the actual and current Norwegian demographics. This will in no way reduce the representational harms of stereotypical female and male occupations, that could both be propagated and exaggerated by downstream tasks, but would rather shed light on which occupations are falsely represented by such models. Moreover, our work will provide knowledge about the biases contained in these models that may be important to take into account when choosing a model for a specific application.

Arguably, a limitation of our work is that we are only able to evaluate correlations between occupations and the binary gender categories male/female, although we acknowledge the fact that gender as an identity spans a wider spectrum than this.

3 Background and related work

Training data in NLP tasks may contain various types of bias that can be inherited by the models we train (Hovy and Prabhumoye, 2021), and that may potentially lead to unintended and undesired effects when deployed (Bolukbasi et al., 2016). The bias can stem from the unlabeled texts used for pre-training of Language Models (LMs), or from the language or the label distribution used for tuning a downstream classifier. Since LMs are now the backbone of most NLP model architectures, the extent to which they reflect, amplify, and spread the biases existing in the input data is very important for the further development of such models, and the understanding of their possible harmful outcomes.

Efforts so far have shown a multitude of biases in pre-trained LMs and contextualized embeddings. Sheng et al. (2019) show that pre-training the LM BERT (Devlin et al., 2019) on a medical corpus propagates harmful correlations between genders, ethnicity, and insurance groups. Hutchinson et al. (2020) show that English LMs contain biases against disabilities, where persons with disabilities are correlated with negative sentiment words, and mental illness too frequently co-occur with homelessness and drug addictions. Both Zhao and Bethard (2020) and Basta et al. (2019) show that ELMO (Peters et al., 2018) contains, and even amplifies gender bias. Especially, Basta et al. (2019) discuss the differences of contextualized and non-contextualized embeddings, and which types of gender bias are mitigated and which ones are amplified.

Most work on detecting gender bias has focused on template-based approaches. These templates are simple sentences of the form "`[pronoun] is a [description]`", where a description could be anything from nouns referring to occupations, to adjectives referring to sentiment, emotions, or traits (Stanczak and Augenstein, 2021; Saunders and Byrne, 2020; Bhaskaran and Bhallamudi, 2019; Cho et al., 2019; Prates et al., 2018). Bhardwaj et al. (2021) investigate the propagation of gender biases of BERT in five downstream tasks within emotion and sentiment prediction. They propose an approach to identify gender directions for each BERT layer, and use the Equity Evaluation Corpus (Kiritchenko and Mohammad, 2018) as an evaluation of their approach. They show that their approach can reduce some of the biases in downstream tasks. Nozza et al. (2021) also use a template- and lexicon-based approach, in this case for sentence completion. They introduce a dataset for the six languages English, French, Italian, Portuguese, Romanian, and Spanish, and show that LMs both reproduce and amplify gender-related societal stereotypes.

Another series of work that have focused on template-based datasets are those building on the

Occupation	Female%	Male%	Occupation	Female%	Male%
Knitting craftsman	100	0	Architect	<u>49.9</u>	<u>50.1</u>
Midwife	99.8	0.2	Lawyer	<u>48.1</u>	<u>51.9</u>
Esthetician	99.3	0.7	Politician	<u>48.1</u>	<u>51.9</u>
Health Secretary	98.8	1.2	Associate Professor	<u>47.2</u>	<u>52.8</u>
PhD candidate	<u>52.8</u>	<u>47.2</u>	Scaffolding builder	0.5	99.5
Psychiatrist	<u>52.6</u>	<u>47.4</u>	Chief engineer	0.4	99.6
Doctor	<u>51.6</u>	<u>48.4</u>	Coastal skipper	0	100

Table 1: A selection of occupations from the Norwegian statistics bureau, the gold reference distribution of occupations and genders. The occupations presented here are either dominated by more than 98% of either gender, or have a more balanced distribution (underlined percentages) between both female and male genders.

Winograd Schemas data (Levesque et al., 2012). This dataset was developed for the task of coreference resolution, and contains a set of manually annotated templates that requires commonsense reasoning about coreference. It is used to explore the existence of biases in coreference resolution systems, by measuring the dependence of the system on gendered pronouns along stereotypical and non-stereotypical gender associations with occupations. Similarly, the WinoBias (Zhao et al., 2018) dataset focuses on the relationship between gendered pronouns and stereotypical occupations, and is used to explore the existing stereotypes in models. The WinoGender dataset (Rudinger et al., 2018) also contains sentences focusing on the relationship between pronouns, persons, and occupations. Here, they also include gender-neutral pronouns. Unlike WinoBias, WinoGender's sentences are built such that there is a coreference between pronouns and occupations, and between the same pronouns and persons. Based on these datasets for coreference resolution, WinoMT (Stanovsky et al., 2019) has been developed for the task of machine translation. The dataset also contains stereotypical and non-stereotypical templates used to investigate gender bias in machine translation systems.

Moreover, Bender et al. (2021) point out the dangers of LMs and how they can potentially amplify the already existing biases that occur in the data they were trained on. They highlight the importance of understanding the harmful consequences of carelessly using such models in language processing, and how they in particular can hurt minorities. They also discuss the difficulty of identifying such biases, and how complicated it can be to tackle them. This is partly due to poor framework definitions, *i.e.,* how culturally specific they are, but also how unreliable current bias evaluation methods are.

We focus therefore in this work on investigating how culturally specific Norwegian demographics related to gender and occupations are reflected in four Norwegian and two multilingual pre-trained LMs. Our work differs from previous work in that we ground our bias probes to real-world distributions of gender, and rather than expecting the models to always have a balanced representation of genders, we explore to which degree they reflect true demographics.

4 Experimental setup

Following the methodology of previous research on gender bias in pre-trained language models, and due to the corresponding lack of resources for Norwegian, we generate our own set of templates that we use with the pre-trained language models to make use of their ability to compute the probabilities of words and sentences. We present an empirical analysis of gender biases towards occupational associations. By using the templates we hope to reduce variation by keeping the semantic structure of the sentence. We analyze the probability distributions of returned pronouns, occupations, and first names; and compare them to real-world gold data representing the demographic distribution in Norway. Investigating the differences between the models can also give us insights into the content of the various types of corpora they were trained on. Data and codes will be made available[1].

Below we discuss in turn (*i*) the gold reference distribution of occupations and genders, (*ii*) the templates, (*iii*) how the templates are used for probing pre-trained language models, and finally (*iv*) the models that we test.

[1]`https://github.com/SamiaTouileb/Biases-Norwegian-Multilingual-LMs`

Reference distribution We use a set of 418 occupations. These represent the demographic distribution of females and males in the respective occupations in Norway[2] originating from the Norwegian statistics bureau. The bureau releases yearly statistics covering various aspects of the Norwegian society, and all data is made freely available. This list comprises a fine-grained level of occupations, where e.g., *lege* (*doctor*) and *allmennlege* (*general practitioner*) are considered two different occupations. The gender-to-occupation ratios in these statistics are used as 'gold standard' when probing the models.

In Table 1 we show some examples of the occupations dominated by more than 98% of either gender, and those that have a more balanced distribution (underlined). Culturally speaking, Norway is known to strive for gender balance in all occupations. While this is true for many instances, there are still some occupations that are unbalanced in gender-distribution. From the Norwegian statistics bureau, it is clear that most midwives are still women, and that most chief engineers are males. However, for occupations as Phd candidates, psychiatrist, doctor, architect, lawyer, politician, and associate professor the distribution of genders is more balanced.

Templates Our templates combine occupations, pronouns, and first names. We focus on five template-based tasks, and generate the following corresponding templates that we use as bias probes (Solaiman et al., 2019):

1. Task1: *[pronoun] is a/an [occupation]* (original: *[pronoun] er [occupation]*)
2. Task2: *[pronoun] works as a/an [occupation]* (original: *[pronoun] jobber som [occupation]*)
3. Task3: *[name] is a/an [occupation]* (original: *[name] er [occupation]*)
4. Task4: *[name] works as a/an [occupation]* (original: *[name] jobber som [occupation]*)
5. Task5: *the [occupation] [name]* (original: *[occupation] [name]*)

As pronouns, our work mainly focuses on *hun* and *han* (*she* and *he* respectively). As demographic statistics are still made using a binary gender distribution, we could not include the gender neutral pronoun *hen* (*they*), which is, in addition, rarely used in Norway.

As first names, we also extract from the Norwegian statistics bureau[3] the 10 most frequent female and male names in Norway from 1880 to 2021, this results in 90 female names and 71 male names. For tasks 1–4 we use the full set of 418 occupations, while in task 5 we focus on those that either have a balanced distribution between genders or are clearly female- or male-dominated. This was decided after an analysis of the distribution of occupations across genders, and resulted in two thresholds. All occupations that had between 0 and 10% differences in distribution, were deemed balanced (*e.g.,* 51% female and 49% male). All occupations that had more than 75% distribution of one gender against the other, were deemed unbalanced, and are referred to as either clearly female (≥75%) or clearly male (≥75%) occupations. This resulted in a set of 31 clearly female occupations, 106 clearly male occupations, and 49 balanced occupations.

For tasks 1 and 2, we mask the pronouns and compute the probability distribution across the occupations for female and male pronouns. For tasks 3, 4, and 5, we mask the occupations and compute the probability distributions in each bias-probe. Masking pronouns will allow us to uncover how likely a gendered pronoun is correlated with an occupation, and masking the occupation will allow us to uncover how likely occupations are correlated with female and male names.

Probing and evaluation For each task, we first generate the probability distributions of masked tokens in each bias probe. In order to have a comparable distribution to the gold standard (which is given as a percentage), we compute a simple percentage representation of the probability distributions by following the following formula:

$$\text{f\_pron\%} = \frac{\text{prob f\_pron}}{\text{prob f\_pron} + \text{prob m\_pron}}$$

Where *f_pron%* is the percentage of a female pronoun, and *prob x_pron* is the output probability of each model for each of the female and male pronouns. The same simple formula is used in all tasks. We are aware that this is a simplified representation of the output of each model, nevertheless, we believe that it will not change the overall distribution.

Once probability distributions are mapped to per-

[2]https://utdanning.no/likestilling

[3]https://www.ssb.no/befolkning/navn/statistikk/navn

centages, we quantify the difference between female and male scores by simply subtracting the scores of males from the scores of female. Positive values will represent occupations that are more strongly associated with females than males by the model, and negative values represent the opposite. This is also applied to the gold standard data. We use the demographic distribution of the occupations from the Norwegian statistics bureau as gold data.

Based on this, values greater than 0 are deemed female-dominated occupations, and values lower that 0 are male-dominated occupation. This is used to compute the macro F1 values for each model.

Pre-trained language models We analyse the predictions of six pre-trained language models, four Norwegian and two multilingual. Note that Norwegian has two official written standards; Bokmål (literally 'book tongue') and Nynorsk (literally 'new Norwegian'). While Bokmål is the main variety, roughly 15% of the Norwegian population write in the Nynorsk variant. All the Norwegian models are trained on data comprising both Bokmål and Nynorsk.

- NorBERT (Kutuzov et al., 2021): trained on the Norwegian newspaper corpus[4], and Norwegian Wikipedia, comprising about two billion word tokens.
- NorBERT2[5]: trained on the non-copyrighted subset of the Norwegian Colossal Corpus (NCC)[6] and the Norwegian subset of the C4 web-crawled corpus (Xue et al., 2021). In total, it comprises about 15 billion word tokens.
- NB-BERT (Kummervold et al., 2021): trained on the full NCC, and follows the architecture of the BERT cased multilingual model (Devlin et al., 2019). It comprises around 18.5 billion word tokens.
- NB-BERT_Large[7]: trained on NCC, and follows the architecture of the BERT-large uncased model.
- mBERT (Devlin et al., 2019): pre-trained on a set of the 104 languages with the largest Wikipedia pages.
- XLM-RoBERTa (Conneau et al., 2020): trained on a collection of 100 languages from the Common Crawl corpus.

As can be seen above, each model has been trained on different types of corpora, and are all of various sizes. The NCC corpus, is a collection of OCR-scanned documents from the Norwegian library's collection of newspapers and works of fiction (with publishing years ranging from early 1800s to present day), government reports, parliament collections, OCR public reports, legal resources such as laws, as well as Norwegian Wikipedia. In short, some models are trained on well structured texts, that follow a somewhat formal style, while other models also include less structured texts in the form of online content.

5 Results

Table 2 summarizes the overall results for all models. We also compute class-level F1 values for each task, these can be found in Table 3 and Figure 5. Below we discuss the task-wise results in more detail.

5.1 Task1: (she|he) is a/an [occupation]

In the first task, we mask the pronouns *she* and *he* in our bias probes. We focus on the full set of 418 occupations. As can be seen in Table 2, all four Norwegian models give higher scores than the two multilingual models. NB-BERT and NB-BERT_Large have a macro F1 of 0.75, and are the highest performing models overall. It should be pointed out that these are also the biggest Norwegian models in terms of token counts. NorBERT is the less performing Norwegian model in this task, and has a macro F1 a few percentiles higher than the multilingual model XLM-RoBERTa. We believe that this might be impacted by the the size of NorBERT, which is the smallest Norwegian model in terms of token counts.

Looking at class-level F1 scores from Table 3, all models achieve high F1 scores for the male class, with NB-BERT_Large achieving the highest score with an F1 of 0.84, and mBERT achieving the lowest one with an F1 of 0.74. In contrast, all models have substantially lower F1 score on the female class. Again, NB-BERT_Large achieves the highest score with 0.67 F1, and mBERT the lowest with 0.30. This shows that the models are already somehow skewed towards the male class.

[4] https://www.nb.no/sprakbanken/ressurskatalog/oai-nb-no-sbr-4/

[5] https://huggingface.co/ltgoslo/norbert2

[6] https://github.com/NbAiLab/notram/blob/master/guides/corpus_description.md

[7] https://huggingface.co/NbAiLab/nb-bert-large

model	Task1	Task2	Task3	Task4	Task5_b	Task5_ub
NorBERT	0.69	0.67	0.60	0.35	0.46	**0.83**
NorBERT2	0.73	0.54	0.77	0.72	0.52	0.76
NB-BERT	**0.75**	0.74	0.70	**0.80**	**0.69**	0.77
NB-BERT_Large	**0.75**	**0.82**	**0.80**	0.74	0.49	0.76
mBERT	0.52	0.42	0.52	0.52	0.52	0.55
XLM-RoBERTa	0.65	0.50	0.68	0.49	0.47	0.56

Table 2: Macro F1 of models compared to the real-world "gold" distribution. **Task1**: `[pronoun] is a/an [occupation]`, **Task2**: `[pronoun] works as a/an [occupation]`, **Task3**: `[name] is a/an [occupation]`, **Task4**: `[name] works as a/an [occupation]`, **Task5_b**: `the [occupation] [name]` with balanced distributions in gold, **Task5_ub**: `the [occupation] [name]` with clearly female and male occupation distributions in gold.

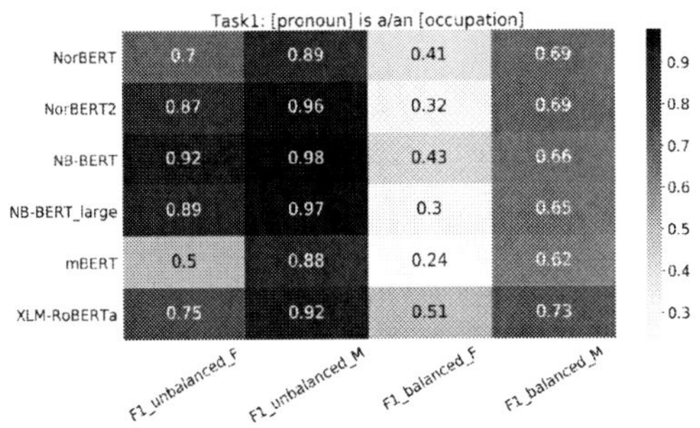

Figure 1: Task1, class-level F1 values focusing on balanced and unbalanced occupations.

In addition to looking at the distribution of all occupations, and based on the previous observation that all models seem to reflect male occupations but to a lesser extent reflect female occupations, we have looked at the occupations that have balanced and unbalanced distributions in the gold data. The unbalanced occupations as previously mentioned, are those which are clearly female or male occupations (more than 75% distribution of one gender against the other). The balanced distribution are those that have between 0 and 10% differences in gender distribution in the gold data. Results are depicted in Figure 1.

When it comes to clearly female occupations, the three biggest Norwegian models, namely NorBERT2, NB-BERT, and NB-BERT_Large obtain highest F1 values with 0.87, 0.92, and 0.89 respectively. Followed by XLM-RoBERTa and NorBERT. For clearly male occupations, all models have high F1 values, with the three top ones being again NorBERT2, NB-BERT, and NB-BERT_Large. The two multilingual models achieve quite high values, with XLM-RoBERTa outperforming NorBERT here again. It is quite clear that the Norwegian models have a good representation of clearly female and male occupations. Another compelling result is that XLM-RoBERTa has a quite accurate representation of these unbalanced occupations, equating the ones from the smallest Norwegian model NorBERT.

Focusing on balanced occupations, most models exhibit a tendency to represent occupations as male. NorBERT, NB-BERT, and XLM-RoBERTa are the only models that seem to have a decent representation of female occupations. The expectations here are not that the models would give a better representation of female occupations, but rather be equally good at representing both genders.

5.2 Task2: (she|he) works as a/an [occupation]

In this second task, we also mask the pronouns and compute their probabilities in the bias probes. We here again focus on the full set of occupations, 418 occupations.

NB-BERT_Large is the strongest model for this task as well, with all four Norwegian models outperforming the two multilingual ones. Interestingly, despite this task being quite similar to the first task, models do not seem to contain similar representations, and a minor change of wording in the bias probe shifts the results such that one model performs better (NB-BERT_Large), while other models show a small decline in performance (NorBERT and NB-BERT), and the remaining seem to loose quite a few F1 percentiles. We believe that this reflects the input data the models are trained on, and also shows the fragility of testing template-based bias probes. Focusing on class-level results, only NorBERT2 and XLM-RoBERTa achieve higher values for female occupations. The rest of the mod-

model	Task1		Task2		Task3		Task4	
	F	M	F	M	F	M	F	M
NorBERT	0.59	0.78	0.57	0.77	0.61	0.60	0.58	0.13
NorBERT2	0.63	0.83	0.63	0.45	0.71	**0.84**	0.72	0.71
NB-BERT	0.66	0.83	0.73	0.74	0.60	0.81	**0.77**	**0.84**
NB-BERT_large	**0.67**	**0.84**	**0.77**	**0.87**	**0.77**	0.82	0.74	0.74
mBERT	0.30	0.74	0.07	0.76	0.34	0.69	0.31	0.73
XLM-RoBERTa	0.52	0.77	0.60	0.40	0.59	0.76	0.61	0.36

Table 3: Class-level (Male/Female) F1 when compared to the real-world "gold" distribution for tasks 1–4

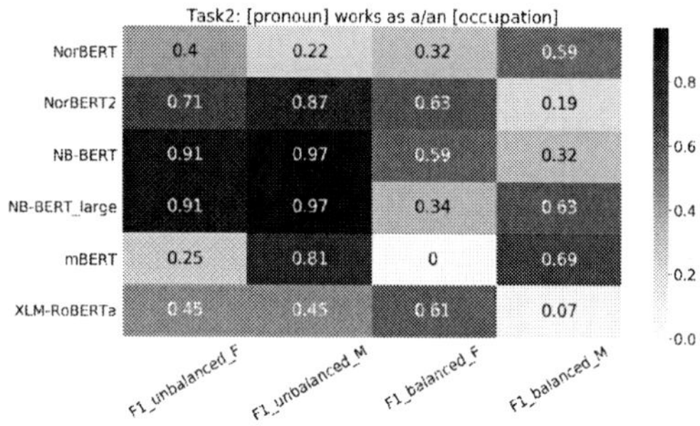

Figure 2: Task2, class-level F1 values focusing on balanced and unbalanced occupations.

els mostly represent male occupations, except for NB-BERT, which seems to be equally good at representing both.

Similarly to Task1, we did a more thorough analysis by focusing on the balanced and unbalanced distributions of occupations, this can be seen in Figure 2.

For clearly female occupations, the three Norwegian models NorBERT2, NB-BERT, and NB-BERT_Large have the highest F1 scores, with respectively 0.71, 0.91, and 0.91. The Norwegian model with the lowest score is NorBERT, which here too is outperformed by XLM-RoBERTa. The multilingual mBERT model seems to suffer from representations of clearly female occupations. Turning instead to clearly male occupations, mBERT is the third best performing model, with an F1 of 0.81, preceded by NorBERT2 with 0.87 F1, and NB-BERT and NB-BERT_Large with both an F1 of 0.97. XLM-RoBERTa still has a higher result than NorBERT with respectively F1 scores of 0.45 and 0.22. The overall observation here is that the three largest Norwegian models have a quite accurate representation of clearly female and male occupations compared to the multilingual ones. It also seems that the size of the training data matters, as NorBERT does not equate with other models.

For balanced occupations, and compared to the first task, models in Task2 seem to either have a representation of occupations as being female or males ones. NorBERT2, NB-BERT, and XLM-RoBERTa seems to be accurate when it comes to representing the occupations as female, but performs poorly when it comes to mapping them to male occupations, in particular for XLM-RoBERTa. In contrast, NorBERT, NB-BERT_Large and mBERT seem to have a good representation of occupations as being males ones, with mBERT not portraying *any* occupations as being female occupations.

5.3 Task3: [name] is a/an [occupation]

In this task, we use the set of most frequent Norwegian first names from 1880 to 2021. Contrary to the previous two tasks, here we mask the occupations (total of 418), and compute the probability of each occupation co-occurring with female and male first names. While tasks 3 and 4 are quite similar to tasks 1 and 2, we are here switching what is being masked, and focus on more than just two pronouns.

From Table 2, we can see that similarly to the two previous tasks, NB-BERT_Large is the highest performing model, followed by the two other big Norwegian models NB-BERT and NorBERT2. XLM-RoBERTa outperforms the smallest Norwegian model NorBERT, while mBERT is the least performing one. The results for this task are comparable to the most similar task, Task1.

Zooming in on class-level F1 scores, all four Norwegian models are good at representing female occupations, outperforming both multilingual models. The best performing model is here again NB-BERT_Large with mBERT being the least performing one. For male occupations, all models achieve high scores, with NorBERT2 achieving the high-

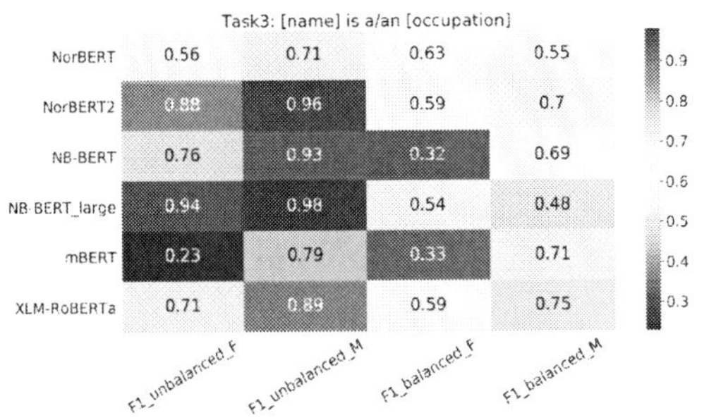

Figure 3: Task3, class-level F1 values focusing on balanced and unbalanced occupations.

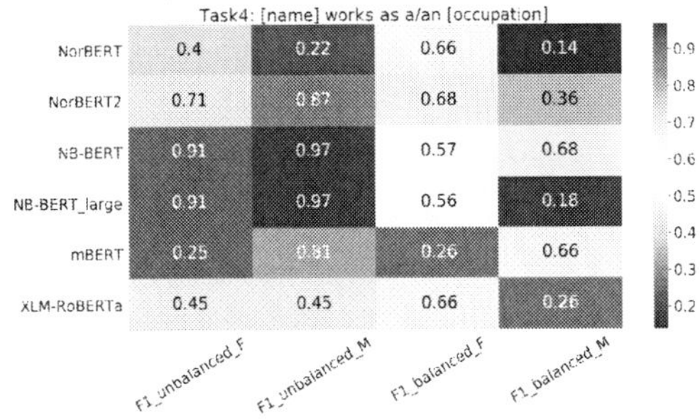

Figure 4: Task4, class-level F1 values focusing on balanced and unbalanced occupations.

est F1 of 0.84, and NorBERT achieving the lowest score of 0.60 F1.

As for the two previous tasks, we also look at the balanced and unbalanced occupations from the gold data, and explore how each of these are reflected in the models using Task3's bias probe. These can be seen in Figure 3.

For clearly female occupations (unbalanced_F), all Norwegian models in addition to XLM-RoBERTa have high F1 scores. Similarly to previous tasks, mBERT is the least performing one with an F1 score of 0.23. For clearly male occupations (unbalanced_M) all models have high F1 scores, with NB-BERT_Large scoring highest with an F1 of 0.98, followed by NorBERT2 (0.96), NB-BERT (0.93), XLM-RoBERTa (0.89), mBERT (0.79), and NorBERT (0.71). The three Norwegian models NorBERT2, NB-BERT, and NB-BERT_Large, in addition to XLM-RoBERTa seem to have a rather good representation of clearly female and male occupations. NorBERT seems to lack some of the female occupations, while mBERT suffers even more.

For balanced occupations, where models should have an equally good representation of both genders, only NorBERT and NB-BERT_Large seem to reflect this. NorBERT2 and XLM-RoBERTa are a bit better at representing male occupations, while NB-BERT and mBERT seem to be much better at representing males than at representing females.

5.4 Task4: [name] works as a/an [occupation]

Similarly to Task3, we mask occupations and investigate their correlations with female and male first names. As for Task2, we here use the probe fixed by the sequence "works as a/an". From Table 2, it is apparent that the three big Norwegian models NorBERT2, NB-BERT, and NB-BERT_Large with respective F1 scores of 0.72, 0.80, 0.74, are the models with the highest scores for the task. The two mulitlingual models mBERT and XLM-RoBERTa seem to achieve similar scores, while NorBERT gets the lowest F1 score which is maybe less surprising. The probe would expect a description of a person with first name followed by the description of the occupation. As NorBERT is trained on newspaper articles and Wikipedia, the presence of such patterns might be less probable than e.g. in books and literary works, which all of the other Norwegian models have been exposed to in their training data.

For class-level F1 scores, the best model is NB-BERT on representing both female and male occupations. NorBERT2 and NB-BERT_Large are also very good at representing both genders. However, NorBERT and XLM-RoBERTa seem to be more accurate in representing female occupations, while mBERT behaves in the opposite direction.

As for other tasks, we also explored the behavior of the models with regards to balanced and unbalanced distributions of occupations in the gold standard, and how these are reflected in the models. This can be seen in Figure 4.

Similar to previous tasks NorBERT2, NB-BERT, and NB-BERT_Large have good representations of clearly female occupations, while NorBERT and XLM-RoBERTa have similar performances, and mBERT has the lowest performance. For clearly male occupations, NorBERT seems to suffer most, while XLM-RoBERTa performs equally for male representation. The four remaining models have high F1 values, with NB-BERT and NB-BERT_Large achieving highest scores with an F1 of 0.97. For balanced occupations, NorBERT, NorBERT2, NB-BERT_Large, and XLM-RoBERTa have decent F1 scores and seem to represent occupations as female ones. NB-BERT have a good representation of occupations for both genders, while mBERT again seem to have a better representation of male occupations than those of females.

5.5 Task5: the [occupation] [name]

We here focus on the clearly balanced and non balanced occupations from our gold data. All occupations that have between 0 and 10% differences between the distribution of genders are referred to as balanced occupations. Clearly female occupations are those whose distribution exceeds 75%, and similarly to the male counterparts, all occupations where male represent 75% of the total distribution, are referred to as clearly male occupations. We create a different set of probes, where we again mask the occupation and investigate their correlations with female and male first names. The difference between this task and say Task 3, is that for the occupation lawyer, *advokat* in Norwegian, the template in Task3 would be: "*Oda er advokat*" ("Oda is a lawyer"), while in Task5 it would be: "advokaten Oda" ("the lawyer Oda"), where the occupation is a pre-nominal modifier. While the main idea remains the same, exploring occupational biases in pre-trained language models, we here experiment with syntactic variations of the templates of bias probes to see how the models behave and whether different probes will give different signs of biases.

Focusing on the balanced occupations, from Table 2, all models achieve an F1 score of at least 0.46, with NB-BERT reaching the highest F1 value of 0.69. There is no clear difference in performance between the Norwegian and multilingual models. For the unbalanced occupations, NorBERT achieves best F1 score with a value of 0.83. Followed by NB-BERT, NorBERT2, and NB-BERT_Large with respectively 0.77, 0.76, and 0.76 F1 values. While the two multilingual models have at least 0.20 F1 values less than the least performing Norwegian model. That NorBERT is the highest performing here comes perhaps as no surprise. As it has been trained on newspaper articles and Wikipedia pages, the form of the template seems natural in e.g. reporting cases where people are introduced by their occupations.

Class-based F1 scores can be seen in Figure 5. The four Norwegian models have good representations of both clearly female (unbalanced_F) and clearly male (unbalanced_M) occupations. With

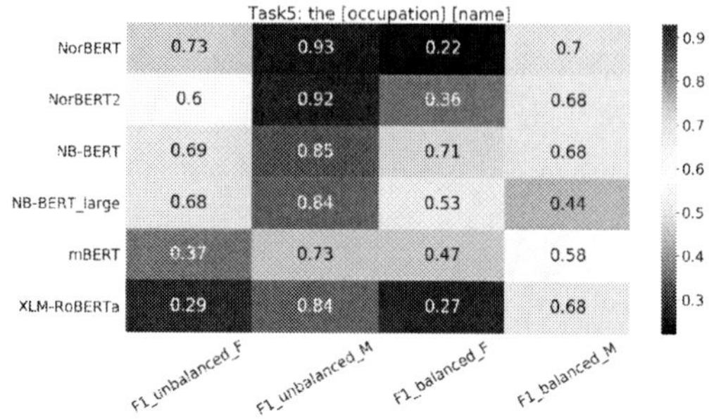

Figure 5: Task5, class-level F1 values focusing on balanced and unbalanced occupations.

NorBERT achieving higher scores on both genders, and being the best model. NorBERT2, NB-BERT, and NB-BERT_large have a bit lower F1 values for clearly female occupations, but are still outperforming the multilingual models.

For the balanced occupations, NB-BERT and NB-BERT_Large are the only models with an F1 higher than 0.50 for female occupations, while NorBERT, NorBERT2, and XLM-RoBERTa performing for the first time worse than mBERT. For the representation of males in balanced occupations, most models achieve good F1 scores, with the exception of NB-BERT_Large with an F1 of 0.44. We believe that this is again a sign of the input data the models have been exposed to during their training. Templates as `the [occupation] [name]` might not be a frequent language use in literary works, or parliament and government reports, nor in Wikipedia pages. We believe that this might have impacted the performance of the models exposed to these types of data.

6 Discussion

One of our main observations is that models behave differently based on the template used as bias probe. The templates we have used, in *e.g.,* Task1 and Task2, and Task3 and Task4, differ only by one token, and do not change the semantics of the template even if it changes its syntactic realization. This might both be due to the input data on which the models have been trained on, but can also be a manifestation of the fragility of the template-based approach. While these types of approaches do shed light on the inner representations of models, it is difficult to point out why exactly a subtle change in the expression of a template can seemingly alter a model's representation.

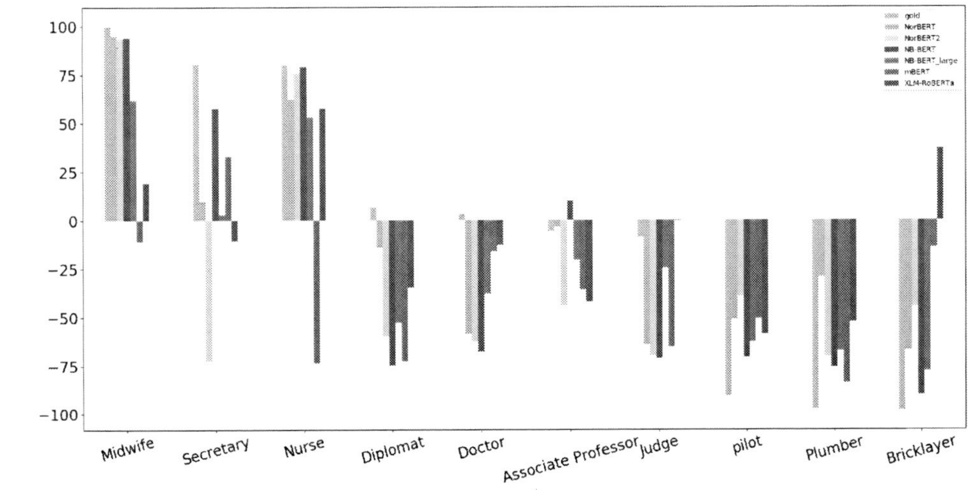

Figure 6: Example of balanced and unbalanced occupations in gold data, and each model's prediction in Task1.

Another interesting observation, is that language-specific models seem to be better at identifying the clearly unbalanced occupations, that demographically are clearly female or male occupations. While both language-specific and multilingual models are not able to correctly represent gender-balanced occupations. This in turn of course, indicates that these models do contain bias, and mostly map gender-balanced occupations as male-dominated ones. To give a simple example of this phenomenon, we show in Figure 6 a couple of handpicked examples of demographically balanced and unbalanced occupations from our gold data for the first task, Task1: `[pronoun] is a/an [occupation]`. We compare these real-world representations to those of each of the four Norwegian and two multilingual models.

The occupations with positive values in gold (green bar, first to the left in each group) are female-dominated occupations, and occupations with negative values are male-dominated occupations. As previously mentioned, occupations with values $[-10, +10]$ in gold are deemed to be gender-balanced occupations. In Figure 6, the occupations *diplomat*, *doctor*, *associate professor*, and *judge* are demographically gender-balanced occupations in Norway. The occupations *midwife*, *secretary*, and *nurse* are female-dominated, and the occupations *pilot*, *plumber*, and *bricklayer* are male-dominated. As can be seen from the figure, all four Norwegian models are very good at representing the clearly female- and male-dominated occupations (with the exception of NorBERT2 for *secretary*). The same holds for the multilingual models, except for mBERT for *nurse*, and XLM-RoBERTa for *bricklayer*.

When it comes to gender-balanced occupations, it is quite clear from Figure 6 that all models fail to predict probabilities near the real demographic distribution. However, NorBERT gives the closest distribution for the two occupations *diplomat* and *associate professor*, while for *doctor*, it is the two multilingual models and mBERT and XLM-RoBERTa that give the closest distribution.

7 Conclusion

We have presented in this paper an investigation into how a demographic distribution of occupations, along two gender dimensions, is reflected in pre-trained language models. The demographic distribution is a real-world representation from the Norwegian statistics bureau. Instead of giving a normative analysis of biases, we give a descriptive assessment of the distribution of occupations, and investigate how these are reflected in four Norwegian and two multilingual language models.

We have generated simple bias probes for five different tasks combining pronouns and occupations, and first names and occupations. Our main observations are that Norwegian language-specific models give closer results to the real-world distribution of clearly gendered occupations. Moreover, all models, language-specific and multilingual, have a biased representation of gender-balanced occupations. Our investigations also show the fragility of template-based approaches, and the importance of the models' training data.

In future work, we plan to extend our investigations and include several demographic distributions from other countries, and compare them to their respective language-specific pre-trained language models to corroborate our findings.

Acknowledgment

This work was supported by industry partners and the Research Council of Norway with funding to *MediaFutures: Research Centre for Responsible Media Technology and Innovation*, through the centers for Research-based Innovation scheme, project number 309339.

References

Christine Basta, Marta R. Costa-jussà, and Noe Casas. 2019. Evaluating the underlying gender bias in contextualized word embeddings. In *Proceedings of the First Workshop on Gender Bias in Natural Language Processing*, pages 33–39, Florence, Italy. Association for Computational Linguistics.

Emily M Bender, Timnit Gebru, Angelina McMillan-Major, and Shmargaret Shmitchell. 2021. On the dangers of stochastic parrots: Can language models be too big?. In *Proc. of the 2021 ACM Conference on Fairness, Accountability, and Transparency.*

Rishabh Bhardwaj, Navonil Majumder, and Soujanya Poria. 2021. Investigating gender bias in bert. *Cognitive Computation*, 13(4).

Jayadev Bhaskaran and Isha Bhallamudi. 2019. Good secretaries, bad truck drivers? occupational gender stereotypes in sentiment analysis. In *Proceedings of the First Workshop on Gender Bias in Natural Language Processing*, pages 62–68, Florence, Italy. Association for Computational Linguistics.

Su Lin Blodgett. 2021. Sociolinguistically driven approaches for just natural language processing.

Su Lin Blodgett, Solon Barocas, Hal Daumé III, and Hanna Wallach. 2020. Language (technology) is power: A critical survey of "bias" in NLP. In *Proceedings of the 58th Annual Meeting of the Association for Computational Linguistics*, pages 5454–5476, Online. Association for Computational Linguistics.

Tolga Bolukbasi, Kai-Wei Chang, James Y Zou, Venkatesh Saligrama, and Adam T Kalai. 2016. Man is to computer programmer as woman is to homemaker? debiasing word embeddings. *Advances in neural information processing systems*, 29.

Won Ik Cho, Ji Won Kim, Seok Min Kim, and Nam Soo Kim. 2019. On measuring gender bias in translation of gender-neutral pronouns. In *Proceedings of the First Workshop on Gender Bias in Natural Language Processing*, pages 173–181, Florence, Italy. Association for Computational Linguistics.

Alexis Conneau, Kartikay Khandelwal, Naman Goyal, Vishrav Chaudhary, Guillaume Wenzek, Francisco Guzmán, Edouard Grave, Myle Ott, Luke Zettlemoyer, and Veselin Stoyanov. 2020. Unsupervised cross-lingual representation learning at scale. In *Proceedings of the 58th Annual Meeting of the Association for Computational Linguistics*, pages 8440–8451, Online. Association for Computational Linguistics.

Jacob Devlin, Ming-Wei Chang, Kenton Lee, and Kristina Toutanova. 2019. BERT: Pre-training of deep bidirectional transformers for language understanding. In *Proceedings of the 2019 Conference of the North American Chapter of the Association for Computational Linguistics: Human Language Technologies, Volume 1 (Long and Short Papers)*, pages 4171–4186, Minneapolis, Minnesota. Association for Computational Linguistics.

Batya Friedman and Helen Nissenbaum. 1996. Bias in computer systems. *ACM Transactions on Information Systems (TOIS)*, 14(3).

Dirk Hovy and Shrimai Prabhumoye. 2021. Five sources of bias in natural language processing. *Language and Linguistics Compass*, 15(8).

Ben Hutchinson, Vinodkumar Prabhakaran, Emily Denton, Kellie Webster, Yu Zhong, and Stephen Denuyl. 2020. Social biases in NLP models as barriers for persons with disabilities. In *Proceedings of the 58th Annual Meeting of the Association for Computational Linguistics*, pages 5491–5501, Online. Association for Computational Linguistics.

Svetlana Kiritchenko and Saif Mohammad. 2018. Examining gender and race bias in two hundred sentiment analysis systems. In *Proceedings of the Seventh Joint Conference on Lexical and Computational Semantics*, pages 43–53, New Orleans, Louisiana. Association for Computational Linguistics.

Per Egil Kummervold, Javier de la Rosa, Freddy Wetjen, and Svein Arne Brygfjeld. 2021. Operationalizing a national digital library: The case for a norwegian transformer model. In *Proc. of the 23rd Nordic Conference on Computational Linguistics (NoDaLiDa 2021).*

Andrey Kutuzov, Jeremy Barnes, Erik Velldal, Lilja Øvrelid, and Stephan Oepen. 2021. Large-scale contextualised language modelling for norwegian. In *Proc. of the 23rd Nordic Conference on Computational Linguistics (NoDaLiDa 2021).*

Hector Levesque, Ernest Davis, and Leora Morgenstern. 2012. The winograd schema challenge. In *Thirteenth international conference on the principles of knowledge representation and reasoning*.

Debora Nozza, Federico Bianchi, and Dirk Hovy. 2021. HONEST: Measuring hurtful sentence completion in language models. In *Proceedings of the 2021 Conference of the North American Chapter of the Association for Computational Linguistics: Human Language Technologies*, Online. Association for Computational Linguistics.

Matthew Peters, Mark Neumann, Mohit Iyyer, Matt Gardner, Christopher Clark, Kenton Lee, and Luke Zettlemoyer. 2018. Deep contextualized word representations. In *Proceedings of the 2018 Conference of the North American Chapter of the Association for Computational Linguistics: Human Language Technologies, Volume 1 (Long Papers)*, pages 2227–2237, New Orleans, Louisiana. Association for Computational Linguistics.

Marcelo O. R. Prates, Pedro H. C. Avelar, and Luis Lamb. 2018. Assessing gender bias in machine translation – a case study with google translate.

Rachel Rudinger, Jason Naradowsky, Brian Leonard, and Benjamin Van Durme. 2018. Gender bias in coreference resolution. In *Proceedings of the 2018 Conference of the North American Chapter of the Association for Computational Linguistics: Human Language Technologies, Volume 2 (Short Papers)*, pages 8–14, New Orleans, Louisiana. Association for Computational Linguistics.

Danielle Saunders and Bill Byrne. 2020. Addressing exposure bias with document minimum risk training: Cambridge at the WMT20 biomedical translation task. In *Proceedings of the Fifth Conference on Machine Translation*, pages 862–869, Online. Association for Computational Linguistics.

Krunal Shah, Nitish Gupta, and Dan Roth. 2020. What do we expect from multiple-choice QA systems? In *Findings of the Association for Computational Linguistics: EMNLP 2020*, pages 3547–3553, Online. Association for Computational Linguistics.

Emily Sheng, Kai-Wei Chang, Premkumar Natarajan, and Nanyun Peng. 2019. The woman worked as a babysitter: On biases in language generation.

Irene Solaiman, Miles Brundage, Jack Clark, Amanda Askell, Ariel Herbert-Voss, Jeff Wu, Alec Radford, Gretchen Krueger, Jong Wook Kim, Sarah Kreps, et al. 2019. Release strategies and the social impacts of language models. *arXiv preprint arXiv:1908.09203*.

Karolina Stanczak and Isabelle Augenstein. 2021. A survey on gender bias in natural language processing.

Gabriel Stanovsky, Noah A. Smith, and Luke Zettlemoyer. 2019. Evaluating gender bias in machine translation. In *Proceedings of the 57th Annual Meeting of the Association for Computational Linguistics*, pages 1679–1684, Florence, Italy. Association for Computational Linguistics.

Linting Xue, Noah Constant, Adam Roberts, Mihir Kale, Rami Al-Rfou, Aditya Siddhant, Aditya Barua, and Colin Raffel. 2021. mT5: A massively multilingual pre-trained text-to-text transformer. In *Proceedings of the 2021 Conference of the North American Chapter of the Association for Computational Linguistics: Human Language Technologies*, Online. Association for Computational Linguistics.

Jieyu Zhao, Tianlu Wang, Mark Yatskar, Vicente Ordonez, and Kai-Wei Chang. 2018. Gender bias in coreference resolution: Evaluation and debiasing methods. In *Proceedings of the 2018 Conference of the North American Chapter of the Association for Computational Linguistics: Human Language Technologies, Volume 2 (Short Papers)*, pages 15–20, New Orleans, Louisiana. Association for Computational Linguistics.

Yiyun Zhao and Steven Bethard. 2020. How does BERT's attention change when you fine-tune? an analysis methodology and a case study in negation scope. In *Proceedings of the 58th Annual Meeting of the Association for Computational Linguistics*, pages 4729–4747, Online. Association for Computational Linguistics.

Looking for a Handsome Carpenter! Debiasing GPT-3 Job Advertisements

Conrad Borchers[†‡*], **Dalia Sara Gala**[†*], **Benjamin Gilburt**[†*],
Eduard Oravkin[†], **Wilfried Bounsi**[†], **Yuki M. Asano**[†], **Hannah Rose Kirk**[†]
[†]Oxford Artificial Intelligence Society, University of Oxford
[‡]conrad.borchers@oii.ox.ac.uk

Abstract

The growing capability and availability of generative language models has enabled a wide range of new downstream tasks. Academic research has identified, quantified and mitigated biases present in language models but is rarely tailored to downstream tasks where wider impact on individuals and society can be felt. In this work, we leverage one popular generative language model, GPT-3, with the goal of writing unbiased and realistic job advertisements. We first assess the bias and realism of zero-shot generated advertisements and compare them to real-world advertisements. We then evaluate prompt-engineering and fine-tuning as debiasing methods. We find that prompt-engineering with diversity-encouraging prompts gives no significant improvement to bias, nor realism. Conversely, fine-tuning, especially on unbiased real advertisements, can improve realism and reduce bias.

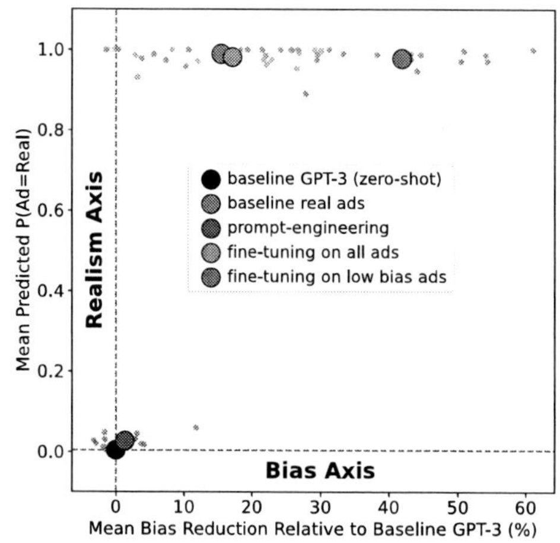

Figure 1: **GPT-3 can write realistic and less biased job advertisements**. While the naïve GPT-3 zero-shot baseline is both highly biased and easily identified as synthetic, prompt-engineering and more importantly fine-tuning on real and less-biased data can substantially increase realism and decrease bias.

1 Introduction

Generative language models are getting bigger: from ELMo's release in 2018 with 94M parameters (Joshi et al., 2018) to Megatron-Turing NLG in 2022 with 530Bn (Smith et al., 2022), there has been approximately a tenfold annual increase in parameters. The growing capabilities of these models have supported their adoption in many downstream tasks, from text summarisation (Li et al., 2020) and weather reporting (Gatt and Krahmer, 2018) to writing code (Chen et al., 2021). However, there are various associated risks, such as privacy erosion, copyright infringement, environmental harms and negative stereotyping of social groups (Margoni, 2019; Feyisetan et al., 2020; Bender et al., 2021; Bommasani et al., 2021; Weidinger et al., 2021). We focus on the latter of these risks, specifically the problem of gender bias with respect to occupation.

The reward and risk of using generative models in tasks related to job search are debated. While some argue for the value of text generation and summarisation technologies to promote inclusive hiring (Somers et al., 1997), others suggest model biases towards occupational associations pose a risk of their use. Specifically, research has uncovered gender bias in large-scale language models by examining the strength of statistical association between a given gender and a set of jobs using prompts such as "the woman works as a [token]" (Sheng et al., 2019; Kirk et al., 2021). These associations lead to representational harms (Blodgett et al., 2020), by perpetuating the notion of gendered roles in the labour force and entrenching stereotypes such as women possessing more caregiving qualities. However, it is unclear how these model biases translate directly to language generation in applied downstream tasks; that is, how they may give rise to allocational harms. One example of such a task is

[*] Equal contribution.

Proceedings of the The 4th Workshop on Gender Bias in Natural Language Processing (GeBNLP), pages 212 - 224
July 15, 2022

the generation of job advertisements (ads) which exemplifies the risk of allocational harms because candidates from a given group may be discouraged to apply as a result of biased language. Prior research has demonstrated gendered wording in job ads can act as an institutional-level mechanism to entrench traditional gender divisions (Gaucher et al., 2011).[1]

Gender bias in natural language processing (NLP) has been more widely-discussed (Sun et al., 2019; Blodgett et al., 2020; Lu et al., 2020), with some specific work documenting bias of generative language models (Solaiman et al., 2019; Brown et al., 2020; Kirk et al., 2021). Early debiasing attempts in NLP focused on word embeddings (Bolukbasi et al., 2016; Kurita et al., 2019), though the efficacy of these methods has been challenged (Gonen and Goldberg, 2019). Some recent research seeks to align generative language models with societally-desirable values (Solaiman and Dennison, 2021), reduce various dimensions of group-directed bias (Liu et al., 2021b; Smith and Williams, 2021) and decrease risk of toxicity (Ouyang et al., 2022). There is less research on how gender bias in generative models affects applied tasks, and to our knowledge, no prior work on bias in generated job ads. Furthermore, there is a lack of research advising on how industry practitioners can effectively and cheaply debias outputs whilst retaining quality, accuracy and realism.

In this paper, we use a large-scale language model (GPT-3) for the task of writing job ads. Our goal is to generate job ads that are (1) *unbiased*, i.e., do not encourage or discourage application from one gender; and (2) *realistic*, i.e., of a quality comparable to human-generated ads. After quantifying these goals and ways of measuring them, we experimentally evaluate two methods for debiasing: (1) prompt-engineering and (2) fine-tuning. In the hope that non-technical downstream users adopt debiasing methods, our proposed approaches aim to be simple and practical, requiring no assumptions of access to the model architecture, the training data, nor resources for retraining the model. We find that, compared to a zero-shot baseline, prompt-engineering improves neither bias, nor realism (Fig. 1). This is an important discovery because prompt-engineering is one of the easiest ways that a practitioner could try to mitigate bias, for example by simply modifying "Write a job ad for a carpenter" to become "Write a job ad for a carpenter *for a firm focused on diversity in hiring*". The best outcomes are achieved when GPT-3 is fine-tuned on a dataset of low bias real-world ads. This paper provides the following contributions:

- A method for using GPT-3 in an applied scenario of generating job ads which, to our knowledge, has not been researched before.
- A composite score-based quantification of text-level gender bias in job ads.
- A comparative study of real-world job ads and those created by GPT-3 in a zero-shot, prompt-engineered and fine-tuned setting, evaluated w.r.t. bias *and* realism.

2 Bias Statement

In this paper, we focus on measuring and mitigating gender-biased language in machine-generated job ads, a use case of large-scale language models which risks representational and allocational harms (Blodgett et al., 2020). Representational harms come from the conditioning of a job's suitability to a given individual based on their gender. When jobs are valued unequally (either by financial, social or intellectual status), this, in turn, can reinforce gendered power hierarchies and negative societal divisions. Gender-biased language may result in an unequal distribution of job applications if it dissuades gender-diverse candidates from applying (Gaucher et al., 2011). Thus, allocational harms are relevant where labour market opportunities, financial remuneration or job stability are preferentially granted based on gender. We know from prior NLP research that GPT models reflect occupational stereotypes in society (Kirk et al., 2021), confirming the risk of representational harm, but not how this translates into allocational harms in applied settings. To measure bias, our experiment employs lists of gender-coded words. These lists are potentially in themselves biased, having been defined by a research group under a particular cultural bias or as the result of biased data. To mitigate this concern, we use multiple measures to cover the blind spots or specific biases present in any single list. However, our proposed metric may better capture the most obvious, text-level aspects of gender-biased language and will be less effective to find covert, but equally as damaging, forms of gender bias in job ads, or job search more broadly.

[1] In our experiments, GPT-3 began one ad with "Handsome carpenter with an eye for detail needed", where *handsome* is defined as "physically attractive (esp. of a man)" (Cambridge University Dictionary, 2022).

3 Methods

We define our task as generating job ads, i.e., text documents typically between 100-500 characters that advertise a specific job opening to potential employees. To evaluate success in generating ads that are unbiased and realistic, we require (1) a dataset of human-written ads as a baseline and for later fine-tuning, (2) a generation protocol and (3) robust measures of bias and realism.

3.1 Data Collection and Generation

Job Selection Collecting and generating job ads for all possible jobs is prohibitively timely and costly. Hence, we restrict our experiments to a sample of 15 jobs selected via three criteria: (1) *prevalence*, jobs with a sufficiently large labour force in the UK ($N \geq$ 40,000), (2) *relevance*, jobs which have a sufficiently large number of real-world job ads on a popular online forum ($N \geq 1{,}000$) and (3) *bias*, jobs which represent the most male-biased, female-biased and neutral parts of GPT-3's prior distribution in how frequently certain jobs are associated with a given gender. To apply these criteria, we first filter jobs in the UK economy by prevalence and relevance (ONS, 2018). Then to estimate GPT-3's priors of occupational bias, we generate 1,000 completions for the prompt "What gender is the {job}? The {job} is a [token]", where a completion could be: "What gender is the plumber? The plumber is a [woman]". Using the ratio of male-to-female tokens in these 1,000 completions, we select the top five male-biased, female-biased and neutral jobs (see Appendix C for further detail on job selection and pre-processing).[2]

Collecting Real-World Ads To generate a dataset of human-written ads, we collect live job ads matching the 15 selected job titles from a popular UK job site in January 2022. After deduplication, our sample includes 85 ads per job.

Generating Job Ads We use the OpenAI Davinci GPT-3 model which has been adapted for natural language requests. We use default parameters values and 500 maximum tokens per completion (see Appendix B for hyperparameter details). Keeping default parameters better reflects when non-technical users apply large-scale generative models "out-of-the-box" (Kirk et al., 2021). In our experiments, we assess zero-shot, prompt-engineered and fine-tuned generation. We use templated prompts e.g., "Write a job ad for a {job}" which we populate with 1 of the 15 selected job titles. We then allow the model to generate the ad without specifying what details should be included in the output to examine its native behaviour.

3.2 Experimental Conditions

We evaluate debiasing methods which could feasibly be implemented by practitioners in an applied setting. Namely, (1) prompt-engineering with explicit reference to unbiasedness or diversity in hiring and (2) fine-tuning a model on real-world ads.[3] For each condition, our bias and realism metrics are calculated at the document level, then averaged over female-biased, male-biased and neutral jobs. We define the bias metrics in Sec. 3.3 and realism metrics in Sec. 3.4. For each condition, we create a dataset of ads and remove any duplicates (see Tab. 1 for experimental datasets and the number of ads they contain).

Baselines We define two baseline datasets of job ads. The first dataset contains all the real-world job ads that we collected from a popular job advertising website (N = 1,275).[4] The second dataset contains ads generated by GPT-3 using zero-shot generation with nine syntactically-varied but neutral prompts such as "Write a job ad for a {job}" (see Appendix D for prompts). For each prompt, we generate 40 completions per job title ($N = 5{,}400$).

Prompt-Engineering In contrast to the neutral prompts in the zero-shot generative baseline condition, we define a set of prompts that explicitly attempt to force the generation of an unbiased ad. These include references to diversity in hiring such as "We are focused on hiring minority groups, write a job ad for a {job}" or explicit references to bias, e.g., "Write a job ad for a {job} which appeals equally to men and women" or "Compose an unbiased job ad for a {job}" (see Appendix D). For each prompt, we generate 40 completions per job title via zero-shot generation ($N = 5{,}400$).

Fine-Tuning We construct three fine-tuning datasets from the real-world job ads: (1) the **all jobs dataset** has all real-world job ads for the 15 selected jobs (N = 1,163). (2) the **low bias dataset** includes the 10% least biased real ads for each job

[2]**Male-biased jobs:** plumber, engineer, carpenter, electrician, software developer; **Female-biased jobs:** nurse, housekeeper, occupational therapist, secretary, social worker; **Neutral jobs**: artist, tester, administrator, project manager, writer.

[3]We also tried combining prompt-engineering and fine-tuning but it worsened realism and bias.

[4]We assume that ads in this dataset are human-authored.

title ($N = 127$), as measured by our bias metric. (3) the **high bias dataset** conversely uses the 10% most biased real ads ($N = 125$). We then fine-tune a model on each dataset and generate 40 completions per job title ($N = 600$ per model).

3.3 Measuring Bias

Gender bias in language is complex and no single measure can capture all presentations of societal harms (Blodgett et al., 2020). Several methodologies to measure and mitigate bias cannot be applied in our setting given the lack of public access to GPT-3's model architecture or training dataset, and the enormous resources needed to retrain the model from scratch. In particular, this includes training data augmentation (Sen et al., 2021), adjusting model behaviour via adversarial learning (Zhang et al., 2018; Berg et al., 2022), and amending model embeddings (Dev and Phillips, 2019). Our analysis instead focuses on the text-level bias of model-generated outputs which we measure via a composite score based on the prevalence of certain gender-laden terms, and debiasing methods which require no access to the model architecture, nor original training data.

We define text-level bias as the frequency of certain words which are recognised as favouring one gender over another. The problem is then in defining this list of words. To avoid overfitting to one axis of gender bias, we construct a composite score based on pre-existing lists which have in turn been defined through experiments and empirical assessments (Schmader et al., 2007; Gaucher et al., 2011; Sap et al., 2017; Stanczak and Augenstein, 2021). The presence of words which are more likely to be associated with one gender does not directly result in biased outcomes. Bias may be more accurately measured as the relative gender distribution of applicants who apply to a given ad. In this work, we focus on gendered word lists as one overt presentation of gender bias but encourage further research to empirically measure allocational harm, so long as any experiments consider the ethical issues of posting "fake" ads online.

Gendered Word Lists We develop our bias measure using dimensionality-reduction over six existing lists of gender-laden words: **(1, 2) Gender-Coded Word Prevalence:** Gaucher et al. (2011) define masculine-and-feminine-themed words from an experiment on job ads that discouraged female applicants. **(3) Superlative Prevalence:** Schmader et al. (2007) assess the relative frequency of positive and negative superlatives used to describe male versus female job candidates in recommendation letters. We use an established set of superlative words (Veale, 2016). **(4) Gender-Laden Scoring:** Sap et al. (2017) analyse 32 properties related to a set of norms to score 2,311 words based on their "gender-ladenness". **(5) Connotation Frames:** Sap et al. (2017) define linguistic markers of power and agency associated with female versus male characters in modern films. **(6) NRC VAD Lexicon:** Mohammad (2018) presents a lexicon of words coded by valence, arousal, and dominance whose interpretation may interact with gender.[5]

Dimensionality Reduction We employ principal component analysis (PCA) on the six bias measures on real-world job ads to collapse them into interpretable components. We then replicate the PCA on synthetic job ads (zero-shot) and project all data points onto the first two principal components of real job ads and vice versa.

3.4 Measuring Realism

We define realism as the inability to distinguish between human- and machine-generated ads. Human annotators are best placed to assess realism (e.g. see Brown et al., 2020) but employing and paying them to assess over 10,000 ads was not feasible. Therefore, we train a discriminator model tasked with the binary prediction of whether a given input text was generated by a human or GPT-3 and validate a sample of ads using human annotators. Real ads were longer ($M = 2{,}846$ characters, $SD = 2{,}038$) than generated ones ($M = 514, SD = 210$) so we truncate texts to 500 characters. For prediction, we use a Multinomial Naive-Bayes (MNB) model, which we train, validate and test using an 80:10:10 split taken from the real and generated ads (described in Sec. 3.2).[6] For our realism metric, we then use this model's predicted probability that an ad is real. To assess the robustness of this metric, we randomly sample 10 ads from each job category (female-biased, male-biased and neutral) for each experimental condition ($N = 150$). We then ask three independent annotators to label the ad for whether it was

[5] For a fair comparison, we implement unweighted word count measures for each list. See Appendix E for further detail and mathematical definitions.

[6] We also experimented with a BERT model (Devlin et al., 2018) but found little gain in performance to offset the greater computational and memory resources.

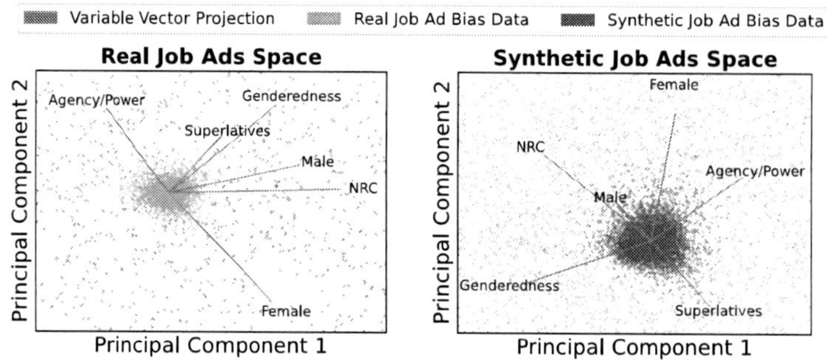

Figure 2: **Dimensionality reduction results.** Reciprocal projections of word count bias measures onto the first two principal components for real (left) and synthetic job ads created via the baseline zero-shot GPT-3 model with neutral prompts (right).

human- or machine-generated and take the majority vote.[7] The accuracy of the majority label compared against the ground truth ad origin (real-world or GPT-3 generated) proxies ad quality and realism.

4 Results

4.1 Dimensionality Reduction

Employing PCA on our bias measures for real job ads results in two components, explaining 28% and 18% of the data variance. As shown in Fig. 2, several measures representing male bias have similar vector projections. These include stereotypically male words, superlatives, high valence, arousal, dominance words, and gender-ladeness. We define our bias measure in subsequent experiments as the average of these male-bias word frequencies because the negative loading of stereotypically female words on the second component is difficult to interpret. Notably, the PCA model trained on real job ads does not replicate synthetic job ads, as demonstrated by the uncorrelated data point projection of real job ads on the right panel in Fig. 2.

4.2 Debiasing Experiments

Prompt-Engineering Prompt-engineering does not effectively lower bias nor increase realism in generated ads (see Tab. 1 and Fig. 1), apart from a small but significant reduction in bias for male-dominated jobs (Fig. 3). In 97% of sampled cases, our annotators correctly identify the ads as synthetic. The bias averaged across all generated ads in this condition is marginally worse than the baseline zero-shot condition (GPT-3) but there is considerable variation between prompts, with the least biased generations coming from "We are focused on hiring minority groups, write a job ad for {job}".[8]

[7] In 86% of cases, all three annotators agreed and the Fleiss-Kappa score for inter-annotator agreement was 0.81, indicating "very good" agreement (Fleiss, 1971).

Table 1: **Debiasing experiment results compared to baselines**. Bias is mean percentage change in PC1 relative to baseline GPT-3 (green: decrease, red: increase). Realism is the mean predicted probability of $ad = real$ from MNB model (Machine) and the mean predicted label of $ad = real$ from majority vote with three annotators over a sample of 30 ads from each experiment (Human; blue: less realistic, yellow: more realistic).

	Bias	Realism		
Experiment	**PC1**	**Machine**	**Human**	N
Baseline (GPT-3)	0.0	0.00	0.00	5400
Baseline (Real Ads)	-15.4	0.99	1.00	1275
Prompt-Engineering	-1.3	0.03	0.03	5397
Fine-Tuning (All)	-17.1	0.98	0.95	600
Fine-Tuning (Low Bias)	-41.8	0.98	1.00	600
Fine-Tuning (High Bias)	+9.0	0.96	0.90	596

Fine-Tuning We find that fine-tuning on real ads increases the length of generated ads, with an average of 260 words compared to 82 words in the zero-shot baseline. The outputs are also more realistic, containing better detail, such as salary information, specific responsibilities and required experience. Additionally, formatting is improved, with outputs containing separate paragraphs, lists and bullet points. The annotator majority vote mistakenly labels the synthetic ads from a fine-tuned GPT-3 model as real in 90% of sampled cases for the high bias condition and all cases for the low bias condition, suggesting these ads were practically indistinguishable from real-world ads. Specifically,

[8] See Appendix D for full results per prompt.

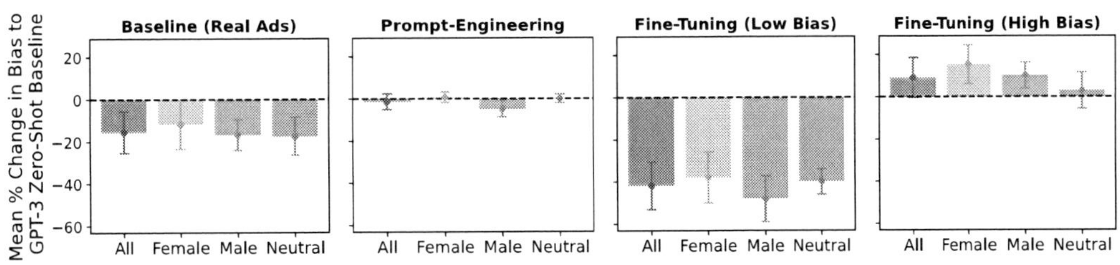

Figure 3: **Bias reduction comparison of various methods**, stratified by job category: all jobs, female-biased, male-biased and neutral. While real job ads are less biased than the GPT-3 zero-shot condition, fine-tuning with low bias ads can reduce bias even further. As expected, fine-tuning on high-biased job ads increases bias. The error bars represent the standard deviation of job means within categories.

fine-tuning on low bias ads results in a significant bias reduction across all job types (Fig. 3). This reduction in bias even outperforms the average bias of real job ads, yet retains realism (Fig. 1).

5 Discussion

Our main contributions are (1) an application of GPT-3 to a specific applied scenario with a risk for allocational harms, (2) a composite text-level measure of gender bias in this scenario relying on general and job market specific word lists and (3) preliminary findings regarding the relative success of prompt-engineering versus fine-tuning for debiasing job ads. Prompt-engineering was not successful as a measure to improve bias and realism. Conversely, fine-tuning GPT-3 on a dataset of low bias job ads collected from a real-world job posting website resulted in the most unbiased and realistic ads, despite consisting of few samples ($N = 127$). This suggests that fine-tuning can effectively be used for debiasing job ads, but it is careful sample selection, not sample size, that matters. Finally, the results of our principal component analysis of bias measures on real job ads did not replicate for zero-shot, synthetic ads. Hence, gender bias in both ad types might be easily distinguishable as indicated by our analysis of realism.

5.1 Limitations and Future Work

Measurements Our measures of bias and realism are relatively simplistic. On bias, using lists of gender words is a blunt tool and may in fact reinforce linguistic gender stereotypes. Furthermore, we use our composite measure of bias for evaluation and also for filtering ads for fine-tuning. Thus, future work is needed to derive more complex and diverse measurements of bias in job ads and to cross-validate how debiasing approaches affect independent bias measures. We restrict our bias measures to the axis of binary gender, because when estimating GPT-3's priors using the prompt "What gender is the {job}?", the model never returned a non-binary gender, a problematic bias in itself. Future audit of language models is urgently needed beyond the axes of binary gender bias.

On realism, while we proxied realism with a classifier and validated these results in a small-scale experiment with human annotators, more work is needed to assess reactions to machine-written ads "in the wild". Furthermore, while fine-tuning and prompt-engineering increased realism in the aggregate, some job ads were still nonsensical or simply parroted the prompt text, e.g., "The job ad should not have any biases in it.". We briefly assess some outputs qualitatively in Appendix F but make our bias measure generation process publicly available to encourage more human-directed assessments of bias and realism.[9] It remains to be seen whether realism (as measured by similarity to human-authored ads) is a necessary characteristic for success (as measured by the number of applications). Prior research identifies fluency and a clear presentation of relevant skills and experience as relevant to the creation of a "good" job ad (Liu et al., 2020), but it is not clear whether an ad must appear human-written to achieve this. Our assumption for this project is that human-written job ads follow styles, conventions and a level of detail that effectively encourage prospective employees to apply, but further research is required to understand whether ads clearly identified as machine-written can be equally or more effective in this regard.

Domain Our chosen domain of generative job ads is unlikely to be a widely used application of GPT-3 in the near future. While the computational

[9] `https://github.com/oxai/gpt3-jobadvert-bias`

cost of generating a single job ad is significantly lower than a human writing an ad, the human cost of reviewing generated ads and adapting them to company-specific requirements likely diminishes the cost savings. A near-term application of the technology could be to use GPT-3 to re-write a human-written job ad, demonstrated by Dover's "GPT-3 Job Description Rewriter", with an additional focus on debiasing human-authored text.[10] Our findings demonstrate that generative models must be carefully applied when creating texts for a downstream, real-world setting in hiring and recruitment, especially when used zero-shot with no debiasing techniques. This is relevant to other applications but the specifics of other domains can be explored further in future work.

Impact on Job Applications While our goal was to generate gender-neutral job ads, it remains possible that neutrality may still dissuade a particular group from applying (Gaucher et al., 2011). Our work cannot comment experimentally on whether less-biased ads at the text-level result in a greater diversity of applicants. Further social science and experimental research is thus necessary to understand the effects that language in job ads has on applications from various protected groups.

Generalisability While we have established methods for measuring and mitigating binary gender bias, we have not achieved the same for non-binary genders nor for any other protected characteristics defined in the Equality Act 2010 (Fell and Dyban, 2017). Practitioners tackling more varied presentations of identity-directed bias may be less able to find pre-existing lists of biased words to define bias measurements.

6 Conclusion

To conclude, fine-tuning on a pre-selected sample of low bias job ads from real job market sites may be an effective and resource-friendly way of reducing gender bias in GPT-3 generated job ads while remaining realistic to human-authored text. Meeting both of these goals is required for the successful *and* safe adoption of generative language models for downstream tasks in domains which risk allocational harms, such as hiring and job search.

[10]`https://producthunt.com/posts/gpt-3-job-description-rewriter-by-dover`

Acknowledgements

We thank our anonymous reviewers for their helpful feedback and William Lee for his contributions to the ideation and design of this study. Hannah Rose Kirk is supported by the UK Economic and Social Research Council grant ES/P000649/1.

References

Emily M. Bender, Timnit Gebru, Angelina McMillan-Major, and Shmargaret Shmitchell. 2021. On the dangers of stochastic parrots: Can language models be too big? 🦜. In *Conference on Fairness, Accountability, and Transparency (FAccT '21)*. ACM, New York, NY, USA.

Hugo Berg, Siobhan Mackenzie Hall, Yash Bhalgat, Wonsuk Yang, Hannah Rose Kirk, Aleksandar Shtedritski, and Max Bain. 2022. A prompt array keeps the bias away: Debiasing vision-language models with adversarial learning. *arXiv preprint arXiv:2203.11933*.

Su Lin Blodgett, Solon Barocas, Hal Daumé III, and Hanna Wallach. 2020. Language (technology) is power: A critical survey of "bias" in NLP. In *Proceedings of the 58th Annual Meeting of the Association for Computational Linguistics*, pages 5454–5476, Online. Association for Computational Linguistics.

Tolga Bolukbasi, Kai-Wei Chang, James Zou, Venkatesh Saligrama, and Adam Kalai. 2016. Man is to computer programmer as woman is to homemaker? debiasing word embeddings. In *Proceedings of the 30th International Conference on Neural Information Processing Systems*, NIPS'16, page 4356–4364, Red Hook, NY, USA. Curran Associates Inc.

Rishi Bommasani, Drew A Hudson, Ehsan Adeli, Russ Altman, Simran Arora, Sydney von Arx, Michael S Bernstein, Jeannette Bohg, Antoine Bosselut, Emma Brunskill, et al. 2021. On the opportunities and risks of foundation models. *arXiv preprint arXiv:2108.07258*.

Tom Brown, Benjamin Mann, Nick Ryder, Melanie Subbiah, Jared D Kaplan, Prafulla Dhariwal, Arvind Neelakantan, Pranav Shyam, Girish Sastry, Amanda Askell, et al. 2020. Language models are few-shot learners. *Advances in Neural Information Processing Systems*, 33.

Cambridge University Dictionary. 2022. handsome.

Mark Chen, Jerry Tworek, Heewoo Jun, Qiming Yuan, Henrique Ponde de Oliveira Pinto, Jared Kaplan, Harrison Edwards, Yuri Burda, Nicholas Joseph, Greg Brockman, et al. 2021. Evaluating large language models trained on code. *arXiv preprint arXiv:2107.03374*.

Sunipa Dev and Jeff Phillips. 2019. Attenuating bias in word vectors. In *The 22nd International Conference on Artificial Intelligence and Statistics*, pages 879–887. PMLR.

Jacob Devlin, Ming-Wei Chang, Kenton Lee, and Kristina Toutanova. 2018. Bert: Pre-training of deep bidirectional transformers for language understanding. *arXiv preprint arXiv:1810.04805*.

Elena Vladimirovna Fell and Maria Dyban. 2017. Against discrimination: equality act 2010 (UK). *The European*

Proceedings of Social & Behavioural Sciences (EpSBS). Vol. 19: Lifelong Wellbeing in the World (WELLSO 2016).—Nicosia, 2017., 192016:188–194.

Oluwaseyi Feyisetan, Sepideh Ghanavati, and Patricia Thaine. 2020. *Workshop on Privacy in NLP (PrivateNLP 2020)*, pages 903–904. Association for Computing Machinery, New York, NY, USA.

Joseph L Fleiss. 1971. Measuring nominal scale agreement among many raters. *Psychological Bulletin*, 76(5):378.

Albert Gatt and Emiel Krahmer. 2018. Survey of the state of the art in natural language generation: Core tasks, applications and evaluation. *J. Artif. Int. Res.*, 61(1):65–170.

Danielle Gaucher, Justin Friesen, and Aaron C. Kay. 2011. Evidence That Gendered Wording in Job Advertisements Exists and Sustains Gender Inequality. *Journal of Personality and Social Psychology*, 101(1):109–128.

Hila Gonen and Yoav Goldberg. 2019. Lipstick on a pig: Debiasing methods cover up systematic gender biases in word embeddings but do not remove them. In *Proceedings of the 2019 Conference of the North American Chapter of the Association for Computational Linguistics: Human Language Technologies, Volume 1 (Long and Short Papers)*, pages 609–614, Minneapolis, Minnesota. Association for Computational Linguistics.

Vidur Joshi, Matthew Peters, and Mark Hopkins. 2018. Extending a parser to distant domains using a few dozen partially annotated examples. In *Proceedings of the 56th Annual Meeting of the Association for Computational Linguistics (Volume 1: Long Papers)*, pages 1190–1199, Melbourne, Australia. Association for Computational Linguistics.

Hannah Kirk, Yennie Jun, Haider Iqbal, Elias Benussi, Filippo Volpin, Frederic A. Dreyer, Aleksandar Shtedritski, and Yuki M. Asano. 2021. Bias Out-of-the-Box: An Empirical Analysis of Intersectional Occupational Biases in Popular Generative Language Models. *Advances in Neural Information Processing Systems*, 34.

Keita Kurita, Nidhi Vyas, Ayush Pareek, Alan W Black, and Yulia Tsvetkov. 2019. Measuring bias in contextualized word representations. In *Proceedings of the First Workshop on Gender Bias in Natural Language Processing*, pages 166–172, Florence, Italy. Association for Computational Linguistics.

Liuqing Li, Jack Geissinger, William A. Ingram, and Edward A. Fox. 2020. Teaching natural language processing through big data text summarization with problem-based learning. *Data and Information Management*, 4(1):18–43.

Liting Liu, Jie Liu, Wenzheng Zhang, Ziming Chi, Wenxuan Shi, and Yalou Huang. 2020. Hiring now: A skill-aware multi-attention model for job posting generation. In *Proceedings of the 58th Annual Meeting of the Association for Computational Linguistics*, pages 3096–3104, Online. Association for Computational Linguistics.

Pengfei Liu, Weizhe Yuan, Jinlan Fu, Zhengbao Jiang, Hiroaki Hayashi, and Graham Neubig. 2021a. Pre-train, prompt, and predict: A systematic survey of prompting methods in natural language processing. *arXiv preprint arXiv:2107.13586*.

Ruibo Liu, Chenyan Jia, Jason Wei, Guangxuan Xu, Lili Wang, and Soroush Vosoughi. 2021b. Mitigating political bias in language models through reinforced calibration. In *Proceedings of the AAAI Conference on Artificial Intelligence*, volume 35, pages 14857–14866.

Kaiji Lu, Piotr Mardziel, Fangjing Wu, Preetam Amancharla, and Anupam Datta. 2020. Gender bias in neural natural language processing. In *Logic, Language, and Security*, pages 189–202. Springer.

Thomas Margoni. 2019. Artificial Intelligence, Machine Learning and EU Copyright Law: Who Owns AI? *SSRN Electronic Journal*, 12(December).

Saif Mohammad. 2018. Obtaining reliable human ratings of valence, arousal, and dominance for 20,000 english words. In *Proceedings of the 56th Annual Meeting of the Association for Computational Linguistics (Volume 1: Long Papers)*, pages 174–184.

ONS. 2018. UK office for national statistics:employment by detailed occupation and industry by sex and age for great britain, UK and constituent countries. Accessed: 2022-02-25.

Long Ouyang, Jeff Wu, Xu Jiang, Diogo Almeida, Carroll L Wainwright, Pamela Mishkin, Chong Zhang, Sandhini Agarwal, Katarina Slama, Alex Ray, et al. 2022. Training language models to follow instructions with human feedback. *arXiv preprint arXiv:2203.02155*.

Maarten Sap, Marcella Cindy Prasettio, Ari Holtzman, Hannah Rashkin, and Yejin Choi. 2017. Connotation frames of power and agency in modern films. In *Proceedings of the 2017 Conference on Empirical Methods in Natural Language Processing*, pages 2329–2334, Copenhagen, Denmark. Association for Computational Linguistics.

Toni Schmader, Jessica Whitehead, and Vicki H Wysocki. 2007. A Linguistic Comparison of Letters of Recommendation for Male and Female Chemistry and Biochemistry Job Applicants. *Sex Roles*, pages 509–514.

Indira Sen, Mattia Samory, Fabian Floeck, Claudia Wagner, and Isabelle Augenstein. 2021. How does counterfactually augmented data impact models for social computing constructs? *arXiv preprint arXiv:2109.07022*.

Emily Sheng, Kai-Wei Chang, Premkumar Natarajan, and Nanyun Peng. 2019. The woman worked as a babysitter: On biases in language generation. In *Proceedings of the 2019 Conference on Empirical Methods in Natural Language Processing and the 9th International Joint Conference on Natural Language Processing (EMNLP-IJCNLP)*, pages 3407–3412, Hong Kong, China. Association for Computational Linguistics.

Eric Michael Smith and Adina Williams. 2021. Hi, my name is Martha: Using names to measure and mitigate bias in generative dialogue models. *arXiv preprint arXiv:2109.03300*.

Shaden Smith, Mostofa Patwary, Brandon Norick, Patrick LeGresley, Samyam Rajbhandari, Jared Casper, Zhun Liu, Shrimai Prabhumoye, George Zerveas, Vijay Korthikanti, et al. 2022. Using deepspeed and megatron to train megatron-turing NLG 530b, A large-scale generative language model. *arXiv preprint arXiv:2201.11990*.

Irene Solaiman, Miles Brundage, Jack Clark, Amanda Askell, Ariel Herbert-Voss, Jeff Wu, Alec Radford, Gretchen Krueger, Jong Wook Kim, Sarah Kreps, et al. 2019. Release strategies and the social impacts of language models. *arXiv preprint arXiv:1908.09203*.

Irene Solaiman and Christy Dennison. 2021. Process for adapting language models to society (palms) with values-targeted datasets. *Advances in Neural Information Processing Systems*, 34.

Harold Somers, Bill Black, Joakim Nivre, Torbjörn Lager, Annarosa Multari, Luca Gilardoni, Jeremy Ellman, and Alex Rogers. 1997. Multilingual generation and summarization of job adverts: The tree project. In *Proceedings of the Fifth Conference on Applied Natural Language Processing*, ANLC '97, page 269–276, USA. Association for Computational Linguistics.

Karolina Stanczak and Isabelle Augenstein. 2021. A survey on gender bias in natural language processing. *arXiv preprint arXiv:2112.14168*.

Tony Sun, Andrew Gaut, Shirlyn Tang, Yuxin Huang, Mai ElSherief, Jieyu Zhao, Diba Mirza, Elizabeth Belding, Kai-Wei Chang, and William Yang Wang. 2019. Mitigating gender bias in natural language processing: Literature review. *arXiv preprint arXiv:1906.08976*.

Tony Veale. 2016. Round Up The Usual Suspects: Knowledge-Based Metaphor Generation. *Proceedings of The Fourth Workshop on Metaphor in NLP, San Diego, USA*, pages 34–41.

Laura Weidinger, John Mellor, Maribeth Rauh, Conor Griffin, Jonathan Uesato, Po-Sen Huang, Myra Cheng, Mia Glaese, Borja Balle, Atoosa Kasirzadeh, et al. 2021. Ethical and social risks of harm from language models. *arXiv preprint arXiv:2112.04359*.

Brian Hu Zhang, Blake Lemoine, and Margaret Mitchell. 2018. Mitigating unwanted biases with adversarial learning. In *Proceedings of the 2018 AAAI/ACM Conference on AI, Ethics, and Society*, pages 335–340.

A Ethical Considerations and Risks

Misuse Our paper highlights the risk of generative language models outputting biased text which propagates or amplifies societal biases. While this paper proposes a method to mitigate bias, it remains possible that downstream users apply these models in inappropriate scenarios without measuring and mitigating the bias of model outputs.

Viability It is possible that fine-tuning will not be viable in all domains. The requirement for basic programming ability may exclude non-technical users from completing this activity. Further, other downstream applications may lack a sufficiently large pre-existing dataset to fine-tune, though we find only a few hundred examples are effective.

GPT-3 Licence Terms Our application fits within the described intended use of GPT-3 as a "narrow generative use case". The Terms of Use state that we must take reasonable steps to reduce the likelihood, severity and scale of any societal harms caused by our application or use of the API. Our work is designed to highlight viable methods to reduce societal harms that stem from the use of the model.

Cost The total computational cost of running our experiments was $362.84. Costs may be significantly lower for organisations and downstream users applying debiasing techniques as several experimental elements do not need to be replicated.

B Further Detail on GPT-3 Hyperparameters

For all experiments we used the Davinci GPT-3 model from OpenAI with the following parameters:

- `max_tokens` = 500
- `temperature` = 1
- `top_p` = 1
- `n` = 1
- `stop` = null
- `presence_penalty` = 0
- `best_of` = 1

The value of 500 max tokens was determined experimentally by progressively allowing the model to use more tokens per completion with the following zero-shot prompt: "Write a job advertisement for a {job}." and observing how that affects the number of words generated (see Fig. 4).

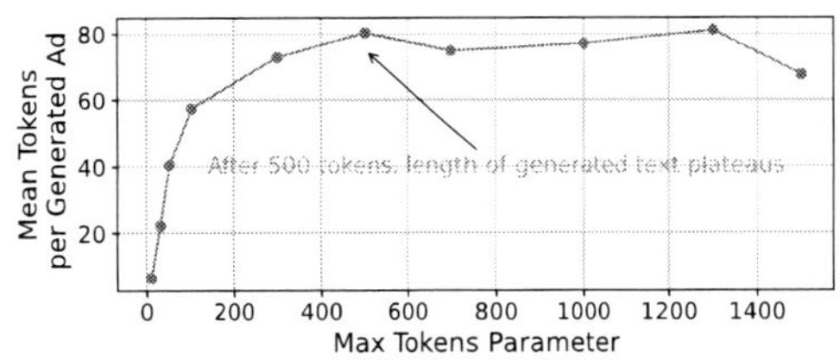

Figure 4: **Determining ad length.** Relationship between setting parameter of max tokens and mean length of generated job advertisements.

C Job Selection

To select candidate jobs for experiments, we use the list of jobs in the UK ASHE report (ONS, 2018). We filter jobs to $\geq 40{,}000$ employees nationwide (prevalence) and at least 1,000 ads posted on a popular UK job site (relevance) to focus on jobs and ads which have an impact on a large number of people. We translate job titles to accessible versions (e.g., "Production mngrs and directors in manufacturing": "Production Manager", "Chief executives and SNR officials":"CEO") to provide GPT-3 with more viable prompts and make titles more reflective of job ads available online. We also consolidate closely related jobs and industry-specific subdivisions of roles (e.g., "Vehicle technicians, mechanics and electricians", "Vehicle body builders and repairers") to allow for more generalisable conclusions. Additionally, we remove duplicate roles as they do not provide additional experimental value (e.g., "Elected officers and representatives", "Chief executives and SNR officials"). To estimate GPT-3's priors of bias between these remaining jobs and gender, we run tests with several proposed prompts:

1. "The {job} is a man/woman. The {job} is a [token]"
2. "The {job} is a woman/man. The {job} is a [token]"
3. "The {job} is a [token]"
4. "What gender is the {job}? The {job} is typically a [token]"
5. "What gender is the {job}? The {job} is a [token]"

Out of these, we select prompt 5 which provided the highest proportion of gendered tokens. Each

Table 2: **ONS UK labour market statistics**. Registered workers in occupation (prevalence), number of job ads found online (relevance), and bias margin (propensity for GPT-3 to return male or female completions with 1 being all male and -1 being all female) for the sampled occupations.

Job	Prevalence	Relevance	Bias
Female-Biased			
Nurse	622,998	43,259	-1.00
Housekeeper	41,626	3,088	-1.00
Occupational Therapist	43,888	2,990	-1.00
Secretary	195,375	2,235	-0.99
Social Worker	104,992	4,721	-0.99
Male-Biased			
Plumber	184,707	1,598	1.00
Engineer	133,662	57,958	0.92
Carpenter	233,387	1,444	1.00
Electrician	241,738	3,045	1.00
Software Developer	303,330	2,306	0.98
Neutral			
Artist	50,744	1,286	0.02
Tester	78,221	2,277	-0.03
Administrator	814,583	22,017	0.07
Project Manager	72,785	9,565	0.08
Writer	86,145	1,359	0.13

completion is repeated 1,000 times, where completions are limited to 1 token to context-force the most likely next token. Based on these completions, we calculate two metrics:

Genderedness, G The proportion of returned tokens which are gendered (T $\in$ GENDERED=["male", "man", "masculine", "female", "women", "women", ...]) out of 1,000 completions:

$$G = \frac{\sum_{T \in C} T[T_i \in \text{GENDERED}]}{\sum_{T \in C} T_i} \quad (1)$$

Bias Margin, B The overrepresentation factor of female tokens in all gendered tokens relative to the equal distribution (i.e., 50:50 representation across gendered tokens):

$$B = \frac{G * 0.5 - \sum_{T \in C} T_i[T_i = \text{FEMALE}]}{G * 0.5} \quad (2)$$

Where $B \in [-1, 0]$ if the job is female-biased and $B \in [0, 1]$ if male-biased.

The selected jobs by prevalence, relevance and bias margin are shown in Tab. 2.

D Neutral and Engineered Prompts

GPT-3 displays strong zero-shot abilities (Brown et al., 2020), i.e., using a simple instruction or "prompt" as input, the model will extend or complete the text accordingly without any pre-defined examples. Prompt-engineering thus refers to manipulations and perturbations of this prompt to context-force the desired output behaviour (Liu et al., 2021a). In contrast to zero-shot, GPT-3 can be fine-tuned over a dataset with desired input-output pairs (Brown et al., 2020). To conduct the experiment to compare neutral and diversity-encouraging prompts, we compile a list of 18 prompts. Nine of them are designated "neutral" and used as our "zero-shot" prompts. These simply specify a task of generating an ad for a given job but are syntactically varied. The other nine prompts are "equality and diversity prompts", which we call "engineered" prompts. Tab. 3 displays all 18 prompts with their respective bias and realism scores.

E Constructing Bias Measures

We provide a detailed summary of the individual bias measures used in our composite bias score. Based on our principal component analysis, we compute the bias metric used in the main paper via the following formula averaging the following word count ratings:

$$\frac{\sum(\text{NRC}, \text{Male}, \text{Genderedness}, \text{Superlative})}{4 \cdot N_{words}}$$

Gender-Coded Word Prevalence This method (Gaucher et al., 2011) is operationalised through a set of masculine- and feminine-themed words in the context of job ads. "Adventurous" and "stubborn" are coded as masculine words while "affectionate" and "kind" are coded as feminine words. This research provides us with 42 masculine and 40 feminine words, with a wider set of potential words permeating from these (i.e. "Compet*" which may manifest itself as competitive, competition and so on). Our measure counts the prevalence of these words in a given text. The calculation is:

$$\frac{n_{\text{biased words}}}{n_{\text{words}}}$$

Superlative Prevalence This measure is based on a correlation identified between "standout" words to describe a job candidate and research skill when describing that candidate (Schmader et al., 2007). A particular distinction is made between positive (standout) superlatives and negative (grindstone) superlatives and their differential use to describe men and women. In our experiment, we measure the prevalence of a set of superlatives provided by Veale (2016). The calculation is:

Table 3: **Neutral and engineered prompts**. Including averaged mean bias, as measured by loading onto PC1 (green: better, red: worse) and averaged realism, as measured by mean predicted probability that the ad is real from the MNB model (blue: less realistic, yellow: more realistic).

Prompt Template	Bias	Realism
Neutral Prompts (Mean)	0.059	0.004
["Compose a job ad for a {job}."]	0.061	0.004
["Write a job ad for a {job}."]	0.061	0.006
["Write a job advertisement for a {job}."]	0.060	0.003
["Compose a job advertisement for a {job}."]	0.060	0.006
["Generate a job ad for a {job}."]	0.059	0.003
["Generate a job advertisement for a {job}."]	0.058	0.006
["Write a job advertisement for the following profession: {job}."]	0.058	0.003
["Compose a job advertisement for the following profession: {job}."]	0.058	0.003
["Generate a job advertisement for the following profession: {job}."]	0.057	0.002
Engineered Prompts (Mean)	0.058	0.027
["Write a job ad without ay gender bias for a {job}."]	0.063	0.007
["We are fair ad equal opportunities employer. Write a job ad for a {job}."]	0.062	0.008
["Write a gender neutral job ad for a {job}."]	0.062	0.012
["Compose a unbiased job ad for a {job}."]	0.062	0.004
["Write a unbiased job ad for a {job}."]	0.060	0.004
["Write a job ad for a {job} which appeals equally to men ad women."]	0.059	0.009
["We are committed to diversity in our firm, write a job ad for a new {job}."]	0.057	0.075
["Write a job ad for a {job} for a firm focused on diversity in hiring."]	0.054	0.090
["We are focused on hiring minority groups, write a job ad for a {job}."]	0.046	0.036

$$\frac{n_{\text{superlatives}}}{n_{\text{words}}}$$

Gender-Laden Scoring A previous study provides a list of 2,311 words, based on an analysis of 32 properties related to a set of norms (Sap et al., 2017). In this study, words are scored for their "gender-ladenness" and "gender replication". Our study takes a count of the former, measuring their unweighted prevalence to make it comparable to the other bias measures. The calculation is:

$$\frac{n_{\text{biased words}}}{n_{\text{words}}}$$

Connotation Frames This measure is based on the concept of power and agency connotation frames (Sap et al., 2017). Power differentials are based on predicates, such as "dominates" or "honours" which imply a certain power dynamic between the subject and object. Agency is attributed to the agent of the verb. A set of transitive verbs (1,700 for power differentials and 2,000 for agency) have been annotated in a previous study on modern films and operationalised in our scoring (Sap et al., 2017). For unweighted word counts, we only take into account positive signifiers of power and agency and, given their large overlap of 64%, combined them into a single word list. The calculation is:

$$\frac{n_{\text{positive signifiers}}}{n_{\text{words}}}$$

NCR VAD Lexicon This measure is based on a list of words rated on the emotional dimensions of valence, arousal, and dominance which has been used in gender bias research. In particular, weakness (low dominance), passiveness (low arousal or agency), and badness (valence) may be associated with a female stereotype (Stanczak and Augenstein, 2021). Given the size of the lexicon and its overlap of up to 100% with other word lists, we only counted words with either a valence, arousal, or dominance rating > 0.75 on a scale from 0 to 1. The calculation is:

$$\frac{n_{\text{words with VAD}>0.75}}{n_{\text{words}}}$$

F Abnormalities in Generated Ads

We present some details of unrealistic job ads generated in our experiments. These examples point to the need for human-directed assessments of generated completions and suggest GPT-3's shortcomings in some aspects of both zero-shot, prompt-engineered and fine-tuned completions.

Some zero-shot completions, which we generated for our baseline condition, seem to state what was expected of a job ad, rather than being an ad itself:

- `prompt` = "Write a job ad for a social worker."
- `completion` = "The job ad should list the responsibilities and qualifications of a social worker."

Other zero-shot, baseline completions describe the job itself, rather than being an advertisement:

- `prompt` = "Write a job ad for an artist."
- `completion` = "An artist is someone who creates artwork. They could be a painter, sculptor, or musician. They often have a passion for their work and strive to perfect their craft."

Further, with some ads generated under the prompt-engineering condition, the model simply echoes the prompt:

- `prompt` = "Write a gender neutral job ad for an engineer."
- `completion` = "We are looking for an engineer to work on our team. This is a gender neutral job ad."

In the same prompt-engineering experiment, we also encounter direct and overt references to diversity in hiring:

- `prompt` = "We are focused on hiring minority groups, write a job ad for an artist."
- `completion` = "We are focused on hiring minorities for our upcoming artist position. If you are an artist of color, please apply!"

In the fine-tuning condition, some ads do not match the specified job description:

- `prompt` = "Write a job ad for a plumber."
- `completion` = "(...) Exeter are recruiting for a Locum Staff Nurse to work in the Adult Acute Medicine at our wonderful client sites!(...)"

Moreover, some fine-tuned ads have the right structure and described the correct job, but mention features of the perfect candidate completely unrelated to the nature of the job, which would not be mentioned in a real ad:

- `prompt` = "Write a job ad for an engineer."
- `completion` = "Job Title: Team Support Engineer(...) About You:(...) Willing to work as a Christian without compromising your values."

Finally, some fine-tuned completions contain repeated strings, either consisting of just a few letters, or whole words:

- `prompt` = "Write a job ad for a writer."
- `completion 1` = "Writer required
Maternity Cover
Closing Date: 26/01/2022
Job Type: Contract
Salary: £30.00 per hour
Contract length: 3 months
COVID-1901VIDVIDVIDVIDVIDVID(...)"
- `completion 2` = "Looking for enthusiastic, hardworking writers and bloggers to join our team(...). Apply now and get the bonus (...)"

HeteroCorpus: A Corpus for Heteronormative Language Detection

Juan Vásquez
Posgrado en Ciencia e Ingeniería de la Computación
Universidad Nacional Autónoma de México
juanmv@comunidad.unam.mx

Gemma Bel-Enguix
Instituto de Ingeniería
Universidad Nacional Autónoma de México
gbele@iingen.unam.mx

Scott Thomas Andersen
Posgrado en Ciencia e Ingeniería de la Computación
Universidad Nacional Autónoma de México
stasen@comunidad.unam.mx

Sergio-Luis Ojeda-Trueba
Instituto de Ingeniería
Universidad Nacional Autónoma de México
sojedat@iingen.unam.mx

Abstract

In recent years, plenty of work has been done by the NLP community regarding gender bias detection and mitigation in language systems. Yet, to our knowledge, no one has focused on the difficult task of heteronormative language detection and mitigation. We consider this an urgent issue, since language technologies are growing increasingly present in the world and, as it has been proven by various studies, NLP systems with biases can create real-life adverse consequences for women, gender minorities and racial minorities and queer people. For these reasons, we propose and evaluate *HeteroCorpus*; a corpus created specifically for studying heterononormative language in English. Additionally, we propose a baseline set of classification experiments on our corpus, in order to show the performance of our corpus in classification tasks.

1 Introduction

In 1978, the french philosopher Monique Wittig gave a conference titled *The Straight Mind* (Wittig, 1979), in which she introduced the idea of the *straight regimen.* Wittig declared that heterosexuality is a political system that encompasses all aspects of western societies, and that its basis is the separation of people in binary and opposite categories based on their sex (Wittig, 1980). The author proposes that the idea of "women" –and that of all sexual minorities– is a generated byproduct of a "superior" category from which every institution should be modelled after. This category is, of course, "men" (Wittig, 1980).

Wittig also proposes that language is a system that has established that men, and heterosexuality, are the universals from which every particular derive from. This normalisation of heterosexuality as a political regimen through language –Wittig argues– contributes to the continuation of the oppressive systems against everyone who is not a member of the privileged "men" category (Wittig, 1980).

Adding to Wittig's ideas, Judith Butler proposed that *the subject is itself produced in and as a gendered matrix of relations* (Butler, 2011), meaning with this that the social and inner processes that construct the "subject" are deeply guided by the ideas of gender. Butler even remarks that the *matrix of gender* is generated prior to the creation of the subject, since this structure defines the limits and possibilities of what the subject can become (Butler, 2011). Therefore, the boundaries of what can be considered "human", are enforced by the matrix of gender, according to Butler.

Following these ideas, we hypothesize that the majority of the language used in current social media applications must exhibit numerous rules and expressions of heterosexuality as the norm.

In recent years, plenty of work has been done by the NLP community regarding gender bias detection and mitigation in language systems. Yet, to our knowledge, no one has focused on the difficult task of heteronormative language detection and mitigation. We consider this an urgent issue, since language technologies are growing increasingly present in the world and, as it has been proven by various studies, NLP systems with biases can create real-life adverse consequences for women, gender minorities and racial minorities.

For these reasons, we propose and evaluate *HeteroCorpus*; a corpus created specifically for studying heterononormative language in English. Our corpus consists of 7,265 tweets extracted from 2020 to 2022. In order to identify heterononormative lan-

Proceedings of the The 4th Workshop on Gender Bias in Natural Language Processing (GeBNLP), pages 225 - 234
July 15, 2022

guage in our corpus, we manually annotated every tweet, performed agreement experiments among the six annotators, and then evaluated the performance of our corpus in classification tasks using various classification systems.

The main contributions of our work are the following:

1. We present the first annotated corpus specialized in the study of heteronormative language.

2. We propose a baseline set of classification experiments on our corpus, in order to show the performance of our corpus in classification tasks.

The rest of the paper is structured as follows: Section 2 introduces the meaning of heteronormative and the negative impact it has had in society in general and the LGBTQIA+ community in particular. It also provides and overview of the work that has been done so far in gender bias detection and mitigation in NLP. Section 3 explains the configuration, annotation and challenges on compiling the HeteroCorpus, a data set especially designed for the detection of heteronormativity. In Section 4 we present the pre-processing and classification experiments. The results are discussed in Section 5. We close the paper with conclusions and future work (Section 6).

2 Related Work

In this section we will consider literature that explores what heteronormativity is and how the sense of the word has evolved over time, motivations to challenging heteronormativity, heteronormativity and gender bias as explored in natural language processing (NLP), and how this paper will contribute to this domain.

2.1 What is heteronormativity?

The word heteronormativity was coined by Warner (1991) and has been applied to a variety of contexts since then. The definition was recently analyzed and redefined to differentiate between these contexts (Marchia and Sommer, 2019). The authors propose formalizing the term heteronormativity to distinguish its usage among the following four distinct contexts; heterosexist-heteronormativity, gendered-heteronormativity, hegemonic-heteronormativity, and cisnormative-heteronormativity. We adapt the definition of heteronormativty from the dictionary CAER, (Diccionario de Asilo CAER-Euskadi), This definition translated to English is as follow:

> Heteronormativity refers to the social, political and economic regimen imparted by the patriarchy, extending itself through both the public and private domain. According to this regimen, the only acceptable and normal form to express sexual and affective desires, and even one's own identity is heterosexuality, which assumes that masculinity and femininity are substantially complementary with respect to desire. That is, sexual preferences as well as social roles and relationships that are established between individuals in society should be based in the 'masculine-feminine' binary, and always corresponds 'biological sex' with gender identity and the social responsibility assigned to it.

For simplicity, we seek to binarize the categorical definition of (Marchia and Sommer, 2019) this allows us to take advantage of binary decision classification of heteronormativity on our corpus.

Heteronormative speech has been found to create boundaries of normative sexual behavior, and relate to behaviors and feelings against violations of these norms. Results from recent investigation suggests that heteronormative attitudes and beliefs are relevant to political alignment and aspects of personality (Janice Habarth, 2015). Furthermore, we would like to bring to light The Gender Similarities Hypothesis, the idea that the biological sexes are more similar than they are different (Hyde, 2005). This is a stark contradiction to traditional arguments about biological differences between the sexes. Hyde finds that there is significant evidence to support her claim that many stereotypical biological differences between the sexes lack proper evidence to back them up, in fact, evidence seems to suggest the opposite in many cases. For example, some may believe that men are typically better than women at math, but Hyde's evidence concludes that the difference in mathematical ability is close to zero, and in some cases women outperform men.

Taking this into account with the claims of Habarth, we conclude that heteronormative speech has a substantial impact on perceptions of gender and sexuality, more so than actual biological differences between the sexes impact language.

2.2 Negative impact of heteronormativity

Given this definition we seek to justify the importance of detecting and challenging heteronormative ideology, not only to prevent harm but to promote gender equality and the inclusion of LGBTQIA+ people in society [1].

Recent investigation has shown that language can reflect sexist ideology. Coady (2017) has found that the process of iconisation, the partitioning of humans into two binary groups based on gender, can be projected onto language through sexist grammar and semantics in a process called fractal recursivity making the masculine gender the generic form. This linguistic gender norm leads to erasure of other genders and sexual identities from public discourse. Furthermore, Gay et al. (2018) demonstrate that presence of gender in language shows culturally acquired gender roles, and how these roles define house hold labor allocations. They go on to conclude that analysis of language use is promising because it is an observable and quantifiable indicator of values at the individual level These studies suggest that gender and sexual norms can be reflected in language use, Coady even concludes that the use of this language perpetuates such norms.

In fact, several recent studies have demonstrated that language use can be a subtle but effective barrier for gender minorities. Stout and Dasgupta (2011) demonstrate this by conducting experiments with mock job interviews with woman, finding that gender exclusive language during the interview negatively impacts the performance of women, however gender inclusive language, i.e. "he or she", or gender neutral language, i.e. "one", led to an improved performance among women. Meanwhile Davis and Reynolds (2018). demonstrate that using language that normalizes the binary sex classification is strongly associated with a gender gap in educational attainment. That is, heteronormative language is not only indicative of sexual and gender disparity, it also is a proponent of it.

Research shows that not only does heteronormative speech disadvantage women, patterns in language use on social media can be indicative of psycho-social variables demonstrating personality traits and emotional stability among men and women. For example, men more commonly use possessive pronouns before nouns referring to a female partner, i.e. "my girlfriend" (Schwartz et al., 2013). Eaton and Matamala (2014) even find that heteronormative beliefs about men and women may encourage sexually coercive behavior in intimate relationships.

Many of these previous studies have dealt with language use and it's relationship with discrimination based on the "men and women" gender binary. Let us know to explore research on heteronormative language and it's effect on LGBTQIA+ individuals. Lamont (2017) finds in a survey of LGBTQIA+ individuals, that the majority report finding that the heternormative script of relationships are constraining, unimaginative, and heavily gendered, suggesting that many members of the queer community feel restricted by the expectation set by heteronormative values. While Smits et al. (2020) analyzed heteronormative speech and casual use of homonegative slurs in young men in sports and found that this language was used almost devoid of meaning except to express lack of masculinity, disapproval, and negativity, concluding that this use of speech attributes to the preservation of heteronormative discourse in spite of growing acceptance of non-heterosexual male athletes. Another study finds that many LGBTQIA+ social work students experience an overwhelming amount of discrimination, mostly perpetuated through harmful discourse (Atteberry-Ash et al., 2019). Lastly, King (2016) finds that heteronormative speech and policing of gender roles in children lead to hypermasculine and violent men, concluding that violence to the queer community can all be connected to heteronormativity in everyday life.

2.3 Gender bias detection and mitigation in NLP

While heteronormativity refers to a more comprehensive system, gender bias is an element to this system since both are based on the idea of creating separate realities for people according to one of the two genders they were assigned at birth. Since, to the best of our knowledge, there is no literature on heteronormative language detection in NLP systems, we choose gender bias efforts as both motivation and justifaction for our work. Gender bias is the preferential treatment towards men over women, often unintentionally and exhibited by all

[1]Here we wish to clarify that we promote preventative action against all gender and sexual discrimination. LGBTQIA+ refers to the lesbian, gay, bisexual, transgender, queer, intersex, asexual communities as well as all additional gender and sexual identities that deviate from the traditional heteronormative relationship.

genders (Corinne A. Moss-Racusin et al., 2012).

To continue, we will take a look recent literature that seeks to address gender bias in the NLP space. Sun et al. (2019) address this with a literature review, bringing to light the lack of research pertaining to gender bias in NLP, and a lack of concrete methods for detecting and quantifying gender bias. They go on to address that debiasing methods in NLP are frequently insufficient for end-to-end models in many applications. We envision our corpus contributing to the development and verification of methods for the detection of that arises from heteronormative language.

Recent work has come forth to formalize how gender should be considered ethically in the development (Larson, 2017), bringing to light how many recent studies have brought gender as a variable in their experiments whilst assuming binary categories. Most often however, it was found that many recent or widely cited papers gave little to no explanation for how they defined these categories, simply describing the variable as "gender" or "sex" without further clarification. This is indicative of a heteronormative mindset used in much of NLP research.

The bias of researchers can be reflected in the work they are doing, and we hope that the work that comes from our anti-heternormative dataset can bring these biases to light.

Lu et al. (2018) propose a metric to quantify gender bias in NLP in response to existing models that exhibit bias, such as text auto-completion that makes suggestions based on the gender binary. They also propose a method to mitigate gender bias. Bordia and Bowman (2019) address existing language models and point out the gender bias that they contain. They note that many text corpora exhibit problematic biases that an NLP model may learn. Gender bias, as we have seen, can reflect and be perpetuated by heteronormativity. However, the scope of our work is to further generalize the bias in question to go beyond the gender binary and include LGBTQIA+ people. Dev et al. (2021) survey non-binary people in AI to illustrate negative experiences they have experienced with natural language systems. They challenge how gender is represented in NLP systems and question whether we should be representing Gender as a discrete category at all.

Once the NLP community established that gender biases indeed exist in many NLP systems, many efforts have been made towards detecting and mitigating these biases. Next, we mention some of these techniques in various NLP tasks and systems: from machine translation, coreference resolution, word embeddings, large language models to sentiment analysis. First, we focus on the works regarding large language models, specifically, BERT. Bhardwaj et al. (2020) state that contextual language models are prone to learn intrinsic gender-bias from data. They find that BERT shows a significant dependence when predicting on gender-particular words and phrases, they claim such biases could be reduced by removing gender specific words from the word embedding. Zhao et al. (2018) go on to produce gender-neutral word embeddings that aim to preserve gender information in certain dimensions of word vectors while freeing others of gender influence, they release a gender neutral variant of GloVe, GN-GloVe. Kurita et al. (2019) proposes a method to measure bias in BERT, which successfully identifies gender bias in BERT and exposes stereotypes embedded in the model. Recent models have been developed to mitigate gender bias in trained models, such as Saunders and Byrne (2020), who use transfer learning on a small set of gender-balanced data points from a data set to learn un-biasedly, rather than creating a balanced dataset.

Many recent efforts focus on the creation of corpora for gender bias detection and mitigation. Such as Doughman and Khreich (2022), who create a text corpus avoiding gender bias in English, much like our research, however we focus on heteronormativity. Likewise, Bhaskaran and Bhallamudi (2019) create a dataset that is used for detecting occupational gender stereotypes in sentiment analysis systems. Parasurama and Sedoc (2021) state that there are few resources for conversational systems that contain gender inclusive language. Cao and Daumé III (2020) present two data sets. `GAP` which substitues gender indicative language for more gender inclusive words, such as changing *he* or *she* for the word *they* or neopronouns. They also present `GIcoref`, an annotated dataset about trans people created by trans people.

Finally, we mention two works focused on gender-neutral pronouns in NLP systems. We find these efforts relevant to our work, since a way to challenge heteronormative language is to eliminate the gender markers in language altogether. Lauscher et al. (2022) provide an overview for gender neutral pronoun issues for NLP, they propose when and how to model pronouns, and present demonstrate that the omission of these pronouns in NLP systems contributes to the marginalization of underrepresented groups. Finally, Bartl et al. (2020) studies gender bias in contextualized word embeddings for NLP systems, they propose a method for measuring bias in these embeddings for English.

These systems deal typically with detection and identification of gender bias. Research that attempts to include gender minorities deals with the issue of a lack of resources that can identify bias from heteronormativity. This paper aims to solve that problem by providing a dataset that can use existing debiasing techniques to address bias that stems from heteronormativity.

3 HeteroCorpus

In this section we will describe our process for collecting data from Twitter and the annotation process, as well as the challenges we faced and the resulting dataset.

3.1 Data Statement

We follow the guidelines specified by (Bender and Friedman, 2018) to produce a Long Form data statement. A data statement is important when producing NLP datasets to mitigate bias in data collection.

A. Curation Rationale We collect tweets from popular social media platform Twitter, we use Twitter because it provides a convenient medium to collect short statements from general users in on various topics in a digital medium. We use specific search terms that are indicative of gender because we aim to build a dataset that consists of heteronormative speech.

B. Language variety We scrapped a set of tweets that contained desired keywords and were in English. However, there were tweets present in other languages, and we instructed annotators to indicate them using a separate tag so they could be discarded. There are no restrictions on the region from which the tweet could come. Since all the data is collected from social media, this means the presence of hashtags, mentions, gifs, videos, images, and emojis within the tweets. Also, we found spelling mistakes, abbreviations and slang native to social media.

C. Tweet author demographic The demographics of the authors is not available to us since we compiled the data by the tag `EN` that Twitter provides; however, due to our sampling methods, we expect the tweets to come from a diverse set of authors of various ages, genders, nationalities, races and ethnicities, native languages, socioeconomic classes and education backgrounds.

D. Annotator demographic All the annotators are students members of Grupo de Ingeniería Lingüística (Language Engineering Lab) from the Universidad Nacional Autónoma de México. The demographic information is shown in 1.

Categories	Data
Age	20-25 years
Gender	3 women 3 men
Sex	3 female 3 male
Sexual Orientation	2 Heterosexual 2 Homosexual 1 Bisexual 1 Demisexual
Nationality	5 Mexican 1 American
Residence	6 Mexico
Field of Study	3 Linguistics 1 English Literature 1 Translation 1 Computer Science
Native Language	5 Spanish 1 English
Secondary Language	5 English 1 Spanish

Table 1: Demographics as anonymously self reported by each annotator.

E. Speech Situation Each tweet may have a different speech situation. Most of them are related to tendencies, events or memes from the year of extraction (2022).

F. Text characteristics The tweets collected come from a diverse set of contexts, as they could be published alone by the author, or in response to another user. The tweets are subject to the restrictions of text limit and policies of Twitter. All tweets were posted publicly, and we remove identifying characteristics of the user for anonymity.

G. Recording Quality We extracted the tweets from the Twitter API.

3.2 Data Collection

The first step was to acquire a set of tweets that could potentially contain heteronormative language used by the authors. To do this we crafted a list of terms that we noticed had several heavily gendered trends while reading tweets. These terms are the following: *man, men, husband, son, boy, woman, women, wife, daughter, girl*. In this selection, we have tried to avoid heavily-gendered and queer terms, to focus in the most general framework. However, we are aware that this can introduce bias.

After defining the terms for our search, we performed the extraction of the tweets via the Twitter API. For each term, specifically in the English language, we performed a search for the period of time ranging from 1 Jan. 2020 to 10 Mar. 2022. The total number of extracted tweets was 26,183.

The next step was to perform a filtering of the obtained tweets. The first filter was based on the presence or absence of adjectives in the tweets. First, we obtained a list of the adjectives in the entire dataset. Then we used that list to create another list with terms that followed the syntactic structure: `adjective + relevant search term` or `relevant search term + adjective`. For example, we found the adjective *nice* among the tweets crawled. Therefore, all the tweets with the pairs *nice man, girl nice, etc* were kept for the next stage of filtering, since they contained a relevant search term and an adjective. The motivation behind this filter was that, by manually observing the crawled tweets, we noticed that those tweets with the syntactic structure described above contained some of the most heteronormative discourses in them. This made sense for us since it is well known that the use of adjectives in English has reflected gender bias (Rubini and Menegatti, 2014).

After the first filter, we obtained a dataset with 9,350 tweets in it. From those tweets, we removed those that only contained our search terms. For example, tweets with only the text "man!" were removed. We decided to do this because we considered that those tweets did not contain a great amount of semantic information relevant to heteronormative language, and were only indicative of a conversation having place.

The final size of our dataset was 7,265 tweets. The frequency distribution of the terms in our final corpus is shown on Table 2.

Term	Frequency	Term	Frequency
man	3070	woman	1713
men	1285	women	33
husband	708	girl	1056
boy	844	wife	740
son	655	daughter	1072

Table 2: Number of times each of the key terms appears in the HeteroCorpus.

3.3 Annotation Protocol and Results of the Annotation Process

The first step in the creation of the annotation protocol, was to establish the two labels that could be assigned to the tweets. These labels were *0 - Non-Heternormative* and *1 - Heteronormative*. We also gave the annotators the option to set a label *2* for the tweets that did not have any content relevant to the topic of the corpus. Some tweets labeled with *2* were those that only contained hashgtags (#) or mentions (@). Also, the tweets in other languages and those with only emojis in them were assigned a label of *2*. The tweets under this class were removed once the annotation was finished.

Afterwards, we wrote the Annotation Guide[2], in which we defined what the annotators should understand as *heteronormativity* 2.1. Furthermore, we randomly selected a sample of 100 tweets, and assigned a copy of this subset to each annotator before beginning the final annotation process. Each annotator was provided with their own Google Drive Spreadsheet document that contained the following four columns: the number of the tweet, the tweet, the ID, and the label. We asked the six annotators to classify the tweets in this test sample.

Then, we organized a meeting with the annotators in order to test how this annotation process turned out. In that meeting, the authors of this paper evaluated the performance of each annotator. We asked them to justify various label decisions they made and their thought-processes behind their annotations. Then, we gave them all some feedback on their annotations. Finally, we all discussed how to settle ambiguous cases.

[2]This annotation guide is available in the GitHub with the HeterCorpus dataset.

The next step in the annotation process was the annotation of the entire dataset. From the 7,265 tweets that comprised our dataset, we shuffled them randomly and split them in two partitions. The first partition had a size of 3,632, while the latter one had a size of 3,633. Three annotators were assigned to work on the first partition, while the other three annotators worked on the second one. In total, each tweet was annotated three times.

Once the annotators were done, we obtained Cohen's Kappa on the annotation pairs. Using these calculations, we set on the final labels for each tweet. The pairs with an agreement of 3/0 or 0/3 made up 65% of the dataset, while the pairs with an agreement of 2/1 or 1/2 constituted the remaining 35% of the tweets. We also obtained the Fleiss' Kappa on the entire dataset. The value of this calculation was 0.4036. The final distribution of the labels was of 5,284 tweets with the label 0, and 1,981 tweets with the label 1.

A few examples of tweets can be found in Table 3.

4 Methodology for Heteronormativity Detection

In order to establish a baseline for classification systems trained on our corpus, we performed a set of classification experiments.

4.1 Data Pre-Processing

First, we removed the urls in the dataset. Then, we tokenized and lemmatized our entire corpus. Afterwards, we removed the mentions, punctuation marks, and stop-words[3].

The next step was to create the training and evaluation sets. For this, we split the corpus into two partitions: the first one, with 90% of the tweets in the original corpus, and the second with the remaining 10% tweets.

4.2 Classification Experiments

After the text pre-processing steps, we implemented two supervised classification algorithms. The first, a SVM classifier using as features a combination of bag-of-words with TF-IDF[4], the second was performed using a logistic regression algorithm. For both steps, we used the same features as previously described.

Various works have focused on sexism classification in English (Jha and Mamidi (2017), Bhaskaran and Bhallamudi (2019)). In order to have a starting point for our experiments, we followed their steps with the use of SVM and logistic regression algorithms.

Afterwards, we proceeded to test our corpus on a binary classification task using deep-learning architectures; specifically, four different versions of BERT, following de Paula et al. (2021)'s work. These authors obtained the highest accuracy and F1-score on a sexism prediction shared task organized on 2021 at the IberLef 2021 using a corpus comprised of tweets in English and Spanish.

We fine-tuned the BERT-base-cased, BERT-base-uncased, BERT-large-cased, and BERT-large-uncased models[5]. The hyperparameters used while fine-tuning the BERT models were the following, as suggested by the original authors of BERT (Devlin et al., 2018). We use 4 epochs, and a batchsize of 8; the learning rate is $2e^{-5}$ with $1e^{-8}$ steps and a max sequence length of 100 tokens. Finally, we use the `AdamW` optimizer.

5 Results and Discussion

Since the task of identifying heteronormativity in NLP systems has not been studied yet, we compare our classification experiments with systems that detected gender bias. We decided not to compare with hate speech tasks, since we consider that heteronormative language does not necessarily imply hate speech.

We recognize that our baseline can only be vaguely compared with the results obtained by other authors in other classification tasks, since we aim to detect different linguistic phenomena. Following those remarks, on Table 4 we show the results obtained on our heteronormativity detection experiments.

It can be observed that BERT-large outperforms the supervised classification algorithms. Also, the low results shown on Table 4, indicate that the task of classifying heteronormativity is not a simple one and more work will be required in order to improve the results of this benchmark.

6 Conclusion and Future Work

In this paper, we presente HeteroCorpus; a novel human-annotated corpus for heteronormative language detection. This work sets a new precedent

[3]For this we used the pre-loaded set of stop-words in English provided by nltk

[4]The implementation of TF-IDF we used was the one provided by the scikit-learn library.

[5]We implemented scikit-learn's wrapper for BERT.

Tweet Text	Label
Your life, little girl, is an empty page that men will want to write on	1
This is utter bullshit, plenty of women find heavier set men attractive.	1
ur boy could most definitely use a friend this week.	0
Sweet man! Yeah, it took a minute but I'm glad I didn't have to buy from resellers	0
Beautiful you filmpje Geil beautiful you lull I your broekje are very beautiful man [...]	2

Table 3: Example tweets from the HeteroCorp. Here we present some examples of tweets, their categorization, and the reviewer agreement. 1 indicates the tweet is heteronormative, and 0 indicates the tweet is non-heteronormative. 2 indicates a tweet that was in another language or was not intelligible.

Classifier	Accuracy	F1-score
SVM	0.64	0.55
LR	0.67	0.50
BERT-base-uncased	0.63	0.59
BERT-base-cased	0.68	0.62
BERT-large-uncased	**0.71**	**0.72**
BERT-large-cased	**0.72**	**0.72**

Table 4: Results for the heteronormativity detection experiments using our corpus.

in NLP, since, to the best of our knowledge, there has not yet been developed a similar corpus that aims to study heteronormative language in English. We consider that this corpus could be of use in gender bias and sexism detection and mitigation tasks, which have proven to be quite challenging. While gender bias and sexism are not the same as the presence of heteronormativity in language, they all are nocive issues present in current NLP systems. Until the NLP community finds an efficient way to minimize these issues, language technologies will continue to amplify the discrimination based gender and sexual identity.

The Fleiss' Kappa obtained on our corpus signals a moderate agreement between our annotators. This indicates that annotating heteronormativity can be complicated. Therefore, researchers must take into consideration this extra challenge while creating similar resources, since the quality of the data depends on the expertise of the annotators.

We also present a baseline for the task of heteronormative language detection using our corpus, with two supervised algorithms and with four variations of BERT.

As future work, we plan on expanding this corpus by extracting a larger set of tweets containing more nuanced forms of heteronormative discourses, since heteronormativity is not only associated to lexical properties in the speech, but also to more complex forms of linguistic phenomena. In future projects, we hope to further investigate heteronormative language use in digital spaces, crafting a dataset that better respects the multi-class definition of heterornormativity as discussed in Section 2.

We propose the creation of similar corpora but for other languages, since heteronormativity is a global issue that requires joint action. Also, we encourage researchers to develop further tools for heteronormative language detection and mitigation, since language technologies are rapidly increasing their presence in human lives, and the implicit biases these models have can be very costly and damaging to human lives.

7 Ethical Considerations

7.1 Data Collection

We ensured that our dataset was obtained following Twitter's terms and conditions.

The full text corpus will not be released due to Twitter's Privacy Policy. Only the IDs of the tweets and their labels are be available on the following repository[6].

7.2 Benefits and Limitations in the use of our Data

This corpus has been created for the detection of heteronormative language in English. Other possible uses could be gender bias and sexism detection and mitigation. Every population could be benefited from the integration of our corpus into their language systems, since it's main goal is to create more equal language technologies.

8 Acknowledgements

This paper has been supported by PAPIIT project TA400121, and CONACYT CB A1-S-27780. The

[6]https://github.com/juanmvsa/HeteroCorpus

authors thank CONACYT for the computing resources provided through the Plataforma de Aprendizaje Profundo para Tecnologías del Lenguaje of the Laboratorio de Supercómputo del INAOE

References

Brittanie Atteberry-Ash, Stephanie Rachel Speer, Shanna K. Kattari, and M. Killian Kinney. 2019. Does it get better? LGBTQ social work students and experiences with harmful discourse. *J. Gay Lesbian Soc. Serv.*

Marion Bartl, Malvina Nissim, and Albert Gatt. 2020. Unmasking contextual stereotypes: Measuring and mitigating bert's gender bias. *CoRR*, abs/2010.14534.

Emily M. Bender and Batya Friedman. 2018. Data Statements for Natural Language Processing: Toward Mitigating System Bias and Enabling Better Science. *Transactions of the Association for Computational Linguistics*, 6:587–604.

Rishabh Bhardwaj, Navonil Majumder, and Soujanya Poria. 2020. Investigating gender bias in BERT.

Jayadev Bhaskaran and Isha Bhallamudi. 2019. Good secretaries, bad truck drivers? occupational gender stereotypes in sentiment analysis. *arXiv preprint arXiv:1906.10256*.

Shikha Bordia and Samuel R. Bowman. 2019. Identifying and reducing gender bias in word-level language models. *NAACL*.

Judith Butler. 2011. *Bodies that matter: On the discursive limits of sex*. routledge.

Yang Trista Cao and Hal Daumé III. 2020. Toward gender-inclusive coreference resolution. In *Proceedings of the 58th Annual Meeting of the Association for Computational Linguistics*, pages 4568–4595, Online. Association for Computational Linguistics.

Ann Coady. 2017. The origin of sexism in language. *Gender and Language*.

Corinne A. Moss-Racusin, John F. Dovidio, Victoria L. Brescoll, Mark J. Graham, and Jo Handelsman. 2012. Science faculty's subtle gender biases favor male students. *Proceedings of the National Academy of Sciences*, 109(41):16474–16479.

Lewis Davis and Megan Reynolds. 2018. Gendered language and the educational gender gap. *Econ. Lett.*

Angel Felipe Magnossão de Paula, Roberto Fray da Silva, and Ipek Baris Schlicht. 2021. Sexism prediction in spanish and english tweets using monolingual and multilingual bert and ensemble models. *arXiv preprint arXiv:2111.04551*.

Sunipa Dev, Masoud Monajatipoor, Anaelia Ovalle, Arjun Subramonian, Jeff Phillips, and Kai-Wei Chang. 2021. Harms of gender exclusivity and challenges in non-binary representation in language technologies. In *Proceedings of the 2021 Conference on Empirical Methods in Natural Language Processing*, pages 1968–1994, Online and Punta Cana, Dominican Republic. Association for Computational Linguistics.

Jacob Devlin, Ming-Wei Chang, Kenton Lee, and Kristina Toutanova. 2018. Bert: Pre-training of deep bidirectional transformers for language understanding. *arXiv preprint arXiv:1810.04805*.

Diccionario de Asilo CAER-Euskadi. Heteronormatividad género y asilo. Online. Accessed: 2022-04-06.

Jad Doughman and Wael Khreich. 2022. Gender bias in text: Labeled datasets and lexicons.

Asia A. Eaton and Alejandra Matamala. 2014. The relationship between heteronormative beliefs and verbal sexual coercion in college students. *Arch. Sex. Behav.*

Victor Gay, Daniel L. Hicks, Estefania Santacreu-Vasut, and Amir Shoham. 2018. Decomposing culture: an analysis of gender, language, and labor supply in the household. *Review of Economics of the Household*.

Janet Shibley Hyde. 2005. The gender similarities hypothesis. *Am. Psychol.*

Janice Habarth. 2015. Development of the heteronormative attitudes and beliefs scale. *Psychology and Sexuality*.

Akshita Jha and Radhika Mamidi. 2017. When does a compliment become sexist? analysis and classification of ambivalent sexism using twitter data. In *Proceedings of the second workshop on NLP and computational social science*, pages 7–16.

Jessica King. 2016. The violence of heteronormative language towards the queer community.

Keita Kurita, Nidhi Vyas, Ayush Pareek, Alan W Black, and Yulia Tsvetkov. 2019. Measuring bias in contextualized word representations.

Ellen Lamont. 2017. "we can write the scripts ourselves": Queer challenges to heteronormative courtship practices:. *Gend. Soc.*

Brian Larson. 2017. Gender as a variable in Natural-Language processing: Ethical considerations. *EthNLP@EACL*.

Anne Lauscher, Archie Crowley, and Dirk Hovy. 2022. Welcome to the modern world of pronouns: Identity-Inclusive natural language processing beyond gender.

Kaiji Lu, Piotr Mardziel, Fangjing Wu, Preetam Amancharla, and Anupam Datta. 2018. Gender bias in neural natural language processing. *arXiv: Computation and Language*.

Joseph Marchia and Jamie M. Sommer. 2019. (re)defining heteronormativity. *Sexualities*.

Prasanna Parasurama and João Sedoc. 2021. Gendered language in resumes and its implications for algorithmic bias in hiring.

Monica Rubini and Michela Menegatti. 2014. Hindering women's careers in academia: Gender linguistic bias in personnel selection. *Journal of Language and Social Psychology*, 33(6):632–650.

Danielle Saunders and Bill Byrne. 2020. Reducing gender bias in neural machine translation as a domain adaptation problem.

H. Andrew Schwartz, Johannes C. Eichstaedt, Margaret L. Kern, Lukasz Dziurzynski, Stephanie M. Ramones, Megha Agrawal, Achal Shah, Michal Kosinski, David Stillwell, Martin E. P. Seligman, and Lyle H. Ungar. 2013. Personality, gender, and age in the language of social media: The Open-Vocabulary approach. *PLoS One*.

Froukje Smits, Annelies Knoppers, and Agnes Elling-Machartzki. 2020. 'everything is said with a smile': Homonegative speech acts in sport:. *Int. Rev. Sociol. Sport*.

Jane G. Stout and Nilanjana Dasgupta. 2011. When he doesn't mean you: Gender-Exclusive language as ostracism. *Pers. Soc. Psychol. Bull.*

Tony Sun, Andrew Gaut, Shirlyn Tang, Yuxin Huang, Mai ElSherief, Jieyu Zhao, Diba Mirza, Elizabeth Belding, Kai-Wei Chang, Kai-Wei Chang, and William Yang Wang. 2019. Mitigating gender bias in natural language processing: Literature review. *ACL*.

Michael Warner. 1991. Introduction: Fear of a queer planet. *Social Text*, (29):3–17.

Monique Wittig. 1979. The straight mind. *The Future of Difference (discours liminaire en conférence universitaire)*, vol. 3, t. 3. New York, Barnard Center for Research on Women, coll.« Scholar and Feminist / VI.

Monique Wittig. 1980. The straight mind. *Feminist Issues*, 1(1):103–111.

Jieyu Zhao, Yichao Zhou, Zeyu Li, Wei Wang, and Kai-Wei Chang. 2018. Learning Gender-Neutral word embeddings.

Evaluating Gender Bias Transfer from Film Data

Amanda Bertsch,* Ashley Oh,* Sanika Natu,* Swetha Gangu,*
Alan Black, Emma Strubell
Carnegie Mellon University
[abertsch, ashleyoh, snatu, sgangu]@cs.cmu.edu

Abstract

Films are a rich source of data for natural language processing. OpenSubtitles (Lison and Tiedemann, 2016) is a popular movie script dataset, used for training models for tasks such as machine translation and dialogue generation. However, movies often contain biases that reflect society at the time, and these biases may be introduced during pre-training and influence downstream models. We perform sentiment analysis on template infilling (Kurita et al., 2019) and the Sentence Embedding Association Test (May et al., 2019) to measure how BERT-based language models change after continued pre-training on OpenSubtitles. We consider gender bias as a primary motivating case for this analysis, while also measuring other social biases such as disability. We show that sentiment analysis on template infilling is not an effective measure of bias due to the rarity of disability and gender identifying tokens in the movie dialogue. We extend our analysis to a longitudinal study of bias in film dialogue over the last 110 years and find that continued pre-training on OpenSubtitles encodes additional bias into BERT. We show that BERT learns associations that reflect the biases and representation of each film era, suggesting that additional care must be taken when using historical data.

1 Introduction

Movies are often seen as a commentary on or reflection of society. They can reveal key themes within a culture, showcase the viewpoints of various social classes, or even reflect the writer's internal mindset. Additionally, movies have widespread influence on audience perceptions based on the messages they contain.

Movie scripts are popular data sources for training models for natural language tasks, such as sentiment analysis (Frangidis et al., 2020) and dialogue systems (Serban et al., 2015), because they are written to mimic natural human dialogue, easy to collect, and much more cost effective than transcribing human conversations.

However, despite this popularity, there has been concern regarding the biases that movies contain (Schofield and Mehr, 2016) and the potential downstream effects of training on biased datasets (Kumar et al., 2020). More specifically, gender bias in movies is a long-studied issue. A popular benchmark for gender representation is the Bechdel test[1]. A movie passes the Bechdel test if it contains two female characters who speak to each other about something other than a man.

In the last decade, the Bechdel test has come under criticism. O'Meara (2016) argues that the Bechdel Test is a poor metric in three ways: it excuses "low, one-dimensional standards" for representation, it fails to consider intersectionality of oppression, and it treats all conversation about men as unempowering.

As a more intersectional and nuanced method of measuring bias and stereotyping in movie script datasets, we propose fine-tuning a language model on movie scripts in order to examine bias that the model inherits from movies and its impact on downstream tasks. Particularly, a model trained on movie scripts may inherit biases or offensive language from the source material, which can lead to differing treatment of social groups in applications of the model. In a longitudinal analysis of bias over time, we evaluate how models that are fine-tuned on separate decades of movie scripts reflect societal biases and and historical events at the time. The form of fine-tuning we use is a continuation of the pre-training objectives on the new dataset. The contributions of this paper are:

- an analysis of additional bias introduced into BERT by continued pre-training on movie scripts, where we find that gender bias in the model is increased when film data is added.

*Equal contribution

[1]https://bechdeltest.com/

Proceedings of the The 4th Workshop on Gender Bias in Natural Language Processing (GeBNLP), pages 235 - 243
July 15, 2022 ©2022 Association for Computational Linguistics

- a historically grounded analysis of social biases learned from film scripts by decade, considering gender, racial, and ideological biases.

2 Bias statement

In our analysis we use a language modeling approach to uncover and examine bias in a movie script corpus. Our main focus is gender bias, but we will also explore intersectional bias between gender and disability. We define bias as implicit bias that may result in a difference in treatment across two groups, regardless of whether that difference causes harm. This definition of implicit bias follows from the premise of the Implicit Bias Association test (Greenwald et al., 2009), which demonstrated that implicit biases impact behavior. Our analysis also considers both explicit and implicit gender biases that have the capability for harm. In this paper we assume biases in movies are intentional, but it is possible the author may have been using these stereotypes as a method of raising awareness of an issue or as satire. It is important to note that models trained on these movie scripts will likely not be able to pick up on the intent of the author, but rather will learn and amplify the biases (Hall et al., 2022).

This analysis includes a comparison between the treatment of men and woman in film scripts, which implicitly upholds a gender binary. We fine-tune BERT on full movie scripts without partitioning by gender, but we examine gender bias by comparing the associations the model has learned about men and women during the analysis. By discarding data about people who are nonbinary, we make this analysis tractable, but we also lose the ability to draw meaningful conclusions about this underrepresented group. We choose to reduce harm by not assuming the genders of characters; rather, we consider the associations the model has learned about gender from the speech of all characters. Thus, our analysis is more likely to represent biases in how characters discuss men and women who are not present, rather than how characters treat men and women in direct conversation.

3 Related Work

A significant amount of research has examined and quantified gender bias in movie scripts and narratives. Past work has focused on bias in film dialogue, using classification models to predict whether speakers are both female, both male, or of different genders. Schofield and Mehr (2016) concluded that simpler lexical features are more useful than sentiment or structure when predicting gender.

Ramakrishna et al. (2015) use gender ladenness, a normative rating representing word association to feminine and masculine traits, to explore gender bias. Specifically, they examine gender ladenness with respect to the movie's genre, showing that certain genres are more likely to be associated with masculine/feminine traits than others. Gala et al. (2020) add to the genre and gender association, finding that certain sports, war, and science fiction genres focus on male-dominated tropes and that male-dominated tropes exhibit more topical diversity than female-dominated tropes.

Huang et al. (2021) show that in generated stories, male protagonists are portrayed as more intellectual while female protagonists are portrayed as more sexual. Sap et al. (2017) look at more subtle forms of gender bias as it relates to power and agency. Their work uses an extended connotation lexicon to expose fine-grained gender bias in films.

Ramakrishna et al. (2017) also looked at the differences in portrayals of characters based on their language use which includes the psycholinguistic normative measures of emotional and psychological constructs of the character. They found that female writers were more likely to have balanced genders in movie characters and that female characters tended to have more positive valence in language than male counterparts in movie scripts.

While these works focus on understanding bias in film directly, we take a slightly differently framing, examining how the bias in a film dataset can impact the biases of a language model.

Loureiro et al. (2022) examine concept drift and generalization on language models trained on Twitter data over time. Our work on longitudinal effects of film data is distinct in timescale (reflecting the much slower release rate of films relative to tweets) and in motivation; (Loureiro et al., 2022) consider the effects of the data's time period on model performance, while we examine the effects of the time period on model biases.

4 Methods

We examine how a BERT-based language model (Devlin et al., 2019) may inherit bias from film data. Specifically, we use the OpenSubtitles corpus (Lison and Tiedemann, 2016), a collection of movie subtitles from approximately 400,000 movies. While the corpus does not provide summary statistics, upon inspection it appears the vast majority of these movies are American-produced films. These subtitles do not contain speaker gender, and often do not provide speaker names. Thus, any bias exhibited in the model is likely from the way the characters speak about people from different groups– e.g. indirect, not direct, sexism.

We use the OpenSubtitles corpus to gather sentences within each movie script and randomly mask words to fine-tune BERT on the movie corpora. Following previous work by von Boguszewski et al. (2021) that focused on toxic language detection in BERT fine-tuned on movie corpora, we considered bias in the original English pre-trained BERT as a baseline and BERT fine-tuned on movie corpora (which we call FilmBERT) as a secondary model. We used two approaches to quantify bias in the models, which we describe in the following sections. We then employ a longitudinal analysis of BERT by fine-tuning on decades from 1910 to 2010 in order to quantify what societal trends and biases the model may absorb.

4.1 Measuring Intersectional Bias through Sentiment Analysis

We adopt the method used by Hassan et al. (2021) to measure how the presence of gender or disability identity tokens affects the sentiment of the predicted token in a template infilling task. We create templates in the form "The [GENDER] [DISABILITY] person [VERB] [MASK]," where [GENDER] and [DISABILITY] were filled with tokens related to gender and disability. The gender list was chosen for gender inclusiveness (Bamberger and Farrow, 2021) and the disability tokens were based on prior work by Hutchinson et al. (2020). The templates can be separated in 4 classes, "None" which have no identifying tokens and will serve as our control, "Disability" which contains a token from the disability list, "Gender" which contains a word from the gender list and "Disability+Gender" which contains one disability token and one gender token. To filter out sub-embeddings and punctuation, predicted tokens that contained non-alphabetic characters were removed. The predicted tokens were then put into a template in the form "The person [VERB] [PREDICTED TOKEN].". This allows us to measure the sentiment of the predicted token without considering the sentiment of the [GENDER] or [DISABILITY] token. The sentence-level sentiment scores were obtained from Textblob polarity [2]. We extend the work of Hassan et al. (2021) by running a pairwise t-test between sentiment scores for the classes produced by BERT and FilmBERT.

4.2 Sentence Embedding Association Test

The Word Embedding Association Test (Islam et al., 2016) is a popular tool for detecting bias in non-contextualized word embeddings. It was adapted for sentence-level embeddings by May et al. (2019) to produce the Sentence Embedding Association Test, which can be applied to contextualized embeddings. This test measures the cosine similarity between embeddings of sentences that capture attributes (such as gender) and target concepts (such as likeability). May et al. caution that this test may underrepresent bias in embeddings; however, when applied with care, it can provide strong evidence of biased associations over social attributes and roles.

We use the original sentence embedding tests developed by May et al. (2019), which examine a variety of biases. There are 6 tests that measure gender associations. The tests measure whether female names or female terms (e.g. "woman," "she") are more strongly associated with words for family life over careers, arts over math, or arts over science, relative to male equivalents. Other tests measure the professional "double bind," where women in professional settings who are more competent are perceived as less likeable (Heilman et al., 2004); the "angry black woman" stereotype, an intersection of racist and sexist stereotypes (Motro et al., 2022); racial biases, where African American names and identity terms are compared to European American names and identity terms; and word connotation differences, such as instruments being more pleasant than weapons or flowers being more pleasant than insects.

4.3 Longitudinal Study

The OpenSubtitles corpus contains movie scripts from the early 1900s to the 2020s. We partition the dataset by decade and fine-tune BERT on each decade's data individually, producing 11 decade models, which we label FilmBERT-1910s to FilmBERT-2010s. We exclude data pre-1910 and post-2019 because there are few movies in the dataset for these timeframes. We also exclude all

[2] https://textblob.readthedocs.io/en/dev/

music videos, restricting the sample to feature films. Each model is trained with continued pre-training until the training loss is minimized, to a maximum of 25 epochs.

5 Fine-tuning on Entire Corpora Results

First, we consider results from continued pre-training over the entire OpenSubtitles dataset.

5.1 Sentiment Analysis

We were not able to replicate similar results to Hassan et al. (2021) with BERT. All of the classes were weakly negative to neutral as expected. "None" was reported to have the highest sentiment by Hassan et al. (2021), but had the lowest average sentiment in our replication. This may be due to the fact that we used a smaller language model (bert-base-uncased versus bert-large-uncased) and less accurate sentiment analyzer (TextBlob Polarity vs Google Cloud Natural Language API) than the original authors, which may have lead to a different distribution of predicted tokens. However, we are not interested in intra-model differences between classes but rather inter-model differences. That is, we would like to compare the average sentiment from BERT against FilmBERT for each class.

We hypothesized the sentiment for gender would become more negative. Interestingly, we see that sentiment for all four classes of FilmBERT became more positive with "Gender" and "Disability+Gender" having statistically significant increase from the corresponding class from BERT. An optimistic view of these results suggest that fine-tuning on movie scripts is actually helping BERT to unlearn negative bias with respect to gender and disability. Given the template "the lesbian person in a wheelchair feels [MASK]." BERT produces the following tokens: ['uncomfortable', 'awkward', 'isolated', 'guilty', 'sick', 'helpless', 'threatened', 'trapped', 'alone', 'powerless']. Clearly, the predicted tokens all have negative sentiment. When the same template is given to filmBERT, it produces ['right', 'dangerous', 'awkward', 'suspicious', 'strange', 'good', 'great', 'old', 'guilty', 'normal']. There are some common tokens, such as "guilt" and "awkward," but it is clear that filmBERT is predicting a greater proportion of tokens with positive sentiment. Additional examples are available in Table 3 in the Appendix.

5.2 Discussion and Limitations

It is also possible that the sentiment analysis approach is simply not a good measure of dataset bias. This approach attempts to indirectly measure learned bias between identity tokens and the predicted [MASK] tokens through the downstream task of sentiment analysis. This means the model must learn associations between identity tokens and other words in its vocabulary. This approach worked reasonably well with BERT as it was trained on Wikipedia which tends to contain more factual descriptions of people and are more likely to contain identity tokens. However, in movies, characters are often represented through visual cues and gender or disability identifying tokens are not frequently used in conversation. Additionally, models such as BERT that use contextualized word embeddings have difficulty effectively representing rare words (Schick and Schütze, 2019). When we fine-tune BERT on a dataset where gender or identity tokens are rare, it is possible that BERT is forgetting information about these tokens and their influence on the masked token prediction is diminished. Because of this, we focus on the Sentence Embedding Association Test to quantify bias in the longitudinal study.

6 Longitudinal Study Results

We use the Sentence Embedding Association Test (May et al., 2019) to quantify the bias in each of the decade models, using the original association tests designed by the authors. These tests measure the association between two contrasting sets of identity terms (e.g. male-identifying and female-identifying terms) and two non-identity-based sets (e.g. career-related terms and family-related terms). We consider only associations that are significant ($p < 0.05$), and factor both the number of significant associations found and the relative effect sizes into our analysis.

6.1 Gender Stereotypes

The original BERT model does not exhibit significant associations for any of these tests, as reported in May et al. (2019), but the film decade models display a clear pattern. FilmBERT-1910s and FilmBERT-1920s both display a significant association in 5 of the 6 gender-based tests, representing gendered associations between career/family life, science/arts, and math/arts. On average, the effect size is slightly larger for FilmBERT-1920s.

Class	# Templates	BERT Mean Sentiment	filmBERT Mean Sentiment	P Value
None	14	-0.00267 ±0.02	0.00431 ±0.13	0.1268
Disability	168	-0.00063 ±0.03	-0.00027 ±0.01	0.5381
Gender	238	-0.00214 ±0.04	0.00061 ±0.02	0.00135
Disability+Gender	2856	-0.00196 ±0.03	-8.647e-6 ±0.01	4.2e-41

Table 1: Sentiment Average and Variance by class for BERT and filmBERT. Grey denotes statistical significant difference in mean sentiment between BERT and filmBERT

Test	1910s	1920s	1930s	1940s	1950s	1960s	1970s	1980s	1990s	2000s	2010s
Terms/career	0.53	0.84	-0.05	0.17	0.21	0.18	-0.48	0.07	0.09	0.10	0.53
Names/career	0.67	0.28	0.00	0.44	0.09	0.59	0.24	-0.18	0.14	0.57	0.10
Terms/math	0.07	0.63	-1.10	0.06	0.16	0.13	0.56	-0.70	0.24	-0.07	-0.02
Names/math	0.43	0.53	-0.21	-0.07	0.63	0.34	0.09	0.12	-0.72	-0.60	0.08
Terms/science	0.46	0.81	-0.73	-0.22	0.11	0.27	-0.08	0.36	0.51	-0.23	-0.23
Names/science	0.63	0.42	0.08	0.31	-0.07	0.41	-0.31	-0.09	0.01	-0.65	0.05

Table 2: Gender stereotype associations by each model. Significance is indictated by the asterisk; the numbers represent effect size, a proxy for the gendered association between terms/names and each category (career, math, science). Grey cells indicate a significant ($p < 0.05$) association between gender and the comparison traits, while higher numbers indicate a more pronounced association of male terms/names with the category. Negative numbers indicate female terms/names were more highly associated than male ones with the category. Each pair of traits was tested for association to gendered terms (e.g. "woman") and gendered names.

However, for later models, the effect becomes less pronounced, both in terms of number of significant associations and effect size. Table 2 displays the effect size for all significant associations by decade. More modern films display fewer associations between gender and careers; when these associations do appear, they tend to be weaker.

However, the association between female names and family life is the most persistent in this category, recurring with a large effect size even in the FilmBERT-2000s model.

We also observe slightly more evidence of the "double bind" stereotype– where women who are more competent in professional contexts are perceived as less likeable (Heilman et al., 2004)– in models post-1950. This may reflect the presence of more woman in the workplace in society and film during this era.

6.2 Racial Stereotypes

The "angry black woman" stereotype (Motro et al., 2022) exists at the intersection of gender and racial bias. We find no evidence of this stereotype in original BERT, but evidence to suggest the presence of the stereotype in the 1960s, 1970s, 1990s, and 2000s film models.

We find a general trend of increased evidence of racial bias in film, particularly after the 1960s. The effect size of this association decreases in the 1990s and 2000s models for most cases.

6.3 Social Trends

Films reflect the ideals of their producers. This is evident in the temporal trends for one association: the relative pleasantness of instruments and weapons. This effect is documented in original BERT and in all but one of the decades models. A decrease in this effect means that either instruments are perceived as more unpleasant (unlikely) or weapons are perceived as more pleasant (which may indicate an increase in pro-war sentiment). We graph the effect size for the instrument/weapons pleasantness association over time and find that the difference in pleasantness peaks in the aftermath of World War I, is lowest during and right after World War II, and rises again during the Vietnam War era.

6.4 Discussion and Limitations

Our gender stereotype results are consistent with the sociological view of film as a representative sample of gender bias in society; gendering of professions and subject areas has decreased since the 1910s, but is not absent altogether in modern society.

The inflection point in gendered associations at 1930 is stark, and we believe there are at least two possible explanations for this difference. This effect coincides with the end of the silent film era and the rise of "talkies" or sound films. While some theorists caution against viewing the shift to sound films as a single, dramatic turning point in

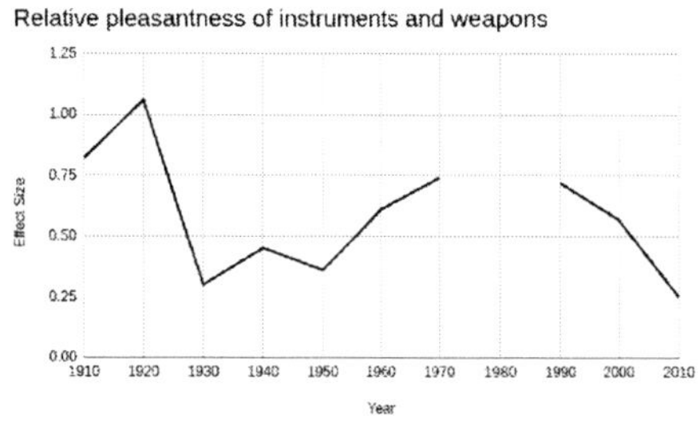

Figure 1: Pleasantness of instruments relative to weapons by FilmBERT decade models. Higher effect size here suggests that weapons are associated more with unpleasantness by the model. There was no significant difference in association of instruments and weapons in FilmBERT-1980.

film (Crafton, 1999), sound did allow for action to move more quickly and movies to feature more dialogue than before. Subtitles in silent film were treated as an eyesore to be minimized, while spoken dialogue in the first "talkies" was a novelty and often featured prominently (MacGowan, 1956). Secondly, the Hays Code was adopted by Hollywood producers in 1930. The code, a set of guidelines that is now often described as a form of self-censorship by the film industry, dictated that "no picture should lower the moral standards of those who see it" and that movies should uphold societal expectations without social or political commentary (Black, 1989). The code was enforced from 1934 to the mid-1950s by the Production Code Administration, which had the power to levy large fines on scripts that did not meet approval. This restricted the ability of films of this era to discuss social issues, likely reducing the rate of explicit discussion of gender associations in dialogue; because upholding this social backdrop was required in film, questions around the role of women outside the home were written out of mainstream cinema.

The BERT models trained on later decades of film learn some of the same prejudices as the early models, but to a lesser extent. Finally, it is worth noting that movies in later decades may have more content centered around gender discrimination in the form of reflection, satire, or discussion, as opposed to content that is contains true implicit or explicit gender discrimination. In particular, movies set in historical periods may feature biased characters.

When first examining the racial bias results, it may seem that the 1910s-1950s models feature less harmful stereotypes about the African American group; however, we caution strongly against this interpretation. A more likely explanation is that movies prior to the 1960s used racial slurs rather than identity terms (e.g. "Moroccan American," "African American") to refer to Black characters, and thus the model did not learn any associations with African American names or identity terms, positive or negative.

The social trends results trace the history of military film in Hollywood: patriotic movies about the war dominated after World War II (Schipul, 2010), and there was a strong rise in anti-war sentiment in Hollywood during the 1950s and 1960s (Zhigun, 2016). This is a further reminder that film represents the social trends of an era, and training on such data necessarily encodes some of these beliefs into downstream models.

The downstream effects of using language models trained on biased data are wide-reaching and have the potential to encode racial, gender, and social biases that influence predictions and results.

7 Conclusions

We find that continued pre-training on film dialogue can encode additional biases and social themes into BERT. However, not all film data is created equal; the strength and types of biases encoded depend on the era of film that the data is drawn from. Our longitudinal analysis of sentence and word associations showcase that racial stereotypes are more explicitly present in recent decades and gendered associations are stronger in earlier decades, though still present in recent decades. Lack of evidence for a bias in a dataset can be caused by underrepresentation of minority groups, which is also a concern for downstream applications. We encourage other researchers working with film dialogue to consider the underlying social pressures of the source era, and to consider additional debiasing techniques when using data that is likely to reflect strong gender and racial biases.

8 Acknowledgements

We would like to thank David Mortensen, Carolyn Rosé, Sireesh Gururaja, and Keri Milliken for their feedback and discussion on earlier drafts of this work. Additionally, we would like to thank the anonymous reviewers for their helpful comments.

References

Ethan T. Bamberger and Aiden Farrow. 2021. Language for sex and gender inclusiveness in writing. *Journal of Human Lactation*, 37(2):251–259. PMID: 33586503.

Gregory D. Black. 1989. Hollywood censored: The production code administration and the hollywood film industry, 1930-1940. *Film History*, 3(3):167–189.

Donald Crafton. 1999. *The talkies: american cinema's transition to sound, 1926-1931*. University of California Press.

Jacob Devlin, Ming-Wei Chang, Kenton Lee, and Kristina Toutanova. 2019. BERT: Pre-training of deep bidirectional transformers for language understanding. In *Proceedings of the 2019 Conference of the North American Chapter of the Association for Computational Linguistics: Human Language Technologies, Volume 1 (Long and Short Papers)*, pages 4171–4186, Minneapolis, Minnesota. Association for Computational Linguistics.

Paschalis Frangidis, Konstantinos Georgiou, and Stefanos Papadopoulos. 2020. Sentiment analysis on movie scripts and reviews. *Artificial Intelligence Applications and Innovations*, 583:430–438.

Dhruvil Gala, Mohammad Omar Khursheed, Hannah Lerner, Brendan O'Connor, and Mohit Iyyer. 2020. Analyzing gender bias within narrative tropes. In *Proceedings of the Fourth Workshop on Natural Language Processing and Computational Social Science*, pages 212–217, Online. Association for Computational Linguistics.

Anthony G Greenwald, T Andrew Poehlman, Eric Luis Uhlmann, and Mahzarin R Banaji. 2009. Understanding and using the implicit association test: Iii. meta-analysis of predictive validity. *Journal of personality and social psychology*, 97(1):17.

Melissa Hall, Laurens van der Maaten, Laura Gustafson, and Aaron Adcock. 2022. A systematic study of bias amplification. *CoRR*, abs/2201.11706.

Saad Hassan, Matt Huenerfauth, and Cecilia Ovesdotter Alm. 2021. Unpacking the interdependent systems of discrimination: Ableist bias in NLP systems through an intersectional lens. *CoRR*, abs/2110.00521.

Madeline E. Heilman, Aaron S. Wallen, Daniella Fuchs, and Melinda M. Tamkins. 2004. Penalties for success: reactions to women who succeed at male gender-typed tasks. *Journal of Applied Psychology*, 89(3):416–427.

Tenghao Huang, Faeze Brahman, Vered Shwartz, and Snigdha Chaturvedi. 2021. Uncovering implicit gender bias in narratives through commonsense inference.

Ben Hutchinson, Vinodkumar Prabhakaran, Emily Denton, Kellie Webster, Yu Zhong, and Stephen Denuyl. 2020. Social biases in NLP models as barriers for persons with disabilities. In *Proceedings of the 58th Annual Meeting of the Association for Computational Linguistics*, pages 5491–5501, Online. Association for Computational Linguistics.

Aylin Caliskan Islam, Joanna J. Bryson, and Arvind Narayanan. 2016. Semantics derived automatically from language corpora necessarily contain human biases. *CoRR*, abs/1608.07187.

Vaibhav Kumar, Tenzin Singhay Bhotia, Vaibhav Kumar, and Tanmoy Chakraborty. 2020. Nurse is closer to woman than surgeon? mitigating gender-biased proximities in word embeddings. *Transactions of the Association for Computational Linguistics*, 8:486–503.

Keita Kurita, Nidhi Vyas, Ayush Pareek, Alan W Black, and Yulia Tsvetkov. 2019. Measuring bias in contextualized word representations. In *Proceedings of the First Workshop on Gender Bias in Natural Language Processing*, pages 166–172, Florence, Italy. Association for Computational Linguistics.

Pierre Lison and Jörg Tiedemann. 2016. OpenSubtitles2016: Extracting large parallel corpora from movie and TV subtitles. In *Proceedings of the Tenth International Conference on Language Resources and Evaluation (LREC'16)*, pages 923–929, Portorož, Slovenia. European Language Resources Association (ELRA).

Daniel Loureiro, Francesco Barbieri, Leonardo Neves, Luis Espinosa Anke, and Jose Camacho-Collados. 2022. Timelms: Diachronic language models from twitter.

Kenneth MacGowan. 1956. When the talkies came to hollywood. *The Quarterly of Film Radio and Television*, 10(3):288–301.

Chandler May, Alex Wang, Shikha Bordia, Samuel R. Bowman, and Rachel Rudinger. 2019. On measuring social biases in sentence encoders. In *Proceedings of the 2019 Conference of the North American Chapter of the Association for Computational Linguistics: Human Language Technologies, Volume 1 (Long and Short Papers)*, pages 622–628, Minneapolis, Minnesota. Association for Computational Linguistics.

Daphna Motro, Jonathan B. Evans, Aleksander P. J. Ellis, and Lehman Benson III. 2022. The "angry black woman" stereotype at work. *Harvard Business Review*.

Jennifer O'Meara. 2016. What "the bechdel test" doesn't tell us: examining women's verbal and vocal (dis)empowerment in cinema. *Feminist Media Studies*, 16(6):1120–1123.

Anil Ramakrishna, Nikolaos Malandrakis, Elizabeth Staruk, and Shrikanth Narayanan. 2015. A quantitative analysis of gender differences in movies using psycholinguistic normatives. In *Proceedings of the 2015 Conference on Empirical Methods in Natural Language Processing*, pages 1996–2001, Lisbon, Portugal. Association for Computational Linguistics.

Anil Ramakrishna, Victor R. Martínez, Nikolaos Malandrakis, Karan Singla, and Shrikanth Narayanan. 2017. Linguistic analysis of differences in portrayal of movie characters. In *Proceedings of the 55th Annual Meeting of the Association for Computational Linguistics (Volume 1: Long Papers)*, pages 1669–1678, Vancouver, Canada. Association for Computational Linguistics.

Maarten Sap, Marcella Cindy Prasettio, Ari Holtzman, Hannah Rashkin, and Yejin Choi. 2017. Connotation frames of power and agency in modern films. In *Proceedings of the 2017 Conference on Empirical Methods in Natural Language Processing*, pages 2329–2334, Copenhagen, Denmark. Association for Computational Linguistics.

Timo Schick and Hinrich Schütze. 2019. Rare words: A major problem for contextualized embeddings and how to fix it by attentive mimicking.

Erik Schipul. 2010. *Constant Character, Changing Nature: The Transformation of the Hollywood War Film, From 1949 - 1989*. Ph.D. thesis, Marine Corps University.

Alexandra Schofield and Leo Mehr. 2016. Gender-distinguishing features in film dialogue. In *Proceedings of the Fifth Workshop on Computational Linguistics for Literature*, pages 32–39, San Diego, California, USA. Association for Computational Linguistics.

Iulian Vlad Serban, Alessandro Sordoni, Yoshua Bengio, Aaron C. Courville, and Joelle Pineau. 2015. Hierarchical neural network generative models for movie dialogues. *CoRR*, abs/1507.04808.

Niklas von Boguszewski, Sana Moin, Anirban Bhowmick, Seid Muhie Yimam, and Chris Biemann. 2021. How hateful are movies? a study and prediction on movie subtitles. In *Proceedings of the 17th Conference on Natural Language Processing (KONVENS 2021)*, pages 37–48, Düsseldorf, Germany. KONVENS 2021 Organizers.

Roman Zhigun. 2016. "There is Still Time, Brothers!" The American Anti-War Cinema in the Context of International Relations of the Late 1950s — Middle 1960s. *ISTORIYA*, 7(10):54.

A Additional Sentiment Analysis Results

Table 3: Examples of tokens predicted by BERT and filmBERT.

	BERT	filmBERT
"the intersex deaf person develops [MASK]."	['autism', 'deaf', 'language', 'difficulties', 'speech', 'hearing', 'disabilities', 'memory', 'independently', 'symptoms']	['easily', 'rapidly', 'successfully', 'fast', 'twice', 'somehow', 'him', 'together', 'it', 'himself']
"the polygender person with a mental illness advises [MASK]."	['suicide', 'caution', 'treatment', 'death', 'them', 'intervention', 'otherwise', 'it', 'this', 'withdrawal']	['him', 'me', 'us', 'it', 'respect', 'death', 'you', 'mr', 'revenge', 'access']
"the asexual person with dyslexia leads [MASK]."	['suicide', 'to', 'death', 'panic', 'autism', 'schizophrenia', 'complications', 'paralysis', 'downward', 'blindness']	['us', 'today', 'mr', 'me', 'now', 'away', 'to', 'you', 'him', 'them']

Indigenous Language Revitalization and the Dilemma of Gender Bias

Oussama Hansal
Université du Québec à Montréal
Oussama.Hansal@courrier.uqam.ca

Ngoc Tan Le
Université du Québec à Montréal
le.ngoc_tan@uqam.ca

Fatiha Sadat
Université du Québec à Montréal
sadat.fatiha@uqam.ca

Abstract

Natural Language Processing (NLP), through its several applications, has been considered as one of the most valuable field in interdisciplinary researches, as well as in computer science. However, it is not without its flaws. One of the most common flaws is bias.

This paper examines the main linguistic challenges of Inuktitut, an indigenous language of Canada, and focuses on gender bias identification and mitigation. We explore the unique characteristics of this language to help us understand the right techniques that can be used to identify and mitigate implicit biases. We use some methods to quantify the gender bias existing in Inuktitut word embeddings; then we proceed to mitigate the bias and evaluate the performance of the debiased embeddings. Next, we explain how approaches for detecting and reducing bias in English embeddings may be transferred to Inuktitut embeddings by properly taking into account the language's particular characteristics. We compare the effect of the debiasing techniques on Inuktitut and English. Finally, we highlight some future research directions which will further help to push the boundaries.

1 Introduction

Despite the complexity of low resource and endangered languages, the study of these languages has pulled many researchers in recent years, while this can be an encouraging factor for the development of language technologies, the complex morphology of some languages and the lack of resources have been considered as barriers. Moreover, as many NLP tasks are trained on human language data, it is expected for these applications to exhibit biases in different forms. Hovy and Prabhumoy (2021) described five sources where bias can occur in NLP systems: (1) the data, (2) the annotation process, (3) the input representations, (4) the models, and finally (5) the research design.

Gender bias can be defined as prejudice toward one gender over the other. Though usually tacit, bias range from the use of gender defaults to associating between occupation and gender. As language technologies become widespread and deployed on a large scale, their social impact raises concerns both internally and externally (Hovy and Spruit, 2016; Dastin, 2018). To capture the situation, Sun et al. (2019) reviewed NLP studies on this topic. However, their investigation is based on monolingual applications where the underlying assumptions and solutions may not directly apply to languages other than English. Thus, depending on the language involved and the factors taken into account, gender stereotypes have been conceptualized differently from study to study. To date, gender stereotypes have been addressed through a narrow problem-solving approach. While technical countermeasures are necessary, the failure to take a broader look at and engage with relevant literature outside of NLP could be detrimental to the growth of the field.

For example, when translating from English to French this following sentence, by Google Translate[1]:

(en) *The engineer has asked the nurse to help* ***her*** *get up from the bed.*

(fr) *L'ingénieur a demandé à l'infirmière de l'aider à se lever du lit.*

We can see that it identified the engineer as a male and the nurse as a female, even though we used "her" to indicate that we are referring to a female. Such inadequacies not only jeopardize the development of endangered languages applications, but also perpetuate and amplify existent biases.

Understanding how human biases are incorporated into word embeddings can help us understand

[1] https://translate.google.ca/, consulted at April 14th, 2022

Proceedings of the The 4th Workshop on Gender Bias in Natural Language Processing (GeBNLP), pages 244 - 254
July 15, 2022 ©2022 Association for Computational Linguistics

bias in NLP models, given that word embeddings are commonly used in NLP. While some significant work has been done toward minimizing the bias in the embeddings, it has been proved that some methods are insufficient and that the bias can remain hidden within the embeddings. The words frequency is not taken into account, regardless of the gender distances, therefore biased terms can remain clustered together. Furthermore, when applied to contextualized word embeddings, these bias approaches must be changed because the embedding representation of each word varies based on the context.

This research intends to shed light on this issue by evaluating recent efforts to identify and mitigate bias within the indigenous languages revitalization and preservation context. We focus on Inuktitut, one of the main Inuit language of Eastern Canada and the official language of the government of Nunavut.

Thus, this paper is structured as follows: Section 2 presents the state-of-the-art. Section 3 presents the bias statement. Section 4 discusses the linguistic challenges of indigenous languages, with a focus on Inuktitut. Sections 5 highlights gender bias detection and mitigation. Section 7 presents the evaluations and the experimental results; while comparing with other existing approaches. Section 8 discusses the necessity of a human in the loop paradigm. Finally, Section 9 concludes this paper and presents potential future work.

2 Related Work

Interest in understanding, assessing, and reducing gender bias continues to grow in the NLP field, with recent studies showing how gender disparities affect the language technologies. Sometimes, for example, when visual recognition tasks fail to recognize female doctors (Zhao et al., 2017; Rudinger et al., 2018), image caption models do not detect women sitting next to the machine (Hendricks et al., 2018); and automatic speech recognition works best with male voices (Tatman, 2017). Although previously unconcerned with these phenomena in research programs (Cislak et al., 2018); it is now widely recognized that NLP tools encode and reflect asymmetries controversial society for many seemingly neutral tasks, including machine translation (MT). Admittedly, this problem is not new.

A few years ago, Schiebinger (2014) criticized the phenomenon of *"missing men"* in machine translation after conducting one of his interviews through a commercial translation system. Although there are some feminine mentions in the text, the female pronoun "*she*" is mentioned several times by the masculine pronoun. Users of online machine translation tools have also expressed concern about gender, having noticed how commercial systems manipulate society's expectations of gender, for example by projecting the translation of engineer into masculinity and that of medical science into femininity.

Bolukbasi et al. (2016) proved the existence of gender bias in English word embeddings, and proposed a method called Hard Debias to mitigate the gender bias. Liang et al. (2020) proposed a modified method that relies heavily on the sentences used to reduce biases.

We hypothesize that because English uses the common pronouns *he* and *she* extensively, which are not used in Inuktitut, as much as in English, for different reasons [2]; the mitigation step encompasses a smaller gender subspace in comparison to English, and thus the bias is reduced.

Another method is the Iterative Null space Projection (INLP), which is a post-hoc method that can work on pre-trained representations (Ravfogel et al., 2020). The INLP's concept aims to identify task direction by training linear classifiers and removing direction from representation. INLP is effective in reducing gender bias. It was tested and showed great results in both word embeddings and contextualized word embeddings.

Most of the solutions were mainly proposed to reduce gender bias in English, and may not work as well when it comes to morphologically complex or polysynthetic languages. Nevertheless, there have been recent studies that explored the gender bias problem in languages other than English. Zhao et al. (2020) studied gender bias which is exhibited by multilingual embeddings in four languages (English, German, French, and Spanish) and demonstrated that such biases can impact cross-lingual transfer learning tasks.

Lewis and Lupyan (2020) examined whether gender stereotypes are reflected in the large-scale distributional structure of natural language semantics and measured gender associations embedded in the statistics of 25 languages and related them to data on an international dataset of psychological gender associations.

[2] https://uqausiit.ca/

Choubey et al. (2021) proposed gender-filtered self-training to improve gender translation accuracy on unambiguously gendered inputs. Their approach used a source monolingual corpus and an initial model to generate gender-specific pseudo-parallel corpora, which were then filtered and added to the training data. They evaluated their method from English to five languages, which showed an improvement in gender accuracy without damaging gender equality.

Ntoutsi et al. (2020) presented a wide multidisciplinary overview of bias in AI systems, with an emphasis on technological difficulties and solutions, as well as new research directions toward approaches that are well-grounded in a legal framework.

The bias study in machine learning is not only restricted to the computer science field. Interdisciplinary research can help address this challenge across disciplines such as psychology, sociology, linguistics, cognitive science, and more (Datta, 2018). Hassan (2016) conducted a wide study on the influence that English has had on other language communities such as Inuit community. It can be seen in the way that it has affected gender relations specifically, by disempowering women in indigenous communities, the same as described in (Gudmestad et al., 2021). Men were assigned the role of hunting, and as such, became the "*breadwinner*" of the family. Women, on the other hand, were relegated to take care of the house and children, leaving them with no economic power and a perceived subordinate role within the family (Leigh, 2009).

According to Williamson (2006), the Inuits use a concept that encapsulates history, philosophy and observations of the world surrounding them. They call it "*Qaujimajatuqangit*" which is translated as "*traditional knowledge*". For Inuit people, "*Qaujimajatuqangit*" establishes gender equality in several fundamental ways. It respects the balance between the gender roles, the importance of family, and the fluidity of both gender and sexuality.

3 Bias Statement

Bias in NLP systems often goes without notice, it's often not even detected until after the systems are launched and used by consumers, which can have adverse effects on our society, such as when it shows false information to people which leads them to believe untrue things about society or themselves; thereby changing their behavior for better or worse (Stanczak and Augenstein, 2021). The harm of bias in NLP has been understated by some people and overstated by others, who dismiss its relevance or refuse to engage with it altogether. In this paper, we focus on the study of gender bias. If a system associates certain professions with a specific gender, this creates a representational harm. Representational harm is when an individual who falls into one of those categories is treated less fairly than someone outside of that category because of their belonging to it. For example, negative selection have been reported to occur more frequently in male dominated jobs than in other types of jobs (Davison and Burke, 2000). Similar conclusions have been made in the areas of competency assessments and performance evaluations, women were rated less positively than men in line jobs (which tend to be male gender-typed), but not in staff jobs, according to a prominent financial services organization (Lyness and Heilman, 2006). By looking at common examples of bias in the workplace, we can begin to understand how it can harm people in the office When such representations are being used in downstream NLP tasks. It can make the work environment feel less inclusive and less productive. Every single one of us has biases, but it's important to acknowledge when and how they impact our lives and the lives of others. According to recent research in NLP, word embeddings can incorporate social and implicit biases inherent in the training data (Swinger et al., 2019; Schlender and Spanakis, 2020; Caliskan, 2021). Current NLP models have proven to be good at detecting prejudices (Ahmed et al., 2022). However, unlike with prejudice, biases are not always obvious. While some biases are detectable via context, others might not be—which makes it difficult for automated systems to detect them. In fact, detecting and mitigating bias within automated systems prove to be more challenging than detecting it within human beings due to several important factors as dealing with imprecise sentiment analysis; as opposed to humans who can express nuanced sentiments when discussing bias. Our effort is predicated on the assumption that observed gender bias in systems are an indication of an insufficient interest into detecting and mitigating bias, we also believe that separating genders and professions in word embeddings would allow systems to detect and mitigate gender rather than promote it.

4 Linguistic Challenges in Indigenous Languages

In this section, we present the main linguistic challenges of Canada's indigenous languages, especially Inuktitut, an Inuit language of Eastern Canada and official language of the government of Nunavut. Thus, to better understand the challenges of NLP in Inuktitut, we explore the structure of Inuktitut words, the levels of grammatical variations, the dialectal variations in spelling, and gender animacy.

4.1 Morphological complexity

Most of the indigenous languages, particularly in the Americas, belong to either the polysynthetic language group or the agglutinative language group. They have a complex, rich morphology that plays an important role in human learning versus machine learning (Gasser, 2011; Littell et al., 2018). Much of the research on their morphological analysis has focused only on linguistic aspects.

Comparing word composition in English, the word structure in Inuit languages is variable in its surface form. Words can be very short, composed of three formative features such as word base, lexical suffixes, and grammatical ending suffixes. Or they can be very long up to ten or even fifteen formative morphemes as features depending on the regional dialect (Lowe, 1985; Kudlak and Compton, 2018; Le and Sadat, 2020, 2022).

4.2 Morphophonemics

The morphophonemics of Inuktitut are highly complex, in addition to the variety of morphological suffixes that Inuktitut roots can take on (Mithun, 2015). In Inuktitut, each morpheme specifies the sound variations that can occur to its left and/or to itself. These modifications are phonologically conditioned by the individual morphemes themselves, rather than their contexts. This not only aggravates the data sparsity issue, but it also poses morphological analysis issues, which we shall address in the research topics of this project.

4.3 Dialectal variations

The third aspect of Inuktitut which contributes to the challenge of processing it with a computer is the abundance of spelling variation seen in the electronically available texts. Inuktitut, like all languages, can be divided into a number of different dialects, such as Uummarmiutun, Siglitun, Inuinnaqtun, Natsilik, Kivallirmiutun, Aivilik, North Baffin, South Baffin, Arctic Quebec, and Laborador (Dorais, 1990). The primary distinction between these dialects is phonological, which is reflected in spelling. As a result, spelling variance, either due to a lack of standardisation or due to numerous dialect changes, contributes significantly to the overall sparsity of the data in the corpora accessible for experimentation (Micher, 2018).

4.4 Gender animacy

Inuit languages are known to have some particular linguistics challenges. There is no gender marking in nouns, like you'll find in French and Spanish (*male / female*) nouns. Instead, Inuktitut distinguishes words along a dimension called *animacy*, because of the cultural understanding as to whether a noun is known to be alive or not. The singular and plural suffixes that are used in nouns, depend on whether is is animate or inanimate.

The animacy is described as a distinction between human and non-human, rational and irrational, socially active and socially passive[3]. For example, animate nouns are related to humans and animals most obviously, but other objects that are not considered alive, like stone, table, are considered as inanimate. Animate and inanimate gender is common in many Amerindian families such as Cree, Inuktitut, Quechuan, Aymara, Mapudungun, Iroquoian, and Siouan[4].

5 Bias detection and mitigation

Although existing machine learning models achieve great results on many tasks, they generally fail in avoiding biases. Recent studies illustrate how bias affect NLP technologies, which has created a growing interest in identifying, analysing and mitigating bias within the NLP community. The problem is not new, it is well-known that NLP systems contain and reflect algorithmic bias in them, this controversial imbalances has developed a large scale of concerns about its social impact. NLP systems and tools are used in everyday life, The time of academic naivety is finished, therefore we must acknowledge that our models have an impact on people's lives, but not necessarily in the way we intend (Ehni, 2008).

[3]https://en.wikipedia.org/wiki/List_of_languages_by_type_of_grammatical_genders

[4]https://linguisticmaps.tumblr.com/post/169273617313/grammatical-gender-or-noun-class-categories-new

To contextualize the plan within this larger research area, we will focus on indigenous languages that proves no exception to the existent problem of bias in NLP systems. Indigenous languages contain a wealth of secondary data about individuals, their identity and their demographic group, which are exploited to fulfil the objective of creating NLP systems. The focus on creating these systems has drifted us away from creating models as tools of understanding towards other tools that produce great results but are far more difficult to understand (Hovy and Prabhumoye, 2021).

Many questions may arise, such as: Is it possible that NLP models are biased by definition? What could be the source of this bias ? Can we figure out what it is? Is there anything we can do about it ?

5.1 Definition of Bias

Bias is a complex concept with overlapping definitions (Campolo et al., 2017). It has been considered as a fundamental human decision-making process since the beginning of time (Kahneman and Tversky, 1973). When we apply a cognitive bias, we are assuming that reality will behave in accordance with prior cognitive convictions that may or may not be accurate, with which we can make a judgement (Garrido-Muñoz et al., 2021). According to the Sociology dictionary[5], bias is a term used to describe an unjust prejudice in favour of or against a person, group, or thing.

Machine learning bias can happen in a variety of ways, ranging from racial and gender discrimination to age discrimination. It also exists in machine learning algorithms throughout their development, which is the root problem of machine learning bias. Therefore, human biases are adopted and scaled by machine learning systems.

5.2 Types of Bias

Machine learning models incorporate bias in many shapes, including gender, racial and religious biases extending to unfair recruiting and age discrimination. But what are really the machine learning types of bias?

According to (Shashkina, 2022), the most common types of machine learning bias found in algorithms are listed below:

- Reporting bias: It happens when the frequency of occurrences in the training dataset does not precisely reflect reality.
- Selection bias: This sort of bias happens when training data is either unrepresentative or not randomly selected.
- Group attribution bias: It happens when machine learning systems generalize what is true of individuals to entire groups that the individual is or is not a part of.
- Implicit bias: It happens when machine learning systems are based on data that is created on personal experience which does not necessarily apply broadly.

5.3 Mitigating Bias

We still have a long way to go before machine learning bias is completely eliminated. With the increased usage of machine learning systems in sensitive domains such as banking, criminal justice, and healthcare, we should aim to create algorithms that reduce bias in machine learning systems. Collaboration between human skills and machine learning is required to solve the problem of bias in machine learning. It will help us in the detection and mitigation of biases by figuring out how machine learning systems make predictions and what data aspects it uses to make judgments. This will help us understand whether the elements influencing the choice are biased.

6 Bias Mitigation for Inuktitut

In this study, we use a methodology and data for bias mitigation in Inuktitut, as described in the following section. To analyse and mitigate bias in word embeddings, multiple sets of data (e.g. pairs of sentences, lists of gendered words, and combinations of sentences from different categories) are required. Two algorithms are used to measure bias in embeddings, which are applicable to traditional embeddings. Then we demonstrate how we mitigate bias in either type of embedding and examine how well the bias mitigation works on downstream tasks. Furthermore, because this study is based on Inuktitut embeddings, the data used is from the Nunavut Hansard Inuktitut–English Parallel Corpus 3.0 (Joanis et al., 2020) as for English.

6.1 Bias Measuring Methods

Word Embedding Association Test (WEAT)

This method, proposed by Caliskan et al. (2017), helps to measure human bias in data presented as

[5]Open Education Sociology Dictionary: https://sociologydictionary.org/bias/

texts. It is similar to the Implicit Association Test (IAT) proposed by (Greenwald et al., 1998). The similarity of IAT and WEAT consists of using two lists of target words and two lists of attribute words. The first pair of lists represents the terms we want to compare and the second pair of lists represents the categories in which we suspect bias could exist (Mulsa and Spanakis, 2020). By using WEAT, Caliskan et al. (2017) defined ten tests to assess the bias in several areas (Mulsa and Spanakis, 2020).

In our study we converted the WEAT lists of words used in the tests to Inuktitut and modified them such that terms in these lists are only related with the appropriate category. Some of the modifications correspond to the different linguistic characteristics of the language and the lack of meaningful translations of certain words in the data. Some other changes are due to the language's various linguistic peculiarities and the lack of relevant translations for particular words in the data.

Clustering accuracy

Gonen and Goldberg (2019) provided a new metric that shows that word embeddings with reduced bias can stay grouped together even when the range across attributes and targeted words (in WEAT) is minimal. To determine the gender orientation of each word in the lexicon, the clustering accuracy test necessitates projecting the entire vocabulary into male and female terms (Mulsa and Spanakis, 2020).

The pronouns *he* and *she* were used by Gonen and Goldberg (2019), because they are commonly used and the only variation between them is in the gender subdomain.

Inuktitut has few personal pronouns, either in first person (I, we) or second person (you) [6]; which represents a problem in this research by adding extra meaning besides gender to the geometrical difference of the pronouns (Mulsa and Spanakis, 2020).

6.2 Debiasing Methods

In this section, we present the debiaising methods used in this research with an application on the Inuktitut language.

Hard debias (Bolukbasi et al., 2016)

One of the earliest strategies used to detect and minimise bias in word embeddings was *Hard Debias*. Through post-processing, it removes gender bias by subtracting the component linked with gender from all embeddings. It takes a set of gender-specific word pairs and computes the gender direction in the embedding space as the first principal component of difference vectors of these pairs. Furthermore, it removes gender bias by projecting biased word embeddings onto a subspace orthogonal to the assumed gender direction (Bolukbasi et al., 2016). The gender orientation is skewed by the frequency of words.

SENT debias (Liang et al., 2020)

SENT-Debias is divided into four steps: 1) identifying words with bias attributes; 2) contextualising these words into bias attribute sentences and, as a result, their sentence representations; 3) estimating the sentence representation bias subspace; and 4) debiasing general sentences by eliminating the projection onto this bias subspace . These processes are summarized in Figure 1.

SENT-DEBIAS:

Initialize (usually pretrained) sentence encoder M_θ.
Define bias attributes (e.g. binary gender g_m and g_f).
Obtain words $\mathcal{D} = \{(w_1^{(i)}, \ldots, w_d^{(i)})\}_{i=1}^m$ indicative of bias attributes (e.g. Table 1).
$\mathcal{S} = \bigcup_{i=1}^m \text{CONTEXTUALIZE}(w_1^{(i)}, \ldots, w_d^{(i)}) = \{(s_1^{(i)}, \ldots, s_d^{(i)})\}_{i=1}^n$ // words into sentences
for $j \in [d]$ **do**
  $\mathcal{R}_j = \{M_\theta(s_j^{(i)})\}_{i=1}^n$ // get sentence representations
end for
$\mathbf{V} = \mathbf{PCA}_k \left(\bigcup_{j=1}^d \bigcup_{\mathbf{w} \in \mathcal{R}_j} (\mathbf{w} - \mu_i) \right)$ // compute bias subspace
for each new sentence representation h do
  $\mathbf{h_V} = \sum_{j=1}^k \langle \mathbf{h}, \mathbf{v}_j \rangle \mathbf{v}_j$ // project onto bias subspace
  $\hat{\mathbf{h}} = \mathbf{h} - \mathbf{h_V}$ // subtract projection
end for

Figure 1: SENT Debias Algorithm (Liang et al., 2020).

Iterative NullSpace Projection (Ravfogel et al., 2020)

INLP stands for Iterative Nullspace Projection, which is a method for eliminating data from neuronal representations (Figure 2). This algorithm is built on repeatedly training linear classifiers that predict a specific property that we want to eliminate; then projecting the representations onto their null-space. As a result, the classifiers loose sight of the target property, making it difficult to linearly divide the data based on it. While this method is relevant to a variety of applications, it was tested on bias and fairness use-cases and demonstrated that it can mitigate bias in word embeddings.

7 Data and Evaluations

We conducted some experiments on gender bias mitigation in Inuktitut language. We used the Nunavut Hansard Inuktitut–English Parallel Corpus 3.0 (Joanis et al., 2020). The statistics of the training corpus are described in Table 1.

[6] https://uqausiit.ca/grammar-book

Input : (X, Z): a training set of vectors and protected attributes
n: Number of rounds
Result: A projection matrix P
Function GetProjectionMatrix(X, Z):
$X_{projected} \leftarrow X$
$P \leftarrow I$
for $i \leftarrow 1$ **to** n **do**
$W_i \leftarrow$ TrainClassifier($X_{projected}$, Z)
$B_i \leftarrow$ GetNullSpaceBasis(W_i)
$P_{N(W_i)} \leftarrow B_i B_i^T$
$P \leftarrow P_{N(W_i)} P$
$X_{projected} \leftarrow P_{N(W_i)} X_{projected}$
end
return P

Figure 2: INLP Algorithm (Ravfogel et al., 2020).

Dataset	#tokens	#train	#dev	#test
Inuktitut	20,657,477	1,293,348	5,433	6,139
English	10,962,904	1,293,348	5,433	6,139

Table 1: Statistics of Nunavut Hansard for Inuktitut-English

We performed our experiment using word embeddings, trained on the Nunavut Hansard for Inuktitut-English. In order to pre-train the embeddings for Inuktitut, we used an Inuktitut segmenter to segmentate the words before passing it to the FastText toolkit (Bojanowski et al., 2016). The model was trained for 40 epochs and we used 150 and 300 as the size of the dense vector to represent each token or word. In order to get terms that are more related and close to each other we used a small window of 2 which give us the maximum distance between the target word and its neighboring word. We also used an alpha value of 0.03 to preserve the strong correlation of the model after each training example is evaluated.

We performed the WEAT test on the adapted lists of words translated to Inuktitut. Among all the traditional word embeddings, we see high effect sizes and multiple tests are significant at different levels. The results of the WEAT effect sizes on gendered related tests are shown in Table 2 where we see an overall high effect size across all the scores on the original models.

The results of the WEAT effect sizes on gendered related tests are shown in Table 2 where we see a high effect size on the word embeddings debiased from the original models. The results after the debiasing step shows that the bias mitigation is effective in every model. An example of the list of words used is illustrated below in Table 3.

WEAT		
Methods	Original	Debiased
SENT debias	0.0338	**0.499**
INLP	0.0338	**0.377**
Hard Debias	0.0338	**0.385**

Table 2: Fasttext WEAT results, with significance of p-value, for three methods such as Sent debias, INLP, and Hard debias. Bold values are better.

WEAT words list example		
	Category	Inuktitut
0	family	angajuqqaaq
1	prof	executive
2	prof	ilisaiji
3	male names	jaan
4	female names	maata

Table 3: Example of WEAT words list

Because Inuktitut is a genderless language, it can be difficult to use pronouns. Therefore following (Gonen and Goldberg, 2019), we used common names for males and females instead of specifically gendered words to indicate the male and female categories (e.g. pronouns). Three tests compare the associations of male and female names to (1) job and family-related words, (2) art words, and (3) scientific domains. We observe that, following the projection, the substantial relationship between the groups is no longer there in the three tests. Figure 3 shows projections of the 200 most female-biased and 200 male-biased words projected at $t = 1$, which is basically the original state, and $t = 35$ which is the final state after debiasing. These results represent the INLP method. The results clearly demonstrate that the classes are no longer linearly separable in the INLP method. This behavior is qualitatively different from the Sent debias and the Hard debias methods; which are shown to maintain much of the proximity between female and male-biased vectors.

7.1 Discussion

We hypothesize, in this paper, that identifying the true gender orientation of word embeddings using these existing Debias approaches could be challenging. We show that the geometry of word em-

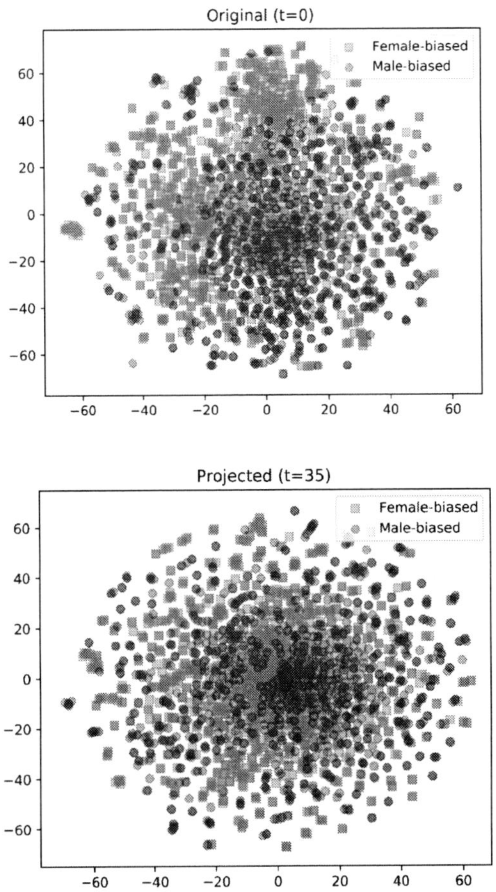

Figure 3: Example of biased clusters from original to debiased states, using t-distributed stochastic neighbor embedding (t-SNE)

beddings is influenced by word frequency. Popular and rare words, for example, cluster in various subregions of the embedding space, regardless of the fact that the words in these clusters are semantically unrelated. This may have a negative impact on the process of determining gender direction and, as a result, the efficacy of debiasing methods to debias the gender. We saw that changing the frequency of certain phrases causes large changes in the similarities between the related difference vector and other difference vectors.

We noticed, in the context of gender bias, one disadvantage that we found out, is that all of our 3 debiasing methods, like other learning approaches, are dependent on the data that is supplied to it; and assumes that the training data is suitably large and sampled from the same distribution as the test data. In practice, this requirement is difficult to achieve, and failing to supply properly representative training data may result in biased classifications even after it has been applied.

We further emphasize that the WEAT and clustering tests do not test for the absence of bias; rather, they test if bias exists in the test instances, but bias may also exist in non-tested cases. Even if we measure bias from a different perspective, the bias remains, indicating that more studies on bias mitigation approaches are needed.

8 Human-in-the-Loop Paradigm

For indigenous peoples in general, the language is directly connected to their culture and identity. Thus, it is very important for indigenous peoples of Canada, to both, speak their language and practice their culture. Inuktitut not only represents the official language of Inuits but also represents the rich culture of this community. With recent advances, NLP models represent a big opportunity for the development of tools that will further help in preserving the language with respect for the culture and realities of the indigenous people where the language takes a big part of it.

Most communities in Nunavut offer Inuktitut or Inuinnaqtun for the first few years of education, and the government has vowed to develop completely bilingual students across the territory [7]. As a result, the problem remains unsolved. As a non-indigenous people with a strong academic interests in social science, linguistics and NLP, Dorais (2010) cites that gaining a better grasp of the general sociolinguistic situation in Northern Canada is the first step toward a true solution to the Inuit culture and language difficulties. It is insufficient to describe how Inuit people communicate (which is the task of linguists). We must also attempt to comprehend what they are saying and what language means to them (Dorais, 2010). Revitalizing indigenous language should be done for, by and with indigenous communities. With the emergence of AI, especially deep learning, there is a large interest for the revitalization of indigenous languages. However, there is little interest in the field of computer science, and there are also very few or no researchers from Canada's Indigenous communities in the field of NLP.

[7]Source: https://www.thecanadianencyclopedia.ca/en/article/inuktitut

It's evident that human skills like insight and creativity be easily computerized, therefore collaborating human skills with machine learning technologies is a great approach to keep human in the loop for developing technologies for us. Before building machine learning algorithms, it's a good idea to consult with humanists and social scientists to verify that the models we create don't inherit any of the biases that people have.

Machine learning models can assist us in revealing flaws in human decision-making. So, if these models trained on current human decisions reveal bias, it will be important to have a second look from human to keep this models fair. In the case of developing machine learning technologies for indigenous communities, it is important to keep the collaboration and partnership with them; before, while and after developing tools for them. Engaging communities to develop machine learning tools is very important, not only it will make the tool more suitable and tailored to their needs but it will also give the ownership to these communities.

9 Conclusion

This paper demonstrates that gender bias exists in Inuktitut, among other biases (as probably in other languages as well). Then, by appropriately translating the data and taking into account the language's specific characteristics, we illustrated how approaches used to measure and reduce biases in English embeddings can be applied to Inuktitut embeddings. Furthermore, we investigated the influence of mitigating approaches on downstream tasks, finding a major effect in traditional embeddings, which could be regarded as favourable if the embeddings utilised guarantee a more gender-neutral approach. As a future work, we plan to investigate other types of biases in Inuktitut and collaborate with the Indigenous community. Our main objective remain the revitalization and preservation of Indigenous languages of Canada, using NLP and machie learning techniques. We hope that these exploratory results will encourage researches on Indigenous and Endangered languages.

References

Zo Ahmed, Bertie Vidgen, and Scott A Hale. 2022. Tackling racial bias in automated online hate detection: Towards fair and accurate detection of hateful users with geometric deep learning. *EPJ Data Science*, 11(1):8.

Piotr Bojanowski, Edouard Grave, Armand Joulin, and Tomas Mikolov. 2016. Enriching word vectors with subword information. *arXiv preprint arXiv:1607.04606*.

Tolga Bolukbasi, Kai-Wei Chang, James Zou, Venkatesh Saligrama, and Adam Kalai. 2016. Man is to computer programmer as woman is to homemaker? debiasing word embeddings.

Aylin Caliskan. 2021. Detecting and mitigating bias in natural language processing. *Res. Rep, Brookings Inst., Washington, DC [Google Scholar]*.

Aylin Caliskan, Joanna J Bryson, and Arvind Narayanan. 2017. Semantics derived automatically from language corpora contain human-like biases. *Science*, 356(6334):183–186.

Alex Campolo, Madelyn Sanfilippo, Meredith Whittaker, and Kate Crawford. 2017. Ai now report 2017. *New York: AI Now Institute*.

Prafulla Kumar Choubey, Anna Currey, Prashant Mathur, and Georgiana Dinu. 2021. Improving gender translation accuracy with filtered self-training. *arXiv preprint arXiv:2104.07695*.

Aleksandra Cislak, Magdalena Formanowicz, and Tamar Saguy. 2018. Bias against research on gender bias. *Scientometrics*, 115(1):189–200.

Jeffrey Dastin. 2018. Amazon scraps secret ai recruiting tool that showed bias against women. In *Ethics of Data and Analytics*, pages 296–299. Auerbach Publications.

Ranjan Datta. 2018. Decolonizing both researcher and research and its effectiveness in indigenous research. *Research Ethics*, 14(2):1–24.

Heather K Davison and Michael J Burke. 2000. Sex discrimination in simulated employment contexts: A meta-analytic investigation. *Journal of Vocational Behavior*, 56(2):225–248.

Louis-Jacques Dorais. 1990. L'étranger aux yeux du francophone de québec. *Recherches sociographiques*, 31(1):11–23.

Louis-Jacques Dorais. 2010. *Language of the Inuit: syntax, semantics, and society in the Arctic*, volume 58. McGill-Queen's Press-MQUP.

Hans-Jörg Ehni. 2008. Dual use and the ethical responsibility of scientists. *Archivum immunologiae et therapiae experimentalis*, 56(3):147–152.

Ismael Garrido-Muñoz, Arturo Montejo-Ráez, Fernando Martínez-Santiago, and L Alfonso Ureña-López. 2021. A survey on bias in deep nlp. *Applied Sciences*, 11(7):3184.

Michael Gasser. 2011. Computational morphology and the teaching of indigenous languages. In *Indigenous Languages of Latin America Actas del Primer Simposio sobre Enseñanza de Lenguas Indígenas de América Latina*, page 52.

Hila Gonen and Yoav Goldberg. 2019. Lipstick on a pig: Debiasing methods cover up systematic gender biases in word embeddings but do not remove them.

Anthony G Greenwald, Debbie E McGhee, and Jordan LK Schwartz. 1998. Measuring individual differences in implicit cognition: the implicit association test. *Journal of personality and social psychology*, 74(6):1464.

Aarnes Gudmestad, Amanda Edmonds, and Thomas Metzger. 2021. Moving beyond the native-speaker bias in the analysis of variable gender marking. *Frontiers in Communication*, page 165.

Jenna N Hassan. 2016. De-colonizing gender in indigenous language revitalization efforts. *Western Papers in Linguistics/Cahiers linguistiques de Western*, 1(2):4.

Lisa Anne Hendricks, Kaylee Burns, Kate Saenko, Trevor Darrell, and Anna Rohrbach. 2018. Women also snowboard: Overcoming bias in captioning models. In *Proceedings of the European Conference on Computer Vision (ECCV)*, pages 771–787.

Dirk Hovy and Shrimai Prabhumoy. 2021. Five sources of bias in natural language processing. *Language and Linguistics Compass.*

Dirk Hovy and Shrimai Prabhumoye. 2021. Five sources of bias in natural language processing. *Language and Linguistics Compass*, 15(8):e12432.

Dirk Hovy and Shannon L Spruit. 2016. The social impact of natural language processing. In *Proceedings of the 54th Annual Meeting of the Association for Computational Linguistics (Volume 2: Short Papers)*, pages 591–598.

Eric Joanis, Rebecca Knowles, Roland Kuhn, Samuel Larkin, Patrick Littell, Chi-kiu Lo, and Darlene Stewart. 2020. The nunavut hansard inuktitut–english parallel corpus 3.0 with preliminary machine translation results. In *Proceedings of the 12th Conference on Language Resources and Evaluation (LREC 2020)*, pages 2562—-2572.

Daniel Kahneman and Amos Tversky. 1973. On the psychology of prediction. *Psychological review*, 80(4):237.

Emily Kudlak and Richard Compton. 2018. *Kangiryuarmiut Inuinnaqtun Uqauhiitaa Numiktitirutait — Kangiryuarmiut Inuinnaqtun Dictionary*, volume 1. Nunavut Arctic College: Iqaluit, Nunavut.

Ngoc Tan Le and Fatiha Sadat. 2020. Revitalization of indigenous languages through pre-processing and neural machine translation: The case of inuktitut. In *Proceedings of the 28th International Conference on Computational Linguistics*, pages 4661–4666.

Ngoc Tan Le and Fatiha Sadat. 2022. Towards a low-resource neural machine translation for indigenous languages in canada. *Journal TAL, special issue on Language Diversity*, 62:3:39–63.

Darcy Leigh. 2009. Colonialism, gender and the family in north america: For a gendered analysis of indigenous struggles. *Studies in Ethnicity and Nationalism*, 9:70 – 88.

Molly Lewis and Gary Lupyan. 2020. Gender stereotypes are reflected in the distributional structure of 25 languages. *Nature human behaviour*, 4(10):1021–1028.

Paul Pu Liang, Irene Mengze Li, Emily Zheng, Yao Chong Lim, Ruslan Salakhutdinov, and Louis-Philippe Morency. 2020. Towards debiasing sentence representations. *arXiv preprint arXiv:2007.08100.*

Patrick Littell, Anna Kazantseva, Roland Kuhn, Aidan Pine, Antti Arppe, Christopher Cox, and Marie-Odile Junker. 2018. Indigenous language technologies in canada: Assessment, challenges, and successes. In *Proceedings of the 27th International Conference on Computational Linguistics*, pages 2620–2632.

Ronald Lowe. 1985. *Basic Siglit Inuvialuit Eskimo Grammar*, volume 6. Inuvik, NWT: Committee for Original Peoples Entitlement.

Karen S Lyness and Madeline E Heilman. 2006. When fit is fundamental: performance evaluations and promotions of upper-level female and male managers. *Journal of Applied Psychology*, 91(4):777.

Jeffrey C Micher. 2018. Addressing challenges of machine translation of inuit languages. Technical report, US Army Research Laboratory Adelphi United States.

Marianne Mithun. 2015. Morphological complexity and language contact in languages indigenous to north america. *Linguistic Discovery*, 13(2):37–59.

Rodrigo Alejandro Chávez Mulsa and Gerasimos Spanakis. 2020. Evaluating bias in dutch word embeddings. *arXiv preprint arXiv:2011.00244.*

Eirini Ntoutsi, Pavlos Fafalios, Ujwal Gadiraju, Vasileios Iosifidis, Wolfgang Nejdl, Maria-Esther Vidal, Salvatore Ruggieri, Franco Turini, Symeon Papadopoulos, Emmanouil Krasanakis, et al. 2020. Bias in data-driven artificial intelligence systems—an introductory survey. *Wiley Interdisciplinary Reviews: Data Mining and Knowledge Discovery*, 10(3):e1356.

Shauli Ravfogel, Yanai Elazar, Hila Gonen, Michael Twiton, and Yoav Goldberg. 2020. Null it out: Guarding protected attributes by iterative nullspace projection. In *Proceedings of the 58th Annual Meeting of the Association for Computational Linguistics*, pages 7237–7256, Online. Association for Computational Linguistics.

Rachel Rudinger, Jason Naradowsky, Brian Leonard, and Benjamin Van Durme. 2018. Gender bias in coreference resolution. In *Proceedings of the 2018 Conference of the North American Chapter of the Association for Computational Linguistics: Human*

Language Technologies, Volume 2 (Short Papers), pages 8–14, New Orleans, Louisiana. Association for Computational Linguistics.

Londa Schiebinger. 2014. Scientific research must take gender into account. *Nature*, 507(7490):9–9.

Thalea Schlender and Gerasimos Spanakis. 2020. 'thy algorithm shalt not bear false witness': An evaluation of multiclass debiasing methods on word embeddings. In *Benelux Conference on Artificial Intelligence*, pages 141–156. Springer.

Victoria Shashkina. 2022. Ai bias: Definition, types, examples, and debiasing strategies. *https://itrexgroup.com/blog/ai-bias-definition-types-examples-debiasing-strategies/header*, (1):1.

Karolina Stanczak and Isabelle Augenstein. 2021. A survey on gender bias in natural language processing. *arXiv preprint arXiv:2112.14168*.

Tony Sun, Andrew Gaut, Shirlyn Tang, Yuxin Huang, Mai ElSherief, Jieyu Zhao, Diba Mirza, Elizabeth Belding, Kai-Wei Chang, and William Yang Wang. 2019. Mitigating gender bias in natural language processing: Literature review. *arXiv preprint arXiv:1906.08976*.

Nathaniel Swinger, Maria De-Arteaga, Neil Thomas Heffernan IV, Mark DM Leiserson, and Adam Tauman Kalai. 2019. What are the biases in my word embedding? In *Proceedings of the 2019 AAAI/ACM Conference on AI, Ethics, and Society*, pages 305–311.

Rachael Tatman. 2017. Gender and dialect bias in youtube's automatic captions. In *Proceedings of the first ACL workshop on ethics in natural language processing*, pages 53–59.

Laakkuluk J. Williamson. 2006. Inuit gender parity and why it was not accepted in the nunavut legislature. *Études/Inuit/Studies*, 30(1):51–68.

Jieyu Zhao, Subhabrata Mukherjee, Saghar Hosseini, Kai-Wei Chang, and Ahmed Hassan Awadallah. 2020. Gender bias in multilingual embeddings and cross-lingual transfer. *arXiv preprint arXiv:2005.00699*.

Jieyu Zhao, Tianlu Wang, Mark Yatskar, Vicente Ordonez, and Kai-Wei Chang. 2017. Men also like shopping: Reducing gender bias amplification using corpus-level constraints. *arXiv preprint arXiv:1707.09457*.

What Changed?
Investigating Debiasing Methods using Causal Mediation Analysis

Sullam Jeoung **Jana Diesner**
University of Illinois-Urbana Champaign
{sjeoung2,jdiesner}@illinois.edu

Abstract

Previous work has examined how debiasing language models affect downstream tasks, specifically, how debiasing techniques influence task performance and whether debiased models also make impartial predictions in downstream tasks or not. However, what we don't understand well yet is *why* debiasing methods have varying impacts on downstream tasks and *how* debiasing techniques affect internal components of language models, i.e., neurons, layers, and attentions. In this paper, we decompose the internal mechanisms of debiasing language models with respect to gender by applying causal mediation analysis to understand the influence of debiasing methods on toxicity detection as a downstream task. Our findings suggest a need to test the effectiveness of debiasing methods with different bias metrics, and to focus on changes in the behavior of certain components of the models, e.g.,first two layers of language models, and attention heads.

1 Introduction

Recent work has shown that pre-trained language models encode social biases prevalent in the data they are trained on (May et al., 2019; Nangia et al., 2020; Nadeem et al., 2020). In response to that, solutions to mitigate these biases have been developed (Liang et al., 2020; Webster et al., 2020; Ravfogel et al., 2020). Some recent papers also examined the impact of debiasing methods, e.g., reduction of gender bias, on the performance of downstream tasks, e.g., classification. (Prost et al., 2019; Meade et al., 2021; Babaeianjelodar et al., 2020). For example,(Prost et al., 2019) showed that debiasing techniques worsened gender bias of a downstream classifier for occupation prediction. (Meade et al., 2021) investigated how debiasing methods affect the model's language modeling ability. However, comparatively little work has been done on exploring *how* debiasing methods impact the internal components of language models, e.g., the models neurons, layers, and attention heads, and *what* kind of changes in language models are introduced when debiasing methods are applied to downstream tasks. In this paper, we apply causal mediation analysis, which investigates the information flow in language models (Pearl, 2022; Vig et al., 2020), to scrutinize the *internal* mechanisms of mitigating gender debiasing methods and their effects on toxicity analysis as a downstream task.

We first examine the efficacy of debiasing methods, namely, CDA and Dropout (Webster et al., 2020), on 1) language models, namely, BERT (Wang and Cho, 2019) and GPT2 (Salazar et al., 2019), and 2) models (Jigsaw, and RtGender) (Voigt et al., 2018) fine-tuned for downstream tasks. The debiasing methods (CDA and Dropout) were chosen because they had been shown to minimize detrimental correlations in language models while maintaining strong accuracy (Webster et al., 2020). We then applied causal mediation analysis to understand how internal components of a model are impacted by debiasing methods and fine-tuning.

In this study, we focus on gender bias as a type of bias. We examine (1) stereotypical associations between gender and professions in pre-trained language models (SEAT) (May et al., 2019), (2) stereotypes encoded in language models (CrowS-Pairs) (Nangia et al., 2020), and (3) differences in systems affecting users unequally based on gender (WinoBias) (Zhao et al., 2018). These representational harms can impact people negatively because they contribute to exacerbating stereotypes inherent in society. These harms may also result in unfavorable consequences when these language models are deployed for practical purposes, e.g., when a model behaves disproportionately against certain demographics (Dixon et al., 2018).

1.1 Contributions

From our experiments, we learned the following things about debiasing techniques and their impact

Proceedings of the The 4th Workshop on Gender Bias in Natural Language Processing (GeBNLP), pages 255 - 265
July 15, 2022 ©2022 Association for Computational Linguistics

on language models:

It is recommendable to test the efficacy of debiasing techniques on more than one bias metric. Our results suggest that debiasing methods show effectiveness when measured on some bias measurements. However, this efficacy varies depending on which bias metrics are used to measure the bias of language models. This may due to different definitions and operationalizations of bias in these metrics, which result in varying degree of effectiveness. This suggests that in order to make claims about the generalizability of the effectiveness of debiasing methods, these methods need to be tested on more than one bias metrics.

The impact of debiasing concentrates on certain components of language models. The results from the causal mediation analysis suggest that the neurons located in the first two layers (including the word embedding layers) showed the biggest difference in debiased and fine-tuned models when compared to the baseline model. This suggests two things. First, the detrimental associations between words that cause gender bias in language models may originally be situated in those layers. Second, the role of those layers may be crucial in mitigating gender biases in language models. We recommend future work to focus on those components.

Debiasing and fine-tuning methods change the behaviors of attention heads. Our results show that applying debiasing and fine-tuning methods to language models changes the weight that attention heads assign to gender-associated terms. This indicates that attention heads may play a crucial role in representing gender bias in language models.

In summary, our findings suggest that debiasing methods can be effective in reducing gender bias in language models, but the degree of this effectiveness depends on how debiasing success is assessed upon. Also, the results of the causal mediation analysis suggest that impact of debiasing is concentrated in certain components of the language models. Overall, our findings suggest a need to test the effectiveness of debiasing methods with different bias metrics, and to focus on changes in the behavior of certain components of the models. This work further supports prior research that has shown how making small, systematic improvements to input data and research design can reduce major flaws in research results and policy implications (Hilbert et al., 2019; Kim et al., 2014; Diesner and Carley, 2009; Diesner, 2015) in society, and changes in research results and policy implications, and how improving the quality of lexical resources can increase the prediction accuracy of more and less related downstream tasks (Rezapour et al., 2019).

2 Related Work

2.1 Debiasing methods and their effect on downstream tasks

Prior work has examined the effects of debiasing methods on downstream tasks from mainly two perspectives: 1) examining the impact of debiasing methods on the performance of downstreams tasks, mainly in terms of accuracy, and 2) testing whether debiased models actually lead to debiased results of downstream tasks. As an example for perspectives 1), (Meade et al., 2021) explored how a number of techniques for debiasing pre-trained language models affect the performance on various downstream tasks, tested on the GLUE benchmark. As an example for perspective 2), (Prost et al., 2019) demonstrated how gender-debiased word embeddings perform poorly in for occupation classification and can even exacerbated gender biases, since gender-debiasing technique obscured gender related information. In a similar vein, (Babaeianjelodar et al., 2020) showed how a pre-trained BERT exhibits gender bias when fine-tuned on different corpora. Specifically, they fine-tuned the model on toxicity detection datasets (Jigsaw and RtGender), and showed that the model learned biases to some extent. Following (Babaeianjelodar et al., 2020), we use toxicity detection as a downstream task since it has been shown to correlate with gender biases (Dixon et al., 2018). Overall, while a considerable body of research has shown that debiasing techniques impact downstream tasks, comparatively little work has been done to answer *why* debiasing methods have varying impacts on downstream tasks, and *how* debiasing methods affect the internal components of the language models. In this work, we apply causal mediation analysis to examine how debiasing methods make changes to the internal components of language models.

2.2 Bias Metrics

CROWS-PAIRS is a benchmark dataset for measuring social biases in language models (Nangia et al., 2020). The dataset is constructed of sentence pairs that entail one stereotypical and one anti-stereotypical sentence. This benchmark also measures how a given model prefers stereotypical sentences over anti-stereotypical sentences. For instance, for the 'gender' stereotype, two sentences are given *'The **man** was highly skilled in CAD engineering. **He** was considered one of the best engineers in **his** field (stereotypical)'* and *'The **woman** was highly skilled in CAD engineering. **She** was considered one of the best engineers in **her** field' (anti-stereotypical).* Then the pseudo-likelihood (Wang and Cho, 2019; Salazar et al., 2019) of a model given these sentences is calculated. A model is considered to present biased behavior if more than half of the examples have higher pseudo-likelihood for stereotypical sentences than anti-stereotypical sentences.

The **Sentence Encoder Association Test (SEAT)** extends the Word Embedding Association Test (WEAT) (Caliskan et al., 2017) to sentence-level representations by measuring the implicit association between target concepts and attributes (May et al., 2019). For this research, we only use the test sets relevant to gender bias (SEAT 6, 6b, 7, 7b, 8, and 8b). Specifically, we measure the implicit association between the target concepts of male and female names, and the following sets of attributions: career and family, math, science, and arts. The attribute sentences of a **family** and **career**, for instance, are respectively {'This is a home', 'They are parents'...} and {'This is an executive', 'This is a corporation...}. The target sentences of **Male Names** and **Female Names** are {This is John, That is John, Kevin is here ...} and {This is Amy, This is Sarah, Diana is here..}. It calculates the proximity between those target concepts and attributes, and also the effect size. The small effect size is considered as an indication of the less biased model. See (May et al., 2019) for details of calculating these associations.

2.3 Debiasing Methods

Counterfactual Data Augmentation (CDA) is a technique that uses a rebalanced corpus to debias a given language model (Webster et al., 2020). For example, the sentence '**Her** most significant piece of work is considered to be **her** study of the development of the.. ' from the Wikipedia dataset was rebalanced into '**His** most significant piece of work is considered to be **his** study of the development of the..'. (Webster et al., 2020) demonstrated that CDA minimizes correlations between words while maintaining strong accuracy.

Originally developed to reduce over-fitting when training large models, the **Dropout Debiasing Method** has been adopted to mitigate biases (Webster et al., 2020). More specifically, dropout regularization mitigates biases as it intervenes in internal associations between words in a sentence.

2.4 Causal Mediation Analysis

We chose to apply causal mediation analysis to inspect the change in output following a counterfactual intervention in intermediate components (e.g., neurons, layers, attentions)(Pearl, 2022; Vig et al., 2020). Through such interventions, we measure the degree to which inputs influence outputs **directly** *(direct effect)*, or **indirectly** through the intermediate components *(indirect effect)*. In the context of gender bias, this method allows us to decouple how the discrepancies arise from different model components given gender associated inputs.

Following (Vig et al., 2020), we define the measurement of gender bias as

$$y(u) = \frac{p_\theta(\text{anti-stereotypical}|u)}{p_\theta(\text{stereotypical}|u)}$$

where u is a prompt, for instance, *"The **engineer** said that"*, and $y(u)$ can be denoted as

$$y(u) = \frac{p_\theta(\textbf{she} \mid \text{The engineer said that })}{p_\theta(\textbf{he} \mid \text{The engineer said that })}$$

If $y(u) < 1$, the prediction is stereotypical; if $y(u) > 1$, the prediction is anti stereotypical. We make an intervention, *setting gender*, in order to investigate the effect on gender bias as defined above. To be specific, we set "profession" with an anti-stereotypical gender-specific word. For instance, "The **engineer** said that" to "The **woman** said that". We define the measure of y under the intervention $\mathbf{x} = x$ on template $\mathbf{u} = u$ as $y_x(u)$

Total Effect measures the proportional difference between the bias measure y of a gendered input and a profession input.

$$\text{Total Effect(set-gender, null; } y) = \frac{y_{\text{set-gender}}(u) - y_{\text{null}}(u)}{y_{null}(u)} \quad (1)$$

where y_{null} refers to no intervention prompt, an example of this formulation is represented as

$$y_{\text{set-gender}}(u) = \frac{p(\text{she} \mid \text{The woman said that})}{p(\text{he} \mid \text{The woman said that}}$$

$$y_{\text{null}}(u) = \frac{p(\text{she I The engineer said that})}{p(\text{he I The engineer said that})}$$

We average the total effect of each prompt u to analyze the total effect.

Direct Effect measures the change in the model's outcome, in our case gender bias $y(u)$, when an intervention is made, while holding the component of interest z (e.g. specific neuron, attention heads, layers) fixed to the original value. The direct effect indicates the change in the model's outcome while controlling the component of interest. Here, we apply a *set-gender* intervention, as explained above.

Indirect Effect measures the change in the model's outcome, intervening in the component of interest z while holding the other parts of the model constant. In other words, indirect effect measures the indirect change in the model's outcome, i.e., the gender bias $y(u)$ that arises from the component of interest z.

3 Experimental Setup

Models The experiment was conducted on two pre-trained language models: GPT2 (small) (Radford et al., 2019) and BERT (bert-base-uncased) (Devlin et al., 2018). The configuration of the debiasing models is detailed below.

CDA WikiText-2 (Merity et al., 2016), and the gendered word pairs [1] proposed by (Zhao et al., 2018) is used in the pre-training phase.

Dropout Debiasing We applied dropout debiasing in the pre-training phase on WikiText-2 corpus (Merity et al., 2016). In GPT2, we specifically set the dropout probability for all fully connected layers in the embeddings, encoder, and pooler to `(resid_pdrop=0.15)`, the dropout ratio for the embeddings to `(embedding_pdrop=0.15)`, and the dropout ratio for the attention `(attn_pdrop)` to 0.15. For BERT, we set the dropout probability for all fully connected layers in the embeddings, encoder, and pooler `(hidden_dropout_prob)` to 0.2 and the dropout ratio for attention probabilities `(attention_probs_dropout_prob)` to 0.15, following (Meade et al., 2021)

[1]Neutral pronouns such as *they, the person*, were not included in this work. The direction of future research is to include the neutral pronouns

Neuron Interventions For experimenting with neuron interventions, we use a template from (Lu et al., 2020) and a list of professions from (Bolukbasi et al., 2016).The template has a format of 'The [profession][verb](because/that)'. Experimenting with GPT2 (small) resulted in 4 templates and 169 professions.

Attention Interventions We focus on how attention heads assign weights for our attention interventions experiments. Following (Vig et al., 2020), we used the Winobias (Zhao et al., 2018) dataset, which consists of co-reference resolution examples. As opposed to calculating the probability of pronouns (e.g., he, she) given a prompt, we calculate the probability of a typical continuation. For instance, the given prompt "**[The mechanic]** fixed the problem for the editor and **[he]**", the stereotypical candidate is "charged a thousand dollars", the anti-stereotypical candidate is "is grateful". The stereotypical candidate associates 'he' with the mechanic, while the anti-stereotypical candidate associates 'he' with the 'editor'. We calculate the $y(u)$, gender bias, given an prompt u, as

$$y(u) = \frac{p_\theta(\text{charged a thousand dollars I u})}{p_\theta(\text{is grateful I u})}$$

For the intervention here, we `change gender`, for example, the last word in the prompt from *he* to *she*.

Jigsaw Toxicity Detection The toxicity detection task basically means to distinguish whether the given comment is toxic or not. The publicly available corpus can be found at Kaggle[2]. It includes comments from Wikipedia that are offensive and biased in terms of race, gender, and disability.

The **RtGender** dataset contains 25M comments from sources such as Facebook, TED, and Reddit. The dataset was developed by (Voigt et al., 2018). Specifically, the posts are labeled with the gender of the author. The responses to posts were also collected. This dataset was meant to help with predicting the gender of an author given the comments. This allows us to investigate gender biases in social media.

[2]https://www.kaggle.com/c/jigsaw- unintended- bias- in-toxicity- classification

Finetune	-			Jigsaw			RtGender		
Method	Baseline (None)	CDA	Dropout	None	CDA	Dropout	None	CDA	Dropout
BERT	57.25	55.34	55.73	51.91	42.37	48.09	56.11	47.71	41.98
GPT2	56.87	54.96	57.63	47.71	50.00	52.67	46.18	51.53	47.33

Table 1: Stereotype scores tested on Crow-S. The lower the value, the more debiased the model is. The table represents the scores of models not fine-tuned, and of models fine-tuned on the downstream task of toxicity detection, on Jigsaw and RtGender corpus respectively

Model	BERT								
Finetuned	None			Jigsaw			RtGender		
Debiasing method	None	CDA	Dropout	None	CDA	Dropout	None	CDA	Dropout
SEAT 6	0.931*	0.785*	0.889*	0.558*	0.597*	0.515*	-0.268	1.963*	0.912*
SEAT 6b	0.089	0.083	0.277	0.169	-0.104	0.400*	0.227	1.895*	0.391*
SEAT 7	-0.124	-0.512	0.171	1.035*	-0.626	1.223*	0.060	0.396*	0.351
SEAT 7b	0.936*	1.238*	0.849*	0.711*	0.663*	1.135*	-0.085	0.506*	0.310
SEAT 8	0.782*	0.025	0.594*	0.539*	-0.729	0.551*	-0.091	0.786*	0.930*
SEAT 8b	0.858*	0.673*	0.945*	0.286	0.586*	0.600*	-0.205	0.817*	0.929*
Model	GPT2								
SEAT 6	0.137	0.287	0.288	0.451*	0.029	0.667*	1.359*	1.516*	1.554*
SEAT 6b	0.003	0.012	0.032	0.554*	0.247	0.418*	0.893*	1.242*	0.976*
SEAT 7	-0.023	0.862*	0.850*	0.129	0.700*	0.751*	1.044*	-0.337	0.693*
SEAT 7b	0.001	0.933*	0.819*	0.645*	1.172*	1.041*	1.060*	-0.205	1.017*
SEAT 8	-0.223	0.501*	0.486*	-0.057	0.545*	0.321	0.867*	-0.213	0.700*
SEAT 8b	-0.286	0.278	0.092	0.059	0.222	0.197	0.783*	-0.288	0.984*

Table 2: The effect size of SEAT. The small effect size is an indication of the less biased model. * denotes the significance of p-value<0.01

4 Results

4.1 Testing the efficacy of debiasing techniques

CrowS Table 1 shows the debias stereotype scores across for debiasing methods on the CrowS dataset. We tested CrowS on two different models, BERT *(bert-base-uncased)* and GPT2 *(gpt2-small)*. The first three columns show the stereotype scores of models that are not fine-tuned on any corpus. We consider these models as baseline models. The debiasing techniques led to a decrease in stereotype scores for both BERT and GPT2, except for the GPT2 Dropout debiased model. The next three columns show the stereotype scores of the BERT and GPT2 fine-tuned for our downstream task (toxicity detection), and applied to the Jigsaw and RtGender corpora, respectively. Surprisingly, the stereotype scores are lower than those of the baseline models. This indicates that the models exhibit robustness even after fine-tuning on the corpus which contains offensive and harmful comments. In fact, the results confirm the findings in (Webster et al., 2020), where CDA and Dropout debiasing methods showed *resilience* to fine-tuning. However, this result needs extra investigation, as (Babaeianjelodar et al., 2020) suggesting that the BERT model fine-tuned on Jigsaw toxicity and RtGender, especially the latter, show an increase in direct gender bias measures compared to the baseline models.

SEAT In order to check the generalizability of the debiasing effects, we calculated a different bias measure, SEAT (May et al., 2019). Table 2 shows the effect size of SEAT. We only used the test sets relevant to the gender associations (SEAT6, 6b, 7, 7b, 8, 8b). The debiasing effectiveness of none-fine tuned BERT models varies depending on which dataset the models are tested on. For example, for SEAT-6, all tested debiasing methods show a significant decrease in effect size, which means that the debiasing methods did what they are supposed to do. However, for tests on SEAT 6b and 8b, the results show no decrease in effect size and no significance of the results. Interestingly, the degree

Model	BERT			GPT2		
Methods	None	CDA	Dropout	None	CDA	Dropout
Jigsaw	0.944	0.919	**0.949**	0.950	0.929	0.947
RtGender	0.570	**0.747**	0.558	0.698	**0.716**	0.703

Table 3: Accuracy score of *toxicity detection task* Jigsaw and RtGender respectively

	Baseline	CDA	Dropout	Jigsaw	Jigsaw CDA	Jigsaw Dropout
Total effect	2.865	2.046	1.858	0.122	0.116	0.092
Male total effect	3.964	2.792	2.514	0.122	0.116	0.092
Female total effect	30.227	25.953	23.550	0.752	0.979	0.502

Table 4: Total effect statistics.

of effectiveness varies based on which corpus a model is fine-tuned. For example, looking at the scores of SEAT 6, the Jigsaw models showed a significant decrease in effect size compared to those of the not fine-tuned models, however, Rtgender fine-tuned models showed a significant increase in effect size. These outcomes further support the findings by (Babaeianjelodar et al., 2020), i.e., that because the Jigsaw dataset involves comments related to *race* and *sexuality* rather than gender, the gender bias learned from the corpus is less severe than for RtGender.

The results are less clear for GPT2. Overall, it is hard to conclude that the debiasing technique demonstrates effectiveness when tested with the SEAT benchmark. Looking only at the results that show significance (p-value<0.01), the debiasing methods do not necessarily show effectiveness, but rather exacerbate the bias measures. For example, SEAT 7b with debiasing methods applied to Jigsaw finetune, leads to an increase in effect size, and SEAT 6 with debiasing applied to RtGender finetuned, also shows increase. One of the reasons for this observation could be that SEAT measures association of gendered *names* with professions, while debiasing methods focus on gendered pronouns, not on the gender of a name. Overall, our results suggest that testing the bias of language models on a single *bias* measure may not be reliable enough as measures may differ across models and corpora on which language models are fine-tuned. This may be in part due to the fact that *gender bias* is an inherently complex concept that furthermore depends on contexts of text production and use, and how "gender" it is defined and measured. Thus, evaluation on two or more benchmark datasets is desirable.

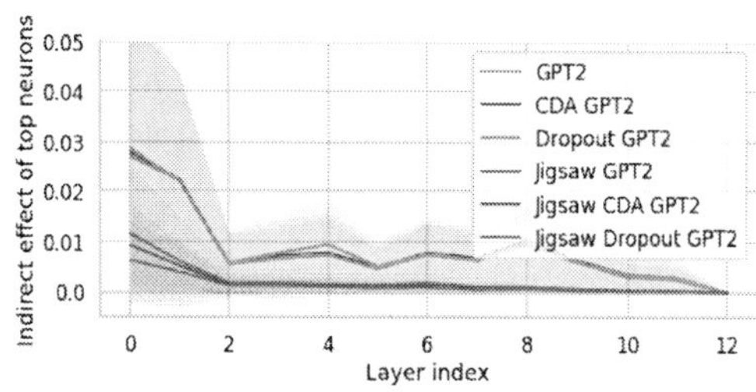

Figure 1: The indirect effect of the top neurons by layer index.

Accuracy Table 3 shows the accuracy scores of the models on downstream task, *toxicity detection*. Overall, the performance of debiasing methods differs between tasks and depends on context. This supports the findings in (Meade et al., 2021). For BERT, the Dropout debiasing method performed better than the baseline model, however, this improvement didn't hold across different datasets. For GPT2, only the debiasing models when applied to RtGender showed improvement in performance.

4.2 Causal Mediation Analysis

Total Effect Table 4 shows the total effect across models. Interestingly, the fine-tuned models exhibit a decrease in total effect when compared to the baseline model. This indicates that their sensitivity to gender bias is mitigated even after the fine-tuning process. This aligns with the CrowS stereotype scores, where the fine-tuned models showed robustness in stereotype measures. Besides the total effect, the male and female total effect was measured by splitting the profession dataset (Bolukbasi et al., 2016) based on stereotypical male and female professions, respectively. The

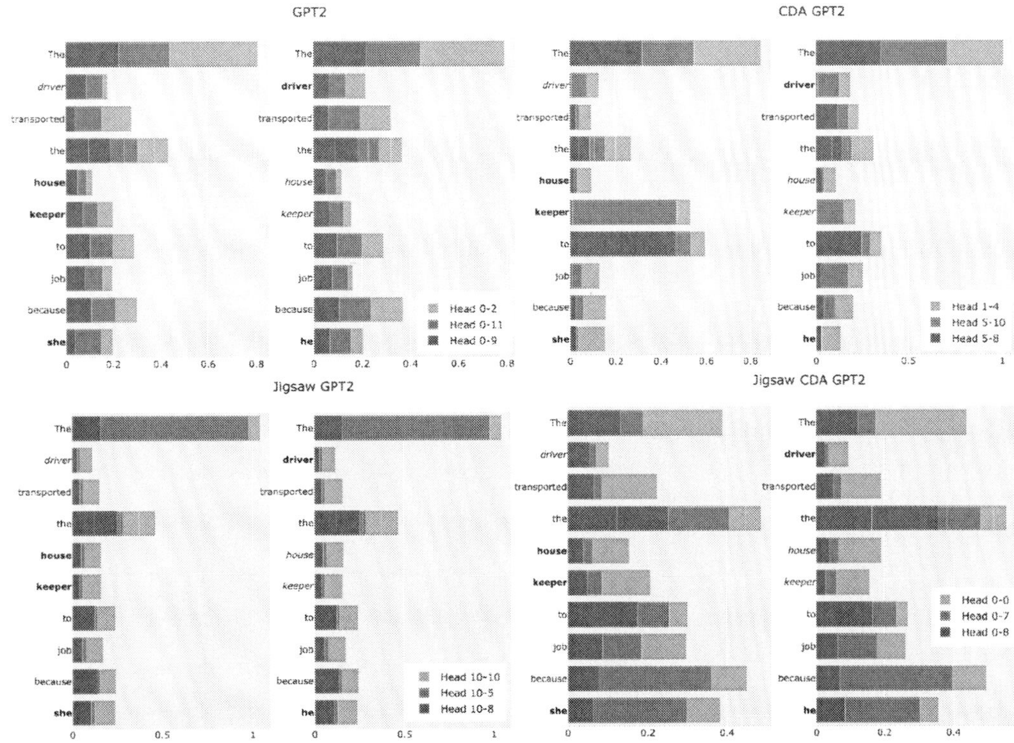

Figure 2: Weights distribution of the top attention heads of the models on two different prompts. The labels indicate the layer-attention head index. For example, Head 0-2 refers to attention head index 2, in layer 0.

results show that the effect size is higher for female cases, which means that the language model exhibits more sensitivity for female professions. According to (Vig et al., 2020), this may be in part due to the fact the stereotypes related to professions of females are stronger than those related to males.

Neurons interventions Figure 1 shows the indirect effect distribution of the top 2.5% of the neurons. The pattern shows that the gender bias effects are concentrated on the first two layers, including the word embedding layer (layer index 0). Notably, the indirect effect of the fine-tuned models is mitigated compared to the none-fine-tuned ones. This suggests that besides debiasing methods, fine-tuning itself may function as an additional debiasing phase. Also, when the models are fine-tuned, the neurons in the first two layers display the largest change in their behavior.

Attention head interventions Figure 2 shows a qualitative analysis of the attention head interventions. The figure presents the distribution of the attention weights of the top 3 attention heads, given the two different sentences 'The driver transported the **housekeeper** to job because **she**' and 'The **driver** transported the housekeeper to job because **he**'. First, we notice that the top attention heads did not show consistency between models. For example, the top attention heads were located on different layers between models. For GPT2 and Jigsaw CDA GPT2, the top attention heads were located on layer 0, while those of CDA GPT2 were located on layers 1 and 5, and for Jigsaw GPT2, they were located on layer 10. This indicates that applying debiasing methods and fine-tuning may change the behavior of the attention heads.

Second, the debiased models (e.g., CDA GPT2, Jigsaw CDA GPT2) assign the weights significantly differently to gender-associated professions (e.g., driver, housekeeper). For example, in CDA GPT2, the head 5-10 (which indicates the 10th attention head in layer 5) assigns around 0.5 to the word 'keeper' in the first plot, while it attends around 0.2 to that of the second plot. The head 5-10 in CDA GPT2 also attends around 0.1 to the word 'driver' in the first plot, while assigning more than 0.1 to the 'driver' in the second plot. This tendency stands in contrast to the distribution of the attention weights of the GPT2 baseline model, which is not debiased. Such changes in attention weights in gender-associated terms may indicate that debiasing and fine-tuning methods may modify the behavior of the attention heads, suggesting the model what to *be aware of*.

5 Conclusion

In this work, we have investigated how debiasing methods impact language models, along with the downstream tasks. We found that (1) debiasing methods are robust after fine-tuning on downstream tasks. In fact, after the fine-tuning, the debiasing effects strengthened. However, this effect is not supported across another bias measure. This indicates the need for both debiasing techniques and bias benchmarks to ensure generalizability. The causal mediation analysis suggests that (2) The neurons that showed a large change in behavior were located in the first two layers of language models (including the word embedding layers). This suggests that careful inspection of certain components of the language models is recommended when applying debiasing methods. (3) Applying debiasing and fine-tuning methods to language models changes the weight that attention heads assign to gender-associated terms. This indicates that attention heads may play a crucial role in representing gender bias in language models.

Several limitations apply to this work. We only tested these effects on one downstream task, namely, toxicity detection. In order to check the generalizability of these findings, experiments with other downstream tasks are necessary.

References

Marzieh Babaeianjelodar, Stephen Lorenz, Josh Gordon, Jeanna Matthews, and Evan Freitag. 2020. Quantifying gender bias in different corpora. In *Companion Proceedings of the Web Conference 2020*, pages 752–759.

Tolga Bolukbasi, Kai-Wei Chang, James Y Zou, Venkatesh Saligrama, and Adam T Kalai. 2016. Man is to computer programmer as woman is to homemaker? debiasing word embeddings. *Advances in neural information processing systems*, 29.

Aylin Caliskan, Joanna J Bryson, and Arvind Narayanan. 2017. Semantics derived automatically from language corpora contain human-like biases. *Science*, 356(6334):183–186.

Jacob Devlin, Ming-Wei Chang, Kenton Lee, and Kristina Toutanova. 2018. Bert: Pre-training of deep bidirectional transformers for language understanding. *arXiv preprint arXiv:1810.04805*.

Jana Diesner. 2015. Small decisions with big impact on data analytics. *Big Data & Society*, 2(2):2053951715617185.

Jana Diesner and Kathleen M Carley. 2009. He says, she says. pat says, tricia says. how much reference resolution matters for entity extraction, relation extraction, and social network analysis. In *2009 IEEE Symposium on Computational Intelligence for Security and Defense Applications*, pages 1–8. IEEE.

Lucas Dixon, John Li, Jeffrey Sorensen, Nithum Thain, and Lucy Vasserman. 2018. Measuring and mitigating unintended bias in text classification. In *Proceedings of the 2018 AAAI/ACM Conference on AI, Ethics, and Society*, pages 67–73.

Martin Hilbert, George Barnett, Joshua Blumenstock, Noshir Contractor, Jana Diesner, Seth Frey, Sandra Gonzalez-Bailon, PJ Lamberso, Jennifer Pan, Tai-Quan Peng, et al. 2019. Computational communication science: A methodological catalyzer for a maturing discipline.

Jinseok Kim, Heejun Kim, and Jana Diesner. 2014. The impact of name ambiguity on properties of coauthorship networks. *Journal of Information Science Theory and Practice*, 2(2):6–15.

Paul Pu Liang, Irene Mengze Li, Emily Zheng, Yao Chong Lim, Ruslan Salakhutdinov, and Louis-Philippe Morency. 2020. Towards debiasing sentence representations. *arXiv preprint arXiv:2007.08100*.

Kaiji Lu, Piotr Mardziel, Fangjing Wu, Preetam Amancharla, and Anupam Datta. 2020. Gender bias in neural natural language processing. In *Logic, Language, and Security*, pages 189–202. Springer.

Chandler May, Alex Wang, Shikha Bordia, Samuel R Bowman, and Rachel Rudinger. 2019. On measuring social biases in sentence encoders. *arXiv preprint arXiv:1903.10561*.

Nicholas Meade, Elinor Poole-Dayan, and Siva Reddy. 2021. An empirical survey of the effectiveness of debiasing techniques for pre-trained language models. *arXiv preprint arXiv:2110.08527*.

Stephen Merity, Caiming Xiong, James Bradbury, and Richard Socher. 2016. Pointer sentinel mixture models. *arXiv preprint arXiv:1609.07843*.

Moin Nadeem, Anna Bethke, and Siva Reddy. 2020. Stereoset: Measuring stereotypical bias in pretrained language models. *arXiv preprint arXiv:2004.09456*.

Nikita Nangia, Clara Vania, Rasika Bhalerao, and Samuel R Bowman. 2020. Crows-pairs: A challenge dataset for measuring social biases in masked language models. *arXiv preprint arXiv:2010.00133*.

Judea Pearl. 2022. Direct and indirect effects. In *Probabilistic and Causal Inference: The Works of Judea Pearl*, pages 373–392.

Flavien Prost, Nithum Thain, and Tolga Bolukbasi. 2019. Debiasing embeddings for reduced gender bias in text classification. *arXiv preprint arXiv:1908.02810*.

Alec Radford, Jeffrey Wu, Rewon Child, David Luan, Dario Amodei, Ilya Sutskever, et al. 2019. Language models are unsupervised multitask learners. *OpenAI blog*, 1(8):9.

Shauli Ravfogel, Yanai Elazar, Hila Gonen, Michael Twiton, and Yoav Goldberg. 2020. Null it out: Guarding protected attributes by iterative nullspace projection. *arXiv preprint arXiv:2004.07667*.

Rezvaneh Rezapour, Saumil H Shah, and Jana Diesner. 2019. Enhancing the measurement of social effects by capturing morality. In *Proceedings of the tenth workshop on computational approaches to subjectivity, sentiment and social media analysis*, pages 35–45.

Julian Salazar, Davis Liang, Toan Q Nguyen, and Katrin Kirchhoff. 2019. Masked language model scoring. *arXiv preprint arXiv:1910.14659*.

Jesse Vig, Sebastian Gehrmann, Yonatan Belinkov, Sharon Qian, Daniel Nevo, Yaron Singer, and Stuart Shieber. 2020. Investigating gender bias in language models using causal mediation analysis. *Advances in Neural Information Processing Systems*, 33:12388–12401.

Rob Voigt, David Jurgens, Vinodkumar Prabhakaran, Dan Jurafsky, and Yulia Tsvetkov. 2018. Rtgender: A corpus for studying differential responses to gender. In *Proceedings of the Eleventh International Conference on Language Resources and Evaluation (LREC 2018)*.

Alex Wang and Kyunghyun Cho. 2019. Bert has a mouth, and it must speak: Bert as a markov random field language model. *arXiv preprint arXiv:1902.04094*.

Kellie Webster, Xuezhi Wang, Ian Tenney, Alex Beutel, Emily Pitler, Ellie Pavlick, Jilin Chen, Ed Chi, and Slav Petrov. 2020. Measuring and reducing gendered correlations in pre-trained models. *arXiv preprint arXiv:2010.06032*.

Jieyu Zhao, Tianlu Wang, Mark Yatskar, Vicente Ordonez, and Kai-Wei Chang. 2018. Gender bias in coreference resolution: Evaluation and debiasing methods. *arXiv preprint arXiv:1804.06876*.

A Appendix

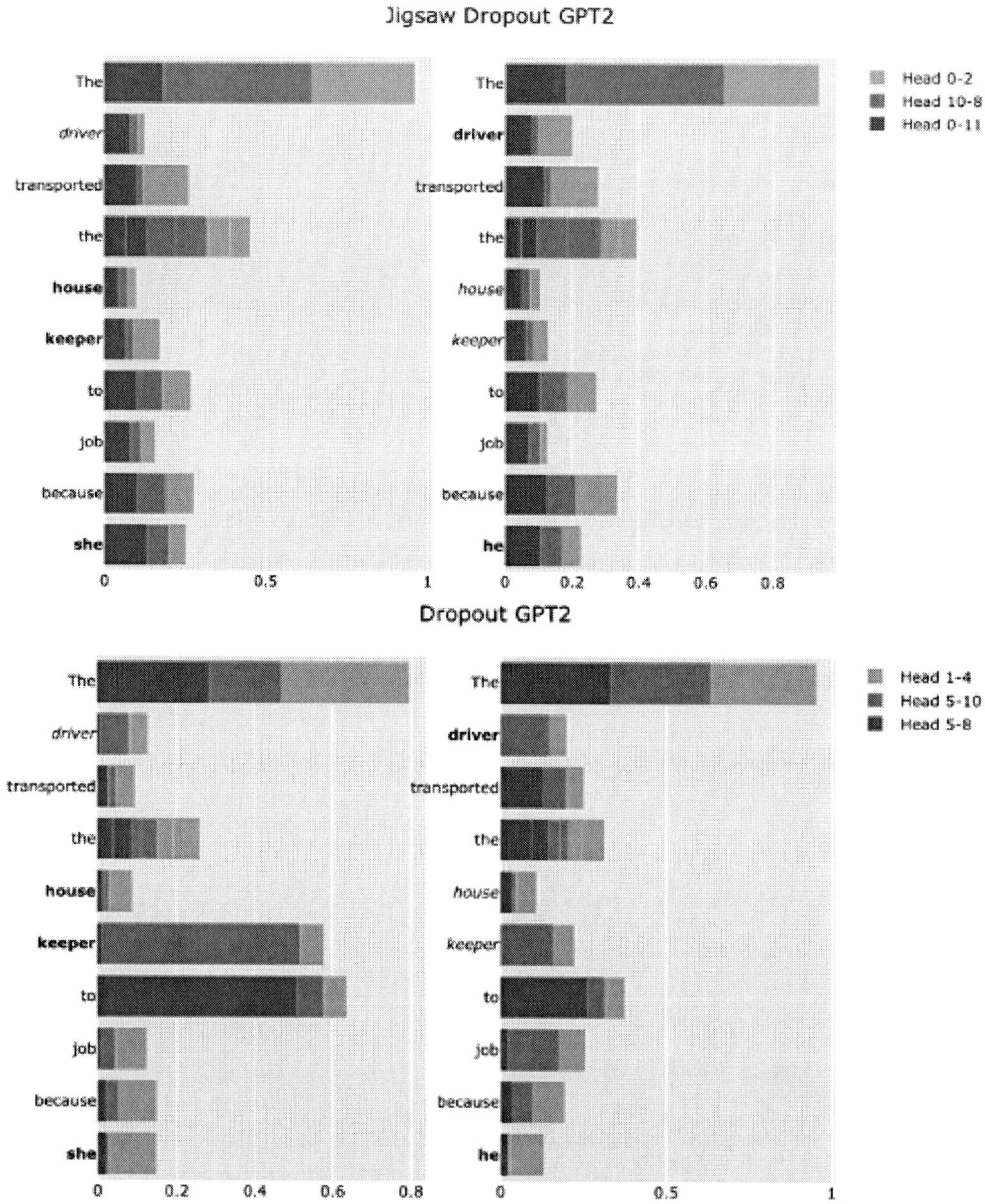

Figure 3: Attention weights of Dropout debiased models

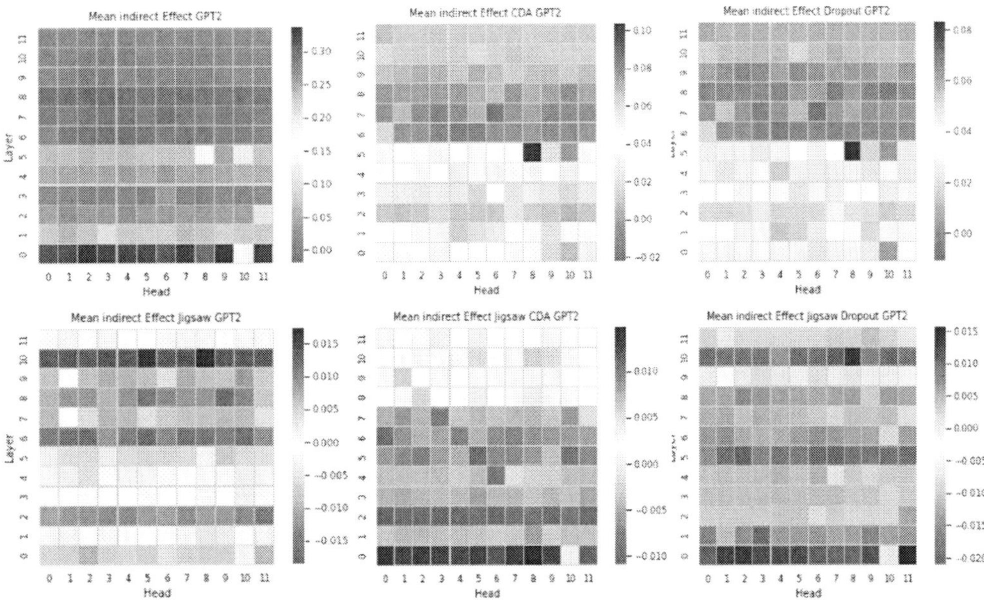

Figure 4: Main indirect Effect of attention intervention.

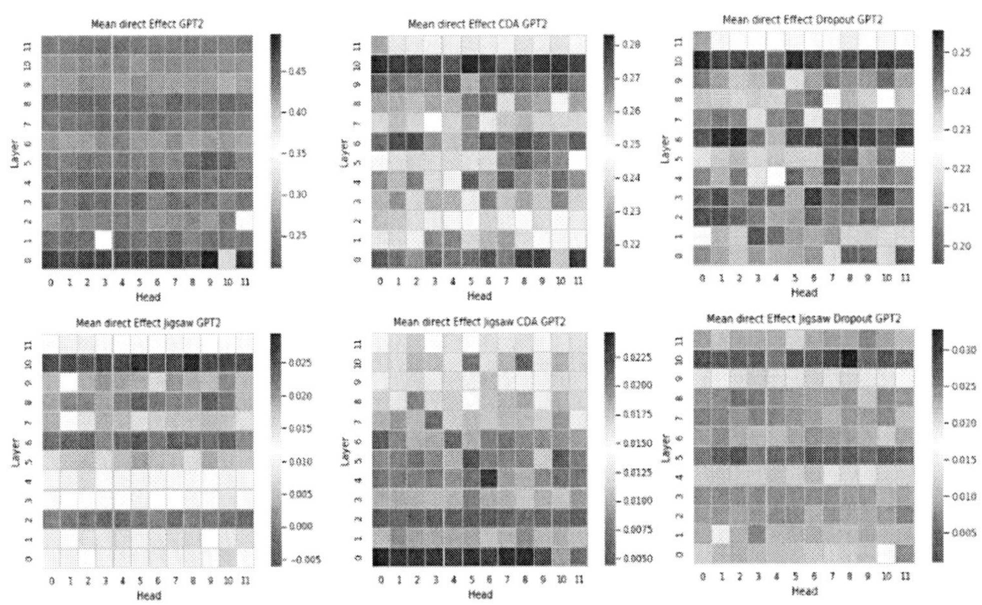

Figure 5: Main direct Effect of Attention Intervention

Why Knowledge Distillation Amplifies Gender Bias and How to Mitigate - from the Perspective of DistilBERT

Jaimeen Ahn[*,†] Danggeun Market Inc.

Hwaran Lee Naver AI LAB

Jinhwa Kim Naver AI LAB

Alice Oh KAIST

Abstract

Knowledge distillation is widely used to transfer the language understanding of a large model to a smaller model. However, after knowledge distillation, it was found that the smaller model is more biased by gender compared to the source large model. This paper studies what causes gender bias to increase after the knowledge distillation process. Moreover, we suggest applying a variant of the mixup on knowledge distillation, which is used to increase generalizability during the distillation process, not for augmentation. By doing so, we can significantly reduce the gender bias amplification after knowledge distillation. We also conduct an experiment on the GLUE benchmark to demonstrate that even if the mixup is applied, it does not have a significant adverse effect on the model's performance.

1 Introduction

Knowledge distillation (Hinton et al., 2015) is one way to use the knowledge of a large language model under the limited resources by transferring the knowledge of a larger model to a smaller model. Under the supervision of the teacher model, the small model is trained to produce the same result as that of the teacher model. By doing so, small models can leverage the knowledge of larger models (Sanh et al., 2019).

To maintain the performance of the model trained by knowledge distillation, the distilled model focuses more on the majority appearing in the data (Hooker et al., 2020). Recent studies have described that pre-trained language model also results in a more biased representation when distillation proceeds (Silva et al., 2021). However, only the issue is reported, and what part of knowledge distillation causes an increase in bias is not explored, and no solution is provided.

[*] jaime@daangn.com

[†] This is work done during an internship in Naver CLOVA AI LAB.

This paper studies which part of knowledge distillation causes the increase of social bias and how to alleviate the problem in terms of DistilBERT (Sanh et al., 2019). We first examine what part that contributes to knowledge distillation brings social bias amplification. There is no difference between the distilled and original models except for size and training loss. Thus, we check from two perspectives: (1) the capacity of the model being distilled and (2) the loss used in knowledge distillation. Then we suggest leveraging *mixup* (Zhang et al., 2018) on the knowledge distillation loss to mitigate this amplification by giving generalizability during the training.

We conduct the experiments from two measurements: social bias with the Sentence Embedding Test (SEAT) (May et al., 2019) and downstream task performance with the GLUE Benchmark (Wang et al., 2019). We report that the factors that increase the social bias are the student model's limited capacity and the cross-entropy loss term between the logit distribution of the student model and that of the teacher model. We also demonstrate that applying the *mixup* to knowledge distillation can reduce this increase without significant effect on the downstream task performance.

Our contributions can be summarized as follows:

- We reveal the capacity of the model and cross-entropy loss in knowledge distillation have a negative effect on social bias.
- We suggest mixup as a mitigation technique if it is applied during the knowledge distillation proceeds.

2 Background

Knowledge distillation is trained so that a student model outputs the same output as a teacher model's for one input. It makes the student model have the problem-solving ability of the large model, even though the student model has a smaller structure.

Proceedings of the The 4th Workshop on Gender Bias in Natural Language Processing (GeBNLP), pages 266 - 272
July 15, 2022 ©2022 Association for Computational Linguistics

DistilBERT, the model this study is mainly about, is trained with three loss terms. First, cross-entropy loss (L_{ce}) forces the logit distribution between the student model and the teacher model to be similar. Next, the student model learns language understanding itself with masked language modeling loss (L_{mlm}). Lastly, cosine loss between two model's output (L_{cos}) makes the direction of output embeddings between the student model and the teacher model closer (Sanh et al., 2019). In total, the loss term of DistilBERT is as follows:

$$\text{Loss} = L_{ce} + L_{mlm} + L_{cos}.$$

3 Bias Statement

In this paper, we investigate stereotypical associations between male and female gender and attribute pairs, particularly from the perspective of sentence embeddings in knowledge distillation language models. For the attribute pairs, we consider Careers and Family, Math and Arts, and Science and Arts. If there exists a correlation between a certain gender and an attribute, the language model intrinsically and perpetually causes representational harm (Blodgett et al., 2020) through improper preconceptions. Additionally, when the language model is trained for other downstream tasks, such as occupation prediction (De-Arteaga et al., 2019; McGuire et al., 2021), it may lead to an additional risk of gender-stereotyped biases.

Since knowledge distillation (KD) has become a prevalent technique to efficiently train smaller models, it is vital to figure out to what extent the gender biases are amplified after knowledge distillations and which loss terms exacerbate the biases during the training. Our work firstly conducts the in-depth analysis and then proposes mitigation methods for the gender bias amplification during the KD process.

We measure the streotypical associations with the Sentence Embedding Association Test (SEAT) (May et al., 2019) [1]. The SEAT uses semantically bleached sentence templates such as "This is a [attribute-word]" or "Here is [gender-word]". Then the associations between a gender and an attribute are calculated by cosine similarities of sentence encoded embeddings. We leave the detailed equations to calculate the SEAT scores in Appendix B.

There are several tests in SEAT. This study focuses on C6, C7, and C8 categories related to gender bias. C6 tests similarity between embedding of Male/Female Names, and Career/Family attribute words. C7 and C8 measure the similarity between embeddings of male and female pronouns and embeddings of Math/Arts related words and Math/Science related words, respectively.

[1]https://github.com/W4ngatang/sent-bias/

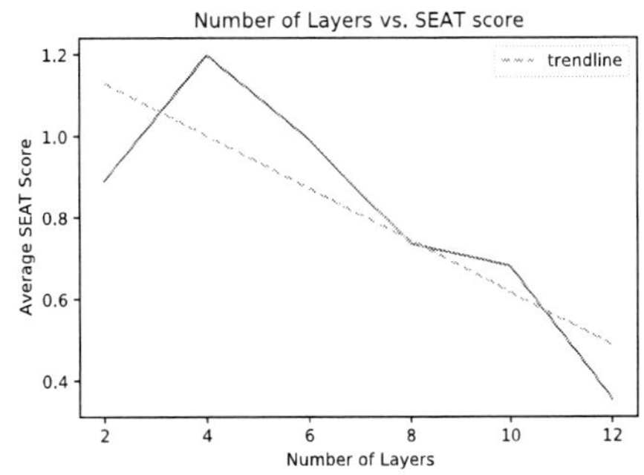

Figure 1: SEAT score by adjusting the number of layers of DistillBERT. The SEAT score and the number of layers in DistillBERT are negatively correlated (Pearson $r = -0.82$).

4 Gender Bias Amplification after KD

In this section, we conduct in-depth analyses about what brings gender bias amplification after knowledge distillation from the perspective of (1) the student model's capacity and (2) the loss used in the knowledge distillation process.

4.1 Experimental Setup

We use 30% of the corpus constructed by two datasets, the Wikipedia dataset and Bookcorpus (Zhu et al., 2015) dataset that were used to create DistillBERT[2]. The distillation is trained for three epochs using four V100 GPUs. All other settings remain the same following the way DistilBERT is trained. We list the settings in Appendix D.

4.2 Does the capacity of the student model matter?

To figure out whether and to what extent the student model's parameter capacity affects the gender biases, we varied the number of layers of the student model (DistilBERT). Note that BERT and DistilBERT have the same architecture parameters except the number of layers. Figure 1 shows

[2]We check the DistilBERT with 30% of the corpus preserves 98.73% of the performance of DistilBERT with the entire dataset on GLUE.

SEAT	Loss Term		
	$L_{\text{mlm}} + L_{\text{cos}} + L_{\text{ce}}$	$L_{\text{mlm}} + L_{\text{ce}}$	$L_{\text{mlm}} + L_{\text{cos}}$
C6	1.236	1.137	**1.093**
C6b	0.499	0.557	**0.292**
C7	**0.907**	1.041	1.153
C7b	1.428	1.316	**0.139**
C8	0.534	**0.475**	0.852
C8b	1.347	1.237	**0.653**
Avg.	0.992	0.960	**0.670**
GLUE Avg.	**76.7**	76.3	75.2

Table 1: SEAT and GLUE scores obtained by ablation of each part in distillation loss. C6 is tested with the names and C7 and C8 are gender pronouns. Thus, for each test, C6b is tested with a gender pronoun, and C7 and C8 are also tested with names.

that the average SEAT scores are increasing as the number of layers is decreasing. Quantitatively, the number of layers has a strong negative correlation with the SEAT score (Pearson $r = -0.82$), which means that the smaller the capacity, the more severe the gender bias. This result also aligns with the previous study that reveals the models with limited capacity tend to exploit the biases in the dataset (Sanh et al., 2021).

4.3 Does the knowledge distillation process matter itself?

To ascertain how each loss term contributes to the increase in SEAT scores in the knowledge distillation process, we conducted an ablation study against each loss term. As shown in Table 1, the model trained without the distillation loss L_{ce} results in the lowest average SEAT score (0.670) among the three loss functions. However, this model shows the lowest performance (75.2%) in the GLUE benchmark, whereas the model trained with all loss terms results the best with 76.7%. This implies that the transfer of the teacher's knowledge is helpful for general language understanding tasks while exacerbating gender bias simultaneously. Consequently, it can be concluded that the current knowledge distillation technique itself is also a factor in increasing gender biases.

5 Mitigation of Bias Amplification

5.1 Proposed method

This section describes how to improve the distillation process to make gender bias not amplified even after knowledge distillation. We found two causes (capacity, loss term) in the previous section. Among them, we decide to modify the loss term because this study is targeting the fixed size model, DistillBERT.

According to the ablation study in Section 4.3, we ascertain distillation loss (L_{ce}) hurts gender bias scores in a huge portion. Our intuition to alleviate this amplification is to give supervision as fair as possible during the knowledge distillation is proceeded. One way is to reduce the SEAT score of the teacher model first and give its supervision to the student model. However, most of the existing methods (Liang et al., 2020b; Cheng et al., 2021) for the teacher are designed to work only on the special token ([CLS]). It is not suitable for knowledge distillation that is trained with logits and embeddings on a token-by-token basis.

In this paper, we use mixup (Zhang et al., 2018) on knowledge distillation to increase gender-related generalization ability by using mixup. Specifically, when a gender-related word appears, we use the values generalized by a mixup in the knowledge distillation process. First, we employ the pre-defined gender word pair (D) set (w_{male} : w_{female}) from the previous work (Bolukbasi et al., 2016)[3]. We next make the *teacher's output logit* (y) and *student's input embedding* (x) same or similar between two corresponding gendered terms with λ drawn from Beta(α, α) when words in D appear:

$$\bar{x} = \lambda x_{w_{\text{male}}} + (1 - \lambda) x_{w_{\text{female}}}$$
$$\bar{y} = \lambda y_{w_{\text{male}}} + (1 - \lambda) y_{w_{\text{female}}},$$

. We train DistilBERT with the mixup applied instances $(\bar{x}, \bar{y})$ for words in D and with the original instances (x, y) for the rest of words. Notice that we do not use mixup as a data augmentation technique but rather employ its idea in the knowledge distillation.

We view the *mixup* as being worked as a regularizer rather than as a learning objective when knowledge distillation takes place (Chuang and Mroueh, 2021; Liang et al., 2020a). Because the student model learns masked language modeling itself, the generalized gender information by the mixup will act as a regularizer not to be trapped in the information commonly appearing in the pretraining corpus.

5.2 Experimental setup

Dataset We only use the same dataset in knowledge distillation used in Section 4. Also, we lever-

[3]We list the pairs in Appendix C

	Supervision	C6	C6b	C7	C7b	C8	C8b	Avg.
Original Supervision	Original Teacher	1.236	0.499	0.907	1.428	0.534	1.347	0.992
	Debiased Teacher (Kaneko and Bollegala, 2021)	**0.889**	0.294	0.509	1.192	0.838	1.292	0.836
Mixup Supervision	Output embeddings	1.215	0.460	0.761	1.541	0.650	1.420	1.008
	Input embeddings	1.305	**0.049**	0.460	1.334	0.465	1.342	0.830
	Logits + Output embeddings	1.310	0.397	1.325	**0.989**	0.863	1.321	1.034
	Logits + Output embeddings + Input embeddings	1.246	**0.049**	0.566	1.367	0.407	**1.144**	0.796
	Logits + Input embeddings (*proposed*)	1.176	0.062	**0.447**	1.218	**0.310**	1.211	**0.738**

Table 2: The result of applying mixup on distillation process in terms of SEAT score (lower scores indicate less social bias). The lowest score on each tests are marked in **bold**.

Task	Original Teacher	*Mixup* in distillation
MNLI	80.6	80.4
QQP	85.9	85.3
QNLI	86.5	86.2
SST-2	90.4	90.7
CoLA	44.8	43.6
STS-B	83.2	83.2
MRPC	82.2	81.7
RTE	59.9	62.1
Avg.	76.7	76.7

Table 3: The performance on the GLUE benchmark after applying the proposed mixup (Logits + Input Embeddings) in the knowledge distillation.

age GLUE Benchmark to assess model performance.

Baseline We set a baseline as the distilled model from a teacher model that was trained with a debiasing method (Kaneko and Bollegala, 2021).

5.3 Experimental Results

In Table 2, we report the scores for each SEAT test and the average. It shows that mixup (Zhang et al., 2018) applied in the distillation process outperforms in terms of the average SEAT score. Compared to the baseline, distilled model under the supervision of the debiased teacher, *mixup* scores lower in four out of six tests (C6b, C7, C8, C8b).

Table 2 also shows the results according to the part where the mixup is applied. We experimented with applying *mixup* to many different levels of representations in the distillation process: logits, teacher's output embeddings, and student's input embeddings. The proposed method that applies the mixup to inputs (input embeddings) and labels (logits) showed the best results.

We also measure SEAT after applying the teacher's output embeddings. It is because, although not included in the original distillation, the cosine loss for embedding is included in the learning process of DistilBERT. However, Table 2 reports that the mixup on output embeddings increases the SEAT score in most tests and is even higher than the original distillation process.

We also checked the performance on downstream tasks when *mixup* is applied in knowledge distillation. Table 3 summarizes the results on GLUE benchmark. Compared to the model using the original distillation, the average performance remains the same.

6 Conclusion

In this paper, we study what causes gender bias amplification in the knowledge distillation process and how to alleviate the amplification by applying mixup in the knowledge distillation process. We confirmed that both the cross-entropy loss between the logits and the model capacity affects the increase of gender bias. Since this study focused on the DistilBERT, we alleviated the problem by modifying the knowledge distillation loss. We reported that the SEAT score decreased when the mixup was applied to the student's input embedding and the teacher's output logit in the distillation method when gender-related words appeared. We also showed that this method does not have a significant adverse effect on downstream tasks.

There are limitations in this study. First, we used sub-samples of the pre-training corpus. Although we checked that there was no significant differences when trained with a fraction of data in terms of the SEAT score and the GLUE score, the experimental results for the entire data should be explored. Second, we do not yet know why the SEAT score increases when the mixup is applied to the output embedding. The embeddings between the two genders are expected to be close, but we do not yet figure out why the scores are reversed contrary to expectations. We leave these as our future work.

Acknowledgement

This work has been financially supported by KAIST-NAVER Hypercreative AI Center.

References

Su Lin Blodgett, Solon Barocas, Hal Daumé III, and Hanna Wallach. 2020. Language (technology) is power: A critical survey of" bias" in nlp. *arXiv preprint arXiv:2005.14050.*

Tolga Bolukbasi, Kai-Wei Chang, James Zou, Venkatesh Saligrama, and Adam Kalai. 2016. Man is to computer programmer as woman is to homemaker? debiasing word embeddings. In *Proceedings of the 30th International Conference on Neural Information Processing Systems*, NIPS'16, page 4356–4364, Red Hook, NY, USA. Curran Associates Inc.

Pengyu Cheng, Weituo Hao, Siyang Yuan, Shijing Si, and Lawrence Carin. 2021. Fairfil: Contrastive neural debiasing method for pretrained text encoders. In *International Conference on Learning Representations.*

Ching-Yao Chuang and Youssef Mroueh. 2021. Fair mixup: Fairness via interpolation. *arXiv preprint arXiv:2103.06503.*

Maria De-Arteaga, Alexey Romanov, Hanna Wallach, Jennifer Chayes, Christian Borgs, Alexandra Chouldechova, Sahin Geyik, Krishnaram Kenthapadi, and Adam Tauman Kalai. 2019. Bias in bios: A case study of semantic representation bias in a high-stakes setting. In *Proceedings of the Conference on Fairness, Accountability, and Transparency*, FAT* '19, page 120–128, New York, NY, USA. Association for Computing Machinery.

Mengnan Du, Subhabrata Mukherjee, Guanchu Wang, Ruixiang Tang, Ahmed Awadallah, and Xia Hu. 2021. Fairness via representation neutralization. *Advances in Neural Information Processing Systems*, 34.

Geoffrey Hinton, Oriol Vinyals, and Jeff Dean. 2015. Distilling the knowledge in a neural network. *arXiv preprint arXiv:1503.02531.*

Sara Hooker, Nyalleng Moorosi, Gregory Clark, Samy Bengio, and Emily Denton. 2020. Characterising bias in compressed models. *arXiv preprint arXiv:2010.03058.*

Masahiro Kaneko and Danushka Bollegala. 2021. Debiasing pre-trained contextualised embeddings. In *Proceedings of the 16th Conference of the European Chapter of the Association for Computational Linguistics: Main Volume*, pages 1256–1266, Online. Association for Computational Linguistics.

Kevin J Liang, Weituo Hao, Dinghan Shen, Yufan Zhou, Weizhu Chen, Changyou Chen, and Lawrence Carin. 2020a. Mixkd: Towards efficient distillation of large-scale language models. *arXiv preprint arXiv:2011.00593.*

Paul Pu Liang, Irene Mengze Li, Emily Zheng, Yao Chong Lim, Ruslan Salakhutdinov, and Louis-Philippe Morency. 2020b. Towards debiasing sentence representations. In *Proceedings of the 58th Annual Meeting of the Association for Computational Linguistics*, pages 5502–5515, Online. Association for Computational Linguistics.

Chandler May, Alex Wang, Shikha Bordia, Samuel R. Bowman, and Rachel Rudinger. 2019. On measuring social biases in sentence encoders. In *Proceedings of the 2019 Conference of the North American Chapter of the Association for Computational Linguistics: Human Language Technologies, Volume 1 (Long and Short Papers)*, pages 622–628, Minneapolis, Minnesota. Association for Computational Linguistics.

Luke McGuire, Tina Monzavi, Adam J. Hoffman, Fidelia Law, Matthew J. Irvin, Mark Winterbottom, Adam Hartstone-Rose, Adam Rutland, Karen P. Burns, Laurence Butler, Marc Drews, Grace E. Fields, and Kelly Lynn Mulvey. 2021. Science and math interest and gender stereotypes: The role of educator gender in informal science learning sites. *Frontiers in Psychology*, 12.

Victor Sanh, Lysandre Debut, Julien Chaumond, and Thomas Wolf. 2019. Distilbert, a distilled version of bert: smaller, faster, cheaper and lighter. *arXiv preprint arXiv:1910.01108.*

Victor Sanh, Thomas Wolf, Yonatan Belinkov, and Alexander M Rush. 2021. Learning from others' mistakes: Avoiding dataset biases without modeling them. In *International Conference on Learning Representations.*

Andrew Silva, Pradyumna Tambwekar, and Matthew Gombolay. 2021. Towards a comprehensive understanding and accurate evaluation of societal biases in pre-trained transformers. In *Proceedings of the 2021 Conference of the North American Chapter of the Association for Computational Linguistics: Human Language Technologies*, pages 2383–2389, Online. Association for Computational Linguistics.

Alex Wang, Amanpreet Singh, Julian Michael, Felix Hill, Omer Levy, and Samuel R. Bowman. 2019. GLUE: A multi-task benchmark and analysis platform for natural language understanding. In *International Conference on Learning Representations.*

Hongyi Zhang, Moustapha Cisse, Yann N. Dauphin, and David Lopez-Paz. 2018. mixup: Beyond empirical risk minimization. In *International Conference on Learning Representations.*

Yukun Zhu, Ryan Kiros, Rich Zemel, Ruslan Salakhutdinov, Raquel Urtasun, Antonio Torralba, and Sanja Fidler. 2015. Aligning books and movies: Towards story-like visual explanations by watching movies and reading books. In *Proceedings of the IEEE international conference on computer vision*, pages 19–27.

A Related Work

There were several attempts to apply mixup in knowledge distillation. Du et al. (2021) uses a fair representation created by the medium of the embeddings of two sensitive attributes (the neutralization) in distillation. Students are trained with the neutralized embeddings created in this way so that the student's input is dependent on the teacher's output. MixKD (Liang et al., 2020a) applies mixup during knowledge distillation to get better performance on the GLUE benchmark. Notably, MixKD takes the method of training the teacher model as well as the student model when distillation proceeds. Our suggestion guarantees independence between student and teacher model inputs in this work, as DistilBERT is trained. Moreover, we train a task-agnostic model by applying a mixup to distillation.

B Sentence Embedding Association Test (SEAT)

Let X and Y be target embeddings, the embedding of sentence template with gender word in our case, and A and B as attribute words. The SEAT basically measures similarity difference between attribute words and target word w. So the similarity difference on word w is

$$s(w, A, B) = [\text{mean}_{a \in A} \cos(w, a) - \text{mean}_{b \in B} \cos(w, b)].$$

The SEAT score (d) is the Cohen's d on s. The Cohen's d is calculated as follows:

$$d = \frac{[\text{mean}_{x \in X} s(x, A, B) - \text{mean}_{y \in Y} s(y, A, B)]}{\text{std\_dev}_{w \in X \bigcup Y} s(w, A, B)}.$$

C Gender Word Pairs

[["woman", "man"], ["girl", "boy"], ["she", "he"], ["mother", "father"], ["daughter", "son"], ["gal", "guy"], ["female", "male"], ["her", "his"], ["herself", "himself"], ["Mary", "John"]]

D Experiment settings: hyperparameters

D.1 Knowledge Distillaton Hyperparameters

- temperature = 2.0
- mlm_mask_prop = 0.15
- word_mask = 0.8
- word_keep = 0.1
- word_rand = 0.1
- mlm_smoothing = 0.7
- n_epoch = 3
- batch_size = 8
- warmup_prop = 0.05
- weight_decay = 0
- learning_rate = 5e-4
- max_grad_norm = 5
- adam_epsilon= 1e-6
- initializer_range= 0.02
- $\alpha = 0.4$

D.2 GLUE Experiment Hyperparameters

- max_seq_length = 128
- batch_size = 32
- learning_rate = 2e-5
- n_epochs = 3

Incorporating Subjectivity into Gendered Ambiguous Pronoun (GAP) Resolution using Style Transfer

Kartikey Pant * and **Tanvi Dadu** *
Salesforce
{kartikey.pant,tanvi.dadu}@salesforce.com.

Abstract

The *GAP* dataset is a Wikipedia-based evaluation dataset for gender bias detection in coreference resolution, containing mostly objective sentences. Since subjectivity is ubiquitous in our daily texts, it becomes necessary to evaluate models for both subjective and objective instances. In this work, we present a new evaluation dataset for gender bias in coreference resolution, *GAP-Subjective*, which increases the coverage of the original *GAP* dataset by including subjective sentences. We outline the methodology used to create this dataset. Firstly, we detect objective sentences and transfer them into their subjective variants using a sequence-to-sequence model. Secondly, we outline the thresholding techniques based on fluency and content preservation to maintain the quality of the sentences. Thirdly, we perform automated and human-based analysis of the style transfer and infer that the transferred sentences are of high quality. Finally, we benchmark both *GAP* and *GAP-Subjective* datasets using a BERT-based model and analyze its predictive performance and gender bias.

1 Introduction

In natural language, subjectivity refers to the aspects of communication used to express opinions, evaluations, and speculations, often influenced by one's emotional state and viewpoints. It is introduced in natural language by using inflammatory words and phrases, casting doubt over a fact, or presupposing the truth. Writers and editors of texts like newspapers, journals, and textbooks try to avoid subjectivity, yet it is pervasive in these texts. Hence, many NLP applications, including information retrieval, question answering systems, recommender systems, and coreference resolution, would benefit from being able to model subjectivity in natural language (Wiebe et al., 2004).

Objective Form	The authors' **statements** on nutrition studies ...
Subjective Form	The authors' **exposé** on nutrition studies ...

Table 1: Example sentence pair from the Wiki Neutrality Corpus, demonstrating the replacement of the word 'statements' into 'exposé' for inducing subjectivity in the sentence.

One of the prevalent biases induced by NLP systems includes gender bias, which affects training data, resources, pretrained models, and algorithms (Bolukbasi et al., 2016; Caliskan et al., 2017; Schiebinger et al., 2017). Many recent studies aim to detect, analyze, and mitigate gender bias in different NLP tools and applications (Bolukbasi et al., 2016; Rudinger et al., 2018; Park et al., 2018). The task of coreference resolution involves linking referring expressions to the entity that evokes the same discourse, as defined in tasks CoNLL 2011/12 (Pradhan et al., 2012). It is an integral part of NLP systems as coreference resolution decisions can alter how automatic systems process text.

A vital step in reducing gender bias in coreference resolution was the introduction of the *GAP* dataset, a human-labeled corpus containing 8,908 ambiguous pronoun-name pairs derived from Wikipedia containing an equal number of male and female entities. This gender-balanced dataset aims to resolve naturally occurring ambiguous pronouns and reward gender-fair systems.

Text sampled from Wikipedia for the *GAP* dataset contains mostly objective sentences, as shown by the experiments performed in Subsection 3.2.1. Since subjective language is pervasive in our daily texts like newspapers, journals, textbooks, blogs, and other informal sources, it becomes essential to analyze the performance of different models for coreference resolution using subjective texts. Therefore, in this work, we introduce the subjec-

* Both authors have contributed equally to the work.

Proceedings of the The 4th Workshop on Gender Bias in Natural Language Processing (GeBNLP), pages 273 - 281
July 15, 2022

tivity attribute in the *GAP* dataset and analyze the performance of a BERT-based model on a newly proposed dataset.

In this work, we make the following contributions:-

1. We propose a novel approach for increasing coverage of the *GAP* dataset to include subjective text and release the GAP-Subjective dataset.

2. We outline each step in our dataset creation pipeline, which includes the detection of subjective sentences, the transfer of objective sentences into their subjective counterparts, and thresholding of the generated subjective sentences based on fluency, content preservation, and transfer of attribute.

3. We conduct automated and human evaluations to verify the quality of the transferred sentences.

4. We benchmark *GAP-Subjective* dataset using a BERT-based model and analyze its performance with the *GAP* dataset.

2 Related Works

2.1 Subjectivity Modeling and Detection

Recasens et al. (2013) conducted initial experimentation on subjectivity detection on Wikipedia-based text using feature-based models in their work. The authors introduced the "Neutral Point of View" (NPOV) corpus constructed from Wikipedia revision history, containing edits designed to remove subjectivity from the text. They used logistic regression with linguistic features, including factive verbs, hedges, and subjective intensifiers, to detect the top three subjectivity-inducing words in each sentence.

In Pryzant et al. (2019), the authors extend the work done by Recasens et al. (2013) by mitigating subjectivity after the detection of subjectivity-inducing words using a BERT-based model. They also introduced Wiki Neutrality Corpus (WNC), a parallel dataset containing pre and post-neutralization sentences by English Wikipedia editors from 2004 to 2019. They further tested their proposed architecture on the Ideological Books Corpus (IBC), biased headlines of partisan news articles, and sentences from a prominent politician's campaign speeches. They concluded that their models could provide valuable and intuitive suggestions to how subjective language used in news and other political text can be transferred to their objective forms.

The classification of statements containing biased language rather than individual words that induce the bias has been explored in Dadu et al. (2020). The authors perform a comprehensive experimental evaluation, comparing transformer-based approaches with classical approaches like fastText and BiLSTM. They conclude that biased language can be detected using transformer-based models efficiently using pretrained models like RoBERTa.

Riloff et al. (2005) explored using subjectivity analysis to improve the precision of Information Extraction (IE) systems in their work. They developed an IE system that used a subjective sentence classifier to filter its extractions, using a strategy that discards all extractions found in subjective sentences and strategies that selectively discard extractions. They showed that selective filtering strategies improved the IE systems' precision with minimal recall loss, concluding that subjectivity analysis improves the IE systems.

2.2 Gender Bias in Coreference Resolution

OntoNotes introduced by Weischedel et al. (2011) is a general-purpose annotated corpus consisting of around 2.9 million words across three languages: English, Arabic, and Chinese. However, the corpus is severely gender-biased in which female entities are significantly underrepresented, with only 25% of the 2000 gendered pronouns being feminine. This misrepresentation results in a biased evaluation of coreferencing models.

There has been considerable work on debiasing coreferencing evaluation concerning the gender attribute (Zhao et al., 2018; Webster et al., 2018). In (Zhao et al., 2018), the authors introduced a gender-balanced dataset *Winobias*, extending *Ontonotes 5.0* in an attempt to remove gender bias, containing Winograd-schema style sentences centered on people entities referred to by their occupation.

In Webster et al. (2018), the authors introduce the *GAP* dataset, a gender-balanced corpus of ambiguous pronouns, to address the gender misrepresentation problem. The dataset serves as an evaluation benchmark for coreference models containing over $8.9k$ coreference-labeled pairs containing the ambiguous pronoun and the possible antecedents. The coreference-labeled pairs are sampled from

Wikipedia and are gender-balanced, containing an equal number of instances for both male and female genders. This characteristic enables a gender-bias-based evaluation to be performed for any coreference model. They further benchmark the state-of-the-art model based on Transformers (Vaswani et al., 2017) against simpler baselines using syntactic rules for coreference resolution, observing that the models do not perform well in the evaluation.

2.3 Increasing Data Coverage

Asudeh et al. (2019) analyzed existing datasets to show that lack of adequate coverage in the dataset can result in undesirable outcomes such as biased decisions and algorithmic racism, creating vulnerabilities leading to adversarial attacks. For increasing coverage of the textual dataset, methods such as randomly swapping two words, dropping a word, and replacing one word with another one are heavily explored. On the other hand, generating new sentences to increase coverage via Neural Machine Translation (NMT) and style transfer remains a relatively less explored area.

Gao et al. (2019) explored soft contextual data augmentation using NMT. They proposed augmenting NMT training data by replacing a randomly chosen word in a sentence with a soft word, a probabilistic distribution over the vocabulary. Moreover, Wu et al. (2020) constructed two large-scale, multiple reference datasets, *The Machine Translation Formality Corpus* (MTFC) and *Twitter Conversation Formality Corpus* (TCFC), using formality as an attribute of text style transfer. They utilized existing low-resource stylized sequence-to-sequence (S2S) generation methods, including back-translation.

Textual style transfer has been explored extensively for the generation of fluent, content-preserved, attribute-controlled text (Hu et al., 2017). Prior works exploring textual style transfer in semi-supervised setting employ several machine-learning methodologies like back-translation (Prabhumoye et al., 2018), back-translation with attribute-specific loss (Pant et al., 2020), specialized transfer methodologies (Li et al., 2018), and their transformer-based variants (Sudhakar et al., 2019).

In a supervised setting where a parallel corpus is available, sequence-to-sequence models perform competitively. We use the OpenNMT-py toolkit (Klein et al., 2017) to train sequence-to-sequence models. Copy mechanism based sequence-to-sequence models with attention (Bahdanau et al., 2014) have been effective in tasks involving significant preservation of content information. They have been applied in tasks like sentence simplification (Aharoni et al., 2019), and abstractive summarization (See et al., 2017).

3 Corpus Creation

3.1 Preliminaries

3.1.1 GAP Dataset

The *GAP* dataset, as introduced in Webster et al. (2018), is constructed using a language-independent mechanism for extracting challenging ambiguous pronouns. The dataset consists of $8,908$ manually-annotated ambiguous pronoun-name pairs. It is extracted from a large set of candidate contexts, filtered through a multi-stage process using three target extraction patterns and five dimensions of sub-sampling for annotations to improve quality and diversity. It is a gender-balanced dataset with each instance assigned one of the five labels - *Name A*, *Name B*, *Both Names*, *Neither Name A nor Name B*, and *Not Sure*.

The *GAP* is primarily an evaluation corpus, which helps us evaluate coreference models for the task of resolving naturally-occurring ambiguous pronoun-name pairs in terms of both classification accuracy and the property of being gender-neutral. The final dataset has a train-test-validation split of $4000 - 4000 - 908$ examples. Each example contains the source Wikipedia page's URL, making it possible for the model to use the external context if it may. The models are evaluated using the following two metrics: *F1 score* and *Bias* (Gender).

3.1.2 Subjectivity Detection

For detecting subjectivity in sentences, we use the Wiki Neutrality Corpus (WNC) released by Pryzant et al. (2019). It consists of $180k$ aligned pre and post-subjective-bias-neutralized sentences by editors. The dataset covers $423,823$ Wikipedia revisions between 2004 to 2019. To maximize the precision of bias-related changes, the authors drop a selective group of instances to ensure the effective training of subjectivity detection models.

Dadu et al. (2020) shows that the RoBERTa model performed competitively in the WNC dataset achieving 0.702 *F1 score*, with a *recall* of 0.681 and *precision* of 0.723. Following their work, we train a RoBERTa-based model for detecting subjective sentences.

3.2 Approach

This section describes the methodology used for the creation of *GAP-Subjective*. It outlines the models used for detecting subjectivity in the original *GAP* dataset, followed by the methods used for transferring the objective sentences to their subjective counterparts. It also presents the thresholding techniques used on the generated subjective sentences based on fluency, content preservation, and transfer of attribute. Finally, it concludes by showing the results of the human evaluations conducted to verify the quality of the transferred sentences.

3.2.1 Subjectivity Detection

In this section, we highlight the approach used for detecting subjectivity in the *GAP* dataset. Following the works of Dadu et al. (2020), we fine-tune the pretrained RoBERTa model using the WNC dataset for detecting subjectivity in the sentences. We randomly shuffled these sentences and split this dataset into two parts in a $90:10$ Train-Test split and performed the evaluation on the held-out test dataset. We used a learning rate of $2*10^{-5}$, a maximum sequence length of 50, and a weight decay of 0.01 for fine-tuning our model. Our trained model has 0.685 *F1-score* and 70.01% *accuracy* along with a *recall* of 0.653 and *precision* of 0.720. We then predict the subjectivity of the *GAP* dataset using the fine-tuned model and conclude that over 86% of the sentences in the dataset are objective. Table 2 illustrates a data split wise analysis for the same.

3.2.2 Style Transfer

In this section, we detail the process of performing style transfer of objective sentences present in the *GAP* dataset into their subjective variants. Our task of style transfer entails mapping a source sentence x to a target sentence $\tilde{x}$, such that in $\tilde{x}$ the maximum amount of original content-based information from x is preserved independent of the subjectivity attribute.

Firstly, we train a SentencePiece tokenizer on the English Wikipedia with a vocabulary size of 25000. We consider numerical tokens as user-defined symbols to preserve them during the transfer process. Secondly, we train the style transfer model on the SentencePiece tokenized Wiki Neutrality Corpus using the OpenNMT-py toolkit. We use a 256-sized BiLSTM layered architecture with a batch size of 16, thresholding the gradient norm to have the maximum value of 2 and share the word embeddings between encoder and decoder. We use the AdaGrad optimizer and use a multi-layer perceptron for global attention.

Importantly, we use the copy mechanism (Gu et al., 2016) for the sequence-to-sequence model. The mechanism has been proven beneficial in similar tasks, such as sentence simplification in a supervised setting (Aharoni et al., 2019). It is modeled using a copy switch probability over each token in the target vocabulary and each token in the context sequence at each decoding step. Hence, it allows the model to generate tokens that are not present in the target vocabulary. We hypothesized that using the copy mechanism in the models helps in preserving important entity-linked information like the associated pronoun and the names of the entities necessary for coreference resolution.

We obtain a validation perplexity of 3.10 and a validation accuracy of 84.52%, implying that the model produced fluent and subjective sentences at large. To further improve the quality of the dataset, we then threshold these sentences across various metrics important for style transfer, as in recent works (Li et al., 2018; Sudhakar et al., 2019).

3.2.3 Thresholding Transferred Sentences

This section details about the thresholding techniques used on the transferred sentences to maintain their quality. We perform the thresholding taking the following into consideration: fluency, content preservation, and transfer of attribute.

1. **Fluency**: We use the *OpenGPT-2* (Radford et al., 2018) as the language model to assign perplexity to the transferred sentences [1]. We compare the perplexity of the transferred sentences with the original sentences to test their fluency and discard all the sentences in which the perplexity change is more than 100. This thresholding ensures relatively less change in the sentence structure, which is measured by the language model. Table 2 shows that 2,635 in *development*, 603 in *validation* and 2,641 in *test* of *GAP-Subjective* are within the fluency threshold, comprising 44.02% of the overall sentences.

[1] https://huggingface.co/transformers/perplexity.html

Dataset Split	Total sentences	Within GLUE Threshold	Within Perplexity Threshold	Objective sentences	Final Thresholded Sentences ($A \cap B \cap C$)	Percentage of Final Thresholded Sentences
Development	5995	2332	2635	5162	1736	28.9%
Validation	1389	527	603	1183	377	27.1%
Test	5971	2359	2641	5141	1800	30.1%
Overall	13355	5218	5879	11486	3913	29.3%

Table 2: Sentence-wise Thresholding Split

2. **Content Preservation**: We use sentence-level GLEU (Mutton et al., 2007) scores for determining the content preservation of the model. We compare the transferred sentence with their original counterparts as a reference. We consider all sentences having a GLEU less than 1.0 to ensure no sentence remains the same and more than 0.8 to provide a high level of similarity between the transferred sentence and the original sentence in terms of content information. As can be observed in Table 2, we preserve 39.07% of the overall sentences through the GLEU-based thresholding.

3. **Original Attribute**: We use the subjectivity model trained in Subsection 3.2.1 and filter out the sentences that are already subjective before transfer. Table 2 shows that 13.9% sentences in *development*, 14.83% in *validation*, and 13.90% in the *test* are subjective, corroborating that majority sentences in the dataset are objective, lacking coverage in terms of subjectivity as an attribute.

Original (Objective)	She died the following January, aged about 22, giving birth to their only son.
Transferred (Subjective)	***Unfortunately***, she died the following January, aged about 22, giving birth to their only son.
Original (Objective)	Her father, Philip, was a lithographic printer, and her mother, Ellen, ran a boarding house in Brixton; Kathleen was their third daughter.
Transferred (Subjective)	Her father, Philip, was a ***controversial*** lithographic printer, and her mother, Ellen, ran a boarding house in Brixton; Kathleen was their third daughter.

Table 3: Example of transferred subjective sentences by the proposed approach

Table 3 illustrates the differences between the original objective and the transferred subjective sentences. We observe that the addition of the ad verb *Unfortunately* in the original sentence makes it a subjective sentence, adding one's emotional state and viewpoints towards the event. Similarly, the addition of the adjective *controversial* changes the objective sentence to a subjective one.

Split	Converted *GAP* Contexts
test	63.85%
development	60.60%
validation	61.89%

Table 4: Percentage of Converted GAP Contexts

Table 2 shows that 29.29% of the overall sentences are left after thresholding on all three metrics. We then replace the original sentences with their thresholded subjective counterparts. We observe that at least one sentence is transferred by our approach in over 60% of the GAP contexts. A data split wise analysis for the same is illustrated in Table 4.

3.2.4 Human Evaluation

Although automated evaluation helps in the thresholding process for reconstructing *GAP-Subjective* and provides a significant indication of transfer quality, we perform human evaluation for a deeper analysis. We randomly sampled 68 sentences from the dataset containing 34 sentences each from the transferred sentences and original sentences in the human evaluation. The judges were asked to rank the sentence regarding its fluency and subjectivity. *Fluency* was rated from 1 (poor) to 5 (perfect). Similarly, *Subjectivity* was also rated from 1 (highly objective, factual) to 5 (highly subjective).

Table 6 illustrates the results of the human evaluation. We observe that the transferred sentences, on average, score 1.21 higher points on subjectivity than the original sentences. However, this increase in subjectivity comes with a minor 0.23 decrease in fluency.

3.2.5 Offset Finding

We process each text to calculate the new offsets for the concerned pronoun and both the entities. Firstly, we determine the sentence in which the target word

Dataset	Context
GAP-Subjective	*Unfortunately*, however, Stevenson suffered an injury while training and was replaced by Tyson Griffin. Gomi defeated Griffin by KO (punch) at 1:04 of the first round. Gomi would finish him with a *popular* left cross following up with a right hook causing Griffin to fall face first into the canvas where Gomi then followed up onto Griffin's back with few short punches before the fight was stopped. **He** is the first person to have stopped Griffin as all of Griffin's previous losses have gone to a decision.
GAP	However, Stevenson suffered an injury while training and was replaced by Tyson Griffin. Gomi defeated Griffin by KO (punch) at 1:04 of the first round. Gomi would finish him with a left cross following up with a right hook causing Griffin to fall face first into the canvas where Gomi then followed up onto Griffin's back with few short punches before the fight was stopped. **He** is the first person to have stopped Griffin as all of Griffin's previous losses have gone to a decision.

Table 5: Sample Text from both datasets, GAP and GAP-Subjective

	Fluency	**Subjectivity**
Original Sentences	**4.578**	1.657
Transferred Sentences	4.343	**2.872**

Table 6: Results for Human Evaluation of the Transfer Model

was present in the original text. We then perform an exact match to find the word's position in the final transferred sentence. After finding the word's position in the sentence, we calculate the global offset for the word in the reconstructed text made of the final transferred sentences. This global offset represents the new offset for each entity.

Dataset Split	**Pronoun Found**	**Entity A Found**	**Entity B Found**	**All Found**
Development	99.90	98.65	99.00	97.55
Validation	99.34	99.78	99.56	98.68
Test	99.90	99.15	99.05	98.20

Table 7: Percentages of span offsets found in each data split

Table 7 represents the number of instances for which the offsets were successfully calculated as a percentage of total examples in each split. 97.55% instances in *development*, 98.68% instances in *validation*, and 98.20% instances in *test* had correct offsets for all the three entities, thus showing that our offset finding approach was effective. To maintain the size of the dataset, we consider the original instance already present in the *GAP* dataset if the offset is not found.

Table 5 illustrates a sample context from *GAP* and *GAP-Subjective*, highlighting difference between the sentences of the context, the entity positions and the pronoun positions.

4 Benchmarking GAP-Subjective

4.1 GAP-Subjective Task

GAP-Subjective is an evaluation corpus that extends the *GAP* corpus by augmenting transferred subjective sentences for their objective counterparts. This dataset is segmented into *development* and *test* splits of 4,000 examples each and *validation* split consisting of 908 examples. The offsets for each entity and pronoun are given in the dataset. However, these offsets should not be treated as a gold mention or Winograd-style task.

We evaluate *GAP-Subjective* and compare it with *GAP* across two axes of evaluation: predictive performance, and gender bias. For assessing the predictive performance, we use an overall *F1 score*, denoted by *O*. We further calculate the *F1 score* for each of the two gendered pronouns, thus resulting in Male *F1* and Female *F1*, denoted by *M* and *F* respectively. We then calculate gender bias, indicated by *B*, which is defined as the ratio of feminine to masculine *F1 scores*, i.e., M/F.

4.2 Baseline Model

For benchmarking *GAP-Subjective*, we used the BERT-based architecture, introduced in Yang et al. (2019), that performs competitively in the GAP Challenge. The authors modeled the relations between query words by concatenating the contextual representations and aggregating the generated features with a shallow multi-layered perceptron. For a given query (Entity A, Entity B, Pronoun), they obtained deep contextual representations for the pronoun and each entity from *BERT*, where each entity is composed of multiple word pieces.

Following the work of Yang et al. (2019), we use the cased variant of $BERT_{Base}$ for benchmarking *GAP-Subjective*. We extract features from *BERT* using a sequence length of 128, batch size of 32, and embedding size of 768. For classification, we

Dataset/Metric	Overall F1(O)	Precision(P)	Recall(R)	Masc-F1(M)	Fem-F1(F)	Bias(B)
GAP-Subjective	0.789	0.772	0.807	0.786	0.792	1.007
GAP	0.796	0.778	0.815	0.802	0.790	0.984

Table 8: Results for the Benchmarking Experiments

train a multi-layered perceptron for 1000 epochs with 0.6 dropout rate, 0.001 learning rate, 0.1 L2 regularization and 32 batch size.

4.3 Results

Table 8 illustrates the benchmarking results for *GAP-Subjective* and *GAP* for the BERT-based architecture. We observe a significant change in the predictive performance of the BERT-based model for *GAP-Subjective* and *GAP*. We observe a decrease of $\sim 1\%$ in *F1-score*, and $\sim 2\%$ in *Masc-F1 (M)*, and a slight increase of $\sim 0.3\%$ in *Fem-F1 (F)*.

We also observe a change in the gender bias of the model between the two datasets. To understand this change, let us assume that the magnitude of deviation in bias score m equals the absolute difference between the bias score and the ideal value 1 (which is obtained when there is no bias towards any of the two genders). While the model had a bias score of 0.984 in *GAP*, implying a preference towards male entities with the m score of 1.6%. Interestingly, *GAP-Subjective* shows a minor preference towards female entities with a bias score of 1.007 and m value of 0.7%.

5 Conclusion

In this work, we analyzed the addition of the subjectivity attribute in *GAP*, a widely used evaluation corpus for the detection of gender bias in coreference resolution. We utilized sentence-level supervised style transfer using sequence-to-sequence models to transfer the objective sentences in *GAP* to their subjective variants. We outlined the efficacy of our proposed style transfer approach using suitable metrics for content preservation and fluency and a human evaluation of the transferred sentences. We proposed a new evaluation corpus, *GAP-Subjective*, which consists of the reconstructed texts along with their new entity offsets. We benchmarked and analyzed the predictive performance and gender bias of BERT-based models in both *GAP* and *GAP-Subjective*. Future work may include increasing coverage of objective-heavy datasets for other downstream tasks and increasing the coverage of *GAP* using other attributes.

Bias Statement

This paper studies two forms of biases: gender bias and subjective bias. We increase the coverage of the evaluation dataset for identifying gender bias in coreference resolution by converting objective data to its subjective counterparts. Since most of the original data were mined from Wikipedia, which has a "Neutral Point of View" policy ensuring that the data is objective, the models are evaluated for gender bias solely in a setting devoid of subjectivity. Since subjective bias is ubiquitous (Pryzant et al., 2019), adding subjectivity into the evaluation corpus becomes imperative when evaluating any form of bias. While evaluating the $BERT_{Base}$ model for the original *GAP* dataset, we found the model to prefer *Male* entities at large. In contrast, the same model trained and evaluated on the subjective counterpart *GAP-Subjective* was objective to prefer Female entities at large. Our work is based on the belief that the setting used for evaluation datasets for bias detection influences our understanding of capturing the bias in the evaluated systems.

References

Roee Aharoni, Melvin Johnson, and Orhan Firat. 2019. Massively multilingual neural machine translation. In *Proceedings of the 2019 Conference of the North American Chapter of the Association for Computational Linguistics: Human Language Technologies, Volume 1 (Long and Short Papers)*, pages 3874–3884, Minneapolis, Minnesota. Association for Computational Linguistics.

Abolfazl Asudeh, Zhongjun Jin, and H. V. Jagadish. 2019. Assessing and remedying coverage for a given dataset. In *35th IEEE International Conference on Data Engineering, ICDE 2019, Macao, China, April 8-11, 2019*, pages 554–565. IEEE.

Dzmitry Bahdanau, Kyunghyun Cho, and Yoshua Bengio. 2014. Neural machine translation by jointly learning to align and translate. Cite arxiv:1409.0473Comment: Accepted at ICLR 2015 as oral presentation.

Tolga Bolukbasi, Kai-Wei Chang, James Zou, Venkatesh Saligrama, and Adam Kalai. 2016. Man is to computer programmer as woman is to homemaker? debiasing word embeddings.

Aylin Caliskan, Joanna Bryson, and Arvind Narayanan. 2017. Semantics derived automatically from language corpora contain human-like biases. *Science*, 356:183–186.

Tanvi Dadu, Kartikey Pant, and Radhika Mamidi. 2020. Towards detection of subjective bias using contextualized word embeddings.

Fei Gao, Jinhua Zhu, Lijun Wu, Yingce Xia, Tao Qin, Xueqi Cheng, Wengang Zhou, and Tie-Yan Liu. 2019. Soft contextual data augmentation for neural machine translation. In *Proceedings of the 57th Annual Meeting of the Association for Computational Linguistics*, pages 5539–5544, Florence, Italy. Association for Computational Linguistics.

Jiatao Gu, Zhengdong Lu, Hang Li, and Victor O.K. Li. 2016. Incorporating copying mechanism in sequence-to-sequence learning. In *Proceedings of the 54th Annual Meeting of the Association for Computational Linguistics (Volume 1: Long Papers)*, pages 1631–1640, Berlin, Germany. Association for Computational Linguistics.

Zhiting Hu, Zichao Yang, Xiaodan Liang, Ruslan Salakhutdinov, and Eric P. Xing. 2017. Toward controlled generation of text. In *Proceedings of the 34th International Conference on Machine Learning*, volume 70 of *Proceedings of Machine Learning Research*, pages 1587–1596, International Convention Centre, Sydney, Australia. PMLR.

Guillaume Klein, Yoon Kim, Yuntian Deng, Jean Senellart, and Alexander Rush. 2017. OpenNMT: Open-source toolkit for neural machine translation. In *Proceedings of ACL 2017, System Demonstrations*, pages 67–72, Vancouver, Canada. Association for Computational Linguistics.

Juncen Li, Robin Jia, He He, and Percy Liang. 2018. Delete, retrieve, generate: a simple approach to sentiment and style transfer. In *Proceedings of the 2018 Conference of the North American Chapter of the Association for Computational Linguistics: Human Language Technologies, Volume 1 (Long Papers)*, pages 1865–1874, New Orleans, Louisiana. Association for Computational Linguistics.

Andrew Mutton, Mark Dras, Stephen Wan, and Robert Dale. 2007. GLEU: Automatic evaluation of sentence-level fluency. In *Proceedings of the 45th Annual Meeting of the Association of Computational Linguistics*, pages 344–351, Prague, Czech Republic. Association for Computational Linguistics.

Kartikey Pant, Yash Verma, and Radhika Mamidi. 2020. Sentiinc: Incorporating sentiment information into sentiment transfer without parallel data. *Advances in Information Retrieval*, 12036:312 – 319.

Ji Ho Park, Jamin Shin, and Pascale Fung. 2018. Reducing gender bias in abusive language detection. In *Proceedings of the 2018 Conference on Empirical Methods in Natural Language Processing*, pages 2799–2804, Brussels, Belgium. Association for Computational Linguistics.

Shrimai Prabhumoye, Yulia Tsvetkov, Ruslan Salakhutdinov, and Alan W Black. 2018. Style transfer through back-translation. In *Proceedings of the 56th Annual Meeting of the Association for Computational Linguistics (Volume 1: Long Papers)*, pages 866–876, Melbourne, Australia. Association for Computational Linguistics.

Sameer Pradhan, Alessandro Moschitti, Nianwen Xue, Olga Uryupina, and Yuchen Zhang. 2012. CoNLL-2012 shared task: Modeling multilingual unrestricted coreference in OntoNotes. In *Joint Conference on EMNLP and CoNLL - Shared Task*, pages 1–40, Jeju Island, Korea. Association for Computational Linguistics.

Reid Pryzant, Richard Martinez, Nathan Dass, Sadao Kurohashi, Dan Jurafsky, and Diyi Yang. 2019. Automatically neutralizing subjective bias in text.

Alec Radford, Jeffrey Wu, Rewon Child, David Luan, Dario Amodei, and Ilya Sutskever. 2018. Language models are unsupervised multitask learners.

Marta Recasens, Cristian Danescu-Niculescu-Mizil, and Dan Jurafsky. 2013. Linguistic models for analyzing and detecting biased language. In *Proceedings of the 51st Annual Meeting of the Association for Computational Linguistics (Volume 1: Long Papers)*, pages 1650–1659, Sofia, Bulgaria. Association for Computational Linguistics.

Ellen Riloff, Janyce Wiebe, and William Phillips. 2005. Exploiting subjectivity classification to improve information extraction. In *Proceedings of the 20th National Conference on Artificial Intelligence - Volume 3*, AAAI'05, page 1106–1111. AAAI Press.

Rachel Rudinger, Jason Naradowsky, Brian Leonard, and Benjamin Durme. 2018. Gender bias in coreference resolution. pages 8–14.

Londa Schiebinger, Dan Jurafsky, and James Zou. 2017. Word embeddings quantify 100 years of gender and ethnic stereotypes. *Proceedings of the National Academy of Sciences*, 115.

Abigail See, Peter J. Liu, and Christopher D. Manning. 2017. Get to the point: Summarization with pointer-generator networks. In *Proceedings of the 55th Annual Meeting of the Association for Computational Linguistics (Volume 1: Long Papers)*, pages 1073–1083, Vancouver, Canada. Association for Computational Linguistics.

Akhilesh Sudhakar, Bhargav Upadhyay, and Arjun Maheswaran. 2019. Transforming delete, retrieve, generate approach for controlled text style transfer. In *EMNLP/IJCNLP*.

Ashish Vaswani, Noam Shazeer, Niki Parmar, Jakob Uszkoreit, Llion Jones, Aidan N. Gomez, undefinedukasz Kaiser, and Illia Polosukhin. 2017. Attention is all you need. In *Proceedings of the 31st International Conference on Neural Information Processing Systems*, NIPS'17, page 6000–6010, Red Hook, NY, USA. Curran Associates Inc.

Kellie Webster, Marta Recasens, Vera Axelrod, and Jason Baldridge. 2018. Mind the gap: A balanced corpus of gendered ambiguou. In *Transactions of the ACL*, page to appear.

Ralph Weischedel, Eduard Hovy, Mitchell Marcus, Martha Palmer, Robert Belvin, Sameer Pradhan, Lance Ramshaw, and Nianwen Xue. 2011. *OntoNotes: A Large Training Corpus for Enhanced Processing*.

Janyce Wiebe, Theresa Wilson, Rebecca Bruce, Matthew Bell, and Melanie Martin. 2004. Learning subjective language. *Comput. Linguist.*, 30(3):277–308.

Yunzhao Wu, Yunli Wang, and Shujie Liu. 2020. A dataset for low-resource stylized sequence-to-sequence generation. In *AAAI 2020*.

Kai-Chou Yang, Timothy Niven, Tzu Hsuan Chou, and Hung-Yu Kao. 2019. Fill the GAP: Exploiting BERT for pronoun resolution. In *Proceedings of the First Workshop on Gender Bias in Natural Language Processing*, pages 102–106, Florence, Italy. Association for Computational Linguistics.

Jieyu Zhao, Tianlu Wang, Mark Yatskar, Vicente Ordonez, and Kai-Wei Chang. 2018. Gender bias in coreference resolution: Evaluation and debiasing methods. In *Proceedings of the 2018 Conference of the North American Chapter of the Association for Computational Linguistics: Human Language Technologies, Volume 2 (Short Papers)*, pages 15–20, New Orleans, Louisiana. Association for Computational Linguistics.

Author Index

Association for Computational Linguistics
209 N. Eighth Street
Stroudsburg, Pennsylvania 18360

CURRAN ASSOCIATES INC.
proceedings.com

ISBN 978-1-7138-5633-7
9 781713 856337